The Pursuit of Racial and Ethnic Equality in American Public Schools

D1569071

The Pursuit of Racial and Ethnic Equality in American Public Schools

Mendez, Brown, and Beyond

Edited by Kristi L. Bowman

Michigan State University Press | East Lansing

KH

Michigan State University Press
East Lansing, Michigan 48823-5245

Printed and bound in the United States of America.

21 20 19 18 17 16 15   1 2 3 4 5 6 7 8 9 10

Library of Congress Control Number: 2014954875
ISBN: 978-1-61186-180-8 (paper)
ISBN: 978-1-60917-467-5 (ebook: PDF)
ISBN: 978-1-62895-239-1 (ebook: ePub)
ISBN: 978-1-62896-239-0 (ebook: Kindle)

Book and cover design by Charlie Sharp, Sharp Designs, Lansing, MI

Visit Michigan State University Press at *www.msupress.org*

11/18/15

Contents

PART I. *Mendez*, *Brown*, and the Civil Rights Act

Mendez (1946)

PART II. Desegregation Unfolds

Milliken (1974)

Jenkins (1995)

Parents Involved and Meredith (2007)

Acknowledgments

A VOLUME LIKE THIS IS THE RESULT OF THE HARD WORK OF MANY, AND PERHAPS most importantly of the exceptionally talented contributing authors whose work makes these issues of equity and equality come alive. In addition to expressing my deep gratitude to each of the contributors, many others deserve thanks as well.

To begin with, Michigan State University Professors Nicholas Mercuro and John Beck led the charge for MSU to commemorate the sixtieth anniversary of *Brown v. Board* and the fiftieth anniversary of the federal Civil Rights Act, resulting in "Project 60/50"—a year-long, cross-campus series of over a hundred events focused on understanding the legacy of these two monumental changes in law. One such event was a unique and memorable symposium hosted at Michigan State University College of Law and the University of Missouri-Kansas City College of Law in April 2014, and shared between these two campuses via a two-day videoconference (MSU technology geniuses Amanda Olivier and Matt Drury have my eternal gratitude for making the whole thing work). Professor Mercuro played a substantial and indispensable role in planning that conference, as did MSU College of Education Associate Dean and Professor Michael Sedlak, Washington University Assistant Professor Michelle Purdy, *Michigan State Law Review* Senior Symposia Editor Shannon Smith (MSU

Law '14), and MSU Events Coordinator Sally Rice. UMKC Professor Daniel Weddle and his team planned and hosted the Kansas City portion of the symposium and in fact the genesis for the format came from his previous conference about student speech. Most of the contributors to this volume came together in person and via videoconference at our symposium. This volume, as well as a *Michigan State Law Review* special issue, are both a direct outgrowth of that event.

The symposium was sponsored by numerous organizations and individuals, including the *Michigan State Law Review*, the MSU College of Education, the MSU Department of Political Science, the MSU LeFrak Forum on Science, Reason, and Modern Democracy, the MSU Office for Inclusion and Intercultural Initiatives, the Education Law Association, the University of Missouri-Kansas City School of Law, the UMKC Joseph Cohen Lecture Fund, Sprint Corporation, UMB, UMKC Student Affairs and student organizations, the Kansas City Metropolitan Bar Association, and the following law firms in Kansas City: Ogletree Deakins; Husch Blackwell; Shook, Hardy & Bacon LLP; Spencer, Fane, Britt & Browne, LLP; Wagstaff & Cartmell; and Hardwick Law Firm LLC. MSU's Project 60/50 also generously continued its support of the symposium by assisting with the publication of this volume.

Many others deserve thanks for their work in helping shape and refine the chapters in this volume. MSU Law students and recent graduates Courtney Soughers (Class of 2014) and Kelsey Brunette (JD expected 2016) provided the bulk of editorial assistance, assisted by Katila Howard (JD expected 2016) and Patrick O'Brien (Class of 2013), and all of their efforts were excellent. MSU Law Librarian Barbara Bean and my assistant Marie Gordon were helpful, as they always are, in countless indispensable ways. Leading scholars across the country graciously agreed to review chapters and provide helpful feedback to the authors, including Scott Bauries, Kevin Brown, Tiffani Darden, Matthew Fletcher, Robert Garda Jr., Molly Hunter, Daniel Kiel, Julie Mead, Eloise Pasachoff, Sarah Reckhow, Victor Romero, William Thro, David Thronson, Kevin Welner, and John Yun.

Additionally, it has been a delight to work with MSU Press. Publisher Gabriel Dotto and Editor in Chief Julie Loehr expressed early enthusiasm for this project; Julie also provided essential advice about many issues. Julia Sullivan shepherded nearly all of the chapters through some, if not all, of the editorial process, and Steven Moore provided particularly helpful copyediting.

To end on a personal note, and to explain in part why I choose to spend my time working on projects like this, it would be remiss if I did not also thank to my family for their support and particularly my parents who taught me by their example that public education is a community responsibility; the talented attorneys with whom I practiced at Franczek Sullivan (now Franczek Radelet) in Chicago who let me share in the awesome responsibility of representing school districts; and the many insightful colleagues and students at MSU and across the country whose questions, comments, and scholarship have continued to influence how and why I think and write about education and equality. Finally, and perhaps most importantly, my husband Gabriel Wrobel and our son Quinn Bowman Wrobel fill each day with small kindnesses and great joy—and have shown such patience when I would be working on this volume and say, again and again, "Just five more minutes."

KRISTI L. BOWMAN
East Lansing, Michigan
October 2014

JAMES E. RYAN

Foreword

In 2014, as our nation celebrated the 60th anniversary of *Brown v. Board of Education*, I was asked—on a number of different occasions—to remark on the legacy of the decision. To be sure, *Brown* gave us much worth celebrating. It overturned *Plessy v. Ferguson* by asserting that separate educational facilities are inherently unequal; it put forth the idea that access to education was a fundamental right; and it delivered a heartening victory to the growing civil rights movement.

But the legacy of *Brown* (as well as *Mendez v. Westminster,* which helped lay the groundwork for the landmark Supreme Court desegregation case) has not been an uninterrupted march toward equality and educational opportunity. In fact, in the decades since, this country has done more than just stumble from the path charted by *Brown* and *Mendez.* From the decision in *Milliken v. Bradley* to restrict the reach of desegregation efforts to the ruling in *Parents Involved v. Seattle* that struck down voluntary district integration plans, the Court has largely turned away from the goal of racially integrated K–12 schools.

And as a people, we have mostly accepted school segregation as the status quo. Rather than work to fulfill the underlying ideal of *Brown,* we have largely accepted the divide between poor, minority, urban districts and middle-class, white, suburban districts. There are some who believe we can continue to educate our children in separate school systems, relying on more money and more testing to equalize opportunity. But 40 years of school finance reform and 30 years of test-based reform tell a much different story. African American and Latino students, despite modest gains, continue to lag behind white students on achievement exams, in high school graduation rates, and in college completion rates. Separate may not inherently be unequal, but isolation based on race and class almost invariably leads to disparate outcomes.

What may be lost in a focus on academic achievement, however, is a deeper social issue that both *Brown* and *Mendez* address. Chief Justice Earl Warren was no doubt correct in claiming that "the impact [of segregation] is greater when it has the sanction of law," but de facto segregation—if we are to accept the somewhat questionable premise that residential segregation is entirely the result of private choice—also threatens our society in a very real way. By 2043, the United States will be majority-minority. The National Center for Education Statistics projected that America's public schools already became majority-minority in fall of 2014. And yet the average white student attends a school that is nearly three-fourths white; the average Latino student attends a school that is 57% Latino; and the average African American student attends a school that is nearly half African American. More than one in three African American children attend a 90–100% minority school, and the percentage of African American students attending these high-density minority schools in the Northeast has actually increased since 1968 (from 42.7% in 1968 to 51.4% in 2011). More and more, this nation is retreating—or being concentrated—into enclaves of "our own kind."

It would be simplistic to lay the weight of all of our society's ills on the shoulders of racial isolation in our schools. But when we are faced with images of race riots in our streets or when we listen to the vitriol spewed at immigrants and their children, can we honestly tell ourselves that none of this hatred or fear is born out of the distance between us? The social and civic mission of schools was once more widely accepted. In the early days of public education, advocates touted schools as training grounds for future citizens—places where the values and knowledge necessary to function in our democratic society could be instilled. Today, our society is becoming increasingly diverse, and that fact will not change just because we refuse to confront it. To be prepared for success in a pluralistic democracy—to be prepared to address the challenges of stereotype, racism, and inequality of resources and opportunities that such a democracy faces—we must learn how to build relationships across racial and ethnic boundaries. Integrated schools can help us do this. They can teach our children to appreciate rather than avoid difference and to understand more fully how similar we really are. Integrated schools can lead, slowly but surely, to a more integrated and just society.

The question becomes—how do we do it? The answer is, of course, as complex as the history that brought us here. This volume captures that complexity. It dismisses the notion that the issue is as simple as "black and white," beginning with a personal and legal exploration of *Mendez v. Westminster* and the educational challenges unique to Latino and Latina students. It details the triumph and tragedies of *Brown* and tells the story of the Civil Rights Act from its roots on the steps of Little Rock Central High School to the tests it faces in the modern era. It provides a sobering review of the Supreme Court's dismantling of the toolkit available to combat racial isolation, from *Milliken* to *Missouri v. Jenkins* to *Parents Involved*. And it turns to the future—to the paths, legal, grassroots, and otherwise, through which we can continue to pursue racial and ethnic equality.

But most importantly, it helps to spark a conversation this nation must have. We have to remove our heads from the sand, accept that separate simply cannot be equal, and start to find a way to come together. The responsibility lies squarely with us. The legacies of *Brown* and *Mendez* do not lie in decisions issued by two courts decades ago; they live in the ongoing struggle for justice this book recounts and in the future it begs us to build.

James E. Ryan is the Dean and Charles William Eliot Professor at the Harvard Graduate School of Education.

KRISTI L. BOWMAN

Introduction

ANNIVERSARIES ARE OFTEN CAUSE FOR REFLECTION AND 2014—THE SIXTIETH anniversary of *Brown v. Board of Education*[1] and the fiftieth of the federal Civil Rights Act[2]—was no different. As we looked back on those two momentous events in U.S. history, we celebrated, criticized, and argued about how far we have come and how far we have yet to go. Over the course of twenty-four chapters, the commentary in this volume captures many of those conversations. Taken together, the chapters trace the narrative arc of school desegregation.

In some ways it is obvious that this volume is part of a discussion that began long ago and that will continue many years in the future—that is the nature of the pursuit of equality, educational or otherwise. But this volume is also part of larger conversations about the significance of law, the importance of education, and the potential to reform educational institutions through law. As such, it is informed by several interrelated premises. First, law and society are in a dynamic relationship and thus constantly influence one another.[3] Second, the meaning of "equality" changes over time, and where a line is drawn can turn something unfair into something unconstitutional overnight.[4] Third, a robust debate exists about the extent to which courts can create social change, with some arguing that litigation victories should be broadly construed, including changing the course of a social movement or influencing policy.[5] Fourth, to engage questions of educational equality effectively, a multidisciplinary approach is necessary, as is a discussion of housing segregation.[6] Fifth and finally, the experiences of people whose education is shaped by the law, and who themselves shape the law, matter.[7] Their stories are important and their voices should be heard.

Accordingly, some of the contributing authors were parties to and attorneys in some of the most significant educational equality cases in U.S. history; many others are leading scholars in law, education, sociology, and public policy. They write from a diversity of perspectives and about a range of issues, and thus make the complexity of the past, present, and future of school desegregation come alive. The pursuit of racial and ethnic equality in education has a complicated history, yet it is also one that is necessary to understand if we are to fully appreciate the space we occupy today.

This volume begins at a point in time and in a place where school desegregation started to gain momentum, in the early 1940s in California. Specifically, we enter the story of the pursuit of educational equality during World War II, when Japanese Americans, including the Munemitsu family in Westminster, California, were forced out of their homes and into internment camps. During the Munemitsus' absence, they rented their farm to Gonzalo and Felícitas Méndez. When the Méndezes sought to enroll their children in the local schools, they were told that their children could not attend Westminster Main Elementary—they should instead attend the "Mexican" school in town. Eventually, the Méndez family and others sued school districts engaged in this practice and in 1946 won a judgment against the districts in *Mendez v. Westminster*.[8] This was the first school desegregation victory for plaintiffs in federal court. Although the precedent created by the decision was binding only in one area of California, the decision was used by many across the state to dismantle the system of separate schools for children of Mexican heritage. In chapter 1, Judge Frederick Aguirre powerfully recounts his own family's history of immigration and segregation and also discusses how his father used the *Mendez* decision to integrate the local schools shortly before Aguirre began kindergarten. In chapter 2, political scientist Philippa Strum draws together historical research and extensive interviews with members of the Méndez family and others to tell the story of *Mendez* in wonderful detail, bringing both the people and the litigation to life. In chapter 3, I discuss the complicated relationship Latinos and Latinas have had with school desegregation from the *Mendez* litigation through the present day and also examine how that relationship has intersected with both immigration law and English-language instruction rights. Together, these chapters ensure that the Méndezes' story is not lost to history, and that we consider Latinos and Latinas not only as part of the present complexity of school desegregation, but also as an important part of the foundation of school desegregation.

In addition to setting into motion the events that would result in *Mendez*, the World War II era influenced the course of school desegregation in many other ways as well. For example: the Supreme Court became increasingly protective of civil rights and started to question *Plessy v. Ferguson*'s "separate but equal" definition of equality;[9] African Americans, especially veterans returning from overseas, began to register to vote and to exercise the franchise in significant numbers, though often in the face of great resistance and violence;[10] and the Supreme Court struck down restrictive housing covenants and invalidated segregation in higher education.[11] In sum, as law professor Michael Klarman has written, "World War II was a watershed in U.S. race relations. The changes in racial attitudes and practices that occurred in the 1940s were more rapid and fundamental than any that had taken place since Reconstruction."[12] Yet, across the country, laws still sanctioned and in some states still required children to be educated separately based on their race.

When the 1950s began, so too did the protests and lawsuits that would eventually lead to the Court's unanimous decision in 1954: *Brown v. Board of Education*.[13] Through the *Brown* decision, the Supreme Court changed the definition of equality, overturning *Plessy* in the context of public schooling. The reaction to *Brown* across much of the American South was appropriately named Massive Resistance, but eventually *Brown* itself became the culture. Today, *Brown* is one of the few Supreme Court decisions most Americans know regardless of their level of education or profession, and it is frequently cited in civil rights and human rights decisions by courts around the world.[14]

Much has been said about *Brown* and this volume captures that discussion and adds to it. In chapter 4, Brown Foundation founding president Cheryl Brown Henderson poignantly remembers the Topeka NAACP's crucial role in the litigation and discusses her family's experiences as the lead plaintiffs in the case. In chapter 5, law professor and former NAACP General Counsel Jack Greenberg, who was one of the attorneys in *Brown*, reflects on *Brown* after the passage of many decades and persuasively concludes that *Brown*'s most important legacy is to have shifted culture by displacing the norm of state-sanctioned segregation. This culture shift did not happen quickly, though, and in chapter 6, education professor Patricia Edwards bravely tells us what the implementation of *Brown* was like by recounting her understandably formative experience as one of the second group of African American children to integrate a formerly all-white high school in Albany, Georgia. In chapter 7, law professor Wendy Parker asks whether school desegregation became easier to realize over time, walking us through the litigation in the four school districts whose school desegregation lawsuits were consolidated into *Brown* and litigation in the Middle District of Alabama, insightfully concluding that although social resistance eventually retreated, the isolation of the judiciary has remained a substantial obstacle to desegregation.

As some of those chapters note, the reaction to *Brown* and to school integration across much of the American South was often intensely hostile and sometimes also violent. The integration of Little Rock Central High School in 1957 exemplifies Massive Resistance, and in chapter 8, former FBI agent John ("Jack") Feeheley recounts with vivid detail his experience as an undercover agent on the scene of the weeks-long integration standoff in Little Rock. The school integration battles there and in other communities were part of the radicalization of Southern politics, and thus part of what demonstrated the necessity of the federal Civil Rights Act of 1964.[15]

Ten years after the Court decided *Brown*, the federal Civil Rights Act cleared the way for the federal government to enforce that decision by allowing the attorney general of the United States to become a plaintiff in a school desegregation case (thus removing that burden from private parties and the nonprofit organizations who had mainly litigated the cases), and by prohibiting racial discrimination in schools that receive federal funds—including not only intentional discrimination, but also government action that has a disparate impact on students.[16] Although often overlooked in favor of a focus on the Supreme Court's decisions, these aspects of the Civil Rights Act have been extraordinarily significant not only in actually desegregating schools, but also in enabling the federal government to continue to combat racial and ethnic inequality as times change. In chapter 9, Allison Brown, a program officer at Open Society Foundations and former Department of Justice attorney, writes compellingly about the contemporary use of Title VI to challenge racial and ethnic disparities in school discipline and proposes ways to reclaim the power of the Act as we move forward. In chapter 10, law professor Derek Black analyzes the Court's 2002 decision in *Alexander v. Sandoval*, which significantly limited the power of Title VI, and offers three nuanced and much-needed proposals to restore Title VI to its original strength.

Thus in the first section of this book, we see that *Mendez, Brown*, and the Civil Rights Act formed a promise of equality. In the second section, we see that the Court stepped back from that promise as school desegregation took hold in the North and the contours of appropriate remedies played out in litigation involving Detroit and Kansas City, and as the voluntary integration policies adopted in Seattle, Washington, and Louisville, Kentucky, were overturned by the Court.

In 1974, by the time the Court decided *Milliken v. Bradley*,[17] it had recognized that intentional segregation could happen even in the absence of statutes requiring or permitting it, which had been prevalent across the South. *Milliken* arose out of Detroit; the district court found that the state and the school district had engaged in unconstitutional action and ordered a cross-district remedy given the racially-isolated nature of the district, and the state's involvement in creating racial isolation. The Court's 1974 decision, the first of its two in the *Milliken* litigation, prohibited the district court from using an inter-district remedy for what it determined were intra-district harms. In chapter 11, retired Judge Nathaniel Jones, who was the NAACP General Counsel at the time of *Milliken*, provides an important window into the NAACP's legal strategy in the case, discussion of the trial, and somber reflections on the Court's decision. In chapter 12, political science professor Joyce Baugh discusses the many dynamics which produced metropolitan areas dominated by residential segregation, and perceptively analyzes the residential and school segregation that came to dominate Detroit by the early 1970s and set the stage for the *Milliken* litigation. *Milliken*'s impact should not be underestimated: in chapter 13, public policy professor Charles Clotfelter convincingly shows that most racial and ethnic isolation in schools today is across district lines, not within districts, and specifically examines school districts in North Carolina. Because *Milliken* prohibits cross-district remedies in the absence of cross-district harm, much of the racial isolation in schools today is beyond the reach of courts.

The *Milliken* case influenced school desegregation remedies across the country, and one of those was in Kansas City, Missouri. The Supreme Court issued three decisions in the Kansas City desegregation litigation, *Missouri v. Jenkins*,[18] the last of which was in 1995. Because the district court could not mandate cross-district integration after *Milliken*, it tried to incentivize white students from surrounding suburban school districts to enroll in the primarily black Kansas City schools by creating exceptional and unique programs. In 1995, the Supreme Court rejected this approach, which it termed "desegregative attractiveness." In chapter 14, the attorney who argued for the state of Missouri before the Supreme Court, John Munich, engagingly shares a first-hand perspective about developing the state's strategy in briefs and for oral argument, and summarizes the state's success in *Jenkins*. In chapter 15, sociologist Kevin Fox Gotham provides crucial context for understanding *Jenkins* by presenting a detailed history of school and housing segregation in Kansas City. In chapter 16, I analyze the legacy of *Jenkins* as seen through over 100 education rights judicial decisions issued since 1995.

After the Court decided three cases about unitary status in the 1990s, including *Jenkins*, more and more school districts were declared unitary and released from court oversight. Many of these districts returned to student assignment systems based on neighborhood schools. Because of existing residential segregation, racial and ethnic isolation in schools often increased. Some school districts in this situation, and also some districts that had never been under court order, employed student assignment plans with the goal of having individual schools reflect the diversity of their communities. Soon after the turn of the millennium, the Court issued decisions that were increasingly skeptical of affirmative action in higher education and race-conscious decision making in higher education admissions.[19] Eventually, the Court agreed to review two cases in which school districts employed voluntary (not court-ordered) student assignment plans that contained race- and ethnicity-conscious measures. These cases, *Parents Involved in Community Schools v. Seattle School District No. 1* from Seattle, Washington, and *Meredith v. Jefferson County Board of Education* from Louisville, Kentucky, were consolidated for argument and decided as one.[20]

In what has become known as the *Parents Involved* decision, the Court held that school districts could seek to create or maintain racial and ethnic diversity in their schools, but that they could not use means that consider individual students' race and ethnicity to do so. Interestingly, the disagreement between the plurality and the dissent was not over whether *Brown* should be upheld or overruled; it was about who could claim to be upholding the true legacy of *Brown*, those who claimed that *Brown* was about anticlassification or those who said it was about antisubordination.[21] In chapter 17, Byron Leet, the trial attorney who represented Jefferson County, provides insight into the social and legal context for the *Meredith* case, including the community's perhaps unexpected reaction to the *Parents Involved* decision. In chapter 18, law professor and dean Erwin Chemerinsky provides a helpful overview of the *Parents Involved* decision and critiques its effect in curtailing voluntary integration policies. In chapter 19, education professor Michael Dumas argues convincingly that although the *Parents Involved* plurality claims to employ a colorblind approach, in reality it reproduces systematic white advantage in school assignment. Like many other authors in this volume, Dumas also explores the connections between housing and school segregation.

By examining the changes in law and society from *Mendez* through *Parents Involved*, we come to understand where we have been, and thus develop a more nuanced understanding of where we are today. So, how do we make our way forward? The five chapters in the third and final section each help us to consider different aspects of the hard work that is required to live up to the ideals of *Mendez, Brown*, and the Civil Rights Act. Some of the chapters advocate for legal change, others seek to describe or influence what Mark Graber describes as "the course of American constitutional politics," showing "the ways in which elected officials and political movements adjust to the possibilities and challenges created by [a] judicial ruling."[22] Of course, at this point it is not just one judicial decision to which they are reacting, but six decades of Supreme Court caselaw and five decades of federal statutory law.

In chapter 20, law professor and dean Danielle Holley-Walker analyzes Southern school districts' response to *Parents Involved*, identifying four types of voluntary integration plans used by those districts. She also helpfully provides a range of policy suggestions to help school districts create or maintain greater diversity in their schools. In chapter 21, education professors Erica Frankenberg and Sarah Diem examine the importance of school boards in enacting voluntary integration and other equity-focused policies through a nuanced study of the school district in Louisville, Kentucky, that gave rise to the *Meredith* litigation. In chapter 22, MALDEF regional counsel David Hinojosa and attorney Karolina Walters explain with great thoroughness the track record of school finance litigation in terms of creating greater educational opportunities for students of color, and identify ways to work around three common roadblocks so that school finance litigation is better able to help us live up to the promise of *Brown*. In chapter 23, education professor Benjamin Superfine and post-doctoral researcher Jessica Gottlieb critically analyze two aspects of education reform sweeping statehouses across the country—teacher evaluation and collective bargaining reforms—and, significantly, examine the potential of those reforms to advance the goals of *Brown* and the Civil Rights Act. Finally, in chapter 24, the capstone of this volume, education professor and cofounder and codirector of the Civil Rights Project/Proyecto Derechos Civiles Gary Orfield perceptively synthesizes the desegregation efforts of the past sixty years, extracting lessons to help us move forward in our vibrant multiracial, multiethnic present.

To be sure, our laws and our society have come a long way since *Mendez, Brown*, and the Civil Rights Act, and the changes that are required to move forward are not all changes that law can produce. But when I see that substantial racial and ethnic achievement gaps persist, that children of color drop out of school more frequently than white children, that our children rarely grow up in schools that reflect the true diversity of our communities, that even very young children of color are suspended and expelled at higher rates than white children, that funding disparities among school districts hamstring districts also burdened by higher student poverty and lower property values, that children are often isolated in their schools by race, ethnicity, poverty, and language, that disadvantage far beyond children's control harms their educational opportunities in so many ways—when I see any of these things and especially when I consider all of them together, I am not satisfied with where we are.[23] Are you?

Kristi L. Bowman is a Professor of Law at Michigan State University, College of Law.

NOTES

1. Brown v. Board of Education, 347 U.S. 485 (1954).

2. Civil Rights Act of 1964, Pub. L. No. 88-352, 78 Stat. 241 (codified as amended in scattered sections of 2 U.S.C., 28 U.S.C., and 42 U.S.C.).

3. See, for example, Robert Post, *Law and Cultural Conflict*, 78 CHICAGO-KENT LAW REVIEW 485, 490 (2003).

4. Jack M. Balkin, Plessy, Brown, *and* Grutter: *A Play in Three Acts*, 26 CARDOZO LAW REVIEW 101, 103 (2005).

5. GERALD ROSENBERG, THE HOLLOW HOPE: CAN COURTS BRING ABOUT SOCIAL CHANGE? (University of Chicago Press 1991); Thomas B. Stoddard, *Bleeding Heart: Reflections on Using the Law to Make Social Change*, 72 NEW YORK UNIVERSITY LAW REVIEW 967, 977–78, 990 (1997); Mary Ziegler, *Framing Change: Cause Lawyering, Constitutional Decisions, and Social Change*, 94 MARQUETTE LAW REVIEW 263, 310 (2010); Scott Barclay, Lynn C. Jones & Anna-Maria Marshall, *Two Spinning Wheels: Studying Law and Social Movements*, 54 STUDIES IN LAW, POLITICS, & SOCIETY 1, 3 (2011); Mark A. Graber, *Hollow Hopes and Exaggerated Fears: The Canon/Anticanon in Context*, 125 HARVARD LAW REVIEW FORUM 33, 37 (2011).

6. GARY ORFIELD & SUSAN EATON, DISMANTLING DESEGREGATION: THE QUIET REVERSAL OF *BROWN V. BOARD OF EDUCATION*, 149–51 (The New Press 1996).

7. See, for example, PATRICIA WILLIAMS, THE ALCHEMY OF RACE AND RIGHTS 3–14 and throughout (Harvard University Press 1991).

8. Mendez v. Westminster, 64 F. Supp. 544 (S.D. Cal. *1946*), affirmed, 161 F.2d 774 (9th Cir. 1947) (en banc); PHILIPPA STRUM, *MENDEZ V. WESTMINSTER*: SCHOOL DESEGREGATION AND MEXICAN-AMERICAN RIGHTS (University Press of Kansas 2010).

9. Plessy v. Ferguson, 163 U.S. 537 (1896); MICHAEL KLARMAN, FROM JIM CROW TO CIVIL RIGHTS 231 (Oxford University Press 2004).

10. KLARMAN, FROM JIM CROW, 236–52.

11. Shelley v. Kramer, 334 U.S. 1 (1948); Sweatt v. Painter, 339 U.S. 629 (1950).

12. KLARMAN, FROM JIM CROW, 288.

13. Brown, 347 U.S. 485.

14. MARTHA MINOW, IN *BROWN'S* WAKE: LEGACIES OF AMERICA'S EDUCATIONAL LANDMARK (Oxford University Press 2010).

15. KLARMAN, FROM JIM CROW, 392-93.

16. Civil Rights Act of 1964; GARY ORFIELD, THE RECONSTRUCTION OF SOUTHERN EDUCATION: THE SCHOOLS AND THE 1964 CIVIL RIGHTS ACT (John Wiley 1969).

17. Milliken v. Bradley, 418 U.S. 717 (1974); PAUL R. DIMOND, BEYOND BUSING: REFLECTIONS ON URBAN SEGREGATION, THE COURTS, AND EQUAL OPPORTUNITY (University of Michigan Press 2005); JOYCE BAUGH, THE DETROIT SCHOOL BUSING CASE: *MILLIKEN V. BRADLEY* AND THE CONTROVERSY OVER DESEGREGATION (University Press of Kansas 2011).

18. Missouri v. Jenkins, 491 U.S. 274 (1989); 495 U.S. 33 (1990); 515 U.S. 70 (1995).

19. Gratz v. Bollinger, 539 U.S. 244 (2003); Grutter v. Bollinger, 539 U.S. 306 (2003).

20. Parents Involved in Community Schools v. Seattle School District No. 1, 551 U.S. 701 (2007).

21. Reva Siegel, *Equality Talk: Antisubordination and Anticlassification Values in Constitutional Struggles Over* Brown, 117 HARVARD LAW REVIEW 1470 (2004).

22. Mark A. Graber, *Hollow Hopes and Exaggerated Fears: The Canon/Anticanon in Context*, 125 HARVARD LAW REVIEW FORUM 33, 37 (2011).

23. See generally PRUDENCE L. CARTER & KEVIN G. WELNER, EDS., CLOSING THE OPPORTUNITY GAP: WHAT AMERICA MUST DO TO GIVE EVERY CHILD AN EVEN CHANCE (Oxford University Press 2013); Gary Orfield & Erica Frankenberg, The Civil Rights Project, Brown *at 60: Great Progress, a Long Retreat, and an Uncertain Future* (2014); CHARLES T. CLOTFELTER, AFTER *BROWN*: THE RISE AND RETREAT OF SCHOOL DESEGREGATION (Princeton University Press 2004); CHARLES J. OGLETREE, JR., ALL DELIBERATE SPEED 260 (W.W. Norton & Company 2004).

PART I

Mendez, Brown,
and the Civil Rights Act

Mendez v. Westminster

64 F.Supp. 544 (S.D. Cal. 1946)

THE HONORABLE FREDERICK P. AGUIRRE

Standing on the Shoulders
of *Mendez v. Westminster*

IN 2014 WE CELEBRATED THE 60TH ANNIVERSARY OF *BROWN V. BOARD OF Education*,[1] undoubtedly the most important civil rights case of the last century. Chief Justice Earl Warren, writing for a unanimous United States Supreme Court in *Brown*, fervently stated that "separate educational facilities are inherently unequal," eventually ordering that all public schools of our nation integrate their classrooms "with all deliberate speed."[2] Over the last half century, *Brown's* sound logic has been extended to housing, employment, voting rights, transportation, public accommodations, parks and recreations, and it initiated a torrent of court decisions and legislation that expanded and protected individual liberties not only for persons of color, but moreover for women, gays and lesbians, the elderly, and our disabled.

Few people know, however, that the 1946 Orange County case of *Mendez v. Westminster*,[3] affirmed on appeal in the Ninth Circuit, provided a key link in the evolutionary chain of school desegregation cases culminating in *Brown v. Board of Education*. The judges found that the Westminster, Santa Ana, Garden Grove, and El Modena (Orange) school districts systematically and intentionally segregated Mexican American children into separate schools solely because of their surname and/or the color of their skin. Therefore the courts ordered the cessation of that unconstitutional conduct. *Mendez* was the first federal court case to hold that separate schools for children of color were not equal; therefore, such conduct violated their constitutional rights. Although *Mendez* is not cited in *Brown*, the National Association for the Advancement of Colored People (NAACP) filed a friend-of-the-court brief in *Mendez* and used *Mendez* as a test case to attempt to topple the "separate but equal" doctrine in public education. Moreover, I know about *Mendez* because it affected me personally. Were it not for the lawsuit I would have attended the same segregated "Mexican" school in Placentia, California, that my father, uncles, aunts, and cousins had to attend.

Like thousands of other Mexicans during the Mexican Revolution (1910–1920), my grandparents came from Mexico and settled in Placentia in 1918. At that time, one grammar school, Bradford Avenue Elementary, served the small city of approximately 800 residents and the neighboring ranches. My uncle and aunt attended Bradford until 1922 when the school board decided to use scarce public funds to construct another grammar school, Baker Street School, a mere five blocks from Bradford. All Mexican American children, including my father, uncles, aunts, and cousins, who are all American-born, were ordered to attend Baker Street School, and all "white" children were instructed to attend Bradford. "White" families like the Hapners, Carltons, Franklins, Steens, Edwardsons, and others lived within two blocks of Baker, but were directed to Bradford, which was a superior school in terms of facilities and teachers. There were no "white" children at Baker. They were all Mexican American. Even the school bus that would pick up "white" and Mexican American children from Santa Ana Canyon and the Richfield area would dutifully leave the "white" children at Bradford and the Mexican American children at Baker.

Then, during World War II, in order to keep Mexican American students from attending Valencia High School, all ninth- and tenth-grade Mexican American children were directed to La Jolla Junior High School. In that manner, those students effectively were discouraged from graduating from high school. My uncles and aunts were forced to board the bus for the one-mile trip to La Jolla, instead of being allowed to walk five blocks to Valencia High School.

By 1948, my father, Alfred V. Aguirre, had served in World War II and then returned home. He formed "Veterans and Citizens of Placentia," a group composed of Mexican American World War II veterans that quickly registered over 300 Placentia citizens to vote. Also in 1948, my father and Ted Duran, a member of the group, consulted with G. W. Marshall, a prominent Los Angeles attorney. They asked Marshall if the 1946 *Mendez v. Westminster*[4] decision could be used to end segregation of Mexican American children in Placentia's schools. Marshall counseled that the same legal principles applied; therefore, such a lawsuit would be successful. But Marshall advised that the group should petition the Placentia School Board one more time before filing the lawsuit. Under threat of a lawsuit, the school officials relented and opened Bradford Elementary School to all students. In 1949, the "Mexican" school closed due to lack of attendance. I entered kindergarten at Bradford in 1951, thus escaping being forced to attend the "Mexican" school.

Since 1971 I have been an attorney, and since 2002 I have been a judge. Because my own experiences are built on the foundations of *Mendez* and *Brown*, I appreciate that *Mendez* and *Brown* exemplify the best in our American cultural values: courage and fairness. The cases displayed the courage of Gonzalo and Felícitas Méndez, of Reverend Oliver Brown, and all the other parents in the *Mendez* lawsuit and the *Brown* lawsuits to challenge the racist educational system through the courts for the benefit of their children and all other children, and the courage of the judges in rendering unpopular, yet morally and legally fair opinions. The cases are a testament to the fairness that can be found in our legal system. Our country displays that rare quality of being able to heal itself, most of the time, from within, without resort to violence and bloodshed. Racism and other important issues have been overcome or resolved largely through our courts where justice ultimately prevails. All of this has culminated in the metamorphic evolution of our society from an ugly caterpillar into a beautiful, multicolored butterfly.

That is the true legacy of *Mendez* and *Brown*.

Frederick P. Aguirre is a judge of the Superior Court, Orange County, California. This piece is excerpted from his article *Mendez v. Westminster School District: How it Affected Brown v. Board of Education*, which first appeared in ORANGE COUNTY LAWYER, February 2005 (Vol. 47 No. 2), p. 30. *Mendez v. Westminster School District: How it Affected Brown v. Board of Education* was also previously published in 4 JOURNAL OF HISPANIC HIGHER EDUCATION 321 (2005).

NOTES

The views expressed herein are those of the author. They do not necessarily represent the views of ORANGE COUNTY LAWYER magazine, the Orange County Bar Association, the Orange County Bar Association Charitable Fund, or their staffs, contributors, or advertisers. All legal and other issues must be independently researched.

1. Brown v. Board of Education, 347 U.S. 483, 494 (1954).
2. Ibid., 495; Brown v. Board of Education, 349 U.S. 294, 301 (1955).
3. Mendez v. Westminster, 64 F. Supp. 544 (S.D. Cal. 1946), *affirmed on appeal*, Westminster v. Mendez, 161 F.2d 774 (9th Cir. 1947).
4. Ibid.

PHILIPPA STRUM

Our Children Are Americans
Mendez v. Westminster and Mexican American Rights

Gonzalo Méndez and his wife Felícitas Méndez were running a café in the small southern California city of Santa Ana when World War II began. The two had met as farm workers in nearby Westminster, in the heart of citrus-growing country. The café was thriving but Gonzalo had long dreamed of running a farm of his own. When the Munemitsus, the Japanese American owners of a farm in Westminster, were sent to a relocation camp and worried about what would happen to the farm during their absence, the Méndezes leased it until the Munemitsus could return. That is why the Méndezes moved back to Westminster, where in 1943 they tried to enroll their three children—Sylvia Méndez, Gonzalo Méndez Jr., and Jerome Méndez—in school.[1]

Their neighborhood school was Westminster Main, an imposing, well-equipped building surrounded by manicured trees and shrubs.[2] The children were turned away at the schoolhouse door when they were taken to register, however, and told they would have to go to Hoover, the small poorly equipped "Mexican" school a few blocks away.[3] Their last name was Mexican; their skin was dark; Westminster Main didn't want them.[4] Two years later the Méndezes would lead a group of Mexican American parents into federal court, challenging the segregation of their children, and legal history would be made. The case would become the first occasion on which a federal court declared that, in education, "separate but equal" was not equal at all.[5]

Mexican Americans and Segregated Education:
The Context for the *Mendez* Case

Mexicans like Gonzalo Méndez had immigrated to the United States in large numbers during the first decades of the twentieth century.[6] Pushed out of Mexico by the political and economic turmoil of its revolution, they were attracted as well by the burgeoning agricultural industry in the Southwest.[7] Railroads had expanded into the American West in the decades after the end of the American Civil War. Simultaneously, advances in irrigation enabled western growers to produce large quantities of fruits and vegetables, which could be transported in the newly invented refrigerator cars on the railroads that now crisscrossed the United States.[8] The result was a much-increased need for cheap labor among both the growers and the railroads.[9]

Official census figures indicated that 661,538 Mexicans entered the United States between 1910 and 1930. Scholars, however, estimate that more than one million came during those years, many of them illegally.[10] By the mid-1920s, Mexican workers constituted the bulk of farm laborers throughout the citrus groves of southern California, the area where the Méndezes would bring their case to court, and accounted for three-quarters of all California farmworkers.[11] By 1930 Mexicans picked more than 80% of the Southwest's crops.[12]

Many of the immigrants settled in poorer neighborhoods—*colonias*—next to citrus groves or vegetable fields, on the outskirts of cities such as Santa Ana, California.[13] Santa Ana is the county seat of Orange County, where the *Mendez* story takes place. They found themselves in neighborhoods that for the most part lacked sewers, gas for cooking and heating, paved streets, or sidewalks. Many families built their own two-room wooden houses. There was little furniture and no refrigerators; heat came from wood-burning kitchen stoves. Clothes were made on pedal-powered sewing machines and cleaned in washtubs. With dirt streets, a lack of flush toilets, and inadequate plumbing and heating, it was difficult to maintain good sanitation. Tuberculosis was a constant threat and affected the Mexican American community at a rate three to five times that of the Anglo community. A survey undertaken in the late 1920s found that the average Mexican couple had buried two children, and many had buried three or more. Wages earned in the citrus groves were substandard, far below the national average, and unemployment was common.[14]

The laborers' children were sent to "Mexican" schools. A nineteenth-century California law specifically gave school districts the authority to create separate schools for "Indian children, excepting children of Indians who are wards of the United States government and children of all other Indians who are descendants of the original American Indians of the United States, and for children of Chinese,

Japanese or Mongolian parentage."[15] The law was enacted before the large-scale Mexican immigration and did not mention Mexicans, but local school authorities interpreted it as a state endorsement of segregated education and acted accordingly when the number of Mexican and Mexican American children increased. Once that happened, school boards began creating "Mexican" schools. By the mid-1920s, there were 15 such schools in Orange County, all but one located in the citrus-growing areas that would be involved in *Mendez v. Westminster.*[16] By 1927 Mexican and Mexican American children—64,427 of them—constituted nearly 10% of all children enrolled in California's public schools, and the 2,869 who were enrolled in Orange County made up 17% of that county's public school population.[17] According to one survey, by 1931 more than 80% of all California school districts with a significant number of Mexican (non-American citizen) and Mexican American students were segregated, usually through the careful drawing of school-zone boundaries by school boards that had been pressured by Anglo residents.[18]

The students in the "Mexican" schools were taught a curriculum quite different from the one offered to Anglo children. The boys studied gardening, bootmaking, blacksmithing, and carpentry to prepare them for the low-paying trades that school authorities assumed would be the only ones such boys could or should follow. The girls studied sewing and homemaking. Their studies took place in substandard buildings, with books and equipment cast off by the Anglo schools.[19] Many of the Mexican schools opened at 7:30 in the morning and ended the day at 12:30, so the children could go to work in the citrus or walnut groves.[20] Teachers and principals were paid markedly less than those in Anglo schools.[21] The unsurprising result was that many students had to repeat grades and gradually dropped out of school altogether. Isabel Martínez's graduation from Fullerton High School in 1931 was so unusual—she was the first Mexican American ever to graduate—that it was written up in the local newspaper.[22]

The rationale for the segregation was twofold. One justification was the children's presumed lack of English. There was, however, no systematic testing of their language skills. As was the case with the Méndez children, students were simply assigned to the Mexican schools on the basis of their last names or their skin color.[23] The second justification was biological determinism. Mexicans had only 58.1% of Anglo students' ability to pursue academic courses, the superintendent of schools in Ontario, California, asserted. "As the Mexicans show considerable aptitude for hand work of any kind, courses should be developed that will aid them in becoming skilled workers with their hands," he continued. "Girls should be trained to become domestic servants, and to do various kinds of hand work for which they can be paid adequately after they leave school."[24] He was not alone. California educator Grace Stanley asserted, in an influential 1920 article entitled "Special School for Mexicans," that Mexican children were happiest in segregated schools where they could thrive with other unfortunates just like themselves. She added that Mexican children had "different mental characteristics" than Anglo children, "showed a stronger sense of rhythm," and "are primarily interested in action and emotion but grow listless under purely mental effort."[25] Other scholars opined solemnly that Mexican children's IQs were far below those of Anglo students.[26]

The Litigation

A CASE TAKES SHAPE

Parents of children in the *colonias* knew that their children's only hope for escape from poverty lay in education. "Our children, all of our children, brown, black, and white, must have the opportunity to be whatever they want to be, and education gives them that opportunity," Felícitas Méndez would say.[27] Many *colonia* parents in Orange County and other parts of California tried to get their children into "Anglo" schools. The *Mendez* trial would demonstrate the refusal of school authorities to acquiesce.[28] Gonzalo Méndez, for example, went to Westminster Main the day after his children were turned away and spoke to the principal, but his children were still not permitted to register. The following day he went to the Westminster school board, where he was equally unsuccessful. Eventually he went to the Orange County school board, again to no avail.[29]

These failures made the Méndezes no less determined to end what they saw as a flagrant injustice. One of their workers told them about attorney David Marcus, a son of Jewish immigrants who had himself experienced anti-Semitism and ran a practice devoted in part to civil liberties cases.[30] Marcus had recently won a case in nearby San Bernardino admitting Mexican Americans to the city's only public park and swimming pool.[31] He suggested that Méndez's case would be stronger if it could be shown that not only Westminster but other school districts in Orange County as well segregated Mexican American students.[32] Was there evidence of that?

Méndez and Marcus began roaming the county, interviewing parents and pulling evidence together. They quickly uncovered the endemic nature of the segregation, as well as the fact that other parents had also protested without success. Some had been told that their children had to be kept out of the Anglo schools because they were dirty; others, that their children knew no English.[33] Some *colonia* families were fearful of having anything to do with the lawsuit Méndez and Marcus were planning; others, however, were excited. The high wartime price of agricultural products meant that the Méndezes could provide much of the money for Marcus's fee and for expenses. Litigation was costly, however, and once four families in the three additional school districts of El Modena, Garden Grove, and Santa Ana agreed to join the suit, volunteers went door to door, collecting a dollar at a time.[34]

While the two men were putting the case together, the Méndezes followed the law by enrolling their children in Westminster's Mexican school. Sylvia Mendez remembered having to eat lunch sitting on the ground outside, because the school had no cafeteria. The school abutted a cow pasture with an electrified wire fence, and that worried her father. Worse, as far as Sylvia was concerned, were the flies that, attracted by the food, settled on the children and their lunches.[35]

Once the plaintiffs were on hand, Marcus had to decide whether to take the *Mendez* case into state court or federal court. Because the California education law permitted the segregation of Indian and Asian students but did not mention Mexican Americans, Marcus could have argued in state court that the Orange County educators were violating state law by adding to it a group of people without authority. That approach, however, assuming it was successful, would have left the door open for California legislators to rewrite the law to include Mexicans. Marcus and the plaintiff families had another reason for bringing the case in federal court. Their concern was not the violation of California law; it was segregation itself. Marcus had won the San Bernardino park case on the basis of the Equal Protection clause of the U.S. Constitution's Fourteenth Amendment.[36] The Méndezes and the other plaintiffs believed that segregated schools violated both their rights, as American citizens, to obtain for their children the best education offered by the government, and their children's rights to have access to that education. "We always tell our children they are Americans," Felícitas Méndez would tell the trial court, "and I feel I am American myself, and so is my husband, and we thought that they shouldn't be segregated like that, they shouldn't be treated the way they are."[37] Marcus planned to bring the case as a class action. If *Mendez* succeeded, the segregation of Mexican American children might conceivably be outlawed throughout California and the nation. Initially, a ruling in the Méndezes' favor would of course apply only to the four Orange County districts. If the districts appealed that decision, however, and if the losing side in the appeals court decided to take the case further, it could wind up in the U.S. Supreme Court.

The problem was *Plessy v. Ferguson*,[38] the 1896 case in which the Supreme Court declared that separate but equal facilities were constitutional, and the subsequent Supreme Court cases that specifically endorsed race-segregated education.[39] The Supreme Court and lower federal courts seemed so unlikely to revisit *Plessy* that in the mid-1940s, when Marcus was planning strategy, the NAACP considered the time not yet ripe to challenge *Plessy*.[40] Marcus decided to take another tack: He would claim that the Mendez case was not about race at all.

THE CASE BEGINS: PRE-TRIAL HEARING

The petition Marcus filed on March 2, 1945 with the District Court for the Southern District of California bore the names of five families in four Orange County school districts and was brought against the districts, their superintendents, and their school boards. It identified the families and their children as American citizens "of Mexican or Latin descent."[41] The question at issue, Marcus would insist throughout the litigation, was not whether the four Orange County school districts segregated students on the basis of race. There was no *racial* segregation, he would tell the court, because Mexicans were members of the white race. The Fourteenth Amendment's Equal Protection clause was being violated by school districts keeping white children from being educated with other white children purely on the basis of ethnicity.[42]

Marcus could make the whiteness claim because the U.S. government classified Mexicans as white. In 1930, after having implicitly assumed for some years that Mexican Americans were white, the U.S. Census Bureau created a new category of "Mexican." The Mexican government was outraged and in 1940, with the Roosevelt administration worried about international relations at a time of impending war, the bureau eliminated the category for Mexicans who were not "definitely Indian or of other nonwhite race."[43] It might be noted that nothing could be better proof of the artificiality of racial categories than the fact that with a few strokes of a pen, Mexicans were white in 1929, nonwhite in 1930, and white again in 1940.

The case was assigned to Judge Paul J. McCormick. As he became the first federal court judge to challenge the separate but equal doctrine, it is worth examining precisely who he was.

McCormick was born in New York City in 1879 and moved to California in 1887. He was initially in private practice, remaining there until he was appointed a deputy district attorney in 1905. Five years later, Governor James N. Gillette named him to fill a position on the California Superior Court in Los Angeles. McCormick was subsequently elected to the court and then reelected, ultimately serving for 13 years and adjudicating civil, criminal, and probate cases. President Calvin Coolidge appointed him to the U.S. District Court for the Southern District of California in Los Angeles in 1924, and he remained on that court on active service until 1951.[44]

McCormick's decisions prior to 1945 reflected a strong moral streak and his solid Catholic faith. In 1923, he was so distressed by what he saw as his duty to pronounce the death sentence on a man convicted of killing a policeman that he consulted his fellow judges beforehand and told the press, "If you had an atheist on the bench he would hang them all. But a man with any religion must feel the awful, tremendous responsibility of such a task."[45] In 1942, with World War II raging, the judge sentenced a conscientious objector to a year in the county jail. "How are we going to insure free exercise of religion," McCormick asked rhetorically from the bench during the sentencing, "if we don't fight for it?"[46] Some years earlier he had written to the RKO movie production company, deploring films that did not contribute to the "social and moral welfare" and recommending the making of more movies such as *Little Women*.[47]

Judge McCormick's Los Angeles courtroom was the scene of relatively mundane citizenship hearings and swearing-in ceremonies but also the swearing-in of actors such as George Sanders and Charles Boyer.[48] In 1939, he dismissed a case in which Charlie Chaplin was accused of plagiarism for his movie *Modern Times*.[49] His docket included a full range of civil and criminal cases and—as in the case of the conscientious objector—his comments from the bench and to the press reflected his beliefs. When he sentenced a Chinese narcotics addict to three years in a federal penitentiary, he said, "It is unfortunate that we have no system of hospitalization for these cases. They are really medical instead of legal problems," thereby indicating that the judge was somewhat ahead of his time. Nonetheless, he demonstrated that in other respects he was very much a man of the moment when he added, "It is particularly vicious to sell narcotics to a white man. Trade in opium between orientals is not as dangerous as this practice."[50] He was firm with people accused of violating Prohibition laws and, as a member of President Herbert Hoover's National Commission on Law Enforcement and Observance, advocated the continuance of Prohibition. He viewed its "outstanding good" as the "abolition of the legalized open saloon." At the same time, McCormick lambasted what he called the "governmental lawlessness" involved in some Prohibition efforts, especially the tendency of law enforcement officers to search homes without a warrant.[51]

Judge McCormick's service on Hoover's commission brought him national attention. So did the part he played in the notorious Teapot Dome scandal, voiding the Pan American Petroleum and Transport Company's contract to the oil in the Elk Hills reserve. His ruling was affirmed by the Ninth Circuit Court of Appeals and by the U.S. Supreme Court.[52]

The jurist who would hear the *Mendez* case, then, was a stern moralist, someone whose feelings about racial differences were mixed at best, a man of stature in his community and in judicial circles generally, and a firm believer in the Constitution. None of that, however, gave any clue as to how he would decide in *Mendez*, and McCormick was in fact not at all certain that the case belonged in his court. He knew that the Constitution gave the federal government no power over education policy, which was implicitly left to the states. The school districts argued that segregated education was legal—the Supreme Court had said so—and all that was at issue was the question of whether the segregation of Mexican American students was warranted. That was a matter of educational policy and so did not belong in federal court. McCormick decided to let the case progress nonetheless while he withheld judgment about his court's jurisdiction.[53]

Marcus, by contrast, was insistent that the court had jurisdiction. His clients had been deprived of their civil rights and the privileges and immunities of American citizens that were guaranteed to each of them by the Constitution and laws of the United States, he asserted. In carrying out a "common plan, design and purpose" to keep the children from specific schools solely because of their "Mexican or Latin descent or extraction," the districts had caused the plaintiffs and their children "great and irreparable damage." He asked the court to declare the practice to be unconstitutional and to issue an injunction prohibiting it.[54]

The lawyer arguing for Orange County was George F. Holden, the Santa Ana County deputy counsel.[55] Holden was a former litigator in private practice, Orange County district attorney, and president of the Orange County bar association. Forty-eight years old in 1945, Holden had behind him years of experience in public office and in litigation as he prepared to face the 41-year-old Marcus.[56] Holden acknowledged that the children in the case were constitutionally entitled to equal treatment, and maintained that they were getting it. The families "of Mexican or Latin descent" in the district spoke Spanish at home, so that their children were "unfamiliar with and unable to speak the English language" when they began school. The districts therefore found it desirable and efficient to educate them separately, the separation being "for the best interests of said pupils of Mexican descent and for the best interests of the English speaking pupils." The Mexican American students were kept in segregated schools "until they acquired some efficiency in the English language." They were taught by teachers with the same qualifications and salary as the teachers in the other schools, and given "all of the facilities and all the instruction" available in them—statements that were patently untrue. The bottom line was that they were being taught separately, but equally, for sound educational reasons, and that they were never separated "solely" because of their ethnicity.[57] He inadvertently implied, however, that the real problem the children faced was that they had been born to Mexican American parents. As he said during the pre-trial hearing,

> Sure, they can speak some English, you know. They have to be able to understand a certain amount of English before they can go from one grade to another, but they cannot grasp it. Where they have lived in the Spanish language, with Spanish customs, and they talk it at home, and as soon as they are out of school they go back to their homes and commence talking. So again, thinking in Spanish, they cannot compete with the other students and advance in the same grade at the same age.[58]

THE TRIAL

The trial began on July 5, 1945. Holden's star witness was James L. Kent, the superintendent of the Garden Grove School District, who agreed absolutely that Mexican American students did not belong in schools with "white" children. In 1941, Kent had written a master's thesis arguing that Mexican Americans were "an alien race that should be segregated socially" and that, happily, segregation had been accomplished in southern California "by designating certain sections where they might live and restricting these sections to them"—in other words, by keeping them out of "white" neighborhoods. "Upon investigation of the mental ability and moral characteristics of the average Mexican school child it is evident that this [housing segregation] is a condition which is advantageous to both the white and Mexican child," he wrote. "Segregation also into separate schools seems to be the ideal situation for both parties concerned."[59] "Mexican" students—whom he repeatedly differentiated from "American" students—were of "a less sturdy stock than the white race" and suffered from health problems as a result of eating nothing but "tortillas, a greasy mixture, or enchiladas and beans."[60] The children suffered from a "racial language handicap," and differences in IQs between the two "races" made it clear that "a separate curriculum . . . based upon their abilities . . . is advisable."[61]

Kent told the court that when Mexican American children first enrolled in school, "We usually find them retarded," meaning unable to work at grade level. Admittedly, some children came to the school speaking English. Of those, "the large percentage of them can speak the English language, or they can understand it, but that does not necessarily mean that they can progress in school . . . by our tests we find they are a year retarded in comparison with the white children. . . . Your Mexican child is advanced, that is, he matures physically faster than your white child, and he is able to do more in games. Therefore, he goes more on physical prowess than he does on mental ability."[62] Richard F. Harris, the Westminster superintendent of schools, added that Mexican American children could not keep up with others because they had not been introduced at home to Mother Goose rhymes and "stories of our American heroes, stories of our American frontier, rhymes, rhythms."[63] A "child of Mexican-speaking families . . . has no conception" of such stories and so had to be educated separately.[64]

Marcus countered the county's case by putting both parents and students on the stand. Parents from each of the four districts testified about their repeated attempts to get their children into the "white" schools, and recounted the denigrating language that school officials used in denying their requests. The parents were frequently told, as noted, that all Mexican American children were dirty and spoke no English, which the officials somehow knew even though the children were given no language tests.[65] Two students testified, demonstrating that they did indeed speak proper English.[66]

Then Marcus anticipated the approach that would be used by the NAACP in *Brown v. Board of Education*. He called two educators to the stand as expert witnesses. Ralph L. Beals was a professor and chairman of the Department of Anthropology at the University of California–Los Angeles. He had done research in Mexico for the National Research Council and the Smithsonian Institution as well as for his university, and he had written roughly 30 books and articles.[67] Marie H. Hughes had been a school principal and curriculum director in New Mexico for 19 years and, in addition, had worked in Los Angeles County for the past five. She had specialized in research about Mexican American children for 20 years.[68] Both testified that separating children with limited English from more fluent children was a poor way to enhance the first group's language proficiency. More importantly, they both argued that the psychological effects of segregation interfered with the segregated students' ability to learn. "Judging by some studies that have been made under my direction," Dr. Beals told the court, "a feeling of antagonism is built up in children, when they are segregated in this fashion. They actually become hostile to the whole culture of the surrounding majority group, as a result of the segregation, which appears to be, to them at least, discrimination. . . . The disadvantage of segregation, it would seem to me, would come primarily from the reinforcing of stereotypes of inferiority-superiority, which exists in the population as a whole."[69] Marie Hughes added,

> Segregation, by its very nature, is a reminder constantly of inferiority, of not being wanted, of not being a part of the community. . . . I would say that any separation of children which prevents free communication among them, on an equal basis, that is, a peer basis, would be bad because of the very fact that segregation tends to give an aura of inferiority. In order to have the people of the United States understand one another, it is necessary for them to live together, as it were, and the public school is the one mechanism where all the children of all the people go.[70]

THE DECISION

Judge McCormick handed down his decision on February 18, 1946, and it was a resounding victory for the plaintiffs. It was more than that, however; it was also a seminal moment in American law. McCormick found the school districts' segregation illegitimate as a matter of both California law and federal constitutional law. A California statute required school districts to admit all children over age six, whether or not their parents were American citizens, and to maintain elementary schools "'with equal rights and privileges as far as possible.'"[71] That, Judge McCormick declared, applied to all children "regardless of their ancestry or extraction" (with the notable exception of Indian and Asian children) and meant that segregation of "pupils of Mexican ancestry" was prohibited. "The common segregation and practices of the school authorities in the defendant school districts in Orange County," however, "pertain solely to children of Mexican ancestry and parentage. They are singled out as a class for segregation." Such segregation violated the state's own laws.[72]

California wanted students to be integrated, according to Judge McCormick's reading of its laws. He found it "noteworthy that the educational advantages of their commingling with other pupils is regarded as being so important to the school system of the State" that education was mandatory for both citizens and noncitizens. California law reflected "a clear purpose to avoid and forbid distinctions among pupils based upon race or ancestry."[73] Further, the Supreme Court had declared in *Hirabayashi v. United States*[74] three years earlier that distinctions made on the basis of race were "by their very nature odious to a free people whose institutions are founded upon the doctrine of equality" and "utterly inconsistent with American traditions and ideals."[75]

Judge McCormick concluded his discussion of "the utter irreconcilability of the segregation practices" with California law and went on to suggest a new interpretation of the federal equal protection clause. "'The equal protection of the laws' pertaining to the public school system in California," he wrote, "is not provided by furnishing in separate schools the same technical facilities, text books and courses of instruction to children of Mexican ancestry that are available to the other public school children regardless of their ancestry."[76] Then came the judge's formulation, so radical for its day: "A paramount requisite in the American system of public education is social equality. It must be open to all children by unified school association regardless of lineage."[77] That, simply stated, was a declaration that "separate but equal" was not equal. The boldness of the language must have made the parties to the litigation catch their breaths. McCormick was implicitly denying the legitimacy of an entire body of equal protection law, and doing so in language that would soon have civil rights organizations all over the country rushing into the case.

The only permissible grounds for the Orange County segregation, McCormick continued, were the children's language difficulties. "But even such situations do not justify the general and continuous segregation in separate schools of the children of Mexican ancestry from the rest of the elementary school population as has been shown to be the practice in the defendant school districts." Instead, there must be "credible examination" of each child, "regardless of his ethnic traits or ancestry."[78] No such examination existed here. "In some instances," McCormick continued with indignation, placement was based on "the Latinized or Mexican name of the child," even though "such methods of evaluating language knowledge are illusory and are not conducive to the inculcation and enjoyment of civil rights which are of primary importance in the public school system of education in the United States."[79] That sentence effectively asserted that civil rights and knowledge about them were key goals of American public education. So was avoidance of artificial distinctions among the students, McCormick said, drawing on the testimony of the experts:

> The evidence clearly shows that Spanish-speaking children are retarded in learning English by lack of exposure to its use because of segregation, and that commingling of the entire student body instills and develops a common cultural attitude among the school children which is imperative for the perpetuation of American institutions and ideals. It is also established by the record that the methods of segregation prevalent in the defendant school districts foster antagonisms in the children and suggest inferiority among them where none exists.[80]

What Judge McCormick did was sufficiently revolutionary to deserve emphasis here. He not only restated the Supreme Court's suggestion in *Hirabayashi* that discrimination based on ancestry was usually suspect; he applied that doctrine in declaring a state's actions to be illegal. He held that Mexican Americans as a group could not legitimately be discriminated against—a holding that would not be echoed by the U.S. Supreme Court until it heard a case involving a Mexican American in 1954.[81] He declared that school segregation impeded learning instead of enhancing it. He insisted, as the NAACP would argue in *Brown v. Board of Education*, that segregated schools fostered unwarranted feelings of inferiority in the students who were segregated. Most importantly, of course, he declared that "separate but equal" education was a violation of the Fourteenth Amendment. There, again, this district court judge anticipated the Supreme Court by almost a decade.

THE APPEAL

The NAACP had known nothing about the *Mendez* case. Once McCormick's decision was handed down, however, the case received nationwide publicity. The school districts promptly announced that they would appeal the verdict, and NAACP Assistant Special Counsel Robert Carter, Thurgood Marshall's second-in-command, knew that he wanted to be involved. Marshall was in the Virgin Islands, recuperating from an illness, so Carter was effectively in charge. The school districts had announced that they would appeal the decision and Carter immediately understood that if the case reached the Supreme Court, it could be the one to attack segregated education on its face. It might even, he thought, signal the beginning of the end for "separate but equal."[82]

Carter had come to believe that sociological evidence, depicting the psychological and pedagogical effects of school segregation, could be a useful weapon in the litigation arsenal. Other lawyers who worked with the NAACP were less sanguine. The social sciences, they said, weren't pure science, and so their findings were too weak to use in cases. Carter nonetheless thought that the *Mendez* case was too good an opportunity to pass up, and he began drafting a brief that he would later call the NAACP's trial brief for *Brown v. Board.*[83] The NAACP entered the case as an *amicus*.

So did the American Jewish Congress, the Japanese American Citizens League, the American Civil Liberties Union, and the Los Angeles chapter of the National Lawyers Guild.[84] The NAACP brief took educational segregation head on. Although Marcus continued to insist that *Mendez* was about ethnicity, not race, the NAACP brief focused on race. There was nothing, Carter wrote, to keep a federal court from declaring that segregation in a public school system was unconstitutional. *Plessy* dealt only with railroad cars, not with education, and a line of cases since indicated that the Court was moving toward a holding that "classifications and distinctions on the basis of race [are] contrary to our fundamental law." The conclusion: "It is clear, therefore, that segregation in our public schools must be invalidated as violative of the Constitution and laws of the United States."[85]

The brief of the American Jewish Congress (AJC) lambasted segregation in general and, in language that echoed that of the experts who had testified at trial, segregation in education in particular. "The value and the desirability of an educational institution is particularly dependent on intangible elements," the AJC asserted. "The physical characteristics of the benches and desks of a school shrink into utter insignificance when compared with the social and psychological environment which the school offers to its children." That "social and psychological environment" could be devastating. Children who were "deemed superior are often, in manifesting their innocent pride, more cruel than normal adults usually are. On the other side, children who feel that they are treated as inferior are more bitterly humiliated by the social stigma that strikes them than adults can be."[86] They are likely to suffer the "deepest and most lasting social and psychological evil results." Segregation based on assumptions of inferiority "perpetuate[s] racial prejudice and contributes to the degradation and humiliation of the minority children."[87]

The state of California also weighed in, and it quickly became apparent that segregation of Mexican American students did not have the state's support. In November 1946, Robert W. Kenny, Governor Earl Warren's attorney general, entered the case as an *amicus*. He argued that any segregation in California schools was unconstitutional, and Warren and the state legislature began the process of implementing that idea.[88] In

January 1947, with the blessing of Governor Warren, four members of the California Assembly introduced a bill to end segregated education in the state.[89] It passed on April 10 which, as it turned out, was only four days before the *Mendez* decision was handed down by a unanimous Court of Appeals on April 14.[90]

Writing for the court, Judge Albert Lee Stephens rejected the county's argument that the Supreme Court's segregation decisions were controlling. His reason was quite different from McCormick's, however. Those decisions, Stephens wrote, were written in cases where the state legislature had mandated segregation. That was not the situation here. "Nowhere in any California law is there a suggestion that any segregation can be made of children within one of the great races." Mexican Americans were neither American Indians nor Asians, and those were the only categories of children whom California law permitted to be segregated. Stephens was willing to concede that California could enact a law permitting the segregation of Mexican Americans but it had not done so, and so the school boards had deprived the plaintiff children of liberty and property without due process of law and the equal protection of the laws.[91]

Stephens specifically declined to get into a discussion of whether racial segregation was constitutional.[92] The country's legal elite, however—at least the part of it outside the South—soon indicated that it was willing to go further than he. Northern and Western law reviews such as the *Yale Law Journal*, the *Michigan Law Review*, the *Columbia Law Review*, and the *Southern California Law Review* saw Judge McCormick's decision as the handwriting on the wall and called for the end of segregated schools.[93]

The school districts involved in the case gave up after the appeals court decision was handed down and integrated their schools, so the case did not make its way to the U.S. Supreme Court. The case nonetheless had ramifications beyond those districts. A few months after Judge McCormick handed down his decision, David Marcus filed suit on behalf of segregated African American and Mexican American school children in Riverside County. The school district promptly ended segregation.[94] At the same time, Orange County's Ontario School Board decided to integrate its formerly all-Anglo Grove School. Anglo parents managed to collect 1,400 signatures on a petition asking the board to rescind its action. The board held firm, however, and once the Anglo parents saw that protest was of no use, they agreed to cooperate. In September of that year the Grove School had 177 Mexican American and 155 non-Mexican-American students.[95] In 1948 scholar Mary Peters surveyed 100 nonurban school districts in southern and central California; 78% of the districts that responded replied that they had segregated Mexican American students; only 18% said that they still did so.[96]

And the Supreme Court did eventually weigh in on the subject that was at the heart of the *Mendez* case. Eight years after Judge McCormick handed down his ruling, Chief Justice Earl Warren wrote for the unanimous court in *Hernandez v. Texas*, the first case argued before that court by Latino attorneys. The decision specifically recognized Mexican Americans as a class entitled to the protection of the Fourteenth Amendment.[97] Mexican American cadre rights had finally been endorsed by the nation's highest court.

Conclusion

The *Mendez* case probably would not have succeeded had it been brought ten years earlier. World War II had a notable effect both on American thinking about racism and on the roughly 350,000 Mexican American soldiers who had fought in the war and returned to begin demanding the same kind of justice at home they believed they had been fighting for abroad.[98] Gilbert Gonzalez has noted that "the California courts heard the *Mendez* case in a period of policy shift toward 'intercultural understanding,'" in which prejudice and discrimination had come to be seen as "negative social forces."[99] There is an ongoing relationship between law and society, and societal attitudes had to change before a judge would write that segregation, with its implication of inferiority, was unjust, or law reviews would publish articles calling for the overturn of *Plessy v. Ferguson*. Law, in turn, affects societal dynamics. *Mendez* clearly heartened the Mexican American community and its activists, encouraging the spate of litigation and pressure on school boards that gradually ended segregation policies in many districts.

Despite its significance, few scholars outside of California knew about the *Mendez* case until the twenty-first century. It was not featured in most constitutional law casebooks; it went unmentioned in the majority of biographies of Earl Warren. One reason may be that most twentieth-century constitutional scholars focused almost entirely on Supreme Court decisions and ignored the work of the lower federal courts. Another possibility is that the orthodox narrative of civil rights in the United States portrayed the African American movement for legal equality as seminal, with other minority groups supposedly piggybacking on the successes of that movement. Little attention was paid to the pre-1950s activism of Mexican American and other Latino/Hispanic communities, although such activism was not at all uncommon.[100]

Mendez is no longer ignored. That is in part due to the efforts of Sylvia Mendez, who has tirelessly taken information about the case to schoolchildren and other audiences around the nation, and in part because of Sandra Robbie's Emmy-winning documentary, *Mendez vs. Westminster: For All the Children/Para Todos los Niños*. It is also because of the emergence of a solid cadre of Chicano and other scholars eager to give Mexican American activism in general and *Mendez v. Westminster* in particular their proper place in United States history.[101] In 2007, the U.S. Postal Service issued a stamp in honor of the case; in 2010, President Barack Obama presented Sylvia Mendez with the Medal of Freedom for her work in publicizing the case; and in 2012, the courthouse in which *Mendez* was tried was declared to be a National Historic Landmark.[102]

Mendez, a seminal moment in American law, deserves all the attention. It also exemplifies the truism that rights are attainable in the American political system—sometimes not early enough, sometimes in no more than small increments, yet attainable all the same—but only if they are fought for. The Méndezes and David Marcus accepted the challenge and, in the process, helped change the definition of equality under the law.

Philippa Strum is a Senior Scholar at the Woodrow Wilson International Center for Scholars. This chapter is based in part on PHILIPPA STRUM, *MENDEZ V. WESTMIN-STER*: SCHOOL DESEGREGATION AND MEXICAN-AMERICAN RIGHTS (University Press of Kansas 2010).

NOTES

1. GILBERT G. GONZALEZ, CHICANO EDUCATION IN THE ERA OF SEGREGATION, 149 (The Balch Institute Press 1990); The Honorable Frederick P. Aguirre, Mendez v. Westminster School District: *How It Affected* Brown v. Board of Education, 4 JOURNAL OF HISPANIC HIGHER EDUCATION 321, 323 (2005); Jennifer McCormick & César J. Ayala, *Felícita "La Prieta" Méndez (1916–1998) and the End of Latino School Segregation in California*, 19 CENTRO JOURNAL 13, 23–24 (2007).

2. A photograph of the Westminster Main school is available at http://www.nps.gov/history/nr/travel/American_Latino_Heritage/Los_Angeles_US_Court_House_and_Post_Office.html.

3. A photograph of Hoover is available at http://www.winifredconkling.com/images/hoover.jpg.

4. Molly Nance, *The Landmark Decision that Faded into Historical Obscurity*, 24 DIVERSE: ISSUES IN HIGHER EDUCATION 28 (2007); McCormick, *Felícita "La Prieta" Méndez*, 24.

5. Transcript of Record, 461–62, Mendez v. Westminister [as in original] School District of Orange County, 64 F. Supp. 544 (S.D. Cal. 1946) (file folders 4292-M, box #740, Civil Cases 4285–4292, RG 221, Records of the District Court of the United States for the Southern District of California, Central Division, National Archives and Records Administration (Pacific Region), Laguna Niguel, California) [hereinafter Trial Transcript] available at http://mendezetalvwestminster.com/court.html. The transcript refers to the lead plaintiff

as "Mendez," without an accent mark, so the case is referred to that way throughout this article.

6. Felícitas Méndez was born in Puerto Rico and thus was an American citizen. By the time of the case, Gonzalo Méndez was a naturalized American citizen.

7. Aguirre, Mendez v. Westminster School District, 322; JUAN GÓMEZ-QUIÑONES, ROOTS OF CHICANO POLITICS, 1600–1940, 303 (University of New Mexico Press 1994).

8. DAVID GUTIÉRREZ, WALLS AND MIRRORS: MEXICAN-AMERICANS, MEXICAN IMMIGRANTS, AND THE POLITICS OF ETHNICITY, 41 (University of California Press 1995); GEORGE J. SÁNCHEZ, BECOMING MEXICAN AMERICAN: ETHNICITY, CULTURE, AND IDENTITY IN CHICANO LOS ANGELES, 1900–1945, 19 (Oxford University Press 1993).

9. GUTIÉRREZ, WALLS AND MIRRORS, 41; GILBERT G. GONZÁLEZ, LABOR AND COMMUNITY: MEXICAN CITRUS WORKER VILLAGES IN A SOUTHERN CALIFORNIA COUNTY, 1900–1950, 19–20 (University of Illinois Press 1994); SÁNCHEZ, BECOMING MEXICAN AMERICAN, 19.

10. Vicki L. Ruiz, *Tapestries of Resistance: Episodes of School Segregation and Desegregation in the Western United States*, in PETER F. LAU, ED., FROM GRASSROOTS TO THE SUPREME COURT: EXPLORATION OF *BROWN V. BOARD OF EDUCATION* AND AMERICAN DEMOCRACY, 56 (Duke University Press 2004); Vicki L. Ruiz, *South by Southwest: Mexican Americans and Segregated Schooling, 1900–1950*, ORGANIZATION OF AMERICAN HISTORIANS MAGAZINE OF HISTORY, 23 (Winter 2001); CHARLES M. WOLLENBERG, ALL DELIBERATE SPEED: SEGREGATION AND EXCLUSION IN CALIFORNIA SCHOOLS, 1955–1975, 109 (University of California Press 1976); GUTIÉRREZ, WALLS AND MIRRORS , 40; SÁNCHEZ, BECOMING MEXICAN AMERICAN, 18; CAMILLE GUERIN-GONZALEZ, MEXICAN WORKERS AND AMERICAN DREAMS: IMMIGRATION, REPATRIATION, AND CALIFORNIA FARM LABOR, 1900–1939 (Rutgers University Press 1994).

11. GUTIÉRREZ, WALLS AND MIRRORS, 45; GONZÁLEZ, LABOR AND COMMUNITY, 7; see also JUAN GÓMEZ-QUIÑONES, MEXICAN AMERICAN LABOR, 1790–1990 (University of New Mexico Press 1994).

12. GONZÁLEZ, LABOR AND COMMUNITY, 7; see also GÓMEZ-QUIÑONES, MEXICAN AMERICAN LABOR.

13. GONZÁLEZ, LABOR AND COMMUNITY, 62.

14. Guerin-Gonzalez, *Mexican Workers*, GUERIN-GONZALEZ, MEXICAN WORKERS 120–21; GONZÁLEZ, LABOR AND COMMUNITY, 32, 59–69; Ruiz, *South by Southwest*, 23.

15. Act of March 12, 1885, California Statutes, Chapter 117, §§ 1–2, Laws and Resolutions passed by the legislature of 1883–84 at its extra session, 99–100; California Education Code § 1662 (Deering 1886); California Education Code §§ 8003–04 (1945).

16. Gilbert G. Gonzalez, *Segregation of Mexican Children in a Southern California City: The Legacy of Expansionism and the American Southwest*, 16 THE WESTERN HISTORICAL QUARTERLY 55, 57 (1985).

17. WOLLENBERG, ALL DELIBERATE SPEED, 110–11; Christopher J. Arriola, *Knocking on the Schoolhouse Door: Mendez v. Westminster, Equal Protection, Public Education, and Mexican Americans in the 1940s*, 8 LA RAZA LAW JOURNAL 166, 170 (1995); GONZALEZ, CHICANO EDUCATION, 137–38; Charles Wollenberg, Mendez v.

Westminster: *Race, Nationality and Segregation in California Schools*, 53 CALIFORNIA HISTORICAL QUARTERLY 319 (1974).

18. NICOLÁS C. VACA, THE PRESUMED ALLIANCE: THE UNSPOKEN CONFLICT BETWEEN LATINOS AND BLACKS AND WHAT IT MEANS FOR AMERICA, 63 (HarperCollins 2003); GONZÁLEZ, LABOR AND COMMUNITY, 99–100; IRVING G. HENDRICK, THE EDUCATION OF NON-WHITES IN CALIFORNIA, 1849–1970, 91–92 (R & E Research Associates 1977).

19. GONZALEZ, CHICANO EDUCATION, 138, 142; GONZÁLEZ, LABOR AND COMMUNITY, 102.

20. Arriola, *Knocking*, 181; GONZALEZ, CHICANO EDUCATION, 146–47.

21. GONZALEZ, CHICANO EDUCATION, 142, 182.

22. GONZÁLEZ, LABOR AND COMMUNITY, 109–11.

23. Pre-Trial Transcript at 21–22, 43–44, Mendez, 64 F. Supp. 544, [hereinafter Pre-trial Transcript] available at http://mendezetalvwestminster.com/pdf/Pre_Trial_Transcript.pdf.

24. Merton Earle Hill, *The Development of an Americanization Program*, 189, 195, passim (Graduate Division of the University of California, doctoral dissertation for Doctor of Education, 1928).

25. Grace Stanley, *Special School for Mexicans*, THE SURVEY, 714 (September 15, 1920).

26. B. F. Haught, *The Language Difficulty of Spanish-American Children*, 15 JOURNAL OF APPLIED PSYCHOLOGY 92 (February 1931) (quoted in GONZALEZ, CHICANO EDUCATION, 72); William H. Sheldon, *The Intelligence of Mexican Children*, SCHOOL AND SOCIETY (February 2, 1924) (cited in WOLLENBERG, ALL DELIBERATE SPEED, 115); Thomas Garth, *The Intelligence of Mexican School Children*, SCHOOL AND SOCIETY (June 28, 1928) (cited in WOLLENBERG, ALL DELIBERATE SPEED, 115).

27. Felícitas Méndez, quoted in English translation from Spanish in VICKI L. RUIZ, FROM OUT OF THE SHADOWS: MEXICAN WOMEN IN TWENTIETH CENTURY AMERICA (Oxford University Press 1998) (cited in McCormick & Ayala, *Felícita "La Prieta" Méndez*, 27).

28. Gonzalez, *Segregation of Mexican Children*, 68–70. These are all quotes from the October 1943 minutes of the Santa Ana Board of Education.

29. Trial Transcript, 79–80, 90–92, 102–103.

30. Author's telephone interviews with Maria Dolores Lane (David Marcus' daughter), January 9, 2008; Stephen DeLapp (grandson), January 6, 2009; Anne K. McIntyre (granddaughter), January 8, 2008; author's email interview with Melissa Marcus (granddaughter), December 10, 2008.

31. Lopez v. Seccombe, 71 F. Supp. 769 (S.D. Cal. 1944).

32. Aguirre, Mendez v. Westminster, 321, 324.

33. Trial Transcript, 64–67, 130, 152, 442, 477.

34. Author's telephone interview with Alex Maldonado, January 22, 2009; GONZALEZ, CHICANO EDUCATION, 152.

35. Author's interview with Sylvia Mendez, February 27, 2009. The Mendez family no longer uses the accent mark in "Mendez."

36. U.S. Constitution, Amendment XIV, Section 1 ("No state shall . . . deny to any person within its jurisdiction the equal protection of the laws").

37. Trial Transcript, 469.

38. Plessy v. Ferguson, 163 U.S. 537 (1896).

39. Cumming v. Board of Education, 175 U.S. 528 (1899); Berea College v. Commonwealth of Kentucky, 211 U.S. 45 (1908); Gong Lum v. Rice, 275 U.S. 78 (1927).

40. Memo from Thurgood Marshall to Roy Wilkins, November 27, 1945, Library of Congress, National Association for the Advancement of Colored People Records, 1842–1999, Part 2 (hereafter NAACP records), Box 136 Folder 11; Thurgood Marshall to Carl Murphy, President, *The Afro-American Newspapers*, December 20, 1946, and Thurgood Marshall speech, Association of Colleges and Secondary Schools for Negroes, Nashville, Tennessee, December 6, 1945, NAACP records, Part 2, Box 136, Folder 3.

41. Petition, 2, 6–7, Mendez v. Westminster School District of Orange County, Civil Action No. 4292 (S.D. Cal. March 1, 1946), available at http://mendezetalvwestminster.com/pdf/Petition.pdf.

42. Trial Transcript, 44, 109.

43. U.S. Department of Commerce, Bureau of the Census, *Abridged Instructions to Enumerators*, 7 (1940) ("Mexicans are to be returned as *white*, unless definitely of Indian or other nonwhite race."), available at http://1940census.archives.gov/downloads/instructions-to-enumerators.pdf. See also U.S. Department of Commerce, Bureau of the Census, *200 Years of US Census Taking: Population and Housing Questions, 1790–1990*, 60 (1989).

44. *Coolidge Picks M'Cormick*, LOS ANGELES TIMES, A5 (February 8, 1924); *Judge's Colleagues Did Not Forget the Day*, LOS ANGELES TIMES, A5 (April 24, 1948); *Fellow Judges Praise Service of McCormick*, LOS ANGELES TIMES, B2 (July 29, 1951).

45. Alma Whitaker, *Death Penalty Brings Emotion*, LOS ANGELES TIMES, A1 (April 8, 1923).

46. *Objector Given Year in Jail*, LOS ANGELES TIMES, A1 (November 10, 1942).

47. *Galaxy of Stars Due at Loew's*, LOS ANGELES TIMES, A9 (January 8, 1934).

48. *Laughton and Elsa File U.S. Citizen Applications*, LOS ANGELES TIMES, A1 (April 23, 1949); *Actor Charles Boyer Becomes U. S. Citizen*, ATLANTA CONSTITUTION, 6 (February 14, 1942).

49. *Chaplin Wins Decision in Plagiarism Suit*, LOS ANGELES TIMES, 3 (November 19, 1939).

50. *Addict Given Sympathy: Judge McCormick Expresses Regret for Lack of Any Hospitalization System for Narcotic Slaves*, LOS ANGELES TIMES, 12 (February 27, 1930).

51. *Commissioners Who Made Exhaustive Prohibition Study*, LOS ANGELES TIMES, 4 (January 21, 1931); *Crime Viewed by M'Cormick: Wickersham Commissioner Returns Home*, LOS ANGELES TIMES, A1 (July 6, 1931).

52. United States v. Pan American Petroleum and Transport Company, 6 F.2d 43 (S.D. Cal. 1925); *Confirms Revoking of Doheny Leases*, NEW YORK TIMES, 6 (July 12, 1925).

53. Pre-trial Transcript, 28, 107.

54. Trial Transcript, 2, 7–8.

55. The defense team was formally headed by Joel E. Ogle, the Santa Ana County Counsel. He effectively turned the case over to Holden, however, and played only a minimal role in it.

56. Email to author from Daniel W. Holden, Mar. 14, 2009; email to author from Chris Jepsen, Assistant Archivist, Orange County Archives, March 10, 2009; email to author from Jack Golden, Senior Assistant County Counsel, Orange County, March 9, 2009; *Mexican Students To Be Unchanged*, ORANGE DAILY NEWS, 1 (September 13, 1946).

57. Pre-trial Transcript, 5.

58. Ibid., 46–47.

59. James L. Kent, *Segregation of Mexican School Children in Southern California*, 3 (University of Oregon, Ed.M. thesis, June 1941).

60. Ibid., 23.

61. Ibid., 67.

62. Trial Transcript, 101, 139.

63. Ibid., 376.

64. Ibid., 377. See also PHILIPPA STRUM, *MENDEZ V. WESTMINSTER*: SCHOOL DESEGREGATION AND MEXICAN-AMERICAN RIGHTS, 82–90 (University Press of Kansas 2010).

65. Trial Transcript, 64–67, 130, 152, 442, 477.

66. Trial Transcript, 258–70. See also STRUM, *MENDEZ V. WESTMINSTER*, 79–80, 90–92, 102–103.

67. Trial Transcript, 660–61. See also Walter Goldschmidt, Ralph H. Turner, & Robert B. Edgerton, *Ralph Leon Beals, Anthropology and Sociology: Los Angeles*, http://texts.cdlib.org/view?docId=hb767nb3z6&doc.view=frames&chunk.id=div00006&toc.depth=1&toc.id=

68. Trial Transcript, 687–89.

69. Ibid., 676.

70. Ibid., 691, 699.

71. Mendez, 64 F. Supp. 548 (quoting California Education Code § 8002).

72. Ibid.

73. Ibid.

74. Hirabayashi v. United States, 320 U.S. 81 (1943).

75. Mendez, 64 F. Supp. 548 (quoting Hirabayashi, 320 U.S. 81, 100, 110).

76. Ibid., 549.

77. Ibid.

78. Ibid., 549, 550.

79. Ibid., 550.

80. Ibid., 549.

81. Hernandez v. Texas, 347 U.S. 475 (1954).

82. Author's interview with Robert L. Carter, October 17, 2008; Robert L. Carter to Claude G. Metzler, December 26, 1946, and Robert L. Carter, Memo to NAACP's Public Relations Department, April 24, 1947, NAACP records, Part 2, Box 136, Folder 3; ROBERT L. CARTER, A MATTER OF LAW: A MEMOIR OF STRUGGLE IN THE CAUSE OF CIVIL RIGHTS, 65–66 (The New Press 2005); RICHARD KLUGER, SIMPLE JUSTICE: THE HISTORY OF *BROWN V. BOARD OF EDUCATION* AND BLACK AMERICA'S STRUGGLE FOR EQUALITY, 400 (Knopf 1975); MARK V. TUSHNET, THE NAACP'S LEGAL STRAGEGY AGAINST SEGREGATED EDUCATION, 1925–1950, 120 (University of North Carolina Press 1987).

83. Author's interview, Robert L. Carter; CARTER, A MATTER OF LAW, 65–66; KLUGER, SIMPLE JUSTICE, 400.

84. The briefs in *Westminster School District v. Mendez* are in Case Files, Ninth Circuit Court of Appeals, Record Group 276, Box 4464, National Archives-Pacific Sierra Region, San Bruno, CA.

85. Brief for the National Association for the Advancement of Colored People as *Amicus Curiae*, 7, 29, Westminster School District of Orange County v. Mendez, 161 F.2d 774 (9th Cir. 1947) (No. 11310).

86. Brief for the American Jewish Congress as *Amicus Curiae*, 13, Westminster, 161 F.2d 774.

87. Ibid., 14.

88. Brief of the Attorney General of the State of California as *Amicus Curiae*, Westminster, 161 F.2d 774; ED CRAY, CHIEF JUSTICE: A BIOGRAPHY OF EARL WARREN, 167 (Simon & Schuster 1997).

89. 1947 California Statute chapter 737, September 10, 1947; WOLLENBERG, ALL DELIBERATE SPEED, 132. Governor Warren signed the bill on June 14.

90. Westminster, 161 F.2d 774. No transcript appears to have been kept of the oral argument.

91. Westminster, 161 F.2d 789–81.

92. Ibid., 780.

93. Note, *Segregation in Public Schools—A Violation of "Equal Protection of the Laws,"* 56 YALE LAW JOURNAL 1059 (1947); Neal Seegert, Comment, 46 MICHIGAN LAW REVIEW 639 (March 1948); Note, *Is Racial Segregation Consistent with Equal Protection of the Laws?* Plessy v. Ferguson *Reexamined*, 49 COLUMBIA LAW REVIEW 629 (May 1949); Harry L. Gershon, Comment, *Restrictive Covenants and Equal Protection*, 21 SOUTHERN CALIFORNIA LAW REVIEW 358 (1947–1948).

94. Lawrence E. Davies, *Segregation of Mexican American Students Stirs Court Fight*, NEW YORK TIMES MAGAZINE, 6 (December 22, 1946).

95. Wollenberg, Mendez v. Westminster, 329.

96. Mary M. Peters, *The Segregation of Mexican American Children in the Elementary Schools of California—Its Legal and Administrative Aspects* (UCLA, M.A. in Education thesis, July 1948).

97. Hernandez, 347 U.S. 477–78, 480.

98. The 350,000 number is in the National WWII Museum, "Latino Americans in WWII At a Glance," http://www.nationalww2museum.org/learn/education/for-students/ww2-history/at-a-glance/latino-americans-in-ww2.html.

99. Gonzalez, *Segregation of Mexican American Children*, 75.

100. Petition for Writ of Mandate No. 66625, Alvarez v. Lemon Grove School District (Superior Court of the State of California, County of San Diego 1931); Salvatierra v. Del Rio Independent School District, 33 S.W.2d 790 (Tex. Civ. App. 1930) (certiorari denied, 284 U.S. 580 (1931)); Lopez v. Seccombe, 71 F. Supp. 769 (S.D. Cal. 1944); Delgado v. Bastrop Independent School District, Civ. No. 388 (W.D. Tex. June 15, 1948); Gonzalez v. Sheely, 96 F. Supp. 1004 (D. Ariz. 1951). GONZÁLEZ, LABOR AND COMMUNITY; GÓMEZ-QUIÑONES, MEXICAN AMERICAN LABOR; RUIZ, FROM OUT OF THE SHADOWS; RICHARD GRISWOLD DEL CASTILLO, ED., WORLD WAR II AND MEXICAN AMERICAN CIVIL RIGHTS (University of Texas Press 2008); MARIO T. GARCIA, MEXICAN AMERICANS: LEADERSHIP, IDEOLOGY, & IDENTITY, 1930–1960 (Yale University Press 1989); Enrique M. López, *Community Resistance to Injustice and Inequality: Ontario, California, 1937–1947*, 17 AZTLAN No. 2, 1–29 (1988).

101. Vicki L. Ruiz, *We Always Tell Our Children They are Americans:* Mendez v. Westminster *and the California Road to* Brown v. Board of Education, 200 THE COLLEGE BOARD REVIEW (Fall 2003) (another version is in 6 THE BROWN QUARTERLY (Fall 2004); Thomas A. Saenz, Mendez *and the Legacy of* Brown: *A Latino Civil Rights Lawyer's Assessment,* 2004 BERKELEY WOMEN'S LAW JOURNAL 395 (2004); Richard Valencia, *The Mexican American Struggle for Equal Educational Opportunity in* Mendez v. Westminster: *Helping to Pave the Way for* Brown v. The Board of Education, 107 TEACHERS COLLEGE RECORD (March 2005); Guadalupe San Miguel, Jr., *The Impact of* Brown *on Mexican American Desegregation Litigation, 1950s to 1980s,* 4 JOURNAL OF LATINOS AND EDUCATION 221 (2005). STRUM, *MENDEZ V. WESTMINSTER;* RICHARD R. VALENCIA, CHICANO STUDENTS AND THE COURTS: THE MEXICAN AMERICAN LEGAL STRUGGLE FOR EDUCATIONAL EQUALITY (New York University Press 2008); JOSÉ F. MORENO, ED., THE ELUSIVE QUEST FOR EQUALITY: 150 YEARS OF CHICANO/CHICANA EDUCATION (Harvard Educational Review 1999); RUBEN DONATO, THE OTHER STRUGGLE FOR EQUAL SCHOOLS (SUNY Press 1997); HERSHEL T. MANUEL, THE EDUCATION OF MEXICAN AND SPANISH-SPEAKING CHILDREN IN TEXAS (The Fund for Research in the Social Sciences 1930); GUADALUPE SAN MIGUEL, JR., "LET ALL OF THEM TAKE HEED": MEXICAN AMERICANS AND THE CAMPAIGN FOR EDUCATIONAL EQUALITY IN TEXAS, 1910–1981 (University of Texas Press 1987).

102. https://about.usps.com/postal-bulletin/2007/html/pb22213/info.4.13.html; http://www.whitehouse.gov/photos-and-video/video/2011/02/16/2010-presidential-medal-freedom-recipient-sylvia-mendez; http://www.nps.gov/history/nr/travel/American_Latino_Heritage/Los_Angeles_US_Court_House_and_Post_Office.html.

KRISTI L. BOWMAN

Pursuing Equity at the Intersection of School Desegregation, English-Language Instruction, and Immigration

IN 1946, A FEDERAL DISTRICT COURT HELD THAT LATINO AND LATINA (LATINO/A) students could not be segregated from "other" white students in public schools. This holding, the outcome of *Mendez v. Westminster*,[1] is one of the earliest victories in school desegregation, and a crucial part of the story of Latinos/as' struggles for equality in the United States. Unfortunately, the story of *Mendez*, and in fact the story of Latinos/as' pursuit of educational equity in general, is not one we often tell. In part this can be explained by demographics: until relatively recently, the Latino/a population was small in number throughout much of the country. Yet, the absence of this story is also due to a more foundational reason: Latinos/as do not fit well within our existing paradigms for conceptualizing (in)equality. The civil rights paradigm is an ill fit because Latinos/as' history and present experiences differ from African Americans' in several material ways—not only because of the importance of language to their experience of immigration, but also because of the very different meaning of race among Latinos/as and African Americans.[2] At the same time, the immigration/assimilation paradigm is inadequate because a presumption of foreignness which often plagues Latinos/as does not attach to the "white" ethnic groups from Europe which historically have constituted the bulk of the U.S. immigrant population.[3]

The importance of theorizing this experience, and of telling this story, is growing because the demographics of U.S. public schools are changing rapidly. Between 1995 and 2011, the number of Latino/a students in our nation's public schools nearly doubled, rising from 6 million to 11.8 million.[4] This group's speedy growth is projected to continue and by 2021—less than a decade from now—is estimated to constitute 15 million students, about 30% of the nation's public school population.[5] By contrast, white enrollment in public schools is expected to continue on the gradual decline that has occurred since at least the mid-1990s. If the federal government's predictions hold true, in fall 2014 white children for the first time comprise fewer than half of the nation's public school students and, in fall 2018, white children will comprise fewer than half of all children under age 18.[6]

In our public schools today, Latinos/as often are concentrated in elementary and secondary schools populated mainly by other Latinos/as and by students in poverty; on average, they continually fail to achieve at the same levels as white children and have higher dropout rates than whites and African Americans; many of them face significant language barriers in education; and their parents often perceive that their children are discriminated against in school.[7] These conditions are complicated by the facts that an increasing number of Latinos/as are moving to parts of the country where few Latinos/as have lived and attended school until recently, and that others' views of them often are tied to ongoing discussion of immigration policy.[8]

The educational challenges that Latinos/as face are complex and must be addressed by a range of litigation and policy initiatives. Beginning with two cases out of California, including *Mendez v. Westminster*,[9] this chapter traces the history of Latinos/as' relationship with school desegregation litigation, which may be considered the most "traditional" legal vehicle in the pursuit of racial/ethnic equity in schools, and also explores the connections between school desegregation, English-language instruction, and immigration. The intersection of these three areas of law demonstrates that educational equity is a complex concept, especially because specific visions of equity may conflict with one another. Additionally, examining each area of law in isolation from the others shows how changes in law have created more equitable educational opportunities for Latinos/as in many ways, and yet those changes have not been nearly enough.

The 1920s–1950s: Early Desegregation Victories for Latinos/as Premised on the "Other White" Strategy

From the 1920s through the 1940s, some aspects of Latinos/as' experiences in the American South were similar to the Jim Crow experiences of African Americans:

Latinos/as were subject to lynching; excluded from white restaurants, parks, swimming pools, and cemeteries; and restricted from buying property owned by whites.[10] Outside of the Southwest, the Latino/a population was relatively small. Immigration law enacted in the early 1920s was based on quotas of individuals from different countries and prioritized white northern and western Europeans; beginning in the 1940s, the federal Bracero program allowed more workers from Mexico, but only granted them temporary status.[11]

Discrimination against Latinos/as also infiltrated public schools. For example, a Texas statute enacted in 1919 provided that "all school business" except foreign language classes must be conducted in English.[12] Under this statute, which was not repealed until 1969, children were punished for speaking Spanish in school, revealing a "public hostility" toward the Spanish language, which continues to some extent today.[13] During the first half of the twentieth century, Texas also did not bother enforcing the mandatory school attendance law for Latinos/as.[14] Furthermore, in Texas and elsewhere, when Latino/as did enroll in public schools, school officials routinely segregated them from white students on the basis of their surnames, purportedly assuming that they needed English-language instruction regardless of whether they actually were English-proficient or not.[15] Interestingly, in 1929, California Attorney General U. S. Webb issued an advisory opinion concluding that the segregation of Latino/a students could not be defended under California law.[16] This advisory opinion clearly did not halt the segregation practices in California public schools, though. In fact, it seems to have had no direct impact on school districts' practices at all.

At that point in time, courts, too, were hostile to school desegregation. Nearly 100 school desegregation or education-related discrimination cases were brought in the nineteenth century, but the first known school desegregation court order was not issued until 1931.[17] That case, *Alvarez v. Owen*,[18] grew out of the Lemon Grove, California, school district's 1930 decision to abandon its previous practice of educating all children together in the same school building, and instead, to educate the Latino/a children in a barnlike structure on the edge of town, separate from the white children. Disputing this decision, Latino/a parents sued the school district. The county court that heard the case ruled in favor of the plaintiffs and made clear that "the laws of the State of California do not authorize or permit the establishment or maintenance of separate schools for the instruction of pupils of Mexican parentage, nationality, and/or descent."[19] To reach this conclusion, the court analyzed the state law permitting the segregation of "African" and "Indian" students and concluded that because Latinos/as were not "African" or "Indian," their segregation was not defensible under state law. The case was not appealed, nor was it ever mentioned in the minutes of a Lemon Grove school board meeting.[20]

Despite the Lemon Grove success and a few other such decisions, the system of widespread Latino/a segregation in the Southwest persisted until the late 1940s and early 1950s when community groups, professional educators, and educational psychologists began opposing school segregation on a large scale.[21] Their opposition was supported by the weight of the federal courts, which quashed school segregation as a violation of the Fourteenth Amendment's Equal Protection Clause. During that time, the most notable battle involving Latino/a students was fought in the federal courts in California: the case was *Mendez v. Westminster*.[22] As political scientist Philippa Strum documents, the facts leading to the *Mendez* case began when Gonzalo Méndez, a Mexican, and Felícitas Méndez, born in Puerto Rico, moved to Westminster, California. Because the Westminster schools were segregated, the school district refused to enroll the Méndez children in the "white" school.[23] The Méndezes were advocates for the children, though, and their activism included joining other Latino/a parents and working with the school board to propose a ballot initiative approving bonds to finance the construction of an integrated school. However, when the bond proposal failed, board action ceased. In nearby Santa Ana, William Guzman and other Latino/a parents attempted to work with their school board to further integrate schools by increasing the size of the transfer program within the district. This school board, too, was unreceptive to the Latino/a parents' proposals. Not only did it refuse to increase the transfer program, it also further restricted the limited number of transfers available. Méndez and Guzman challenged the repeated decisions of these school boards to perpetuate segregation by becoming two of the five primary plaintiffs in *Mendez v. Westminster School District*.[24]

In 1946, a federal district court concluded in *Mendez* that because the practice of segregating Latinos/as in public schools violated the state and federal constitutions, the plaintiffs were entitled to the injunctive relief of an integrated education. Specifically, the court held:

> The "equal protection of the laws" pertaining to the public school system in California is not provided by furnishing in separate schools the same technical facilities, text books and courses of instruction to children of Mexican ancestry that are available to the other public school children regardless of their ancestry. A paramount requisite in the American system of public education is social equality. It must be open to all children by unified school association regardless of lineage.[25]

Importantly, the district court discussed a state statute under which schools could legally segregate students but were not required to do so. This statute was the successor to the one reviewed in the Lemon Grove case and was titled "Schools for Indian children, and children of Chinese, Japanese, or Mongolian parentage."[26] The federal district court deciding *Mendez* concluded that the statute was "not pertinent to this action" because "[i]t is conceded by all parties that there is no question of race discrimination in this action."[27] While the plaintiff class was described as those of Mexican "extraction," "descent," or "ancestry," the court presumed that the Latino/a plaintiffs were racially white.[28] The NAACP filed a cautious amicus brief in *Mendez* at the appellate level, introducing social science evidence about the general harm of segregation. Another amicus brief filed by lawyer and historian Carey McWilliams focused on the specific harm of segregation in the educational context.[29] The Ninth Circuit Court of Appeals affirmed the district court in 1947, but the social science evidence was not part of its reported decision.[30]

The connections between *Mendez* and *Brown v. Board of Education*[31] (1954), are numerous. Most obviously, the legal reasoning was parallel, especially the emphasis on social science evidence to prove the harm of segregation.[32] Oddly enough, another common theme was Earl Warren's involvement in or proximity to both decisions. First, as attorney general of California, Warren played a leading role in the internment of Japanese Americans during World War II—and of course it was the internment of the Munemitsu family that led the Méndez family to rent the Munemitsu farm in Westminster and attempt to enroll their children in Westminster Main Elementary School.[33] Second, the *Mendez* decision led to the repeal of California's school segregation statutes that became effective upon Warren's signature because, by then, he had become governor of California.[34] Third, less than a decade after *Mendez* was decided, Warren had become the Chief Justice of the United States Supreme Court and, during his first term, penned the Court's unanimous opinion in *Brown*.

Although *Mendez* was groundbreaking in many ways, it did not take long for the decision's limitations to become apparent. The *Mendez* plaintiffs had been successful because they relied on the classification of Latinos/as as white by law for U.S. Census and citizenship purposes, resulting in a holding that school districts could not justifiably segregate some white students (Latinos/as) from other white students (Anglos). This became known as the "other white" strategy. Although the strategy resulted in significant short-term gains for Latinos/as, as in *Mendez*, it also turned out to have major drawbacks. First, the strategy clearly did not reflect the reality of Latinos' and Latinas' lived experiences. As the Supreme Court acknowledged in its 1954 decision *Hernandez v. Texas*,[35] Latinos/as were systematically segregated in public schools and discriminated against in public life; they did not have the social privileges of whiteness, even if they were legally white.

Second, throughout the 1950s and 1960s and especially after the Supreme Court's decisions in *Brown I*[36] in 1954 and *Brown II*[37] in 1955, segregationists came to employ the "other white" strategy, designating Latinos/as as white and enrolling them in schools with African American students to create schools they claimed were racially integrated.[38] However, in communities with a critical mass of both African

Americans and Latinos/as, this practice regularly created one set of schools in which African Americans and Latinos/as were concentrated and another set for whites.

Although the shortcomings of the "other white" strategy were significant, Latinos/as had still come a long way from where they had started the century.

The 1960s: Trading the "Other White" Strategy for the Protections of Federal Civil Rights Legislation, and Witnessing Major Immigration Reform

In part because the "other white" strategy began to backfire, Latino/a activists more or less abandoned it during the 1960s in favor of a distinctly Latino/a, nonwhite/nonblack categorization. Latinos/as argued that they should be considered as an independent and identifiable group in the same way that whites and African Americans were, and not conflated with whites or African Americans in school desegregation litigation or remedies.[39] These arguments, occurring in the context of the Civil Rights Movement, coincided with major immigration reform that was also driven by a focus on equality. The Immigration and Nationality Act of 1965[40] rescinded the system of national-origin quotas that had been in place since the 1920s, and which had clearly favored white western Europeans over immigrants from most of the rest of the world.[41] Eventually, these immigration reforms would help to substantially diversify the United States population, including that in its public schools, particularly by opening up immigration from Latin America and Asia—but at the time of the Act's passage, these long-term effects appear to have been unanticipated.[42]

Even at the end of the 1960s, the Latino/a student population was still small (only around 2 million students) and Latinos/as were rarely included in the rapidly growing number of Southern school desegregation plans.[43] Latinos/as' marginality in educational equity struggles was not limited to desegregation litigation, however. In 1964 the Civil Rights Act became federal law.[44] The Act invested the U.S. Department of Health, Education, and Welfare (the predecessor to the current Department of Education) with the authority to enforce Title VI of the Civil Rights Act, a provision prohibiting intentional discrimination and policies that have a disparate impact in federally funded education settings. The Civil Rights Act, like the Civil Rights Movement out of which it grew, focused primarily on African Americans' rights; thus, at first the Department of Health, Education, and Welfare did not interpret Title VI to protect Latinos/as nor did it even keep records identifying Latinos/as as a group separate from whites.[45]

By contrast, during this time, advocates began to achieve success in their struggles to secure some English-language instruction for English Language Learner (ELL) students, the vast majority of whom were (and continue to be) Latino/a. Up until the 1950s and 1960s, students who did not speak English were expected to acquire English fluency through "submersion."[46] This practice is what it sounds like: children who spoke little or no English were placed into classes conducted entirely in English, were submersed in the language, and would effectively sink or swim. Although submersion meant that ELL students were taught in classrooms alongside students of other races and ethnicities, it also meant that ELL students did not receive any specific instruction in the English language.

During the 1960s, some schools began to provide ELL students with English-language instruction that was actually structured and, among other things, these new programs used the students' native language to help teach them English. This shift was immensely important in the long term, but in the short term it generated some backlash: communities with ELL Latino/a students at times were reluctant to provide bilingual education for fear that their towns would be overrun by Latinos/as and would suffer white flight as a result.[47] However, the emerging English-language instructional norms eventually would have staying power in part because they were buttressed by a new federal law. The Bilingual Education Act of 1968[48] was the first piece of federal legislation to provide funding for schools to teach English to students who were not English-proficient, although it did not obligate states and schools to accept the funding or provide such instruction.[49]

In sum, during the 1960s, major immigration reform set the stage for long-term changes in the racial and ethnic diversity of the U.S. population. Additionally, racial and ethnic integration, and separate structured English-language instruction, were emerging as distinct aspects of what it meant to create equitable educational opportunities for nonwhite students. By the end of the 1960s, these latter two strands would start to intertwine as Latinos/as brought lawsuits alleging that school districts in Corpus Christi, Texas, and Denver, Colorado, illegally segregated Latino/a students and provided them insufficient English-language instruction.[50] These two cases were the first to draw national attention to the interplay between these issues, and both cases would play out throughout the next decade.

The 1970s: Desegregation and Bilingual Education Litigation Take Off, and Some Conflicts Emerge

Building on the legal and social progress of the 1960s, the 1970s saw substantial change in immigration, school desegregation, and bilingual education. By the end of the decade, the interactions among these three issues would start to become clearer.

Since the 1970s, immigrant children have changed the dynamics of public schools in substantial ways, perhaps most obviously by often having English-language instruction needs and also by increasing the racial and ethnic diversity of schools. This is true both for first- and second-generation immigrants. Even though most first-generation immigrants are adults, all second-generation immigrants are, by definition, initially children. Thus, consider the following: In 1960 (prior to the 1965 Immigration and Nationality Reform Act), seven of the ten largest immigrant groups in the U.S. were from Europe; together, these groups constituted about half the immigrants that year. By contrast, only 6% of immigrants in 1960 were from Mexico.[51] In 1970, five years after the major legal change, fewer than 40% of immigrants were from Europe and a combined 13% (about 1.2 million people) were from Mexico (8%) and Cuba (5%).[52] By the beginning of the next decade, in 1980, only about 20% of immigrants (nearly 3 million people) would be from Europe, while the same number were from Latin American/Caribbean countries (Mexico 16% and Cuba 4%). Also by 1980, substantial numbers of immigrants from Asia had started to arrive (Philippines 4% and Korea 2%).[53] Additionally, the 1970s immigration changes were not felt evenly throughout the country, because until the 2000s most of the Latin American/Caribbean immigrants were concentrated in the Southwest and in parts of Florida and New York.

Meanwhile, it was not until 1970 that courts formally rejected the "other white" designation of Latinos/as in school desegregation cases. That year, two federal district courts held that Latinos/as were protected by *Brown v. Board of Education*. In the Corpus Christi school district, nearly half the students were Latino/a, nearly half were white, and approximately 4% were African American. In the desegregation case arising out of this school system, *Cisneros v. Corpus Christi Independent School District*,[54] the district court held that the segregation of both nonwhite groups (Latinos/as, and African Americans) from white students resulted in a constitutionally impermissible dual school system. The Fifth Circuit affirmed this decision two years later in 1972, correctly anticipating the Supreme Court's 1973 decision in *Keyes v. School District No. 1*.

As in Corpus Christi, the demographic composition of the Denver public school system in 1968 did not fit the black-white binary: approximately 71% of the students were white, 13% were African American, and 16% were Latino/a. Aware of racial and ethnic isolation within the district, the school board adopted resolutions to desegregate the Denver schools by changing attendance boundaries. Before the resolutions were fully implemented, however, a newly elected school board rescinded the resolutions and implemented a voluntary exchange program. In *Keyes*, the Denver school desegregation lawsuit, the district court found the school system liable for intentional segregation and entered a remedial order.[55] The district court considered

Latinos/as nonwhite and concluded that a Denver school with 70–75% Latino/Latina or African American students would be considered impermissibly racially identifiable. It distinguished between Latino/a and African American students, and noted the "desirability (even though it is not constitutionally mandated) of having both Negroes and Hispanos in the desegregated schools on as close to an equal basis as possible."[56] The Tenth Circuit affirmed in part, reversed in part, and remanded the case, but it did not question the designation of Latinos/as as nonwhite.[57]

When *Keyes* was argued before the Supreme Court in 1972, 66% of students in the Denver school system were white, 14% were African American, and 20% were Latino/a. The Supreme Court held in part that on remand the district court in *Keyes* should consider African Americans and Latinos/as to be part of the same group for purposes of school desegregation. As a result, Denver schools that had 70–75% Latino/a students, African American students, or a combination of Latino/a as well as African American students were held to be impermissibly racially identifiable.[58] The Court relied on its 1954 decision in *Hernandez v. Texas*[59] for the principle that Latinos/as can constitute a constitutionally protected class but relied upon the report of the United States Commission on Civil Rights to conclude that "though of different origins, Negroes and Hispanos in Denver suffer identical discrimination in treatment when compared with the treatment afforded Anglo students."[60] Not surprisingly, lower courts in subsequent years applied *Keyes* by classifying African Americans and Latinos/as together as nonwhite.[61] The Supreme Court's decision in *Keyes* did not make any preliminary statements about the contested relationship between racial/ethnic integration and English-language instruction, which was left to the mercy of the lower courts.[62]

However, a few years earlier, in 1970, the Department of Health, Education, and Welfare had issued a memorandum to school districts interpreting Title VI of the Civil Rights Act as protecting ELL students. Most importantly, the Department required school districts to "take affirmative steps to rectify the language deficienc[ies]" when those deficiencies effectively barred children from receiving an education.[63] The gaps were immense: a 1972 U.S. Commission on Civil Rights study determined that "6.5 percent of the public schools in the Southwest offered bilingual education; 2.7 percent of the Chicano student population was being served in these programs ... [and thus] about one in forty Chicano students in the five Southwestern states were being served in bilingual education classes, although about one in two first graders were likely in need of such services. . . ."[64]

Then, in 1974, three significant events occurred. First, in January, the Supreme Court decided *Lau v. Nichols*,[65] upholding the Office of Civil Rights' (OCR) interpretation that Title VI of the Civil Rights Act required school districts to take "affirmative steps" to remedy students' language deficiencies.[66] *Lau* was based on national origin discrimination, not racial or ethnic discrimination, though; in part because of this framing, its impact would reach beyond schools, perhaps most significantly ensuring courtroom interpreters for nonnative English speakers.[67] Second, in August, Congress reauthorized and amended the Bilingual Education Act, for the first time explicitly permitting English-*proficient* students to enroll in bilingual classes in order to advance cultural understanding and to reconcile the goals of desegregation and bilingual education.[68] This change also suggested that bilingualism was an asset for native English speakers (three decades later, this theme would emerge as popular among middle-class whites). Third, as part of the same bill that reauthorized the Bilingual Education Act, Congress passed the Equal Educational Opportunities Act (EEOA).[69] The EEOA codified the Court's "affirmative steps" holding from earlier that year in *Lau*. Because of these three events, in less than a year the formal legal regime affecting ELL students—the vast majority of whom were Latinos/as—changed radically.

Soon thereafter, in 1975, OCR issued guidelines interpreting *Lau* as favoring bilingual programs that included native-language instruction, arguably going further than the requirements of *Lau*.[70] For several years, the Department of Health, Education, and Welfare used these guidelines when formulating hundreds of consent agreements, and federal courts applied these guidelines as well.[71] In 1978, shortly before the end of this tumultuous decade, Congress again reauthorized the Bilingual Education Act. In a measure that some regarded as a step back from earlier policy declarations, the reauthorization emphasized that the purpose of bilingual education should be transitioning nonnative-English speakers into English-language classrooms.[72]

Thus, English-language instruction programs and services grew throughout the 1970s, and during this time many language minority communities began to benefit from the first comprehensive English-language instruction programs school districts had ever offered. Yet, because these programs usually required nonnative English speakers to be concentrated with one another for purposes of English-language instruction, they conflicted with some aspects of aggressive desegregation remedies that sought systemic racial and ethnic balance of students within school districts. Toward the end of the 1970s, parents of language minority students publicly opposed desegregation decrees in some communities in favor of more concentrated English-language instruction programs; in other communities, parents attempted to intervene in desegregation litigation to ask courts to balance the interests of desegregation and ELL students. Latino/a parents were granted intervenor status in ongoing desegregation suits in Denver, Colorado; Detroit, Michigan; Los Angeles, California; Madison Park, Massachusetts; New York, New York; Waterbury, Connecticut, and likely other places, as well.[73] Chinese American parents were granted intervenor status in San Francisco, California.[74] In some school districts, courts struggled to balance bilingual education needs with integration goals. In other districts, bilingual programs were framed as segregating students and gave way to the goal of racial and ethnic integration.[75] Ultimately, between 1972 and 1975, the Mexican American Legal Defense and Educational Fund (MALDEF) initiated 39 school desegregation lawsuits—not an insignificant number, especially for this type of case—but even when considering this litigation activity, scholars describe the organization as prioritizing bilingual education policy and litigation over school integration.[76]

Finally, perhaps reflecting the public's and courts' ambivalence about how Latinos/as fit within the goals of school desegregation, social science desegregation research during this time did not identify Latino/a students as a distinct group. Unfortunately for them, this was the "most productive period of empirical research on the effects of desegregation on school outcomes," and it completely passed them by.[77]

1980s Through the Present: Immigration Expands, Education Rights Contract

During the 1960s and 1970s, Latinos/as began to benefit from expanding educational equity rights via legislative statutes, judicial doctrine, and administrative regulations. In the three and a half decades since, many progressive social changes have occurred, but in general the rights-based framework provided by law has contracted for Latinos/as and African Americans alike, even while immigration from Latin America has grown rapidly.

1980s: ONE STEP FORWARD, ONE STEP BACK, ONE STEP SIDEWAYS

During the 1980s, laws regulating English-language instruction changed substantially, resulting in less curricular and cultural space for students' native languages. At the same time, undocumented immigrant students gained substantial educational access rights. Finally, although school desegregation cases were litigated and remedies played out across the country, the governing jurisprudence changed little.

In 1984, the Supreme Court decided one of the most notable cases of the decade, *Plyler v. Doe*,[78] which held that undocumented immigrant children had a right to elementary and secondary education on the same terms as U.S. citizens. A defining feature of immigration law is to treat citizens quite differently from noncitizens and thus to tolerate inequality between the two groups. In *Plyler*, however, the Court invoked *Brown*'s "apparently absolute command of equality" and rejected the idea that states could refuse to enroll undocumented immigrant children in public schools and thus eventually create a permanent underclass.[79] *Plyler*'s full impact would not be apparent for another two decades.

Although *Plyler* had also involved Latino/a ethnic isolation and language segregation, the Court was silent on both of those issues. The other two branches of the federal government, however, were not. Legal changes with regard to English-language instruction during the 1980s were substantial. First, in the early 1980s, the U.S. Department of Education withdrew the *Lau* guidelines that had stated that instruction in a student's native language was an important part of English-language instruction.[80] Second, around the same time, Congress amended the Bilingual Education Act to explicitly accept Structured English Immersion (SEI) pedagogy, thus endorsing a method of English-language instruction that involved very little communication in the student's native language.[81] Third, during the late 1980s, Congress amended the Bilingual Education Act to increase funding for SEI programs and also to put a three-year limit on students' enrollment in bilingual programs, thus restricting financial support for English-language instruction programs which in part used a student's native language.[82] Research about English-language instruction generally has demonstrated that students in traditional bilingual programs acquire English more slowly but also acquire more content, while students in immersion programs acquire English more quickly but lose content along the way. However, these changes were driven more by the political climate of the time, in which a renewed interest in "English-only" statutes and regulations took root in various regions of the country.

The retreat from the progressive legal changes of prior decades was not a complete one. For example, the Fifth Circuit's 1981 decision in *Casteneda v. Pickard*,[83] the most well-known ELL case of the 1980s, permitted a great deal of deference to school districts' English-language instruction choices. While this could allow for the possibility that an SEI program could satisfy the EEOA, it also led to deference to districts that retained bilingual instructional approaches. Additionally, throughout the 1980s OCR investigated alleged EEOA violations and, when appropriate, negotiated binding compliance agreements with school districts to remedy the deficiencies—an activity it continues to this day.[84]

Finally, Latinos/as' as well as ELL students' relationships with school desegregation cases continued to be tenuous. In 1980, the Sixth Circuit declared in the Detroit desegregation case *Bradley v. Milliken*[85] that "when the choice is between maintaining optimal conditions in a bilingual education program and desegregating all-black schools, desegregation must prevail."[86]

1990s: SCHOOL DESEGREGATION JURISPRUDENCE EMBRACES UNITARY STATUS

The 1990s saw increasing racial and ethnic diversity through immigration that continued in line with previous trends, and little change regarding English-language instruction rights. In fact, except for the routine reauthorization of the Bilingual Education Act in 1994, Congress had little to say about English-language instruction during the 1990s. Toward the end of the 1990s, though, some major English-language instructional changes started happening at the state level: for example, California voters approved a proposal requiring SEI (colloquially known as "English-only instruction") for ELL students across California.[87] The resulting widespread changes in law would belong to the new century.

Regarding desegregation litigation, the most significant legal changes in the 1990s were three Supreme Court decisions that made it easier for school districts under court oversight to achieve unitary status. This created precedent that could work to the disadvantage of Latino/a students. For example, in 1991, the Supreme Court's decision in *Board of Education v. Dowell*[88] changed the landscape for school desegregation, sanctioning piecemeal unitary status declarations. However, *Dowell* did not discuss the rights of Latino/a children in Oklahoma City, which was significant because the school district's demographics had changed much during the course of court oversight.[89] Thus, in Oklahoma City and in school districts across the country, unitary status could be granted without considering new issues of inequality presented by a growing Latino/a student population.

2000–PRESENT: LAW AND POLICY PULLING IN VARIOUS DIRECTIONS

Since the turn of the century, school desegregation, English-language instruction, and immigration have collectively and individually been plagued by interesting tensions. Sometimes, law has moved in one direction while voluntary policy decisions have trended in another. Other times, the long-term impact of decades-old legal changes has finally become apparent.

To begin with immigration, since 2000, Mexicans have accounted for about 30% of immigrants into the United States, by far the single largest immigrant group; additionally, in 2012, immigrants from Cuba, El Salvador, the Dominican Republic, and Guatemala totaled an additional 10% of immigrants.[90] During this same time, immigrants from Southeast Asia and the Indian subcontinent have increased from roughly 16% in 2000 to about 20% in 2012.[91] Of course, as noted previously, most immigrants are adults: in 2011, the Pew Research Center reported that about 6% of documented immigrants and 13% of undocumented immigrants were children.[92]

Also as noted earlier, immigration and a high birthrate among a young population are the major factors in the rapid growth of the Latino/a population in U.S. public schools. The first year in which U.S. public schools had more Latino/a than African American students was 2001, and the gap has only widened since then.

Although the Latino/a population had been concentrated in a few states for quite some time, since 2000 this has changed significantly: in 2012, Latinos/as comprised at least one-fifth of public school kindergarteners in 17 states, including Massachusetts, New Jersey, Kansas, Nebraska, Washington, and Idaho.[93] As a result of changing migration patterns, the impact of the Supreme Court's 1984 decision in *Plyler* is now being felt across the country—public schools must accept the estimated 1 million undocumented immigrant children who live in the U.S.[94] The enrollment of these students can create challenges for schools and communities because undocumented immigrant children in particular are likely to be performing below grade level, in need of English-language instruction, and in need of a host of other social and personal support the school cannot provide.[95] These services are expensive and schools are hardly flush with cash, which can lead to conflict on the local level.

Federal law has not forgotten ELL students, which is important because, even today, an estimated 20–40% of Latino/a students are ELLs.[96] In 2001, Congress passed the No Child Left Behind Act (NCLB), which is still in effect in 2014.[97] NCLB repealed the Bilingual Education Act (1968) but left the EEOA (1974) untouched. Pursuant to NCLB, ELL students must participate in standards-based testing, and they may be tested in their native language only during the first three years they are enrolled in public schools in the United States. After that, they must be tested in English.[98] Some argue that because of these changes as well as changes in grant-funding, NCLB has the effect of favoring SEI over other bilingual and language instruction programs.[99]

Additionally, in 2009, the Supreme Court decided an EEOA case, *Horne v. Flores*,[100] by a vote of 5–4. On the whole, the majority approached the case as one chapter in a storied dispute among judges, lawyers, scholars, and policymakers about the extent to which increased funding can improve education. First, the *Horne* majority focused on the multiple ways in which the EEOA "appropriate action" standard can be satisfied—and, curiously, not only discussed the nonmonetary means for such satisfaction but also emphasized those means. This language about the extent to which "money matters" is likely to influence EEOA, school finance, and school desegregation cases for years to come. Second, the Court rejected the lower courts' "rigid" view of when the state could be released from court oversight, evoking its desegregation cases from the 1990s that facilitated courts' grants of unitary status. Third, in the only aspect of the decision that Latino/a advocates celebrated, the Court preserved EEOA as a meaningful cause of action when it held that compliance with EEOA and NCLB are not interchangeable.

Although NCLB and *Horne* are seen as retreats from English-language instruction rights, dual language instruction programs are becoming increasingly popular throughout the U.S. as white middle-class parents often push for programs that enroll half native English speakers and half native speakers of a target language (usually Spanish, sometimes Mandarin, occasionally another language). Unlike SEI, dual language programs have the goal of educating all students so that they are fluent in both languages. In 2000, 260 such programs operated; by 2010, an estimated 2,000 programs were in existence.[101] The exact number of programs currently operating in the U.S. is unknown, but they appear to have increased even since 2010 as more states and local school districts have enacted these programs; for example, Utah has promoted the rapid growth of these programs and in the 2014–15 school year, it will have dual language programs in 118 schools across its state.[102] Even though law protecting ELL students does not prioritize preserving their native language, dual language programs view nonnative English speakers as an asset to the educational environment. In many communities, these programs also present one way to reconcile the goal of racial and ethnic integration with English-language instruction for nonnative speakers.

However, because of changes in school desegregation jurisprudence, if dual language programs create racially and ethnically diverse classrooms, the diversity is likely to be a coincidence. The Supreme Court's most recent elementary and secondary school integration decision was issued in 2007. In that case, *Parents Involved in Community Schools v. Seattle School District No. 1*,[103] the Court reviewed the voluntary student assignment plans that school districts in Seattle, Washington, and Louisville, Kentucky, had implemented with the goal of increasing the racial/ ethnic diversity within their public schools. The Court was split 4–1–4, with Justice Kennedy concurring and dissenting in part.[104] Kennedy's opinion thus joined with the dissenters to create a holding that the pursuit of racial diversity could be a compelling government interest, and joined with the plurality to create a holding that the voluntary transfer plans at issue were not narrowly tailored to achieve the goal of diversity.[105] The decision was a blow to civil rights advocates.

Even more recently, the Supreme Court has decided two higher education affirmative action cases: *Fisher v. University of Texas*[106] (2013) and *Schutte v. Coalition to Defend Affirmative Action*[107] (2014). Although it is never precisely clear how the holding of a higher education affirmative action case will apply to elementary and secondary schools (indeed, even after the Court's 2003 decisions in *Gratz*[108] and *Grutter*,[109] federal appellate circuits still interpreted Supreme Court precedent to permit race-conscious voluntary integration of elementary and secondary schools, which was then struck down in 2007 in *Parents Involved*), the decisions point in an important direction. First, *Fisher* continues on the path of analyzing affirmative action and voluntary integration in a manner that is "strict in theory but fatal in fact."[110] This suggests that the few school districts that employ voluntary integration plans face an even higher hurdle when justifying the narrow tailoring of their consideration of race and ethnicity. Second, in *Schutte* the Court upheld via a 6–2 decision a state constitutional amendment that prohibited affirmative action by focusing on the amendment's application to higher education admissions, although the amendment at issue was written in a way that it arguably prohibits voluntary integration plans in elementary and secondary schools. Both of these decisions involved white plaintiffs, and neither presented issues of Latino/a educational equity squarely.

Interestingly, during this same time, Latinos/as have been able to bring successful school desegregation lawsuits in which they alleged that a school district had engaged in unconstitutional intentional discrimination. Some of these lawsuits have incorporated English-language instruction claims, and they seem connected to conflicts emerging as Latinos/as, whether immigrants or not, are diversifying communities across the country. For example, in 2005, nearly all of the Latina and Latino students at one North Dallas elementary school were assigned to bilingual and English as Second Language (ESL) classrooms even though many of them were proficient in English.[111] The school principal authorized these student assignment practices so the school could market a racially isolated educational experience to affluent white families in the school's surrounding neighborhood attendance zone via word of mouth and also brochures that contained almost no black or brown faces.[112] Not surprisingly, the district was held liable for violating the Fourteenth Amendment.[113] Although Texas has been home to a substantial Latina/o population for many years, it appears that this particular school had not.

Thus, taken together, the legal and social changes since the turn of the century present a complex picture. The Latino/a student population in this country has grown rapidly through migration and a high birthrate, yet school desegregation litigation and voluntary integration plans—the most traditional way to use law and policy in pursuit of educational opportunity for a racially and ethnically marginalized group—have become of limited utility for nonwhites, except in situations like the hopefully rare North Dallas example. As a result of the changes in Supreme Court doctrine—the Court's hostility toward considering racial/ethnic difference even for the purpose of benefiting a historically marginalized group—most Latino/a students are now much more likely to benefit from facially race/ethnicity-neutral laws and policies such as those that guarantee English-language instruction, though of course the majority of Latinos/as (the vast majority, by some counts) are English-proficient.

Conclusion

From the "other white" strategy through recent Supreme Court decisions about voluntary integration and the EEOA, we see the power of the law to create social change and also the limits of the law in doing so. From the battles over English-language instruction rights and policies over the past half-century we see tensions between wanting our classrooms to reflect our increasingly diverse communities, and separating particular sub-groups of students for purposes of English-language instruction. From the changes in immigration law and resulting changes in our society, we see a country that is growing increasingly diverse and will soon not even have a majority racial or ethnic group. Changes in each of these three areas have affected educational opportunities for Latino/a students profoundly. Going forward, each of these three areas of law will contribute substantially to how we define and pursue educational equity for the most rapidly growing racial/ethnic group in the country.

And yet, as cases and conflicts from *Mendez* through the present day demonstrate, the three areas of law do not operate in isolation. In fact, they are necessarily intertwined. To discuss educational equity for Latinos/as means engaging school desegregation and also English-language instruction with their at-times contradictory goals of integration, on one hand, and temporary separation, on the other hand—and also being aware of the ways in which over-identification of Latinos/as as ELLs has been a cover for unconstitutional segregation. The discussion also cannot happen without awareness of the influence of immigration permitted by law and immigration outside the law because the rapid growth of the Latino/a population owes so much to immigration, and also because the politics of immigration influence perceptions of Latinos/as more generally.

Understanding these connections complicates our conceptions of educational equity, and yet it also paints a more nuanced picture that acknowledges the fullness of Latinos/as' experiences in schools across the country 100 years ago, and today.

Kristi L. Bowman is a Professor of Law at Michigan State University College of Law. Portions of this chapter are adapted from *The New Face of School Desegregation,* 50 DUKE LAW JOURNAL 1751 (2001) and *Pursuing Educational Opportunities for Latino/a Students,* 88 NORTH CAROLINA LAW REVIEW 911 (2010), which received the Education Law Association's Steven J. Goldberg Award for Distinguished Scholarship in Education Law.

NOTES

For helpful comments on the current chapter and its previous iterations, the author thanks Erica Frankenberg, Rachel Moran, David Thronson, and participants at conferences where she presented this work. For research and editing assistance she thanks Courtney Soughers, Maria Lapetina, Caitlin Salazer-Reid, and Lauren Foley.

1. Mendez v. Westminister School District of Orange County, 64 F. Supp. 544 (S.D. Cal. 1946).

2. Cristina Rodriguez, *Latinos: Discrete and Insular No More*, 12 HARVARD LATINO LAW REVIEW 41, 43–49 (2009); Rachel F. Moran, *Neither Black Nor White*, 2 HARVARD LATINO LAW REVIEW 61, 69 (1997); Douglas J. Massey, *Latinas/os, Poverty, and the Underclass: A New Agenda for Research*, 15 HISPANIC JOURNAL OF BEHAVIORAL SCIENCES 449, 453 (1993).

3. Moran, *Neither Black Nor White*, 69.

4. National Center for Education Statistics, Digest of Education Statistics, *Table 203.50. Enrollment and percentage distribution of enrollment in public elementary and secondary schools, by race/ethnicity and region: Selected years, fall 1995 through fall 2023* (December 2013).

5. Ibid.

6. Ibid.

7. In 2008, nearly half of Latino/a students were concentrated in high-poverty schools, a slightly higher percentage than African Americans overall. National Center for Education Statistics, U.S. Department of Education, *The Condition of Education 2008*, 49, 152. When schools were disaggregated by community type, this same dynamic held true in cities and suburbs, but not in towns and rural areas where a greater percentage of African Americans were concentrated in high-poverty schools. The dropout rate for Latinos/as, though high, was in 2008 the lowest recorded for this group since record-keeping started in 1972. U.S. Department of Education, National Center for Education Statistics, Fast Facts, *Question: What Are the Dropout Rates of High School Students?* (2008). Latinos fare better than Latinas, though: Only 59% of Latinas graduate from high school on time; the remaining 41% drop out, finish high school in five years or more, or get a GED. Catherine Gewertz, *Report Probes Educational Challenges Facing Latinas*, EDUCATION WEEK, 10, 52, 56, 59, 61 (September 2, 2009). Of all students' homes in which English is not spoken, Spanish is spoken in nearly three-quarters of the homes. Richard Fry & Felisa Gonzales, Pew Hispanic Center, *One-in-Five and Growing Fast: A Profile of Hispanic Public School Students* 11 (2008).

8. Richard C. Jones, *The Ambiguous Roles of Suburbanization and Immigration in Ethnic Segregation: The Case of San Antonio*, 29 URBAN GEOGRAPHY 196, 197 (2008); Daniel T. Lichter et al., *National Estimates of Racial Segregation in Rural and Small-Town America*, 44 DEMOGRAPHY 563, 563, 574–75 (2007).

9. *Mendez*, 64 F. Supp. 544.

10. Lupe S. Salinas, *Linguaphobia, Language Rights, and the Right of Privacy*, 3 STANFORD JOURNAL OF CIVIL RIGHTS & CIVIL LIBERTIES 53, 65–66 (2007).

11. Hiroshi Motomura, *Who Belongs? Immigration Outside the Law*, 2 UNIVERSITY OF CALIFORNIA-IRVINE LAW REVIEW 359, 369–70 (2012).

12. Act of May 13, 1933, Ch. 125, § 1, 1933 Texas General Laws 325, 325–36, *repealed* by Act of

May 22, 1969, Ch. 289, § 4, 1969 Texas General Laws. 871, 872.

13. Salinas, *Linguaphobia*, 65 n.65, 66; Margaret E. Montoya, *Law and Language(s): Image, Integration and Innovation*, 7 LA RAZA LAW JOURNAL 147, 148 (1994); Steven W. Bender, *Direct Democracy and Distrust: The Relationship Between Language Law Rhetoric and the Language Vigilantism Experience*, 2 HARVARD LATINO LAW REVIEW 145, 150, 167 (2007).

14. James Thomas Tucker, *The Battle Over "Bilingual Ballots" Shifts to the Courts: A Post-Boerne Assessment of Section 203 of the Voting Rights Act*, 45 HARVARD JOURNAL ON LEGISLATION 507, 563 (2008).

15. Ibid., 563–65 (Texas and Arizona); Kristi Bowman, *The New Face of School Desegregation*, 50 DUKE LAW JOURNAL 1751, 1773 (2001) (California).

16. CHARLES WOLLENBERG, ALL DELIBERATE SPEED: SEGREGATION AND EXCLUSION IN CALIFORNIA SCHOOLS, 1855–1975, 123 (University of California Press 1976).

17. Caroline Hendrie, *In Black and White*, EDUCATION WEEK 31 (March 24, 1999).

18. Alvarez v. Owen, No. 66625 (California Superior Court, San Diego County, filed April 17, 1931).

19. Alvarez v. Owen, No. 66625 (California Superior Court, San Diego County, filed April 21, 1931) (order issuing peremptory writ of mandate) (the court's decision and order are reprinted in Bowman, *The New Face of School Desegregation*, Appendix).

20. Robert R. Alvarez, Jr., *The Lemon Grove Incident: The Nation's First Successful School Desegregation Court Case*, 32 JOURNAL OF SAN DIEGO HISTORY 131 (Spring 1986).

21. GILBERT G. GONZALES, CHICANO EDUCATION IN THE ERA OF SEGREGATION, 22 (Balch Institute Press 1990); WOLLENBERG, ALL DELIBERATE SPEED, 118–23. Consider the many groups participating as amici in *Brown*: the United States, the ACLU, the American Federation of Teachers, the American Jewish Congress, the American Veterans Committee, Inc., the Congress of Industrial Organizations, and the many social scientists who provided the appendix to the appellant's brief.

22. Phoebe C. Godfrey, *The "Other White": Mexican Americans and the Impotency of Whiteness in the Segregation and Desegregation of Texan Public Schools*, 41 EQUITY & EXCELLENCE IN EDUCATION 247, 250–51, 253 (2008); Richard R. Valencia, *The Mexican American Struggle for Equal Educational Opportunity, in* Mendez v. Westminster: *Helping to Pave the Way for* Brown v. Board of Education, 107 TEACHERS COLLEGE RECORD 390, 418 (2005); Steven H. Wilson, *Brown Over "Other White": Mexican Americans' Legal Arguments and Litigation Strategy in School Desegregation Lawsuits*, 21 LAW & HISTORY REVIEW 145 (2003); Steven Harmon Wilson, *Some Are Born White, Some Achieve Whiteness, and Some Have Whiteness Thrust upon Them: Mexican Americans and the Politics of Racial Classification in the Federal Judicial Bureaucracy, Twenty-Five Years After* Hernandez v. Texas, 25 CHICANO-LATINO LAW REVIEW 201, 213 (2005).

23. PHILIPPA STRUM, *MENDEZ V. WESTMINSTER*: SCHOOL DESEGREGATION AND MEXICAN-AMERICAN RIGHTS (University Press of Kansas 2010); Philippa Strum, *Our Children Are Americans:* Mendez v. Westminster *and Mexican American Rights* in this volume.

24. Mendez, 544; WOLLENBERG, ALL DELIBERATE SPEED, 123–25.

25. Mendez, 64 F. Supp. 549.

26. Ibid., 545 n.5.

27. Ibid., 546, 548.

28. Ibid., 546; GONZALES, CHICANO EDUCATION, 152.

29. Richard Delgado, *Derrick Bell's Toolkit—Fit to Dismantle That Famous House?*, 75 NEW YORK UNIVERSITY LAW REVIEW 283, 304 (2000).

30. Westminster School District v. Mendez, 161 F.2d 774, 781 (9th Cir. 1947).

31. Brown v. Board of Education, 347 U.S. 483 (1954).

32. Frederick P. Aguirre, Mendez v. Westminster School District: *How it Affected* Brown v. Board of Education, 47 ORANGE COUNTY LAWYER 30 (2005).

33. STRUM, *MENDEZ V. WESTMINSTER*; Strum, *Our Children Are Americans*; Mendez v. Westminster: *For All the Children* (documentary film, Sandra Robbie, producer, 2003).

34. California AB 531, An act to add Section 51204.6 to the Education Code, relating to the public school curriculum §1(c) (Amended January 7, 2008).

35. 347 U.S. 475 (1954).

36. Brown, 347 U.S. 483.

37. Brown v. Board of Education, 349 U.S. 294 (1955).

38. Gary Orfield & Chungmei Lee, The Civil Rights Project, *New Faces, Old Patterns? Segregation in the Multiracial South*, 5 (2005); Phoebe C. Godfrey, *The "Other White": Mexican Americans and the Impotency of Whiteness in the Segregation and Desegregation of Texas Public Schools*, 41 EQUITY & EXCELLENCE EDUCATION 247, 254 (discussing desegregation in Houston); Rachel F. Moran, *Milo's Miracle*, 29 CONNECTICUT LAW REVIEW 1079, 1086 (1997); Valeriano Saucedo, *Civility, Respect, and Life Experience: A Latino Perspective from the Bench*, 13 LA RAZA LAW JOURNAL 51, 51 (2002); Richard R. Valencia, Martha Menchaca & Ruben Donato, *Segregation, Desegregation, and Integration of Chicano Students: Old and New Realities, in* RICHARD VALENCIA, ED., CHICANO SCHOOL FAILURE AND SUCCESS: PAST, PRESENT, AND FUTURE, 71, 90 (Routledge 2002).

39. Tom I. Romero, II, *MALDEF and the Legal Investment in a Multi-Colored America*, 18 LA RAZA LAW JOURNAL 135, 137 (2007).

40. Public Law 89-236, 79 Stat. 911, enacted June 30, 1968.

41. Jennifer Ludden, *1965 Immigration Law Changed Face of America*, npr.org (May 9, 2006).

42. Ibid.

43. Gary Orfield & Chungmei Lee, The Civil Rights Project, *Historic Reversals, Accelerating Resegregation, and the Need for New Integration Strategies*, 16, 23 (2007); Erica Frankenberg, Chungmei Lee & Gary Orfield, The Civil Rights Project, *A Multiracial Society with Segregated Schools: Are We Losing the Dream?*, 32 (2003).

44. Civil Rights Act of 1964, Public Law No. 88-352, 78 Stat. 241 (codified in scattered sections of 42 U.S.C.).

45. Tom I. Romero, II, *¿La Raza Latina?: Multiracial Ambivalence, Color Denial, and the Emergence of a Tri-Ethnic Jurisprudence at the End of the Twentieth Century*, 37 NEW MEXICO LAW REVIEW 245, 271–74 (2007).

46. Kelly Bikle, Kenji Hakuta & Elsa S. Bilings, *Trends in Two-Way Immersion Research, in* JAMES A. BANKS & CHERRY MCGEE BANKS, EDS., HANDBOOK OF RESEARCH ON MULTICULTURAL EDUCATION (Jossey-Bass 2004).

47. Michelle R. Wood, *ESL and Bilingual Education as a Proxy for Racial and Ethnic Segregation in U.S. Public Schools*, 11 JOURNAL OF GENDER, RACE & JUSTICE 599, 617 (2008).

48. Elementary and Secondary Education Amendments of 1967, Public Law No. 90-247, 81 Stat. 783, 816–20 (1968) (codified as amended in scattered sections of 20 U.S.C.).

49. James Crawford, *Obituary: The Bilingual Ed Act, 1968–2001*, RETHINKING SCHOOLS ONLINE (Summer 2002).

50. Cisneros v. Corpus Christi Independent School District, 324 F. Supp. 599, 606 (S.D. Tex. 1970); Keyes v. School District No. 1, 303 F. Supp. 279, 289 (D. Colo. 1969) (granting preliminary injunction); modified, Keyes v. School District No. 1, 303 F. Supp. 289 (D. Colo. 1969).

51. Migration Policy Institute, *Top Ten Immigrant Groups, 1960* (2014).

52. Migration Policy Institute, *Top Ten Immigrant Groups, 1970* (2014).

53. Migration Policy Institute, *Top Ten Immigrant Groups, 1980* (2014).

54. Cisneros, 324 F. Supp. at 606.

55. Keyes v. School District No. 1, 313 F. Supp. 61, 69 (D. Colo. 1970). The district court's opinion in Keyes was reported in two parts: Keyes v. School District No. 1, 313 F. Supp. 61, 69 (D. Colo. 1970) (making findings of fact and law) and Keyes v. School District No. 1, 313 F. Supp. 90 (D. Colo. 1970) (prescribing a remedy).

56. Keyes, 313 F. Supp. 100.

57. Keyes v. School District No. 1, 445 F. 2d 990, 1007 (10th Cir. 1971).

58. Keyes v. School District No. 1, 413 U.S. 189, 197–98 (1973).

59. Hernandez v. State of Texas, 347 U.S. 475 (1954).

60. Keyes, 413 U.S. 197–98.

61. Bowman, *The New Face of School Desegregation*, 1777–81.

62. M. Beatriz Arias, *The Impact of Brown on Latinos: A Study of Transformation of Policy Intentions*, 107 TEACHERS COLLEGE RECORD 1974, 1980 (2005).

63. Identification of Discrimination and Denial of Services on the Basis of National Origin, 35 Fed. Reg. 11595, 11595 (Office of Civil Rights July 17, 1970).

64. Richard Valencia, *The Plight of Chicano Students: An Overview of Schooling Conditions and Outcomes*, in CHICANO SCHOOL FAILURE AND SUCCESS: PAST, PRESENT, AND FUTURE, 3, 8.

65. Lau v. Nichols, 414 U.S. 563 (1974).

66. Ibid., 568; Rachel F. Moran, *Undone by Law: The Uncertain Legacy of Lau v. Nichols*, 16 BERKELEY LA RAZA LAW JOURNAL 1, 4–5 (2005). OCR was then a division of the Department of Health, Education, and Welfare and is a subdivision of the Department of Education today.

67. Thomas E. Perez, Assistant Attorney General of the United States, *Dear Chief Justice/State Court Administrator Letter* (August 16, 2010).

68. Education Amendments of 1974, Public Law 93-380, §§ 702(a), 703(a)(6), 88 Stat. 474, 503, 505 (codified as amended in scattered sections of 20 U.S.C.); Bethany Li, *From Bilingual Education to OELALEAALEPS: How the No Child Left Behind Act Has Undermined English Language Learners' Access to a Meaningful Education*, 14 GEORGETOWN JOURNAL ON POVERTY LAW & POLICY 539, 551 (2007).

69. Equal Educational Opportunities Act of 1974, Public Law 93-380, § 259, 88 Stat. 514, 521 (1974) (codified at 20 U.S.C. §1232g (2006)).

70. Rachel F. Moran, *The Politics of Discretion: Federal Intervention in Bilingual Education*, 76 CALIFORNIA LAW REVIEW 1249, 1280–83 (1988).

71. The Federal General Educational Provisions Act authorizes the Department of Education

    [T]o enter into a compliance agreement with a recipient that is failing to comply substantially with Federal program requirements. . . . In order to enter into a compliance agreement, the Department must determine, through written findings, that the recipient cannot comply with the applicable program requirements until a future date and that a compliance agreement is a viable means of bringing about such compliance.

    Notice of Written Findings and Compliance Agreement with the New Hampshire Department of Education, 73 Fed. Reg. 4319, 4320 (Jan. 23, 2009). If the recipient agrees to modify its actions, policies, etc. to come into compliance, the Department may enter into this informal compliance agreement with the recipient rather than withholding funds or ultimately litigating against the recipient. 20 U.S.C. § 1234(c) (2006). Thus, the compliance agreement process is an important part of the Department's law enforcement activities. For a further description of this process, see Notice of Written Findings and Compliance Agreement with the New Hampshire Department of Education, 73 Fed. Reg. 4319–31. Moran, *The Politics of Discretion*, 1283.

72. Education Amendments of 1978, Public Law No. 95-561, 92 Stat. 2268–69 (codified at 20 U.S.C. § 3222 (2001)).

73. Rachel F. Moran, *Rethinking Race, Equality, and Liberty: The Unfulfilled Promise of Parents Involved*, 69 OHIO STATE LAW JOURNAL 1321, 1338 (2008); Joaquin G. Avila, *Equal Educational Opportunities for Language Minority Children*, 55 UNIVERSITY OF COLORADO LAW REVIEW 559, 561–62 (1984); Bryant G. Garth, *Conflict and Dissent in Class Actions: A Suggested Perspective*, 77 NORTHWESTERN UNIVERSITY LAW REVIEW 492, 518–19 (1982); Moran, *Rethinking Race*, 1338, 1340; Moran, *Mio's Miracle*, 1086.

74. Moran, *Rethinking Race*, 1338, 1340.

75. RUBEN DONATO, THE OTHER STRUGGLE FOR EQUAL SCHOOLS: MEXICAN AMERICANS DURING THE CIVIL RIGHTS ERA, 129 (SUNY Press 1997); Joaquin G. Avila, *Equal Educational Opportunities for Language Minority Children*, 55 UNIVERSITY OF COLORADO LAW REVIEW 559, 561–62; Tom I. Romero II, *Our Selma is Here: The Political and Legal Struggle for Educational Equality in Denver, Colorado, and Multiracial Conundrums in American Jurisprudence*, 3 SEATTLE JOURNAL FOR SOCIAL JUSTICE 73, 115 (2004); Bowman, *The New Face of School Desegregation*, 1791–92.

76. Arias, *The Impact of Brown*, 1979; Romero, *MALDEF and the Legal Investment*, 142; Marie C. Scott, *Resegregation, Language, and Educational Opportunity: The Influence of Latino Students in North Carolina Public Schools*, 11 HARVARD LATINO LAW REVIEW 123, 127. MALDEF was in strange company, joined by the Nixon administration, among others. Frankenberg, Lee, & Orfield, *A Multiracial Society*, 19–20.

77. Arias, *The Impact of Brown*, 1978.

78. Plyler v. Doe, 457 U.S. 202 (1982); Nina Rabin, Mary Carol Combs & Norma Gonzalez, *Understanding Plyler's Legacy: Voices from Border Schools*, 37 JOURNAL OF LAW & EDUCATION 15, 51 (2008).

79. Hiroshi Motomura, Brown v. Board of Education, *Immigrants, and the Meaning of*

Equality, 49 NEW YORK LAW SCHOOL LAW REVIEW 1145, 1147 (2005).

80. Moran, *The Politics of Discretion*, 1293–96.

81. Eugene E. Garcia & Ann-Marie Wise, *Language, Public Policy, and Schooling: A Focus on Chicano English Language Learners, in* CHICANO SCHOOL FAILURE AND SUCCESS: PAST, PRESENT, AND FUTURE, 149, 154–55 (Routledge 2002); Moran, *The Politics of Discretion*, 1306–14.

82. Garcia & Wise, *Language, Public Policy, and Schooling*, 155.

83. Castaneda v. Pickard, 648 F.2d 989, 1009–10 (5th Cir. 1981). *Castaneda*'s three-part analysis has remained the seminal test for determining EEOA compliance for over 25 years, although it was modified somewhat by the Supreme Court's 2009 decision in *Horne v. Flores*, 557 U.S. 433 (2009).

84. Ibid.; Mary Ann Zehr, *Under Federal Pressure, District Addresses ELLs*, EDUCATION WEEK, 1, 12 (June 10, 2009).

85. Bradley v. Milliken, 620 F.2d 1143 (6th Cir. 1980).

86. Ibid., 1154.

87. In an unusual, fleeting step, a federal district court prevented the implementation of Proposition 227 in the San Jose school district for which it was overseeing a remedy. Wendy Parker, *The Supreme Court and Public Law Remedies: A Tale of Two Kansas Cities*, 50 HASTINGS LAW JOURNAL 475, 571 n.420 (1999).

88. Board of Education of Oklahoma City Public Schools, Independent School District No. 89, Oklahoma County, Oklahoma v. Dowell, 498 U.S. 237, 246, 249–50 (1991).

89. Orfield & Lee, *Historic Reversals*, 9, 14.

90. Migration Policy Institute, *Top Ten Largest U.S. Immigrant Groups, 2000* (2014); Migration Policy Institute, *Top Ten Largest U.S. Immigrant Groups, 2012* (2014); Migration Policy Institute, *Top Ten Largest U.S. Immigrant Groups, 2012* (2014).

91. Ibid.

92. Jeffrey S. Passel & D'Vera Cohn, Pew Research Center, *Unauthorized Immigrant Population: National and State Trends* (2011).

93. Jens Manuel Krogstad, Pew Research Center, *A View of the Future Through Kindergarten Demographics* (July 8, 2014).

94. Passel & Cohn, *Unauthorized Immigrant Population*.

95. Lesli A. Maxwell, *Schools Brace for Influx of Immigrants*, EDUCATION WEEK 1, 19 (July 9, 2014).

96. According to the Pew Hispanic Center, 18% of Latina/o students are LEP; the National Council on Education Statistics (NCES) reports that 36.3% of Latina/o students are LEP; and the National Council of La Raza contends that 45% of Latina/o students are LEP. Richard Fry & Felisa Gonzales, Pew Hispanic Center, *One-in-Five and Growing Fast: A Profile of Hispanic Public School Students*, iv (2008); National Center on Education Statistics, *Status and Trends in the Education of America Indians and Alaskan Natives: 2008, Table 5.4b. Percentage of students who qualify for limited-English-proficient (LEP) services, by LEP enrollment status and race/ethnicity: 2006* (2008); Melissa Lazarin, *Improving Assessment and Accountability for English Language Learners in the No Child Left Behind Act*, 1 (2006). Much of this nearly 20-point discrepancy is likely explained by the organizations' different definitions of what constitutes "proficiency." Using varying definitions is understandable given that neither the U.S. Department of Education's

regulations nor relevant federal statutes define "ELL" or "proficiency." Rather, these terms are defined at the state and local level.

97. No Child Left Behind Act, 20 U.S.C. §§ 1041–44, 3427, 6052, 6053e, 6054b, 6055h, 6056a (2006) (amending the Elementary and Secondary Education Act of 1965, 20 U.S.C. §§ 6301–6578).

98. Drew H. Gitomer, Jolynne Andal & Derek Davison, *Using Data to Understand the Academic Performance of English Language Learners*, 21 POLICY ISSUES 1, 3 (2005). Additionally, ELL students' performance on standards-based tests is disaggregated from other students' performance; students also are disaggregated from race/ethnicity, disability, and poverty. Ibid.

99. STEVEN W. BENDER ET AL., EVERYDAY LAW FOR LATINO/AS, 3, 78 (Paradigm Publishers 2008).

100. Horne v. Flores, 129 S.Ct. 2579 (2009).

101. David McKay Wilson, *Dual Language Programs on the Rise*, 27 HARVARD EDUCATION LETTER (March/April 2011).

102. Utah Dual Language Immersion Program, *2014–2015 School Year* (July 15, 2014).

103. Parents Involved in Community Schools v. Seattle School District No. 1, 551 U.S. 701 (2007).

104. Ibid., 720–34.

105. Parents Involved, 551 U.S. 783, 787 (Justice Kennedy, concurring).

106. Fisher v. University of Texas at Austin, 133 S.Ct. 2411, 570 U.S. __ (2013).

107. Schuette v. Coalition to Defend Affirmative Action, Integration and Immigrant Rights and Fight for Equality By Any Means Necessary (BAMN), 134 S.Ct. 1623, 572 U.S. __ (2014).

108. Gratz v. Bollinger, 539 U.S. 244 (2003).

109. Grutter v. Bollinger, 539 U.S. 306 (2003).

110. Adarand Constructors, Inc. v. Pena, 515 U.S. 200, 237 (1995).

111. Santamaria v. Dallas Independent School District, Memorandum and Order, 18, 22–23, 25, 67, 69, 100 (N.D. Tx. Nov. 16, 2006, 3:06-CV-692-L)

112. Ibid., 38–44.

113. Ibid., 19, 21, 22–23, 25, 26, 30–31, 34, 35–36, 68, 79, 100–101 ("In reserving certain classrooms for Anglo students, Principal Parker was, in effect, operating, at taxpayer's expense, a private school for Anglo children within a public school that was predominantly minority").

Brown v. Board of Education

347 U.S. 483 (1954)

CHERYL BROWN HENDERSON

The Rest of the Story
of *Brown v. Board of Education*

IN THE 1940S AND 1950S, MY FAMILY LIVED IN AN INTEGRATED NEIGHBORHOOD along First Street in Topeka, Kansas. Every morning, the African American children who lived there would head off to school in one direction, and the white children living next door would head off to school in another. Like the white schools, the African American schools were good schools. The facilities were built by the same person, so the African American schools were not substandard buildings with leaky roofs and outhouses, as in the South. The teachers were well-trained; many of them had advanced degrees, so the African-American children were not receiving a poor education. Unlike in South Carolina where African American children walked ten miles to school, in Topeka they walked a few blocks and caught a bus. Thus, in what would become the case *Oliver Brown et al. v. Board of Education of Topeka, Kansas,*[1] my family and others were not disputing the quality of their children's education—they were disputing the principle of segregation.

The families did not initially turn to the courts, though. From 1948 to 1950, McKinley Burnett, the Topeka NAACP chairperson, issued a public rallying cry against school segregation. Burnett attended every single school board meeting during that time. He would take petitions with him on occasion, but really he was trying to speak during the public comment part of the agenda about opting to integrate the public elementary schools in Topeka. Unfortunately, over the course of two years, Burnett never had a chance to say his piece. The local NAACP chapter then turned to a new strategy: spending the summer of 1950 recruiting people so that by the fall of 1950, when school was about to start, they would have a class of plaintiffs ready to challenge school segregation. At the end of that summer after talking to fellow church members, NAACP members, and personal friends, as well as knocking on doors, they had assembled a group of 13 families, including a total of 20 children. Of course, because local teacher and NAACP member Lucinda Todd was at the strategy meeting, she was able to say right away, "Sign me up," which in many ways makes her the first plaintiff in the Topeka case.

In the fall of 1950, each of the 13 families was instructed by the NAACP legal team to locate the nearest white school to their home; take their child or children and a witness and try to enroll; and then come back and report what transpired. At that point, the soon-to-be-plaintiffs, after their children were denied enrollment in the white schools, pretty much got to go back to their everyday lives. It was left to the legal team to come up with the legal strategy and do all the research to put together a case. In February 1951, *Brown v. Board of Education* was filed. It was at that point that the case became associated with my father, Oliver Brown.

When the case was tried in federal district court, it was heard by a three-judge panel.[2] The presiding judge, Walter Huxman, had been the governor of Kansas before he became a judge. Consequently, he was very familiar with the state's school segregation law, which had been enacted in 1879. That law, in essence, was two-tiered. It said that only cities of a certain size (15,000 or more) could have segregated schools and, even then, they could only segregate elementary schools. Many of the early cases were from small towns and thus plaintiffs were successful in the state supreme court because the statutory permission to segregate did not apply to the smaller districts. The larger communities, including Topeka, had segregated elementary schools and that is what the *Brown* case in Kansas challenged, unlike its companion cases in the other states, which challenged segregation in elementary *and* secondary schools, and large and small districts, alike.

Judge Huxman was probably aware that Alfred Fairfax, one of Kansas's first African American legislators, had challenged the state's school segregation law unsuccessfully. Especially after hearing expert testimony from psychologist Dr. Louisa Holt, Judge Huxman likely thought long and hard about how he could craft his opinion in such a way that the Supreme Court would have to make a definitive decision about the permissibility of segregated public schools. It was politically savvy on his part to not go against custom or against the current law but still to write the opinion in such a way that left the question of school segregation open.

Eventually, four cases were on the Supreme Court's docket, all seeking the same judicial remedy. The court combined those cases and decided they would all be heard under the heading of one of the cases.[3] It is my understanding that the court very purposely selected *Brown v. Board of Education* because Kansas was not a Southern state. The Supreme Court wanted to take segregation out of the context of North and South.

We all know how the Supreme Court decided *Brown v. Board of Education.* For many years, people would come to Topeka looking for a wonderful little story, because it is what they believed *Brown* was: a little girl wanted to go to school down the block but she could not because she was African American; her father was angry about that and he sued the school board; Thurgood Marshall rode in and decided to represent them; the Supreme Court did the right thing. That story is sadly incomplete. It trivializes all the sacrifices that were made to bring about *Brown v. Board of Education.* It keeps people in the dark about the nearly 200 plaintiffs out there—many of whom lost jobs, had their homes burned, or were run out of their communities because they signed a petition to be part of a court case. It negates the role played by and the legal brilliance of the team that developed the strategy of how best to attack Jim Crow.

The truth is that all of these people, through the *Brown* decision, made the country start talking about racism, segregation, discrimination, and second-class citizenship. The Montgomery bus boycott, the Civil Rights Act of 1964, the Voting Rights Act of 1965, the Supreme Court decision that ended segregation in transportation—all of those things, and so many more, emanate from the *Brown* decision. *Brown* broke the silence.

Cheryl Brown Henderson is the Founding President of The Brown Foundation for Educational Equity, Excellence and Research, and the owner of Brown & Associates, an educational consulting firm. This piece is adapted from Cheryl Brown Henderson's comments in the 2004 documentary *Black/White & Brown:* Brown versus the Board of Education of Topeka, produced by KTWU in Topeka, Kansas.

NOTES

1. Brown v. Board of Education, 347 U.S. 483 (1954).
2. Brown v. Board of Education, 98 F. Supp. 797 (D. Kan. 1951).
3. Briggs et al. v. Elliott, 103 F. Supp. 920 (E.D.S.C. 1952); Davis v. County School Board of Prince Edward County 103 F. Supp. 337 (1952); Belton v. Gebhardt, 87 A.2d 862 (Delaware

Chancery Court 1952), affirmed as Gebhardt v. Belton, 91 A.2d 137 (Supreme Court of Delaware 1952). *Bolling v. Sharpe*, 347 U.S. 497 (1954), arose out of the District of Columbia, and thus was decided under the Fifth Amendment instead of the Fourteenth.

JACK GREENBERG

Brown v. Board of Education
An Axe in the Frozen Sea of Racism

IN THE EARLY 2000S, I VISITED BUDAPEST, SOFIA, AND SMALL TOWNS IN BULGARIA to work with Columbia Law School's Public Interest Law Initiative (PILI), lawyers, and nongovernmental organizations on integrating Roma (gypsy) children into the public schools. While it had not been the purpose, the experience turned out to be much like learning a foreign language, a process through which one understands one's own language better. *Brown v. Board of Education*[1] took on new meaning for me.

A year earlier, Bulgaria had integrated 2,400 Roma schoolchildren into the majority school population.[2] This first step in a program that will cover all of Eastern Europe was smooth and successful. In contrast, our desegregation in the United States was tumultuous, sometimes violent, and fraught with difficulty for decades. Indeed, it has not fully recovered from this beginning. Even as small a start as that in Bulgaria, attempted almost anywhere in the South circa 1954, would have met violent, strident resistance. Angry opposition poured forth in the South for more than a decade and a half following 1954, even though almost nothing was desegregated.[3]

I have pondered the reason for the difference, and think it is that Eastern Europe has been politically hospitable toward—or has at least accepted—integration. Not that there has been widespread enthusiasm for the change. Indeed, there has been a great deal of inertia and some attempts to evade it. But, there has been nothing like the Massive Resistance, aptly named, that obstructed desegregation in the United States. I came to believe that *Brown*'s key role—not at all anticipated when it was filed or decided—more than any school desegregation that it eventually accomplished, was to contribute to creating a political environment in which race relations could change fundamentally. Only in the new ambience was it possible for school desegregation and other racial transformation to evolve.

Blacks, Roma; United States, Eastern Europe Compared

Comparisons are far from exact, given the many dissimilarities between the two societies. The United States is a single nation, with differences among states and regions, a constitution, and its own history. Europe—including Eastern Europe, where desegregation is beginning—has a very different political relationship among and between its constituent states and the European community: different international rules, governmental systems, languages, antagonisms, economies, and so forth.

African Americans are somewhat more than 13% of the United States population, although in some regions the proportion is higher than in others.[4] The overall fraction of Roma population in Eastern Europe is less. Roma are distributed differently in different countries and regions within them: estimates are as high as 10% in Romania, where there is the largest concentration, but the official statistics put the figure at approximately 4%.[5] Estimates are complicated by the widely acknowledged problem of self-identification. Roma are often not easily distinguishable by physical features; because of stigma and prejudice many self-report as majority population. They once were nomadic, but nowadays are mostly sedentary. Roma speak a number of different language variants. Some Roma speakers can understand some versions but not others, although one fairly dominant version is fairly widespread. Most Roma probably also speak the language of the countries in which they live.[6]

Like African Americans, Roma have been subordinated.[7] Their economic and social situation has been substandard by every measure. Despite the lack of reliable data, employment discrimination against them is commonplace; unemployment in some places is almost 100%.[8] Wealth among the Roma is virtually nonexistent. They often live in segregated shantytowns, suffer higher incidence of disease and illness, and have a lower life expectancy than non-Roma. Further, they frequently are victims of racially motivated violence; their crime commission and victimization rates are extraordinarily high, as is maltreatment by the criminal justice system.[9] As of 2001, approximately 70% of school-age Roma children were segregated in Bulgaria.[10] The rate varied significantly country by country, although in most places it was high.[11]

Roma children recently have been segregated by being placed in separate schools or separate classrooms within a school, or by diagnosis as handicapped for placement in separate rooms, a practice we know in the United States as well.[12]

But Roma do not share the worldwide brand of color that sets apart darker-skinned people in most, if not all, societies across the globe. Many resemble their non-Roma neighbors. On the other hand, one encounters frequent reference to Roma as irremediably criminal and incapable of learning or working, a view somewhat resembling the ideology of black inferiority.[13] While Roma speak a common language or languages in some regions and have their own culture and traditions, they also share in the culture and traditions of the places in which they live. Other characteristics unique to each group defy comparison: on the one hand, complex regimes of segregation followed forced migration and enslavement of African Americans; on the other, decades of communist rule prohibited Roma from traveling from place to place, as had been their custom, and they therefore have become mostly sedentary. Yet, in meaningful ways, the segregation that separates Roma schoolchildren from other children closely resembles the segregation that has separated African American schoolchildren from other children in the United States.

The quality of Roma education can only be described as execrable. For example, only 5% graduate from secondary school, fourth-graders commonly are illiterate, only 0.3% show interest in taking national exams for admission to elite schools after seventh or eighth grade, and in Bulgaria, more than half of Roma school windows are covered by cardboard, an occurrence that is probably representative of other countries in the region.[14]

But the United States and Eastern Europe are similar in important ways. Both acquiesce in the rule of law. They recognize the superior status of human rights principles, including racial equality. Our Constitution, Eastern European domestic constitutions, and the European Convention for the Protection of Human Rights largely embody the same rights.[15] The European Commission has issued a Race Equality Directive, according to which the European Union (EU) will not admit countries unless they desegregate Roma schoolchildren.[16] At the same time, for many years, notwithstanding constitutions and laws, the United States and Europe tolerated subordination of African Americans and Roma, although both societies now are engaged in remedying that violation.

Notwithstanding much successful school desegregation in the United States, defiance and evasion accompanied the process from the beginning. In contrast, at the outset, six towns in Bulgaria had recently desegregated before I visited, all uneventfully, some highly successfully. To be sure, this has been only the start. As time goes on, Roma desegregation will display greater variety and all of it might not be so accepting of the demand for change.

In Hungary, even in advance of the desegregation that is scheduled to take place soon, some evasion resembling what we have seen in the United States has occurred. In September 2003, Hungary required phasing out all 700 Roma classes in the country by 2008.[17] But, Jászladány, 56 miles south of Budapest, established a private school in a city building, supported by the municipal government, resembling the segregated academies that sprang up in the southern United States following *Brown*.[18] Forty percent of the Jászladány population, but only 17% of the private school's students, are Roma.[19] However, unlike public officials' averted gaze in the United States, the Hungarian national ombudsman for minority rights announced that such schools will be closed. In the American South, politics and legal obstacles protected private white schools for years, although in time, lawsuits cut back some subsidies such as free books, and blacks eventually won the theoretical right to attend.[20]

A further caveat about forming judgments too quickly about Eastern European desegregation is that innovative social programs often cannot be replicated on a large scale. Roma desegregation might progress differently in the future. How it will evolve, however, does not have much impact on my conclusions. The differences in the beginnings of the two countries' desegregation experiences have helped me understand our history as I had not before.

The Origins of Desegregation in Eastern Europe

In 2000, the European Union adopted the Race Equality Directive, a directive that requires schools to desegregate, and has roots in the Universal Declaration of Human Rights, international covenants and conventions, and the European Convention on Human Rights.[21] It requires that member states achieve race equality.[22] In order to join the EU, Eastern European countries must comply with the Directive. It is inconceivable that there would be attacks on its legitimacy in the same way that there were attacks on the Supreme Court's decision in *Brown v. Board of Education*. Given the geopolitics of European Union enlargement, political leaders are too committed to the process (based on theories of how it will bring economic prosperity as well as psychological factors tied to collective historical memory) to generate opposition to EU standards. The general public is caught up in the "idea" of Europe and what it represents (the opposite of communism and Soviet domination). Before the Race Equality Directive was promulgated, Bulgaria enacted a "Framework Program" by which it will implement the Directive.[23]

Among Roma, race equality and integration have been seen as synonymous. There has been no inclination to follow the route of separate but equal. Roma and non-Roma recognize that, without equal education, efforts to close the Roma/ white gap cannot succeed.[24] They believe that the only way to achieve equality is to integrate. A recent example can be found in teacher training. The Roma integration effort in Bulgaria has the goal of increasing the number of trained educators for Roma children. Twenty-eight Romany educational desegregation supervisors are enrolled in a new university-level pedagogy training program that will award teaching certificates.[25] In committing to integration, Roma leadership points to factors like those that persuaded United States civil rights advocates to seek integration rather than equalization: for example, the harmful effect of isolation on learning, the fact that separate Roma school funding would most likely remain unequal to white school funding, that contacts with majority children can establish useful relationships, and that integration helps Roma children develop lifestyles and manners of the majority community, facilitating wider acceptance and opportunities.[26]

In addition to legal requirements, a practical consideration has supported Bulgarian integration: the Eastern European population is falling because of low birthrates and emigration. But Roma population is not falling. Schools are funded on a per capita basis, and consequently teachers and administrators in the white schools welcome the income new Roma students provide. Indeed, the main source of opposition to desegregation, weak as it is, comes from teachers and administrators in Roma schools (who are not Roma) because they will lose funding.[27] The only other reservations I have heard about integration is that some Roma families feared that white schoolchildren would introduce theirs to drugs. I have also heard passing mention of a desire to maintain cultural identity.

The integrated Bulgarian public schools—2,400 Roma children in six Bulgarian towns about ten years ago—suggest what is possible in Eastern Europe. In this case, integration was administered and funded by a private foundation and supported by nongovernmental organizations (NGOs), the financial clout of George Soros, and the World Bank, but the schools were public and the integration was an expression of public policy.[28] I visited two of the towns that had desegregated, Montana and Vidin. My role was not to give advice, but to describe American desegregation, issues it posed, responses, and the consequences. At one desegregated school, I attended a meeting of three or four hundred parents, pupils, teachers, and administrators, Roma and non-Roma, who were overwhelmingly in favor of desegregation. One person after another stood up and spoke about the success of desegregation for perhaps three hours. I think that only one speaker disapproved of integration. One of my hosts was particularly proud that a Romany boy who was attending a desegregated school had been ranked number two in the national mathematics examination. Such a meeting would have been inconceivable anywhere in the South in 1954. I thought of Potemkin Villages and Soviet demands for public avowals of conformity and asked questions to find out the genuineness of the assertions of support. Even with reservations concerning my capacity to judge attitudes expressed in a foreign language (translated, plus a few English speakers) in a foreign place, I believe that I heard statements of genuine belief.

Even more inconceivable was the community effort that went into making integration successful, the likes of which never occurred in connection with any United States desegregation. Social workers visited every Romany family that had school-age children; tutors were available for children who needed help; teachers received special training; and families that needed food or clothing received assistance. Roma and non-Roma children shared outings, social events, and cultural experiences together as part of facilitating integration.[29] The project received major political support, and the press publicized the advantages of integration. In April 2001, the president of Bulgaria congratulated the organization that sponsored the desegregation.[30] In one town, by the end of the school year the number of students participating in the program increased from 275 to 460 as of the beginning of the second school term. Improved results showed how well the children had adjusted by the end of the first year. The second school year began with more than 600 children registered in mainstream schools.[31] Roma reside on the periphery of towns, a housing pattern opposite of minority housing patterns in the United States. The techniques employed to redistribute students are those used in the United States: pairing and clustering of schools in either Roma or white neighborhoods so that children from the entire community must go to a single school for specified grades. They bus children to school if it is a distance from their homes.[32]

Two additional differences might contribute to the different reactions. First, Roma children who attend integrated schools travel to them by bus from their homes, but white children do not travel by bus or otherwise to the Roma schools in Roma neighborhoods. In the United States, school desegregation was begun in a similar way. However, black families soon objected to the fact that they had to travel to white schools, whereas whites did not have to travel to black schools. Black and white children should be treated the same, they argued. Moreover, it was insulting to black teachers and administrators to designate black schools as off-limits to whites. Therefore, two-way busing, uncongenial for many white families, was used. I have wondered whether two-way busing is being contemplated by Eastern Europeans. Those I asked believe that the Roma schools, often one- and two-room buildings accommodating many more grades, are so dilapidated that neither Roma nor whites would want to occupy them in the future.

Another factor is the size of the Roma population. While it is large in some places, overall it is smaller than the black population in the United States, particularly in the South. Typically, the number of Roma integrated into a Bulgarian system would be smaller than the number of blacks integrated into a Southern community. United States desegregation specialists believe that, to permit proper acculturation, approximately 20% minority population is needed, although a population as low as 5% might work. I am not well-informed enough about the distribution of Roma population, nor do I or anyone else know at this time whether such a factor might be at work in Roma desegregation.

I do not want to suggest that all of Eastern Europe has embraced desegregation so positively. There has been inertia and some anticipatory efforts to evade it, but nothing like the barrage of hostility that greeted *Brown*. The Budapest-based European Roma Rights Center filed cases before domestic and international courts challenging school segregation in the Czech Republic and Croatia as well as in Sofia, Bulgaria.[33] Sometimes, egregious anti-Roma activity occurs, although it has not so far been linked to the expected school transition. In the 1990s, there were pogroms against Roma in Romania.[34] Vigilantes burned Roma houses, at least a couple of times with the residents inside.[35] In the Czech Republic, one town built a wall around a Roma ghetto.[36] Skinheads have attacked Roma from time to time in Hungary and in other Central European countries.[37] Nevertheless, I did not see anything connected to school integration in Eastern Europe resembling commonplace reactions during a comparable period in the American South. I think of the case of African American Mack Charles Parker, who was jailed on a charge of having raped a white woman in Poplarville, Mississippi. In April 1959, a mob broke into the jail and lynched him.[38] In editorials, the local newspaper linked the lynching to campaigns for civil rights: "Reprehensible as the act [of lynching] is, . . . it served to emphasize again the fact that force must not be used in pushing revolutionary changes in social custom. Every such action produces an equal and opposite reaction."[39]

One major difference between current integration efforts in Bulgaria, anticipated integration elsewhere in Eastern Europe, and integration efforts in post-1955 United States is that the president of the United States did not support school integration. In Europe, government at the international, national, local, and school levels supports what is being done.[40]

The Beginnings of Desegregation in the United States

President Eisenhower disagreed with *Brown*.[41] The United States government did not support desegregation even though it filed a brief on behalf of the plaintiff black children.[42] Until the solicitor general made his position clear, however, the plaintiffs' lawyers were anxious about what it might be. Following the Supreme Court decision, Eisenhower said only that the law should be obeyed.[43] He personally wrote part of a friend-of-the-court brief for the solicitor general's office that asked the court in its implementation decision to take into account the psychological difficulties that would attend the end of racial segregation in schools. Obviously, he meant the difficulties that whites would have with blacks.

A South-wide policy of "massive resistance" launched Resolutions of Interposition and Nullification and created well-funded State Sovereignty Commissions devoted to preventing desegregation.[44] State supreme court judges, state attorneys general, even federal judges denounced the Supreme Court.[45] States prosecuted civil rights organizations and tried to disbar civil rights lawyers, enacted legislation that would close integrated schools, and created complex administrative procedures through which black children would have to go for a nonsegregated education.[46]

Distinguished scholars attacked the reasoning of the *Brown* opinion, lending credibility to some of its cruder critics. Legal luminaries like Learned Hand and esteemed scholars like Herbert Wechsler, who personally opposed segregation, delegitimized the *Brown* decision.[47] A 2001 book about *Brown* consists of essays by law professors who think that the Court did not effectively justify its conclusion; they have written opinions to show how they could have done it better.[48]

In 1955, in *Brown II*, the implementation opinion, the Court held that desegregation might be implemented "with all deliberate speed."[49] But there was very little desegregation. Scattered areas in border states had some, allowing black children to enroll in white schools, usually in a single grade or several grades, during a period of years. In a number of communities, even this provoked violence.[50] There was some litigation by blacks aimed at admission to white schools, but the few civil rights lawyers were overcommitted and could not bring more cases or press vigorously the cases they filed.[51] Defendant school boards litigated existing cases to a fare-thee-well, further consuming energies of civil rights groups. Opponents of integration mounted frequent violence. The Department of Justice did not yet have statutory authority to engage in school desegregation litigation.

Opposition to *Brown* No Surprise

That the South would ignore and even disobey court orders to cease discrimination did not surprise plaintiffs' lawyers in *Brown*. No one, however, anticipated the intensity of the response. Civil rights litigation had, until then, produced many paper victories. Courts had ordered universities to admit blacks, interstate buses and railroads to stop segregating, voting officials to cease prohibiting black voting, jury commissioners to cease excluding blacks from pools of jurors, and courts to cease enforcing agreements among property owners not to sell to blacks.[52] These decisions produced only slight changes. Visible, substantial reform was very, very slow in coming.

Southern officials and institutions typically treated a court decision as though it applied only to the plaintiff and defendant in that case. Bus companies did not act as if a Supreme Court decision about seating on the bus controlled their terminals. One bus company did not treat a decision directed at another as relevant to its own situation. Railroad companies did not treat a decision governing sleeping or dining cars as applicable to coaches, or a decision affecting one company as applicable to another. Voting officials evaded outright court orders that invalidated laws or practices that excluded blacks by adopting fresh registration or voting criteria that once again shut them out. One case after another overturned convictions because blacks had been excluded from juries, but their exclusion from juries continued. Prosecutors assumed that lawyers in the next case might not know or care to raise the issue.

Decisions that required admitting blacks to higher education prefigured the reaction that would occur at the elementary and high school level. Despite Supreme Court decisions beginning in 1939—and an earlier 1936 Maryland Court of Appeals decision[53]—it was virtually impossible for more than a small handful of blacks, without first filing a lawsuit, to attend an accredited law, medical, or other professional school or get a PhD in the South until the 1960s.[54] In 1939, the Supreme Court in *Missouri ex rel. Gaines v. Canada* ordered the University of Missouri to admit a black applicant to its law school because Missouri had no law school for blacks.[55] But no other school within the university acted as though that decision applied beyond law school. A subsequent case had to be filed to secure admission of blacks to the Missouri School of Journalism.[56]

In 1948, the United States Supreme Court required that the University of Oklahoma admit a black woman to its law school.[57] But immediately thereafter, the Oklahoma Graduate School of Education rejected an applicant because he was black.[58] The University of Texas Law School rejected a black plaintiff and set up a two-room law school for him instead.[59] The Supreme Court ordered that the Oklahoma and Texas plaintiffs be admitted in 1950.[60]

The degree of recalcitrance is illustrated by the fact that, even after *Brown* was decided in 1954, as late as the 1960s the University of Alabama, the University of Georgia, and the University of Mississippi all came under court orders to admit blacks, enforced by troops at the campus.[61] Indeed, before blacks were admitted, suits had to be filed in every single Southern state with the exception of Arkansas. I participated in suits against universities in Delaware, Maryland, Virginia, North Carolina, South Carolina, Georgia, Alabama, Florida, Louisiana, Mississippi, Texas, and other states.

We might ask an anachronistic question: Was there some way that the attack on segregation could have been directed so that American integration then would have unfolded as smoothly (so far) as Roma integration has today? In view of the resistance to integration in higher education and the likelihood of even stiffer opposition at the elementary and high school level, might it not have been better initially to direct efforts at some target other than education? Opportunities would be increased if there were integration in housing, employment, and public accommodations. What about litigation to integrate them? Would it have been easier and provided a transition to educational issues? Two main obstacles discouraged such an alternative approach. First, the state action doctrine, and second, whether a legal right to integrate those options could translate into genuine social change.[62]

The state action doctrine pronounced in the Civil Rights Cases of 1883 held that the Fourteenth Amendment prohibited discrimination only by the state, not by private persons.[63] It used the term "state" in a very narrow sense.[64] Because the overwhelming part of housing, employment, and public accommodations was private in a constitutional sense, the state action doctrine would have been an insurmountable barrier to almost anything that mattered in those categories.[65]

Second, even suits against state-owned or state-operated employment, housing, and public accommodations would be limited in what they could accomplish. The restrictive covenant cases allowed blacks to buy property in some all-white areas.[66] These areas turned all black, and did not integrate. Housing units are discrete. To move into a white neighborhood as the first black is a daunting prospect. Government jobs were virtually impossible to obtain, even with successful litigation. Too much discretion in selection was involved. Jobs are different from one another; wholesale litigation was unlikely to change very much very soon. And, in any event, only a small handful of jobs would be in play. There was an infinitesimally small number of government-owned public theaters, golf courses, and other places of amusement and entertainment. No suit could open them up with the impact of desegregating a school district.

Some considered enforcing the "equal" part of the "separate but equal" formula.[67] But if a case were to be won, there would be the problem of compelling governmental agencies to tax and appropriate court-ordered funding; and, if that succeeded, there would be the need to sue again as black schools slid back into physical inequality. Out of that recognition, Nathan Margold, who drafted the policy paper that launched the desegregation campaign, argued for striking at the heart of the "evil"—segregation.[68]

There was every reason to expect a hostile reception for cases that ordered elementary and high school integration. Thurgood Marshall said that he thought that, in Georgia, we would have to sue the schools in every county. The rest of the South, with spotty exceptions, would be no easier.

Shouldn't Politics Be the Mode of Attack?

During the 1930s there had been a debate among black leadership—almost two decades before the school cases were filed—regarding the path to pursue in the quest for equality. They discussed briefly, but dismissed, emigration to Africa and revolution. The first was undesirable and the second was doomed, as they realized. In a democracy, politics, of course, would be the preferred way to proceed. Again, an anachronistic comparison with Roma desegregation suggests that social and governmental institutions, rather than courts, could better effect social changes such as desegregation. Of course, in the United States, social and governmental institutions were not interested then in changing the status of African Americans. They fiercely tried to hold on to the status quo, sometimes referred to as the South's "heritage."

While the NAACP was a political organization, it could not even persuade Congress to enact an anti-lynching bill. Franklin Roosevelt did not fight for one because, if he had, Southern senators would not have supported his efforts to overcome the Depression, or support the Allies before the United States entered World War II.[69] Unless blacks could vote, politics would be hopeless. It should have been easy to gain the vote; legal rules prohibiting voting discrimination abounded. The Fourteenth and Fifteenth Amendments and related statutes had secured the right to vote. But repeated litigation, usually successful, made hardly a dent in Southern voting practices.

When the Voting Rights Act of 1965 was enacted, only a small percentage of blacks in the 100 counties with the highest black populations could vote.[70] In the deep South, the percentage was even smaller. Without the vote, the political option was illusory.

Courtroom action seemed to be the only viable option. But why go to court after having experienced such resistance to judicial decrees, and recognizing the limits on what they had achieved? The definitive answer is not in any document, nor was the question asked. There was no place else to go. It was like seeking one's way out of a maze: when one path turned out to be unpromising, they tried another. Attacking school segregation in court was the only apparent effort that possibly might be worth the trouble.

The Effect of the School Segregation Decisions

We won *Brown*. But almost nothing happened with schools. The South threw up a wall of "massive resistance," as noted previously. There was a great deal of nonproductive litigation; or, we thought it was nonproductive.[71] Finally, in 1969, after a decade and a half of marginally effective lawsuits, in *Alexander v. Holmes County Board of Education*, the Supreme Court struck down all of the school board defendants' tactical ploys that had amounted to a program of "litigation forever."[72] School desegregation in earnest began. Southern schools changed from almost no black students in predominantly white schools in 1954, with the proportion of black students jumping to 33.1% in 1970 and to 43.5% by 1988.[73] Then a retreat set in, which continues to this day. The rate was 32.7% in 1998.[74] This chapter is not the place to account for the decline. Suffice it to say that maintaining desegregation was difficult in the face of newly fashioned legal doctrines and demographic changes.

But something else was happening. In retrospect, the struggle to desegregate schools was about more than schools. The opponents of *Brown* were proved to have been right in claiming that victory for plaintiffs would spell doom for segregation in all its manifestations.

The implications of *Brown* went beyond school integration, and raised a legal and moral imperative that was influential even when it was not generally obeyed. It set a standard of right conduct. It might be argued that law does not necessarily set standards or induce compliance; take, for example, laws that are widely disobeyed or in disrepute or subject to conflicting views. But *Brown* was not merely a pronouncement by the Court. As the brief for the United States on implementation stated, "The right of children not to be segregated because of race or color is not a technical legal right of little significance or value. It is a fundamental human right, supported by considerations of morality as well as law."[75] Or, as the United States argued in another brief:

> It is in the context of the present world struggle between freedom and tyranny that the problem of racial discrimination must be viewed. The United States is trying to prove to the people of the world, of every nationality, race, and color, that a free democracy is the most civilized and most secure form of government yet devised by man.[76]

The arguments of those who wanted to maintain segregation did not involve claims about right and wrong. They were couched in terms of federalism, local control, original intent of the Constitution, the sanctity of precedent, the role of the judiciary in a democracy, the difficulty of compliance, or the academic inadequacy of blacks.[77] In briefs on the question of implementing desegregation decrees, states argued "unfavorable community attitude," "health and morals" of the black population, that local school boards were "unalterably opposed," and the like. North Carolina argued that integration would create the "likelihood of violence," and that "[p]ublic schools may be abolished."[78] Oklahoma urged that desegregation would create "financial problems."[79] Florida argued that approximately 2% of white births in Florida compared to 24% of Negro births were "illegitimate."[80] Florida also reported that of more than 11,000 cases of gonorrhea, more than 10,000 were among blacks.[81] There were some claims that the Bible intended the races to be separate. I have scoured the briefs of defendants and have reviewed the public debates. There were no claims that segregation was right and moral.

Second, enforcing *Brown* had implications that established national, not regional, standards as the measure of equality. Efforts at school desegregation were opposed by a steady drumbeat of physical resistance. That, in turn, was almost always overcome by superior police and military force. There could be no more authoritative endorsement of desegregation than the government's determination to suppress forcible resistance by force. In border states—for example, in Milford, Delaware; Clay and Sturgis, Kentucky; Clinton, Tennessee; and Greenbrier County, West Virginia—violent public demonstrations against desegregation were suppressed or contained by police, troops, and/or the National Guard.[82] In 1957, in Little Rock, Arkansas, the president had to summon the armed forces to assure black children's entry to Little Rock High School.[83] The next president summoned troops to secure admission of James Meredith to the University of Mississippi and Vivian Malone and James Hood to the University of Alabama in the early 1960s.[84] In a few instances, school officials withdrew segregation plans.[85] But, ultimately, national rule established its superiority by physical force over physical resistance.

Third, a people's movement embraced the principles that underlie *Brown* and demonstrated vigorously for their implementation. By 1960, the sit-ins began. Leaders of the first sit-ins had been inspired by *Brown*. Freedom rides began in 1961, partly in homage to *Brown*, with the first ride scheduled to arrive in New Orleans on May 17, 1961, its anniversary.[86] Martin Luther King Jr. annually held prayer pilgrimages on May 17.[87] King often preached and spoke about the role of the Supreme Court, signifying *Brown*. Rosa Parks, whose act of defiance launched the Montgomery bus boycott, was an NAACP administrator, steeped in *Brown*. The boycott was resolved by *Gayle v. Browder*, in which the Supreme Court, citing *Brown*, held unconstitutional the segregation law that was the subject of the boycott.[88] Symbolic defiance of segregation laws and customs, like sit-ins, were not new. The black press had run stories about sit-ins and sitting in prohibited sections of buses and so forth as far back as the 1930s. But, for the first time, there was national network television, which inspired emulation everywhere. Soon, thousands of demonstrators were demanding equal rights—blacks and whites, North and South.

Together, the moral imperative of the *Brown* decision, the physical suppression of resistance, the Civil Rights Movement, and Massive Resistance and its defeat culminated in the Civil Rights Acts of the 1960s.[89] Those acts marked the beginning of a political transformation of the United States. It has been manifested in ways too numerous to set forth here, but epitomized in the election of 40 black Congressmen and of the election of black mayors at one time or another in every major American city and most smaller ones. Its implications, of course, go beyond race relations. Lyndon Johnson, upon signing the civil rights bills, observed that they meant the end of the Democratic Party in the South. He was right.

Europeans took centuries and many wars to recognize that national and ethnic antagonisms are too destructive to tolerate. The Second World War and the Cold War imparted immediacy to human rights commitments. There was a Roma "holocaust" alongside the Jewish Holocaust.[90] While brotherly love has not pervaded Roma and non-Roma relationships, virulence has subsided perhaps to within range of what English, French, Germans, and Italians think of each other. Apart from soccer matches, where worst inner feelings come to the surface, and in such places as former Yugoslavia, populations get along, sometimes very well. What lies in the hearts and minds of mankind may be unknowable, and Eastern Europe or parts of it might break up like the former Yugoslavia. But we would not expect something of that sort to erupt in Western Europe and, I think, among countries that are, or aspire to be, part of the EU.

We might conceive of the political situation in the United States in the mid-twentieth century as frozen until 1954. Southern white racist hegemony was dominant. It kept blacks in subordinate caste-like status. The school integration decision, if a metaphor may be permitted, acted like a powerful icebreaker. It made America accept racial change. *Brown* was not merely a school case. Supreme Court Justice Robert H. Jackson used this metaphor in describing the path-breaking role of the Nuremberg trials: he told his staff that they had to produce "an ice pick to break up the frozen sea within us."[91] Scholar Stanley Corngold has suggested that Jackson might have found the metaphor in Kafka, who wrote that "[a] book must be the axe for the frozen sea inside us."[92]

Like my metaphorical icebreaker or Kafka's metaphorical axe, *Brown* created pathways over which America could arrive at racial change. *Brown* was not merely a school case.

So when I saw smooth, easy, agreeable, successful school desegregation in Bulgaria and wondered why *Brown* had not gone so smoothly in the United States, the answer was that *Brown*, while a school case, did different work in different circumstances. Schools could not desegregate in the racially hostile atmosphere of the South in the 1950s or even later than that. The laws, state and local legislatures, Congress, state and federal judges, society, and the economy all did not want to change the racial arrangements that privileged whites. There was no way to change them in the face of opposition with vested interest in the status quo. *Brown* was a first step in cracking open that frozen sea by changing and energizing minds, creating a social movement that became political, enlisting parts of the country and the world, and enacting basic laws that affected power relationships between black and white, North and South.

Then South Carolina or Mississippi could receive our version of the Race Equality Directive and respond like Vidin.

Jack Greenberg is a Professor of Law at Columbia University Law School. This chapter is adapted from an article by the same title originally published in the SAINT LOUIS UNIVERSITY LAW JOURNAL © 2004, St. Louis University School of Law, St. Louis, Missouri.

NOTES

Jack Greenberg served as assistant counsel to the NAACP Legal Defense and Educational Fund from 1949 to 1961 and as director-counsel from 1961 to 1984. He is grateful to Moez M. Kaba, Columbia Law School 2005, for his superb assistance in writing this chapter as well as in other matters.

1. Brown v. Board of Education, 347 U.S. 483 (1954).
2. Krasimir Kanev, Bulgarian Helsinki Committee, Open Society Institute, *The First Steps: An Evaluation of the Nongovernmental Desegregation Projects in Six Bulgarian Cities*, 4 (2003).
3. See generally HARVIE WILKINSON, III, FROM *BROWN* TO *BAKKE*: THE SUPREME COURT AND SCHOOL INTEGRATION (Oxford University Press 1979); Frank T. Read, *Judicial Evolution of the Law of School Integration Since* Brown v. Board of Education, 39 LAW & CONTEMPORARY PROBLEMS 7, 29 (1975); Charles L. Zelden, *From Rights to Resources: The Southern Federal District Courts and the Transformation of Civil Rights in Education, 1968–1974*, 32 AKRON LAW REVIEW 471 (1999).
4. U.S. Census Bureau, Race Alone or in Combination: 2000 (table of population), http://factfinder.census.gov/servlet/QTTable?_bm=y&-geo_id=01000US&-qr_name=DEC_2000_SF1_U_QTP5&-ds_name=DEC_2000_SF1_U&-_lang=en&-redoLog=false&_sse=on (created February 26, 2004).
5. Kanev, *The First Steps*, 10; The World Bank Group, *The Roma*, http://lnweb18.worldbank.org/ECA/ECSHD.nsf/ecadocbylink/the+roma? (2003).
6. EU Accession Monitoring Program, Open Society Institute, *Monitoring the EU Accession Process: Minority Protection*, 57–58 (2002); *The Roma People from Barathan to the Rest of the World*, www.romaversitas.edu.mk/eng_zaromite_istorijat.asp (2002).
7. Kanev, *The First Steps*, 8.
8. Ibid., 8–9; World Bank Group, *The Roma*.
9. EU Accession Monitoring Program, *Minority Protection*, 45–49; Kanev, *The First Steps*, 9; see also Maxine Sleeper, *Anti-Discrimination Laws in Eastern Europe: Toward Effective*

Implementation, 40 COLUMBIA JOURNAL OF TRANSNATIONAL LAW 177, 178, 181 (2001) (explaining that violence toward Roma in Eastern and Central Europe is often ignored by law enforcement).

10. EU Accession Monitoring Program, *Minority Protection,* 93.

11. See, for example, Branimir Plese, *Racial Segregation in Croatian Primary Schools: Romani Students Take Legal Action,* (2002) (explaining that 59.07% of Roma primary school students attended segregated classes in the 2000–2001 school year); Mihai Surdu, *The Quality of Education in Romanian Schools with High Percentages of Romani Pupils* (2002) (describing the high incidence of segregation in schools in Romania).

12. Kanev, *The First Steps,* 8.

13. EU Accession Monitoring Program, *Minority Protection,* 46–49.

14. Kanev, *The First Steps,* 9.

15. The European Convention for the Protection of Human Rights and Fundamental Freedoms, 213 United Nations Treaty Series 222 (November 4, 1950).

16. Council Directive 2000/43/EC of 29 June 2000 Implementing the Principle of Equal Treatment Between Persons Irrespective of Racial or Ethnic Origin, 2000 O.J. (L 180) 22. Interestingly, following the United States Civil War, seceding states were not permitted to rejoin the Union without first submitting their constitutions to Congress. No Southern state added a school segregation provision to its constitution until after it was readmitted.

17. Address by Bálint Magyar, Minister of Education on the Regional Roma Conference, June 30, 2003.

18. European Roma Rights Centre, *Private School in Hungary Declared Unlawful* (November 7, 2002).

19. I should note one important difference between the United States and Hungary: in the United States, all the students would have been white.

20. See generally, JACK GREENBERG, CRUSADERS IN THE COURTS: HOW A DEDICATED BAND OF LAWYERS FOUGHT FOR THE CIVIL RIGHTS REVOLUTION (Basic Books 1994).

21. Council Directive, 2000 O.J. (L 180) 22; Universal Declaration of Human Rights, General Assembly Resolution 217A (III), United Nations GAOR, 3d Session, Articles 1–2, United Nations Document A/810 (1948); Convention for the Protection of Human Rights, 213 United Nations Treaty Series 222.

22. Council Directive, 2000 O.J. (L 180) 22, Article 2.

23. For a description of the law, see Kanev, *The First Steps,* 7. When this chapter was originally published, the Bulgarian government had yet to officially publish the law. The full text of the law is available at www.bghelsinki.org. One United States Department of Justice argument in *Brown* was that racial segregation created serious foreign policy difficulties, placing the United States outside of the norms of the modern industrialized world. Brief for the United States as Amicus Curiae (October Term 1952), 5–8, Brown v. Board of Education, 347 U.S. 483 (1954) (Nos. 8 et al.). Eastern Europe, conforming to EU demands, similarly looked to external standards of equality. But the South has clung to its traditions more than Eastern Europe seems to be continuing in its ancient modes of treating Roma, at least so far.

24. "White" is the term for non-Roma nationals of the country in which Roma live.

25. VIKTORIA BORISOVA, SUPERVISORS IN THE EDUCATIONAL DESEGREGATION STARTED THEIR UNIVERSITY TRAINING IN PEDAGOGY (on file with author).

26. In Eastern Europe, national identity plays a role unknown in the American South. Persons of Turkish descent who live in Hungary, for example, attend Turkish schools and apparently have no interest in going to Hungarian schools. This is not segregation in the sense that we know it or as it is practiced against Roma. There is no comparable Roma homeland.

27. Kanev, *The First Steps*, 6, 10; see also Ekkehard Kraft, *Demographic Changes in Southeastern Europe: Declining Birth Rates, Rising Emigration*, www.nzz.ch/english/ background/2002/12/05_southeast_europe.html (November 30, 2002) (explaining that birthrates in Bulgaria have dropped and now stand at 1.14 children per woman and explaining further that emigration has contributed to Bulgaria's declining population).

28. The private foundation is known as The Open Society Foundation—Sofia. It supports efforts among Bulgarian and Yugoslav nongovernmental organizations to stabilize the region. See Open Society Foundation—Sofia, www.soros.org/natfound/bulgaria. The nongovernmental organization responsible for implementing the first desegregation efforts in Bulgaria is known as the Drom Organization, a Roma non-profit that carries out various human rights-oriented projects throughout Bulgaria. Kanev, *The First Steps*, 11.

29. Kanev, *The First Steps*, 4.

30. Open Society Institute, European Roma Rights Center, Bulgarian Helsinki Committee, and the Human Rights Project, Press Release, *Conference: The Desegregation of the "Romani Schools" in Bulgaria a Condition for an Equal Start of Roma* (April 28, 2001).

31. Kanev, *The First Steps*, 11.

32. Ibid., 4.

33. European Roma Rights Centre, *The ERRC Legal Strategy to Challenge Racial Segregation and Discrimination in Czech Schools* (2000) (describing a suit filed in the Constitutional Court of the Czech Republic challenging and seeking remedies for school racial segregation and discrimination and subsequent application to the European Court of Human Rights in Strasbourg); Plese, *Racial Segregation in Croatian Primary Schools* (describing a suit filed by a group of Roma students in Croatian court challenging school segregation policies).

34. European Roma Rights Centre, *Roma in Romania* (October 1999).

35. Ibid.

36. European Roma Rights Centre, *City Authorities Build Ghetto Wall in Usti nad Labem, Czech Republic* (October 14, 1999).

37. European Roma Rights Centre, *Skinheads Attack Roma in Hungary* (November 4, 1999).

38. GREENBERG, CRUSADERS IN THE COURTS, 217.

39. *Mississippi: Officials Express Concern at Poplarville Incident*, SOUTHERN SCHOOL NEWS (May 1959) (quoting editorial comments from the combined issue of Jackson, Mississippi's CLARION LEDGER and DAILY NEWS (April 26, 1959)).

40. As I was completing this piece in 2004, I received an update reaffirming the broad support for desegregation from Edwin Rekosh, Executive Director of Public Interest Law Initiative at Columbia University's Budapest Law Center. (Mr. Rekosh and PILI work closely with the desegregation movement.) A local organization in Southern Serbia has found data suggesting that segregation exists and is working with local government authorities to address it. The Romanian Ministry of Education is drafting a policy directing all schools to identify and eradicate segregation. However, elsewhere, the situation does not seem quite as bright. Not all segregated schools are being embraced by the Ministry of Education's

integration program in Hungary. In Bulgaria, some activists complain that there is much rhetoric but little action on the integration front; in response, they are litigating and strategizing ways to protest.

41. Stanley K. Schultz & William P. Tishler, *Civil Rights in an Uncivil Society* (1999) (explaining that Eisenhower disagreed with the decision, but knew he was obligated to enforce it).

42. Brief for the United States on the Further Argument of the Questions of Relief, 7–8, 19, Brown v. Board of Education, 347 U.S. 483 (1954) (Nos. 8 et al.). This might have been because the government had supported the plaintiffs in the Truman administration and realistically could not change its position.

43. GREENBERG, CRUSADERS IN THE COURTS, 204; Schultz & Tishler, *Civil Rights*, 3.

44. Davison M. Douglas, *The Rhetoric of Moderation: Desegregating the South During the Decade After* Brown, 89 NORTHWESTERN LAW REVIEW 92, 93, note 4 (listing states that enacted interposition resolutions claiming *Brown* to be illegitimate); ibid., 93 n.5 (providing examples of state legislation aimed at resisting efforts to integrate).

45. GREENBERG, CRUSADERS IN THE COURTS, 199–202, 226–27, 381–82.

46. Ibid., 217–24 (discussing legal efforts to destroy the National Association for the Advancement of Colored People (NAACP) and the Legal Defense Fund, including an attack by the Internal Revenue Service on the NAACP's tax exemption status).

47. *See* LEARNED HAND, THE BILL OF RIGHTS: THE OLIVER WENDELL HOLMES LECTURES (Harvard University Press 1958); Herbert Wechsler, *Toward Neutral Principles of Constitutional Law*, 73 HARVARD LAW REVIEW 1 (1959).

48. JACK M. BALKIN, ED., WHAT *BROWN V. BOARD OF EDUCATION* SHOULD HAVE SAID: THE NATION'S TOP LEGAL EXPERTS REWRITE AMERICA'S LANDMARK CIVIL RIGHTS DECISION (New York University Press 2001).

49. Brown v. Board of Education, 349 U.S. 294, 301 (1955).

50. Claude Sitton, *2,000 Youths Riot in New Orleans*, NEW YORK TIMES A1 (November 17, 1960); *Peaceful Transition, Mob Activity Marks Kentucky's School Month*, SOUTHERN SCHOOL NEWS (October 1956). See generally, GREENBERG, CRUSADERS IN THE COURTS.

51. GREENBERG, CRUSADERS IN THE COURTS, 253.

52. Cases about universities included *McLaurin v. Oklahoma State Regents for Higher Education*, 339 U.S. 637 (1950) (holding that an African American graduate student was entitled to receive the same treatment from the state as students of other races); *Sweatt v. Painter*, 339 U.S. 629 (1950) (holding that the petitioner was entitled to be admitted at Texas law school); *Sipuel v. Board of Regents of University of Oklahoma*, 332 U.S. 631 (1948) (holding that the petitioner was entitled to be admitted to Oklahoma law school); and *Missouri ex rel. Gaines v. Canada*, 305 U.S. 337, 352 (1938) (holding that the petitioner was entitled to be admitted to the state law school "in the absence of other and proper provision for his legal training within the State").

 Cases about the integration of interstate buses and railroads included *Boynton v. Virginia*, 364 U.S. 454 (1960) (holding that a diner is viewed as an integral part of interstate commerce and could not discriminate); *Henderson v. United States*, 339 U.S. 816 (1950) (holding that railroad dining cars cannot refuse service to customers based on their race); and *Mitchell v. United States*, 313 U.S. 80, 94 (1941) (stating that "The denial to a rail passenger of equality of accommodations because of his race would be an invasion of a fundamental individual right which is guaranteed against state action by the Fourteenth

Amendment, and in view of the nature of the right and of our constitutional policy, it cannot be maintained that such discrimination is not essentially unjust").

Cases about voting rights included *Terry v. Adams*, 345 U.S. 461 (1953) (holding that a voting scheme that included a white-only primary deprived certain citizens of the right to vote based on race); *Smith v. Allwright*, 321 U.S. 649 (1944) (declaring that a resolution of a political party limiting membership to whites only was unconstitutional where membership in a political party was an essential qualification for voting in a primary); *Lane v. Wilson*, 307 U.S. 268 (1939) (invalidating an Oklahoma statute providing that citizens who had not voted in 1914 were required to register within a short period and exempting from such provisions those who had registered in 1914 under a state constitutional provision that had been declared invalid); *Nixon v. Herndon*, 273 U.S. 536 (1927) (striking down a Texas law prohibiting African Americans from participating in the Democratic primary election); and *Guinn v. United States*, 238 U.S. 347 (1915) (invalidating an Oklahoma constitutional amendment imposing a test of reading and writing a section of the state Constitution as a condition to voting for anyone who had not been entitled to vote on or before January 1, 1866).

Cases about exclusion from juries included *Batson v. Kentucky*, 476 U.S. 79 (1986) (holding that the Equal Protection Clause forbids a prosecutor from challenging potential jurors solely on account of race); *Alexander v. Louisiana*, 405 U.S. 625, 628 (1972) (stating that a "criminal conviction of a Negro cannot stand under the Equal Protection Clause of the Fourteenth Amendment if it is based on an indictment of a grand jury from which Negroes were excluded by reason of their race"); *Swain v. Alabama*, 380 U.S. 202, 203–204 (1965) (stating that "a State's purposeful or deliberate denial to Negroes on account of race of participation as jurors in the administration of justice violates the Equal Protection Clause"); and *Shepherd v. Florida*, 341 U.S. 50 (1951) (reversing a conviction of African American defendants where the method of jury selection discriminated against African Americans).

Cases about racially restrictive covenants included *Shelley v. Kraemer*, 334 U.S. 1 (1948) (holding that the judicial enforcement of private restrictive covenants is unconstitutional).

53. Pearson v. Murray, 182 A. 590 (Maryland Court of Appeals 1936).

54. African Americans could, however, attend Meharry Medical School in Nashville.

55. Missouri ex rel. Gaines v. Canada, 305 U.S. 337 (1938).

56. State ex rel. Bluford v. Canada, 153 S.W.2d 12 (Supreme Court of Missouri 1941).

57. Sipuel v. Board of Regents of University of Oklahoma, 332 U.S. 631 (1948).

58. McLaurin v. Oklahoma State Regents for Higher Education, 87 F. Supp. 526 (W.D. Okla. 1948).

59. Sweatt v. Painter, 339 U.S. 629 (1950).

60. McLaurin v. Oklahoma State Regents for Higher Education, 339 U.S. 637 (1950); GREENBERG, CRUSADERS IN THE COURTS, 55, 64.

61. GREENBERG, CRUSADERS IN THE COURTS, 225–26, 304, 323.

62. To consider but one example, the right to integrated housing would mean little during a housing shortage.

63. The Civil Rights Cases, 109 U.S. 3, 26 (1883).

64. Ibid., 10–12.

65. There is an interesting contrast, in this regard, with Eastern Europe. Having been socialized during the past half-century under Soviet domination, life there is accustomed

to state intrusion in social activity that, in the United States, we consider private.

66. See, for example, Shelley v. Kraemer, 334 U.S. 1 (1948) (holding that the judicial enforcement of private restrictive covenants is unconstitutional).

67. Plessy v. Ferguson, 163 U.S. 537 (1896).

68. GREENBERG, CRUSADERS IN THE COURTS, 58–59.

69. If one needs a modern history lesson on the reasons for this, read Robert Caro's third volume on Lyndon Johnson in which he describes the operation of the Senate. ROBERT A. CARO, MASTER OF THE SENATE: THE YEARS OF LYNDON JOHNSON (Knopf 2002).

70. 42 U.S.C. § 1973 (2000) et seq.; see GREENBERG, CRUSADERS IN THE COURTS, 361–62, 514.

71. Ibid., 201–202, 227.

72. Alexander v. Holmes County Board of Education, 396 U.S. 19 (1969).

73. Erica Frankenberg, Chungmei Lee & Gary Orfield, Civil Rights Project, *A Multi-Racial Society with Segregated Schools: Are We Losing the Dream?* (2003).

74. Ibid.

75. Brief for the United States on the Further Argument of the Questions of Relief at 6, Brown v. Board of Education, 347 U.S. 483 (1954) (Nos. 8 et al.).

76. Brief for the United States as Amicus Curiae (October Term 1952) 6, Brown, 347 U.S. 483 (Nos. 8 et al.); See generally, MARY L. DUDZIAK, COLD WAR CIVIL RIGHTS: RACE AND THE IMAGE OF AMERICAN DEMOCRACY (Princeton University Press 2000).

77. GREENBERG, CRUSADERS IN THE COURTS, 166.

78. Brief for Virginia as Amicus Curiae at 3, 15, Appendix A,1, Brown, 347 U.S. 483 (Nos. 8 et al.); Brief of Harry McMullan, Attorney General of North Carolina, Amicus Curiae 8, 36, Brown, 347 U.S. 483 (Nos. 8 et al.).

79. Brief of Mac Q. Williamson, Attorney General of Oklahoma, Amicus Curiae 14, Brown, 347 U.S. 483 (Nos. 8 et al.).

80. Amicus Curiae Brief of the Attorney General of Florida 21, Brown, 347 U.S. 483 (Nos. 8 et al.).

81. Ibid.

82. GREENBERG, CRUSADERS IN THE COURTS, 135–39, 226–27.

83. *U.S. Troops Sent to Little Rock; Three Districts Desegregate*, SOUTHERN SCHOOL NEWS (October 1957).

84. *Troops Dispatched*, NEW YORK TIMES A1 (May 13, 1963); *Alabama Admits Negro Students; Wallace Bows to Federal Force; Kennedy Sees "Moral Crisis" in U.S.*, NEW YORK TIMES A1 (June 12, 1963).

85. GREENBERG, CRUSADERS IN THE COURTS, 302.

86. TAYLOR BRANCH, PARTING THE WATERS: AMERICA IN THE KING YEARS, 1954–63, 427 (Simon & Schuster 1988).

87. GREENBERG, CRUSADERS IN THE COURTS, 285–88.

88. Browder v. Gayle, 142 F. Supp. 707 (M.D. Ala. 1956) affirmed, Gayle v. Browder, 352 U.S. 903 (1956).

89. Civil Rights Act of 1964, 42 U.S.C. § 2000E et seq. (2000); Civil Rights Act of 1968, 42

U.S.C. § 3601 et seq. (2000).

90. *Minority Protection*, 58.

91. Anthony Lewis, *Never Again*, NEW YORK TIMES A19 (April 3, 1995).

92. FRANZ KAFKA, LETTERS TO FRIENDS, FAMILY, AND EDITORS 17 (Richard & Clara Winston trans., Schoken 1977).

PATRICIA A. EDWARDS

Integrating an All-White High School in the Segregated South

Memories, Challenges, and Lessons Learned

I AM AN AFRICAN AMERICAN WHO GREW UP IN THE SEGREGATED DEEP SOUTH, in Albany, Georgia, a midsized community. Growing up, I often wondered why black people were so disliked and treated like second-class citizens. My family could not check into hotels or eat in restaurants, and I remember the signs over water fountains, bathrooms, bus stations, and doctors' offices that said "white only" or "colored only." This was the environmental print of my early literacy.[1] I could not understand why there was only one swimming pool in the city of Albany for black children. I did not understand why we were not supposed to go in certain places like movie theaters, restaurants, and hotels. As a young child, I found racism confusing and disheartening; I remember asking myself if I were being punished for something.

As I grew older, I pondered the paradox of black people being expected to respect a country that didn't respect us. I often thought to myself that our money was green; we were Americans; and black people defended our country in wars. If we were citizens of this great nation, why were we treated so unfairly? Even today, the legacy of plantation culture, slavery, and share cropping are permanent insignia in the South.[2] The visual remnants bring back unpleasant memories about ways of life that repelled me even as they formed my young self, and experiences in my life that continue to impact my life as a teacher and scholar even today.

Lessons from All-Black Schools

I entered kindergarten a few years after the 1954 U.S. Supreme Court landmark decision *Brown v. Board of Education*,[3] which declared segregation in education unconstitutional. But until 10th grade, I attended segregated schools. I had black teachers only, who taught despite the dismal, unfair, discriminatory situations and inferior textbooks and resources. However, as many researchers have discussed, black teachers did not allow themselves to become victims of their environments.[4] Instead, they viewed themselves as trained professionals who embraced a series of ideas about how to teach African American children. My teachers taught us to be proud of being black and that the color of our skin wasn't a hindrance, but that we represented a race of people from African descent that came from kings and queens. My black teachers connected with my classmates and me and conveyed to us the urgent value of getting an education in the coming years. My teachers said that their generation had not made it to Dr. Martin Luther King Jr.'s promised land, but someday my classmates and I would.[5] "If you get an education," said my teachers, "nobody can take it away from you."

While the later integration of schools provided a public stance against racism, for me integrated schools severed the connection and innate understanding between black students and their black teachers. From my vantage point, segregated schools were Afrocentric schools; teachers and students were one people in a struggle against racism. And, indeed, the schools I attended prior to integration had many examples of what is now called Afrocentrism.[6] For example, every day our black teachers led us in singing the National Anthem but we also sang "Lift Every Voice and Sing."[7] The Afrocentrism of my days in segregated schools reflected, naturally, what we today call "culturally relevant teaching."[8] Black people shared an unspoken understanding of our struggles, goals, pride, and perseverance as a race. Many of my black teachers came from poor backgrounds and understood the range of the black students in their classrooms.

Black teachers in the segregated schools I went to—and black teachers in segregated schools everywhere—desired to help black children reach their maximum potential so that they would be ready to meet the challenges of a very difficult world. Black teachers of that time exemplified consciousness, risk-taking, and bravery that has been lost since the 1960s. My black teachers fought against the Eurocentric hegemony by consistently exalting the value of education, since education could be the factor that tipped the scales. They focused on making us students adopt, live with, and thrive with a consciousness of yes-we-can excellence, high standards, and academic rigor. We took pride in being held to a high standard and having a curriculum on par with what was expected of white students.

However, I also recall becoming ever more aware of how segregation of schools was unequal, unfair, and wrong for all of the moral reasons we know it is wrong. I also saw the wrongness on a level not talked about so much by historians. The textbooks, equipment, and supplementary materials in all-black schools were often outdated and inferior to what was provided at all-white schools. This awareness was undoubtedly influenced by my experience as a young girl of age of nine or ten, attending mass meetings with my family and listening to Dr. King preach about hope. Dr. King dared us to think unthinkable thoughts, and to be "maladjusted" when it came to segregation and discrimination.[9] Even as a young child, I could feel the frustration that black folks felt. I saw in Dr. King what the world would soon come to see, and heard a voice that I knew had the ability to articulate all the confusion and pain I had already felt because of the color of my skin and the doors it seemed to shut. I became emboldened by what I now know as emancipatory talk. Dr. King said that we did not have to put up with racism and segregation. He told us to stand up against Jim Crow laws in all the ways we knew how. I remember sitting in a pew, my mind going a mile a minute, wondering what I could do and how I might help. Something that touched me, specifically as a child, was that Dr. King said not everyone could march in protest; he said we needed people to actively do all different kinds of work for our cause. I took this to heart, and it gave me the strength to stand up for what I knew was right several years later.

1965: Transfer to All-White Albany High

During my 11th-grade year, in 1965, I was thrust into the Civil Rights Movement when I transferred to an integrated school. I was a member of the second group of black students to transfer to Albany High, an all-white high school. My experiences at the all-white high school were filled with what Gwendolyn Thompson McMillon would describe as "victories, setbacks, tensions, overt acts of racism, and hypocrisy."[10]

In the summer of 1965, my mother and father told me that they had received a letter from the school board office indicating that a "freedom of choice" plan was in effect. At that time, these plans were common integration tools used by school districts across the South, but they would be struck down by the Supreme Court in 1968 because they rarely resulted in anything more than token desegregation.[11] As in other communities, the plan in Albany would allow black parents the opportunity to send their children to one of the three all-white high schools. After my parents received this letter, jubilation, optimism, and hope filled my home. Through a child's eyes, I could see the weight of oppression lift from my parents' shoulders. I believed at that moment that I was making history. I would have an equal chance and taste the sweetness of the American pie. However, another set of emotions filled my home too. My mother was in favor of me attending an all-white school. My father was not. "We're just asking for trouble," he said. He thought things weren't going to change, and blacks and whites would never be treated as equals. Mama thought I would have an opportunity to get a better education if I went to the new school—and a chance for a good job later in life. My parents argued about it and prayed about it. Eventually, my mother convinced my father that despite the risks, they had to take this step forward, not just for their own children, but for all black children. My parents then asked me if I wanted to attend Albany High School. I said, "Yes. I feel that I should go." I entered an all-white school eight years after President Eisenhower intervened to allow the Little Rock Nine to enroll in Little Rock Central High school in 1957.

I can vividly recall the first day I caught the bus at the all-black high school to be driven the ten miles to all-white Albany High School. While on the bus, I experienced a range of emotions: excitement, nervousness, fear, doubt, and wondering whether I had made the right decision. What if I didn't like it? Would I be treated in different ways by teachers and students? I thought about what I might be missing at my former high school. I wondered whether any of the students would physically and verbally attack me in the hallways or bathrooms. I worried that my last two years of high school would be filled with racial confrontations. To quiet my fears, I began singing quietly to myself "I Ain't Gonna Let Nobody Turn Me Around." A calmness washed over me as I thought, "Too many people are counting on me. Stand strong, Pat."

Even though I was very confident in my academic ability, I was not sure whether I had the stamina to deal with the social, political, and cultural struggles that I might encounter on a daily basis at this all-white high school. Nevertheless, I felt compelled to disprove the stereotypes about my intellectual ability. It was certainly a message I received from my parents, neighbors, and friends: "Pat, make us proud." My parents, teachers, neighbors, and other community folks encouraged me to push against the grain and never give up, and this chorus of support got me through some shaky times.

Upon my arrival at Albany High School, I noted the number of police officers and a line of white students in front of the school yelling "Two, four, six, eight, we don't want to integrate," a common chant of segregationists across the South.[12] I heard the "N" word and shouting that carried the message to return to my own high school:

"This is our school! We don't want you here." I, along with the other black students, walked silently into the building. I was horrified to learn that no two black students would be assigned to the same class during the same time period. In other words, I would be the only black student in my classes all day long.

Life at Albany High

My childhood memories are the source from which I started to form my beliefs about the world. I constantly heard statements like "Unless our children begin to learn together, there is little hope that our people will ever learn to live together."[13] I was cautioned not to allow "unfinished business," "unresolved conflicts," "ghosts of the past," and "nightmares of yesterdays" to prevent me from pursuing my goals in life. I learned to build inner strength, handle rejection, develop my own uniqueness, keep my flaws in perspective, make friends with different kinds of people, and help others become more confident. Three particular experiences at Albany High School had an indelible impact on my life. These experiences were hard-fought victories that made me a more resilient person and that strengthened my faith. Though I did not know it at the time, these three experiences also would provide the platform for me to be extremely successful in my career.[14]

A PLEA FOR A SPANISH PARTNER

Most days I came to school full of fear. However, I was inspired by the words of President John F. Kennedy: "Let us never negotiate out of fear, but let us never fear to negotiate."[15] I learned to negotiate in this setting. For example, I was the only black student in my Spanish class, as in all my other classes. Consequently, I had to perform both halves of an in-class Spanish conversation by myself. Determined not to fail my Spanish class, I would say to myself, "Buenos días, cómo está usted?" and then answer with, "Muy bien, gracias." My classmates laughed. My teacher appeared frustrated with my classmates, but she did nothing to help me get a Spanish conversational partner. I understood why she did not assign me a conversational partner. During this period of time, had my teacher assigned me a partner, she would have had serious repercussions from parents.[16] At the end of the first six weeks of school, I walked in front of my Spanish class and told my classmates that it had been extremely difficult to have conversations with myself and that I would greatly appreciate it if someone would volunteer to be my Spanish conversational partner. My classmates surprised me: six students volunteered. I accepted all six.

YOU CAN'T BE ON THE DEBATE TEAM

No black student had ever been on the debate team and I desperately wanted to participate because I knew I could perform. In a discussion with my parents, I shared with them that I might not be accepted on the debate team because of my race. My parents noted that I was depressed and frustrated. My mother talked with our neighbors about this; one of them who taught history at the predominately black high school gave my mother a copy of Langston Hughes's poem "Mother to Son."[17] My mother personalized it to include a conversation between the two of us. Mama said:

> Well, Pat, I'll tell you:
> Life for black folk ain't been no crystal stair.
> It's had tacks in it,
> And splinters,
> And boards torn up,
> And places with no carpet on the floor—
> Bare.
> But all the time
> Black folk been a climbin' on
> And reachin' landin's,
> And turnin' corners,
> And sometimes goin' in the dark
> Where there ain't been no light.
> So, Pat, don't you turn back.
> Don't you set down on the steps
> 'Cause you finds it's kinder hard.
> Don't you fall now—
> For black folk still goin', honey,
> Black folk still climbin',
> And life for black folk ain't been no crystal stair.

I held on to these words. On Monday, I went back to school. The debate team advisor told me that I could join the debate team but would not travel to the state meet in Atlanta. Of course, I knew why. All across the South, blacks could not stay in hotels.[18] I was crushed and I told my mama who replied, "Let me see what I can do," while also reminding me that I *had* made the debate team.

We did figure out a solution to the state meet. My parents drove me to Atlanta the morning of the debate and waited in the car until the debate was over then drove me back home. Consequently, I was able to participate in the State Debate Team meet. That year we won the state debate competition. As the saying goes, "Don't wait for your ship to come; swim out to get it." This perfectly characterizes my feelings at the time. I did swim out to get my ship.

YOU WON'T WIN THE GIRLS' PRESIDENCY

In the late '60s, many girls grew tired of the notion that only boys could hold the student government presidency. Students at my high school decided to run two sets of officers—a slate for boys and a slate for girls. This was done to provide girls equal representation on the student council. At the end of my 11th-grade year, I ran for girls' president. I had no chance of winning because there were only 13 black girls including myself in my grade level, and I had two strong and popular white female competitors also vying for the presidency. But, I made the decision to run anyway. It was painful putting myself out there. I had to think about the verbal attacks on me and on my friends. I had to think about threats being made about bombing my house. I was fully aware of the fact that Dr. Martin Luther King Jr.'s house had been bombed.[19] I was fully aware of the fact that four young black girls in Birmingham, Alabama, had lost their lives when their church was bombed.[20] I had to do some painful thinking about the students who stared as they passed me in the halls.

The student body at Albany High School also did some painful thinking. Many of them questioned why I wanted to run for this office in the first place. Many openly said to me that that I had no business running for this office. Dr. King once wrote that "nothing pains some people more than having to think."[21] Perhaps one of the most painful last minute things that I had to think about was getting someone to introduce me. I could not convince any of the black girls to introduce me to the student body because of their fear of the repercussions. As a result, I asked one of my white female classmates to introduce me and she agreed. I am sure she engaged in some painful thinking, also.

I really wanted to win, but I had already decided that I would not be hurt if I did not win because there is more than one way to win. I said to myself if I did not win at least I could begin again more intelligently and at least I would get the experience of competing. I gained a lot of confidence by saying to myself, "My mother brought me a new blue suit, the entire community is behind me, and I have gotten the opportunity to do something that I wanted to do."

At the assembly, I had to face 2,500 students—many of whom chose to act as hecklers; but I stood firm. The principal came to the stage and warned the hecklers that he was going to send them home for three days. They laughed and said in unison "That's OK, we will have three extra days at the beach." After the principal and teachers calmed the students down, I was able to speak. I addressed the student body by saying: "If you vote against me only because I am black, I guess I lost. But that's not fair. It is genetically too late for me to change what color I am. I have a permanent suntan and it won't come off. Why are you going to Panama Beach, Florida, to get a suntan?" The students laughed and then they began to listen. I continued, "We have a Vietnam War going on and we have no time to have a war here at home in the United States and in Albany, Georgia. If you elect me as your president, I will fight for some of the things that we want to improve here at Albany High School. For example, I will work for us to have a smoking area, better food choices in the lunch room, and work to allow seniors to leave at 2:30 each day." I did not expect to win, so I did not initially write an acceptance speech. Because my speech went so well, the day after the election I came prepared with an acceptance speech, which I delivered, telling the student body "This is a new day"—and it was. It was also a new day in my life. On this day, two of the childhood songs I always sang resurfaced clearly in my mind: "I Ain't Gonna Let Nobody Turn Me Around" and "We Shall Overcome." I was very happy that day.

LESSONS LEARNED

During my first year at Albany High School, I was knocked down again and again, yet I kept getting back up. I acted as a trailblazer during a tumultuous and critical time of the transition from a segregated to integrated school situation. Although I earned much praise and at times even acceptance, I had to fight hard to achieve these things every single day I was there. After I completed my high school education, teachers, students, family members, and community folks told me that I could go to college at the University of Georgia or anywhere else. I listened to what they had to say, but in consultation with my parents I made the decision to attend a historically black college. Even though I was very confident in my academic ability, I was not sure whether I had the strength and stamina to deal with the social, political, and cultural struggles that I might encounter on a predominately white college campus and still do well in my academic studies. In high school, my parents were there to calm my feelings and help solve my problems. I thought if I were to leave home and attend a predominately white college, I could not call home every night and I certainly could not come home every weekend. I was strong, but still fragile.

Becoming an Educator with a Focus on Students and Families

Growing up in Albany, Georgia, and being told all my life that teaching was a good career for women, especially black women, I felt destined to become a teacher. I attended Albany State University, a small black teachers' college in the South, and was constantly reminded of how important my role would be as a black educator in the lives of boys and girls of color. My professors often informed me that black students needed to see positive role models in the classroom. Specifically, they needed teachers who understood something about their cultural heritage/background as well as their learning styles.

My professors, who themselves had taught only in segregated settings and were unsure of what it would mean to teach in integrated settings, cautioned me that before I completed my undergraduate education I would be faced with the challenges of teaching in such settings. They warned that I would not only have to build a learning community for students of color, but for a diverse group of learners as well. My professors also sensed a slow decline in the number of minority students entering the teaching profession and explored with me the possibility of being the only black teacher in a school. They informed me that I might be charged with the responsibility of helping my white colleagues think about teaching black students, and my white colleagues could in turn help me think about teaching white students. My undergraduate professors' predictions have become a reality. As a scholar and teacher educator, I have helped white teachers gain a better understanding of teaching black students and creating a learning community for diverse learners, which has become increasingly important because of the continued slow decline in the number of minorities entering the teaching profession.[22] I have helped both white teachers and teachers of color understand the complexities of teaching in today's classrooms and the difficulties that might occur in communicating with children and families different from themselves.

My teaching spans over 35 years in classrooms. All of my experiences in a range of educational contexts shape and frame my work as a teacher, as a researcher, as a learner, and as a mentor. I have been committed to helping both in-service and pre-service teachers better understand their relationship with children and families. I have been committed to the generation and integration of knowledge and to the application of knowledge in authentic situations. I have been committed to making visible how contexts outside of the classroom can influence one's classroom. I have been committed to conveying that what goes on in the classroom is influenced by experiences beyond the classroom door, including the larger school, family, religious, and neighborhood contexts. In each of these commitments, I have sought to bridge the cultures of parent and teacher perceptions of one another and of home, school and community literacies.[23]

My work with families and children was launched when I served as a W. K. Kellogg National Fellow from 1983 through 1986. Given the transdisciplinary nature of my research and its broad impact on the study of family, intergenerational, and emergent literacy, some might be surprised that I began my work with families and children in a Head Start Center in a rural north Louisiana community (Ruston) and conducted a follow-up study in one elementary school located in a small rural southeast Louisiana community (Donaldsonville). Moreover, my research was motivated both by my work in these two rural Louisiana communities and by my passionate concern for the large number of children from poor and minority families who struggle to succeed in our nation's schools. This research was first reported in a paper entitled "Supporting Lower SES Mothers' Attempts to Provide Scaffolding for Book Reading" and it broke new ground by highlighting the need for teachers to shift from telling to showing low-literate mothers how to share books with their children.[24] The 1990 publication of my books *Parents as Partners in Reading: A Family Literacy Training Program* (which was later published in Spanish), and also *Talking Your Way to Literacy: A Program to Help Nonreading Parents Prepare Their Children for Reading*, ushered in more than a decade of scholarly activity that dramatically changed the way we think about the relationship between home and school.[25]

As a pioneer in my field of study, I bridged the worlds of families and schools, applying my knowledge of the lives and cultures of these people so that they could have the potential to discover, restructure and transform education for low-income children. The resulting programs were implemented in schools and libraries—Even Start, Head Start, and Chapter I programs—as well as in teenage parent and family centers across the nation. Moreover, these programs go to the heart of the literacy problem: to the home, where the problem often begins, and to the parents, from whom the most effective and long lasting solutions come.

Conclusion

While reading my childhood stories and assessing the development of my professional life, one may ask, "How did I make it in such hostile environments?" I have pondered the answer to that question and believe it is imperative that I conclude this chapter by sharing how I made it over.

Dr. King was a national hero who significantly impacted my thinking. However, Dr. King's words came to life in my home where my parents were visible role models of the values he talked about. Several factors attributed to my educational and professional success. First of all, my parents were involved in my education in and out of school. They were my first role models from whom I learned the importance of education and service to others. Mom was PTA president and advocated for students and parents. Dad owned the neighborhood barbershop and gave free haircuts to men and boys of meager means. Secondly, my parents taught me about my rich family history and encouraged me to continue our family legacy. As previously noted, I come from a family that values education, and my parents had high expectations for my sisters and me. We were expected to get good grades in school, go to college, and pursue a productive career. Getting a good education was not an option, but an expectation.

Lastly, my parents encouraged me to take risks and supported me through the risk-taking process. Some of my colleagues have told me that they were sheltered from the fight for equality that was taking place during my childhood and young adulthood. They were not allowed to attend meetings and participate in activities in their racist surroundings. I believe one of my greatest assets is my firsthand involvement in the Civil Rights Movement. My parents took me to meetings, talked to me about racism, and encouraged me to use my gifts and talents to improve the quality of life for myself and other African Americans. Whether representing the black community in a quest to integrate Albany High School, negotiating for a Spanish partner, campaigning to become the girls president of an all-white high school, implementing an urban initiative as the African American president of a predominantly white international organization, or presenting speeches around the world, the lessons learned from my parents during my formative childhood years are the messages that continuously play in my mind. *I won't let nobody turn me around*, because Mom and Dad taught me to be a risk-taker, and to finish whatever I start.

In summary, my parents raised me to be an advocate for the disadvantaged and a community servant; they expected me to succeed; and stood side-by-side with me as we participated in activities that would improve the quality of life for me and for others. As I reflect back over my life, I can see how my parents literally took me by the hand and led me to Dr. King's promised land.

Patricia A. Edwards is a Professor in the Department of Teacher of Education in the College of Education at Michigan State University.

NOTES

1. Richard G., Lomax & Lea M. McGee, *Young Children's Concepts about Print and Reading: Toward a Model of Word Reading Acquisition*, 22 READING RESEARCH QUARTERLY 2 (1987); Lea M. McGee, *Young children's Environmental Print Reading*, 63 CHILDHOOD EDUCATION 118 (1986); Elfrieda H. Hiebert, *Preschool Children's Understanding of Written Language*, 49 CHILD DEVELOPMENT 1231 (1978).

2. KARI FREDERICKSON, COLD WAR DIXIE: MILITARIZATION AND MODERNIZATION IN THE AMERICAN SOUTH (University of Georgia Press 2013); MARK SMITH, MASTERED BY THE CLOCK: TIME, SLAVERY, AND FREEDOM IN THE AMERICAN SOUTH (University of North Carolina Press 1997); JAMES OAKES, THE RULING RACE: A HISTORY OF AMERICAN SLAVHOLDERS (Knopf 1982); C. VANN WOODWARD, THE STRANGE CAREER OF JIM CROW (Oxford University Press 1955); Nancy Virts, *Change in the Planation System: American South, 1910–1945*, 43 EXPLORATIONS IN ECONOMIC HISTORY 153 (2006).

3. Brown v. Board of Education, 347 U.S. 485 (1954).

4. ADAM FAIRCLOUGH, A CLASS OF THEIR OWN: BLACK TEACHERS IN THE SEGREGATED SOUTH (Harvard University Press 2007); MICHELE FOSTER, BLACK TEACHERS ON TEACHING (The New Press 1997); Vanessa Siddle-Walker, *African American Teaching in the South: 1940–1960*, 38 AMERICAN EDUCATIONAL RESEARCH JOURNAL 751 (2001); Arlette Willis, *Literacy at Calhoun Colored School 1892–1945*, 37 READING RESEARCH QUARTERLY 8 (2002).

5. Martin Luther King., Jr., *I Have a Dream* (Washington, DC, August 28, 1963).

6. MWALIMU J. SHUJAA, TOO MUCH SCHOOLING, TOO LITTLE EDUCATION: A PARADOX OF BLACK LIFE IN WHITE SOCIETIES (Africa World Press 1994); MOLEFI K. ASANTE, THE AFROCENTRIC IDEA (Temple University Press 1987); MOLEFI K. ASANTE, AFROCENTRICITY: A THEORY OF SOCIAL CHANGE (Amulefi Press 1980).

7. This song, written by brothers James Weldon Johnson and John Rosamond Johnson to commemorate forty years of African American freedom, is known as the African American national anthem. Mary A. Love, National Council of Christian Churches USA, *"Lift Every Voice and Sing"* (1995).

8. ALTHIER M. LAZAR, PATRICIA A. EDWARDS, & GWENDOLYN T. MCMILLON, BRIDGING LITERACY AND EQUITY: THE ESSENTIAL GUIDE TO SOCIAL EQUITY TEACHING (Teachers College Press 2012); GENEVA GAY, CULTURALLY RESPONSIVE TEACHING: THEORY, RESEARCH, AND PRACTICE (Teachers College Press 2000); Gloria Ladson-Billings, *But That's Just Good Teaching! The Case for Culturally Relevant Pedagogy*, 34 THEORY INTO PRACTICE 3 (1995).

9. See, for example, Martin Luther King, Jr., *The Role of Social Scientists in the Civil Rights Movement*, 24 JOURNAL OF SOCIAL ISSUES 1 (1968).

10. Gwendolyn Thompson McMillon, *A Tale of Two Settings: African-American Students' Literacy Experiences at Church and at School*, 26 (Doctoral dissertation, Michigan State University (2001)).

11. Green v. County School Board of New Kent County, Virginia, 391 U.S. 430 (1968).

12. Wilbur C. Rich, *Putting Blacks Kids into a Trick Bag: Anatomizing the Inner-City Public School Reform*, 8 MICHIGAN JOURNAL OF RACE & LAW 159, 162 (2002); Robert

Cohen, *"Two, Four, Six, Eight, We Don't Want to Integrate": White Student Attitudes Toward the University of Georgia's Desegregation*, 80 GEORGIA HISTORICAL QUARTERLY 616 (1996).

13. Milliken v. Bradley, 418 U.S. 717, 783 (1974) (Justice Thurgood Marshall, dissenting).

14. For example, I served as a member of the International Reading Association Board of Directors from 1998–2001; in 2006–2007 as the first African American President of the Literacy Research Association (formerly the National Reading Conference); as the fourth African American President of the International Reading Association (2010–2011); additionally, I served as a People to People Language and Literacy Delegation Leader to China, South Africa, and Russia.

15. John F. Kennedy, *Presidential Inaugural Address* (January 20, 1961).

16. Kimberly Jenkins Robinson, *Resurrecting the Promise of Brown: Understanding and Remedying How the Supreme Court Reconstitutionalized Segregated Schools*, 88 NORTH CAROLINA LAW REVIEW 787, 798–801 (2010).

17. Langston Hughes, *Mother to Son*, in THE COLLECTED POEMS OF LANGSTON HUGHES (Vintage Books 1994).

18. Theodore M. Hesburgh, *The End of Apartheid in America*, 54 GEORGE WASHINGTON LAW REVIEW 244, 246 (1986).

19. CLAYBORNE CARSON, THE AUTOBIOGRAPHY OF MARTIN LUTHER KING, JR., 78–82 (Grand Central Publishing 1998).

20. Chris Pruitt, *16th Street Baptist Church Bombing (1963)*, U.S. NATIONAL PARK SERVICE (November 2011).

21. MARTIN LUTHER KING, JR., STRENGTH TO LOVE 14 (Fortress Press 1981).

22. Tia C. Madkins, *The Black Teacher Shortage: A Literature Review of Historical and Contemporary Trends*, 80 JOURNAL OF NEGRO EDUCATION 417 (2011); Jacqueline J. Irvine, *An Analysis of the Problem of Disappearing Black Educators*, 88 ELEMENTARY SCHOOL JOURNAL 503 (1988).

23. LAZAR, EDWARDS, & MCMILLON, BRIDGING LITERACY AND EQUITY; PATRICIA A. EDWARDS, GWENDOLYN T. MCMILLON, & JENNIFER D. TURNER, CHANGE IS GONNA COME: TRANSFORMING LITERACY EDUCATION FOR AFRICAN AMERICAN STUDENTS (Teachers College Press 2010); PATRICIA A. EDWARDS, CHILDREN'S LITERACY DEVELOPMENT: MAKING IT THROUGH SCHOOL, FAMILY, AND COMMUNITY INVOLVEMENT (Allyn & Bacon 2004).

My research on parent involvement, especially parent-child book reading, has propelled me to the forefront of the reading profession and as a national expert on family/intergenerational literacy. Few professors have been so rewarded by hearing personally from former First Lady Barbara Bush, working with governors, giving professional testimony to policymakers, or appearing on TV or radio as I have. I have given more than 1000 speeches for teachers, administrators, daycare providers, adult educators, legislators and governors around the country and throughout the world. I have also been invited to apply for an endowed chair at many of the institutions that I was afraid to attend when I finish high school, including the University of Alabama and the University of Georgia.

As an African American researcher and educator, I have done much to build bridges and cross boundaries that have traditionally constrained African American children and youth. Through my leadership, mentorship, research and service, I have contributed significantly to moving the field forward in addressing literacy problems that plague our diverse society. The legacy of my career has not been built around easy ideas to explore, as matters of mind and process have never been straightforward things to observe. Nonetheless, my notions about families and children as well as my notions about culturally and linguistically diverse children have not been based on armchair speculations.

24. Patricia A. Edwards, *Supporting Lower SES Mothers' Attempts to Provide Scaffolding for Book Reading*, in JOBETH ALLEN & JANA MASON, RISK MAKERS, RISK TAKERS, RISK BREAKERS: REDUCING THE RISKS FOR YOUNG LITERACY LEARNERS (Heinemann 1989).

25. PATRICIA A. EDWARDS, PARENTS AS PARTNERS IN READING: A FAMILY LITERACY TRAINING PROGRAM (Children's Press 1990) (Spanish edition 1992); PATRICIA A. EDWARDS, TALKING YOUR WAY TO LITERACY: A PROGRAM TO HELP NONREADING PARENTS PREPARE THEIR CHILDREN FOR READING (Children's Press 1990).

WENDY PARKER

Brown's 60th Anniversary
A Story of Judicial Isolation

> One vehicle can carry only a limited amount of baggage.
> —Chief Justice Warren E. Burger, *Swann v. Charlotte-Mecklenburg*
> *Board of Education*, 402 U.S. 1, 22 (1971)

SIXTY YEARS AGO THE SUPREME COURT ANNOUNCED, "IN THE FIELD OF PUBLIC education, the doctrine of 'separate but equal' has no place."[1] In 1954, no one doubted the significance of that command, even among those who actively resisted it.

Brown v. Board of Education[2] has now outlasted *Plessy v. Ferguson*,[3] which for 58 years sanctioned "separate but equal." Does that necessarily mean, however, that *Brown* has eclipsed *Plessy* in significance? Has the power of *Brown* instead waned in its advancing age? Granted, few publically decree *Plessy* as the best guide to race relations in the twenty-first century; yet, our schools are still segregated and unequal in ways reminiscent of *Plessy*.[4] That naturally leads one to question the lasting significance of *Brown*, particularly as it turns 60.

This chapter examines the legacy of *Brown* through the lens of two sets of school desegregation cases. The first are four cases that the Supreme Court considered in its *Brown v. Board of Education* decision—cases from Delaware, Kansas, South Carolina, and Virginia.[5] The second are school desegregation cases litigated in the Middle District of Alabama. The Alabama cases are unique because of the active role taken by federal judges in managing their school desegregation dockets.[6]

From these cases, a story of judicial isolation emerges. In the four original *Brown* cases, parties bring issues to federal courts for resolution, and the federal courts make their rulings, which are most often approving what the parties have already decided. In the Alabama cases, the federal courts tell the parties to bring issues to their attention, and the judges then issue their decisions, which again are typically not disputed by the parties. Throughout these proceedings, the federal judges are crafting remedies to achieve desegregation "to the extent practicable," with proper deference to local control, as the Supreme Court has told them to do.[7]

Yet, their desegregative efforts are isolated; they lack connection to any other governmental body. Today, no other government action actively supports or facilitates school desegregation. That task remains only for federal judges. A state may be present as a party defendant, and the United States may be a party plaintiff. In the litigation, however, these government entities are acting as litigants—they seek judicial resolution, but they themselves take little responsibility outside their party status in facilitating school desegregation.

Even more troubling, states and the United States often undercut school desegregation outside the courtroom, thereby further isolating federal judges. The Obama Administration, for example, has encouraged states to expand their charter school offerings—even though their educational value is disputed and their segregative effect is well documented.[8] At the state level, the original *Brown* cases and the Middle District of Alabama cases show how states, outside of federal court, also act in ways that undercut the possibility of achieving desegregation. The State of Delaware, for example, today mandates neighborhood schools despite its persistent housing segregation.[9] These actions validate and permit the presence of segregated schools, contrary to *Brown*'s central premise and all too consistent with *Plessy*.

This is not to argue that Massive Resistance has returned. Massive Resistance presupposes a power to be defeated. Instead, Massive Resistance has given way to judicial isolation, where other decision makers pursue agendas at odds with the judicial goal of desegregation to the extent practicable. Education reform today simply ignores the idea of inherent inequality of segregation.[10] Federal judges stand alone when it comes to that idea (and even they do not seem that willing to spearhead efforts to eradicate school segregation).[11]

To tell the tale of lonely school desegregation judges, I begin with the four original *Brown* districts and then turn to the Middle District of Alabama. What emerges is a story of other government entities undercutting the judges' ability to create lasting school integration. The districts also reflect what is true in many other school districts: an increasing Hispanic student population and the continued presence of predominately white private schools.

The Original *Brown* Districts

The Supreme Court consolidated four cases into one when it decided *Brown v. Board of Education.* The cases involved Clarenton County, South Carolina; New Castle County, Delaware; Topeka, Kansas; and Prince Edward County, Virginia.[12] Although these four cases were not the first to seek an end to K–12 school segregation, their success before the Supreme Court makes them an interesting place to analyze the present-day impact of *Brown*.[13]

Table 1 presents one way to view the impact of school desegregation litigation in these four school districts: the number of schools disproportionately white or disproportionately minority.[14] I define schools as disproportionately white or minority by a standard commonly used in litigation, the standard of plus or minus 15%.[15] That is, a school is deemed to be disproportionately white if the student body is greater than 15% points of the school district's white population. Similarly, a school is deemed to be disproportionately minority if the student body is not within 15% points of the school district's white population. The numbers for two school districts (Clarenton County, South Carolina, and New Castle County, Delaware) are listed

Table 1. Current Conditions in Original Brown School Districts*

SCHOOL DISTRICT	NO. SCHOOLS	% WHITE	NO. DISPROP. WHITE SCHOOLS (%)	NO. DISRPROP. MINORITY SCHOOLS (%)
Clarendon County, SC	**12**	**34%**	**2 (17%)**	**4 (33%)**
Clarendon No. 1, SC	4	3%	0 (0%)	0 (0%)
Clarenton No. 2, SC	6	29%	0 (0%)	0 (0%)
Clarenton No. 3, SC	2	69%	0 (0%)	0 (0%)
Prince Edward County, VA	**3**	**38%**	**0 (0%)**	**0 (0%)**
Topeka, KS	**28**	**40%**	**2 (7%)**	**3 (11%)**
New Castle County, DE	**85**	**41%**	**19 (22%)**	**22 (26%)**
Brandywine, DE	15	50%	1 (7%)	4 (27%)
Christina, DE	27	33%	3 (11%)	6 (22%)
Colonial, DE	14	32%	0 (0%)	0 (0%)
Red Clay, DE	29	47%	8 (28%)	11 (38%)

*This table is based on data reported during the 2012–2013 school year.

twice: once as the original, single district they were when the Supreme Court decided *Brown*, and also as the multidistricts they became. The numbers in bold reflect the original four *Brown* districts.

The table demonstrates both success and failure. Two school districts can boast significant student integration: Prince Edward County in Virginia and Colonial School District in Delaware, an entity created after *Brown*. Both districts comply with the plus or minus 15% standard, and the districts are demographically diverse.

The three school districts created out of Clarenton County, South Carolina, are desegregated by the standard of the districts they became. Their extremely small size for a single South Carolina county (the three school districts together educate around five thousand K–12 students) and their creation as a hostile response to *Brown*, however, makes their very existence suspect. These districts cannot truly boast of successful school integration given the continued isolation of black students in Clarenton County District No. 1.

The remaining school districts have lost their status of black and white schools coexisting. Instead, the districts have schools of various degrees of integration, and segregation. The story of the four schools districts is explored in more detail below.

CLARENTON COUNTY, SOUTH CAROLINA

As it was in the 1950s, Clarenton County, South Carolina, today is a rural county with about 35,000 residents.[16] While the county was predominately African American in the 1950s, it is now evenly split between African Americans and whites.[17] It was the first of the *Brown* cases to reach the Supreme Court docket, but change came slowly. Before *Brown*, the county had three black schools and two white schools.[18] That pattern continued until the 1960s.[19]

The initial school desegregation remedies for Clarenton County were the best the defendants could have hoped for. The first remedy was simply the elimination of explicit *de jure* laws.[20] That remedy was replaced with an ineffective freedom of choice plan. In a divided, en banc decision, the Fourth Circuit ended that in 1970 by approving a plan that compelled actual integration.[21]

The state of South Carolina and white Clarenton citizens were not pleased with *Brown*, and their reactions limited the reach of the 1970 desegregation order. First, after *Brown* was decided, South Carolina divided Clarenton County School District into three very small school districts along racial lines. Two were overwhelming white (Clarenton County District Nos. 2 and 3), and one was overwhelmingly African American (Clarenton County District No. 1).[22] Since then, the districts have been treated separately for the purposes of school desegregation litigation.

The black district, No. 1, today educates only 808 K–12 students, and almost all are black.[23] Of the two original white districts, one is now overwhelmingly black (No. 2) and the other is still predominately white (No. 3); both are still small, but neither district is one-race. District No. 2 was declared unitary and its school desegregation suit dismissed in 2004. Nos. 1 and 3, on the other hand, are still under court order, but with no apparent intention of seeking unitary status.[24]

The second action impeding court-ordered integration was the establishment of private schools.[25] The two predominately black districts have practically all-white schools founded in the backdrop of desegregation. A white academy (Clarendon Hall) opened in District No. 1, the 95% black school district, in 1965. It remains today as a virtually all-white school, with almost 300 students.[26] A second private academy (Laurence Manning Academy) opened in District No. 2 in 1972. Its student population of 1,000 students is 98% white.[27] As at the birth of school integration, those private schools continue to provide a place for white flight and impede school integration.

The division of the school district into three districts predominately of one race and the creation of private, white academies effectively nullified the Fourth Circuit's 1970 order compelling school integration. The state of South Carolina and white parents used their power to undercut the efficacy and importance of the desegregation order. That resistance locks in segregation today, and no one seems interested in changing that segregation. The 1970 order mandating actual school integration is an isolated point in time.

NEW CASTLE COUNTY, DELAWARE

Brown also considered efforts to desegregate schools in New Castle County, which encompasses Wilmington, Delaware. As of 1897, the Delaware constitution required separate schools for black and white children.[28] In 1952, a state court judge ordered the admission of black students to white schools because of inequalities between black and white schools.[29]

Like Clarenton County, desegregation came slowly to New Castle County.[30] In 1954, Wilmington public schools were 28% African American. By 1974, that percentage had increased to 83%, with a slight increase in overall enrollment. Half of Wilmington's twenty schools in 1974 were almost all black, and one school was virtually all white. The all-black schools in 1954 Wilmington remained that way in 1974.[31]

In 1981, a federal court approved a state plan to divide the county into four districts: Brandywine, Christina, Colonial, and Red Clay.[32] All four districts were declared unitary in 1995.[33] The schools were fairly integrated at the time. All the traditional schools in Brandywine, Christina, and Colonial met a plus or minus 10% standard.[34] Red Clay had a harder time demonstrating full compliance with this standard, but all of its elementary and middle schools and two of its four high schools did.[35] Plaintiffs contested unitary status not on student assignment issues, but on within-school issues.[36]

Since unitary status, New Castle County schools have resegregated.[37] While all but two schools in the county met a ±10 standard in 1995 at the time of unitary status, now only Colonial's schools all comply with a ±15 standard. One-third of the schools in Brandywine and Christina school districts fail this standard. Red Clay, which initially had the hardest time demonstrating integration of its student bodies, now has two-thirds of its schools outside of this band.

White flight, which began even before unitary status, caused part of that resegregation.[38] Yet, white flight is not the complete story. The state of Delaware must be held responsible as well. It intentionally undercut school integration with its Neighborhood Schools Act, a law aimed at the New Castle County school districts and a law reminiscent of the efforts of states to evade the force of *Brown* in the 1960s.[39]

After unitary status, the four New Castle County school districts continued their pre-unitary status student assignment practices, including busing.[40] That ended in 2000 with the Neighborhood Schools Act, which required students be assigned to their closest neighborhood school.[41] Specifically, the law required the four New Castle County school districts to assign students based on their geographical proximity and natural neighborhood boundaries.[42] The law essentially mandated the creation of segregated schools. Nor can the consequences of the act be deemed unknown or unknowable to the legislators. Wilmington's segregated neighborhoods are neither new nor a secret. A study attributes that act to increased segregation of Delaware schools, particularly in New Castle County.[43]

Like school districts throughout the United States, New Castle County is also changing demographically in ways that make integration of minority students with white students more difficult. [44] The four school districts have at least doubled their Hispanic student population since unitary status.[45] That has come at the cost of white student enrollment. The number of white students has declined, while the African American population has remained constant.[46] While the increase in minority population creates more opportunities for diverse student bodies in predominately white schools, it also increases the opportunities for isolated minority schools.

PRINCE EDWARD COUNTY, VIRGINIA

Prince Edward County is the site of one of the most notable acts of Massive Resistance. Here, Virginia closed public schools for five years instead of desegregating them.[47] Prince Edward Academy, a private school in name only, opened to educate white students.[48] When the public schools reopened, whites continued to enroll in the white academy.[49] Today, however, Prince Edward County is as close as one can find to a desegregation success story. That success is largely attributable to white parents eventually returning to the public school system.[50]

In 1971–72 only 6% of the students in the public schools were white; the number increased to 23% in 1980.[51] By 1999, the enrollment had returned to its 1952 demographics, 39% white and 59% African American.[52] That racial makeup continues today; the overall student population is 54% African American and 38% white.[53] Those students are also evenly distributed across schools—a relatively easy task given that today Prince Edward County has only one elementary school, one middle school, and one high school.

This is not to say that Prince Edward County's legacy of segregation is gone. The infamous Prince Edward Academy has been renamed Fuqua School, after J. B. Fuqua donated $10 million in 1993.[54] The school is still overwhelming white, although in 2008 it offered an African American football high school student a scholarship and enrolled a handful of African American students.[55] The school, however, had significant financial difficulties before the infusion of Mr. Fuqua's money. Today it has fewer than 500 students; it enrolled over a thousand students before it lost its tax-exempt status over its racially exclusionary admissions policies in 1978.[56]

I found no indication of any school desegregation litigation in the county after the schools reopened in 1964. The return of white parents to the school system appears to be driven not by court order but by a private campaign of white parents to return to public schools.[57] The courts set up the possibility for desegregated schools by requiring integration and ordering the schools reopened. Yet, the courts do not appear to be involved in getting the white parents to return to the schools. That effort came from outside the courts.

TOPEKA, KANSAS

Integration came more quickly to Topeka than elsewhere. In 1951, Topeka, Kansas had 22 elementary schools: 18 for its white students, and four for its black students, who made up 8.4% of the student population.[58] Its junior and high schools already had some integration.[59] By 1953, before *Brown* was decided, the school district admitted black students to formerly all-white elementary schools. This integration was reflected in the school district's 1955 enrollment numbers.[60]

Progress toward integration, however, eventually slowed. By 1966, schools were still strongly associated with one race, and the schools were reorganized in 1974 to redress the continued segregation of schools.[61] Over the plaintiffs' objections, the district court granted the school district unitary status in 1987 because of the lack of a causal link between past illegality and current school segregation.[62] The Tenth Circuit, however, reversed.[63]

The dispute over unitary status, however, was gone by 1999. Then the parties agreed to unitary status, which the district court granted in a six-paragraph opinion.[64] The court found that all schools met a plus or minus 15% standard, and that staff and faculty had been evenly distributed as well.[65] No one appealed, and the case most strongly associated with *Brown* had ended.

More than a decade after unitary status, however, schools outside of the plus or minus 15% band have returned.[66] Two schools are disproportionately white under that standard, and three schools are disproportionately minority. That makes for 18% of the schools demonstrating more segregation than at the time of unitary status.

The more profound change, perhaps, is the increase in the Hispanic population. Hispanic students were practically nonexistent in the 1980s, and today are more than a quarter of the student population.[67] The black population is virtually the same (18.6% black in 2012–13, compared to 18.5% black in 1985). The number of white students has decreased to 40%.

These demographic changes, found throughout the United States, make white enclaves more difficult to maintain. Today, the two Topeka schools with the highest proportion of white students are an elementary and high school, each with a 61% white student population.[68] As is true in all four *Brown* districts, there are more schools with a disproportionately minority student population than schools with a disproportionately white student population.[69]

Continued school segregation in Delaware, Kansas, and South Carolina (and throughout the United States) calls into question the lasting significance of *Brown*. School desegregation jurisprudence and white flight are typically blamed for continued segregation.[70] The original *Brown* districts reveal another cause as well: the lingering acceptance outside the federal courtroom of *Plessy*'s approval of separate but equal.

School segregation remains partly because other government bodies continue to accept the existence of schools separated by race. Executive and legislative entities try to fix any inherent inequality in separate schools instead of eradicating the segregation itself. Inside the courtroom, the quest of states is typically to end a school desegregation case as quickly as possible, with as little change as possible. Outside the courtroom, states go far to act in ways at odds with *Brown*'s explicit disapproval of separate but equal in the schoolhouse. This indicates not a defect in *Brown* but a lack of commitment outside the federal judiciary to *Brown*'s central premise that separate schools are inherently unequal.

The acceptance of *Plessy*'s separate but equal approach is perhaps most surprising in Delaware, which in the beginning was not nearly resistant as other states to *Brown*. Delaware's Neighborhood Law specifically prevents assignment to achieve racial integration in schools, despite the persistent pattern of segregated neighborhoods. This reflects a state decision that schools *should* be separate if the cost is busing.[71] The state has chosen a reality of separate schools consistent with *Plessy*'s acceptance of separate railway carriages. As a result, the state of Delaware aided the resegregation of New Castle County schools. The federal courts in the Delaware case compelled racially balanced schools as the price of ending the school desegregation lawsuit, but that achievement was quickly undercut.

The history of South Carolina also indicates that the actions of Massive Resistance continue to affect schools today. South Carolina's division of a single county school system along racial lines is an early example of effective state action undercutting the efficacy of school desegregation orders, but one with lingering effects today. Countywide school districts are well known for increasing the chances of school segregation by making white flight harder.[72] South Carolina provided opportunities for segregation by creating school districts strongly associated with one race, and effectively thwarted the integrative aspects of *Brown*. The continued presence of private schools, originally founded as white academies to prevent racial mixing in schools, is another indicator of how Massive Resistance continues to lock in segregation.

The cases from Kansas and Virginia, however, are different and indicate the difficulty of lasting desegregation through judicial action. Here we have a state that led the cause of Massive Resistance (Virginia) and a state that quickly enrolled black students in formerly all-white schools (Kansas). From this distinct history comes school districts with more enduring integration than Delaware or South Carolina. Prince Edward County boasts diverse, integrated schools. Topeka does as well, for almost four-fifths of its schools.

The federal courts in both situations were instrumental in creating opportunities for integration. The federal courts were critical in getting the public schools reopened to children of all races in Prince Edward County.[73] The Tenth Circuit was adamant that the Topeka school district could achieve higher levels of student and teacher integration, and the school district complied.[74]

This work of the judiciary deserves praise, but even in Kansas and Virginia the federal courts continue to be an isolated part of the quest for equality. No court order mandated white parents to return in Prince Edward County; the white parents choose to do so, when they were ready to do so. No court order also addresses the very new district Topeka, Kansas, is becoming. It started as a 90% white district in 1952; it is now less than 40% white. The work of the federal courts—because it has a time limit and because courts have limited themselves to redressing only present-day effects caused by de jure segregation—has little impact on addressing changes like the increase in minority population in our schools. Here the courts have had almost no role.

The Middle District of Alabama

This section turns from the original *Brown* districts to *Lee v. Macon County Board of Education*.[75] This set of cases provides an opportunity to evaluate how an unusually proactive judiciary can affect the end of the school desegregation process.

Macon originally sought only the integration of a small, rural school in Tuskegee, Alabama. Two former law school classmates, on opposite sides of the issue, used the case to decide the fate of desegregating almost all Alabama schools. Within weeks of the suit's filing, Judge Frank M. Johnson Jr. ordered immediate enrollment of black students in the white school for the school year starting the following month, to be followed by a more expansive desegregation plan for the next school year.[76] After the school district assigned thirteen black students to the white school, Judge Johnson's law school classmate, Governor George Wallace, ordered the school closed.[77] An arsonist thought that was insufficient, and set the school on fire.[78] Six African American students admitted to the school—its entire enrollment for the 1963–64 school year—finished the school year in "makeshift classrooms."[79] Macon Academy, a "private" school with public funding, opened for white students.[80]

The state of Alabama quickly paid a judicial price for its resistance. Within a year, a three-judge court joined Governor Wallace and other state officers as defendants to the original lawsuit against Macon County, and held them legally responsible for desegregating the ninety-nine Alabama public school districts not already under court order.[81] That led to 35 school districts in the Middle District of Alabama being covered by *Lee v. Macon County Board of Education*.[82]

Today, *Lee v. Macon* stands out not because of its attending violence and resistance, but because of two current district court judges of the Middle District of Alabama, Judge W. Harold Albritton III and Judge Myron H. Thompson. Starting with Judge Albritton in 1995, these two judges have issued orders in their pending, but inactive, school desegregation cases requiring the parties to show cause why the school districts should not be declared unitary and the cases dismissed.[83] The show cause orders affected the descendants of the original *Lee v. Macon* lawsuit, and school desegregation cases in the Middle District of Alabama pending at the time *Lee v. Macon* was filed.

Judge Albritton and Judge Thompson are unique in managing their school desegregation dockets. Despite *Brown II*'s command to district court judges to continue their jurisdiction during the school desegregation process, school desegregation cases are known to languish on court dockets, with little activity, for decades.[84] Judge Albritton and Judge Thompson set up a process that required the parties to justify continued court jurisdiction—and this in turn meant the parties had to evaluate the progress toward ending segregation to the extent practicable and thereby achieving unitary status.[85] The federal judges insisted that the lawsuit would one day end, but only when the schools had been adequately desegregated, thereby holding out benefits for both plaintiffs and defendants.

The judges set this goal before parties representing a variety of viewpoints and experiences. Judge Thompson continued the state's legal liability for statewide issues, and the Department of Justice had intervened in the *Lee* litigation in 1963 as plaintiffs.[86] That meant four sets of parties: the private plaintiffs (represented by experienced Alabama school desegregation lawyers, including lawyers from the original *Lee* filing), the United States, the local school districts, and the state defendants.

From a process standpoint, judicial involvement was confined largely to two tasks: starting the discussion on attaining unitary status and encouraging settlement of issues preventing unitary status.[87] Resolution of the show cause orders typically started with a consent decree allowing partial unitary status in some matters, and mandating remedies for the remaining issues. After that, schools were either declared fully unitary or, more typically, awarded partial unitary status in additional areas. This sometimes meant that schools districts were at times denied their requests for full unitary status. Instead, courts would award partial unitary status in additional areas, while reserving a few issues for continued judicial oversight. Throughout the process, the judges encouraged settlement of the outstanding issues, turning at times to a magistrate judge. Annual status conferences were held to monitor and resolve any outstanding compliance issues. Only rarely were the parties unable to agree. [88]

Almost 20 years later, the process has largely come to an end. All school districts save two have been declared fully unitary.[89] By 2008, all but three districts had been declared completely unitary.[90] Most school districts achieved full unitary status after around ten years of actively litigating unitary status issues. The predominant judicial influence was forcing the parties to address outstanding issues, and the parties did so. In the end, all grants of full unitary status were done without party objection—a remarkable ending to a case that began with such acrimony.

That the process took a decade for most cases partly reflects the number of cases simultaneously being litigated by the same set of lawyers and the expansive approach the judges took to the scope of *Brown*. The reach of *Brown* was fully present: quality of education was at issue, and not just student assignment. These issues took time to resolve because they needed and received additional work.

Interestingly, student assignment was usually not at issue at unitary status proceedings.[91] Most of the schools districts are small, rural districts with only a few schools.[92] In three cases, black parents protested that enrollment changes would unduly burden their children, but only once successfully.[93] Black parents also sometimes protested about the lack of inclusion in extracurricular activities.[94]

The achievement most often mentioned in the unitary status proceedings was the increase in minority teachers—a fitting end perhaps given the number of minority teachers who lost their jobs in the immediate aftermath of *Brown*.[95] While the parties did not object to full unitary status by the time it was awarded, community members often did, but not always.[96]

Perhaps the order with the biggest impact was the statewide consent decree on special education. Black students had been overrepresented in particular special education categories, while underrepresented in others. In the agreement, Alabama agreed to revamp its special education procedures and policies and implement those changes throughout the state to address these disparities.[97] Six years later, the state demonstrated successful compliance with the consent decree, including substantial reduction (albeit not elimination) of the inequalities.[98]

The inclusion of the community in unitary status proceedings also deserves praise. The judges required broad notice of unitary status proceedings, and took community complaints seriously.[99] For example, in Elmore County, community members objected to the school district's response to a report of a racial slur by a substitute teacher.[100] After the fairness hearing, the school district investigated the matter and took corrective action. Parents also complained that the school district's dress code allowed display of the Confederate flag.[101] To resolve this issue, the school board enlisted the help of the Southeastern Equity Center and local community focus groups, and adopted a new policy. All this was done before unitary status was awarded. The courts gave the local community the opportunity for official complaints, which had to be addressed to the court's satisfaction before unitary status. The community gained power through that process, if only for a moment in time.

While the judges deserve praise for their process and commitment to achieving desegregation to the extent practicable, the cases also demonstrate the very real limits of *Brown*. For example, white flight destroyed whatever chance Macon County, the original *Lee* defendant, had of diverse schools. The county transitioned from a school system with separate public schools for black and white students in 1963 to a system with all-black schools in 2013.[102] In the 2013–14 school year, not a single white student was enrolled at a public school in Macon County.[103] All 2,177 students also qualified for free and reduced lunch.[104] The private academy continues to enroll white students, but not many.[105] In 2006, Judge Thompson declared the Macon County school system unitary, and the lawsuit ended.

The federal courts diligently worked to forestall white flight in Macon County, but without success. In 1993, the federal courts prevented the closing of a small, public school with a significant white population to prevent white flight, but the efforts eventually failed.[106] Twenty years later, the school was all black as well.

The other school district in the Middle District of Alabama that once garnered national attention is Randolph County.[107] In 1994, the principal of a high school in the small, rural county made national news for his statements on interracial marriage and biracial students.[108] Today, it is one of the two pending school desegregation cases in the Middle District, and the only school desegregation issue left concerns personnel. Solomon Seay, one of the original *Lee* attorneys, praised the Randolph County consent decree negotiated in the backdrop of the national outcry over the principal's statements as the "very best" school desegregation remedy he had ever achieved.[109] Despite all of these efforts, African American students still perform, however, worse than their white counterparts on end-of-year testing.[110] As Chief Justice Burger recognized in *Swann*, *Brown* should not be expected to solve all educational inequities.

Conclusion

Despite the limited capacity of the federal judiciary to create lasting integration, I would still give *Brown* the diamond often attending a 60th anniversary. *Brown* is not a mere historical marker, holding a place in time when something important happened. *Brown* puts the issue of race in education on the table, front and center. Even as the United States turns to methods other than school desegregation to effectuate educational equality, no one can ignore race in education after *Brown*. And no one has; no one argues race is irrelevant in judging educational equity. Instead, we argue about *how* to use race in achieving racial equity in schooling. *Brown* forces the conversation, even if it does not force a particular result. Its simple message of the inherent inequality in segregation stands out among other civil rights markers. The question remains, as it always has, whether we can accept that message.[111]

Wendy Parker is the James A. Webster Professor of Public Law at Wake Forest University School of Law.

NOTES

1. Brown v. Board of Education, 347 U.S. 483, 495 (1954) (*Brown I*).
2. Ibid.
3. Plessy v. Ferguson, 163 U.S. 537, 544 (1896). That opinion effectively lasted for 58 years, until 1954 when *Brown* was decided. *Brown* rejected *Plessy*'s applicability to public education, but did not explicitly overrule it. The Supreme Court first specifically overruled *Plessy* in 1970, although appellate courts had earlier deemed it overruled. Oregon v. Mitchell, 400 U.S. 112, 133 (1970).
4. But see, Derrick A. Bell, *Bell, J., Dissenting*, in DERRICK A. BELL, WHAT *BROWN V. BOARD OF EDUCATION* SHOULD HAVE SAID (New York University Press 2001) (arguing that a strict adherence to *Plessy* would have been a more effective remedy for minority school children than the unenforceable promise of *Brown*). See generally, Sean F. Reardon & Ann Owens, *60 Years after* Brown: *Trends and Consequences of School Segregation*, 40 ANNUAL REVIEW OF SOCIOLOGY 199 (2014).
5. I do not examine the District of Columbia schools, which the Supreme Court also ruled unconstitutionally segregated the same day it decided *Brown*. Bolling v. Sharpe, 347 U.S. 497, 500 (1954). The political structure of the District of Columbia and its overwhelming African American student population make it exceptionally unique. *See generally* Washington, DC, State Advisory Committee to U.S. Commission on Civil Rights, *Public Education in the District of Columbia: the Need to Ensure Equal Access to a High Quality Education for All Children* (2010).
6. Wendy Parker, *The Future of School Desegregation*, 94 NORTHWESTERN UNIVERSITY LAW REVIEW 1157, 1205 (2000).
7. Board of Education v. Dowell, 498 U.S. 237, 248, 250 (1991).
8. Wendy Parker, *From the Failure of Desegregation to the Failure of Choice*, 34 WASHINGTON UNIVERSITY JOURNAL OF LAW AND POLICY 117, 125, 138–42 (2012). For other critiques of the Obama Administration's record on civil rights, see Olatunde C.A. Johnson, *Stimulus and Civil Rights*, 111 COLUMBIA LAW REVIEW 154 (2011); Michael Selmi, *The Obama Administration's Civil Rights Record: The Difference an Administration Makes*, 2 INDIANA JOURNAL OF LAW AND SOCIAL EQUALITY 108 (2013).
9. William J. Glenn, *A Quantitative Analysis of the Increase in Public School Segregation in Delaware: 1989–2006*, 46 URBAN EDUCATION 719, 730 (2011).
10. See generally JAMES E. RYAN, FIVE MILES AWAY, A WORLD APART: ONE CITY, TWO SCHOOLS, AND THE STORY OF EDUCATIONAL OPPORTUNITY IN MODERN AMERICA (Oxford University Press 2010).
11. This is perhaps most obvious at the Supreme Court level. Erwin Chemerinsky, *The Rehnquist Court & Justice*, 1 WASHINGTON UNIVERSITY JOURNAL OF LAW AND POLICY 37, 49 (1999).
12. Brown, 347 U.S. 486 n.1.
13. Westminster School District v. Mendez, 161 F.2d 774, 781 (9th Cir. 1947) (en banc) (holding that segregation of Mexican American students in California violated the Fourteenth Amendment).
14. The data can be found on websites maintained by the states' boards of education. State of Delaware, *District Enrollment by Race/Ethnicity 2012–13* [hereinafter *2012–13 New*

Castle County Data], available at: http://profiles.doe.k12.de.us/SchoolProfiles/State/
Default.aspx; Kansas State Department of Education, Kansas ᴋ–12 Reports, *Topeka
Public Schools USD 501 Statistics 2012–13* [hereinafter *2012–13 Topeka Data*], available
at: http://svapp15586.ksde.org/k12/CountyStatics.aspx?org_no=D0501; South Carolina
State Department of Education, *45-Day Active Headcount, School Headcount by Gender
and Race 2012–13, Clarenton County Districts Nos. 1, 2, 3* [hereinafter *2012–13 Clarenton
County Data*], available at: https://ed.sc.gov/data/student-counts/Student_Headcounts/
ActiveStudentHeadcounts.cfm; Virginia Department of Education, *Fall Membership
Reports, Prince Edward County 2013–14* [hereinafter *2013–14 Prince Edward County
Data*], available at: http://bi.vita.virginia.gov/doe_bi/rdPage.aspx?rdReport=Main&subRp
tName=Fallmembership.

15. Brown v. Board of Education, 892 F.2d 851, 870 n.54 (10th Cir. 1989), vacated and
remanded, 503 U.S. 978, on remand reinstated with additions, 978 F.2d 585 (10th Cir.
1992).

16. Compare U.S. Census Bureau, *Clarenton County, South Carolina Quick Facts*, http://
quickfacts.census.gov/qfd/states/45/45027.html, with PETER IRONS, JIM CROW'S
CHILDREN: THE BROKEN PROMISE OF THE *BROWN* DECISION (Viking Penguin
2002).

17. IRONS, JIM CROW'S CHILDREN, 46; U.S. Census Bureau, *Clarenton County, South
Carolina Quick Facts*, http://quickfacts.census.gov/qfd/states/45/45027.html.

18. Briggs v. Elliot, 98 F. Supp. 529, 539 (E.D.S.C. 1951) (Judge Waring, dissenting), reversed as
part of Brown, 347 U.S. 483 (1954).

19. Brunson v. Board of Trustees of School District No. 1, 244 F. Supp. 859, 861 (E.D.S.C.
1965).

20. Briggs v. Elliott, 132 F. Supp. 776, 777 (E.D.S.C. 1955) (three-judge court) (per curiam).
That opinion articulated the infamous "Parker Doctrine": "The Constitution . . . does not
require integration—it merely forbids discrimination"; J. HARVIE WILKINSON, III,
FROM *BROWN* TO *BAKKE*: THE SUPREME COURT AND SCHOOL INTEGRATION:
1954–1978, 81–82 (Oxford University Press 1979).

21. The freedom of choice plan produced only "token" integration. Brunson v. Board of
Trustees of School District No. 1, 429 F.2d 820, 821 (4th Cir. 1970) (Judge Craven,
concurring in part and dissenting in part). Four schools were all-black, and a few black
students attended white schools. The original suit considered by the Supreme Court in
Brown I concerned the constitutionality of de jure school segregation laws and was tried
to a three-judge court. Once the laws were declared unconstitutional, a new suit was filed
before a single district court judge. Ibid., 823 n.1 (Judge Sobeloff, concurring). This suit
about the constitutionality of a freedom of choice plan was filed against Clarenton County
District No. 1.

22. IRONS, JIM CROW'S CHILDREN, 331.

23. The current data for Clarenton County is for the 2012–13 school year. *2012–13 Clarenton
County Data*.

24. Today District No. 3 has a 69% white student population and District No. 2 is 29% white in
its student population. Ibid. The demographics of the three districts have been fairly stable
since at least 1993. South Carolina Advisory Committee to the U.S. Commission on Civil
Rights, *Desegregation of Public School Districts in South Carolina* 7, 17 (December. 2008)
[hereinafter *South Carolina Desegregation*], available at: http://www.eusccr.com/SC%20
school%20deseg%20report--Dec%202008.pdf.

25. IRONS, JIM CROW'S CHILDREN, 331 ("Almost every white family in Summerton abandoned the public schools rather than consent to integration").

26. Great School Home Page for Clarendon Hall School, http://www.greatschools.org/south-carolina/summerton/1138-Clarendon-Hall-School/. The school educates 235 K–12 graders, and 95% of the students are white. African Americans make up 1% of the student body.

27. Great School Home Page & Student & Teacher Page for Laurence Manning Academy, http://www.greatschools.org/south-carolina/manning/1165-Laurence-Manning-Academy/?tab=enrollment.

28. Leland B. Ware, *Educational Equity and* Brown v. Board of Education: *Fifty Years of School Desegregation in Delaware*, 47 HOWARD LAW JOURNAL 299, 300 (2004).

29. Belton v. Gebhart, 87 A.2d 862, 871 (Delaware Court of Chancery), affirmed, 91 A.2d 137 (Delaware Supreme Court 1952), decided as Brown, 347 U.S. 483 (1954). The state of Delaware was eventually held liable for segregation in New Castle County. Evans v. Buchanan, 379 F. Supp. 1218, 1221–22 (D. Del. 1974) (three-judge court).

30. A 1960 opinion deemed the state's desegregation plan insufficient for not desegregating all grades in Delaware by 1961. Evans v. Ennis, 281 F.2d 385, 389–90 (3d Cir. 1960).

31. Between 1954 and 1974, the school district grew in size from 12,875 students to 14,688 students. Evans, 379 F. Supp. 1222, 1223 ("All of the pre-*Brown* colored schools that remained open continued to be operated as virtually all-black schools").

32. Evans v. Buchanan, 512 F. Supp. 839, 874 (D. Del. 1981).

33. Coalition to Save Our Children v. State Board of Education, 901 F. Supp. 784 (D. Del. 1995), affirmed, 90 F.3d 752 (3d Cir. 1996) (2–1).

34. Coalition to Save Our Children v. Board of Education, 90 F.3d 752, 762 n.8 (3d Cir. 1996).

35. Ibid.

36. Ibid., 762. Plaintiffs argued many within-school issues, including extra-curricular activities, discipline, special education, and tracking. Ibid., 763–64, 768, 775. The dissent also agreed on the finding of unitary status on student assignment, but not on all the within school issues. Ibid., 781 (Judge Sarokin, dissenting).

37. *2012–13 New Castle County Data.*

38. Glenn, *A Quantitative Analysis*, 731 ("School segregation essentially doubled in Wilmington between 1992 and 2006"). The increase in segregation was true in other parts of Delaware as well, but at a lower rate. This study found that resegregation in Wilmington predated unitary status, beginning in 1991–92. Ibid., 734.

39. Neighborhood Schools Act, Delaware Code Annotated Title 14, §220.

40. Glenn, *A Quantitative Analysis*, 722.

41. Leland Ware & Cara Robinson, *Charters, Choice, and Resegregation*, 11 DELAWARE LAW REVIEW 1, 7 (2009). The law allowed limited exceptions.

42. Ibid. The law was amended in 2004 to exempt middle and high schools if 40% of the 6–12 enrollment was by choice. Glenn, *A Quantiative Analysis*, 722.

43. Ware & Robinson, *Charters, Choice, and Resegregation*, 7–8; Glenn, *A Quantitative Analysis*, 730 (demonstrating that "the Neighborhood Schools Act led to a greater than expected level of isolation of White students").

44. Gary Orfield, John Kucsera, & Genevieve Siegel-Hawley, The Civil Rights Project, *E Pluribus. . . . Separation Deepening Double Segregation for More Students*, 8 (2012) ("In 1970, nearly four out of every five students across the nation were white, but by 2009, just

over half were white").

45. Between 1997 and 2013, the Hispanic student population doubled in Brandywine (from 1.9% to 5.3%) and in Red Clay (from 12.4% to 23.8%). The population more than quadrupled in Christina (from 4.3% to 18.8%) and in Colonial (from 4.2% to 19.7% (Colonial). These numbers can be found on the Fall Enrollment Reports for the school districts for the applicable years. State of Delaware, Department of Education, *School Profiles,* http://profiles.doe.k12.de.us/SchoolProfiles/CommonControls/.

46. Ibid.; Glenn, *A Quantitative Analysis,* 735 ("The decline in the number of White students in the Wilmington area played what appears to be the largest role in resegregating the schools").

47. Griffin v. County School Board, 377 U.S. 218, 231 (1964). The story of the school closing is well told in BOB SMITH, THEY CLOSED THEIR SCHOOLS: PRINCE EDWARD COUNTY, VIRGINIA, 1951–1964 (University of North Carolina Press 1965).

48. For a history of the academy, see Jennifer E. Spreng, *Scenes From the Southside: A Desegregation Drama in Five Acts,* 19 UNIVERSITY OF ARKANSAS AT LITTLE ROCK LAW REVIEW 327, 351–54, 369–70, 393–97, 401–404 (1997).

49. Ibid., 369–70.

50. Ibid., 371–76. The integration is not without complaint. Ibid., 379 ("Some [black parents] continued to object to ability grouping, disciplinary policies that they claimed discriminated and forced blacks to accommodate white sensibilities, and the loss of a culturally black focus in the schools") (footnotes omitted).

51. Ibid., 382.

52. Compare Davis v. County School Board, 103 F. Supp. 337, 338 (E.D. Va. 1952) (three-judge court), decided as Brown, 347 U.S. 483 (1954) with James L. Hunt, Brown v. Board of Education *After Fifty Years: Context and Synopsis,* 52 MERCER LAW REVIEW 549, 571 (2001).

53. *2013–14 Prince Edward County Data.*

54. Spreng, *Scenes From the Southside,* 401–404.

55. Kevin Sieff, *Fuqua School Looks to African American Football Star to Shatter Racist Legacy,* WASHINGTON POST (December 11, 2011).

56. Spreng, *Scenes From the Southside,* 393–96. Its tax-exempt status was restored in 1986.

57. That story is told in Spreng, *Scenes From the Southside.*

58. Brown, 892 F.2d 85.

59. The secondary schools were racially identifiable in 1951, but the schools were not always of one race. Ibid., 857–58.

60. Ibid., 854, 895–98 nn.8–10, 898–99 (Judge Baldock, dissenting).

61. Ibid., 855, 877 (majority opinion). For example, 65% of white students attended 90+% white schools, and an additional 18.7% attended 80–90% white schools. Close to half of all minority students attended 50+% minority schools.

62. Brown v. Board of Education, 671 F. Supp. 1290, 1311 (D. Kan. 1987), affirmed in part, reversed and remanded in part, 892 F.2d 851 (10th Cir. 1989), vacated and remanded, 503 U.S. 978, on remand reinstated with additions, 978 F.2d 585 (10th Cir. 1992).

63. Brown, 892 F.2d 851, 853.

64. Brown v. Unified School District No. 501, 56 F. Supp. 2d 1212, 1213 (D. Kan. 1999).

65. Ibid., 1213–14.

66. The following recent school district data can be found at *2012–13 Topeka Data*.

67. Brown, 892 F.2d at 857 n.9 ("The parties are in agreement that the difference in analysis between black students and minority students is not significant in this case"). Specifically, the Hispanic student population for 2012–13 was 28%. *2012–13 Topeka Data*.

68. The two schools are Topeka West High School (60.9% white) and Randolph Elementary School (60.5% white). The schools were predominately white schools in 1985. Ibid., 858 n.13 (showing Topeka West as the high school with the smallest minority population, at 7.9%); ibid., 857 n.8 (reporting that Randolph Elementary was 14.8% minority).

69. Table 1.

70. Federal courts are often blamed for taking a limited view of their authority in school desegregation cases. For example, the Supreme Court set an exacting standard for interdistrict remedies and does not require that desegregation be lasting before unitary status is attained. Dowell, 498 U.S. 251 (Justice Marshall, dissenting); Milliken v. Bradley, 418 U.S. 717, 745 (1973). Resistance of white parents (and sometimes minority parents) is commonly blamed as well for perpetuating school segregation. Parker, *The Future of School Desegregation*, 1180–84.

71. The law is similar to the Supreme Court's recent decision invalidating a voluntary integration plan that considered race in admissions. Parents Involved in Community School v. Seattle School District No. 1, 551 U.S. 701, 710 (2007).

72. RYAN, FIVE MILES AWAY, 115.

73. Griffin v. County School Board, 377 U.S. 218, 231 (1964).

74. The Tenth Circuit took over 100 pages of Federal Reporter pages to disagree over whether the Topeka schools were sufficiently desegregated, and then re-affirmed that decision after a remand from the Supreme Court. Brown, 892 F.2d 851 (10th Cir. 1989), vacated and remanded, 503 U.S. 978, on remand reinstated with additions, 978 F.2d 585 (10th Cir. 1992).

75. 221 F. Supp. 297, 300 (M.D. Ala. 1963) (ordering an "immediate start" to desegregation for the 1963–64 school year).

76. Ibid.

77. Lee v. Macon County Board of Education, 267 F. Supp. 458, 462 (M.D. Ala. 1967) (three-judge court) (per curiam).

78. Lee v. Macon County Board of Education, 970 F.2d 767, 768 (11th Cir. 1992), opinion vacated on other grounds, 987 F.2d 1521 (11th Cir. 1993) (en banc).

79. Ibid., 768.

80. Lee, 267 F. Supp. 462–63.

81. Lee v. Macon County Board of Education, 231 F. Supp. 743, 758 (M.D. Ala. 1964) (three-judge court) (per curiam). The suit also expanded to trade schools, junior colleges, and athletic conferences. Lee v. Macon County Board of Education, 317 F. Supp. 103 (M.D. Ala. 1970) (three-judge court) (per curiam) (requiring disestablishment of dual systems for trade schools and junior colleges); Lee v. Macon County Board of Education, 283 F. Supp. 194 (M.D. Ala. 1968) (three-judge court) (per curiam) (mandating integration of athletic conferences and associations for high schools and junior colleges and recognizing voluntary integration of collegiate conferences); Lee, 267 F. Supp. 458 (ordering desegregation of trade schools, vocational schools, and state colleges).

82. Five other school districts in the Middle District of Alabama were already subject to other school desegregation litigation at the time of *Lee v. Macon*. Parker, *The Future of School Desegregation*, 1203–1204.

83. Ibid., 1205.

84. Brown, 349 U.S. at 301 (*Brown II*); Parker, *The Future of School Desegregation*, 1199.

85. At the time, two school districts had already been granted unitary status, and four other school districts were in various stages of achieving unitary status. Parker, *The Future of School Desegregation*, 1204–1205. The other school desegregation cases were largely inactive. Ibid., 1204 ("Like the school districts in Georgia and Mississippi, thirty-one of the forty districts in Alabama had no meaningful litigation activity for at least one ten-year period").

86. Lee v. Lee County Board of Education, 963 F. Supp. 1122, 1128–30 (M.D. Ala. 1997); Lee v. Macon County Board of Education, 231 F. Supp. 744.

87. The progress of school desegregation in the Middle District of Alabama is based on published opinions and on docket sheets and court filings available online via PACER (Public Access to Court Electronic Records). Wendy Parker, *Lessons in Losing: Race Discrimination in Employment*, 81 NOTRE DAME LAW REVIEW 889, 904 nn.68–69 (2006) (detailing PACER).

88. For example, a mere month after the private plaintiffs and the United States filed motions for contempt against Covington City, the parties in 2005 agreed to a consent decree.

89. The two are Chambers County and Randolph County. Chambers County filed a status report on October 22, 2013, but apparently has never sought unitary status. Randolph County in a 2013 consent decree has undertaken additional efforts to achieve unitary status in personnel issues; the school district has achieved unitary status in all other respects.

90. Barbour County was declared unitary in 2013, without party opposition. It first achieved partial unitary status in 1997.

91. In two cases (Lee County and Tallapoosa County), the judges were stricter on ensuring the even distribution of teachers than students. Lee v. Lee County Board of Education, No. 3:70CV845-T, 2005 WL 2850111, *1 (M.D. Ala. Oct. 25, 2005) (granting full unitary status after holding compliance with standards on faculty assignment at two predominately black schools); Lee v. Tallapoosa County Board of Education, No. 3:70CV849-T, 2004 WL 1368876, *1 (M.D. Ala. June 16, 2004) (awarding full unitary status after faculty assignment at all-black school was addressed); Lee v. Tallapoosa County Board of Education, No. 70-T-849-E, 2002 WL 31757973, *12 (M.D. Ala. Nov. 22, 2002) (allowing unitariness on student assignment despite the presence of a small, all-black school, but not on teacher assignment because of a disproportionate number of black teachers at the school); Lee v. Lee County Board of Education, No. 70-T-845-E, 2002 WL 1268395, *8, 11 (M.D. Ala. May 29, 2002) (granting partial unitary status on student assignment despite the presence of two predominately black schools, but denying unitary status on faculty assignment because of high numbers of black teachers at the two schools).

92. Most of the Alabama school districts had a large physical size and a small number of schools (but often more than one per grade). Given the large physical size of the school districts and the possibility of rural housing segregation, I did not include a table similar to the one done for the original *Brown* districts describing the demographic distribution of students.

93. Lee v. Macon County Board of Education, No. 2:70CV846-T, 2005 WL 1899360 (M.D.

Ala. Aug. 5, 2005) (over the objections of black parents, approving the closure of two all-black schools); Lee v. Autauga County Board of Education, 59 F. Supp.2d 1199, 1209–10 (M.D. Ala. 1999) (at the request of private plaintiffs, denying school district's motion to close small, predominately black school because of the burden it would place on black students); Lee v. Geneva County Board of Education, 892 F. Supp. 1387 (M.D. Ala. 1995) (over objections by black parents, allowing movement of grades 6–12 after a fire destroyed the school building).

94. Lee v. Dothan City Board of Education, No.70CV1060-WHA, 2007 WL 1856928, *2 (M.D. Ala. June 27, 2007) (noting community concerns over the selection of cheerleaders); Lee v. Roanoke City Board of Education, No. 3:70CV855-MHT, 2007 WL 1196482, *10 (M.D. Ala. Apr. 23, 2007) (reporting that a white girls club left the high school after objections were raised); Lee v. Elmore County Board of Education, No. 2:70CV3103-T, 2004 WL 1809877, *9 (M.D. Ala. Aug. 11, 2004) (detailing objections to a dress code allowing the Confederate flag and to the selection of cheerleaders).

95. Dothan, 2007 WL 1856928, *2; Roanoke, 2007 WL 1196482, *5; Lee v. Covington City Board of Education, No. 2:70CV3102-MHT, 2006 WL 269942, *4 (M.D. Ala. Feb. 6, 2006); Elmore, 2004 WL 1809877, *7; Lee v. Opelika City Board of Education, No. 70-T-853-E, 2002 WL 237032, *6 (M.D. Ala. Feb. 13, 2002). Private attorney Solomon Seay, one of the original *Lee* lawyers, mentioned the importance of this issue in the unitary status proceedings. Joseph Mark Bagley, *School Desegregation, Law and Order, and Litigating Social Justice in Alabama, 1954–1973*, 751 (January 5, 2014) (unpublished PhD dissertation, Georgia State University). The same was also true for administrators. One school district had not had a black principal since 1968, when the schools were desegregated. That prevented full unitary status in 2002. Lee v. Alexander City Board of Education, No. 70-T-850-E, 2002 WL 31102679, *7, 12 (M.D. Ala. Sept. 13, 2002).

96. For example, many people protested unitary status in Butler County, Chilton County, Elmore County, and Tallapoosa County. Other districts had no objections by their community noted on their respective docket sheets: Alexander City, Auburn City, Coosa County, and Phenix City.

97. Lee v. Lee County Board of Education, 476 F. Supp. 1356, 1360, 1362–64 (M.D. Ala. 2007) (opinion of Judge Thompson). Black students were overrepresented in the categories of mental retardation and emotional disturbance, but underrepresented in the categories of specific learning disability and gifted.

98. Ibid., 1364. Granted, disparities continued. For example, the ratio of black to white students in the mental retardation program, where the greatest disparities previously existed, fell from 3.24:1 to 2.18:1. The proportion of black students identified as gifted increased as well. The parties had no objections to unitary status on the issue. The state was also required to address state-wide inequalities in facilities, and the parties entered into a consent decree to resolve these issues as well and to use facilities funds to assist rather than hinder desegregation. Ibid., 1364, 1365. Lee, 2006 WL 1041994 *1, 8. The state has achieved unitary status on this issue as well, without party objection. Lee, 2009 WL 1231497 *1.

99. Notice typically was posted in various school offices, published in local newspapers, sent home with students, and mailed to parents. Lee v. Elmore County Board of Education, No. 2:70CV3103-T, 2004 WL 1809877, *3 (M.D. Ala. Aug. 11, 2004).

100. Ibid., *10.

101. Ibid.

102. Lee v. Macon County Board of Education, 221 F. Supp. 297 (M.D. Ala. 1963). Specifically, in

1963 the school system had 17 schools for its 5,317 black students and three schools for its 970 white students.

103. This is a new status for the school district. Notasulga High School (a K–12 school) just one year ago had eleven white male students (but no female white students). Alabama State Department of Education, *Enrollment by Ethnicity and Gender, Macon County 2013–14, 2012–13*, available at: http://web.alsde.edu/PublicDataReports/Default.aspx.

104. Ibid., Free Lunch by School and System.

105. In 1995, Macon Academy moved and renamed itself to address declining enrollment. Macon East Academy, About Us, http://www.maconeast.net/about-us.

106. In 1991, Notasulga High School, a small K–12 school, had a 42% white student population. In 1992–93 the federal courts ordered that it remain open, denying the school board's request to move the high school years to a new high school building planned for the entire county (which would have been 6% white). Lee v. Macon County Board of Education, 970 F.2d 767, 775 (11th Cir. 1992), original opinion vacated upon rehearing, 987 F.2d 1521 (11th Cir.), affirmed, 995 F.2d 184 (11th Cir. 1993). The Eleventh Circuit protected the school because it alone in the county "fulfilled the objective of racial harmony that is the very spirit of *Brown*." Lee, 970 F.2d at 774. That effort to prevent white flight failed. Today, the school is entirely black.

107. ProPublica reporter Nikole Hannah-Jones investigated the resegregation of schools in Tuscaloosa, Alabama through three generations of one family—a grandfather who attended segregated schools, a mother who benefited from desegregation, and a talented granddaughter struggling in a resegregated school. Nikole Hannah-Jones, *Segregation Now . . . Sixty Years After* Brown v. Board of Education, *The Schools In Tuscaloosa, Alabama Show How Separate And Unequal Education Is Coming Back*, THE ATLANTIC (April 17, 2014).

108. Parker, *The Future of School Desegregation*, 1204.

109. Bagley, *School Desegregation*, 751 (quoting attorney Seay as saying that the Randolph County consent decree was "'the very best public school desegregation plan that [he] had gotten in any system,'" a plan which "'touched on every facet of education in a public school system'").

110. For example, in 2001–2002, 36% of black students passed the third grade reading test, compared to 49% of white students. Stanford Achievement Test 9th Edition, Randolph County, Grade 3, Reading, 2001–2002, available at: http://www03.alsde.edu/Accountability/Accountability.asp. In 2012–13, the percentage of black students achieving a IV (out of IV) on the Alabama Reading Test for Grade 3 was 20%, compared to 46% for white students. *2012–2013 Alabama Reading and Mathematics Test, Randolph County, Grade 3, Reading, 2012–13*, available at: http://www03.alsde.edu/Accountability/Accountability.asp.

111. Only during a brief period in the 1960s, when school desegregation efforts were most successful, have all three federal branches of the government together sought actual desegregation of schools. Wendy Parker, *Connecting The Dots:* Grutter, *School Desegregation, and Federalism*, 45 WILLIAM AND MARY LAW REVIEW 1691, 1718–22 (2004).

Civil Rights Act of 1964

Public Law No. 88-352, 78 Stat. 241

JOHN J. (JACK) FEEHELEY

Massive Resistance before the Civil Rights Act
The Integration of Little Rock Central High School

At two o'clock in the morning of August 2, 1957, I received a telephone call from the New Orleans FBI office. The night superintendent advised me that he had just finished talking to the SAC (Agent in Charge) of the office and that I was to be sent on a special undercover assignment.

I was not to tell my wife or anybody where I was going. I should plan on being gone for at least two months. I was to take a good car and leave immediately for Little Rock, Arkansas. I was not to go near the Little Rock FBI office but was to get a motel room and report in by phone for instructions. My wife had just delivered our first baby some months earlier. All that I could tell her was that I was leaving and would not be back for possibly two months or more, and that fellow agents and their wives would be checking on her for whatever she might need.

I drove straight through to Little Rock. When I arrived, I was advised that large crowds of hostile citizens and Governor Orval Faubus were strongly resisting the integration of Central High School. The strength of the resistance had not been anticipated because in 1949 the University of Arkansas School of Law had been integrated without incident. Also, in 1956 the city's public buses were desegregated without incident and, in 1955, the school board had voted unanimously on a plan of gradual integration of Central High that would start in September 1957. So, city officials were caught off guard when hundreds of angry citizens surrounded the school to prevent the students from entering.

What the FBI was looking for was "organized resistance" to the court order. My job was to infiltrate the crowd each day and try to determine if the resistance was organized and by whom. It was suspected that Governor Faubus's office had helped organize some resistance as an excuse to call out the National Guard, who, "in the interest of public safety," had been sent to surround the school and prevent black students from entering. I was to report to the FBI twice a day, and to phone immediately if I came up with anything. I was told that three other agents like me, not known in Little Rock, had been called in from three other field offices. The Bureau did not want the press or anyone else to know that they were following events very closely because at this point the integration was still a state matter, not a federal one.

Early the next morning, I drove the very short distance from my motel to Central High and parked a couple of blocks from the school. The school was a very classical high school building: brick, about four stories tall, as school buildings used to be, with an enrollment of some two thousand students. What was unusual about Central High that morning was that it was surrounded by a few hundred Arkansas National Guardsmen. They were obviously "at ease" as some were standing, some were sitting, some had their helmets off, and some had their rifles leaning against trees. However, they did have the school tightly surrounded.

It was about 7:00 A.M., but already a crowd was gathering. Within the next couple of hours, a very large crowd, numbering in the hundreds and at times estimated at more than a thousand, had assembled. A lot of the guardsmen were local young men, so there was some bantering back and forth between the guardsmen and the crowd. About 10:00 A.M., four police cars pulled up in front of the school. The policemen attempted to escort the black students into the school. Two things happened: the guardsmen immediately closed ranks very tightly, and the crowd immediately surrounded the police and the students. The crowd shouted epithets at both the police and the students. Fearing for the safety of the black students, the police placed them back into the police cars and drove off. This same scene was repeated each day for the next five or six days. The police were not able to get the black students into the school, and had they done so, the students would have been in jeopardy.

The crowd was gradually turning into a mob and getting very aggressive. A *Life* magazine photographer had his camera smashed and was beaten. Whenever one of the many reporters there were spotted, their notes were torn up, and they were beaten and told to go back to where they came from. The mob began to push through the guardsmen's line and run through the school looking for any black students. The mob was in total control.

Some three weeks after Governor Faubus had ordered the Arkansas National Guard to the school, the U.S. District Court for the Eastern District of Arkansas in Little Rock granted the injunction requested by the Justice Department and ordered the governor to withdraw the National Guard. At that point, on September 20, Governor Faubus withdrew the Guard. We found out later that he correctly thought he would be arrested by the FBI if he defied the federal order. Now the school was surrounded by Little Rock policemen who actually were trying to integrate the school.

About a thousand people were gathered in front of the school one day when the police escorted the nine black students through a side door into the school just as classes were to begin. When the mob learned that the black students were inside, they went berserk. They surged through the police line and ran into the school with shouts and threats. The police could not contain them so the black students were taken out through a back door. And thus it went day after day.

Each day I came to the school about 7:00 A.M. and worked my way through the crowd. I listened to conversations and observed groups to see if any individuals seemed to be giving directions or orders. Every so often, cars would pull up and eight or ten men would get out and join the crowd. Each day, the mob became more aggressive and violent. They had control of the school and would charge in and out of the building. More and more individuals in the crowd believed to be reporters and outsiders were being singled out and assaulted. I was getting more anxious by the day. If I had been singled out and targeted, I could not identify myself as an FBI agent. I was given the once-over more than a few times but was never accosted. Then, a new phase developed. Groups of whites would drive through the black districts at night, honking horns and shouting insults. They started to fire-bomb black churches and the police could not prevent it. So far, there was much evidence in regard to individual actions, but I had not come up with anything indicating a conspiracy or organized resistance to the court order.

Finally, we got the break we were looking for. We had been looking for evidence of "organized" resistance or conspiracy to justify federal troops, and we hadn't come up with anything. The break in the stalemate came from a different direction. Late one evening, Little Rock Police Chief Gene Smith, who had been coordinating closely with the Little Rock FBI Office, came to the office to announce that he was no longer responsible for the safety of the citizens of Little Rock. With the fire-bombings of the churches and violence spreading beyond the school and into the black neighborhoods, the situation was out of control. He requested assistance from the governor by way of the state police but had been told no state help was available.

The chief was asked if he and Mayor Woodrow Mann would give the FBI a signed statement in this regard along with a request for federal assistance by way of U.S. Marshals. As soon as we had this crucial statement late the evening of September 24, the Little Rock FBI office sent a teletype to the Bureau in Washington. Director J. Edgar Hoover was immediately notified of the statement—that it had been verified by the agents on the scene (myself and three others)—and that the situation was out of control. Without delay, Director Hoover advised President Dwight Eisenhower, who immediately federalized the ten thousand-member Arkansas National Guard, which eliminated Governor Faubus's authority over those troops. President Eisenhower ordered those troops to remain "standing down" and to play no further role. Then he ordered the 101st Airborne Division of the United States Army to be dispatched to Little Rock to establish law and order and to enforce the court order to integrate Central High. Within hours, a thousand troops of the 101st Airborne were loaded onto transport planes from their base at Ft. Campbell, Kentucky. At about 5:00 A.M., I heard the giant transports arriving at Little Rock Airport. The troops went immediately to the armory on the edge of town where they were to be quartered. Half were then deployed to the school; they were under strict orders to be either on duty at the school or to be in the armory, nowhere else.

By 7:00 A.M., when I made my appearance at the school, the scene was entirely different. The troops stood shoulder to shoulder in a tight perimeter completely encircling the school. A second perimeter, some 50 feet outside the first perimeter, encircled the front perimeter and the entire school. Every 20 feet inside the second perimeter was a squad of 15 soldiers. All the soldiers were in full battle dress; all were at the ready with fixed bayonets ready to charge; all were deadly serious about their mission; and all their eyes fixed straight ahead at the gathering mob.

The mob began to gather as it had been doing for days on end. After a sufficient number showed up, they began to shout and taunt the soldiers. They called them Nazis and Gestapos, shouted for them to get out of Little Rock, and to mind their own business. As soon as five or six would gather in a group, a 101st Airborne officer would step out with an electric bullhorn and say, "I order you to cease and desist. Comply with the court order and return to your homes." The group would respond with the same taunts and insults. The officer would step back into the ranks and order out a squad. The ranks would part, and the squad would come out on the double, fan out into a straight line, lower their bayonets, and charge into the group. The ranks would immediately close behind them. As the squad charged, the mob would scatter and run. The officer picked out the biggest and loudest members of the mob and ordered them arrested. This same scene was repeated throughout the day all around the perimeter. Three men suffered bayonet wounds. I interviewed one of them, who said that, as he was running away, he turned to see how close the trooper was to him and hung himself up on the bayonet. We interviewed everybody who had been arrested to determine motives, and if federal charges against them were in order.

By the end of the day, whenever an officer would step out and order the mob to "cease and desist," it would immediately break up, and individuals would leave the scene. The mob psychology of defiance had been broken. They did as they were ordered, or they would be arrested. The mob no longer controlled the school, nor could they any longer threaten the black students. The next day, some 24 days after integration had first been attempted, military vehicles with armed soldiers pulled up to the school and escorted the nine black students into Central High School.

The situation remained tense for weeks as a few incidents occurred between students in the school, but integration had been accomplished. A very loud and clear message had been sent throughout the nation and the world that the court order to integrate the schools would be enforced by the federal government.

Some six weeks after getting that early morning telephone call notifying me of a special assignment in Little Rock, I returned home. The mob scenes in Little Rock and what was happening there had been national and international news for weeks on end. History had been made there, and I am glad to have played a significant role in this historical event.

John J. "Jack" Feeheley is a former FBI agent.

ALLISON R. BROWN

Equity in Education
The Present and Future of the Civil Rights Act of 1964

THE CIVIL RIGHTS ACT OF 1964[1] IS ALIVE, THOUGH NOT NEARLY AS WELL AS IT once was. Recently, especially under the Obama Administration, the federal agencies charged with enforcement of the Act have done so with a vigor that harkens back to the days of the Act's passage when the executive branch of the federal government came together with civil rights advocates and youth, lobbyists, legislators, clergy, and business leaders in unified fashion to craft and support the Act. I begin this chapter with a brief overview of how the Civil Rights Act's education provisions came into being in order to convey why they remain important. I then discuss the Obama Administration's use of the Act to focus on inequality as manifested through school discipline, and project my hopes for the future use of the Act in the continued pursuit of educational equity.

The Civil Rights Act: Creation and Continued Importance

In 1963, the Department of Justice's initial draft of the Civil Rights Act of 1964 focused on two core tenets: school desegregation and public accommodations.[2]

Unlike its predecessors, the Civil Rights Acts of 1957 and 1960, the Civil Rights Act of 1964 was sweeping legislation with strong enforcement language.[3] Though the Civil Rights Act of 1957 did create the Civil Rights Division of the Department of Justice, which then as now has the ability to enforce civil rights provisions in federal law, no law other than the Civil Rights Act of 1964 had ever attempted to prohibit racial discrimination in nearly every facet of American society.

The Department of Justice focused on school desegregation for obvious reasons. Although *Brown v. Board of Education* declared in 1954 that "separate but equal" has no place in public education," after *Brown*, most school districts adopted freedom of choice plans, which essentially maintained the status quo because residential segregation and hostile attitudes prevented any real integration.[4] As the U.S. Commission on Civil Rights reported in the early 1970s, "[d]uring the 10-year period between 1954 and 1964, many desegregation lawsuits were filed, numerous decrees were issued, but little school desegregation occurred."[5] Thus, in 1964, after mass social protest, the Civil Rights Act came to be, and it was the nation's strongest hope for salvation. Although it has been parsed and battered by the courts, it remains and is still standing in the custody and care of the executive branch of the federal government.

The continuing utility of the Civil Rights Act of 1964 is important for many reasons, including the current ineffectiveness of equal protection litigation. Using education as their proxy, the nation's federal courts have allowed for the co-opting of race-based discrimination claims, now scrutinizing voluntary racial diversity admissions programs for racial "discrimination" against whites.[6] In 2007, the Supreme Court in *Parents Involved in Community Schools v. Seattle School District No. 1* essentially took voluntary racial integration off the table for public schools.[7] While some characterize the Supreme Court's 2013 opinion in *Fisher v. the University of Texas* as a punt, the Court actually made the strict scrutiny standard of review stricter than it ever has been before.[8] Additionally, it is clear that after the *Schuette v. Coalition to Defend Affirmative Action* decision in 2014, the Supreme Court will move aside when states choose to take it upon themselves to eliminate and prohibit the consideration of race in higher education admissions.[9] Civil rights advocates have been boxed into a rapidly shrinking corner and must avoid the use of race or explicit discussion of race in seeking diversity in programming and equal educational opportunity for students of color.

As race-consciousness is removed from the table as a viable legal strategy for attaining equity in education, education practitioners are left confused and frustrated, and advocates are left in the untenable position of among other things using socioeconomic status as a proxy for race in educational equity cases. Many times, discussions about education reform intentionally conflate race and class. There are a few reasons for this, including that the federal courts have slowly closed the courthouse doors to claims of race discrimination in education. Courts also have almost completely prohibited deliberate and voluntary efforts to create racial diversity in schools. This often leaves educators, community members, and others thinking about poverty only in terms of race. But race and socioeconomic status are not the same. The Department of Education revealed in 2012 that, for the first time in history, American schools reported more than one million homeless students.[10] Thirty-eight percent of black children live below the poverty line. Even so, research has demonstrated that when controlling for poverty, racial disparities in academic performance remain.[11] This is a symptom of this country's seemingly intractable racial illness.

According to the UCLA Civil Rights Project, nationally, the average black or Latino student now attends school with a substantial majority of children in poverty, double the level in schools of whites and Asians. A recent piece in *The Nation* by Greg Kaufman and Elaine Weiss discussed this problem:

> Concentrated poverty plays a key role in explaining why poor white students perform better on tests, on average, than African-American students with similar family incomes. Not only are white children much less likely than their black peers to live in poverty, among those who are poor, only 12 percent of white children live in concentrated poverty, while nearly half of poor African-American children do. Black students are thus much more likely to attend schools in which most of their classmates are also poor.[12]

For too many children, contending with the nation's infected racial narrative is compounded by the negative effects of living in concentrated poverty. On November 27, 1963, when Lyndon B. Johnson took the podium in the House chambers for the first time as president after John F. Kennedy's assassination, he implored the nation to help him, to work together to "write the next chapter [for equal rights], and to write it in the books of law."[13] Advocates and enforcement authorities can use the history of the Civil Rights Act as a frame to help equip stakeholders with the necessary tools to navigate between the overlapping worlds of race and poverty so that education advocacy efforts can be tailored for students based on their unique needs.

The Civil Rights Act, Contemporary Federal Action, and Strategic Alliances around School Discipline

Today, there are many, including the executive branch of the federal government, who still are doing their part to stamp out the malignant forces that have dispersed and regrouped since the Act's passage in 1964 so that black children and the black community might realize their potential and finally and fully, as a collective, contribute to the economic, political, and social success of this nation. Equity in education remains advocates' frontier, and school discipline their focal point.

In-school suspensions, out-of-school suspensions, expulsions, law-enforcement referrals, and school-based arrests exact a toll on the students who experience them and on the school environment for students and teachers. Persistent racial disparities in each of these categories of discipline nationwide and in numerous schools and school districts are the modern-day manifestation of the racial mindset that so spurred the need for creation of the Civil Rights Act of 1964. These exclusionary discipline practices also inflict an actual cost on the government and society at large: In a study that followed over 900,000 middle- and high-school students in Texas, researchers at Texas A&M University observed a strong correlation between exclusionary discipline practices and grade retention, and exclusionary discipline and students dropping out of school. They found that dropouts cost the state of Texas between $5.4 and $9.6 billion. Grade retentions cost the state $146,546,614.[14]

Under legal authority granted by the Civil Rights Act, the U.S. Departments of Education and Justice are taking an active role in addressing the problem of exclusionary discipline and racial disparity in public education. The agencies have issued guidance to schools, explaining the meaning and present-day implications of the Act for particular issues, including for instance school discipline; they collect and publicly release data, which quantifies inequity based on race and other protected categories; they work together to proactively encourage school districts to engage in equitable practices; and, when necessary, they enforce students' rights through litigation.

SCHOOL DISCIPLINE GUIDANCE

Responding to years of collaboration with, and information and pressure from, civil rights groups and individual complaints by students and their families, the U.S. Departments of Justice and Education in January 2014 jointly issued a set of guidance documents to schools and school districts. The joint guidance makes clear school districts' obligations under the Civil Rights Act to prevent and eliminate racial discrimination in school discipline that may show up as disparate impact on students of color.[15] In May 2014, the Department of Education clarified that the Act's requirements are applicable to public charter schools, too.[16]

As the agencies explained in the joint discipline guidance, the Civil Rights Act prohibits intentional discrimination against students of a protected class based on their status in that group. Title IV of the Civil Rights Act is the desegregation provision of the Act and prohibits discrimination on the basis of race, color, sex, religion, or national origin by public elementary and secondary schools and public institutions of higher learning.[17] Title VI, Adam Clayton Powell's contribution to the Act, prohibits discrimination by recipients of federal funds on the basis of race or national origin.[18]

Intentional discrimination can be found explicitly written into a school's discipline policies if, for example, they expressly require certain discipline actions for students of particular racial groups. However, intentional discrimination is more likely to be found in a school's practices. For instance, if a black student comes to school wearing flip-flops in violation of the school's facially neutral uniform dress code and is suspended from school for a period of time while a white student who is similarly situated—committing the same infraction, in the same grade, with a similar discipline history—wears flip-flops to school and does not receive any consequence or is treated with a lesser punishment, the school may have engaged in intentional discrimination under the law and thus could be in violation of Title IV and Title VI of the Civil Rights Act. Similarly, a school discipline policy that is developed with the intent of punishing only students of one race is a policy in and of itself that could be in violation of the Civil Rights Act. For instance, a written provision of the school discipline code that punishes students of one race for wearing styles of hair that are particular to that race—for example: cornrows, dreadlocks, or braids—regardless of whether students are similarly situated and who ultimately gets punished under that provision, may constitute intentional discrimination under the law.

Finally, intentional discrimination may be imputed to a school or school district if the motivations of the educator enforcing the discipline code are racial in nature, such as if the educator uses racial epithets when administering punishment against students of a particular race. In *People Who Care v. Rockford Board of Education*,[19] the district court found that the school district intentionally discriminated against a group of black students by assigning them to lower-level classes even though they had received the same qualifying test scores as white students who were assigned to higher-level classes. The school district offered no reason for this disparity. This was intentional discrimination as defined under the Fourteenth Amendment of the U.S. Constitution, a definition shared by interpretation of discrimination under the Civil Rights Act.[20] Racial disparities and evidence of intentional discrimination in educational treatment are only the beginning of the legal inquiry for the Departments of Justice and Education, but trigger their Civil Rights Act jurisdiction.

Relatedly, the implementing regulations for Title VI make clear that federal enforcement of Title VI should include inquiry as to whether school practices disparately impact protected classes of students.[21] The federal agencies thus investigate (1) whether a school's discipline policy results in an adverse impact on students of a particular race as compared to students of other races, (2) whether the policy is necessary to meet an important educational goal, and (3) whether there are comparably effective alternative policies or practices that would meet the stated goal but that would exact less of a burden or adverse impact on the affected group or, if the school indicates the policy is necessary, whether the reason offered is a pretext for discrimination.[22]

Data about the school or school district in question is typically what the agencies use to assess the first prong of disparate impact analysis, whether students of a particular race have been adversely impacted by the school's discipline policy, and thus the federal government's data collection is essential.

DATA COLLECTION

Federal collection of civil rights-related data in education has expanded to include unprecedented levels of data and information in the Civil Rights Data Collection (CRDC), released most recently in March 2014 by the United States Department of Education Office for Civil Rights (OCR) about the 2011–12 school year.[23] When the expanded collection was first released in March 2012 for the 2009–10 school year, it electrified advocacy efforts to bring equity to students of color, students with disabilities, students who were limited English proficient, and others.[24] All of a sudden, advocates had access to data and information on a scale not before seen and were anxious for more data to share with communities and to validate perceptions of injustice.

OCR, for the first time ever and in response to heartbreaking requests from civil rights advocates, published suspension and expulsion data for preschoolers—three- and four-year-old children—in the most recent CRDC.[25] That data indicate that black preschoolers accounted for only 18% of preschool students in the nation, and they were 48% of students suspended out of school more than once. White students were 43% of preschool enrollment and 26% of preschool students who were suspended out of school more than once. Moreover, 5% of all white students in public elementary and secondary schools were suspended in 2011–12, and 16% of black students were. For students of color with disabilities, that number jumps to 25%. Black students were 16% of students enrolled in public schools, but they were 27% of students referred to law enforcement in school and 31% of students arrested out of school. White students were 51% of student enrollment, 41% of students referred to law enforcement, and 39% of those arrested.

Under Title IV and Title VI of the Civil Rights Act, quantitative data can go only so far. Anecdotal evidence, qualitative data, is also important to inform the investigations of the Departments of Justice and Education and to change hearts and minds that hold mistakenly and detrimentally negative beliefs about children of color. Here is a true story of a young man and a young woman, both of whom were popular high-school students killed in their prime.[26] They didn't know each other; one lived in DC, the other in Iowa. There were significant parallels between them—their friends demonstrated their grief by making t-shirts with their likenesses and names and packed their funerals to pay their respects; they were both talented, he as a musician, she as an athlete. There was one significant difference between them. He was black and was shot dead for his shoes. She was white and was killed when her motorbike struck a tree. His death was barely a blip in the local newspaper. Hers made national news.

We afford certain children an assumption of childhood purity and privilege that we do not allow other children. Death at the age of 18 or 19 is not something we expect and, for some children, it shocks our conscience so much that even national media outlets have to stop and take some time to focus on just that. For other children, it is what we expect—that they will die a violent death before they reach maturity. There is nothing in this example that would violate the Civil Rights Act of 1964, 50 years ago or today. And, yet, there is a level of humanity that is missing still for too many children. Not grieving the same for the black boy gunned down in the streets of DC as we do for the white girl killed on her motorbike is not against the law, but there is something wrong there.

While data will necessarily undergird any federal investigation of potential Civil Rights Act violations in schools, stories like these, of inequitable treatment based on race, are what light the match for coordinated involvement in righting racial wrongs. Communities get involved, practitioners do, and so does the federal government.

SUPPORTIVE SCHOOL DISCIPLINE INITIATIVE

On July 21, 2011, the Departments of Justice and Education demonstrated their collective commitment to combine their enforcement authority under the Civil Rights Act in order to combat the "school-to-prison pipeline." On that day, after convening two joint conferences specifically focused on racial disparities in student discipline for their respective agencies, Secretary of Education Arne Duncan and Attorney General Eric Holder announced the launch of the Supportive School Discipline Initiative (SSDI), a collaboration between the Department of Education and Department of Justice to address racial disparities and other factors in school discipline that contribute to the school-to-prison pipeline.[27] The school-to-prison pipeline is a cacophonous mash-up of numerous factors, including zero-tolerance student discipline policies, that contribute to (1) in the short term, the exclusion of children, disproportionately children of color, from the regular classroom environment as a means of punishment; and (2) in the long term, the entanglement of children, again disproportionately children of color, in the criminal justice system.[28] The SSDI has been working to address racial disparities in student discipline and encourage the use of positive school discipline methods that reinforce good behavior, gently redirect when students are off-task, appropriately assign consequences for bad behavior, and, most importantly, create healthy and nurturing learning environments for all students.

ENFORCEMENT THROUGH LITIGATION

The Civil Rights Act has been buoyed of late by the work of the U.S. Departments of Justice and Education, which have invested like no time in recent history in an unprecedented collaborative fashion to wield the Act as a sword and a shield for children of color. In Meridian, Mississippi, for example, as late as 2010, black children routinely were being suspended, expelled, and arrested out of school for minor infractions. Students were arrested out of school for being late to class, wearing the wrong color socks in violation of the school's dress code, talking back to a teacher—things for which grown people could not be arrested in the streets. Between 2006 and 2010, every one of the children arrested out of school was black, and black students were punished more harshly than white students for the same behavior.[29]

Under Title IV of the Civil Rights Act and with multifaceted cooperation from parents and students, community members, faith leaders, and others, the Department of Justice, Civil Rights Division, Educational Opportunities Section investigated and litigated the school discipline issues in this long-standing school desegregation case, and ultimately was successful in negotiating with the school district a long-term, comprehensive consent decree that will bring the students and their families one step closer to racial equity. By its own terms, the consent decree in Meridian "reflects the District's obligations under Title IV of the Civil Rights Act of 1964 to administer discipline without discrimination on the basis of race and in a manner that does not perpetuate or further the segregation of students on the basis of race."[30] Pursuant to the terms of the decree, the school district must modify its school discipline policies and practices to "incorporate culturally responsive techniques, support and reinforce positive behavior and character development, employ corrective strategies and interventions to keep students in the classroom, and resort to exclusionary discipline only in limited circumstances."[31]

The Meridian case also inspired unprecedented robust, coordinated activity from the various sections of the Department of Justice, Civil Rights Division. In August 2012, after working with the Educational Opportunities Section of the Division to conduct an investigation, the Special Litigation Section of the Division filed its own lawsuit against the state of Mississippi and its Department of Human Services and Division of Youth Services; the city of Meridian; Lauderdale County, where Meridian is located, and which operates the Lauderdale County Youth Court; and the local Youth Court judges Frank Coleman and Veldore Young.[32] The complaint alleges, under the Violent Crime Control and Law Enforcement Act of 1994, 42 U.S.C. § 14141, that the defendants "engage in a pattern or practice of unlawful conduct through which they routinely and systematically arrest and incarcerate children, including for minor school rule infractions, without even the most basic procedural safeguards, and in violation of these children's constitutional rights."[33] The same types of efforts by the government to aggressively enforce the Civil Rights Act related to discipline and educational equity have taken place in Palm Beach County, Florida and in other cities across the country.[34]

The spirit of the Civil Rights Act still lives.

The Civil Rights Act in the Next Fifty Years

Inequity remains this country's biggest albatross. With the Civil Rights Act of 1964 as a tool and a moral guide, we can support educators with the technical assistance and training they need to nurture all of our children to success, and shape new advocacy frameworks such as that developed in the Meridian school discipline case.

TECHNICAL ASSISTANCE

As government and advocates identify disparities that could result in the withholding of federal funds under Title VI and/or litigation under Title IV of the Civil Rights Act, the first priority should be to provide technical assistance to educators, particularly where there is no intent to discriminate. Title IV was originally intended to provide technical assistance to schools and school districts that were under desegregation orders to help them to desegregate their schools.[35] Recent federal actions related to Title IV have been primarily enforcement-oriented,[36] but schools continue to need technical assistance.[37] The federal government and service providers can and should offer and provide equity-focused technical assistance to schools as a preemptive measure that would be less costly than initiating litigation against school districts for violating the law and more desirable than cutting off federal funds to schools whose students are likely most in need.

Working through their consent decrees and settlement agreements, the Department of Justice often requires that schools seek technical assistance to remedy violations of the Civil Rights Act and move toward equity for all students.[38] The Department of Education relies on its Office for Civil Rights regional offices and Equity Assistance Centers to provide racial equity-related technical assistance to schools in need of such services.[39] These actions usually occur at the back end of an investigation. Schools need an avenue, through both the Department of Education and Department of Justice, for proactive and pre-emptive resolution of possible violations of the Act and to ensure that they are creating healthy school environments that embrace all students and their families.

NEW ADVOCACY FRAMEWORKS

As we have seen, the federal government continues to use the Civil Rights Act to address racial inequity in schools. A range of policies present opportunities for the federal government to continue to use its enforcement power, and also for communities and advocates to work together to push for change in their communities. Two important avenues for policy reform involve rethinking how we ensure school safety, and reconsidering assumptions about black communities and children.

In 2011, Aaron Kupchik, associate professor at the University of Delaware, and Geoff Ward, professor at University of California, Irvine, presented to the American Sociological Association their findings that the placement and location of school security—armed police officers, metal detectors, even police dogs—is "more closely related to student race and ethnicity and to socio-economic status than to actual criminal behavior."[40] This is despite the fact that the mass killings and shootings that take place in schools occur in white, middle-class communities.[41] Specifically, in elementary and middle schools, where security measures are typically fewer than at the high-school level, poverty is a "significant predictor" of the use of security measures.[42] Kupchik concluded, "the experience of policing in school and the criminalization of student misconduct begins earlier for students attending schools with concentrated poverty, potentially contributing to short- and long-term disparities in educational achievement."[43] Their findings held after controlling for student misbehavior and crime, location in an urban setting, and perceived area crime rates.[44]

Instead of such a heavy emphasis on school security personnel and equipment, particularly in urban schools, school climate and overall achievement and conditions for learning are important. All students need an environment with high expectations, where they are engaged and challenged, their natural ability and inclination to learn is nurtured rather than redirected or extinguished, and they are treated with respect.[45] This is also often easier to discuss than racial disparity and eliminating racial disparity since creating classroom environments that embrace the whole child and support the individualized needs of every child is universal. As a real-life example of what happens when schools focus on creating a safe and nurturing school environment for the safety, security, and academic well-being of children, we need look only as far as Boston, Massachusetts. In 2010, the principal of the Orchard Gardens School fired the security guards and replaced them with art instructors.[46] Ninety percent of the school's students lived at or below the poverty line, and some were homeless. Since the principal reinvigorated the school's arts and music program, discipline incidents are down, attendance and student performance are up. Although it is notoriously difficult to replicate effective school reform, this anecdote reflects a larger emphasis on the importance of building relationships and emotional support for children in schools. Creating safe and nurturing learning environments will not only help schools to meet their legal obligations under the Civil Rights Act to identify, reduce, and eliminate racial disparity in educational opportunity, it also will help them to abide by the hefty moral compass educators carry as they instruct the nation's children.

Like the need to rethink how we pursue school safety, there is also a need to evaluate the impact of the assumptions we make about black communities and children, and to reconsider those assumptions. When civil rights analysis and evaluation of potential violations of the Civil Rights Act begin with racial disparity and data to show racial gaps in academic performance, there is a danger of creating self-fulfilling trenches from which children and families find it difficult to extract themselves: Children will be what they see and understand themselves to be. Yet, counternarratives exist. For example, Ivory Toldson, Deputy Director of the White House Initiative on Historically Black Colleges and Universities and Howard University professor of education, has conducted research that debunks myths about black communities, demonstrating for example that more black men are in college than in prison and black students are as likely as other students and more to value education and to consider smart kids "cool," none of which is part of the mainstream racial narrative.[47] Toldson uses that counternarrative as a starting point to demonstrate the inherent ability of any person, regardless of race, to succeed, and he advocates from that starting point for ways to ensure such success for all. In other words, a civil rights frame that starts with creative consideration of all children's abilities that can enhance our society as a whole is the right course to pursue and delivers us back to the original intent of the Civil Rights Act. So, while we know, for instance, from the Educational Testing Service that middle-income children hear 1500 more words per hour at four years old than low-income children, starting with success means that intelligence can be conveyed in various ways and there are strong teachers and school support teams that have picked up on these various ways that intelligence is expressed to help children overcome societal barriers to opportunity.[48]

It is imperative as we embark on the next chapter for civil rights and racial equity that we do all we can to change the nation's mindset about black and brown people. This mindset has quantifiable results: For example, studies demonstrate that students of color are eligible for Advanced Placement courses at the same rate as whites but are not counseled to enroll in A.P. courses and are not participating in A.P. courses at the same rate.[49] The current racial narrative has summarily relegated groups of people by race to a category of unworthiness and then defined them as people who supposedly do not care about education or value education for their children. This gives others permission, in some school reform efforts for instance, to judge those groups unfavorably, attempt to erase their identity, and ultimately try to assimilate them to the dominant culture of white, affluent "mainstream." We have seen this before in Native American schools of the past and Japanese internment camps that sought to erase students' cultural identity in boarding schools.

What the Civil Rights Act did not and could not do was to legislate that the nation undertake a close examination of its racial beliefs, an examination that does not begin with assessing the failures of students by racial category and the shortcomings of communities and parents who are raising children in difficult circumstances. Instead, the starting point for self-examination must be from an assumption of competence about the populations most in need of civil rights advocacy and the Civil Rights Act's protections.

Conclusion

While we celebrate victories such as the Civil Rights Act of 1964, those celebrations must be short-lived as there is still much work to do. Civil rights law is but one tool to change practices in hopes of eventually changing mindsets. So, the work continues—in courtrooms and classrooms and boardrooms, in philanthropy and in science labs, in the voting booth and at police precincts. What we have learned from the Civil Rights Act is that the law alone isn't enough. True equality requires systemic change and a shift in mindset, such as President Lyndon B. Johnson's eventual view that the Civil Rights Act and the civil rights movement were a moral imperative. When we look carefully at the teachers, parents, youth, community members, faith leaders, business leaders, and legislators whose work brought us the Civil Rights Act and *Brown v. Board*, we see proof that if we all keep doing our part, we can pick up where they left off and continue their work to finally achieve equity.

The spirit of *Brown* and the Civil Rights Act has been violated at nearly every turn, and yet the Act survives.

Allison R. Brown is the Program Officer for Racial Justice at the Open Society Foundations. She has been an education consultant and is a former attorney at the U.S. Department of Justice, Civil Rights Division, Educational Opportunities Section.

NOTES

1. 42 U.S.C. Sections 2000c *et seq.* & 2000d *et seq.*, Pub.L. 88–352, 78 Stat. 241, enacted July 2, 1964.

2. CLAY RISEN, THE BILL OF THE CENTURY: THE EPIC BATTLE FOR THE CIVIL RIGHTS ACT, 47 (Bloomsbury 2014).

3. Ibid., 15.

4. Richard W. Brown, *Freedom of Choice in the South: A Constitutional Perspective*, 28 LOUISIANA LAW REVIEW 455 (1968).

5. U.S. Commission on Civil Rights, *Title IV and School Desegregation: A Study of a Neglected Federal Program*, 1 (January 1973).

6. Parents Involved in Community Schools v. Seattle School District No. 1, 551 U.S. 701 (2007); Grutter v. Bollinger, 539 U.S. 306 (2003); Regents of the University of California v. Bakke, 438 U.S. 265 (1978); Fisher v. University of Texas, 631 F.3d 213 (5th Cir. 2011), 133 S. Ct. 2441, 570 U.S. ___ (2013), No. 11-345; Hopwood v. Texas, 78 F.3d 932 (5th Cir. 1996).

7. 551 U.S. 701 (2007).

8. Fisher, 133 S. Ct. 2411.

9. 134 S. Ct. 1623, 572 U.S. ___ (2014).

10. Saki Knafo & Joy Resmovits, *Homeless Students Top 1 Million, U.S. Says, Leaving Advocates 'Horrified'*, HUFFINGTON POST (June 28, 2012); National Center for Homeless Education, *Education for Homeless Children and Youths Program, Data Collection Summary* (June 2012).

11. The black and Latino poverty rate is two times that of whites. National Poverty Center, *Poverty in the United States: Frequently Asked Questions* (2014). Robert Balfanz, Vaughan Byrnes, & Joanna Fox, The Civil Rights Project, *Sent Home and Put Off-Track: The Antecedents, Disproportionalities, and Consequences of Being Suspended in the Ninth Grade* (April 2013); Russell J. Skiba et al., *Race Is Not Neutral: A National Investigation of African American and Latino Disproportionality in School Discipline*, 40 SCHOOL PSYCHOLOGY REVIEW 85 (2011).

12. Greg Kaufman & Elaine Weiss, *This Week in Poverty: Time to Take on Concentrated Poverty and Education*, THE NATION (February 2013).

13. Lyndon Baines Johnson, *Address Before a Joint Session of the Congress* (November 27, 1963).

14. The Council of State Governments Justice Center, *Breaking Schools' Rules: A Statewide Study on How School Discipline Relates to Students' Success and Juvenile Justice Involvement* (2014).

15. Catherine Lhamon, Assistant Secretary, Office for Civil Rights, U.S. Department of Education & Jocelyn Samuels, Acting Assistant Attorney General, Civil Rights Division, U.S. Department of Justice, *Dear Colleague Letter on the Nondiscriminatory Administration of School Discipline* (January 8, 2014).

16. Catherine E. Lhamon, Assistant Secretary, Office for Civil Rights, U.S. Department of Education, *Dear Colleague Letter: Charter Schools* (May 14, 2014).

17. 42 U.S.C. § 2000(c) (2000); Pub. L. 88-352, Title IV, §§ 407, 409-10 (July 2, 1964), 78 Stat. 248-9.

18. 42 U.S.C. § 2000(d) (2000); Pub. L. 88-352, Title VI, §§ 601-02 (July 2, 1964), 78 Stat. 252.

19. 851 F. Supp. 905, 958-1001 (N.D. Ill. 1994).

20. See, e.g., Elston v. Talladega County Board of Education, 997 F.2d 1394, 1405 n.11, 1407 n.14 (11th Cir.), rehearing denied, 7 F.3d 242 (11th Cir. 1993).

21. 34 C.F.R. § 100.3(b)(1).

22. U.S. Department of Justice, *Title VI Legal Manual*, 47-53 (January 2001).

23. U.S. Department of Education, *Expansive Survey of America's Public Schools Reveals Troubling Racial Disparities* (March 21, 2014) ("The U.S. Department of Education's Office for Civil Rights released today the first comprehensive look at civil rights data from nearly every public school in the country in nearly 15 years"). The data is available on the U.S. Department of Education's website for Civil Rights Data Collection, at: http://ocrdata. ed.gov/Home.

24. See, e.g., National Women's Law Center, *How to Use the Civil Rights Data Collection Online Tool to Check Your School's Record on Title IX Issues* (Webinar) (September 2012), available at http://www.nwlc.org/resource/how-use-civil-rights-data-collection-online-tool-check-your-school%E2%80%99s-record-title-ix-issues; The Capitol Insider, *Civil Rights Data Collection Released* (March 2012).

25. U.S. Department of Education, Office for Civil Rights, *Civil Rights Data Collection, Data Snapshot: School Discipline* (March 2014).

26. HBO Real Sports: Iowa Girls High School Volleyball (October 2012); Matt Zapotosky, *Teen Slain During Possible Attempted Robbery* (August 2012), available at http://www.washingtonpost.com/blogs/crime-scene/post/teen-slain-during-attempted-robbery/2012/08/06/ae2c22ee-dfd3-11e1-a19c-fcfa365396c8_blog.html.

27. U.S. Department of Education & U.S. Department of Justice, *Supportive School Discipline Initiative* (2014).

28. See, e.g., American Civil Liberties Union, *What is the School-to-Prison Pipeline?*, available at: https://www.aclu.org/racial-justice/what-school-prison-pipeline.

29. Proposed Consent Decree, Barnhardt, et al. & U.S. v. Meridian Municipal Separate School District, 65-cv-01300-HTW-LRA, (March 23, 2013); Julianne Hing, ColorLines, *What the DOJ Can't Do on School Discipline Reform* (April 3, 2013); Julianne Hing, ColorLines, *The Shocking Details of a Mississippi School-to-Prison Pipeline* (November 26, 2012).

30. Barnhardt Proposed Consent Decree, 4.

31. Ibid., 9.

32. Complaint, U.S. v. City of Meridian et al., 4:12-cv-00168-HTW-LRA (October 24, 2012).

33. Ibid., 1.

34. Agreement between the United States of America and the School District of Palm Beach County (February 26, 2013); Agreement to Resolve Oakland Unified School District OCR Case Number 09125001 (September 17, 2012) (Title VI resolution with Oakland, California school district); Memorandum of Agreement (April 24, 2013) (Title IV resolution with Decatur, Indiana school district).

35. U.S. COMMISSION ON CIVIL RIGHTS, TITLE IV AND SCHOOL DESEGREGATION, 3.

36. U.S. Department of Justice, Civil Rights Division, Educational Opportunities Section home page, http://www.justice.gov/crt/about/edu/.

37. School districts' need and desire for technical assistance became apparent to me while I was an attorney in the U.S. Department of Justice's Civil Rights Division, Educational

Opportunities Section from 2006–12. Additionally, schools and districts have repeatedly indicated to me, in my capacity as an education equity consultant from 2012–14, a need for this assistance.

38. See, e.g., Palm Beach County Agreement and Barnhardt Proposed Consent Decree.

39. Equity Assistance Centers, http://www.equityassistancecenters.org/; About OCR: Overview of the Agency, http://www2.ed.gov/about/offices/list/ocr/aboutocr.html.

40. Daniel Fowler, *Race and Poverty Often Unjustifiably Tied to School Security Measures* (August 20, 2011) (press release). Aaron Kupchik & Geoff K. Ward, *Reproducing Social Inequality Through School Security: Effects of Race and Class on School Security Measures* 3-9 (2011) (unpublished manuscript).

41. David J. Leonard, *The Unbearable Invisibility of White Masculinity: Innocence in the Age of White Male Mass Shootings* (January 2013), available at http://gawker.com/5973485/the-unbearable-invisibility-of-white-masculinity-innocence-in-the-age-of-white-male-mass-shootings.

42. Kupchik & Ward, *Reproducing Social Inequality,* 2.

43. Ibid., 22.

44. Ibid., 21.

45. David Osher, *School Climate, the Conditions for Learning and Academic Achievement* (June 15, 2010) (Congressional briefing).

46. Katy Tur, *Principal Fires Security Guards to Hire Art Teachers – and Transforms Elementary School*, NBC News (May 1, 2013).

47. Ivory Toldson and Janks Morton, *Cellblock vs. College*, EMPOWER MAGAZINE (April 20, 2011); Ivory Toldson and Delila Owens, *Acting Black: What Black Kids Think About Being Smart and Other School-Related Experiences* (July 1, 2012).

48. David Shenk, *The 32-Million Word Gap*, THE ATLANTIC (March 9, 2010).

49. College Board, *Eighth Annual AP Report to the Nation* (2012).

DEREK W. BLACK

Defining Discrimination
Intent, Impact, and the Future of Title VI of the Civil Rights Act of 1964

THE CIVIL RIGHTS ACT OF 1964 HAS HAD THE LARGEST IMPACT ON RACIAL equality of any legislation passed. Although the Supreme Court had declared school segregation unconstitutional a decade earlier in *Brown v. Board of Education*,[1] no significant school desegregation occurred prior to the Act. In fact, a mere 2% of African American children in the South attended schools with white majorities in 1964.[2] With the passage of the Civil Rights Act of 1964, things changed quickly. School desegregation began occurring at a rapid pace, and those titles of the Act aimed at employment and public accommodations, likewise, began to fundamentally change opportunity for African Americans and other minorities across the country.

The Civil Rights Act included eleven different titles, each aimed at discrimination in some different context or granting the federal government authority to address it. Title VI was one of the most sweeping. It prohibits racial discrimination in any program receiving federal funds.[3] As federal money began to flow more widely to education during the 1960s, Title VI's prohibitions quickly applied to all of the nation's public schools, and eventually applied to a substantial number of private schools as well. It, likewise, extended its reach beyond education to various other public and private industries, such as transportation, health, and environment, that receive federal funds. The strategy was simple: the further the federal government spread its money, the greater its leverage to address racial equity and discrimination in all facets of public life.

For nearly four decades, Title VI did more than just root out obvious invidious discrimination; it helped promote racially equitable results. Under Title VI, complainants could pursue administrative and litigation remedies for racial inequality, even when they could not demonstrate the existence of malevolent design by some particular actor. It was enough that a federal funding recipient had enacted a policy or engaged in a practice that produced racially disparate results that could not be justified by the practical necessity of achieving some important goal. Complainants relied on agency regulations that prohibit disparate impact.[4] Agencies had enacted those regulations pursuant to their authority under section 602 of the Civil Rights Act, which provides that agencies shall enforce section 601's prohibition on discrimination and guarantee of equal access by enacting regulations.[5]

Then, in 2002, the Supreme Court, by a vote of five to four in *Alexander v. Sandoval*, reversed course. It brought an end to private individuals' ability to use litigation as means to challenge racial inequality in federally funded programs, save those instances when they could demonstrate intentional discrimination. The Court held, contrary to prior case law, that violations of disparate impact regulations do not give rise to a private cause of action.[6] The Court did not alter agencies' authority to enforce their regulations administratively, but for private individuals seeking recourse in court, Title VI became largely redundant. It provided no more protection than the Fourteenth Amendment, to which state actors were already subject. The only meaningful vestige was litigants' ability to continue to sue private entities that received federal funds and engaged in intentional discrimination.

The effects of the loss were enormous in education. Extreme racial imbalances in school and classroom assignments have continued unchallenged. As we move further from de jure segregation, proof that intentional segregation is the cause of or motivates segregation has become almost impossible to show. Likewise, racial disparities in discipline, special education, student achievement, and funding are rampant, and likely caused by implicit biases, but presenting that bias in a way that meets the intentional discrimination standard—or convinces courts that the standard is met—has been so difficult that litigants have almost stopped bringing litigation challenges.

Such a monumental loss in education and elsewhere demands a response, particularly as we pass the 50th anniversary of the Civil Rights Act. Three major and distinct responses are possible: administrative action, litigation to evolve new doctrine, and legislative reform. Administrative action is immediately available to enforce disparate impact. The Department of Education, for instance, announced its intent to enforce its disparate impact regulations in discipline in 2014. Administrative action, however, can vary significantly based on changes in administration and the political climate of any given year. Strategic litigation has not yet been explored, but may also be possible based on decisions that followed *Sandoval* and implicitly expressed uneasiness with cutting off too many litigation remedies for inequality and discrimination. Yet, best case litigation outcomes would still fall short of a complete reversal of *Sandoval*. The only complete solution is legislative reform, but given the current political environment, legislation is, at best, several years away. In short, each of the options offers its own set of significant benefits and limitations. If Title VI of the Civil Rights Act of 1964 is ever to regain a modicum of its prior glory, the best strategy for civil rights advocates is to press on all three fronts.

From the Civil Rights Act of 1964 to *Sandoval*

THE AMBIGUITY OF DISCRIMINATION AND THE RESPONSIBILITY TO DEFINE IT

The impact of *Sandoval* on the attempts of litigants to protect the Constitution's guarantee of equality regardless of race cannot be fully appreciated without an understanding of what the Civil Rights Act of 1964 sought to achieve and how courts interpreted Title VI prior to *Sandoval*. The key issue in Title VI is what constitutes discrimination. From the Act's passage, some level of uncertainty pervaded the issue, but the definition tended toward a broader concept. In the decades following the Act, the definition of discrimination gradually shifted from a prohibition on policies and actions that result in a disparate impact on vulnerable groups to a prohibition only on those policies that are motivated by racial or gender animus. This emergent intent standard eventually came to be embodied in the Court's holding in *Sandoval*, eliminating previously significant limitations on racial inequality.

The debate over the meaning of discrimination and who has the authority to address it, however, long predates *Sandoval* and even the Civil Rights Act itself. This debate stretches back to the enactment of the Fourteenth Amendment. Section five of the Fourteenth Amendment provides that Congress shall have the "power to enforce, by appropriate legislation, the provisions of this [amendment]" and, thus, interpret the meaning of equal protection. The potential for an expansive interpretive power aroused significant concern during the debates surrounding the Fourteenth Amendment.[7] Some feared Congress would have a blank check to police states' treatment of their citizens.[8] Others were concerned Congress might abandon its responsibility and leave equality empty of meaning or subject to an "accidental majority of Congress."[9] The final language of the Fourteenth Amendment represents a compromise between these two positions. It guaranteed rights that are not subject to congressional fiat, but also extended power to Congress to further specify how these rights might be protected.

Despite this wide power, Congress never fully clarified the Amendment's central right of equal protection under the law. The most expansive implementation of the Fourteenth Amendment's promise of equality is the Civil Rights Act of 1964, but the Act again failed to define the core terms of equality and discrimination. The Act did not even use the term equal protection and, instead, shifted the legal paradigm to one of prohibiting discrimination. In Title VI of the Civil Rights Act, Congress provided that "[n]o person in the United States shall, on the ground of race, be excluded from participation in, be denied the benefits of, or be subjected to discrimination under any program or activity receiving Federal financial assistance."[10] Like the Fourteenth Amendment, the Act did not provide any guidance as to what amounts to discrimination or equal protection, although the inclusion of the language "excluded from participation in" and "denied the benefits of" hints at a potentially broader meaning. Regardless, the Supreme Court has repeatedly indicated that Title VI is inherently ambiguous.[11]

The legislative history and statutory structure of Title VI, however, suggest that the lack of definitiveness served important ends. To prevent the Civil Rights Act from being endlessly bogged down in debate and amendments, Congress chose to avoid some issues and condemn others to generality. Because the meaning of discrimination was so important and subject to intensely different views, the only realistic way for the Act to secure a majority within a reasonable amount of time was for Congress to leave the language in Title VI vague.[12] Congress did, however, create the means by which to further define the contours of Title VI's discrimination prohibition by authorizing agencies to interpret the Act and pass regulations to further that interpretation.[13] Nonetheless, this convenient choice has created unanticipated problems over time. The Court has proven unwilling to respect this delegation of authority to agencies, substituting its own interpretation, but rarely offering any more substance or reasoning than Congress.

FROM IMPACT TO INTENT AND BACK AGAIN

In the first case to address the scope of Title VI, *Lau v. Nichols*[14] in 1974, the Court recognized a violation of Title VI based solely upon evidence of disparate impact. Four years later in *Regents of University of California v. Bakke*,[15] the Court seemingly reversed course, holding that Title VI only prohibits intentional discrimination, regardless of impact. But shortly after *Bakke*, the Court undercut the practical effect of *Bakke's* holding. In 1983 in *Guardians Association v. Civil Service Commission*,[16] the Court held that although Title VI itself only prohibits intentional discrimination, its implementing regulations create a cause of action for disparate impact. Thus, evidence of intent is unnecessary to sustain a claim under Title VI.

While stated succinctly above, the holdings of these cases were subject to varying interpretation and framing because of the absence of a single majority opinion in *Bakke* or *Guardians*. Members of the Court issued 12 separate opinions between the two cases, ten of which formed some part of the holdings. In 1985, the Court offered some clarification of this line of cases in *Alexander v. Choate*[17] by reiterating *Guardians'* disparate impact holding. *Choate*, however, was a disability discrimination case interpreting Section 504 of the Rehabilitation Act. Although portions of Section 504 are modeled after Title VI, Section 504 is distinct from Title VI in important ways, making *Choate's* reference to Title VI less instructive. Regardless, in none of these cases was there a serious discussion as to the ambiguity of the statutory language "discrimination." Only in *Bakke* was it raised at all. Even there, only a minority took up the issue and they disagreed amongst themselves as to the ambiguity and meaning of discrimination.[18]

Over the next 25 years, the Court avoided the inconsistencies in its previous holdings and made no attempt to clarify the meaning of discrimination. Finally, in *Alexander v. Sandoval* in 2001, the Court admitted that "[a]lthough Title VI has often come to this Court, it is fair to say (indeed, perhaps an understatement) that our opinions have not eliminated all uncertainty regarding its commands."[19] But the Court's analysis in *Sandoval* again neglected to confront the source of the incoherence: the inherent ambiguity of discrimination and equal protection. The Court indicated that the ambiguity arose from its fractured opinions and holdings, rather than the unexplored and undefined meaning of discrimination that caused the fractured decisions. As a result, the Court in *Sandoval* answered only the narrow issue it framed: whether the implementing regulations of Title VI can create a private cause of action for disparate impact.

ALEXANDER V. SANDOVAL AND ITS DEFINITIVE ANSWER

The Court's holding in *Sandoval*, as understood by lower courts, brought a complete and final end to disparate impact challenges under Title VI of the Civil Rights Act. The plaintiff in *Sandoval* challenged an Alabama policy of administering drivers' license tests only in English, claiming that the law had a disparate impact based on ethnicity.[20] The Supreme Court, however, found that no implied private cause of action existed to enforce Title VI regulations. In its analysis of sections 601 and 602 of the Civil Rights Act, the Court concluded that section 601 creates individual

rights with the language "no person . . . shall . . . be subject to discrimination . . . ,"
and this language prohibits only intentional discrimination.[21]

While the language of section 602 authorizes federal agencies to enact regulations to further the purposes of section 601 and ensure that recipients of federal
funds do not engage in discrimination, the Court found that section 602 does not
confer any private rights or cause of action beyond those already created by section
601. Because section 601 prohibits only intentional discrimination and section 602
furthers only rights granted in section 601, section 602 cannot create an independent
private cause of action for disparate impact. Thus, insofar as section 602 regulations
proscribe activities permitted by section 601, they are not enforceable by an implied
private right of action.[22]

The silver lining, if there was one, was that the Court assumed that regulations
prohibiting disparate impact were in themselves valid.[23] Private individuals could
no longer bring causes of action to enforce these regulations, but agencies remained
free to enforce the regulations administratively. The Court's explicit holding—that
no implied private right of action exists under section 602—does not address this
apparent inconsistency. As a practical matter, this contradiction is reasonable. If one
believes that some disparate impact is problematic, bring it before an agency, not a
court. But doctrinally, the notion that agencies can enforce principles beyond the
scope of section 601 is potentially hard to justify.

Regardless, in cutting off private litigation for disparate impact, *Sandoval* closed
a door that was once essential to ensuring the enforcement of civil rights legislation
and providing equal opportunity in education. Without an avenue through which
individuals can enforce section 602 privately, many would argue that civil rights
have taken a step backward. Although an intent standard is theoretically aligned
with eliminating racial animus, a subjective intent doctrine is difficult for plaintiffs
to satisfy and easy enough for defendants to skirt. This problem has manifested
itself time and time again with school segregation in particular. The effect of such
a standard is to protect the status quo of segregation and inequality and, in many
instances, permit it to grow. Because the standard requires active racial motivations,
it insulates the perpetuation, continuation, and benign neglect of inequities by
government actors, whether in the context of the classroom, the criminal justice
system, housing patterns, or various other structural disparities. Neither courts
nor plaintiffs can intrude on, second-guess, or invalidate governmental discretion
in decision-making, absent evidence of intentional discrimination.

Salvaging What Was Lost

Three options, of varying viability, exist to salvage what was lost in *Sandoval*: a litigation strategy designed to narrowly construe the doctrine of *Sandoval*; a more forceful agency enforcement of disparate impact regulations; and a legislative amendment to the Civil Rights Act. Of the three, agency action is the most readily viable, but that solution could be fleeting. Agency actions are necessarily subject to retraction as presidential administrations change. Amending the Civil Rights Act to specifically reinstate rights either consummate with pre-*Sandoval* law or evolved understandings of discrimination and equality would yield the most effective and lasting change, but this option is the least likely due to the legislative gridlock that has persisted since 2008. A litigation strategy rests somewhere in between. Litigation remedies are currently more likely than legislative action, but less effective. Litigation success is less likely than administrative action, but would be more effective and lasting if secured. The following sections address each of these options.

LITIGATION TO EVOLVE DOCTRINE

Although *Sandoval* definitively held that disparate impact regulations cannot create a private cause of action and that plaintiffs must demonstrate intentional discrimination to sustain a cause of action under the statute itself, *Sandoval* did not address the scope and meaning of intentional discrimination. *Sandoval* can be understood as but one among a series of cases where the Court has recently explored liability for intentional discrimination under Title VI and Title IX of the Education Amendments of 1972.[24] Title IX addresses gender discrimination in education, rather than race, but the Court has long since treated doctrines recognized under either of those two statutes as extending to the other.[25] A series of Title IX school cases, including *Gebser v. Lago Vista*,[26] *Davis v. Monroe County*,[27] and *Jackson v. Birmingham*,[28] demonstrate that intentional discrimination need not be a narrow concept restricted solely to instances where race or gender played an active or malevolent role in a funding recipient's decision. This line of cases demonstrates that a defendant also violates Title VI and Title IX when it intentionally acts or fails to act in a way that causes, perpetuates, or contributes to discrimination or disadvantages that occur within its programs. Such a violation occurs if the discrimination and disadvantage continue to occur because the defendant knowingly refuses or fails to intervene, even when the defendant did not initially desire or act to create discrimination or disadvantage.

Under this approach, the scope of actionable violations under Title VI and Title IX expands significantly beyond the traditional narrow understanding of "intentional discrimination." For instance, staff members or students, neither of whom is an agent of the school, may harass female students, or teachers might adopt pedagogically unsound or unjustified practices that unfairly exclude minorities from an education opportunity. A school official might play no role in these situations, but if the official learns of them and takes no action to limit their continuation, the Court has held that a school intentionally violates Title IX's prohibition against discrimination. The same would be true with Title VI.

For instance, in *Gebser v. Lago Vista*, the Court held that a school district could be liable for a teacher's harassment of a student if it knew of the harassment and took no action to stop it.[29] The Court reasoned that to hold otherwise would "frustrate the purposes' of Title IX."[30] Title IX was enacted "'[t]o avoid the use of federal resources to support discriminatory practices' and 'to provide individual citizens effective protection against those practices.'"[31] When a school fails to respond to known discrimination within its programs, that discrimination becomes the policy or action of the school itself, even if the school is not directly committing the discrimination.[32] The Court labeled this "deliberate indifference to discrimination"[33] that is "the cause" of the deprivation of federal rights.[34] The Court further built on this doctrine in *Davis v. Monroe County*,[35] holding that a district could also be liable for student-on-student harassment when it was deliberately indifferent to it. The important point in both of these cases is that the Court transformed discrimination by third parties into discrimination by the school, and was willing to accept the school's deliberate indifference as intentional discrimination.

If the broadening of intentional discrimination was subtle in *Gebser* and *Davis*, it became obvious in *Jackson v. Birmingham*.[36] The issue in *Jackson* was whether an individual who complains about discrimination has a private cause of action when a school retaliates against that person in response to the complaint. The case presented a difficult issue because it followed *Sandoval*'s holding eliminating all private causes of action for anything short of intentional discrimination. On that basis, lower courts had rejected a cause of action for retaliation.[37] The Supreme Court, however, found that *Sandoval* did not bar the claim because retaliation is a form of intentional discrimination.

The Court emphasized that Title IX's prohibition against action that subjects students to gender discrimination is sweeping. The Court explained that "'[d]iscrimination' is a term that covers a wide range of intentional unequal treatment,"[38] and proceeded to delve into what intentional discrimination could entail. The Court wrote, "[r]etaliation is, by definition, an intentional act" and "is a form of 'discrimination' because the complainant is being subjected to differential treatment."[39] Furthermore, retaliation must be understood as a form of discrimination "'on the basis of sex' because it is an intentional response to the nature of the complaint:

an allegation of sex discrimination."[40] In comparison to deliberate indifference, "retaliation represents an even easier case" because "[i]t is easily attributable to the funding recipient, and it is always—by definition—intentional."[41]

The Court emphatically argued that this broad interpretation was necessary for the statute's prohibitions to have practical effect. If those who are best suited to reveal discrimination—teachers—are not protected, discriminatory violations would too often go unremedied and "Title IX's enforcement scheme would unravel."[42] The Court in *Davis* and *Gebser* had held that a school district is liable only for harassment of which it has previous actual knowledge. If a district were free to retaliate against those who provide notice, employees and students would soon refrain from providing notice, and sexual harassment could flourish in schools with no prospect of legal intervention. Thus, Title IX must provide a private cause of action to prohibit it. The dissenters, however, made it quite clear that, while the Court's decision may be practically enticing, intentional discrimination, as traditionally understood, is distinct from retaliation and, thus, the majority opinion was a retreat from the holding in *Sandoval*.[43]

Collectively, these cases offer strong precedent and reasoning for the notion that intentional discrimination, within the context of Title VI and Title IX, is broader than its traditional connotation of race- and gender-motivated action by a defendant. The *Gebser* line of cases demonstrates that the statutory bar of discrimination in federally funded programs—which the Court has interpreted to mean "intentional" discrimination—also prohibits volitional actions that effectively perpetuate discrimination, undermine congressional intent, or subject individuals to inequality. Although the Court has given no sign that discrimination under the constitution is anything other than a narrow inquiry into whether the decision-maker harbored a race- or gender-based bias or motive, the *Gebser* line of cases demonstrates a more fluid statutory inquiry. If nothing else, these cases indicate that *Sandoval* cannot be read narrowly or in isolation; rather, the Court's deliberate indifference, intent, and retaliation cases must be synthesized to arrive at a single and generally applicable standard for intentional discrimination.

Close analysis of these cases reveals that certain factors and indicia are consistently referenced in these cases and could form the theoretical foundation and justification for an evolved concept of intentional discrimination. A full analysis of those cases and factors can be found in *The Mysteriously Reappearing Cause of Action: The Court's Expanding Concept of Intentional Discrimination in Gender and Race Discrimination Statutes*.[44] Given the scope of this chapter, it suffices to simply outline the factors and indicia. First, the Court was motivated by whether a defendant had made a value choice in regard to the existence of discrimination or inequity. Outside of the *Gebser* line of cases, the Court, of course, has made clear that although choice is part of intent, merely making a choice does not involve the type of intent the Court requires to justify liability. But something more than volitional choice occurred in the *Gebser* line of cases: the defendants' choices manifested *value* judgments regarding discrimination and inequality. They made official value choices to allow discrimination or inequality—and the potential for more in the future—to go unaddressed.

Second, the Court focused on whether that choice directly caused discrimination or inequity to continue. In the sexual harassment cases, a school's choice to disregard the harassment played a causal role in the continuation of discrimination. With retaliation, causation was less evident, although if the complaining party's allegations were correct and the party was terminated, it is safe to assume that the discrimination continued and was indirectly encouraged.

Third, the Court assessed whether the continued existence of that discrimination or inequity in a federally funded program is inconsistent with congressional objectives and, as a practical matter, whether the defendant's action would affirmatively further congressional objectives. The entire line of cases emphasized that to permit the district to make the choices it had would frustrate the purpose of the underlying statute and allow federal money to support programs in which discrimination and inequality were occurring, rather that protect against it.[45] Certain processes, like the protection against retaliation, are simply indispensable to achieving those ends. Without protection, individuals would rarely, if ever, report discrimination and Title IX violations would go unremedied.[46]

The foregoing analysis should allow litigants to bring broader discrimination claims, including some premised on facts demonstrating disparate impact (though the claim would not be articulated as disparate impact). Thus far, no one has brought litigation based on this analysis. Litigants have brought other claims that attempt to narrow the impact of *Sandoval* on other grounds, but lower courts have rejected them.[47] The foregoing analysis, however, is based on the Court's precedent and there is little reason to forego utilizing it. For the Supreme Court to reject it, it would have to disavow the doctrinal path it created. With that said, the risk of such a disavowal is not insubstantial.

The *Gebser* line of cases involves facts of sexual harassment and official hostility to addressing discrimination that the Court likely finds normatively objectionable. To the extent these cases are motivated by normative objections rather than a broadened understanding of intentional discrimination, a plaintiff friendly doctrine may be hard to replicate in other contexts. For instance, the majority of the Court does not seem to intuit any normative problem with policies that produce disparate impact. If anything, the majority normatively objects to interfering with government policy simply because of its impact. To overcome this normative bias—if it exists—litigants would need test cases that similarly represent normatively egregious circumstances. Disparate impact cases can represent these types of circumstances, but courts predisposed against the claims can also just dismiss or justify the circumstances as statistical anomalies rather than discrimination or inequality. In short, a litigation victory could produce a significant and lasting solution to *Sandoval*, but it is far from clear that lower courts or the Supreme Court are willing to entertain claims designed to do so.

ADMINISTRATIVE ENFORCEMENT OF DISPARATE IMPACT

While *Sandoval*'s explicit rejection of disparate impact regulations as creating a cause of action was of enormous significance, so too was the Court's willingness to assume the validity of the disparate impact regulations. Federal agencies remain able to enforce their own definitions of discrimination administratively. The Court could revisit the validity of the regulations themselves and conclude that an agency's interpretation of Title VI as authorizing disparate impact regulations is unreasonable.[48] The Court's insistence on intentional discrimination in various cases makes that outcome more than an insignificant risk, but the more likely outcome is that the Court would uphold the regulations based on longstanding principles of deference to agency interpretations. In *Chevron v. Natural Resources Defense Council, Inc.*[49] and subsequent cases, the Court held that when Congress has charged an agency with enforcing a statute, the Court must defer to the agency's interpretation so long as it is reasonable.[50] This deference is particularly appropriate—if not mandated—in regard to statutory prohibitions on race and, by extension, gender discrimination. Neither Title VI nor Title IX provides any explanation of or context for what is entailed by the guarantee that "[n]o person in the United States shall, on the ground of race [or sex] be excluded from participation in, be denied the benefits of, or be subjected to discrimination under any program or activity receiving Federal financial assistance."[51] Per congressional intent, regulatory agencies fill in this need for context and explanation. The legislative history shows that Congress refrained from defining discrimination, in part, because Congress itself was uncertain as to what "discrimination" meant.

A high level of deference toward agencies in combating educational inequality was also implicit in the Court's holdings in *Gebser, Davis*, and *Jackson*. Each of those cases relied heavily upon regulations in justifying the schools' liability. *Sandoval* marks the sole exception in the Court's willingness to defer to agencies in the *Gebser* line of cases. The other cases routinely reached holdings that rest upon and are consistent with agencies' interpretations of the statutes' prohibitions, even when that interpretation does not fit precisely within the traditional intent doctrine.

Agencies, nonetheless, appeared reluctant to press their authority to enforce disparate impact following the Court's decision in *Sandoval*, thereby eliminating the opportunity for the Court to strike down the validity of the regulations themselves.[52] Not until Barack Obama's second term did agencies seriously reassert their authority. The most notable step in that direction may be the Department of Justice and Department of Education's joint guidance on school discipline.[53]

The Departments' guidance very poignantly waded into the topic of disparate impact in school discipline and defended its willingness to do so. The guidance was specifically directed at reducing racial disparities in discipline even where there is no clear evidence of disparate treatment. The guidance indicated that the first question the agencies would ask of school districts is whether "the discipline policy resulted in an adverse impact on students of a particular race as compared with students of other races."[54] That racial disparities were not the result of intentional discrimination would be beside the point. It is enough that "students of a particular race, as compared to students of other races, are disproportionately . . . sanctioned at higher rates; disciplined for specific offenses; subjected to longer sanctions or more severe penalties; removed from the regular school setting to an alternative school setting; or excluded from one or more educational programs or activities."[55]

If a disparity exists, a school must justify the disparity by demonstrating that its policy is designed to achieve some important educational goal and that its chosen method for achieving that goal is necessary.[56] If some other policy might be equally effective in achieving the district's goal without creating the same level of racial disparities, "then the Department would find that the school had engaged in discrimination."[57]

The foregoing framework is a reiteration of the disparate impact analysis that courts and agencies applied prior to *Sandoval*. Notable, however, is the Department's willingness to not simply label disparities that can be avoided as disparate impact, but as "discrimination." By doing so, the Department is defining discrimination independently from and differently than the Court. The Department is saying that, when a district creates racial disparities without a good reason or could achieve its objectives through some other equally effective policy, the school is engaging in discrimination. While the Court has rejected this concept of discrimination, this concept is an equally reasonable definition of discrimination. A school that persists in a policy that fails the Department's analysis is necessarily placing administrative convenience or some other low level interest above racial equity. This disregard for inequality could easily be labeled discriminatory.[58]

With the continual growth of the administrative state, agency enforcement of disparate impact or alternative concepts of discrimination has the capacity to fill much of the gap left by *Sandoval*. In many ways, administrative action is preferable to litigation. The cost to individuals to bring an agency complaint is minimal, whereas litigation is time-consuming and expensive. Agencies also have the capacity to resolve complaints much quicker than courts. They have more personnel and unique remedial options available. Agencies also have the authority to act unilaterally and initiate investigations of schools where no complaint has even been lodged.

Administrative enforcement in education, however, comes with three significant drawbacks. First, complainants have less control and play a less active role in administrative complaints. Once they lodge a complaint, how the investigation proceeds is almost entirely dictated by the agency. It can pursue and not pursue issues and theories largely as it sees fit. Second, the agency's goal is not necessarily to remedy any harm that an individual complainant or class might have suffered, but, in the context of education, to bring the school back into compliance moving forward. Courts similarly enjoy wide discretion in their final opinions and remedies, but prior to that point, litigants control how a case is framed. And although a court's decision is out of the litigants' hands, that decision is still heavily constrained by existing case law and subject to direct appellate review. Agencies, in contrast, set their own rules, and the scope of challenges to those rules and agency decisions pursuant to them are relatively narrow.

Third, the previously noted efficacies of administrative action all hinge on agency discretion, motivations, and politics. An agency need not enforce disparate impact or any other aggressive interpretation of discrimination, nor need it do so in a timely manner. During George W. Bush's administration, agencies seemed to have no impetus to enforce disparate impact at all, even though disparate impact regulations were in place at all the major agencies. The Bush administration seemed to understand discrimination as a narrow concept. When Barack Obama was elected, many expected a sharp reversal from the Bush Administration's approach. They were disappointed. Not until Obama's second term was there a clear willingness to rely on disparate impact theory to address racial disparities. To the administration's credit, however, policy guidance like that in regard to school discipline may indicate a willingness to go even further than pre-*Sandoval* agencies would have. Regardless, the overarching lesson is that administrative strategies, while potentially powerful, can be subject to more limits than litigation. During certain administrations, administrative victories can be as difficult to secure as litigation, and old victories can be cut short.

AMENDING THE CIVIL RIGHTS ACT OF 1964

The last time Congress passed any comprehensive civil rights legislation was in the Civil Rights Act of 1991.[59] The 1991 amendments were designed to overturn the

Supreme Court's narrowing of actionable employment discrimination claims.[60] This reversal of the Court was not unusual. Just a few years prior to the 1991 amendments, Congress, in response to Supreme Court decisions, passed the Civil Rights Restoration Act of 1987 to expand private causes of action for gender, race, age, and disability discrimination in federally funded programs.[61] Similarly, Congress had amended the Voting Rights Act in 1982 to overturn the Court's rejection of voting rights claims based on discriminatory effects in *City of Mobile v. Bolden*.[62]

Since the 1991 civil rights amendments, the Supreme Court has issued numerous decisions other than *Sandoval* that have narrowed the scope of other civil rights claims. With the exception of the Lilly Ledbetter Fair Pay Act of 2009,[63] Congress has not responded to any of these decisions. In 2004, a coalition endorsed omnibus civil rights legislation to reverse those decisions. The legislation, titled the Fairness and Individual Rights Necessary to Ensure a Stronger Society: Civil Rights Act of 2004 (Fairness Act), addressed negative decisions in the areas of race, gender, age, disability, and employment, along with a few other idiosyncratic civil rights issues.[64] Over 100 United States representatives and 25 senators sponsored the Fairness Act, as well as over 60 national nonprofit and advocacy organizations. On January 24, 2008, Senator Edward Kennedy reintroduced this legislation as the Civil Rights Act of 2008.[65] Then-Senators Barack Obama and Hillary Clinton joined in cosponsoring this legislation.

On the campaign trail for the presidency, Barack Obama, Hillary Clinton, and John Edwards acknowledged the need for change in civil rights and promised to take action if elected. With Obama's election and the retention of democratic majorities in both the House and the Senate, some sort of civil rights restoration legislation was all but a foregone conclusion among those closest to the issue. The legislation, of course, never came to be. It suffices to say that the recession, the controversy surrounding the Affordable Health Care Act, and the change in the composition of the House of Representative took civil rights reform off the legislative agenda. Nothing has changed since, leaving legislation the least likely of the three post-*Sandoval* strategies, at least, in the short term.

Putting aside its short-term prospects, legislation may be the best solution. If civil rights reform becomes possible again, the challenge will be one of substantive policy choices. If past is prologue, the debate will be framed as intent versus impact, and polemic sides will form. Rather than redraw old lines, the better approach may be to promote a discussion focused solely on what we mean by "intent." In the context of antidiscrimination, the Court, with the exception of the *Gebser* line of cases, has insisted that intent, or intentional discrimination, entails a subjective motivation to advantage or disadvantage based on race.[66] A mere awareness of race or racial consequences is insufficient. This understanding of intent is premised on the construct of "good guys" and "bad guys," which promotes a problematic moralistic discussion.

If antidiscrimination law were policy-driven, the debate could become less about pointing fingers at particular activities and people as being racists, and more about how to create programs that function fairly. In federally funded programs, the goal could become one of promoting racial equity, rather than conceding to the perpetuation of inequity. The best way to foster this type of discussion is to turn the debate to the less emotional and politically charged lessons found in tort law, leaving the past frames for discrimination behind.

Such a turn makes doctrinal sense as well when one considers that antidiscrimination law is but a species of tort. In tort, one finds that no sacrosanct or inherent form of fault justifies imposing or alleviating liability. The mens rea, intent, or substituted standards vary widely across torts.[67] Neither context nor circumstances can explain this variance. Instead, the variance itself demonstrates the nonexistence of an inherent concept of fault in tort. Particular liability standards or mental states are chosen for certain torts and in certain contexts, not because they reflect fault, but because they produce desired results.

Tort law does not distract itself, as has antidiscrimination law, with the notion that it is punishing "wrongdoers" or morally unacceptable "faulty" conduct. Tort law determines the ends that the law should produce and then shapes standards of legal liability to achieve them. Thus, nothing is particularly significant or indicative of inherent culpability in a standard based, for instance, on foreseeability, substantial certainty, or deliberate indifference, other than the fact that these standards regulate society in a manner that will produce desirable outcomes. This is not to suggest that people who accidentally kill and those who intentionally kill are morally indistinguishable from one another. A difference certainly exists and criminal law takes that difference into account. But a tort system need not take that difference into account if, for instance, its only purpose is to compensate family members for their loss of support. In that case, the defendant's motives are irrelevant. Likewise, if the goal of antidiscrimination law is to reduce racial inequity, segregation, or barriers, a defendant's motives are irrelevant.

As this analogy suggests, understanding how and why tort liability standards are sculpted is instructive in analyzing antidiscrimination standards. A comparison between the two is invaluable in considering any new meaningful, effective, and appropriately conceptualized civil rights legislation. Thus far, neither courts nor legislatures have done much, if anything, to foster this policy oriented approach to discrimination and civil rights legislation. If society has changed in the ways that the Court and various legislators claim, then visiting this conversation is crucial, regardless of the position on which anyone might want the final legislation to land.[68]

A transparent conversation about intent and goals would likely lead to a debate over no less than three alternatives to the current intent standard: adopting a pure disparate impact standard, adopting a modified disparate impact standard, or adopting some form of deliberate indifference. A "pure" disparate impact standard—one that determines liability primarily based on the extent of the impact rather than the defendant's ability to articulate a legitimate or nondiscriminatory explanation—is essentially concerned with ameliorating racial harms and burdens. In general, it renders irrelevant the question of subjective motive or intent and establishes liability irrespective of the blameworthiness of a defendant's conduct. It represents a determination that society should be ordered and operated along a particular line—a racially equitable distribution of burdens, benefits, and opportunities.

In federally funded programs, recipients would be agreeing to make certain types of decisions and produce certain types of results by accepting funds. For instance, in education, a school would be agreeing to eliminate disparities in discipline or adopt student assignment policies that produce equal access to resources and racially balanced schools. When a school's policies or decisions produce results contrary to those desired by federal legislation or regulation, liability would be imposed. As with strict liability for abnormally dangerous products, if a resulting harm occurs—here, a racially disparate impact—the defendant is liable. Benevolent motivations, extraordinary precautions, and reasonable care are simply irrelevant, unavailable defenses. Such a standard maximizes equality and places the cost of achieving it on those institutional actors who are the best position to deliver it.

A "modified" disparate impact standard would provide more flexibility than a "pure" standard. A modified standard would permit defendants to continue their course of action, even if it caused disparate impacts, so long as they can establish an acceptable explanation for the disparate impact. The requirements placed on that explanation depend on the results one wants to produce and the party one wants to favor. The explanation could be as permissive as requiring a legitimate nondiscriminatory explanation—which would allow most impacts to remain in place—or as strict as requiring the defendant to demonstrate that the particular course of action is a necessity—which would overturn numerous policies. For instance, a school district might justify a student assignment policy that produces racial imbalance in schools with an explanation as simple as a preference for neighborhood schools, or be required to justify it with a more compelling explanation such as unsustainable financial costs of cross-neighborhood transportation or new school construction.

While discriminatory purpose is facially irrelevant under a modified impact standard and the standard would prohibit unintentional discrimination, a modified impact standard is not necessarily inconsistent with an intent standard. Rather, a modified impact standard is a reasonable response to the fact that proving intent is difficult and can produce unreliable results. If one wants to ensure that intentional discrimination does not slip through the cracks, a standard that requires a defendant to justify the disparate impacts it causes is advantageous. In other words, although a modified impact standard does not require an explicit inference of intent, it may often impose liability in those instances where intent likely exists, but is not easily demonstrated. In particular, it would capture cases where the policy is not consciously race-motivated, but is the result of subconscious biases and irrational beliefs.

With that said, a modified impact standard is primarily aimed at furthering a concept of discrimination distinct from malevolent subjective intent. Modified impact is premised on the notion that discrimination occurs when one's actions treat racial groups differently without any justification. The lack of a justification for the inequality, rather than intent, makes it discrimination. A modified impact standard would prohibit this type of discrimination by assessing whether alternative courses of action are available and reasonably feasible. In short, a modified disparate impact standard operates to seriously reduce otherwise avoidable racial inequities.

The third option, some form of a deliberate indifference standard, would be similar in many ways to the modified intent standard discussed above in the synthesis of the *Gebser* line of cases. Deliberate indifference could focus on objective factors and overcome the problems of proof that currently limit the intent standard. First, it could ask whether the government was or should have been aware of the racial harm or impact that its actions caused or the benefits or opportunities that it denied. A "should have" approach eliminates the problem of discerning a defendant's actual knowledge, but remains fair by not holding a defendant responsible for all impacts. Second, the standard, like modified disparate impact, could evaluate whether other less harmful reasonable alternatives were or became available. Third, it would not impose liability simply because alternatives were available, but could explore why those alternatives were not implemented. Finally, the standard could weigh any competing interests that a defendant might offer as justifying the racial harm. Overall, if the defendant could not justify the choice to perpetuate a racial harm—in spite of available alternatives—with some governmental purpose that outweighs the racial harm, the defendant would be deliberately indifferent to inequality and subject to liability.

Of the three options, this final one—deliberate indifference—probably comes closest to reflecting current societal norms. A standard that required complete racial equality in federally funded programs goes further than many would accept. For them, fairness to defendants would require an opportunity for defendants to explain their actions and the burdens of promoting greater equality. Pure disparate impact ignores these concerns; modified disparate impact and deliberate indifference do not. Modified disparate impact, however, still focuses heavily on outcomes and has the capacity to discount defendants' intent, making it highly undesirable for those committed to traditional concepts of discrimination. Deliberate indifference, in contrast, may thread the needle between merely prohibiting traditional intentional discrimination and imposing robust racial equality. Deliberate indifference analysis is triggered by disparate results, but still requires an element of choice—something short of intentional discrimination—by the defendant to trigger liability. By couching liability in terms of choice, it accommodates some concerns about fairness to defendants, while, at the same, time requiring defendants to make racially equitable choices. After all, even the currently conservative Court has been willing to endorse versions of deliberate indifference liability in Title IX.

Conclusion

Equal protection and discrimination have always eluded easy definition. Thus, the key question for victims of discrimination and inequality is who gets to define the terms. With equal protection claims brought under the Fourteenth Amendment, the answer is that the Court decides (although there has been some disagreement on this point).[69] In the Civil Rights Act, Congress and, through delegated authority, agencies decide. Courts, of course, play a role in ensuring Congress's legislation was constitutionally permissible and agencies' interpretations of the legislation are reasonable. In recent decades, however, the Court appears to have resisted the interpretative authority of agencies and, instead, defined statutory discrimination the same as it has defined equal protection discrimination. By doing so, the Court has cut short remedies and rights that plaintiffs have enjoyed since Congress passed the Civil Rights Act and agencies enacted various implementing regulations. One of the most damaging decisions was the Court's holding in *Sandoval* that plaintiffs could not enforce Title VI disparate impact regulations through litigation.

Nothing short of a legislative amendment to the Civil Rights Act will salvage all that was lost in *Sandoval*, and a legislative amendment is implausible in the current political environment. Political environments, however, can change quickly. Just six years ago, amendments to the Civil Rights Act seemed immediately forthcoming. Regardless, other meaningful options remain immediately viable. Agencies can still enforce disparate impact regulations administratively. The vigorousness with which they enforce those regulations will necessarily be subject to external politics and changes in the presidency, but when predisposed, agencies have the capacity to place serious limits on racial inequality. Plaintiffs, under certain circumstances, may also find it possible to expand the meaning of intentional discrimination through litigation. Intent is no more of a fixed term than discrimination. The Court has been unwilling to permit claims alleging anything short of intentional discrimination, but it has proven willing to expand what it means by intentional discrimination.

As the 50th anniversary of the Civil Rights Act comes and goes, it is important that we not rest on its past success, but press forward with new strategies and reforms. The Civil Rights Act, even more than the initial decision in *Brown v. Board of Education*, drove the desegregation of schools and helped foster racial equality in various aspects of education, as well as other federally funded programs. Staggering racial disparities in discipline, academic achievement, and school assignment, however, reveal that far too much work is left undone. These continuing challenges, nonetheless, pale in comparison to the entrenched de jure segregation that the Act first confronted. Through reinvigorated litigation, administrative action, and legislation, the Act might finally complete the work it began some 50 years ago.

Derek W. Black is a Professor of Law at the University of South Carolina School of Law. This chapter is an original work, but draws heavily upon portions of three of the author's previously published articles: *A Framework for the Next Civil Rights Act: What Tort Concepts Reveal about Goals, Results, and Standards*, 60 RUTGERS LAW REVIEW 259 (2008); *The Mysteriously Reappearing Cause of Action: The Court's Expanding Concept of Intentional Discrimination in Gender and Race Discrimination Statutes*, 67 MARYLAND LAW REVIEW 358 (2008); and *The Contradiction Between Equal Protection's Meaning and Its Legal Substance: How Deliberate Indifference Can Cure It*, 15 WILLIAM & MARY BILL OF RIGHTS JOURNAL 533 (2006).

NOTES

1. 347 U.S. 483 (1954).

2. See, for example, Erica Frankenberg, Chungmei Lee, & Gary Orfield, The Civil Rights Project, *A Multiracial Society with Segregated Schools: Are We Losing the Dream?* 37 (2003) (analyzing the increase in school segregation as a result of Supreme Court decisions).

3. Civil Rights Act of 1964, Public Law Number 88-352, 78 Stat. 241 (1964) (codified as amended at 42 United States Code §§ 2000a to 2000h-6 (2000)).

4. See, for example, Guardians Association v. Civil Service Commission, 463 U.S. 582 (1983); see also Powell v. Ridge, 189 F.3d 387, 399–400 (3d Cir. 1999); New York Urban League v. New York, 71 F.3d 1031, 1036 (2d Cir. 1995); Roberts v. Colorado State Board of Agriculture, 998 F.2d 824, 832 (10th Cir. 1993); United States v. Yonkers, Number. 80 Civ. 6761, 1995 Westlaw 358746, *5 (Southern District of New York June 14, 1995) (interpreting *Guardians* to create a private cause of action).

5. 42 U.S.C. §§ 2000d-1 (2000).

6. Alexander v. Sandoval, 532 US. 275, 285–86 (2001).

7. UNITED STATES CONSTITUTION, AMENDMENT XIV, § 5.

8. CHARLES FAIRMAN, RECONSTRUCTION AND REUNION 1864–88, 1278 (The Macmillan Co. 1971).

9. Ibid., 1281 (quoting Representative Giles W. Hotchkiss).

10. 42 United States Code § 2000d (2000).

11. Guardians, 436 U.S. 592 ("The language of Title VI on its face is ambiguous; the word 'discrimination' is inherently so"); ibid., 622–23 (Justice Marshall dissenting) ("The word 'discrimination' was nowhere defined in Title VI." Rather, "the antidiscrimination principle of § 601 of the Act '[w]as a general criterion to follow"); Regents of University of California v. Bakke, 438 U.S. 265, 337–38 (Justices Brennan, White, Marshall, & Blackmun, concurring in part and dissenting in part).

12. See generally, Charles F. Abernathy, *Title VI and the Constitution: A Regulatory Model for Defining "Discrimination,"* 70 GEORGETOWN LAW JOURNAL 1, 20–32 (revealing Congress's awareness of the ambiguity, uncertainty as to how to define it, and its ultimate "compromise" of delegating the issue to agencies).

13. 42 United States Code § 2000d-1, 1–402; Abernathy, *Title VI and the Constitution*, 3.

14. 414 U.S. 563 (1974).

15. 438 U.S. 265 (1978).

16. 463 U.S. 582 (1983).

17. 469 U.S. 287 (1985).

18. Justice Powell concluded that although discrimination "is susceptible of varying interpretations," Bakke, 438 U.S. 284, the legislative intent is "clear" that Title VI "proscribe[s] only those racial classifications that would violate the Equal Protection Clause or the Fifth Amendment," ibid., 287, which in his opinion were only those motivated by intentional discrimination. Brennan tied discrimination's meaning to the Constitution as well, but focused on the flexible and evolving meaning of discrimination, leaving room for the notion that Title VI and the Constitution could diverge. Ibid., 338–40 (Justices Brennan, White, Marshall & Blackmun, concurring in part and dissenting in part). Stevens concluded that Title VI contains "plain language" that produces a "crystal clear" ban on exclusion and answers the question before the Court. Ibid., 412, 418 (Justice Stevens, concurring in part and dissenting in part). Thus, although he recognizes discrimination was a contested term during the passage of the Act, his opinion suggests that he may not even agree that discrimination lacks an inherent meaning in the Act.

19. Sandoval, 532 U.S. 279 (2001).

20. Ibid., 278–79.

21. Ibid., 289.

22. Ibid.

23. Ibid., 281–82.

24. See generally, Derek W. Black, *The Mysteriously Reappearing Cause of Action: The Court's Expanded Concept of Intentional Gender and Race Discrimination in Federally Funded Programs*, 67 MARYLAND LAW REVIEW 358 (2008).

25. Jackson v. Birmingham, 544 U.S. 167, 177–78 (2005) (applying *Sandoval's* Title VI holding to Title IX); Grove City College v. Bell, 465 U.S. 555, 566 (1984) (noting that Title IX was patterned after Title VI); North Haven Board of Education v. Bell, 456 U.S. 512, 514

(1982) (same); Cannon v. University of Chicago. 441 U.S. 677, 694–99 (1979) (arguing that because the drafters of Title IX assumed it would be interpreted as Title VI had been, and because Title VI had been construed as creating a private remedy, Title IX also includes an implied private remedy).

26. 524 U.S. 274 (1998).

27. 526 U.S. 629 (1999).

28. 544 U.S. 167 (2005).

29. Gebser, 524 U.S. 283.

30. Ibid., 285 (quoting Guardians Association v. Civil Service Commission, 463 U.S. 582, 595 (1983)).

31. Ibid., 286 (quoting Cannon v. University of Chicago, 441 U.S. 677, 704 (1979)).

32. Ibid., 290.

33. Ibid.

34. Ibid., 291 (citing Board of Commissioners v. Brown, 520 U.S. 397 (1997); Collins v. Harker Heights, 503 U.S. 115, 123–24 (1992); Canton v. Harris, 489 U.S. 378, 388–92 (1989)).

35. Davis v. Monroe County Board of Education, 526 U.S. 629 (1999).

36. Jackson, 544 U.S. 167 (2005).

37. Ibid., 172.

38. Ibid., 175, 183 (noting that Title IX provides a cause of action that "encompass[es] diverse forms of intentional sex discrimination").

39. Ibid., 173–74.

40. Ibid., 174.

41. Ibid., 183.

42. Ibid., 180.

43. Ibid., 188–89 (Justice Thomas, dissenting).

44. Black, *The Mysteriously Reappearing Cause of Action.*

45. Jackson, 544 U.S. 180 (majority opinion) (quoting Cannon v. University of Chicago., 441 U.S. 677, 704 (1979)).

46. Ibid.

47. For example, prior to the Supreme Court's holding in *Jackson*, many lower courts dismissed claims of retaliation for a racially hostile environment because such claims did not clearly or explicitly demonstrate intentional discrimination. See, e.g., Bryant v. Independent School District, 334 F.3d 928, 929 (10th Cir. 2003) (restating the lower court's holding that "there is no private right of action under Title VI to remedy non-intentional forms of discrimination such as disparate impact and permitting the existence of a hostile environment"); Jackson v. Birmingham Board of Education, 309 F.3d 1333, 1347–48 (11th Cir. 2002), reversed, 544 U.S. 167 (2005) (holding that Title IX permits retaliation claims only from persons that have experienced intentional discrimination).

48. Even if a reasonable interpretation, the Court could declare disparate impact regulations unenforceable because Title VI's prohibition on intentional discrimination does not put states on clear notice of the potential of administrative enforcement based on disparate impact, which Spending Clause precedent requires. See generally, Terry Jean Seligmann, *Muddy Waters: The Supreme Court and the Clear Statement Rule for Spending Clause*

Legislation, 84 TULANE LAW REVIEW 1067 (2010).

49. 467 U.S. 837 (1984).

50. See also, United States v. Mead Corporation, 533 U.S. 218, 226–27 (2001) (qualifying but reaffirming Chevron).

51. 42 U.S.C. § 2000d (2000); 20 U.S.C. § 1681(a) (2000).

52. David J. Galalis, *Environmental Justice and Title VI in the Wake of* Alexander v. Sandoval: *Disparate-Impact Regulations Still Valid Under* Chevron, 31 BOSTON COLLEGE ENVIRONMENTAL AFFAIRS LAW REVIEW 61, 64–65 (2004) (noting speculations that the Sandoval decision would eliminate the ability to enforce agency regulations); Benjamin Labow, *Federal Courts:* Alexander v. Sandoval: *Civil Rights Without Remedies*, 56 OKLAHOMA LAW REVIEW 205, 230 (2003) (concluding if that were the issue before the Court it would likely hold the regulations themselves to be an invalid exercise of power).

53. Civil Rights Division, United States Department of Justice & Office for Civil Rights, United States. Department of Education, *Dear Colleague Letter: Nondiscriminatory Administration of School Discipline* (2014), http://www2.ed.gov/about/offices/list/ocr/letters/colleague-201401-title-vi.pdf.

54. Ibid., 11.

55. Ibid.

56. Ibid.

57. Ibid.

58. David Benjamin Oppenheimer, *Negligent Discrimination*, 141 UNIVERSITY OF PENNSYLVANIA LAW REVIEW 899, 969 (1993).

59. Civil Rights Act of 1991, Public Law Number 102-166, 105 Statute 1071 (codified as amended in scattered sections of 42 United States Code).

60. Congress explicitly indicated that its purpose for the Act was "to respond to recent decisions of the Supreme Court by expanding the scope of relevant civil rights statutes in order to provide adequate protection to victims of discrimination." Ibid., 1071. *See generally* Robert Belton, *Mixed-Motive Cases in Employment-Discrimination Law Revisited: A Brief Updated View of the Swamp*, 51 MERCER LAW REVIEW 651 (2000) (discussing the 1991 amendments and other changes in employment discrimination).

61. Civil Rights Restoration Act of 1987, Pub. L. No. 100-259, 102 Stat. 28 (1988). In *Grove City College v. Bell*, 465 U.S. 555 (1984), the Court had held that a plaintiff only had a cause of action if the specific program in which he faced discrimination had received federal funds. Ibid., 573–74. Thus, if the school received only federal funds for its special education program, and no other program, the school would have been free to discriminate against students in other programs. The Civil Rights Act of 1987 overturned this holding. See, for example, Leake v. Long Island Jewish Medical Center., 695 F. Supp. 1414, 1415–16 (E.D.N.Y. 1988).

62. 446 U.S. 55, 70 (1980). See Voting Rights Act of 1965, Public Law No. 91-285, § 2, 84 Stat. 314 (codified as amended at 42 U.S.C. § 1973 (1982)); see also, Thornburg v. Gingles, 478 U.S. 30 (1986) (discussing and applying the amendment).

63. Lilly Ledbetter Fair Pay Act, Public Law No. 111-2, 123 Stat. 5 (2009).

64. *Fairness and Individual Rights Necessary to Ensure a Stronger Society: Civil Rights Act of 2004*, House Resolution 3809, 108th Congress (2004), http://www.thomas.gov/cgi-bin/bdquery/z?d108:HR03809:@@CC@D&summ2=m&. In general, the bill would

"restore, reaffirm, and reconcile legal rights and remedies under [the varying] civil rights statutes." 150 Congress Record H514 (daily edition February 11, 2004). Specifically, it would amend the Civil Rights Act of 1964, the Education Amendments of 1972, and the Age Discrimination Act of 1975 to permit plaintiffs to establish discrimination based on disparate impact. In addition, the bill would amend the Uniformed Services Employment and Reemployment Act of 1967, and the Fair Labor Standards Act of 1938 to provide that a state's receipt or use of federal financial assistance for a state program or activity shall constitute a waiver of sovereign immunity to a suit under such Acts by a program employee. Finally, it would authorize civil actions in federal court for discrimination based on disability by amending the Air Carrier Access Act of 1986.

65. Civil Rights Act of 2008, Senate 2554, 110th Congress (2008).

66. See, for example, Massachusetts v. Feeney, 442 U.S. 256 (1979) ("'Discriminatory purpose,' however, implies more than intent as volition or intent as awareness of consequences.") (citation omitted).

67. For example, the tort of malicious prosecution requires a showing of specific motive. RESTATEMENT (SECOND) OF TORTS § 653 (1977). In products liability cases, however, motive is irrelevant; the primary inquiry is concerned with whether the burden of preventing the harm is less than the probability of harm resulting, multiplied by the gravity of the harm. See DAN B. DOBBS, THE LAW OF TORTS 340 (2000). In intentional torts, a plaintiff need only show that a defendant knew that there was a substantial certainty that his acts would bring about a result. Ibid., 48. With negligence, motive and specific intent are also of minimal importance. The key questions are whether harm was foreseeable and whether the likelihood and gravity of harm outweigh the cost of avoiding it. Ibid., 341.

68. See, for example, Shelby County, Alabama. v. Holder, 133 S. Ct. 2612, 2625 (2013) (positing that discrimination, at least as the Court understands it, is largely gone from the voting process).

69. Compare Katzenbach v. Morgan, 384 U.S. 641, 651 (1966) with City of Boerne v. Flores, 521 U.S. 507, 526–27 (1997).

PART II

Desegregation Unfolds

Milliken v. Bradley

418 U.S. 717 (1974)

Milliken v. Bradley
A Judicial Betrayal of *Brown*

WHILE I WAS SERVING AS COUNSEL TO THE KERNER COMMISSION IN 1968, AND shortly after I became the general counsel of the NAACP in 1969, the extent of the spread of Northern school segregation was becoming increasingly apparent. In particular, the officers of the Detroit branch of the NAACP were concerned by these patterns. I met with these officers, at their request, during the 1970 NAACP annual national convention to discuss developments in that city.

They informed me about recently signed legislation in Michigan (Act 48[1]), signed into law by Governor William Milliken, which virtually enjoined the Detroit school board from implementing a very modest desegregation plan that would have affected 10,000 white students out of a school system of about 300,000. This desegregation plan created a political firestorm. Additionally, the inferior quality of education that was being provided to black children was a cause of deep concern to the local NAACP officers. For example, Michigan law required that children be exposed to six hours of education a day, but in overcrowded schools black children were limited to just half that time. Rather than reassign the students in the overcrowded black schools into the adjacent white schools that had excess capacity, the state policy shortened the educational day for black children.

When I returned from the convention to my office in New York, I called a meeting of my legal team and the Detroit school board lawyers, who were interested in having the NAACP intervene. At the meeting, I concluded that the legislation was a clear case of interposition and nullification by the state because when the state passed Act 48, it halted the actions of the Detroit school board to comply with the command of *Brown*. That was tantamount to Governor George Wallace of Alabama standing in the schoolhouse door, and to Governor Orval Faubus of Arkansas interfering with the order of the district court to integrate Little Rock High School.

I made it clear to the Detroit school board lawyers that our strategy would have to include joining the Detroit school board as a defendant. That infuriated them and their lawyer. In fact, when the lawyer for the Detroit school board, George Bushnell Jr., who had been an ally of the NAACP, realized that his client would be a nominal defendant, he said: "I'll whip your asses in court." I responded, "You'll have to do that, because we have no choice but to join you as a party."

There were, however, two Sixth Circuit precedents that stood in our way. We decided that we would have to develop a strategy that would allow us to distinguish *Craggett v. Cleveland Board of Education*[2] and *Deal v. Cincinnati Board of Education*.[3] In those cases, the Sixth Circuit, in the 1960s, had held that the racial imbalance in schools that was being complained of by black plaintiffs did not result from state action, and without state action the federal courts had no jurisdiction.

We drafted our lawsuit to indicate that we could prove that the racial imbalance in Detroit's schools was a result of official action by the state of Michigan as well as by the Detroit school board. The initial reaction by the trial judge, Stephen Roth, was skeptical, if not hostile. He made it clear to us that he was a long-time resident of Michigan, had been the Attorney General of Michigan, knew the "good people" of Michigan, and that the allegations we made in that complaint with regard to the conduct of the officials in Detroit and in Michigan just could not be sustained. Therefore, he was not going to grant us any temporary relief. On appeal, the Sixth Circuit later did grant temporary relief, and took a different view of our complaint.

Eventually, Judge Roth became a convert. He made it very clear, as we proceeded on the merits, that he thought we could make our case. We had to show that discriminatory housing policies and school policies combined to form a nexus. For instance, we offered proof of restrictive housing covenants and their effect in maintaining segregated owner-occupied neighborhoods in Detroit. Additionally, we offered proof of public housing policies that ensured when public housing was constructed in Detroit, it was constructed on a segregated basis, and that the school board accommodated the practice by committing to build schools where the housing authorities were planning to put the segregated housing. Without such a commitment from the school board, the public housing would not have been built.

Furthermore, the policies of the real estate industry, the banking industry, and the FHA had all worked together to create and maintain residential segregation.

We also developed a huge map of Detroit as an exhibit in the case, which Judge Roth allowed us to post on a wall in the courtroom. It had overlays of every five years, which showed racial population shifts, student assignment changes, and transfer policies of the Detroit school board. As the black citizens of Detroit were being moved around the city through discriminatory housing policies, the school boundary lines also shifted. It was irrefutable that the student assignment policies had a racial motive.

Judge Roth made specific findings on the interaction that occurred between school officials, housing officials, and banking officials to create the racial isolation that existed in schools. The Sixth Circuit's decisions in the *Deal* and *Craggett* cases in the 1960s had held that the policies of housing were separate and apart from school policies—that school officials had no control over what the housing industry did. We proved that there was a connection. Our evidence tied them together, showing the interrelationship between the housing industry and the policies of the school board. That was sufficient for Judge Roth, and for the Sixth Circuit. But, unfortunately, the Sixth Circuit did not include that as a factor in its affirmance of the district court holding that there were enough other segregative acts by the state and Detroit officials to establish their culpability.[4]

After Judge Roth made his findings with regard to the intentional acts that provided jurisdiction to the federal courts, we then proceeded to have hearings on the remedy. After taking considerable testimony, Judge Roth concluded that a remedy limited to the political boundaries of Detroit would not last very long because of the massive nature of the constitutional violations he identified. The evidence showed that the state of Michigan, through the application of its policies or the failure to enforce its proclaimed non-discrimination policies, was a participant in creating segregation and isolation in Detroit. Therefore, as a joint tortfeasor, the state could be required by the Court to participate in the remedy. When Judge Roth made his finding, he directed the state of Michigan to join with the Detroit school district in formulating a desegregation plan. He didn't say what the plan should be, but he indicated that the plan should not be hemmed in by the political boundaries between Detroit and the various suburban communities. That was where things stood at the time an appeal was taken to the United States Supreme Court.

The issue placed before the Supreme Court was: Could the suburban districts be required to participate in a remedy, of a two-way nature, that would have students in suburban schools being assigned to some schools in Detroit and some children in Detroit being assigned to some schools in the suburbs? As Professor Joyce Baugh's book *The Detroit School Busing Case:* Milliken v. Bradley *and the Controversy over*

Desegregation suggests, neither Justice Potter Stewart nor Chief Justice Burger could bring themselves to affirm a plan that was going to disturb suburban white children.[5] Thus, what the Supreme Court did was ignore the fact that the state of Michigan was the parent of education. Local school districts were sub-units of the state, created by the state. In fact, we offered evidence that in one fell swoop, the state had dissolved some 300 school districts without the consent of the affected citizens—an action that was consistent with the state's power. So, we argued, the state had the power to participate in a remedy that would realign student attendance policies so as to enhance desegregation. Ultimately, this argument was unsuccessful.

The significance of the case to me has only grown since the time it was litigated. I knew then that we had the ability to break the back of urban segregation. We had devised a means by which, if the precedents established in the South were followed in the Northern cases, we could achieve a significant reformation of Northern and urban conditions. In the 1973 decision of the Sixth Circuit that was appealed to the Supreme Court, the Honorable George Edwards, then the Chief Judge of the Sixth Circuit, wrote an opinion that stated: "The instant case calls up haunting memories of the now long overruled and discredited separate but equal doctrine of *Plessy v. Ferguson*. If we hold that school district boundaries are absolute barriers to a Detroit school desegregation plan, we would be opening a way to nullify *Brown v. Board of Education*, which overruled *Plessy*."[6] But when the Supreme Court issued its first decision in *Milliken* in 1974, the Court rejected and abandoned the precedents it had established in the Southern cases.[7] It retreated from *Brown*.

If we look at the condition of education today in urban America, we see that Judge Edwards was absolutely right. If one more justice had followed the Court's clearly established precedents, the educational landscape of this country would be dramatically different, all to the good of America and its children.

Nathaniel R. Jones is Of Counsel at Blank Rome LLP, a retired judge on the U.S. Court of Appeals, Sixth Circuit, and the former general counsel of the NAACP.

NOTES

1. Act approved July 7, 1970, 1970 Michigan Public Acts 136 (repealed by Act of January 13, 1977, 1976 Michigan Public Acts 1541).

2. Craggett v. Cleveland Board of Education, 338 F.2d 941 (6th Cir. 1964).

3. Deal v. Cincinnati Board of Education, 369 F.2d 55 (6th Cir. 1966), certiorari denied 389 U.S. 847 (1967), appeal after 1966 decision remanded to the district court, 419 F.2d 1387

(6th Cir. 1969), certiorari denied 402 U.S. 962 (1971).

4. Bradley v. Milliken, 338 F. Supp. 582 (E.D. Mich. 1971); Bradley v. Milliken, 345 F. Supp. 914 (E.D. Mich. 1972). Both district court opinions were affirmed by *Bradley v. Milliken* 484 F.2d 215 (6th Cir. 1973), which was reversed and remanded by *Milliken v. Bradley* 418 U.S. 717 (1974).

5. JOYCE A. BAUGH, THE DETROIT SCHOOL BUSING CASE: *MILLIKEN V. BRADLEY* AND THE CONTROVERSY OVER DESEGREGATION (University Press of Kansas 2011).

6. Bradley v. Milliken, 484 F.2d 215, 249 (6th Cir. 1973).

7. Milliken v. Bradley, 418 U.S. 717 (1974).

JOYCE A. BAUGH

School Desegregation in Metropolitan Detroit

Struggling for Justice in a Divided and Troubled Community

I have a dream this afternoon, that one day, right here in Detroit, Negroes will be able to buy a house or rent a house anywhere that their money will carry them, and they will be able to get a job.

—Dr. Martin Luther King Jr., June 23, 1963

DR. MARTIN LUTHER KING JR. UTTERED THESE WORDS TO A LARGE CROWD gathered in Detroit, Michigan on June 23, 1963, two months before his famous "I Have a Dream" speech at the March on Washington. Dr. King, along with Mayor Jerome Cavanagh, had just led a march of 125,000 strong up Woodward Avenue to a rally at Cobo Hall. But why was Dr. King leading a civil rights march in Detroit, a Northern city; and what led him to make these remarks?

Despite the fact that Jim Crow laws (de jure segregation) that existed in the South were not present in Detroit in 1963, Detroit, like other Northern cities, was as tightly segregated as its Southern counterparts. The causes and manifestations, however, were different. As Alan Anderson and George Pickering noted in *Confronting the Color Line: The Broken Promise of the Civil Rights Movement in Chicago*, "In the

North, the issues were different. Legally mandated segregation and discrimination had been mostly eliminated by midcentury, but the color line continued in the form of segregated and inferior schools and housing for blacks and in black poverty and unemployment. This 'de facto' segregation was not legally mandated, but many of its major causes were legally sanctioned."[1] Legal scholars and commentators have distinguished between de jure and de facto segregation, but Anderson maintains that this is a distinction without a difference because of the role played by public officials in creating and preserving both housing and school segregation in northern communities.

Milliken v. Bradley (1974)[2] arose after civil rights activists turned their attention to the "metropolitan color line" in the North following their efforts to eradicate Jim Crow segregation and disenfranchisement in the South. This color line, reflected particularly in segregated housing and segregated schools, illustrated longstanding conflicts both within central cities and between cities and suburbs. The attempt to desegregate schools in the Detroit metropolitan area in the early 1970s occurred as the city was mired in economic and racial strife, and as politics at the local, state, and especially national levels became increasingly conservative. This chapter focuses first on the mechanisms that created and have maintained residential segregation in metropolitan areas, with special attention to the city of Detroit and its suburbs. The emphasis then shifts to discussions about school segregation in Detroit, the city's economic decline, school reform and integration efforts, and the conservative political climate.

Racially Segregated Housing

Reynolds Farley and Walter R. Allen, Douglas S. Massey and Nancy A. Denton, and Thomas Sugrue provide valuable insights into the development of residential segregation in the United States, including Detroit.[3] As table 1 illustrates, the turning point was the first Great Migration, from about 1910 to 1930, when large numbers of black migrants first arrived in northern cities.

There was considerable hostility in the North to black migration, including the frequent use of terms such as "nigger" and "darky" in Northern newspapers, the regularity of stories about black crime and vice, and an upsurge in racial violence.[4]

After a drop-off in black migration during the Great Depression, the black population in Northern cities increased dramatically between 1940 and 1970 due to increased black migration and white flight to the suburbs, as illustrated in table 2.

As black residents tried to move into all-white neighborhoods, several interlocking mechanisms kept them out.

Table 1. Migration of Southern Blacks to Northern Cities, 1870–1970

1870–1880	71,000	1920–1930	877,000
1880–1890	80,000	1930–1940	398,000
1890–1900	174,000	1940–1950	1,468,000
1900–1910	197,000	1950–1960	1,473,000
1910–1920	525,000	1960–1970	1,380,000

Source: U.S. Census Bureau

Table 2. Change in Black Population Percentages in Several Northern Cities, 1950–1970

	1950	1970		1950	1970
Chicago	14	33	Detroit	16	44
Cleveland	16	38	Philadelphia	18	34

Source: U.S. Census Bureau

RESTRICTIVE COVENANTS

After the United States Supreme Court struck down local segregation ordinances in its 1917 decision in *Buchanan v. Warley*,[5] restrictive covenants became an important tool for ensuring residential segregation. These covenants are private contractual agreements among property owners, specifying that the buyer and seller may not sell or lease property to blacks and sometimes other groups, such as Jews or Catholics, for a designated period of time. Provisions in the covenants called for enforcement by courts if they were violated. When the Supreme Court first reviewed the constitutionality of restrictive covenants in *Corrigan v. Buckley* (1926), the high court refused to hold that they violated the Fourteenth Amendment, concluding that private individuals were not prohibited from entering into contracts "in respect to the control and disposition of their own property."[6]

The issue of restrictive covenants returned to the Supreme Court in 1948, in *Shelley v. Kraemer* and *McGhee v. Sipes*, companion cases from St. Louis, Missouri, and Detroit, respectively.[7] The justices did not invalidate the covenants themselves but instead ruled that *state enforcement* of race-specific restrictive covenants violated the Fourteenth Amendment's Equal Protection Clause. The ruling did not mean the end of this practice, however, as properties in white communities continued to be covered by restrictive covenants. In fact, for two years after *Shelley*, the federal government, which aided in the development of suburbs in the 1940s and 1950s, actually advocated that these agreements be honored in the appraisal process. And real estate agents who violated racial covenants and other discriminatory practices that were supported by their national and local boards faced the wrath of white customers and other agents.[8]

HOLC RATING SYSTEM AND RESIDENTIAL SECURITY MAPS

Policies instituted by the federal government, in conjunction with private sector practices, have helped to create and maintain racially segregated housing in cities and suburbs.[9] For example, in 1933 the Home Owners' Loan Corporation (HOLC) was created to provide mortgage assistance to homeowners who were facing foreclosure during the Great Depression. The program was operated in a racialized way, in accordance with the rating system established by HOLC for determining loan risks. The system designated four categories of neighborhood quality, with these letter and color codes:

- First Category A Green
- Second Category B Blue
- Third Category C Yellow
- Fourth Category D Red

Most loans went to the top two categories, while the bottom two received the fewest. The HOLC system "undervalued older central city neighborhoods that were racially or ethnically mixed,"[10] and every neighborhood with black residents, no matter how few, was coded red. HOLC ratings covered every block in the city, and this information was used to prepare color-coded "Residential Security Maps." This marked the origin of the term and practice called "redlining."

But the greatest impact of the HOLC mortgage program was its use by private banks and public sector loan programs. The HOLC system was institutionalized in the loan programs of the Federal Housing Administration (FHA), established in 1937, and in the Veterans Administration programs, authorized in the G.I. Bill. These two programs are now recognized as major forces that drove suburbanization in the United States. The FHA and VA housing initiatives generally favored suburban development and—because they were based on the HOLC rating system—they encouraged racial segregation. The FHA provided substantial loans for the construction of new homes in the suburbs, but not for purchasing or remodeling homes in the inner city.

The 1939 FHA *Underwriting Manual* also promoted residential segregation. It contained this language: "If a neighborhood is to retain stability, it is necessary that properties shall continue to be occupied by the same social and racial classes."[11] Finally, private builders and developers, relying on the availability of FHA and VA loans for prospective home buyers, complied with these racially restrictive practices.

HIGHWAY DEVELOPMENT AND URBAN RENEWAL POLICIES

Charles M. Lamb explains how federal policies regarding highway development and urban renewal also contributed to the color line in housing, both urban and suburban.[12] The interstate highway system that began during the Eisenhower admin- istration (1953–1961), along with the dramatic expansion of automobile use in the 1960s, made it possible for white suburbanites to commute to downtown areas for work or recreation while maintaining racially exclusive communities in the suburbs. In addition, some of these federally funded highway projects removed minorities from certain neighborhoods and segregated them elsewhere. As a result of federal and local highway projects in the late 1940s and 1950s, densely populated black neighborhoods in Detroit were destroyed to make room for the Chrysler, Lodge, and Ford freeways, without providing sufficient alternative housing for the displaced residents. Also devastating to black neighborhoods were urban renewal programs in the 1950s and 1960s, which condemned large areas of Detroit inhabited by poor and working-class blacks to make room for private development of middle-class housing. Like the highway projects, these "slum clearance" programs razed "blighted areas" without providing the residents with alternative places to live.[13]

PUBLIC HOUSING

The primary means for addressing the displacement problem became the construc- tion of public housing developments, but this proved to be contentious. Even before the urban renewal projects of the 1950s and 1960s, there was significant conflict over using public housing developments as a means of dealing with housing shortages. President Roosevelt's New Deal programs provided federal assistance for building low-income housing but left program implementation to local officials, who generally maintained racial segregation in the developments.

In Detroit, working- and middle-class whites were able to beat back efforts to build public housing in their neighborhoods, as were all-white or nearly all-white suburban communities. In the 1940s, the city of Dearborn, and its long-time mayor Orville Hubbard, epitomized the hostility to public housing in suburban Detroit. Although a major Ford plant that employed a significant number of black workers during World War II was located in Dearborn, black workers did not live there. When federal officials proposed a project to house these workers, Dearborn officials vehemently protested. In 1944, the city council passed an anti-public housing resolution, and Hubbard consistently pledged to keep Dearborn "lily white."

STEERING AND BLOCKBUSTING

Real estate agents practiced a policy of "steering" blacks and whites to separate neighborhoods strictly defined by race. The national association's Code of Ethics steering policy commanded that real estate agents "should never be instrumental in introducing into a neighborhood . . . members of any race or nationality, or any industry whose presence will be clearly detrimental to real estate values."[14] This policy, originally enacted in 1924, was amended slightly in 1950, but it had the same meaning. Blockbusting, another exclusionary tool, changed racial boundaries while simultaneously increasing profits for real estate brokers. After helping a black family move to an all-white neighborhood—thus "breaking" the block—brokers would create a panic among white homeowners, informing them that their property values would decrease. Subsequently, brokers would persuade them to sell their homes at lower prices and then would resell them to black buyers at higher prices. With blockbusting, the racial character of the neighborhood changed as well, as it shifted from all-white, to predominantly black, to all-black within a short period of time.[15]

NEIGHBORHOOD IMPROVEMENT ASSOCIATIONS/HOMEOWNERS' ASSOCIATIONS

Another important element in maintaining racially segregated communities in Northern cities was the creation of neighborhood "improvement associations."[16] In Detroit, these were also known as civic associations, protective associations, and homeowners' associations. The ones in Detroit were not initially created for the purpose of racial exclusion; but for working-class whites who became homeowners, the issues of race and housing became interconnected. Blacks who moved into formerly all-white neighborhoods faced harassment, mass demonstrations, picketing, effigy-burning, window-breaking, arson, vandalism, and physical attacks. These attacks peaked between 1953 and 1957 and again in the early 1960s, and were organized and widespread.

The homeowners' groups had a strong influence on local politics. They were key to the election of Albert Cobo, a Republican, as mayor, in a Democratic, pro-union city. The groups were successful in getting a Homeowners' Rights Ordinance placed on the ballot in 1964, which was meant to preserve their right to segregated housing and to discriminate in real estate sales. This effort was a tremendous success, as voters approved the proposal by a margin of 55–45%, but the Wayne County District Court declared the ordinance unconstitutional, and it never was implemented.

According to Massey and Denton, "The most salient feature of postwar segregation is the concentration of blacks in central cities and whites in suburbs."[17] Population figures from 1970, the year that *Milliken* began, bear this out. Dearborn, Warren, and Livonia were the three largest Detroit suburbs. Of 400,000 residents in these three communities, only 186 were black—13 in Dearborn, 41 in Livonia, and 132 in Warren. In addition, for the other 24 suburbs with populations of 35,000 or more, in all but two—Inkster and Highland Park—the black population was less than 3%; most had fewer than 1%. As noted earlier, FHA and VA housing initiatives contributed significantly to this. Real estate agents worked with the officials of suburban governments and school systems to convey the message that black homeowners or renters were not welcome in Detroit's suburbs. Racial violence was not as prevalent in the suburbs as it was in the city because public policies and real estate practices, municipal boundaries that kept services contained within each suburban community, and the refusal of suburban governments to participate in regional/metropolitan government projects made violent attacks less necessary.

School Segregation and Economic Decline in Detroit

At the time of the 1954 ruling in *Brown v. Board of Education*,[18] racial segregation in public education was as widespread in the North as in the South, although this received little to no attention. Davison Douglas's pathbreaking book sheds important light on this subject.[19] He chronicles conflicts over school segregation in states and territories in the Northeast, Midwest, and West, from before the Civil War until 1954. Douglas describes statutes and court decisions that explicitly required or permitted segregation in public schools in these non-Southern states, as well as the roles of school board policies and rigid residential segregation in maintaining racially segregated schools after statutes had been repealed.

In the mid-nineteenth century, Detroit school officials initially refused to provide public education for black children at all, but they finally succumbed to pressure and created separate schooling for them.[20] A Michigan Supreme Court decision (*People ex rel. Workman v. Board of Education of Detroit* 1869),[21] along with continued pressure from the black community and its white allies, finally led to a change in board policy. Jeffrey Mirel reports that for the last three decades of the 1800s, Detroit's public schools remained integrated.[22] In fact, the city's schools were still integrated as late as 1922. But by the mid-1930s, the school system was becoming resegregated as a result of changing housing patterns, especially because of restrictive covenants and the other factors described earlier. In addition, however, the school board itself initiated resegregation policies that began in the 1930s and continued into the 1960s.

For example, in 1933 the board transformed Sidney D. Miller Intermediate School into a high school, changing its role as a feeder school for Eastern High. Eastern was integrated and, like other high schools in the city, was experiencing severe overcrowding. In addition to changing Miller to a high school, the board adopted a policy permitting students in the Miller attendance area to transfer to other schools. The Miller attendance zone was overwhelmingly black, so this resulted in the transfer of the few white students remaining there to other schools. Mirel emphasizes the significance of race in the board decisions, noting that "despite the severe overcrowding of all the high schools in the city in the 1930s, no other intermediate schools were elevated to senior high status and, with the exception of Western High School (which was rebuilt after a fire in 1936), no new high schools were constructed during this period. In short, the creation of Miller High School was a clear case of deliberate school segregation."[23]

Detroit's African American community had additional concerns about the school system, including a paucity of black teachers and curriculum issues. From the 1930s to 1950s, the black community, in alliance with the Detroit Federation of Teachers (DFT) and the United Auto Workers Union (UAW), continued its fight to reform the system, especially with respect to increasing the number of black teachers and counselors and improving the curriculum for black students. This liberal-labor-black coalition, although not unified on all issues, succeeded in getting several of its favored candidates elected to the school board in the late 1940s and 1950s, including the first black elected official in Detroit, Dr. Remus Robinson, a prominent local surgeon. The alliance also worked on school funding issues and sought to influence personnel decisions made by the school board. By 1960, the coalition had made considerable progress on personnel and curriculum matters, but not on the matter of segregation. In fact, beginning in the 1950s, the school board created optional attendance zones in neighborhoods that were experiencing racial transition, thus allowing white students to flee predominantly black schools. Other board policies helped to establish or maintain segregation. These included gerrymandering of attendance lines, racialized feeder patterns (the assignment of elementary school attendance zones for junior high schools and junior high attendance zones to high schools), school transportation policies, and school construction decisions, including the selection of sites for new schools.

In the midst of these developments in the 1950s and early 1960s, the Detroit school system was experiencing major financial shortfalls. Defeats of school millage renewals/increases and bond proposals, along with a significant cut in the school allocation from the County Tax Allocation Board and decreases in revenue from property assessments, created ongoing financial crises. Indeed, the difficulties faced by the public school system were part of the larger social and economic changes in the metropolitan area that had begun years earlier.

In the early 1940s, Detroit had been the center of military production for the World War II effort. Auto companies and other manufacturers produced military hardware, airplanes, tanks, and other vehicles, and thus created thousands of good-paying as well as entry-level manufacturing jobs. Sugrue notes, "Almost overnight, Detroit had gone from one of the most depressed urban areas in the country to a boomtown, a magnet that attracted workers from all over the United States. . . . Between 1940 and 1943, the number of unemployed workers in Detroit fell from 135,000 to a mere 4,000."[24]

By the early 1950s, however, the local economy had undergone a major restructuring, ushering in a long period of economic decline, and with it the loss of thousands and thousands of good-paying and especially entry-level manufacturing jobs. The latter had provided both whites and blacks who had little education and fewer skills an opportunity to move up the economic ladder. According to census figures, the number of manufacturing jobs declined from 338,400 in 1947 to just 204,400 in 1958—a drop of nearly 40%. The elimination of manufacturing jobs, combined with persistent employment discrimination, was particularly devastating to Detroit's black residents. Worker layoffs, relocations, and dismissals had a ripple effect on the local economy. Local businesses closed, and the city began filling with abandoned storefronts and restaurants, burned-out homes, and vacant lots. Working-class and middle-class whites who had adequate resources and skills relocated to the suburbs, taking those resources with them. The white population in suburban Detroit grew from 732,000 in 1940 to 1,106,000 in 1950 and to 2,015,000 in 1960. Due to white flight in the 1950s, along with white resistance to blacks moving to the suburbs, Detroit became "poorer and blacker," characterized by fiscal distress due to disinvestment and the departure of much of its tax base.

Sugrue cites several factors as responsible for the economic restructuring of Detroit after World War II, with automation in the automobile, auto parts, and machine tool industries as the "most important force."[25] With the institution of automated assembly lines, manufacturers were able to increase productivity and reduce their labor costs. This had an especially significant impact on Detroit-area workers because so many of the most labor-intensive production jobs were located in Detroit area plants. In addition, independent automobile manufacturers as well as parts suppliers were driven out of business by the heavy automation used by General Motors (GM) and Ford. Even small companies not affected by automation left Detroit and relocated to areas where they could hire cheap, nonunion labor.

Plant location decisions by the "Big Three" automobile manufacturers—Ford, GM, and Chrysler—also contributed to Detroit's economic decline. During the 1940s and 1950s, they closed, downsized, and relocated numerous plants. More than 20 new plants were built in the Detroit suburbs, and new facilities were built in small- and medium-sized cities in other states. As a result, other auto-related companies also left the city: machine tool companies, metalworking companies, and parts manufacturers.

According to Sugrue, Detroit's industrial job loss also can be attributed to federal government policies during World War II and the postwar period. Some military projects were established in suburban areas, and tank and tank engine production was shifted to cities outside of Michigan, including New Orleans, Chicago, and Cleveland. By the early 1950s, members of Congress from Sunbelt states were successful in directing extensive military spending to their communities, away from states in the Northeast and Midwest.

Also contributing to the economic difficulties were complaints by business owners about taxes. Despite the city's failure to increase property taxes for a ten-year period between 1948 and 1958, corporate executives used threats of leaving the city to extract favorable changes in tax laws. At the same time, Detroit officials were faced with an aging infrastructure, an expensive social-welfare program, and an increasing number of indigent residents—many of whom were black—without sufficient tax revenue to meet these needs. In this climate, Detroit lost out to small towns and rural areas in neighboring states that could offer lower tax rates.

Community Control, Integration, and Act 48

Consequently, reformers faced serious headwinds as they continued efforts to reform the school system and end segregation. The year 1965 proved to be a major turning point, as candidates supported by the liberal-labor-black coalition gained control of the school board. In two years, the board increased the number of African American school administrators and teachers, adopted a more multicultural curriculum, and hired a new superintendent, Norman Drachler, who was committed to integration. At the same time that Drachler and the board were pushing for integration, however, another segment of the black community, led by Reverend Albert Cleage, called instead for "community control" of black schools as the only way to improve them. According to Cleage, the school system was deliberately miseducating black children and this would not end until black teachers and administrators were in charge of black schools. Cleage and his community control advocates found two allies in the Michigan House of Representatives, James Del Rio (a black Democrat) and Jack Faxon (a white Democrat), who each introduced bills on the subject in 1968. These bills did not attract much support, but others in the community, including the Detroit branch of the NAACP, appeared receptive to some level of decentralization of the school system, although not "community control" as espoused by Cleage and his allies.

Subsequently, in 1969, Coleman Young, who later became Detroit's first black mayor, introduced a decentralization bill in the state senate. Young's bill divided the city into several regions, each with its own governing board, and maintained the central city board with authority to adopt guidelines for the regional boards to follow. As Young's bill was debated in the legislature, Abraham Zwerdling, school board chair, looked for a way to promote integration, even while accepting that some level of decentralization was inevitable.

Young's bill, which became Public Act 244, was passed by the state house and senate and signed into law by Governor William Milliken in August 1969.[26] As a result, the school board was forced to develop a decentralization plan, the first task being to determine the regional boundaries. The board held a series of public hearings on this issue. The community control advocates argued for establishing regional boundaries that would ensure black control of black schools, while many white Detroiters advocated drawing the boundaries along existing administrative lines. This scenario, along with neighborhood schools, would preserve racial segregation in the school system. After the hearings, early in 1970, Zwerdling encouraged his Board colleagues to create integrated regions that could be the basis for future integration of the schools. At this point, the Board was split into three groups: four pro-integration liberals, two anti-integration conservatives, and one community control advocate.

Superintendent Drachler, as directed by Zwerdling, drafted a modest two-way integration plan that would significantly change the racial composition of 11 of the city's 22 high schools, and a substantial number of black students would be assigned to the three remaining schools that were predominantly white. This would be the first attempt in the district's history at two-way integration. At its meeting on April 7, 1970, in a chaotic atmosphere, the board heard statements about the plan from supporters and opponents before voting to approve it by a 4–2 vote. Several days later, a white citizens group initiated a campaign to recall the four members who supported what became known as the April 7 plan.

The state legislature also rejected the school board's "decentralization with integration" plan, albeit through different approaches. Again, Senator Coleman Young stepped in to find a compromise. He was concerned that some legislators wanted to pass an anti-integration law, but he was also upset with the school board for what he termed a "chicken-shit integration plan."[27] He worked with legislative leaders in the house and senate on a bill that preserved decentralization but that also repealed the April 7 plan. The new law, Act 48, also included an "open enrollment"

provision permitting white students left in neighborhood schools that were changing from white to black to transfer out of the black schools. Act 48 was signed into
law by Governor Milliken on July 7, 1970.[28] In addition, although the law contained
provisions shortening the terms of the pro-integration school board members with
the understanding that the citizens group would stop the recall effort, the group
went back on its word. On August 4, the Detroit school board experienced the first
successful recall effort in its 128-year history.

Following the passage of Act 48, local and national NAACP officials and
attorneys engaged in behind-the-scenes negotiations with Detroit school officials
to coordinate a response. After a series of talks, NAACP officials determined that
a coordinated strategy would not be successful because the recall and subsequent
election left the school board without any members who would promote integration.
Consultations between local and national NAACP leaders, therefore, resulted in a
comprehensive suit challenging school segregation citywide.

Racial Uprising and Conservative Politics

Two additional factors are important in setting the context for the *Milliken* case: the
1967 racial uprising and the rise of conservatism in local, state, and national politics.
Detroit had escaped the kind of disorder that swept through Harlem in 1964 and
the Watts area of Los Angeles in 1965, and, for a variety of reasons—in spite of its
economic, political, social, and racial problems—it was thought to be immune from
a major race riot. It was the only city in the nation at the time with more than one
African American member of the United States House of Representatives (John
Conyers and Charles Diggs). In 1966, *Look* magazine and the National Municipal
League named Detroit an All-America city, and Jerome Cavanagh, who was elected
mayor in 1962 with strong support from black voters, was successful in bringing
in millions of dollars in federal funding for local programs. Cavanagh also worked
to integrate the predominantly white police force, which had been a longstanding
source of tension and hostility in the black community. Furthermore, despite the
problems of economic decline and workplace discrimination, some black Detroiters
managed to obtain relatively secure, good-paying jobs and were able to purchase
their own homes, albeit on a segregated basis. In addition, Detroit was a center
of civil rights activism in the early 1960s. The Detroit branch of the NAACP, with
20,000 members, was the largest in the country. The Detroit Council for Human
Rights organized the successful freedom march in June of 1963 described at the
beginning of this chapter. At the time, it was the largest rally on behalf of civil rights
in the nation's history.

These outward appearances, however, masked reality. As noted earlier, much of the city's federal funding was devoted to urban renewal and highway projects, programs that destroyed black neighborhoods and displaced black residents. As a result, frustration and anger built in the black community. The 1967 "riot" began after the Detroit police raided a "blind pig," an illegal after-hours nightclub, in one of the city's largest black neighborhoods in the wee hours of a Sunday morning in July. Tempers flared, and before long, fires, looting, and vandalism rocked a six-block area of the city. Over a five-day period, the police arrested over 7,200 people, 43 individuals (33 blacks and 10 whites) were killed, and property damage was in the millions. The violence caught many Detroit residents off guard; for others, however, the rebellion was not only unsurprising but in many respects was predictable. In an interview for the *Eyes on the Prize* television documentary series, Ron Scott, a black Detroiter described the situation this way: "Inside of most black people there was a time bomb. There was a pot that was about to overflow, and there was rage that was about to come out. And the rebellion just provided an opportunity for that. I mean, why else would people get upset, cops raiding a blind pig. They'd done that numerous times before. But people just got tired of it. And it just exploded."[29] The Kerner Commission's report on civil disorder in the cities affirmed Scott's observation. "Many grievances in the Negro community result from the discrimination, prejudice and powerlessness which Negroes often experience. They also result from the severely disadvantaged social and economic conditions of many Negroes as compared with those of whites in the same city and, *more particularly, in the predominantly white suburbs.*"[30] Whatever the origins, the uprising only hardened racial lines between blacks and whites in the city and between Detroit blacks and white suburbanites.

Civil rights activities directed at the metropolitan color line, along with these urban uprisings in the mid-to-late 1960s, contributed to a backlash among whites. In 1966, during a march for open housing in Chicago, Dr. King and other civil rights activists were met by an angry mob of 5,000 whites, some of them holding up swastikas while others threw bricks and set off cherry bombs. In addition, Richard Nixon was elected president in 1968 (and reelected in 1972) based in significant measure on his opposition to federal enforcement of civil rights laws. This was different from his 1960 presidential campaign, which Edward Carmines and James Stimson assert "was still part of the racially progressive tradition of the Republican Party."[31] By contrast, Charles Lamb notes that by 1968, although his campaign was repudiating discrimination and racism, "Nixon was promising whites that his administration would not forcefully push for desegregation, that busing to achieve a racial balance in public schools was out of the question, and that he was opposed to federal intervention in local education."[32] His public shift was partly a reaction to the success that George Wallace, Alabama's prosegregation governor, was having in his third-party bid for the presidency. Conservative racial politics was also seen at the local level. Throughout the mid-1960s, white homeowners' groups exerted considerable influence on local and state politics. Sugrue reports that they "pressured local politicians to oppose civil rights legislation. Their votes played a crucial role in the defeat of Michigan's Democratic governor, G. Mennen Williams, in 1966, and in the defeat of local referenda to raise taxes to pay for Detroit's increasingly African American public schools."[33] And they provided significant support to George Wallace in his 1968 (and 1972) presidential campaign. (Wallace won the 1972 Michigan Democratic primary.)

Conclusion

It is in this context that *Milliken* arises. Rigid housing segregation defined the entire Detroit metropolitan area, city and suburbs. Black and white neighborhoods were created and maintained through discriminatory policies and practices of realtors and banks, as well as those of the federal and local governments. These included restrictive covenants, redlining, highway development and urban renewal programs, the placement of public housing, steering, blockbusting, and suburban resistance to integrated housing. Detroit school officials maintained racially segregated schools by utilizing optional attendance zones, gerrymandered attendance lines, and racialized feeder patterns, and by their decisions regarding school transportation and construction.

After becoming a boomtown in the early 1940s during World War II, the city suffered from severe economic distress in the decades that followed. The manufacturing sector, the lifeblood of Detroit's economy, lost thousands upon thousands of jobs due to automation, the relocation of auto plants and related industries to the suburbs and to other states, and the shift of federal military contracts to other Midwest cities and Sunbelt states. These factors, along with the flight of working- and middle-class whites to the suburbs beginning in the 1950s, dramatically reduced the tax revenue available for city services, including public education. City schools were also harmed by the failure to pass important millages and bond proposals.

In the 1960s, as reformers in the black community and their allies worked toward improvements in curriculum and instruction and fought to integrate the schools, they faced resistance from other black leaders advocating for total "community control" of black schools. Adding fuel to the tense atmosphere was the 1967 racial uprising, which intensified the racial resentments and hostility between blacks and whites in the city and between Detroit blacks and white suburbanites. And the increasingly conservative politics at the local, state, and national levels reflected significant opposition to federal policies to integrate public schools, with the Nixon administration being particularly hostile to these efforts.

When *Milliken* reached the Supreme Court, President Nixon's four appointees—Warren Burger, Harry Blackmun, Lewis Powell, and William Rehnquist—were joined by Potter Stewart in striking down the multidistrict remedy ordered by U.S. District Judge Stephen Roth. Roth had concluded that the Detroit public schools were illegally segregated because of both housing segregation by the private and public sectors and de jure school segregation by the Detroit board and state officials. He ordered a metropolitan-wide remedy after concluding that, because of the racial demographics, a plan limited to the city schools would be ineffective. This was because by the time the case was filed, the Detroit school population was 70% black.

In July 1974, by a 5–4 vote, the high court held that before a metropolitan-wide remedy could be imposed for the segregation in Detroit schools, there must be evidence that the other school districts engaged in unconstitutionally racially discriminatory acts. Chief Justice Burger wrote, "The record before us, voluminous as it is, contains evidence of *de jure* segregated conditions only in the Detroit schools. . . . With no showing of significant violation by the 53 outlying school districts and no evidence of any interdistrict violation or effect, the court went beyond the original theory of the case."[34] The majority's ruling, in effect, ignored the rigid housing segregation that made specific discriminatory policies by suburban districts unnecessary.

Joyce A. Baugh is a Professor in the Department of Political Science at Central Michigan University. Some of the information contained in this chapter is from the author's book THE DETROIT SCHOOL BUSING CASE: *MILLIKEN V. BRADLEY* AND THE CONTROVERSY OVER DESEGREGATION, 24–25, 30–34, 38–42, 60 (2011). This copyrighted material is published with the permission of the University Press of Kansas. Some additional material appeared in Joyce A. Baugh, *A Wrong Without a Remedy:* Milliken v. Bradley *and the Controversy Over School Desegregation*, 18 THE COURT LEGACY 18 1 (November 2011).

NOTES

1. ALAN B. ANDERSON & GEORGE W. PICKERING, CONFRONTING THE COLOR LINE: THE BROKEN PROMISE OF THE CIVIL RIGHTS MOVEMENT IN CHICAGO, 2 (University of Georgia Press 1986).

2. Milliken v. Bradley, 418 U.S. 717 (1974).

3. REYNOLDS FARLEY & WALTER R. ALLEN, THE COLOR LINE AND THE QUALITY

OF LIFE IN AMERICA, Chapter 5 (Oxford University Press 1989); DOUGLAS S. MASSEY & NANCY A. DENTON, AMERICAN APARTHEID: SEGREGATION AND THE MAKING OF THE UNDERCLASS, Chapter 2 (Harvard University Press 1993); THOMAS SUGRUE, THE ORIGINS OF THE URBAN CRISIS: RACE AND INEQUALITY IN POSTWAR DETROIT, Chapters 2 and 3 (Princeton University Press 2005).

4. MASSEY & DENTON, AMERICAN APARTHEID, 30.

5. Buchanan v. Warley, 245 U.S. 60 (1917).

6. Corrigan v. Buckley, 271 U.S. 323, 331 (1926).

7. Shelley v. Kraemer, 334 U.S. 1 (1948); McGhee v. Sipes, 334 U.S. 1 (1948).

8. MASSEY & DENTON, AMERICAN APARTHEID; SUGRUE, THE ORIGINS OF THE URBAN CRISIS.

9. REYNOLDS FARLEY, SHELDON DANZIGER, & HARRY J. HOLZER, DETROIT DIVIDED (Russell Sage Foundation 2000); MASSEY & DENTON, AMERICAN APARTHEID.

10. MASSEY & DENTON, AMERICAN APARTHEID, 51.

11. Ibid., 54.

12. CHARLES M. LAMB, HOUSING SEGREGATION IN SUBURBAN AMERICA SINCE 1960: PRESIDENTIAL AND JUDICIAL POLITICS (Cambridge University Press 2005).

13. SUGRUE, THE ORIGINS OF THE URBAN CRISIS, 48.

14. ANDERSON & PICKERING, CONFRONTING THE COLOR LINE, 464.

15. FARLEY, DANZIGER, & HOLZER, DETROIT DIVIDED; SUGRUE, THE ORIGINS OF THE URBAN CRISIS.

16. MASSEY & DENTON, AMERICAN APARTHEID, 35.

17. Ibid., 67.

18. Brown v. Board of Education, 347 U.S. 483 (1954).

19. DAVISON M. DOUGLAS, JIM CROW MOVES NORTH: THE BATTLE OVER NORTHERN SCHOOL SEGREGATION, 1865–1954 (Cambridge University Press 2005).

20. DAVID M. KATZMAN, BEFORE THE GHETTO: BLACK DETROIT IN THE NINETEENTH CENTURY, Chapter 1 (University of Illinois Press 1973).

21. People ex rel. Workman v. Board of Education of Detroit, 18 Mich. 400 (Michigan Supreme Court 1869).

22. JEFFREY MIREL, THE RISE AND FALL OF AN URBAN SCHOOL SYSTEM: DETROIT, 1907–1981 (University of Michigan Press 1993).

23. Ibid., 188.

24. SUGRUE, THE ORIGINS OF THE URBAN CRISIS, 19.

25. Ibid., 130.

26. Act approved August 11, 1969, 1969 Michigan Public Acts 475 (amended and repealed in part by Act approved July 7, 1970, 1970 Michigan Public Acts 136).

27. JEFFREY MIREL, THE RISE AND FALL OF AN URBAN SCHOOL SYSTEM: DETROIT 1907–1981, 342 (University of Michigan Press 1993).

28. Act approved July 7, 1970, 1970 Michigan Public Acts 136 (repealed by Act of January 13, 1977, 1976 Michigan Public Acts 1541).

29. Quoted in HENRY HAMPTON & STEVE FAYER, VOICES OF FREEDOM: AN ORAL HISTORY OF THE CIVIL RIGHTS MOVEMENT FROM THE 1950s THROUGH THE 1980S, 376 (Bantam Books 1990).

30. THE REPORT OF THE NATIONAL ADVISORY COMMISSION ON CIVIL DISORDERS, 111 (Bantam Books 1968) (emphasis added).

31. EDWARD G. CARMINES & JAMES A. STIMSON, ISSUE EVOLUTION: RACE AND THE TRANSFORMATION OF AMERICAN POLITICS, 53 (Princeton University Press 1989).

32. LAMB, HOUSING SEGREGATION, 114.

33. SUGRUE, THE ORIGINS OF THE URBAN CRISIS, 265.

34. Milliken v. Bradley, 418 U.S. 717, 745 (1974).

CHARLES T. CLOTFELTER

Milliken and the Prospects for Racial Diversity in U.S. Public Schools

"IMPEACH EARL WARREN" SIGNS APPEARED IN THE SOUTH IN ANGRY REACTION to the Supreme Court's historic 1954 decision in *Brown*. But the era of muscular Court decisions attacking school segregation turned out to be a relatively brief interlude, lasting only two decades. Whereas *Swann v. Charlotte-Mecklenburg Board of Education* (1971)[1] might be considered the high water mark for judicial endorsement of proactive racial balance in public schools, the Court's decision in *Milliken v. Bradley* (1974)[2] marked the end of this era, and the beginning of judicial retreat.

In *Milliken* the Court drew a bright line, limiting subsequent segregation remedies, for all intents and purposes, to whatever could be accomplished within a school district's boundaries. This chapter examines the prospects for racially diverse public schools across the country, focusing on the restrictions set down by the *Milliken v. Bradley* decision. It describes the racial disparities that exist across school districts in many metropolitan areas. It reviews previous analysis of changes in metropolitan segregation that occurred between 1970 and 2000, wherein segregation within school districts generally declined and segregation between school districts generally increased. To bring the story up to date, the chapter extends this analysis by applying a similar approach to data beyond 2000. In addition, it draws on detailed analysis of segregation in school districts in North Carolina; although these districts were not much affected by the *Milliken* constraint, analysis of enrollment patterns in that state vividly illustrate implications of rulings since *Milliken.*

The first section of the chapter reviews the concept and measurement of segregation in social science. The second section summarizes previously published research examining changes in racial segregation in the public schools of U.S. metropolitan areas. The third section presents new findings summarizing changes over the first decade of the twenty-first century. The fourth section discusses implications arising from research on school segregation in North Carolina. The chapter's last section draws conclusions based on the analysis.

Measures and Determinants of School Segregation in Metropolitan Areas

As employed these days by social scientists, the term *segregation* refers not to government-sanctioned separation, but rather to unevenness or imbalances in racial composition. The term is used most often to describe racial disparities across residential areas such as census tracts or across schools within a district or metropolitan area. A district whose schools all have the same racial composition would clearly not be segregated in this or any other sense, and numerical indices such as the one used in the present chapter would assign to such an unlikely scenario a value of zero. At the other extreme would be an entirely segregated district: a district where every school's student body is composed exclusively of students from one racial category or the other, but not both. Such a district would have a numerical index value of one. Virtually all actual districts in the United States today lie somewhere between these two polar extremes, and calculated numeric indices will accordingly produce values between zero and one, allowing researchers or policy makers to compare districts or metropolitan areas according to their degree of racial segregation, or imbalance, in schools.

The primary numerical index of segregation used in this chapter measures the percentage gap that exists between actual and potential contact between white and nonwhite students in public schools. It is calculated using information on the number of white and nonwhite students in each one of the public schools in some 330 metropolitan areas in the United States.[3] Consistent with other widely used indices, this index can range from zero, signifying racially balanced schools throughout a metropolitan area, to one, signifying total racial separation in the metropolitan area's schools.[4] To illustrate its use, consider the metropolitan area of Detroit. In 2000 it had the dubious distinction of having the most severely segregated schools in the country, with an index value of 0.68. That is to say, in the Detroit metropolitan area's public schools white and nonwhite students attended the same schools at a rate that was 68% below the rate that would have been the case if white and nonwhite students had been spread evenly across all the schools in the metropolitan area.[5] The next most segregated metropolitan areas were Cleveland (with an index of 0.66) and Gary (0.64). In 2010, the metropolitan areas with the least segregated schools, were Laredo, Texas (a nearly all-nonwhite area with an index value of 0.10), followed by two almost all-white areas, Glen Falls, NY (with an index of 0.02) and Bangor, ME (0.02).

It is worth highlighting one feature of such indices: In contrast to measures of racial contact or isolation, these segregation indices are not influenced by the overall racial composition of metropolitan areas. They attempt to correct for overall racial composition. In contrast, one widely used measure that does not attempt to do this is "the percentage of black students attending schools with 90–100% minority enrollment," a measure that is readily calculated and easily understood.[6] If a high percentage of black students attend such schools, it is clear that the students in such schools are not having the experience of attending schools with white students, whatever that experience might imply, thus suggesting a situation of racial isolation. Yet in a metropolitan area like Laredo, no amount of effort to end school segregation could avoid having a metropolitan area full of schools that are 90 to 100% minority. By contrast, even if school officials tried their best to segregate schools in Glen Falls or Bangor, they would be hard put to have even one school with more than 90% minority enrollment. By focusing on imbalances, the current measure of segregation compares actual racial enrollment patterns to potential ones, putting all metropolitan areas on an equal footing, numerically speaking.

What factors determine how segregated the schools will be in a metropolitan area? The first thing that might come to mind is the degree of segregation that exists in residential patterns. Indeed, if all students simply attended the public school closest to their home, it would be true that residential segregation would determine school segregation. Many things go into the determination of residential housing patterns and residential segregation, including choices by households about where to live, government policies affecting lending and the placement of public housing, and discriminatory practices in the real estate market. For the purpose of the present analysis, I will summarize these aspects as *residential choices* made by households.[7] Such choices, made hundreds or thousands of times a year, exert a profound effect on patterns of school segregation.

As much as school attendance patterns depend on residential patterns, however, a simple housing-school connection wherein students attend the closest school does not describe contemporary American urban areas, for two main reasons. For one, metropolitan areas are typically carved up into different school districts, sometimes a multitude of them, and students are rarely allowed to cross district borders to attend school, even if it is close by. If school districts differ by racial composition, then a certain amount of racial segregation simply cannot be avoided under these circumstances, since racially imbalanced districts will inevitably produce racially imbalanced schools, even if every district racially balanced the schools under its control. Nor can students be forced to attend the schools of another district, a prohibition made official by the Supreme Court in its 1974 *Milliken v. Bradley* decision.[8] Thus the second factor determining the extent of school segregation in a metropolitan area is the degree to which areas are divided up into districts with different racial compositions. Call this factor *jurisdictional balkanization.* The more districts there are and the wider the divergence there is in racial compositions, the greater the imbalance across schools in a metropolitan area will be.

The other reason school segregation may not follow directly from residential segregation is that, within these districts, students may not be assigned to the closest school, depending on the district's rules for student assignment. The most infamous departure from the closest-school assignment rule occurred during the era of de jure segregation, when no student was allowed to attend the closest school if that student's race did not match the school's official racial designation. Other departures from the closest-school assignment rule characterized school desegregation orders involving such policies as minority-to-majority transfers, magnet schools, or "crosstown busing" to achieve racial balance. Although policies such as these may now be prohibited, as a result of the Supreme Court's 2007 *Parents Involved in Community Schools*[9] decision, historically they were important during the period of pro-active school desegregation.

In sum, three factors determine school segregation in a metropolitan area: household residential choices, jurisdictional balkanization, and student assignment policies within districts. Of these, only the last can be modified by way of school desegregation orders. Most of the famous school desegregation cases, such as *Brown v. Board of Education,*[10] *Green v. County School Board of New Kent County,*[11] and *Swann v. Charlotte-Mecklenburg Schools,* relate to the last of these factors—the rules that school districts follow in assigning students to schools. If there are racial disparities between the various districts in a metropolitan area, then eliminating segregation, or imbalances, within districts can only go so far in eliminating all racial imbalance in the metro area. This is a central issue, if not *the* central issue, in *Milliken v. Bradley.* That decision limited remedies, in almost all cases, to those that involved student assignment within districts, but said the racial disparities across districts would remain outside the reach of policymakers, be they federal, state, or local. The maximum amount of interracial contact one could strive for, then, would be limited by the two remaining factors: balkanization of jurisdictions and household choices about where to live.

In my 2004 book *After* Brown: *The Rise and Retreat of School Desegregation,* I divided the school segregation in metropolitan areas between segregation *within* districts (and thus subject to desegregation orders) and segregation *between* districts (influenced by jurisdictional balkanization and household choices).[12] To illustrate the application of these ideas, I illustrated this decomposition with the example of South Bend-Mishawaka, Indiana. In 2011, this metropolitan area contained some 38,600 public school students distributed across five different school districts. The percentage of nonwhite students in those districts ranged from 3% in the Union-North United district to 62% in the South Bend Community school district. By virtue of such large racial disparities, my calculated segregation rates imply that more than three-fourths of this metropolitan area's school segregation can be attributed to racial disparities between districts, the rest being due to disparities within districts.[13] In other words, racial disparities between the schools within districts are much less important in explaining contemporary school segregation in South Bend-Mishawka than are the large racial disparities that exist between the area's school districts.

The Legacies of *Brown* and *Milliken*: 1970 to 2000

The numerical indices of segregation described above can be used to measure the combined impact of the unprecedented efforts taken in the wake of *Brown v. Board of Education*[14] and the 1964 Civil Rights Act[15] by federal courts and the executive branch to encourage local desegregation efforts as well as the limits imposed by *Milliken.* In my 2004 book I presented indices of school segregation in metropolitan areas for 1970 and 2000, dividing each metro area index into a between-district and a within-district component. My calculations led me to conclude that two factors—district balkanization and household choices—had the effect of offsetting a significant portion (but not all) of the gains achieved by desegregation within school districts. This general offsetting can usefully be illustrated by the metropolitan area cited earlier, South Bend-Mishawaka. In 1970, 18% of the students enrolled in the South Bend city school district were nonwhite. Three decades later that share had increased to 47%, reflecting the aggregate effect of thousands of decisions by white families to move out of the district to one of the four surrounding districts or to choose to locate in one of those outlying districts when first moving into the metropolitan area. Due largely to desegregation efforts within the city district, segregation *within* the metro area's districts declined significantly over the three-decade period. But, because of the declining number of white students in the city district, segregation *between* districts increased.[16]

For all metropolitan areas in the country, the increase in between-district segregation had the effect of offsetting, on average, about one quarter of the decrease in segregation that was achieved through desegregation efforts. By size of metropolitan area, segregation declined more in larger areas (those with more than 200,000 students) than smaller ones. By region, segregation declined the most in metropolitan areas in the South and Border states. It decreased the least in metro areas in the Northeast.

Changes in School Segregation Since 2000

I have undertaken a similar analysis of metropolitan areas between 2000 and 2011. Using the same numerical index based on imbalances across schools of white and nonwhite students, I found that the average level of racial segregation in public schools has continued to go down, and this was driven by declines in both within- and between-district segregation. On average, the decline in overall segregation during those 11 years was about a third of that over the previous three decades. In other words, the degree of white-nonwhite segregation declined in the first decade of the twenty-first century at about the same rate per decade that it had fallen in the previous three decades. It is noteworthy that over this same 40-year period, roughly 1970–2010, there was a parallel decline in white-black residential segregation.[17]

Table 1 summarizes my findings for segregation over these four decades. The table's first column of numbers is based on my previous analysis, and the second is based on the similar analysis for 2000 to 2011.[18] The last column gives the calculated average segregation index in 2011. For all metropolitan areas, the changes show that the 1970–2000 period was one of offsetting trends in school segregation. Thanks to vigorous efforts to root out the vestiges of racially separate assignment policies, segregation within districts fell markedly during those years. Partially offsetting this decline, however, was an increase in between-district segregation, as white households increasingly opted for suburban school districts, as was the case in South Bend-Mishawaka. All told, the net decline in segregation was about three-fourths what it would have been had there been no change in racial disparities across school districts.

Contrast these offsetting effects with what occurred between 2000 and 2011. In this more recent period, segregation actually decreased along both dimensions. Between-district segregation, which had increased in the decades before 2000, reversed direction after 2000. Within-district segregation also decreased, but only

Table 1. Change in White-Nonwhite School Segregation in Metropolitan Areas

	1970 to 2000	2000 to 2011	2011
All metropolitan areas			
N	332	333	
Within districts	−0.190	−0.005	0.085
Between districts	0.051	−0.044	0.208
Total	−0.139	−0.049	0.292
Large			
N	48	42	
Within districts	−0.198	−0.002	0.094
Between districts	0.034	−0.066	0.230
Total	−0.164	−0.068	0.325
Smaller			
N	284	291	
Within districts	−0.180	−0.010	0.073
Between districts	0.072	−0.018	0.181
Total	−0.108	−0.027	0.254
Northeast			
N	67	68	
Within districts	−0.127	−0.010	0.061
Between districts	0.092	−0.025	0.314
Total	−0.035	−0.035	0.374
Border			
N	22	23	
Within districts	−0.189	−0.003	0.085
Between districts	−0.068	−0.067	0.195
Total	−0.257	−0.070	0.281
South			
N	107	107	
Within districts	−0.333	−0.012	0.118
Between districts	0.065	−0.031	0.146
Total	−0.268	−0.043	0.264
Midwest			
N	78	78	
Within districts	−0.223	−0.012	0.051
Between districts	0.112	−0.073	0.292
Total	−0.111	−0.085	0.343
West			
N	58	57	
Within districts	−0.103	0.004	0.085
Between districts	0.050	−0.028	0.151
Total	−0.053	−0.024	0.235

Source: Author's calculations, CLOTFELTER, AFTER *BROWN* (Table A2.3).
Note: For 1970–2000 change, totals exclude public/private disparity. Large metropolitan areas are defined as those with public school enrollments of 200,000 or more. Weighted Averages (0402142).

Table 2. Most Segregated Metropolitan Areas, 2000 and 2011

	Within district segregation index	Between district segregation index	Overall segregation index
Most Segregated Districts, 2000			
Detroit, MI PMSA	0.020	0.661	0.681
Cleveland, OH PMSA	0.068	0.588	0.656
Gary-Hammond, IN PMSA	0.028	0.608	0.636
Birmingham, AL MSA	0.060	0.567	0.627
Flint, MI MSA	0.080	0.506	0.586
Cincinnati, OH-KY-IN PMSA	0.082	0.498	0.580
Beaumont-Port Arthur, TX MSA	0.089	0.488	0.577
Chattanooga, TN-GA MSA	0.450	0.127	0.576
Providence, RI PMSA	0.034	0.538	0.573
Milwaukee, WI PMSA	0.059	0.513	0.572
Most Segregated Districts, 2011			
Monroe, LA MSA	0.323	0.237	0.560
Cleveland, OH PMSA	0.028	0.526	0.555
Beaumont-Port Arthur, TX MSA	0.042	0.500	0.542
Reading, PA MSA	0.004	0.531	0.535
Providence, RI PMSA	0.035	0.495	0.529
Buffalo, NY PMSA	0.065	0.445	0.510
Lawrence-Haverhill, MA-NH PMSA	0.012	0.490	0.502
Springfield, MA MSA	0.019	0.482	0.502
Newark, NJ PMSA	0.022	0.480	0.501
Birmingham, AL MSA	0.090	0.409	0.499

Source: Common Core of Data, author's calculations

a bit, as efforts to balance schools racially more or less ended after 2000. By 2011, as shown in the last column, most racial segregation in urban America's public schools can be attributed to differences in racial makeup between school districts, not to disparities across schools within districts.

The remainder of the table highlights differences by size and region. As in the previous period, large metropolitan areas (those with more than 200,000 students in 2000) saw larger declines in segregation than smaller ones. By region, metropolitan areas in the Midwest had the biggest declines in segregation, followed by those in Border states. By 2011, however, the Midwest, along with the Northeast, had the most segregated metropolitan areas. The region with the lowest segregation rates was the West.

Table 2 shines a spotlight on the metropolitan areas exhibiting the most extreme segregation in 2000 and 2011. Detroit, which had been the most severely segregated metropolitan area in 2000, experienced a precipitous drop in its city district's enrollment and fell out of the top ten in 2011. In that year, the tenth most segregated metropolitan area was Monroe, Louisiana. All told, four of the most segregated metropolitan areas in 2011 had also been in the top ten a decade before.

Although it is the primary measure of segregation used in this chapter, the index of white-nonwhite imbalance is by no means a perfect or comprehensive measure of school segregation or its ramifications. Other measures that are attentive to absolute levels of interracial contact reveal other important aspects of segregation. In an attempt to reflect the different insights that can be gleaned from alternative measures, Table 3 presents weighted averages of a variety of measures, all computed using school-level data on enrollment by race.

The table illustrates four important facts. First, the student population in American metropolitan areas has become less white. Between 2000 and 2011, the nonwhite percentage rose from 42.3% to 51.8%. Second, racial imbalances generally declined over the period. This conclusion is supported not only by changes in the white-nonwhite index highlighted in this chapter but also by changes in the dissimilarity index, as defined in terms of different pairs of racial groups. Third, trends are mixed when using the share of black students attending 90–100% minority schools, but for Hispanic students the trends are all in the direction of increasing segregation. Fourth, owing to the rising percentage of nonwhites in public schools the extent that nonwhites tend to be in school with others in the same category, has generally gone up. For the typical white student, however, the overall percentage of white students at the same school has declined, reflecting the long-running decline in white share among the country's public school students.

By 2011, public schools in the metropolitan areas of the Northeast and Midwest were most segregated, owing to the tendency of metro areas in those regions to have numerous and racially distinct school districts. By contract, metropolitan areas in the West and South, where school districts tend to cover bigger land areas and be less racially distinct, had the lowest rates of segregation.

Three Lessons from North Carolina

In work with Helen Ladd and Jacob Vigdor, I have applied several versions of the segregation index to schools in North Carolina. This research has three major implications for understanding the significance of modern day school segregation beyond those spelled out in the previous sections. I summarize these points briefly here.

Table 3. Comparison of School Segregation and Interracial Exposure

Measure and Year	All MSAs	Smaller MSAs	Larger MSAs	Northeast	Border	South	Midwest	West
Percent Nonwhite								
1999	42.3%	33.8%	49.4%	36.2%	35.0%	48.8%	28.9%	52.0%
2010	51.8%	43.8%	58.6%	42.6%	44.1%	59.0%	36.6%	63.0%
Segregation, 1999								
Within Districts	0.090	0.083	0.096	0.070	0.088	0.131	0.062	0.081
Between Districts	0.251	0.198	0.296	0.339	0.262	0.176	0.365	0.179
Total	0.341	0.280	0.393	0.409	0.350	0.307	0.428	0.259
Segregation, 2010								
Within Districts	0.085	0.073	0.094	0.061	0.085	0.118	0.051	0.085
Between Districts	0.208	0.180	0.230	0.314	0.195	0.146	0.292	0.151
Total	0.423	0.338	0.494	0.362	0.350	0.488	0.289	0.520
Dissimilarity Index								
White-Nonwhite								
1999	0.534	0.489	0.572	0.607	0.527	0.493	0.616	0.463
2010	0.493	0.453	0.527	0.561	0.459	0.473	0.522	0.460
White-Black								
1999	0.600	0.543	0.647	0.686	0.616	0.543	0.705	0.512
2010	0.579	0.524	0.625	0.664	0.593	0.547	0.656	0.498
White-Hispanic								
1999	0.519	0.470	0.559	0.631	0.462	0.464	0.528	0.502
2010	0.503	0.454	0.544	0.595	0.458	0.458	0.496	0.512
Black-Hispanic								
1999	0.478	0.422	0.526	0.437	0.543	0.479	0.579	0.416
2010	0.433	0.384	0.473	0.400	0.474	0.427	0.512	0.397

Measure and Year	All MSAs	Smaller MSAs	Larger MSAs	Northeast	Border	South	Midwest	West
Percentage of black students in schools 90–100% nonwhite								
1999	40.5%	27.0%	49.7%	51.9%	40.5%	35.6%	46.7%	28.6%
2010	40.8%	27.5%	50.3%	49.8%	39.3%	38.7%	41.9%	33.9%
Percentage of Hispanic students in schools 90-100% nonwhite								
1999	39.5%	31.0%	43.7%	46.2%	12.0%	43.4%	28.6%	37.7%
2010	44.0%	36.5%	48.4%	44.6%	17.2%	46.0%	30.8%	47.2%
Homogeniety Rates (Percent own race in one's own school)								
Whites								
1999	77.7%	80.6%	74.5%	84.2%	80.1%	71.2%	86.0%	68.6%
2010	69.9%	73.4%	65.9%	78.2%	72.1%	62.4%	78.3%	59.3%
Blacks								
1999	54.9%	51.2%	57.3%	53.4%	61.4%	57.0%	65.0%	23.0%
2010	48.5%	46.4%	50.1%	45.9%	54.1%	52.3%	54.5%	16.6%
Hispanics								
1999	54.7%	53.1%	55.6%	44.7%	19.7%	58.8%	42.3%	58.8%
2010	56.6%	54.8%	57.7%	46.3%	29.3%	58.4%	42.6%	63.6%
Nonwhites								
1999	69.6%	62.0%	73.9%	72.2%	63.1%	69.7%	65.7%	71.0%
2010	72.0%	65.8%	75.9%	70.6%	64.6%	73.9%	62.5%	76.1%

Source: Author's calculations

*The index of segregation measures the degree of imbalance in racial composition across schools, specifically, in the percentage of students in each school who are nonwhites. The dissimilarity index is an alternative index that measures the imbalance between students in the specified pairs of categories. For each index, a value of zero indicates balanced schools and a value of one indicates complete separation of the two groups. See the Methodological Appendix for precise definitions. Homogeneity rates show the weighted average percentage of students in the school who are in a typical student's same racial category.

THE IMPORTANCE OF LOCAL DECISIONS

Despite the significance of both state and federal bodies in affecting public schools, it remains the local school board that is the lynchpin for determining school segregation in urban areas. Actions by local school boards have led to varying degrees of racial imbalance in schools. To be sure, the ability of a school board to change the racial balance of its schools is limited. Comparatively low levels of residential segregation in North Carolina have meant that, even with pure neighborhood-based assignment, county-level school imbalance measures would remain well below those encountered in many locales across the country. Moreover, the influence of school boards is also necessarily limited by the racial and ethnic makeup of its school-aged population.

In North Carolina, patterns of school segregation have traditionally reflected those in the South at large. Although some previously all-white schools had become formally desegregated beginning in the early 1960s, it was not until 1968 that the long-standing racial distinctions between schools began to disappear. After 1968, for example, the vestiges of the previously segregated schools almost vanished in Charlotte-Mecklenburg. Its public schools quickly became racially balanced, thanks to a comprehensive assignment plan that involved transporting students between city and suburban neighborhoods. That plan was made famous by the Supreme Court's 1971 decision in *Swann v. Charlotte-Mecklenburg Board of Education*[19] upholding busing as a constitutional means of achieving racial desegregation. That decision would later be seen as the high-water mark for judicial action to push schools to desegregate. By 1990, federal courts had begun to release districts from further affirmative efforts to balance schools racially.[20]

Some local school boards, including Charlotte-Mecklenburg, responded to the removal of federal pressure by ending comprehensive desegregation plans. First came Forsyth County, whose consolidated Winston-Salem/Forsyth district had operated a busing plan since 1971 that resulted in quite racially balanced schools. As late as the fall of 1994, not a single public school in that district had an enrollment more than 90% nonwhite. In 1995, a newly elected school board voted to adopt a new student assignment plan dividing the district into eight attendance zones and allowing parental choice within those zones. As a result of the new plan, racial disparities among schools increased, and by the fall of 2000 a fifth of all nonwhite students attended schools that were 90–100% nonwhite.[21]

In Charlotte-Mecklenburg—which as a result of the earlier court case had pursued an aggressive policy of crosstown busing for the purposes of racial desegregation—the school board replaced its strict racial balance assignment plan in 1992 with one that used magnet schools in the district's downtown neighborhoods to attract suburban whites, relying on quotas to keep the magnet schools racially balanced. In the fall of 1994 the percentage of black and Hispanic students attending 90–100% nonwhite schools was 2.5%, and by 2000 that percentage had risen to 7.2%. Following a decision by the Fourth Circuit Court of Appeals striking down racial quotas in 1999, however, the school board adopted a new assignment plan in 2002 that, like the one in Winston-Salem/Forsyth, put greater emphasis on neighborhood schools and offered parents greater choice about which schools their children would attend.[22] The result was a broad shift to neighborhood schools and a dramatic increase in the isolation of students by race. By 2006, some 39.9% of the district's nonwhite students attended schools that were 90–100% nonwhite, and by 2012 that share stood at 43.1%.[23]

By contrast, Wake County (containing Raleigh) has managed to maintain a high degree of racial balance in its schools, thanks to policies that have aimed to avoid concentrations of low-income students. While the percentage of black and Hispanic students in Charlotte-Mecklenburg attending 90–100% minority schools was rising from 7.2% to 43.1%, the comparable shares in Wake increased from 1.0% to 5.0%. These vastly different histories are largely the result of differences in local school assignment policies.

ECONOMIC SEGREGATION

Along with concerns about the growing economic inequality in the U.S., some observers have noted with concern the apparent increase in residential segregation by economic status. Using data for North Carolina, Ladd, Vigdor, and I applied the same index previously used for racial segregation in North Carolina schools to economic segregation instead. We divided students according to whether they were eligible to participate in the federal free lunch program, which requires a family income not too much higher than the income cutoff for poverty status. Using the same formula underlying the segregation index, we calculated the imbalance across schools in each county between students eligible for free lunch and those not eligible. We found that this index increased between the 1994–1995 school year and the 2010–2011 school year. The increase was about twice as fast in Charlotte-Mecklenburg, the district that abandoned its previous policy of racial balance. By contrast, economic segregation in Wake County, which maintained a policy of avoiding concentrations of low-income students, saw an increase slightly less than that for the state as a whole.[24]

TEACHER CHARACTERISTICS

Among the reasons school imbalance is an important issue of public policy is that the quality of teachers in a school tends to correlate with that school's racial composition or income level. In our research we found that schools with higher concentrations of minority students or students on free lunch also tend to have teachers with weaker credentials.[25]

Specifically, we compared teachers using five proxies of quality. For example, teachers in schools with minority shares in the highest quarter of all schools, as compared to those in schools with shares in the lowest quartile, had less teaching experience, had scored lower on standardized tests for teachers, were more likely to have graduated from an unselective college, were more likely to have an irregular teaching certificate, and were less likely to have national board certification. All of these differences were statistically significant. We found similar disparities when comparing schools in the highest and lowest quartiles by percentage of students eligible to receive free lunch. These findings apply to both elementary and middle schools. Not only do segregated schools reduce the opportunities for students to benefit from diversity, they also tend to advantage white and affluent students by exposing them to teachers with stronger credentials.

Conclusion

Not only were the 1960s a tumultuous decade of change, they were also a decade of sweeping policy change in civil rights, instigated and carried out by all three branches of the federal government. No realm of American life was more profoundly shaped than the racial enrollment patterns in the nation's public schools. Most dramatic was the transformation of public schools in the formerly segregated schools in the 11 states of the former Confederacy. The process of racial desegregation in public schools continued beyond the decade of the 1960s—haltingly, to be sure, but firmly backed by the federal government's resolve to end what had been a national disgrace. With the dawning of the 1970s, however, resistance to desegregation grew and solidified, and not just in the South. Parents in South Boston loudly denounced the court order that brought black students to their beloved high schools, and presidential candidate George Wallace took the issue national. President Nixon and his successor Gerald Ford made no secret of their misgivings about "forced busing."

In this altered landscape, the Supreme Court in 1974 handed down a decision in *Milliken v. Bradley*[26] rejecting a desegregation plan that would have transported students in Detroit from one school district to another, a ruling that would become the beginning of the Court's gradual retreat from assertive efforts to balance schools racially. The admonitions in *Brown v. Board of Education*[27] and *Green v. County School Board of New Kent County*[28] had not exactly been undone, but they had been defanged and more tightly circumscribed.

Against this policy backdrop, the quotidian mechanisms of urban housing markets continued to do their unremarkable but transformative work. Families formed, had children, and found housing, often moving between and within urban areas. Highways, rising incomes, and moving job centers all encouraged families to move to the suburbs. So did concerns about crime and attitudes about schools. This process of continual residential churning meant that school segregation became, in a sense, a moving target. In the three decades between 1970 and 2000, the uncounted individual decisions that drove this process had the aggregate effect of offsetting, partially, the decreases in racial segregation that were achieved by assertive desegregation policies. Based on my calculation of indices of racial segregation in public schools, I estimate that households' residential choices offset about a quarter of the decrease in segregation brought about through desegregation policies. In this chapter I extended my previous research into the first decade of the twenty-first century. I found that racial segregation between white and nonwhite students—that is, imbalance in the public schools in metropolitan areas—continued to decline, mostly because city and suburban districts have converged, rather than diverged, in their racial composition.

This reduction in measured racial segregation should not be a source of celebration or great comfort, however, for two reasons. First, there lurks behind the convergence by race a persistent divergence by economic status. All available indicators suggest that segregation by income is increasing. Second, disparities by race or income have real educational and social consequences. Not only do they deprive young people of the chance to experience diverse environments, such disparities usually bring with them disparities in teacher quality, given the freedom that teachers often possess to move from school to school. If these disparities are to be minimized, however, it will not be enough to look to federal authorities to intervene. Instead, it will be up to local school boards and voters to assert the value of diversity in the public schools.

Charles T. Clotfelter is the Z. Smith Reynolds Professor of Public Policy and Professor of Economics and Law, and the Director for the Center for the Study of Philanthropy and Voluntarism at Duke University.

Methodological Appendix

DEFINITIONS OF METROPOLITAN AREAS

So that metropolitan areas would have the same definitions for the various years, the Census Bureau's 1990 definitions of metropolitan areas were used. For all regions except New England, metropolitan areas are defined as groups of adjoining counties. The 1990 definitions are given here: http://www.census.gov/population/metro/files/lists/historical/90mfips.txt

MEASURES OF SCHOOL SEGREGATION

Segregation in metro area k is defined as the percentage gap between the maximum exposure rate, which would result from racial balance throughout all schools and classrooms in the metro area, and actual exposure rate E_k:

$$S_k = (n_k - E_k)/n_k,$$

This segregation can be decomposed into two components: (1) the portion due to racial disparities within districts,

$$S_{kw} = (E_k^* - E_k)/n_k,$$

and (2) the portion due to racial disparities between districts:

$$S_{kB} = (n_k - E_k^*)/n_k,$$

where E_k^* is the exposure rate that would occur if every school district were racially balanced.

Calculated exposure rates and imbalance indices employ data on schools (denoted i) and districts (j) within metro areas (k). The white-nonwhite exposure rate for any metro area k is:

$$E_k = (\Sigma_i \Sigma_j W_{ijk} n_{ijk})/(\Sigma_i \Sigma_j W_{ijk}),$$

where n_{ijk} is the percentage of school i in district j and metro area k that is nonwhite, and W_{ijk} is the corresponding number of white students in that school.

A comparison, hypothetical exposure rate would occur if all schools in each district were racially balanced:

$$E_k^* = (\textstyle\sum_j W_{jk}\, n_{jk})/(\textstyle\sum_j W_{jk})$$

where n_{jk} = percentage nonwhite in district j in metro area k and W_{jk} is the number of white students in district j in metro area k.

NOTES

This chapter was written when the author was on sabbatical leave at the New York University Law School. He is grateful to Lucas Westmaas for research assistance and to NYU and Duke University for financial support. The views expressed here are the author's and do not necessarily reflect those of any institution.

1. Swann v. Charlotte-Mecklenburg Board of Education, 402 U.S. 1 (1971).

2. Milliken v. Bradley, 433 U.S. 267 (1977).

3. The analysis is based on data for metropolitan areas in the lower 48 states. Charter schools, which are public schools run independently of local public school districts, are not included in the analysis.

4. See the methodological appendix for the definition of the segregation index used in this paper.

5. To be more precise, the segregation is based on the gap between the actual and the maximum percent nonwhite in the average white student's school. In 2000, 31.1% of Detroit's public school students were nonwhite, but the average white student was in a school where the percentage of nonwhite students was only 9.9%. The gap between those two percentages is 68.1%, or 0.681 [= (0.311−0.099)/0.311], which is the segregation index.

6. For example, see Gary Orfield, John Kucsera, & Genevieve Siegel-Hawley, The Civil Rights Project, *E Pluribus . . . Separation: Deepening Double Segregation for More Students* (September 2012).

7. A related dimension of household choice involves decisions about whether to send children to private schools. As noted above, this set of decisions had a relatively small aggregate impact in the period 1970 to 2000 in most metropolitan areas and is not reflected in the calculations reported in the current chapter.

8. The *Milliken* decision does allow for exceptions to this general rule, where it can be shown that official decisions beyond the district were responsible for existing segregation, but the understanding is that such circumstances will be rare.

9. Parents Involved in Community Schools v. Seattle School District No. 1, 551 U.S. 701 (2007).

10. Brown v. Board of Education, 347 U.S. 483 (1954).

11. Green v. County School Board of New Kent County, 391 U.S. 430 (1968).

12. CHARLES T. CLOTFELTER, AFTER *BROWN*: THE RISE AND RETREAT OF SCHOOL DESEGREGATION (Princeton University Press 2004). That decomposition of metropolitan school segregation contained a third part, segregation attributable to any racial disparity between students attending public schools compared to those attending private schools. Quantitatively, that component was not large. In any case, it is not reflected in the current chapter's calculations.

13. Of the metropolitan area's total segregation index in 2011 of 0.292, 0.062 is due to within-district racial disparities and 0.230 is due to between-district disparities.

14. Brown, 347 U.S. 483.

15. Civil Rights Act of 1964, Public Law No. 88-352, 78 Stat. 241 (codified as amended in scattered sections of 2 U.S.C., 28 U.S.C., and 42 U.S.C.).

16. Between 1970 and 2000, the index of within-district segregation in South Bend-Mishawaka fell from 0.374 to 0.052. Meanwhile, the index for between-district segregation increased from 0.054 to 0.200. The overall index thus fell, from 0.428 to 0.252.

17. This decline in residential segregation, using the dissimilarity index for black and white residents, was documented in Edward Glaeser & Jacob Vigdor, Manhattan Institute Civic Report No. 66, *The End of the Segregated Century: Racial Separation in America's Neighborhoods, 1890-2010* (2012).

18. CLOTFELTER, AFTER *BROWN*.

19. Swann, 402 U.S. 1.

20. Charles T. Clotfelter, Helen F. Ladd & Jacob L. Vigdor, *Federal Oversight, Local Control, and the Specter of "Resegregation" in Southern Schools*, 8 AMERICAN LAW AND ECONOMICS REVIEW 1 (Summer 2006).

21. Clotfelter et al., *Federal Oversight*, 369–70.

22. Capacchione v. Charlotte-Mecklenburg Schools, 57 F. Supp. 2d 228 (W.D.N.C. 1999).

23. Charles T. Clotfelter, Helen F. Ladd, & Jacob L. Vigdor, *Racial and Economic Diversity in North Carolina's Schools: An Update*, Table 4 (Sanford School, Working Paper SAN13-03, 2013); Charles T. Clotfelter, Helen F. Ladd, & Jacob L. Vigdor, Racial and Economic Imbalance in Charlotte's Schools: 1994–2012, in ROSLYN ARLIN MICKELSON, STEPHEN SAMUEL SMITH, & AMY HAWN NELSON, EDS., YESTERDAY, TODAY, AND TOMORROW: THE PAST, PRESENT, AND FUTURE OF (DE)SEGREGATED EDUCATION IN CHARLOTTE (Harvard Education Press forthcoming).

24. Economic segregation appears to be growing in residential areas as well. Paul A. Jargowsky, *Changes in Segregation by Race and Class: The Implications for Schools*, in ANNETTE LAREAU & KIMBERLY GOYETTE, EDS., CHOOSING HOMES, CHOOSING SCHOOLS: RESIDENTIAL SEGREGATION AND THE SEARCH FOR A GOOD SCHOOL (Russell Sage Foundation 2014) finds that black-white residential segregation has been declining since 1990, but segregation between poor and non-poor is rising among whites, blacks, and Asians. Refer to table 1.

25. We next calculated, separately for elementary and middle schools, for the schools above and below their respective county median racial composition, the average values for five objective measures of teacher quality: the percentage of teachers with less than three years of teaching experience, the percentage of teachers who graduated from undergraduate institutions deemed "less competitive" by *Barrons*, the percentage of teachers with irregular teaching licenses, the average normalized teacher test score (expressed as the difference from the state average, in standard deviation units), and the percentage of teachers who were nationally board-certified.

26. 433 U.S. 267 (1977).

27. 347 U.S. 483 (1954).

28. 391 U.S. 430 (1968).

Missouri v. Jenkins

515 U.S. 70 (1995)

JOHN R. MUNICH

Missouri v. Jenkins
A Remedy without Objective Limitation

Two years before the Supreme Court decided *Missouri v. Jenkins*[1] in 1995 (*Jenkins III*) and began the process of closing what was likely the most ambitious and expensive school desegregation remedy in the nation's history, I became the Chief Litigation Counsel in the Missouri Attorney General's Office. When I began my position with the Office, the attorney general initially assigned two cases to me for my personal docket: the St. Louis (*Liddell v. Board of Education*[2]) and Kansas City (*Jenkins v. Missouri*) desegregation cases. At the time, I had absolutely no experience in such cases apart from studying them in law school.

In the attorney general's office, I headed up a small team of lawyers dedicated to defending the two cases. In the spring and summer of 1993, as we were making very initial plans to begin an effort to obtain the state's dismissal from the St. Louis case, the lower court issued rulings that were ultimately reversed in *Jenkins III*. In denying the state of Missouri's motion for partial unitary status, the district court ruled that because Kansas City Metropolitan School District (KCMSD) student achievement was below "national norms" in many grades, the goals of its *Milliken II* remedial component had not been met, thus introducing for the first time an educational achievement component in addition to the traditional "*Green* factors" analysis the courts had used.[3] The Eighth Circuit affirmed this ruling, and the state subsequently sought rehearing *en banc*, which the Eighth Circuit also denied, albeit with a comprehensive dissenting opinion from five judges.

Those rulings, combined with the addition of a fifth possible vote on the Supreme Court (Justice Thomas, ironically, an alumnus of the Missouri Attorney General's Office), provided a potential path to persuading the Supreme Court to take another look at the *Jenkins* remedy and the state's massive financial obligations there. As a result, I turned a substantial part of my time to the briefing on rehearing and rehearing en banc, and thereafter to the state's petition for certiorari. The Supreme Court granted the certiorari in fall 1994, ordered expedited briefing, and set the argument for January 11, 1995. The attorney general informed me that I would be arguing for the state in my first appearance before the Supreme Court. That began the most intensive preparation process I have ever undertaken in any case (before or after) as we worked on the merits briefs and then prepared for argument. As argument day drew near, the case garnered immense national interest, with numerous parties filing amicus briefs, a standing-room-only courthouse on argument day, and extensive media coverage.

The argument took place against the backdrop of two other relatively recent desegregation decisions of the Court, the 1992 decision in *Freeman v. Pitts*,[4] and the 1991 decision in *Board of Education v. Dowell*.[5] Both of these decisions had lowered the bar for the termination of desegregation remedies and made clear that a majority of the justices were wary of unlimited terms of federal court oversight of desegregating school districts. Mindful of Justice Brennan's frequent observation to his clerks that the most important rule of constitutional law was counting to five, it was important in looking at the case to try to determine the source of the five votes needed to overrule the Eighth Circuit. The case had already been heard on the merits by the Court in *Jenkins II*, decided in 1990, where the Court held 5–4 that the trial court erred in imposing a local tax rate to fund the desegregation remedies but could order local authorities, as part of the remedy, to secure the necessary funding via enactment of sufficient tax increases.[6] Notably, in *Jenkins II* the Court declined to examine the scope of the remedy ordered by the lower courts, although four dissenting justices expressed their alarm over the broad scope and expense of the desegregation plan. From *Jenkins II*, it was clear that four sitting members of the Court harbored serious concerns about the breadth of the Kansas City remedy: Chief Justice Rehnquist and Justices Kennedy, Scalia, and O'Connor. But since that 1990 decision, Justice Thomas had joined the Court.

Jenkins III would allow us to argue directly about the remedy ordered by the district court, which was unique in a number of respects. The first distinguishing characteristic traces to the alignment and positioning of the parties. KCMSD, originally a plaintiff when the case was first filed, became realigned as a defendant, along with the state of Missouri and surrounding suburban school districts. As the case progressed through the liability phase, KCMSD was found to be jointly and severally liable with the state as a constitutional violator. The adjoining suburban districts, however, were dismissed from the case and thus never became responsible for financing a remedy. In the end, KCMSD, although adjudged a liable defendant, argued with the plaintiffs for an ever-expanding remedy because this became a vehicle for the massive infusion of state dollars into the district. As Justice Kennedy described the arrangement in *Jenkins II*: "[t]he plaintiffs and KCMSD might well be seen as parties that have 'joined forces apparently for the purpose of extracting funds from the state treasury.'"[7]

Second, because the suburban districts had been dismissed from the case, the remedy necessarily proceeded as an *intra*district remedy—as opposed to an *inter*district or metropolitan-wide remedy. The implications of this point would be one of the linchpins of the Supreme Court's decision in *Jenkins III*, but more on that later.

The third point of distinction was the sheer size and breadth of the remedy.[8] Because of this, the remedy in *Jenkins* stands out for its extraordinary expense. Not only was the state ordered to essentially rebuild and upgrade the entire physical plant of KCMSD, but it was also required to fund a host of *Milliken II*-type remedies. In its peak years, the state of Missouri was funding nearly half of KCMSD's operating budget—in addition to the regular state aid distributed through the state's public school funding formula.[9] As described by dissenting Eighth Circuit judges:

> The remedies ordered go far beyond anything previously seen in a school desegregation case. The sheer immensity of the programs encompassed by the district court's order—the large number of magnet schools and the quantity of capital renovations and new construction—are concededly without parallel in any other school district in the country.[10]

The last unique aspect of the remedy was a product of the suburban districts' dismissal from the case. Explaining that "[t]o accomplish desegregation within the boundary lines of a school district whose enrollment remains 68.3% black is a difficult task," the district court pursued a remedy of "desegregative attractiveness," on the theory that the only way to "desegregate" the KCMSD was to entice suburban white children to attend KCMSD schools through the creation of unique magnet schools, world-class capital facilities, academic and extracurricular programs not readily available in most public schools, and so on.[11] This ambitious goal of making the district "attractive" to suburban white children was largely responsible for the expense and breadth of the remedy, but ultimately led to the Supreme Court's ruling in *Jenkins III* striking down the remedy as beyond the scope of the district court's remedial authority.

Thus, our argument in the Supreme Court focused on three issues. First, we emphasized that the lower court's remedy was inherently an interdistrict remedy, intended to effect the movement of school children across district boundaries, while the trial court had long ago determined that the constitutional violation was purely intradistrict in nature—occurring solely within KCMSD.

Second, we argued that the student achievement element introduced into the unitary status calculus by the lower courts demonstrated that those courts had not used the proper test for determining when a constitutional violator could be released from its desegregation obligations. Further, we argued that because student achievement is so closely tied to factors in the home and community and outside the direct control of the schools and the state, it was not, consistent with the Court's holding in *Freeman* and other cases, an appropriate unitary status criterion.

Last, a discrete part of the case involved a court-ordered salary increase in the range of $70 million in annual cost—to be paid by the state—for nearly all KCMSD employees. We argued that this component of the remedy was not properly designed to cure any vestiges of segregation that had been identified in the case and therefore was beyond the power of the local courts to order. While the $70 million annual sum was certainly not insignificant, it paled in comparison to other components of the remedy in cost. However, as many supporters of the remedy privately acknowledged pre- and post-argument, this component of the remedy provided credence to the state's central argument—that the remedy ordered in KCMSD was out of control.

The Supreme Court issued its 5–4 decision on June 12, 1995. The Court agreed with the state on the three arguments we presented. The central premise of the Court's ruling is summarized in one passage of the opinion:

> The District Court's pursuit of "desegregative attractiveness" cannot be reconciled with our cases placing limitations on a district court's remedial authority. It is certainly theoretically possible that the greater the expenditure per pupil within the KCMSD, the more likely it is that some unknowable number of nonminority students not presently attending schools in the KCMSD will choose to enroll in those schools. Under this reasoning, however, every increased expenditure, whether it be for teachers, noninstructional employees, books, or buildings, will make the KCMSD in some way more attractive, and thereby perhaps induce nonminority students to enroll in its schools. But this rationale is not susceptible to any objective limitation.[12]

The Court went on to note that:

> Each additional program ordered by the District Court—and financed by the State—to increase the "desegregative attractiveness" of the school district makes the KCMSD

more and more dependent on additional funding from the State; in turn, the greater the KCMSD's dependence on state funding, the greater its reliance on continued supervision by the District Court.[13]

Thus, in broad terms, *Jenkins III* broke little new ground, but instead simply reinforced what the Court had already ruled in *Freeman* and *Dowell*—desegregation remedies were finite and were to be measured against the objective *Green* factors when courts were deciding a unitary status motion. Moreover, many of the unique and far-reaching aspects of the KCMSD remedy meant that the ruling would not apply to many of the more mainstream desegregation remedies that were still in place at the time. Viewed more closely, however, the Court's decision strongly intimated that the outside durational limit on *Milliken II* remedies was one full student cohort:

> The remedial quality education program should be tailored to remedy the injuries suffered by the victims of prior *de jure* segregation. Minority students in kindergarten through grade 7 in the KCMSD always have attended AAA rated schools; minority students in the KCMSD that previously attended schools rated below AAA have since received remedial education programs for a period of up to seven years.[14]

The Court also stated that on remand, the plaintiffs' burden to demonstrate actionable educational vestiges of segregation was to be a heavy one. It criticized the district court because "it never has identified the incremental effect that segregation has had on minority student achievement."[15] In other words, going forward, generic comparisons of all KCMSD students' achievement results to the scores of other districts' children would not suffice. Plaintiffs (and the trial court) were to identify the "incremental effect" that de jure segregation that ended some years prior had visited upon the achievement of current-day "minority" students (not all students) in the KCMSD. As a matter of proof, given the data difficulties and the passage of time, this was a burden nearly impossible to meet.

By the time the federal district court declared that the Kansas City Metropolitan School District had attained unitary status in 2003, the federal courts had supervised the remedy in the district for 25 years and ordered remedial programs in the district that cost in excess of $1.5 billion, with most of that money paid under court order by the state of Missouri.[16]

John R. Munich is a partner at Stinson Leonard Street, LLP. From 1993 to 1995, he was the Chief Counsel for Litigation in the Missouri Attorney General's Office; from 1996 through January 1999, he was the Deputy Attorney General for the state of Missouri.

NOTES

1. Missouri v. Jenkins, 515 U.S. 70 (1995).

2. Liddell v. Board of Education, Case No. 4:72-CV100-SNL (Eastern District of Missouri). A settlement agreement was entered in 1999; a consent decree was entered in 2011. The case remains open.

3. Order of April 16, 1993, at 11; Green v. County School Board of New Kent County, Virginia, 391 U.S. 430 (1968).

4. Freeman v. Pitts, 503 U.S. 467 (1992).

5. Board of Education v. Dowell, 498 U.S. 237 (1991).

6. Missouri v. Jenkins, 495 U.S. 33 (1990).

7. Missouri v. Jenkins, 495 U.S. 33, 76 (1991) (Justice Kennedy, concurring) (quoting Milliken v. Bradley, 433 U.S. 267, 293 (1977) (Justice Powell, concurring in judgment)).

8. Denial of the State's Motion for Rehearing and Rehearing En Banc, No. 90-2238 et al. (8th Cir., March 15, 1994) (Judge Beam, dissenting).

9. The District Court stated that it had "gone to great lengths to provide the KCMSD with facilities and opportunities not available anywhere else in the country." Order of July 30, 1993, 4, Jenkins v. State of Missouri, 1993 WL 566488 (W.D. Mo. 1993) (No. 77-0420-CV-W-4).

10. Jenkins by Agyei v. State of Missouri, 855 F.2d 1295, 1318-19 (8th Cir. 1988), affirmed in part and reversed in part under a slightly different name, Missouri v. Jenkins, 495 U.S. 33 (1990).

11. Jenkins v. State of Missouri, 639 F. Supp. 19 (W.D. Mo. 1985) affirmed as modified under a slightly different name. Jenkins by Agyei v. State of Missouri, 807 F.2d 657 (8th Cir. 1986).

12. Jenkins, 515 U.S. 98.

13. Ibid., 99.

14. Ibid., 102.

15. Ibid., 101.

16. At the time of the St. Louis, Missouri, unitary status trial in 1996, an expert witness for the state concluded that Missouri had been ordered to pay more for desegregation remedies—in Kansas City and St. Louis—than all other states combined (of those that had been ordered to make such payments). Liddell v. Board of Education, Trial Testimony of Dr. Christine Rossell (1996).

KEVIN FOX GOTHAM

Missed Opportunities, Enduring Legacies
School Segregation and Desegregation in Kansas City, Missouri

"I think *Plessy v. Ferguson* was right and should be reaffirmed."
—William Rehnquist, Chief Justice of the U.S. Supreme Court.[1]

OVER THE LAST CENTURY, FEW ISSUES HAVE GENERATED MORE CONTROVERSY in U.S. metropolitan areas than school "desegregation." "Busing," "magnet schools," and "controlled choice" have become familiar academic and popular vocabulary and reflect a long history of struggles to integrate schools and ameliorate racial inequalities. These issues are particularly significant in Kansas City, Missouri, the site of one of the nation's most controversial and expansive desegregation orders during the 1980s and 1990s. Racial segregation in housing and schools have been defining features of the Kansas City metropolitan area for over a century. The Kansas City, Missouri, School District (KCMSD) was racially segregated from its creation in September 1867. In the ensuing decades, school officials provided separate education facilities for blacks and whites, and the city and metropolitan area developed clearly defined patterns of racial segregation. By 1940, the block-level "index of dissimilarity" for nonwhite-white segregation stood at 88.0, indicating that at least

88% of all minorities would have had to change their place of residence in Kansas City to live in an integrated neighborhood.[2] This high segregation level remained relatively fixed throughout the postwar era, ranging from 91.3 in 1950 and to 90.8 in 1960, and 88.0 by 1970.[3] In the 1990s, Douglas Massey and Nancy Denton identified Kansas City as one of the nation's *hypersegregated* metropolitan areas due to the high degree of segregation in housing patterns on a range of indices.[4] While the index of dissimilarity for the metropolitan area declined slightly to 73.15 in 1990 and 69.12 in 2000, Kansas City continues to be one of the most segregated metropolitan areas in the nation, a situation that is reinforced by continuing suburbanization, inner city disinvestment, and school segregation.[5]

This chapter has three goals. First, the historical narrative developed in this chapter points to the key events and decisions underlying the origin of school segregation, identifies crucial turning points and missed opportunities in the struggle to desegregate schools, and reveals how a historical trajectory set long ago still molds contemporary responses to the problems of racial segregation in schools. My second goal is to illustrate the reflexive relationship between schools and housing, especially the impact of school administrative decisions on racial housing patterns. Finally, I examine the significance of Kansas City, Missouri's school desegregation plan and the 1995 U.S. Supreme Court decision that effectively ended the desegregation effort that had begun in 1984.

School Segregation from *Plessy* (1896) to *Brown* (1954)

During the Civil War, the Kansas and Missouri state line that bisects the Kansas City metropolitan area was a front of intense warfare between pro- and anti-slavery groups. The pro-slavery forces in Missouri, called the "bushwhackers," sought to impose slavery on Kansas through coercion and ballot stuffing. On the Kansas side, free-state proponents, the "Jayhawkers," sought the state's admission to the Union with slavery prohibited. This North/South conflict also affected public schools.[6] As was typical throughout the South, the Missouri state constitution required segregated schools for whites and blacks. Indeed, Missouri was the northern-most of the states to require separate schools for whites and blacks by state constitution. Under mandates enacted in 1865, 1868, 1869, 1875, and 1889, the state of Missouri made it a criminal offense for "any colored child to attend a white [public] school" and extended the bar to private schools in 1909.[7] The Missouri Supreme Court upheld the constitutionality of these provisions in 1891 and, in 1910; the state attorney general alerted all Missouri school districts that the state would prosecute school officials operating racially integrated schools. Until 1929, the state of Missouri

Table 1: Total and Black Population for Kansas City, Missouri, 1880–1930.

Year	Total Population	Percent Increase	Black Population	Percent Increase	Percent Black of Total
1880	55,785		8,143		14.6
1890	132,716	137.9	13,700	67.6	10.3
1900	163,752	23.4	17,567	28.2	10.7
1910	248,381	51.7	23,566	34.1	9.5
1920	324,410	30.6	30,719	30.4	9.5
1930	399,746	23.2	38,574	25.6	9.7

exempted school districts from providing schools for African American children whose enumeration dropped to below 15 and required school districts to eliminate African American schools if attendance fell below eight. After 1929, the state gave school districts the option to discontinue schools for blacks, no matter what their enumeration.[8]

The development of racially segregated schools in Kansas City stemmed from a series of discriminatory government actions, U.S. Supreme Court decisions, and dramatic demographic shifts during the late-nineteenth and early-twentieth centuries.[9] Table 1 shows total and black population for Kansas City, Missouri between 1880 and 1930.

Table 1 shows that the city experienced a dramatic population increase during the decades after 1880. The total population increased from 55,785 in 1880 to almost 400,000 by 1930. Black population increased from 8,143 in 1880, to 23,566 in 1910, to 38,574 by 1930, the result of the beginnings of the Great Migration of Southern blacks to Northern and Midwestern cities from 1915 to 1930.[10] During this period, the percentage of blacks living in the city declined from 14.6% in 1880, to 10.7% in 1900, to 9.5% in 1920.[11]

After the *Plessy v. Ferguson*[12] decision in 1896 that institutionalized the doctrine of "separate but equal" in education, the state of Missouri imposed a racially segregated school system on a widely dispersed and largely rural African American population. Table 2 summarizes total and black school enumeration in Kansas City, Missouri, and the counties surrounding the city on the Missouri side of the state line: Clay County, Jackson County (excluding Kansas City, Missouri), and Platte County. The Kansas City, Missouri, city limits are contained within Jackson County.[13]

As table 2 shows, as of 1900, African Americans made up about the same proportion of school children in rural Clay, Platte, and Jackson Counties. Yet, from 1900–1954, the percentage of blacks attending schools in Kansas City, Missouri, skyrocketed while the total school population increased more modestly. During the same time, the total

Table 2: Total and Black School Enumeration, 1900–1954 (Kansas City, Missouri, Clay County, Jackson County [excluding Kansas City, Missouri], and Platte County, Missouri).

	Kansas City, Missouri	Jackson County	Clay County	Platte County
1900				
Total Pop.	59,407	10,538	5,997	4,871
Black Pop.	5,248	655	429	351
% Black	8.8	6.3	7.1	7.2
1954				
Total Pop.	103,085	44,009	13,103	4,054
Black Pop.	14,527	153	153	62
% Black	14	0.3	1.1	1.5
Percent Change, 1900–1954				
Total Pop.	+76	+318	+118	−17
Black Pop.	+177	−77	−64	−82

Source: Annual Reports of the Superintendent of Public Schools of Missouri, 1881, 1900, 1910, 1920, 1930, 1940, 1950; X53E. Box 200. KC250; Arthur A. Benson, II. Legal Papers. WHMC-KC.

school population of Jackson County (outside Kansas City, Missouri) and rural Clay County, followed this same pattern. In Platte County, the total school population declined modestly but the black school population plunged dramatically.

The demographic effect of this racially segregated system of schools is even more graphic when comparing white and black school enumeration. Table 3 shows white school enumeration in Jackson County (excluding Kansas City, Missouri), Clay County, and Platte County in Missouri at five-year intervals from 1935 to 1954. As table 3 shows, from 1935 to 1954 the number of white students attending schools in all three counties rose.

For decades, scholars have documented the historically strong African American commitment to education in the face of considerable economic hardship and racial discrimination.[14] The experience of African Americans in the Kansas City metropolitan area between World War I and 1954 demonstrated the tenacity of that commitment. During this era school districts in only six of the 61 African American settlements in Jackson, Clay, and Platte Counties provided elementary schools for African American children, creating pressures for parents either to move to areas where schools were located or make their children travel long distances to schools. At the secondary level, access to schools was even more limited for African American students. Until 1954, Lincoln High School in Kansas City, Missouri and its feeder

Table 3: White School Enumeration in Jackson County (excluding Kansas City, Missouri), Clay County, and Platte County, Missouri. 1935–1954.

	Jackson County	Clay County	Platte County
1935	14,429	7,118	3,361
1940	14,441	6,857	3,041
1945	16,082	7,443	3,914
1950	32,340	9,174	2,982
1954	43,856	12,950	3,992
Percent of Loss (−) or Gain (+) in School Population, 1935–1954			
	+204	+82	+19

Source: Annual Reports of the Superintendent of Public Schools of Missouri, 1935, 1940, 1945, 1950, 1954. X49A. *School Enumeration in Jackson (Excluding Kansas City, Missouri), Clay, and Platte Counties, 1935–1954*; X53E. *Black School Enumeration as a Percentage of Total Enumeration in Clay, Jackson (excluding Kansas City, Missouri), and Platte Counties, 1881–1954.* Box 200. KC 250. Arthur A. Benson, II. Legal Papers. WHMC-KC.

junior high schools in the city were the only schools in the three-county area that provided post-elementary education to blacks.

Thus, for most of the decades before *Brown,* Missouri's interdistrict system of racially segregated schools required African American families who wanted their children to receive an education to attend schools in Kansas City.

While black and white schools were "separate," they were not "equal." Of the elementary schools that rural school districts provided for blacks, many were dilapidated, infested with rodents, and inadequate for education. In 1929, a Missouri Education Commissioner reported:

In these schools, if they may be so called, education opportunities are practically non-existent. The typical school is in operation for about six months a year. The teacher, usually . . . young and immature . . . , has had little if any training above high school and frequently not so much. The building is usually a miserable shack totally unfit for human habitation. Textbooks and reference books are scarce and usually dilapidated. They are unsanitary, totally unattractive and generally unsuitable.[15]

In some cases, African American children endured long bus rides past neighborhood schools and over district school boundaries to attend schools in Kansas City. Unlike the intense controversies that busing elicited during the 1970s and 1980s, few blacks or whites protested against busing African American children during the 1930s and 1940s. Whites viewed busing as an easy way to segregate without maintaining a costly dual school system while blacks saw it as the only available means of obtaining an education in an era of rampant racial exclusion. School records, newspaper reports, and testimony in the *Jenkins v. Missouri*[16] case suggest that the typical bus ride was anywhere from 20 miles for African American children living within the city limits of Kansas City to 60 miles for African American children traveling to Kansas City from rural areas.[17] In Kansas City, from 1945 to 1954, approximately 100 African American schoolchildren from Independence, Missouri, were bused each year to attend schools in Kansas City, Missouri. African American children living in Park Hill in north Platte County, and Pleasant Hill and Harrison in rural Cass County, were transported to the KCMSD by bus or private car up to 1954.

For every child who was transported daily, there were many sent by poor families in rural towns to live with relatives in the KCMSD. Overall, the interdistrict system of segregated education in the metropolitan area meant that rural blacks were forced to travel long distances to attend schools or uproot themselves and move to Kansas City to have any reasonable hope for any kind of education. As one local resident put it,

> [The segregated school system] affected everyone that was trying to get [an] education. . . . [F]amilies and school children that wanted to receive a high school education in this area were sent to central Kansas City, which was about the only place to get a high school education. . . . We also know that there were areas like North Kansas City that did not maintain elementary schools for children. They had to come into Kansas City. Lee's Summit closed the elementary school down in 1910. They first went to Kansas City then to Independence. Independence closed Young High School [in the 1920s]. They came into the city. . . . In all the areas that did not maintain schools for blacks, it had an effect because [blacks] could not live there and have any access to education.[18]

The process of black in-migration to Kansas City and white exodus to the suburbs was reinforced by a wide range of discriminatory mechanisms, especially the housing policies of the Home Owners' Loan Corporation (HOLC), the Federal Housing Administration (FHA), and the Veterans Administration (VA) that barred blacks from purchasing homes in the suburbs.[19] From the 1920s through the 1950s, the Kansas City Real Estate Board (formed in 1900) subscribed to a national code of real estate ethics that endorsed the view that all-black and racially mixed neighborhoods were inferior to all-white homogenous neighborhoods.[20] During this time, the FHA's underwriting manuals referred to the "infiltration of inharmonious racial or national-ity groups" as "adverse" to neighborhood stability and advised appraisers to lower the rating of properties in racially mixed or all-black neighborhoods.[21] Although the FHA removed explicitly racist language from its manuals in the 1950s, later manuals continued to refer to the necessity of maintaining "homogenous" neighborhoods and warned of the risk of "dissimilar" groups as "unstable" and "inharmonious."[22]

In short, the systematic housing discrimination by private and public actors, which reinforced the state-enforced segregated school system, restricted both the housing and educational choices of blacks and influenced their decisions to move from rural areas to the inner city.

African Americans migrating from rural areas in Missouri, as in many areas of the country without racially segregated school systems, such as Michigan, Indiana, and Iowa, were drawn by jobs to the metropolitan areas but were prevented from settling in the suburbs because of widespread housing segregation, which was supported and bolstered by the federal government. Yet part of the lure of Kansas City, Missouri, was that the rural school systems available to blacks were rudimentary at best and nonexistent at worst. While jobs and economic opportunities might pull people into the city, the availability of schools would more specifically influence housing choices. In short, discriminatory federal housing policies and de jure segregated school systems formed a mutually reinforcing set of institutional barriers that prevented blacks from participating in the suburbanization process that benefitted millions of whites. While the promise of employment opportunities may have lured blacks to migrate to Kansas City, once in the city housing discrimination relegated them to racially segregated neighborhoods, where their children attended racially segregated schools.

School Segregation and Desegregation after *Brown*, 1955–1977

The U.S. Supreme Court's historic 1954 *Brown v. Board of Education*[23] decision ruled that the "separate but equal" precept of *Plessy v. Ferguson*[24] was unconstitutional and that state-sanctioned segregated school systems are "inherently unequal." A year later, in *Brown II*, the Supreme Court ruled that school districts should begin desegregating their schools with "all deliberate speed" but set no standard or deadline for desegregation to occur. In response, in 1955, the KCMSD eliminated explicitly *racial* attendance zones, replacing them with *neighborhood* attendance zones. This decision to adopt neighborhood attendance zones was based on the state of Missouri's decision to relinquish state control over how and where local school districts educated African American children after 1954. Before the Supreme Court's decision, the education of African American children, including their separation from white children, was considered a state government responsibility. After *Brown*, the state of Missouri adopted the policy that school desegregation was a matter of local discretion, choice, and control. A month after the *Brown* decision, the Missouri attorney general ruled that local districts "may . . . permit 'white and colored' children to attend the same schools," but left it up to local school districts to decide "whether

[they] must integrate."[25] After maintaining a policy of explicit racial segregation in schools for more than 50 years, the state now delegated to local school districts responsibility for remedying the problem.

Pursuant to the neighborhood attendance zone plan, the KCMSD school board eliminated explicit racial school attendance zones and drew new attendance zones using ostensibly nonracial criteria such as building capacity and student travel distance. Over the next two decades, from 1955 through the mid-1970s, the school board made frequent shifts in the attendance areas of its schools, typically removing white areas from the western-most portions of its racially transitional zones and attaching them to all-white zones farther west. While north/south school attendance boundaries changed often, the east/west boundary along Troost Avenue—a major north/south boulevard—remained fairly constant, setting in motion a process of rapid racial transition in neighborhoods and schools east of Troost.[26]

According to U.S. Census Bureau data, from 1950 through 1970 the number of white residents living in neighborhoods east of Troost plunged dramatically, declining from 126,229 in 1950 (75% of the total population) to 33,804 (25%) two decades later. In contrast, the number of black residents living in this area increased from 41,348 (25% of the total) in 1950 to 102,741 (75%) by 1970.

As tables 4 and 5 show, almost all schools located east of Troost experienced dramatic racial turnover at various times over the two decades after *Brown*. Specifically, by the mid-1970s, every high school east of Troost was more than 90% black and 16 out of 18 elementary schools located east of Troost were more than 90% black. In contrast, every elementary school and high school west of Troost was less than 50% black.[27]

Segregative school actions in this crucial period established Troost Avenue as a cognitive racial boundary—later to be referred to by local residents as the "Troost Wall"—that real estate "blockbusters" manipulated to stimulate white flight from neighborhoods east of Troost Avenue. "Blockbusting" is a practice in which real estate agents attempt to move nonwhite, usually African American families, into an all-white neighborhood for the purpose of exploiting white fears of impending racial turnover and property devaluation to buy up other property on the block at depressed prices.[28] Newspaper reports from the 1950s through the 1970s reveal that city council members, neighborhood coalitions, and civil rights groups were well aware of the destabilizing effects of blockbusting and panic selling, yet neither the state of Missouri nor the Kansas City Real Estate Board investigated or halted blockbusting or other profiteering real estate practices, including racial real estate steering and redlining, that affected southeast neighborhoods.[29]

On June 20, 1963, a group of African American and white residents staged a protest at a KCMSD Board meeting, charging that the district, via its attendance zone

Table 4. Racial Makeup of Kansas City, Missouri School District Elementary Schools at Five-Year Intervals, 1955–56 to 1974–75.

Elementary Schools located East of Troost Avenue, West of the Blue River, South of 31st Street.

School	1955–56 % Black	1960–61 % Black	1965–66 % Black	1970–71 % Black	1974–75 % Black
Linwood	18.2	89.9	98.8*	99.8	98.4
Ladd	4.7	99.0*	99.8	99.8	99.6
Moore	2.3	45.2	72.1	92.6	93.2
Faxon	0.7	11.5	54.6*	92.5	95.6
Seven Oaks	0*	65.1	96.8*	99.4	98.7
Melcher	not open	0.2	38.6	89.9	96.7
Mann	0	84.2	97.9*	99.1	98.9
Bancroft	0	1.2	28.5	66.6	84.4
Kumpf	0	62.2	96.8*	99.4*	100.0
Meservey	0	13.5	76.7	98.2	97.5
Graceland	28.8	43.4	89.6	99.0	99.6
Chick	0	10.8	51.2	83.6	90.8
Willard	0	0	7.3	92.2	98.7
Troost	0	1.3	3.3	42.2	93.3
Pershing	0	2.7	42.7	99.5	98.7
Pinkerton	0	0	18.0	84.3	94.9
Blenheim	0	0	20.9	53.9	92.3
Marlborough	0	0.2	30.6*	21.6	73.8

Elementary Schools Located West of Troost Avenue, East of the Missouri-Kansas State Line, South of 31st Street.

School	1955–56 % Black	1960–61 % Black	1965–66 % Black	1970–71 % Black	1974–75 % Black
Longan	0	1.5	2.7	4.2*	10.1
Volker	0	0	0	5.6	13.3
Swinney	0*	0.5*	18.6*	6.6	18.8
Nelson	0*	0*	1.1	14.6*	41.5
Bryant	0	0	0	1.1	15.4
Border Star	0	0	4.1	8.4	19.7
Cook	0	0	0	7.2	25.1

*Boundary change occurred within noted five-year interval.
Source: XK2. *Kansas City, Missouri (KCMO) School Districts, Total Enrollment, High School Enrollment, Junior College Enrollment, Elementary School Enrollment, 1954–1983*, Box 213. KC 250 Arthur A. Benson, II. Legal Papers. WHMC-KC.

Table 5. Racial Makeup of Kansas City, Missouri School District High Schools Located West of Troost Avenue and East of Troost Avenue at Five-Year Intervals, 1954–55 to 1974–75.

| School Year | High Schools West of Troost Avenue | | | | | | High Schools East of Troost Avenue | | | | | |
| | Westport | | Southwest | | Lincoln | | Central | | Pasco | | Southeast | |
	Total Enrolled	% Black	Total Enrolled	% Black	Total Enrolled	% Black	Total Enrolled	% Black	Total Enrolled	% Black	Total Enrolled	% Black
1954–55	1461	0	2031	0	1100	100.0	1604	0	1657	0	1575	0
1960–61	1684	2.5	1772	0.1	927	100.0	1522	90.2	1893	9.7	1883	1.7
1965–66	1862	10.9	2469	0.7	1121	99.9	2648	99.4	1597	62.4	1781	22.2
1970–71	1766	38.0	2387	0.8	1323	100.0	2115	99.9	1545	99.4	1463	79.6
1974–75	1361	47.6	2017	12.0	1312	99.9	2204	100.0	1466	99.9	2114	97.7

Source: Kansas City Missouri School District Annual Fall Membership Report 1954–55 and Annual Desegregation Reports, 1954–55 to 1974–75. High schools south of Interstate 70.

policies, was reinforcing neighborhood segregation by adopting "the unwritten law of the Troost line" as the boundary separating white and African American populations in Kansas City. More protests followed, and on August 1, 1963, the board adopted a policy statement declaring "that integration is a factor to be taken into account within the school system whenever it is possible to do so without destroying the fundamental principle of the school as a major service unit to the neighborhood of which it is part."[30]

Throughout the early 1960s, editorials in the local African American-owned newspaper, the *Kansas City Call*, repeatedly condemned the school board's segregative practices, drawing attention to how racially identifiable schools contributed to the maintenance of segregated neighborhoods.[31] Early on, the *Call* recognized that segregative school board policies interlocked with the discriminatory activities of local real estate firms and agents to perpetuate Troost Avenue as a racially identifiable school attendance boundary. Over the next decade, local civil rights groups and a number of neighborhood coalitions staged numerous protests at KCMSD board meetings demanding that the school board extend attendance zones across Troost Avenue. During this time, the school board repeatedly justified its segregative school attendance boundary policies on the grounds that "neighborhood unity," "neighborhood autonomy," and "neighborhood stability" had to be preserved before school integration could go forward. These claims provided the justification for changes in school district boundaries, which were redrawn dozens of times throughout the late-1950s and the 1960s to segregate blacks in schools east of Troost Avenue while maintaining the predominantly white composition of schools west of Troost. Not surprisingly, virtually every school the KCMSD built after 1954 opened either all-white or all-black.[32]

Until 1976, attendance zones did not cross Troost, despite overcrowding in African American schools east of Troost and underutilization of white schools west of Troost. Interestingly, the decision to eliminate the Troost Avenue attendance boundary came only after the Department of Health, Education, Welfare (HEW) investigated the district in 1973 and compelled it to adopt a comprehensive desegregation plan.[33] Until 1968, no African Americans served on the school board, and the racial composition of the board remained predominantly white throughout the 1970s.

During the 1960s, the state of Missouri and KCMSD board officials considered a number of school desegregation measures, including busing, equalizing funding across school districts, changes in school boundaries, and student transfer policies. However, school board officials refused to implement any of the proposed school desegregation measures, and, in the process, allowed attendance patterns to continue on a segregated basis.

In response to continued racial segregation both between and within schools, a number of civil rights groups mounted protests attacking what they perceived as efforts by an intransigent school board to maintain the racial segregation of Kansas City schoolchildren. In September 1964, a group calling itself the Citizens Coordinating Committee (CCC) staged a protest at a school board meeting, accusing the board of disregarding "the welfare of our children and callously ignoring the expressions of concern by apprehensive parents."[34] Later that month, the school district changed its policy and allowed bused students to mix into the regular enrollment. Justifying its actions as implementing the requirements of the 1955 *Brown II* decision to move with "all deliberate speed," the school board maintained that the purpose of its new busing policy was to integrate schools "as expeditiously as possible," a stance that the *Kansas City Call* immediately denounced as another "high-sounding phrase which really means 'any old time' or 'maybe not at all.'"[35] More protests followed in 1965. In October 1965, Freedom, Inc. issued a "Black Paper" setting out points of "frustration and discontent" among blacks of Kansas City, listing wrongs that should be corrected by local political officials. According to one point in the paper:

We protest the continuing refusal of the Board of Education to provide adequate education facilities; the continuing over crowded conditions which the vast majority of Negro children are required to seek an education; the continuing refusal to appoint qualified Negroes to administrative and supervisory positions in the school system; the continuing refusal to assign the best qualified teachers to those schools with the greatest need; and the aggravation of this situation by transferring the best and most skilled teachers to schools and areas where the need for their special talents is slight; . . . Freedom Incorporated and the Negro community will no longer be content or silent when we receive only the dregs of the tax dollars which we pay for the education of our children.[36]

Throughout the 1960s and into the 1970s, opponents of racial mixing in the schools, busing, and the elimination of racially identifiable school boundaries repeatedly voiced their resistance to school integration and equalization of school funding across districts on ostensibly non-racial grounds. For example, in 1969, State Representative James Spainhower introduced legislation to equalize school funding throughout the state by consolidating small school districts into larger regional school districts throughout the state. The objective of the "Spainhower Plan," as it became known, was not to promote racial integration but to relieve overcrowding in smaller districts and to redistribute educational resources across school districts. However, opponents vehemently denounced his plan on the grounds that it would exacerbate inequalities between school districts, impoverish education in the suburban school districts, and lead to more harm than good. Spainhower remembered dozens of conversations with fellow state legislators concerning his school equalization proposal in which "there were some things they would talk about with me in private that they would not talk about in public."

Privately they would discuss the detrimental effects upon their own political careers if our proposals for school district reorganization were pursued . . . , that it would compel them to take positions which could be harmful to them politically. The racial question was one which was discussed privately [but] was really not discussed publicly. It would cause them to have to face up to the issue of integration and they would just as soon not face up to that because to them it was a no-win issue.[37]

As Spainhower remembered, opponents of the plan perceived it as a policy for racial desegregation, though they never explicitly referred to it this way. He recalled that "generally it was phrased that, 'We like our school district like it is, it is doing a good job, we don't want to get part of Kansas City in our school district.'"[38]

From *Jenkins v. Missouri* (1977) to *Missouri v. Jenkins* (1995)

By the early 1970s, the segregative policies of the KCMSD were coming under heavy and sustained attack by local civil rights groups such as the National Association for the Advancement of Colored People (NAACP), the Congress of Racial Equality (CORE), the Southern Christian Leadership Committee (SCLC), and by the federal government.[39] In January 1973, the SCLC filed suit asking for desegregation of all KCMSD secondary schools.[40] A 1974–75 federal investigation of the KCMSD by the Department of Health, Education and Welfare (HEW) found that the school district had illegally segregated schools, had taken actions in the past to perpetuate segregation, and had ignored and passed up previous opportunities to desegregate its schools. Under threat to cut off federal funds to the district, HEW required that the school board dismantle its Troost Avenue attendance zone boundary and establish a long-range and comprehensive plan for school desegregation.[41] In 1976, a district task force submitted to HEW an integration plan entitled "Plan 6-C" that would realign attendance zones and bus students until every school within the school district was at least 30% minority. In July 1977, HEW responded that Plan 6-C did not "satisfy constitutional standards because it would continue a substantially large number of schools which are either racially isolated or substantially disproportionate in their racial composition." However, HEW could not accept or reject the KCMSD's plan because Congress had not yet acted on proposed antibusing legislation that affected HEW's powers. School board officials decided to implement Plan 6-C, and schools opened in fall 1977 with the plan in place.[42]

The school board designed Plan 6-C to attract federal money for the financially starved school district. "I may be the only person in this town that will admit that, but that's what it was in the truest sense of the word, the school district needed dollars," remembered Emanuel Cleaver, executive director of the Kansas City branch of the SCLC in 1981 and later mayor. "I don't think any of us operated under the assumption that Plan 6-C would desegregate the system." When board officials implemented Plan 6-C in 1977, eight out of every ten African American children in the district attended schools that were at least 90% black while the majority of white students attended schools that were more than 90% white. Four years later, enrollment figures showed virtually no significant change in the numbers and percentages of African American and white students attending KCMSD schools. By 1981, nonwhites made up 72.6% of the district's enrollment, up from 68.6 in 1977–78. White flight continued to cripple desegregation efforts as white enrollment plummeted by more than 4,000 students in four years, declining from 14,207 in 1977–78 to 10,191 in 1981.[43]

Racial conflicts over schools reached a crescendo in the late-1970s and 1980s, setting the stage for a protracted and bitter controversy over whether the problem of school desegregation required a local or a metropolitan solution. Protest and opposition against Plan 6-C busing plans were widely reported in the local Kansas City media. Some white activists and teachers opposed busing plans, believing that the quality of schools would decline as African American students were bused in from overcrowded black schools. One white resident living in Kansas City, Missouri, at the time asserted that "I'm afraid I'm going to sound pompous by saying this but we're paying for our ancestors' sins."[44] Meanwhile, civil rights leaders such as Emanuel Cleaver (leader of SCLC), Vertis Swinton (NAACP), Alvin Brooks (CORE), and Charles Briscoe (a school board official) called for a metropolitan-wide solution to the problem of school segregation.

In May 1977, in what would become Kansas City's landmark desegregation case, *Jenkins v. State of Missouri*,[45] the KCMSD sued 18 suburban school districts in Kansas and Missouri, the states of Kansas and Missouri, and the federal government. Initially, the school district positioned itself as the plaintiff in the suit, claiming that an interdistrict (city/suburban) *and* interstate (Kansas/Missouri) desegregation remedy was necessary to integrate racially isolated city schools. In October 1978, the U.S. District Court dismissed the cases against the state of Kansas and its suburban districts, and the school district was realigned as a defendant. The case proceeded to trial with a group of plaintiff schoolchildren suing both the KCMSD and the state of Missouri and the KCMSD cross-claiming against the state.

In 1984, the district court judge Russell Clark found the state of Missouri and the KCMSD had "violated the Constitution by failing to eliminate vestiges of a racially segregated dual system previously required under law."[46] The state was found liable for causing segregation through its laws and other acts that "had the effect of placing the state's imprimatur on racial discrimination." The school district was castigated for the segregative intent and effects of its school attendance boundary changes, its 1960s "intact busing" policy that kept black students separate from white students, and its repeated disregard for considering integration plans when they were proposed.[47]

However, Judge Clark dismissed the suburban school districts from responsibility for Kansas City's segregated school system, finding that "there is no credible or substantiated evidence of a constitutional violation by these suburban school districts."[48] With this decision, the problem of school desegregation was redefined as a local, rather than a metropolitan, problem. Any desegregation remedy would have to be accomplished within the geographical limits of the KCMSD, rather than through a metropolitan solution. Interestingly, after 1957, the geographical size of the Kansas City, Missouri, school district remained basically the same while the city annexed over 219 square miles of outlying land, creating new school districts for suburban whites. Without the state's 1957 enactment of H.B. 171, the KCMSD board officials would have automatically expanded school boundaries to become coterminous with city boundaries following annexations in 1958, 1959, 1961, 1962, and 1963. Because of H.B. 171, however, the KCMSD was unable to expand into all-white suburban areas to create a more racially balanced school district after 1957.

Moreover, that the Kansas City metropolitan area is split by the state line with Kansas made a true metropolitan desegregation difficult. Indeed, the historically bifurcated nature of the metropolitan area provided for the growth of suburban bedroom communities, especially in Johnson County, Kansas, to which Kansas City whites could flee.[49] Judge Clark's decision to release the suburban school districts from the desegregation suit was one he would later regret: "The very minute I let those suburban school districts out, I created a very severe problem for the court and for myself, really, in trying to come up with a remedial plan to integrate the Kansas City, Missouri, School District," the chief judge reflected years later. "The more salt you have, the more white you can turn the pepper. And without any salt, or with a limited amount of salt you're going to end up with a basically black mixture."[50]

Based on the 1984 district court decision, Kansas City's school desegregation efforts between 1985 and 1987 focused on rebuilding the KCMSD's schools and developing a comprehensive magnet school plan designed to attract suburban white students to the city school district within a system of controlled choice.[51] The guiding principle was that Kansas City schools would have to be improved substantially, both in image and substance, before whites from suburban districts could be persuaded to voluntarily enroll their children in the inner city school.[52]

The court also directed that the state of Missouri pay the costs of renovating or replacing all schools in the KCMSD in an effort to remedy the deleterious effects of deteriorating educational facilities and to avoid financial bankruptcy. After the KCMSD's enrollment had become majority African American in 1970, the district's voters, who remained majority white, rejected school funding initiatives 19 times while schools crumbled and the district faced fiscal insolvency. During the two decades after 1970, schools fell into chronic disrepair and deteriorated to the point that broken toilets, leaky ceilings, and rodents became commonplace in inner city schools.

In 1977, a *Kansas City Star* editorial referred to the KCMSD as "a neglected and financially starved entity that is merely awaiting official notice of its death."[53] As a result of the 1984 district court order, however, by February 1996, $1.7 billion had been spent by the school district and the state of Missouri to rebuild the district's crumbling schools, a process that in less than a decade brought a dramatic facelift to inner-city schools surrounded by poverty, deteriorating neighborhoods, and decaying infrastructure.

In June 1995, the U.S. Supreme Court struck down the central legal tenet of Kansas City's desegregation plan, ruling 5–4 in *Missouri v. Jenkins*[54] that the district court had had no authority to order expenditures for the purpose of attracting suburban whites. Not surprisingly, by the fall of 1996, the percentage of white students in the KCMSD dropped to a record low 22.1% as the percentage of minority students surged to a record high 77.9%. In 1996, the school board officials began closing schools, ended free transportation to schools for suburban white students, and initiated a series of staff layoffs, thus marking a return to the days of fiscal uncertainty and financial turmoil for the poverty-impacted school district. In November 1999, U.S. district court judge Dean Whipple dismissed the Kansas City, Missouri, school desegregation lawsuit and refused to block a state decision to strip the KCMSD of accreditation. While an appellate panel reinstated the desegregation case in March 2000, in October 2000, the state of Missouri revoked the district's accreditation and effectively ended the state's responsibility for paying the costs of desegregation.[55]

Conclusion

It has been over a century since the U.S. Supreme Court decided *Plessy v. Ferguson*,[56] the landmark case that legitimated public policies of "separate but equal." Two generations later, the Supreme Court ruled in *Brown v. Board of Education*[57] that state-sanctioned segregated schools are "inherently unequal" and ordered that school districts integrate their schools. For decades after *Brown*, many state governments and school boards throughout the nation worked to evade *Brown*'s anti-segregation doctrine. Even after the passage of civil rights laws, fair housing, and court-ordered busing in the 1960s and 1970s, school desegregation proceeded at a snail's pace. In the 1970s and 1980s, a broad-based conservative backlash against school desegregation gained momentum and was successful in recasting desegregation as symptomatic of "big government" and a threat to democracy and free choice.[58] Today, the Supreme Court has divested *Brown* of much of its scope and reach. As Gary Orfield and Susan Eaton have noted, "The Supreme Court decisions of the 1990s offer instruction not about how to further desegregation but how to dismantle it."[59] Indeed, the 1995 Supreme Court decision in *Missouri v. Jenkins*[60] requires that desegregation policies be limited in time and extent and requires the restoration of local control as the primary goal in desegregation cases. In short, by tacitly supporting the "separate but equal" doctrine that *Brown* outlawed, the Supreme Court is embracing a return to unequal public schools, a trend that is exacerbated by persistent racial inequalities in housing, employment, and other areas of American society.[61]

Clearly, the Kansas City case belies any notion that the historical development of racial segregation in schools and housing was "natural," accidental, immutable, or caused by remote and uncontrollable demographic forces or migration processes. For decades before *Brown,* the state of Missouri and local school board officials—in both Kansas City, Missouri, and the surrounding Missouri counties that form its metropolitan area—engaged in practices explicitly intended to create and maintain a racially segregated school system in the city. School districts in the surrounding counties discriminated against African American students in ways that both encouraged and forced the migration of students into the racially segregated Kansas City school system. These segregative practices interlocked with intentionally and explicitly discriminatory housing policies and real estate practices to create the racially identifiable neighborhoods and schools that came to characterize Kansas City.[62] After the *Brown* decision, school boundary decisions established Troost Avenue as a racial boundary separating white neighborhoods to the west of Troost and black neighborhoods to the east of Troost. During this time, the school board wielded the "neighborhood" school policy as a shield with which to ward off claims of intentional school segregation leveled by civil rights groups. The KCMSD's insistence upon preserving the almost all-white composition of its schools west of Troost made it impossible to keep its schools east of Troost racially integrated, putting pressure on white families to move out of the area and resulting in virtually complete racial turnover in the southeast part of the city.[63]

These school actions were felt throughout the metropolitan area and exerted a profound influence on the residential development of the metropolitan area in the post-World War II era. Segregative school policies combined with discriminatory public and private housing actions restricted the choices of blacks to inner city housing and schools. In turn, the creation of quality schools in the suburbs combined with new housing primed by FHA and VA housing subsidies expanded the housing and school choices of whites and stimulated them to move out of the city. Yet the Kansas City experience is not unique. With slight variations, what happened in Kansas City and its surrounding metropolitan area during the past century occurred in cities throughout the entire country—indeed, in almost every metropolitan area where racial minorities have sought to gain access to quality education and housing.[64]

Today, the fragmentation of local government, including school districts, has powerfully influenced the pattern of racial segregation in metropolitan areas. In Kansas City, the existence of the Kansas/Missouri state line exacerbates this political fragmentation and, more important, has effectively shut off the option of drawing from the heavily white suburbs on the Kansas side of the state line (in Johnson County) to integrate city districts. More than three decades ago, Karl Taeuber noted that the system of school districts in a metropolitan area "creates and sustains the identification of residential neighborhoods that vary in perceived quality. . . . Just as a good neighborhood tends to create and sustain a good school, a good school tends to create and sustain a good neighborhood."[65] In *Place Matters: Metropolitics for the Twenty-First Century,* Peter Dreier, John Mollenkopf, and Todd Swanstrom maintain that suburban municipalities have become powerful sorting mechanisms for racial and class divisions.[66] Where people live, as Dreier and colleagues point out, has a profound influence on the choices people have, the economic resources they have access to, and their capacity to achieve a high quality of life. Racial segregation has always been America's "dilemma," as Gunnar Myrdal observed decades ago, and the vast racial differences in resources and school financing across metropolitan areas mean that segregated schools will continue to be unequal schools because segregation concentrates poverty and disadvantage.[67]

Kevin Fox Gotham is Associate Dean for Academic Affairs in the School of Liberal Arts and Professor of Sociology at Tulane University. This chapter is adapted from an article by the same title previously published in 43 AMERICAN STUDIES 5 (2002).

NOTES

I thank Farrah Gafford, Jessica Pardee, and anonymous reviewers of *American Studies* for comments on an earlier draft of this chapter. When conducting research for this piece, in addition to accessing the primary sources in the *Jenkins v. Missouri* case, I consulted hundreds of pages of court testimony, depositions, and the plaintiffs' exhibits themselves. The citations used in this paper take the following form: plaintiff's exhibit (X) followed by the exhibit number, title of the exhibit, box containing the exhibit, the archive number for collection (KC 250), the name of the collection (e.g., the Arthur Benson papers), and the location (Western Historical Manuscript Collection-Kansas City (WHMC-KC)).

1. Gary Orfield, *Turning Back to Segregation*, 10 in GARY ORFIELD & SUSAN E. EATON, EDS., DISMANTLING DESEGREGATION: THE QUIET REVERSAL OF *BROWN V. BOARD OF EDUCATION* (The New Press 1996).

2. The index of dissimilarity measures the proportion of a racial group that would have to move in order to live in a racially mixed neighborhood. A value of 60 or above is considered very high and implies extreme segregation. A value of 40 or 50 suggests moderate segregation and a value of 30 or below means that only a minority of residents need to move to a different census tract in order for racial groups to be evenly distributed. *See* Lewis Mumford Center. *Ethnic Diversity Grows, Neighborhood Integration Is at a Standstill*, www.albany.edu./mumford/census (April 3, 2001); DOUGLAS S. MASSEY & NANCY A. DENTON, AMERICAN APARTHEID: SEGREGATION AND THE MAKING OF THE UNDERCLASS, 54–55 (Harvard University Press 1993).

3. Aage B. Sorensen, Karl E. Taeuber, & Leslie J. Hollingsworth Jr., *Indexes of Residential*

Segregation for 109 Cities in the United States, 8 SOCIOLOGICAL FOCUS 125, 128–30 (1975).

4. Hypersegregation is based on the measurement of five dimensions of residential segregation: uneven distribution of African Americans within a metropolitan area, geographic isolation of African Americans, concentration of African Americans within spatially dense areas, clustering of black neighborhoods into one large ghetto, and centralization of African Americans near the Central Business District. MASSEY & DENTON, AMERICAN APARTHEID, 75–77. A racial group is said to be "hypersegregated" if it is segregated on at least four of the five above indices. The hypersegregation of African Americans is important for three reasons. First, not only are African Americans more segregated than other racial groups on any single dimension of segregation, but they are more segregated on all dimensions simultaneously. Second, African Americans are the only racial/ethnic group that was hypersegregated in selected American cities according to analyses of 1980 and 1990 census tract data. Third, hypersegregation operates as a "multiplier effect" that concentrates disadvantage in the urban core and deprives predominantly African American communities of the social supports and opportunities for socioeconomic betterment. Not only does living in hypersegregated neighborhoods restrict opportunities for upward mobility through access to jobs and income, quality schools, and housing equity, but it is also closely associated with higher crime and poor living conditions. ROBERT D. BULLARD, J. EUGENE GRIGSBY, & CHARLES LEE, RESIDENTIAL APARTHEID: THE AMERICAN LEGACY (The Regents of the University of California Center for Afro-American Studies Publication 1994); JOHN YINGER, CLOSED DOORS, OPPORTUNITIES LOST: THE CONTINUING COSTS OF HOUSING DISCRIMINATION (Russell Sage Foundation 1995).

5. The Kansas City metropolitan statistical area (MSA) is a bi-state, 11-county area, containing more than 460 municipalities. The counties that have traditionally made up the urban core of the metropolitan area include Johnson County and Wyandotte County in Kansas; Cass County, Jackson County, and Platte County, in Missouri. The Kansas City, Missouri School District (KCMSD) is located within Kansas City, Missouri, which is in Jackson County. Over the last few decades, Johnson County, Platte County, and Cass County, have experienced tremendous economic growth and burgeoning suburban housing construction as jobs, wealth, and people have flowed to these outlying regions. In contrast, both Wyandotte and Jackson Counties exhibit declining economic fortunes, with declining population, blue collar work force, rising poverty rates, and increasing percentage of minority residents. KEVIN FOX GOTHAM, RACE, REAL ESTATE, AND UNEVEN DEVELOPMENT: THE KANSAS CITY EXPERIENCE, 1900–2000 (State University of New York Press 2002); Mumford Center *Ethnic Diversity Grows, Neighborhood Integration Is at a Standstill* (April 3, 2001).

6. In the South, school districts were generally coterminous with county lines. In the North, however, school districts served children within walking distance. After the Civil War, 17 states, including Missouri, superimposed patterns of racial segregation upon their school districts, requiring that schools be kept separate for blacks and whites. Four states, including Kansas, allowed towns with more than 15,000 people to set up segregated schools only through elementary schools. In 1904, Kansas City, Kansas, passed an ordinance that required separate schools for blacks and whites, and Sumner High School opened as the city's only black high school. SUSAN D. GREENBAUM, THE AFRO-AMERICAN COMMUNITY IN KANSAS CITY, KANSAS: A HISTORY (Kansas Department of Public Development 1982).

7. 1889 Missouri Laws 226; 1909 Missouri Laws 770; 1909 Missouri Laws 790; 1909 Missouri Laws 820.

8. 1865 Missouri Laws 177; 1869 Missouri Laws 86–7; 1870 Missouri Laws 149; 1877 Missouri Laws 264; 1893 Missouri Laws 247; 1909 Missouri Laws 790–91; 1929 Missouri Laws 382.

9. Kevin Fox Gotham, *Constructing the Segregated City: Housing, Neighborhoods, and Racial Division in Kansas City, 1880–2000* (Ph.D. Dissertation, University of Kansas (1997)); Homer Clevenger, *The Building of the Hannibal and St. Joseph Railroad*, 36 MISSOURI HISTORICAL REVIEW 32 (1941); CHARLES N. GLAAB, KANSAS CITY AND THE RAILROADS: COMMUNITY POLICY IN THE GROWTH OF A REGIONAL METROPOLIS (University Press of Kansas 1993).

10. JACQUELINE JONES, THE DISPOSSESSED: AMERICA'S UNDERCLASS FROM THE CIVIL WAR TO THE PRESENT (Basic Books 1992); NICHOLAS LEMANN, THE PROMISED LAND: THE GREAT BLACK MIGRATION AND HOW IT CHANGED AMERICA (Random House 1991); CAROLE MARKS, FAREWELL, WE'RE GOOD AND GONE: THE GREAT MIGRATION (Indiana University Press 1989).

11. During these decades, Jim Crowism was extended to almost all public and private organizations and institutions in Kansas City. Local ordinances in Kansas City, St. Louis, and elsewhere mandated racially separate public parks, restaurants, hotels, theaters, department stores, swimming pools, and health care facilities. Dwayne R. Martin, *The Hidden Community: The Black Community of Kansas City, Missouri during the 1870s and 1880s* (M.A. Thesis, University of Missouri, Kansas City (1982)). In Kansas City, Missouri, for example, the city council passed an ordinance in 1914 making it illegal to establish "any school . . . for . . . persons of African descent" within one-half mile of a school for "persons not of African descent." Lehew et al. v. Brummell et al., 15 S.W. 765 (Missouri Supreme Court 1891).

12. Plessy v. Ferguson, 163 U.S. 537 (1896); LORENZO J. GREENE, GARY R. KREMER, & ANTONIO F. HOLLAND, MISSOURI'S BLACK HERITAGE, 107–108 (University of Missouri Press 1993).

13. In 1873, the city limits of Kansas City, Missouri spread over only 5.25 square miles. Land annexations in 1873, 1885, 1897, and 1909 increased the city's size to approximately 60 square miles. The next annexation drive would not occur until 1947, which increased the city limits to 62 miles. From 1887 to 1950, the KCMSD school board consistently and repeatedly expanded its school district territory after the city expanded its boundaries by annexation. 1957 Missouri Laws 454; 1965 Missouri Laws 275, 276–77, codified at Missouri Revised Statute § 162.71 (1965).

14. HENRY ALLEN BULLOCK, A HISTORY OF NEGRO EDUCATION IN THE SOUTH: FROM 1619 TO THE PRESENT (Harvard University Press 1967); Leslie Baham Inniss, *Historical Footprints: The Legacy of the School Desegregation Pioneers*, in MICHAEL PETER SMITH & JOE R. FEAGIN, EDS., THE BUBBLING CAULDRON: RACE, ETHNICITY, AND THE URBAN CRISIS (University of Minnesota Press 1995); Harvey Kantor and Barbara Brenzel, *Urban Education and the 'Truly Disadvantaged': The Historical Roots of the Contemporary Crisis*, in MICHAEL KATZ, ED., THE "UNDERCLASS" DEBATE: VIEWS FROM HISTORY (Princeton University Press 1992); Walter R. Allen & Joseph O. Jewell, *The Miseducation of Black America: Black Education Since AN AMERICAN DILEMMA*, in OBIE CLAYTON, JR, ED., AN AMERICAN DILEMMA REVISITED: RACE RELATIONS IN A CHANGING WORLD, 169 (Russell Sage Foundation 1996).

15. X210 (1929 Report, 122–23); ibid. (1922 Report, 33, 1927 Report, 147), 1858, 212 (1945

Report, 37), 189. Box 201. Kansas City 250, Arthur A. Benson, II. Legal Papers. Western Historic Manuscript Collection-Kansas City.

16. Jenkins v. Missouri, 593 F. Supp. 1485 (W.D. Mo. 1984), affirmed, 807 F.2d 657 (8th Cir. 1986), certiorari denied, 484 U.S. 816 (1987).

17. *Expert Witness Still Contends that Availability of Education Caused Concentration of Blacks in K.C.*, KANSAS CITY CALL (December 9–15 1983); *Trial Tales Continue on Blacks Being Forced out of Rural Schools to KC*, KANSAS CITY CALL (November 11–17, 1983); *Blacks Recall Long Trips to Segregated Schools*, KANSAS CITY STAR E-1 (May 5, 1977); T434; Tl82, 324, 474, 539, 548, 708, 761, 855, 920, 933, 951, 1021, 1053, 1292, 1339, 1400, 1656, 1689, 3167, 3598. Jenkins, 593 F. Supp. 1485 (1985).

18. Dr. James Anderson Testimony, A1-4. Joint Addendum A (Excerpts from Record) of Kalima Jenkins, et al. and the School District of Kansas City, Missouri (KCMSD), Appellants. Folder 13, KC 250, Arthur A. Benson, II. Legal Papers. Western Historic Manuscript Collection-Kansas City.

19. GOTHAM, RACE, REAL ESTATE, AND UNEVEN DEVELOPMENT; Kevin Fox Gotham, *Racialization and the State: The Housing Act of 1934 and the Origins of the Federal Housing Administration (FHA)*, 43 SOCIOLOGICAL PERSPECTIVES 291–317 (2000); Kevin Fox Gotham, *Urban Space, Restrictive Covenants, and the Origin of Racial Residential Segregation in a U.S. City, 1900–1950*, 24 INTERNATIONAL JOURNAL OF URBAN AND REGIONAL RESEARCH, 616–33 (2000); KENNETH T. JACKSON, CRABGRASS FRONTIER: THE SUBURBANIZATION OF THE UNITED STATES (Oxford University Press 1985); MASSEY & DENTON, AMERICAN APARTHEID, 54–55; JILL QUADAGNO, COLOR OF WELFARE: HOW RACISM UNDERMINED THE WAR ON POVERTY, 90–91 (Oxford University Press 1994); MARC A. WEISS, RISE OF THE COMMUNITY BUILDERS: THE AMERICAN REAL ESTATE INDUSTRY AND URBAN LAND PLANNING, 151 (Columbia University Press 1987); CHARLES ABRAMS, FORBIDDEN NEIGHBORS: A STUDY OF PREJUDICE IN HOUSING, 230–37 (Kennikat 1971).

20. Gotham, *Urban Space*, 616–33.

21. QUADAGNO, COLOR OF WELFARE, 90–91; JACKSON, CRABGRASS FRONTIER; MASSEY & DENTON, AMERICAN APARTHEID, 54–55; ROSE HELPER, RACIAL POLICIES AND PRACTICES OF REAL ESTATE BROKERS, 201–16 (University of Minnesota Press 1969).

22. Federal Housing Administration 1936; 1938; 1947; 1952.

23. Brown v. Board of Education, 347 U.S. 483 (1954).

24. Plessy, 163 U.S. 537 (1896).

25. X583. *A Study of the Problems Involved in the Desegregation of Public Schools in Kansas City, Missouri.* Research Department Kansas City Missouri School District. 7115/54; X585. *Policy Statements: Policies for Transition from System of Separate Schools to a Desegregated School System.* Kansas City Missouri School District. 3/3/55. Box 202. Kansas City 250, Arthur A. Benson, II. Legal Papers. Western Historic Manuscript Collection-Kansas City.

26. Jenkins, 593 F. Supp. 1493; See, 2/21184 Stipulation, Numbers. 12, 39, 42, 43, 48; X7211 D. *Analysis of School Boundary Changes, Kansas City, Missouri School District, 1953–4 – 1974–5.* Box 210. Kansas City 250, Arthur A. Benson, II. Legal Papers. Western Historic Manuscript Collection-Kansas City.

27. X20. *Racial Make-up of KCMSD Elementary Schools in the Southeast Corridor at Five Year*

Intervals Between 1955 and 1975. Box 200; XK2. *Kansas City, Missouri School Districts, Total Enrollment, High School Enrollment, Junior College Enrollment, Elementary School Enrollment, 1954–1983.* Box 213. Kansas City 250. Arthur A. Benson, II. Legal Papers. Western Historic Manuscript Collection-Kansas City.

28. W. EDWARD ORSER, BLOCKBUSTING IN BALTIMORE: THE EDMONDSON VILLAGE STORY (University Press of Kentucky 1994); Joe. R. Feagin, *Urban Real Estate Speculation in the United States: Implications for Social Science and Urban Planning,* in RACHEL BRAT, CHESTER HARTMAN, & ANN MEYERSON, EDS., CRITICAL PERSPECTIVES ON HOUSING (Temple University Press 1986); Helper, Racial Policies and Practices, 201–16; David A. Snow & Peter J. Leahy, *The Making of a Black Slum-Ghetto: A Case Study of Neighborhood Transition,* 16 JOURNAL OF APPLIED BEHAVIORAL SCIENCE 459–81 (1980).

29. Kevin Fox Gotham, *Separate and Unequal: The Housing Act of 1968 and HUD's Section 235 Program,* 15(1) SOCIOLOGICAL FORUM 13–37 (2000).

30. Kansas City, Missouri School District. 6/20/63. *Minutes of Meeting;* Kansas City, Missouri School District. 6/25/63. *Minutes of Meeting;* Kansas City, Missouri School District. 7/2/63. *Transcript of Proceeding;* Kansas City, Missouri School District, *Racial Policy,* Report Number 16 (1963); Kansas City, Missouri School District. *Integration and the Kansas City Missouri, Schools: A Statement of the Board of Education of the School District of Kansas City, Missouri, Acknowledging Requests Made by the Kansas City Congress of Racial Equality.* X716. Box 202. KC 250, Arthur A. Benson, II. Legal Papers. Western Historic Manuscript Collection-Kansas City.

31. *Study Four Areas of Community Problems,* KANSAS CITY CALL 12 (March 3, 1961); *Southeast Picture Confused,* KANSAS CITY CALL 17 (October 19, 1962); *Parents Stand Pat Against Segregation,* KANSAS CITY CALL 2 (December 14, 1962).

32. X2711 H. Office of Civil Rights, *School Site Construction* (1975). Box 21 0; XK2. *Kansas City, Missouri School Districts, Total Enrollment, High School Enrollment, Junior College Enrollment, Elementary School Enrollment, 1954–1983.* Box 213; XK54. *Schools Which Were Planned or Existing as One Race Schools in 1954, and which Remained 90 Percent or More of the Same Race until 1977–78.* Box 213. KC 250, Arthur A. Benson, II. Legal Papers. Western Historical Manuscript Collection–Kansas City.

33. *Desegregation Proceeds Warily Under Federal Eye,* KANSAS CITY STAR (December 27, 1974); *'Watered Down' Desegregation Plan to HEW; One-Way Busing,* KANSAS CITY CALL (June 13–19, 1975); *School District Submits Poorly Prepared Plan to HEW,* KANSAS CITY CALL (June 20–26, 1975); *HEW Flatly Turns Down K.C. Desegregation Plan,* KANSAS CITY CALL (July 18–25, 1975); *School Officials Muff Chances to Desegregate,* KANSAS CITY CALL (December 12–18, 1975); *School District Failures Coming Back to Haunt It,* KANSAS CITY CALL (December 12–18, December 1975).

34. *Make 9 School Demands,* KANSAS CITY CALL (September 25, 1964); *Events in K.C. School Controversy: Where Are We Headed in the School Bussing Situation,* KANSAS CITY CALL 15 (September 25, 1964).

35. *Phrases, Local and National,* KANSAS CITY CALL 17 (November 6, 1964).

36. *Issue K.C. 'Black Paper,'* KANSAS CITY CALL (October 15–21, 1965).

37. Sherry Lamb Schirmer, *Landscape of Denial: Space, Status and Gender in the Construction of Racial Perceptions Among White Kansas Citians, 1900–1958,* 4 (Ph.D. dissertation, University of Kansas (1995)).

38. Ibid.

39. *Argue Over School Integration,* KANSAS CITY CALL (January 12–18, 1974); *Black Leaders Plead for School Integration,* KANSAS CITY CALL (January 19–25, 1973); *Rally Behind Briscoe Resolution: Integration Official District Policy Now,* KANSAS CITY CALL (January 26–31, 1973); *Schools May Lose Funding, Judge Orders Investigation,* KANSAS CITY CALL (July 13–19, 1973); *Nearly 55 Percent Black Majority in K.C Schools,* KANSAS CITY CALL (July 13–19, 1973); *School Board Members Try to Reverse Policy on Integration—But Lose,* KANSAS CITY CALL (July 13–19, 1973); *Teacher Integration Goes Smoothly as Foes Protest,* KANSAS CITY CALL (July 27–July 2, 1973); *Dr. Metcalf Causes Stir With Talk of 'Easing Integration',* KANSAS CITY CALL (August 10–16, 1973); *689 Teachers Shifted In Integration Move, Protests Minimum,* KANSAS CITY CALL (August 17–23, 1973); *School Opens Next Week With Teacher Integration Still 'Bone of Contention',* KANSAS CITY CALL (August 24–30, 1973); *Citizens and Teachers Lambast School Board,* KANSAS CITY CALL (March 22–28, 1974); *Board Balks At Shifting Four High School Principals for Integration,* KANSAS CITY CALL (August 16–22, 1974); *School Board Action (Or Inaction) Gets District Into Difficulty,* KANSAS CITY CALL 14 (February 14–20, 1975); *Freedom Issues Statement Against Desegregation Plan,* KANSAS CITY CALL 3 (July 18–25, 1973); *Are School Boards Needed?,* KANSAS CITY CALL 10 (July 25–31, 1975); *No Desegregation in Schools This Fall,* KANSAS CITY CALL (August 8–14, 1975); *Schools Go Fumbling Along,* KANSAS CITY CALL 10 (September 5–11, 1975).

40. *S.C.L.C. Not Dropping School Suit-Cleaver,* KANSAS CITY CALL (February 1–7, 1974); *S.C.L.C. To Hold Second Hearing on Integration,* KANSAS CITY CALL (March 22–28, March 1974).

41. *Desegregation Proceeds Warily Under Federal Eye,* KANSAS CITY STAR (December 27, 1974); *School Board Asks for Desegregation Delay,* KANSAS CITY CALL 10 (May 16–22, 1975); *New Desegregation Plan-E Leaves Much to be Desired,* KANSAS CITY CALL (June 6–12, 1975); *'Watered Down' Desegregation Plan to HEW; One-Way Busing,* KANSAS CITY CALL (June 13–19, 1975); *Coalition of Black Ministers, Opposition to School Board,* KANSAS CITY CALL (June 13–19, 1975); *School District Submits Poorly Prepared Plan to HEW,* KANSAS CITY CALL 6 (June 20–26, 1975); *HEW Flatly Turns Down K.C. Desegregation Plan,* KANSAS CITY CALL (July 18–25, 1975); *HEW's Rejection of School Plan Sends Board into Sunday Sessions,* KANSAS CITY CALL (July 18–25, 1975); *Board Ducks Issue, Votes to Sue HEW,* KANSAS CITY CALL (July 25–31, 1975); *School Officials Muff Chances to Desegregate,* KANSAS CITY CALL (December 12–18, 1975); *School District Failures Coming Back to Haunt It,* KANSAS CITY CALL 18 (December 12–18, December 1975); *HEW Ends Testimony in School Board Hearing; Defense on in January,* KANSAS CITY CALL (December 19–25, 1975); *School Presents Case in HEW Hearings,* KANSAS CITY CALL (January 9–15, 1976); *Former School Superintendent Takes Stand at HEW Hearing,* KANSAS CITY CALL (January 9–15, 1976).

42. *Chairman of Task Force Bitterly Opposed to Desegregation Plan 6-C,* KANSAS CITY CALL (December 10–16, 1976); *Desegregation Plan 6-C, Adopted by School Board, Leaves All Black 'Corridor',* KANSAS CITY CALL (December 10–16, 1976); *HEW Finds School Desegregation Plan 6-C to be 'Unconstitutional',* KANSAS CITY CALL (July 8–12, 1977); *Schools Gearing Up for Opening of Fall Term Under Desegregation Plan,* KANSAS CITY CALL (August 12–18, 1977); *Public School Open Wednesday with Desegregation Plan 6C in Operation,* KANSAS CITY CALL (September 2–8, 1977).

43. *Figures Make KC District Appear to be Resegregating,* KANSAS CITY STAR (November 15, 1981).

44. *In the Suburbs: Bussing Presents Philosophical Dilemma for Father-Teacher in Favor of Integration,* KANSAS CITY STAR, (August 28, 1977); *In the City: Black Parents View*

Plan for Desegregation as Mindless Shuffling of Children's Bodies, KANSAS CITY STAR, (August 28, 1977).

45. Jenkins v. Missouri, 593 F. Supp. 1485 (W.D. Mo. 1984).

46. Ibid., 1487.

47. Ibid.

48. *Area Integration Suit Turns on District; Kansas Freed*, KANSAS CITY TIMES (July 10, 1978); *Suburban Districts Dismissed in School Desegregation Trial*, KANSAS CITY CALL (April 6–12, 1984); *U.S. Judge Deals Blow to Metropolitan Desegregation Plan*, KANSAS CITY CALL, (July 6–14, 1984).

49. The population of Johnson County increased dramatically after 1940, from 33,327 in 1940 to 62,783 in 1950; 143,792 in 1960; 220,073 in 1970; 270,269 in 1980; and 335,034 in 1990; a ten-fold increase in 50 years. By 2000, the population of the county was over 450,000 people. By this time, less than 10% of the population of the county was minority and less than 5% was black.

50. *The End of Integration*, TIME, 41 (April 29, 1996).

51. Alison Morantz, *Money and Choice in Kansas City: Major Investments With Modest Returns*, in ORFIELD & EATON, DISMANTLING DESEGREGATION.

52. Arthur Benson, *School Segregation and Desegregation in Kansas City*, Unpublished Manuscript (1995).

53. *Metropolitan Desegregation: Not a War Declaration*, KANSAS CITY STAR (April 20, 1977).

54. Missouri v. Jenkins, 515 U.S. 70 (1995).

55. *Enrollment of Whites Drops*, KANSAS CITY STAR C-1 (November 10, 1995); *Court Ends Desegregation Case; Loss of Accreditation Stands; Relief, Dismay Follow Decision*, KANSAS CITY STAR, (November 18, 1999); Catherine Gewertz, *U.S. Appellate Panel Reinstates Kansas City Desegregation Case*, EDUCATION WEEK (March 8, 2000); Catherine Gewertz, *A Hard Lesson for Kansas City's Troubled Schools*, EDUCATION WEEK, (April 26, 2000).

56. Plessy v. Ferguson, 163 U.S. 537 (1896).

57. Brown v. Board of Education, 347 U.S. 483 (1954).

58. BRUCE FULLER & RICHARD F. ELMORE, WHO CHOOSES? WHO LOSES? CULTURE, INSTITUTIONS, AND THE UNEQUAL EFFECTS OF SCHOOL CHOICE (Teachers College Press 1996); GARY ORFIELD & CAROLE ASHKINAZA, CLOSING THE DOOR: CONSERVATIVE POLICY AND BLACK OPPORTUNITY (University of Chicago Press 1991); THOMAS B. EDSALL & MARY D. EDSALL, CHAIN REACTION: THE IMPACT OF RACE, RIGHTS, AND TAXES ON AMERICAN POLITICS (W.W. Norton 1991).

59. ORFIELD & EATON, DISMANTLING DESEGREGATION, xv.

60. Jenkins, 515 U.S. 70 (1995).

61. Gary Orfield, Plessy *Parallels: Back to Traditional Assumptions*, in GARY ORFIELD & SUSAN E. EATON, EDS., DISMANTLING DESEGREGATION: THE QUIET REVERSAL OF *BROWN V. BOARD OF EDUCATION* (The New Press 1996); Kevin Fox Gotham, *Blind Faith in the Free Market: Urban Poverty, Residential Segregation, and Federal Housing Retrenchment, 1970–1995*, 68 SOCIOLOGICAL INQUIRY 1–31 (1998); Kevin Fox Gotham & James D. Wright, *Housing Policy*, in JAMES MIDGLEY,

MICHELLE LIVERMORE, & MARTIN B. TRACY, EDS., HANDBOOK OF SOCIAL POLICY, 237–55 (Sage Publications 2000).

62. Gotham, *Urban Space*, 616–33.

63. GOTHAM, RACE, REAL ESTATE, AND UNEVEN DEVELOPMENT.

64. MASSEY & DENTON, AMERICAN APARTHEID, 54–55.

65. Karl Taeuber, *Housing, Schools, and Incremental Segregative Effects*, 441 THE ANNALS OF THE AMERICAN ACADEMY OF POLITICAL AND SOCIAL SCIENCE 158 (1979).

66. PETER DREIER, JOHN MOLLENKOPF, & TODD SWANSTROM, PLACE MATTERS: METROPOLITICS FOR THE TWENTY-FIRST CENTURY (University of Kansas Press 2001).

67. GUNNAR MYRDAL, AN AMERICAN DILEMMA: THE NEGRO PROBLEM AND MODERN DEMOCRACY (Harper & Bros. 1944); Gary Orfield & John T. Yun, The Civil Rights Project, *Resegregation in American Schools* (1999); MASSEY & DENTON, AMERICAN APARTHEID, 54–55.

KRISTI L. BOWMAN

The Legal Legacy
of *Missouri v. Jenkins*

THE SUPREME COURT'S 1995 DECISION IN *MISSOURI V. JENKINS* IS ONE OF THE many middle children of school desegregation jurisprudence. Born long after the celebrated civil rights victories in *Brown v. Board of Education*[1] and *Green v. County School Board of New Kent County*,[2] and a generation before *Parents Involved in Community Schools v. Seattle School District No. 1*[3] and the higher education affirmative action cases brought by white plaintiffs, *Jenkins* has merited comparatively little sustained scholarly attention in its own right. *Jenkins* has not been forgotten, but most often it is mentioned in the literature merely as part of the arc of school desegregation jurisprudence, or as the last of three decisions in the 1990s in which the Court defined what it meant for a school district to "eliminate the vestiges of segregation root and branch" and paved the way for courts across the country to close school desegregation cases.[4]

Those three decisions were part of a long trajectory of retrenchment on school desegregation by the Court, starting with *Milliken v. Bradley*[5] in 1974 and continuing most recently in 2007 with *Parents Involved*.[6] Although the Court has not decided a school desegregation or voluntary integration case since 2007, it has decided two higher education affirmative action cases, both of which indicate that the retrenchment has continued: in 2013 the Court reinforced the narrowness of narrow tailoring in *Fisher v. Texas*,[7] and in 2014 it held that a state constitutional amendment could prohibit the consideration of race in higher education admissions in *Schuette v. Coalition to Defend Affirmative Action*.[8] *Jenkins* is, at the very least, one point on an arc trending in a very definite direction. *Jenkins* might be more than just one step in a long journey, though.

The Kansas City desegregation story that gave rise to *Jenkins* has captured our attention in large part because of the expense of the court-ordered remedy. Interestingly, this was not the remedy the plaintiffs sought; as Alison Morantz has written, "[t]he plaintiffs had originally asked that segregated minority students in the city be given access to the already effective white schools in the suburbs."[9] But *Milliken* prevented the district court from ordering a cross-district remedy outright, so the district court took a different approach, trying to create a school district of such high quality that white students from surrounding suburbs would be drawn to the mostly black school district. Nearly 20 years after the Court decided *Jenkins*, is the expense of the remedy the primary legal legacy of *Jenkins*, though? In this chapter I answer that question by analyzing how courts have used *Jenkins* in a total of 104 education rights judicial decisions issued from the time *Jenkins* was decided through August 2014.

To establish a framework for this analysis, I first discuss the *Jenkins* decision and summarize the most influential commentary about it. Then I analyze four groups of judicial decisions that have cited *Jenkins*, beginning with the subsequent decisions in the Kansas City litigation, continuing with school desegregation litigation in other school districts, turning to school finance litigation across the country, and concluding with two Supreme Court decisions. In the conclusion I discuss ways in which the legal landscape would be the same had the Court not granted certiorari in *Jenkins* a third time—and ways in which it would be different.

The Supreme Court's 1995 Decision

When *Jenkins* came before the Court in 1995, the Kansas City case was not a stranger to the Court's hallowed halls. Many school desegregation cases are under court oversight for decades without ever making their way to the Supreme Court, but the 1995 appearance was *Jenkins*'s third. In 1989, the Court decided a dispute related to attorney fees in *Jenkins*.[10] Then, in 1990, the Court held that the district court in Kansas City should not have imposed a tax increase to subsidize the court-ordered desegregation remedy, although the district court had properly ordered that the school district finance its share of the remedy.[11] Finally, in 1995, the Court had something to say about the substance of the expansive (and expensive) remedy that had, in large part, been upheld by the Eighth Circuit Court of Appeals.

FIVE OPINIONS BY THE JUSTICES

The Supreme Court's decision in *Jenkins* was the result of a 5–4 split. Chief Justice Rehnquist wrote for the majority in an opinion joined by Justices O'Connor, Scalia, Kennedy, and Thomas. Justices O'Connor and Thomas each wrote a separate concurrence. Justice Souter wrote a dissenting opinion that was joined by Justices Stevens, Ginsburg, and Breyer. Justice Ginsburg also dissented separately.

The majority opinion was focused on three issues. First, the Court held that the court-ordered remedy went too far when it pursued the goal of making the majority-black district attractive to white students from neighboring school districts. To do so was an *inter*district remedy for an *intra*district harm, which exceeded the "admittedly broad discretion of the district court" to pursue the goal of "restor[ing] the victims of discriminatory conduct to the position they would have occupied in the absence of such conduct."[12] Second, and relatedly, court-approved salary increases for district staff, which were part of the "desegregative attractiveness" focus of the remedy, also exceeded the district court's authority. Third, the district court erred when it compared the achievement of students in the district to national norms rather than "decid[ing] whether the reduction in achievement by minority students attributable to prior *de jure* segregation has been remedied to the extent practicable."[13] The Court admonished the district court to "sharply limit, if not dispense with, its reliance on this factor."[14] It continued:

> Just as demographic changes independent of *de jure* segregation will affect the racial composition of student assignments, so too will numerous external factors beyond the control of the [Kansas City Municipal School District (KCMSD)] and the State affect minority student achievement. So long as these external factors are not the result of segregation, they do not figure in the remedial calculus. Insistence upon academic goals unrelated to the effects of legal segregation unwarrantably postpones the day when the KCMSD will be able to operate on its own.[15]

With its eyes already on unitary status, the Court quoted its 1992 decision in *Freeman v. Pitts*, which had quoted its 1991 decision in *Board of Education v. Dowell* in the following statement: "The ultimate inquiry is 'whether the [constitutional violator has] complied in good faith with the desegregation decree since it was entered, and whether the vestiges of past discrimination [have] been eliminated to the extent practicable."[16] Encouraging the lower court to wind up its oversight, the Court emphasized several times the idea that "our cases recognize that local autonomy of school districts is a vital national tradition."[17] The majority opinion concluded that "On remand, the District Court must bear in mind that its end purpose is not only 'to remedy the violation' to the extent practicable, but also 'to restore state and local authorities to the control of a school system that is operating in compliance with the Constitution.'"[18]

Justice O'Connor's concurrence focused mainly on responding to Justice Souter's dissent. She emphasized that the majority properly considered whether "desegregative attractiveness" could guide a court-ordered remedy, and that the majority's decision, with which she agreed, was not a departure from precedent.[19]

Justice Thomas's concurrence engaged the whole of school desegregation jurisprudence. It demonstrated the significance of the change that had occurred when, in 1991, he assumed the seat on the Court previously held by Justice Thurgood Marshall. Thomas's opinion rested on two bases. First, he questioned the Supreme Court's (and lower courts') reliance on social science evidence that segregation harms black children, describing that approach as relying "upon questionable social science research rather than constitutional principle."[20] Relatedly, he discussed how private choices can create de facto segregated schools and asserted that de facto segregation does not necessarily produce inferior education. The constitutional harm in *Brown*, in Thomas's view, was that "the State classified students based on their race."[21] Thomas thus laid the groundwork for what would become his insistence later on that *Brown* and the Fourteenth Amendment promise color-blindness, not color-consciousness. Second, he criticized the expansive and extensive nature of school desegregation remedies as inconsistent with traditional principles of federalism and also inconsistent with courts' traditional equitable powers.[22]

Justice Souter's dissent was joined by Justices Stevens, Ginsburg, and Breyer. After recounting the history of the school district's actions, the court-ordered remedy, and the litigation, Souter contended that the propriety of "desegregative attractiveness" as the guiding light in a school desegregation remedy was beyond the scope of the issues the Court had agreed to review, and thus an inappropriate basis to support the majority's holding. Even assuming the issue was properly considered, though, Souter argued that the majority's holding on this issue was "flatly contrary to established precedent."[23] Souter then turned to the issue of unitary status, reviewing the procedures for seeking partial unitary status and contending that while student achievement test scores should not be the cornerstone of a unitary status decision, they could (and should) play an important role in such a determination.[24] Additionally, he argued that the court-ordered salary increases were appropriate in terms of ensuring that a desegregation remedy was implemented effectively by well-qualified, seasoned educators.[25]

Finally, Justice Ginsburg dissented separately, emphasizing the "evanescent" nature of the remedy as compared to the centuries-long duration of the harm.[26] Her brief opinion concluded: "to curtail desegregation [in Kansas City schools] at this time and in this manner is an action at once too swift and too soon."[27]

In 2003, eight years after the Court issued its last decision in *Jenkins*, the district court granted unitary status and closed the case.

SCHOLARLY COMMENTARY

The five opinions by the justices demonstrate the deep divisions on the Court about school desegregation, a division that reflects many of the divisions in our country about racial and ethnic inequality, and about the propriety of race- and ethnicity-conscious remedies. Lower courts are bound to apply the majority opinion in *Jenkins*, but the majority opinion alone stretched across 31 pages in the U.S. Reports and so there is a lot from which to choose when citing *Jenkins*. Although *Jenkins* has received comparatively little sustained scholarly attention, as mentioned previously, there was a brief flurry of scholarly activity soon after *Jenkins* was decided, and then after several years had passed there emerged a few especially important contributions about *Jenkins*'s lasting significance, which I group into three categories.

First is a focus on the Court's strong encouragement that the district court move the school district quickly toward unitary status—even though unitary status had not been sought prior to *Jenkins* coming before the Court. About a decade after *Jenkins*, federal appeals judge David Tatel observed:

> Stepping back from the details of . . . *Jenkins*, I am struck by the virtual absence . . . of any concern about the seriousness of the Fourteenth Amendment violations or the educational harms of segregation, particularly when compared to the majority's emphasis on the virtues of local control.[28]

This aspect of *Jenkins* is important, as demonstrated by law professor Kimberly Jenkins Robinson's identification of *Jenkins* as the culmination of a series of cases in which the Court embraced "educational federalism," a deference by federal courts to state and local authority which, she argues, has been a "critical impediment to school desegregation."[29] Examples include the Court's focus on "good faith" as a portion of the unitary status test, starting in the 1990s; the Court "sanction[ing] termination of . . . a desegregation decree if a school district attempted unsuccessfully to integrate its schools"; the "Court openly acknowledg[ing] the continued effects of past discrimination but disclaim[ing] any need or responsibility for the school board to remedy those effects despite prior opinions that placed this responsibility on intentionally discriminatory school boards"; and, the Court's "silence about the large number of single-race schools that would result under [a] school board's proposed neighborhood assignment plan" after unitary status.[30] As Robinson argues, each of these changes was driven by a focus on returning education to local control, rather than a focus on creating equal educational opportunity for students whose experiences were shaped by unconstitutional segregation.

Second, as Tatel and law professor Wendy Parker have separately argued, *Jenkins* also was significant because it revived the "incremental effect" standard of causation, holding school districts responsible only for remedying the portion of current disparities that plaintiffs could prove were a result of defendants' unconstitutional action, and ensuring that a remedy was tailored precisely to the harm.[31] As Parker writes, "Before the rise of incremental effects analysis, in the heyday of causation presumptions, defendants were held responsible for all current disparities for which defendants could not prove their lack of responsibility."[32] The ultimate consequence of placing the burden of proof on plaintiffs and requiring particular findings about causation is that the incremental effect standard, in Parker's words, "makes it difficult to hold a defendant responsible for current disparities because defining the precise, current effects of a past illegality is exceedingly difficult, if not impossible."[33] This issue can present itself at multiple points during the life of a school desegregation case, and in slightly different ways.

Third, also about a decade after *Jenkins*, education professors Preston Green and Bruce Baker wrote that *Jenkins* was understood to support the argument in school finance litigation that "there is no correlation between funding and academic outcomes"—or, to use the more colloquial phrase, that "money doesn't matter."[34] Indeed, the *Wall Street Journal* had said as much.[35] It is easy to understand how *Jenkins* can be read to support this argument; in fact, in 1997, the federal district court judge who had presided over the *Jenkins* litigation since 1977 compiled a list of many of the Supreme Court's comments about the financial expenditures in the case:

- "The total cost for these quality education programs has exceeded $220 million."
- "Since its inception, the magnet school program has operated at a cost, including magnet transportation, in excess of $448 million."
- "As of 1990, the District Court had ordered $260 million in capital improvements... Since then, the total cost of capital improvements ordered has soared to over $540 million."
- "The District Court's desegregation plan has been described as the most ambitious and expensive remedial program in the history of school desegregation. ... As a result, the desegregation costs have escalated and now are approaching an annual cost of $200 million."

- "The State, through the operation of joint-and-several liability, has borne the brunt of these costs."[36]

Without question, the costs of the remedy in Kansas City were substantial and the gains in academic achievement were, to put it kindly, modest. In 1997, five years before unitary status was granted, the district court noted that "the total cost of the desegregation effort [so far has been] $1.8 billion."[37] Yet, as Green and Baker determined, it is highly problematic to use *Jenkins* in support of the claim that "money doesn't matter" in education reform. In their words:

[The Kansas City school district] was a very high spending district for only five years, and . . . when adjusted for student needs, [the district] was already below average in its metropolitan area by 1998. Coincidentally, it was not until 1998 that Missouri implemented its current and first statewide system of outcome assessment. It would be difficult if not impossible to evaluate the effects of funding that no longer existed on outcomes that were not yet being measured. . . . [Additionally,] the primary goal of the . . . desegregation plan was to increase the "desegregative attractiveness" of the school district. Accordingly, Judge Clark did not target the additional educational spending on remedies, such as reducing class sizes in grades K–3 or improving the quality of the district's teachers, which might have reduced the district's racial achievement gap.[38]

These three aspects of the *Jenkins* decision seem significant—but do courts see *Jenkins* the same way these commentators do? The next section engages this question.

Interpreting and Applying *Jenkins*

Jenkins could be said to stand for many things, and its legacy after nearly 20 years has many facets. In this chapter I examine one of those facets: the legal legacy, as understood through subsequent written judicial decisions citing *Jenkins*. An analysis of these decisions tells us many things. Most importantly, when examining lower court decisions, we see how those courts are interpreting and applying *Jenkins*. When examining subsequent Supreme Court decisions, we learn how the Court is continuing to refine the meaning of *Jenkins*. As such, this analysis is an important part of measuring *Jenkins*'s impact.

The snapshot of decisions examined here is as follows: from the date *Jenkins* was decided (June 12, 1995) through August 26, 2014, 221 judicial decisions cited *Jenkins* and about half those decisions were in educational rights cases: ten were in the Kansas City, Missouri, desegregation litigation of which *Jenkins* was a part;

88 were in other school desegregation cases; six were in school finance cases; and two were issued by the Supreme Court, one in a voluntary integration case, and the other in an English Language Learner (ELL) and school finance case. The 104 post-*Jenkins* judicial decisions analyzed in this chapter do not include one opinion that was later vacated and reissued in part by the same panel, and do not double-count an opinion that was reprinted as an appendix in another opinion; they do include two decisions issued by magistrate judges. A decision was not removed from the analysis if it was reversed on appeal. To analyze the four groups of judicial decisions, I employ a summative approach to qualitative content analysis, analyzing the text of judicial decisions by tabulating the frequency of citations to *Jenkins* to support various specific propositions and thus identifying themes in courts' use of *Jenkins*.[39]

HOW *JENKINS* PLAYED OUT IN THE SUBSEQUENT KANSAS CITY DESEGREGATION LITIGATION

The Supreme Court decision this chapter refers to as *"Jenkins"* was in fact one of 75 decisions in the long-running Kansas City desegregation litigation. The Court's 1995 decision came toward the end of the litigation; only ten decisions were subsequently issued in that case which cited to the Court's 1995 decision, and three of those mentioned *Jenkins* only in passing.[40] As the Eighth Circuit described *Jenkins* in 2008, the Court's decision "changed the direction of the case, refocusing the court and the parties on the goal of ending court supervision of the District."[41]

Soon after the Court decided *Jenkins*, the district and the state filed a motion for unitary status and in 1996 the state negotiated an agreement that it would pay the district $320 million and be dismissed from the case.[42] Also in 1996, the district court ordered an interim desegregation remedy and budget for the 1996–97 school year, which the state appealed. In January 1997, the Eighth Circuit Court of Appeals issued the first decision in the case to interpret and apply *Jenkins*. This decision laid the groundwork for the subsequent federal district court and appellate decisions that would be issued as the case wound its way towards unitary status. Citing *Jenkins*, the Eighth Circuit emphasized that the primary test for unitary status was to examine whether the school district had complied with the remedy in good faith and had eliminated the vestiges of discrimination to the extent practicable; all seven of the subsequent decisions in the Kansas City litigation which substantively engaged *Jenkins* focused on this test. The Eighth Circuit also made frequent mention of the Supreme Court's instruction that the district court conclude its oversight and return the district to local control; six of the seven decisions in this group emphasized this aspect of *Jenkins*. However, the Eighth Circuit also noted that the return to local control was not an unqualified goal:

The Court in *Jenkins III* certainly refers to the restoration of local control on several occasions, and the Court emphasizes the goal of returning the school district to local control, but the other part of the equation is that the district court must consider whether the previously segregated district has achieved partial unitary status.[43]

Additionally, the Eighth Circuit mentioned the *Jenkins* holdings about student achievement, but did not engage this issue as much as subsequent decisions in the Kansas City litigation would do (including this decision, five of the seven decisions in this group would mention the student achievement debate in *Jenkins*). Relatedly, five of the seven decisions, including this one, would cite *Jenkins* for the proposition that the remedy was limited to the constitutional violation, with three noting that external factors could influence student achievement disparities, although only four of the decisions mentioned the *Jenkins* Court's instruction that a remedy be precise. Finally, four of the seven decisions, including this one, cited *Jenkins* for the holding that pursuing desegregative attractiveness was not an appropriate goal. Thus, the first opinion in the Kansas City litigation to engage *Jenkins* stayed true to the course the Court had set, and the rest of the decisions would follow suit.

When the district court issued its first lengthy post-*Jenkins* decision two months later in March 1997, it granted partial unitary status to the district regarding student extracurricular activities, approved the privately negotiated settlement agreement that dismissed the state from the litigation, and made clear that it expected the school district to make rapid progress towards unitary status, pending the completion of a capital investment campaign. The district court demonstrated that it was mindful of the Supreme Court's admonition in *Jenkins* that it end its oversight and return the school district to local control, making mention of this aspect of the Court's decision several times and noting critically that *Jenkins* was part of a "change in direction that the Supreme Court has taken in recent years in their decisions regarding desegregation," describing the retrenchment without naming it as such.[44]

In this decision, the district court also made two other notable contributions to the interpretation and application of *Jenkins*, the first of which was to add to the "money doesn't matter" debate by quoting with implied criticism the Court's lengthy comments on the cost of the Kansas City remedy.[45] (Only one other decision in the post-*Jenkins* Kansas City litigation would enter this debate, and it would be written by the district court judge's successor.) The second contribution was to engage the question about the proper role of student achievement in a desegregation remedy. The district court acknowledged the Supreme Court's instruction that it "'sharply limit' its reliance on the comparison of [the district's] students . . . to national norms" but responded that no such comparison was necessary, because "a gap exists between the test scores of black and white children *within* [the district]."[46] This was the last decision Judge Clark issued in the *Jenkins* litigation.

Two months later, in May 1997, Judge Clark's successor, Judge Whipple, issued a decision with a tone that differed substantially from that of his predecessor. Judge Whipple relied on *Jenkins* to emphasize that "the Constitution does not obligate school systems to eradicate every racial disparity and every lingering effect of prior discrimination. . . . Lingering disparities [between racial groups] are not dispositive of a wrongdoer's continued individual liability nor of a school district's achievement of unitary status."[47] Judge Whipple cited to Justice Thomas's *Jenkins* concurrence at three different points, including to support the statement that "a causal link may be absent where present disparities result from discriminatory forces, such as socio-economic factors, which operate independently of the State" or the school district.[48] The change in judges at the district court level was evocative of the change in justices at the Supreme Court level.

In August of that same year, the Eighth Circuit issued a decision in the appeal from Judge Clark's March 1997 decision. Among other things, the Eighth Circuit noted that the district court had followed the Supreme Court's "incremental effects" instruction in *Jenkins* that it "quantify the vestige" of segregation in the racial student achievement gap and seek to remedy only that portion of the gap. It emphasized that *Jenkins* had not prohibited courts from finding that a racial student achievement gap was a vestige of a de jure segregated system. [49] Thus, when supported by the proper findings, an achievement gap could be relevant in the creation of a school desegregation remedy.

Nineteen ninety-seven continued to be a very busy year in the *Jenkins* litigation. In November, Judge Whipple upheld the state's decision to designate the Kansas City school district as "unaccredited," and sua sponte—meaning on the court's own motion, not on a motion from the parties or with the full hearings that normally attend this stage of school desegregation litigation—the district court granted unitary status in the case.[50] This decision quoted *Jenkins* when noting that the Kansas City desegregation plan "has been described as 'the most ambitious and expensive remedial program in the history of school desegregation.'"[51]

In 2000, the Eighth Circuit sitting en banc reversed the district court's grant of unitary status in a decision that produced six separate opinions, a rarity in most circuits and certainly in that one. In short, the Eighth Circuit held that the district court could not grant unitary status "without taking evidence or hearing arguments."[52] Some of the judges debated whether *Jenkins* permitted courts to recognize that an achievement gap was a vestige of unconstitutional segregation, with the majority concluding that it did.[53] Three years later, after proper hearings, the district court granted unitary status and the parties did not appeal.

In sum, throughout the remainder of the Kansas City litigation, the federal district court and the Eighth Circuit, taken together, followed *Jenkins* closely. After *Jenkins*, the federal district court quickly changed the course of the remedy, no longer pursuing desegregative attractiveness; it also made specific findings about the incremental effect of de jure segregation on student achievement. The district court (both Judge Clark and Judge Whipple) responded to the Supreme Court's invocations of federalism and local control, with Judge Clark moving the district toward unitary status, and Judge Whipple going so far as to grant unitary status prematurely, according to the Eighth Circuit. Although none of the subsequent decisions in the *Jenkins* litigation cited *Jenkins* to question the correlation between spending and student achievement, they did not need to, given the revised scope of the remedy and the rapid march toward unitary status. During what remained of the litigation, the courts engaged in an internal dispute about only one significant issue—at a general level it was a dispute about how the incremental effects test applied, and at a specific level it was a disagreement about whether *Jenkins* permitted a district court to consider student achievement as a vestige of de jure segregated schools.

JENKINS'S APPLICATION IN OTHER SCHOOL DESEGREGATION CASES

In the post-*Jenkins* Kansas City litigation, *Jenkins* was applied in a way that continued in the direction of the Supreme Court's decision. Thus, evaluating the Kansas City litigation does not produce any results that are particularly surprising. The next question is: what is *Jenkins's* legacy in the broader world of school desegregation litigation? Eighty-eight judicial decisions in school desegregation cases engaged *Jenkins* for a variety of principles—some surprising, some not. The decisions are listed in an Appendix to this chapter and these decisions' use of *Jenkins* is summarized and analyzed in this section.

Before turning to a substantive analysis of how courts used *Jenkins*, it is worth noting the procedural posture of the decisions analyzed in this section. Of this group of 88 decisions, 53 (60%) were issued in response to motions for unitary status, with 48 of those 53 decisions (91%) resulting in a grant of full or partial unitary status by the district court or on appeal. This is not unusual given *Jenkins's* focus on winding up court oversight or the timing of *Jenkins* vis-à-vis the arc of school desegregation, in which decades-old cases have been coming to a close, especially since the turn of the millennium.[54] Indeed, more than one decision in the group of 48 begins with the words "This longstanding desegregation case began in 1963 . . . " and concludes by granting unitary status.[55] Only 32 of the decisions (36%) in this group were issued in ongoing desegregation litigation. The small remaining number of decisions were issued in cases in which plaintiffs disputed school districts' voluntary integration plans.

Given that the majority of decisions in this group involve unitary status, it is not surprising that 27 of the 88 decisions—nearly one-third of this group—cite *Jenkins* to emphasize the importance of winding up court oversight and returning control to the school district. As mentioned above, this was a significant theme in *Jenkins*, as Tatel noted, and indeed many of the Supreme Court's school desegregation cases employ this idea of education federalism, as Robinson has convincingly argued.

However, that is not why *Jenkins* is most often cited; in 38 decisions it was cited for the proposition that the district should eliminate the vestiges of segregation "to the extent practicable." In only three decisions did the court also explicitly say that "to the extent practicable" did *not* mean "to the maximum extent practicable," although that was the subtext in many of the decisions. Similarly, in 22 decisions, some of which are also counted in the group of 38, *Jenkins* was cited for a three-part test for evaluating unitary status that included the "extent practicable" language, the "good faith" requirement, and consideration of whether a school district had "fully and satisfactorily complied . . . for a reasonable period of time."[56] Nearly three-quarters of these 22 decisions (16) were from the Middle District of Alabama, which often used the three-part test language as boilerplate.[57] It makes sense that courts cite *Jenkins* for these tests because it was the third of three early-to-mid 1990s cases about the appropriate scope of court-ordered remedies and, as such, engaged the question of unitary status and the Court's education federalism along with it.

The reason *Jenkins* is most often cited is, however, not the reason it is perhaps most widely feared—as Green and Baker recognized, *Jenkins* easily can be used to argue that "money doesn't matter" in education reform. It is likely that dozens of defendants, at the very least, have cited *Jenkins* in support of this principle in school desegregation motions and briefs, in addition to the media and scholarly commentary that employs *Jenkins* to this effect. However, as mentioned above, Green and Baker have documented why this mantra was inaccurate in the context of the Kansas City desegregation situation and therefore why it is especially dangerous as a legacy of *Jenkins*. Fortunately, given this context, in only three school desegregation decisions have courts employed *Jenkins* to suggest that "money doesn't matter," and one of those was merely noting the debate about the impact of spending. Indeed, more courts (six) have cited *Jenkins* to define magnet schools, or suggest the potential that magnet schools can increase integration, than have cited *Jenkins* to argue against expensive desegregation remedies.

So then, what of the Court's determinations regarding the issues that were the focus of the majority opinion in *Jenkins*? The "desegregative attractiveness" holding (including the decision about court-ordered salary increases for district staff) was one of the most significant aspects of *Jenkins*. Yet, in this group of 88 decisions, only five decisions cited *Jenkins* for the idea that courts may not order remedies designed to create "desegregative attractiveness"; five decisions cited *Jenkins* to underscore the impropriety of cross-district remedies to address within-district harm; and one decision cited *Jenkins* for both of these propositions. At first glance, it might seem that the relative paucity of citations to *Jenkins* for these principles might mean that *Jenkins* had a limited impact in this regard. In fact, the opposite is likely true. The "desegregative attractiveness" aspect of *Jenkins* was a clear holding, and thus just as it was clear that courts could not order cross-district busing after *Milliken*, it was clear that they could not try to create "desegregative attractiveness" after *Jenkins*. Relatedly, by addressing this specific issue, the Court was also emphasizing that a remedy should be limited to addressing the constitutional harm originally found, and 16 decisions in this group have cited *Jenkins* for that principle.

Similarly, the student achievement aspect of *Jenkins* has proven important in lower courts' decisions, and in this way the incremental effects standard from *Jenkins* could be said to have played out in 25 different decisions, although in only a couple of those decisions do courts cite *Jenkins* in a discussion with the level of specificity of Parker and Tatel's analyses, discussing the burden and standard of proof, for example. Still, the cases in this group of 25 are close enough to issues of incremental effects that it is fair to include them in this larger category. Thus of this group of 25, 17 decisions cited *Jenkins*'s discussion of student achievement components of a remedy, including nine decisions that cited *Jenkins* for the proposition that external factors influence student achievement, four decisions that cited *Jenkins* for the idea that the remedy must be precise (and therefore based on a precise finding of harm for which the state is responsible), and three decisions that cite *Jenkins* for the principle that remaining racial imbalances can be permissible. In addition, seven other decisions cited *Jenkins* for the "external factors" principle alone. Almost all of the decisions discussing the student achievement issue referred to the difficulty of determining what portion of an achievement gap is a vestige of unconstitutional discrimination, with some of the decisions discussing the *Jenkins* decision and even the subsequent district court and federal appellate decisions in the *Jenkins* litigation at great length.

Similarly, almost all of the decisions to discuss student achievement noted courts' limited jurisdiction over the student achievement issue. In 2000, a federal district court opined: "Most federal courts looking at the achievement gap issue have declined to even consider it as a vestige."[58] The following passage illustrates a typical decision in this group:

> Although our remedies have not addressed test scores directly, they provide significant
> evidence that a racial disparity in achievement unfortunately remains. Courts considering
> scores on standardized tests as evidence of an achievement gap, however, generally accord

them little weight in determining the question of unitary status, and the Supreme Court has suggested that measuring student achievement against national norms may not be the proper test to use. Other federal courts considering the achievement gap in the context of school desegregation have determined that socioeconomic factors and family background explain most if not all of the difference in students' test scores.[59]

Thus courts have often applied the incremental effect test Parker and Tatel identified in *Jenkins*, but their discussions of *Jenkins* on this topic are unfortunately imprecise.

Finally, Justice Thomas's and Justice O'Connor's concurring opinions were cited in a handful of lower courts' post-*Jenkins* decisions, with Thomas's concurrence appearing in six and O'Connor's in three. Although the citation frequency is not high, it still seems unusual, considering that the majority opinion is the only one with precedential effect and that the lower courts almost always cited Thomas's and O'Connor's opinions with approval, or to support a substantive principle in the lower court's decision. In one way or another, all six cases citing Thomas's *Jenkins* concurrence employed the idea that racial isolation by itself can result from private choices and is not necessarily a constitutional harm.[60] The citations to O'Connor's concurrence varied in terms of topic and were nearly all in footnotes.[61]

In sum, this group of 88 decisions rarely relies on *Jenkins* for the idea that money doesn't matter, or that desegregative attractiveness is not an acceptable remedial focus, but it does cite *Jenkins* much more frequently for the idea that the remedy must be tailored to the constitutional harm. It also engages *Jenkins* to discuss student achievement, and with varying levels of specificity is influenced by the "incremental effects" test from *Jenkins* that Parker and Tatel have described. But, more than either of these two propositions, this group of decisions emphasizes the need to wind up court oversight and return schools to local control, consistent with what Tatel and Robinson both have observed. Finally, and perhaps somewhat ironically because *Jenkins* was not a unitary status case, the decisions in this group cite *Jenkins* more than anything else for a unitary status test, whether general or specific.

JENKINS'S APPLICATION IN SCHOOL FINANCE CASES

There are many similarities between school desegregation litigation and school finance litigation: both seek to create more equitable educational opportunities for disadvantaged students, both focus on structural reform to achieve their goals, and if litigation is successful, both involve substantial expenditures in the remedial phase.[62] But, while school desegregation litigation is focused on racial and ethnic equality within one school district, school finance litigation is focused on revenue and expenditure disparities among school districts within a given state and thus targets the statewide school finance scheme. Despite the differences, it makes sense that precedent from one line of cases would be influential in the other.

As discussed above, nearly a decade ago Green and Baker demonstrated that the *Jenkins* litigation did not prove that financial expenditures are irrelevant to educational quality, even though some commentators have used *Jenkins* to argue that it proves just that.[63] Thus it is worth asking whether courts hearing school finance cases have employed *Jenkins* to support that proposition. In addition to the Court's decision in *Horne v. Flores*, discussed in the following section, six judicial decisions in school finance cases have cited *Jenkins*.

Although two of these decisions could be characterized as citing *Jenkins* for the proposition that "money doesn't matter," in one of those decisions the only citation to *Jenkins* was in a dissenting opinion.[64] The other decision is more significant: it is a 1995 decision of the Rhode Island Supreme Court that the state's school finance system was constitutional.[65] Even though the majority hedges, noting that "money alone *may never* be sufficient . . . huge expenditures do *not necessarily* result in improved educational achievement," the end result in the case—sustaining the existing system—suggests what the majority likely thinks of the question.[66] Additionally, one other state supreme court opinion, an early decision in the long-running *Leandro* litigation in North Carolina, mentioned *Jenkins* and the Kansas City experience as supporting the view that "money doesn't matter," but did so while noting the extreme level of judicial and scholarly disagreement about the link between funding and educational quality.[67] Of course, other decisions in school finance litigation and other scholars and media commentators have concluded that there is little connection between expenditures and student achievement, but they did not cite *Jenkins* to do so.[68]

The other three opinions are of little significance, at least as far as their use of *Jenkins* is concerned. One was issued in the Missouri school finance litigation that began in 1990; in that decision, the court neutrally acknowledged the *Jenkins* litigation that had also arisen out of the same state and at times formed a sort of double-helix with the Missouri school finance case.[69] The other two opinions were issued in ELL litigation in Texas and cited *Jenkins* to support statements about the extent of courts' remedial powers (one of these decisions vacated the other).[70]

Thus, in traditional school finance litigation, *Jenkins* has made surprisingly few appearances in judicial decisions. Of its limited appearances, thankfully only one—nearly twenty years ago in a small state—relied even somewhat on *Jenkins* for the proposition that Green and Baker have since disproven.

THE SUPREME COURT'S REFLECTIONS ON *JENKINS*

Examining lower courts' decisions gives us a window into how courts have interpreted and applied *Jenkins*. Examining Supreme Court decisions suggests how justices are continuing to refine the principles articulated nearly twenty years ago in *Jenkins*.

The Supreme Court does not often hear school desegregation cases these days—indeed, the three most recent cases about racial or ethnic preferences in education have all involved affirmative action at colleges or universities or voluntary integration in K–12 public schools. Thus it is not unusual that over a decade passed before any of the justices cited *Jenkins* in a written opinion in another education case focused on racial or ethnic inequality. The first mention occurred in 2007, when the Court issued its decision in *Parents Involved in Community Schools v. Seattle School District No. 1*, holding via a fractured set of opinions that while school districts could consider the pursuit of diversity a compelling governmental interest, they were limited in doing so to policies that did not consider the race or ethnicity of individual students.[71] The plurality decision regarding the narrow-tailoring issue was written by Chief Justice Roberts, with Justice Thomas joining that opinion and also writing separately.

Of the five opinions published in *Parents Involved*, it was only Thomas's that mentioned *Jenkins*. Thomas could have cited to the *Jenkins* majority for many of his propositions, but instead he cited other decisions as well as his own lengthy concurrence in *Jenkins*. (It is not unusual for justices to continue to develop and advance a specific position, and sometimes justices are even able to persuade colleagues to agree them over time, eventually turning a concurring opinion into a majority opinion; Justice O'Connor did this successfully in the Establishment Clause context, for example.[72]) Citing his *Jenkins* concurrence, Thomas emphasized twice that racial "imbalance" can stem from private decision rather than state action; implied approval of the result that a narrow tailoring analysis is often "automatically fatal" to the policy at issue; stated that the goal of diverse classrooms is not supported by a pedagogical interest much less a compelling governmental interest; and, in a lengthy footnote, explained the outdated approach of desegregation remedies.[73] Thomas's opinion in this voluntary integration case did not mask his hostility to race-conscious government action, even when in pursuit of more racially and ethnically diverse classrooms, or his hostility to school desegregation litigation in general.

Two years later, in 2009, the Court decided *Horne v. Flores*,[74] a case about English Language Learners' statutory rights under the Equal Educational Opportunities Act.[75] *Horne* also involved questions about the proper extent of the court-ordered remedy, whether the state was funding ELL programs adequately, and how the EEOA intersected with NCLB. Although the case was clearly not a school desegregation or voluntary integration case, the state defendants invoked dicta and guiding principles from the Court's many school desegregation cases, especially ones that, like *Jenkins*, civil rights advocates perceived as part of a retreat from *Brown*.

In *Horne*, Justice Alito wrote for the Court in a 5–4 decision. The majority's discussion of *Jenkins* was curious. First, it cited the *Jenkins* majority for the principle that preserving local control is vitally important in institutional reform litigation—and then it also cited Thomas's concurrence for more specific discussion on the same point.[76] Second, when criticizing the lower court for "improperly substitut[ing] its own educational and budgetary policy judgments for those of the state and local officials," the majority again relied on Thomas's *Jenkins* concurrence for support.[77] Third, the *Horne* majority relied on the *Jenkins* majority when discussing the impropriety of a court ordering a remedy that geographically exceeded the district where a violation was proven.[78] Thus, in *Horne*, the Court continued to develop the meaning of *Jenkins*, most importantly by emphasizing the education federalism that Tatel observed in *Jenkins* and which Robinson has traced throughout many of the Court's education cases. By citing to Thomas's concurrence on this point, the Court gave that opinion more credibility and arguably limited precedential value.

Taken together, the Court's discussions in *Parents Involved* and *Horne* do not shed much light on *Jenkins*, although *Horne* suggests that Thomas may be picking up votes for some of his opinions about school desegregation litigation. And, more generally, *Parents Involved* and *Horne*, taken together with *Fisher* and *Schutte*, suggest that *Jenkins* is solid precedent.

Conclusion

Nearly twenty years after *Jenkins*, it appears that the case is here to stay. In large part, school desegregation decisions cite *Jenkins* for a test when determining unitary status and, again and again, courts cite *Jenkins* for the virtues of returning control to the local school district. Thus the education federalism that Robinson has traced in the Court's jurisprudence, and on which Tatel also commented, has come to life in these lower court cases. However, the propositions for which *Jenkins* is most frequently cited are in fact not unique to *Jenkins*. Similarly, other principles for which *Jenkins* is less frequently cited also appear in the Court's other school desegregation decisions, such as: a remedy must be tailored to a constitutional harm; external factors can influence racial and ethnic inequality and imbalance within a district; cross-district remedies are not permissible; remaining racial or ethnic imbalance is not necessarily unconstitutional. With regard to these issues, *Jenkins* is valuable as precedent because it marks yet another point on a consistent trajectory, not because it articulates anything new in the law. If the Court had never granted certiorari in *Jenkins*, lower courts could cite other Supreme Court decisions for all of these principles.

Although none of those legal principles are part of *Jenkins*'s independent legacy, *Jenkins* is significant in its own right in some ways which are consistent with what we might expect, and some which are not. First, and perhaps most significantly, lower courts' have applied the "incremental effects" standard Parker and Tatel identified, most often with regard to student achievement, although most of the discussion of this principle has been at a very general level. This change anticipated by Parker and Tatel has marked yet another way in which *Jenkins* embodies education federalism. Second, turning to an expected effect that turns out to be absent, the dicta that supports the "money doesn't matter" argument is unique to *Jenkins* among the Court's school desegregation cases because of the scope of the remedy. However, lower courts in school desegregation and school finance cases have almost never relied on *Jenkins* to support that argument, although media and scholarly commentary has not been so reluctant.Third and finally, the holding in *Jenkins* that a court could not order remedies designed to create "desegregative attractiveness" was unequivocal and inevitably has had a significant impact on the remedies plaintiffs sought and courts ordered. Although the number of courts willing to order such remedies may have been relatively small, the absence of any disputes about this issue from judicial decisions suggests widespread understanding and acceptance of this holding.

Jenkins is one point on the arc of school desegregation litigation, to be sure, and yet it is more than that—it also bends the arc a bit, though not toward justice.

Kristi L. Bowman is a Professor of Law at Michigan State University College of Law.

Appendix: List of 88 School Desegregation Decisions Citing *Jenkins*

Ahern v. Board of Education of the City of Chicago, 1996 WL 134257 (N.D. Ill. 1996).

Application of County Collector of County of Winnebago, Illinois, 96 F.3d 890 (7th Cir. 1996).

Belk v. Charlotte-Mecklenburg Board of Education, 269 F.3d 305 (4th Cir. 2001).

Belk v. Charlotte-Mecklenburg Board of Education, 233 F.3d 232 (4th Cir. 2000).

Berry v. School District of City of Benton Harbor, 195 F.Supp.2d 971 (W.D. Mich. 2002).

Berry v. School District of City of Benton Harbor, 141 F.Supp.2d 802 (W.D. Mich. 2001).

Berry v. School District of City of Benton Harbor, 184 F.R.D. 93 (W.D. Mich. 1998).

Berry v. School District of City of Benton Harbor, 56 F.Supp.2d 866 (W.D. Mich. 1999).

Brown v. Unified School District No. 501, 56 F.Supp.2d 1212 (D. Kan. 1999).

Capacchione v. Charlotte-Mecklenburg Schools, 57 F.Supp.2d 228 (W.D. N.C. 1999).

Cleveland v. Union Parish School Board, 2009 WL 1491188 (W.D. La. 2009).

Cleveland v. Union Parish School Board, 570 F.Supp.2d 858 (W.D. La. 2008).

Coalition to Save Our Children v. State Board of Education of State of Delaware, 901 F.Supp. 784 (D. Del. 1995).

Coalition to Save Our Children v. State Board of Education of State of Delaware, 90 F.3d 752, 760 (3rd Circuit 1996).

Cowan ex rel. Johnson v. Bolivar County Board of Education, 923 F.Supp.2d 876 (N.D. Miss. 2013).

Cowan ex rel. Johnson v. Bolivar County Board of Education, 914 F.Supp.2d 801 (N.D. Miss. 2012).

Crawford v. Huntington Beach Union High School District, 121 Cal.Rptr.2d 96 (California Court of Appeals, 4th District 2002).

Davis v. School District of City of Pontiac, 95 F.Supp.2d 688 (E.D. Mich. 2000).

Edgerson on Behalf of Edgerson v. Clinton, 86 F.3d 833 (8th Cir. 1996).

Fisher v. Tucson Unified School District, 652 F.3d 1131 (9th Cir. 2011).

Fisher v. U.S., 2014 WL 4106322 (D. Ariz. 2014).

Fisher v. U.S., 2007 WL 2410351 (D. Ariz. 2007).

Gensaw v. Del Norte County Unified School District, 2008 WL 1777668 (N.D. Cal. 2008).

Goodwine v. Taft, 2002 WL 1284228 (S.D. Ohio 2002).

Graham v. Evangeline Parish School Board, 2012 WL 1833400 (W.D. La. 2012)

Graham v. Evangeline Parish School Board, 223 F.R.D. 407 (W.D. La. 2004).

Hampton v. Jefferson County Board of Education, 102 F.Supp.2d 358 (W.D. Ky. 2000).

Hampton v. Jefferson County Board of Education, 72 F.Supp.2d 753 (W.D. Ky. 1999).

Harris v. Crenshaw County Board of Education, 2006 WL 2590592 (M.D. Ala. 2006).

Ho by Ho v. San Francisco Unified School District, 965 F.Supp. 1316 (N.D. Cal. 1997).

Holton v. City of Thomasville School District, 425 F.3d 1325 (11th Cir. 2005)

Hoots v. Pennsylvania, 118 F.Supp.2d 577 (W.D. Pa. 2000).

Keyes v. Congress of Hispanic Educators, 902 F.Supp. 1274 (D. Colo. 1995).

Lee v. Alexander City Board of Education, 2002 WL 31102679 (M.D. Ala. 2002).

Lee v. Auburn City Board of Education, 2002 WL 237091 (M.D. Ala. 2002).

Lee v. Autauga County Board of Education, 2005 WL 1868745 (M.D. Ala. 2005).

Lee v. Autauga County Board of Education, 2004 WL 2359667 (M.D. Ala. 2004).

Lee v. Autauga County Board of Education, 2004 WL 1699068 (M.D. Ala. 2004).

Lee v. Butler County Board of Education, 183 F.Supp.2d 1359 (M.D. Ala. 2002).

Lee v. Covington County Board of Education, 2006 WL 269942 (M.D. Ala. 2006).

Lee v. Dothan City Board of Education, 2007 WL 1856928 (M.D. Ala. 2007).
Lee v. Elmore County Board of Education, 2004 WL 1809877 (M.D. Ala. 2004).
Lee v. Lee County Board of Education, 963 F.Supp. 1122 (M.D. Ala. 1997).
Lee v. Lee County Board of Education, 476 F.Supp.2d 1356 (M.D. Ala. 2007)
Lee v. Lee County Board of Education, 2002 WL 1268395 (M.D. Ala. 2002).
Lee v. Macon County Board of Education, 2006 WL 1381873 (M.D. Ala. 2006).
Lee v. Opelilka City Board of Education, 2002 WL 237032 (M.D. Ala. 2002).
Lee v. Phenix City Board of Education, 2005 WL 2850392 (M.D. Ala. 2005).
Lee v. Roanoke City Board of Education, 2007 WL 1196482 (M.D. Ala. 2007).
Lee v. Russell County Board of Education, 2002 WL 360000 (M.D. Ala. 2002)
Lee v. Tallapoosa County Board of Education, 2002 WL 31757973 (M.D. Ala. 2002).
Liddell by Liddell v. Board of Education of City of St. Louis, 126 F.3d 1049 (8th Cir. 1997).
Liddell by Liddell v. Board of Education of the City of St. Louis, 121 F.3d 1201 (8th Cir. 1997).
Liddell by Liddell v. Board of Education of City of St. Louis, 142 F.3d 1103 (8th Cir. 1998).
Liddell v. Special School District, 149 F.3d 862 (8th Cir. 1998).
Little Rock School District v. Arkansas, 664 F.3d 738 (8th Cir. 2011).
Little Rock School District v. North Little Rock School District, 451 F.3d 528 (8th Cir. 2006).
Little Rock School District v. Pulaski County Special School District, 237 F.Supp.2d 988 (E.D. Ark. 2002).
Little Rock School District v. Pulaski County Special School District, 2011 WL 1935332 (E.D. Ark. 2011).
Manning ex rel. Manning v. School Board of Hillsborough County, 244 F.3d 927 (11th Cir. 2001).
Manning v. School Board of Hillsborough County, 1997 WL 33479029 (M.D. Fla. 1997).
McFarland v. Jefferson County Public Schools, 330 F.Supp.2d 834 (W.D. Ky. 2004).
Mills v. Freeman, 942 F.Supp. 1449 (N.D. Ga. 1996).
Monroe v. Jackson-Madison County School System Board of Education, 2010 WL 3732015 (W.D. Tenn. 2010).
NAACP, Jacksonville Branch v. Duval County School, 273 F.3d 960 (11th Cir. 2001).
Parents Involved in Community Schools v. Seattle School District No. 1, 426 F.3d 1162 (9th Cir. 2005).
Paynter v. State, 720 N.Y.S.2d 712 (New York Superior Court 2000).
Pennsylvania Human Relations Commission v. School District of Philadelphia, 681 A.2d 1366 (Supreme Court of the Commonwealth of Pennsylvania, 1996).

People Who Care v. Rockford Board of Education, School District No. 205, 1996 WL 364802 (N.D. Ill. 1996).

People Who Care v. Rockford Board of Education, School Dist. 205, 246 F.3d 1073 (7th Cir. 2001).

People Who Care v. Rockford Board of Education, School Dist. No. 205, 171 F.3d 1083 (7th Cir. 1999).

People Who Care v. Rockford Board of Education, School Dist. No. 25, 153 F.3d 834 (7th Cir. 1998).

People Who Care v. Rockford Board of Education, 2000 WL 1855107 (N.D. Ill. 2000).

Reed v. Rhodes, 934 F.Supp. 1533 (N.D. Ohio 1996).

Reed v. Rhodes, 179 F.3d 453 (6th Cir. 1999).

Reed v. Rhodes, 1 F.Supp.2d 705 (N.D. Ohio 1998).

Reed v. Rhodes, 934 F.Supp. 1492 (N.D. Ohio 1996).

San Francisco NAACP v. San Francisco Unified School District, 413 F.Supp.2d 1051 (N.D. Cal. 2005).

Stanley v. Darlington County School District, 1996 WL 294369 (D. S.C. 1996).

Stanley v. Darlington County School District, 915 F.Supp. 764 (D. S.C. 1996).

Tasby v. Moses, 265 F.Supp.2d 757 (N.D. Tex. 2003).

U.S. v. Board of Public Instruction of St. Lucie County, 977 F.Supp. 1202 (S.D. Fla. 1997).

U.S. v. Board of School Commissioners of City of Indianapolis, 128 F.3d 507 (7th Cir. 1997).

U.S. v. Caldwell Parish School Board, 2011 WL 2634086 (W.D. La. 2011).

U.S. v. City of Yonkers, 197 F.3d 41 (2nd Cir. 1999).

U.S. v. Mississippi (Choctaw County School District), 941 F.Supp.2d 708 (N.D. Miss. 2013).

U.S. v. State of Texas, 158 F.3d 299 (5th Cir. 1998).

U.S. v. Unified School District No. 500, Kansas City (Wyandotte County), 974 F.Supp. 1367 (D. Kan. 1997).

U.S. v. Yonkers Board of Education, 123 F.Supp.2d 694 (S.D.N.Y. 2000).

NOTES

1. 347 U.S. 483 (1954).
2. 391 U.S. 430 (1968).
3. 551 U.S. 701 (2007).
4. CHARLES J. OGLETREE, JR., ALL DELIBERATE SPEED 260 (W.W. Norton & Company 2004). The three decisions were *Board of Education of Oklahoma City v. Dowell*, 498 U.S.

237 (1991), *Freeman v. Pitts*, 503 U.S. 467 (1992), and *Missouri v. Jenkins*, 515 U.S. 70 (1995).

5. Milliken v. Bradley, 418 U.S. 717 (1974).

6. Parents Involved, 551 U.S. 701.

7. Fisher v. University of Texas at Austin, 133 S.Ct. 2411 (2013).

8. Schuette v. Coalition to Defend Affirmative Action, Integration and Immigrant Rights and Fight for Equality by Any Means Necessary (BAMN), 134 S.Ct. 1623 (2014).

9. Alison Morantz, *Money and Choice in Kansas City: Major Investments with Modest Returns*, 241, 243 in GARY ORFIELD & SUSAN E. EATON, EDS., DISMANTLING DESEGREGATION: THE QUIET REVERSAL OF *BROWN V. BOARD OF EDUCATION* (The New Press 1996).

10. Missouri v. Jenkins by Agyei, 491 U.S. 274 (1989).

11. Missouri v. Jenkins, 495 U.S. 33 (1990).

12. Ibid., 99, 101 (in part quoting Milliken v. Bradley).

13. Ibid., 92, 100–101.

14. Ibid., 101.

15. Ibid.

16. Missouri v. Jenkins, 515 U.S. 70, 81, 90 (1995) (quoting Freeman v. Pitts, 503 U.S. 467, 492 (1992) (quoting Board of Education of Oklahoma City Public Schools v. Dowell, 498 U.S. 237, 249–50 (1991))).

17. Ibid., 100 (citations omitted).

18. Ibid., 102.

19. Ibid., 103–14 (Justice O'Connor, concurring).

20. Ibid., 114–18 (Justice Thomas, concurring).

21. Ibid., 121.

22. Ibid., 118–23 (Justice Thomas, concurring).

23. Ibid., 139–48, 158–75 (Justice Souter, dissenting).

24. Ibid., 154, 156 (Justice Souter, dissenting).

25. Ibid., 154, 156 (Justice Souter, dissenting).

26. Ibid., 175–76 (Justice Ginsburg, dissenting).

27. Ibid., 176.

28. David S. Tatel, *Judicial Methodology, Southern School Desegregation, and the Rule of Law*, 79 NEW YORK UNIVERSITY LAW REVIEW 1071 (2004).

29. Kimberly Jenkins Robinson, *The High Cost of Education Federalism*, 48 WAKE FOREST LAW REVIEW 287 (2013).

30. Ibid., 300–301.

31. Wendy Parker, *The Future of School Desegregation*, 94 NORTHWESTERN UNIVERSITY LAW REVIEW 1157, 1172–73 (2000); Wendy Parker, *The Supreme Court and Public Law Remedies*, 50 HASTINGS LAW JOURNAL 475, 531–33 (1999); Tatel, *Judicial Methodology*.

32. Parker, *The Supreme Court and Public Law Remedies*, 1173.

33. Parker, *The Future of School Desegregation*, 1173.

34. Preston C. Green, III & Bruce D. Baker, *Urban Legends, Desegregation and School Finance:*

Did Kansas City Really Prove that Money Doesn't Matter?, 12 MICHIGAN JOURNAL OF RACE AND LAW 57, 58, 80 (2006).

35. Ibid., 58.

36. Jenkins v. Missouri, 959 F. Supp. 1151, 1154 (W.D. Mo. 1997), affirmed, 122 F.3d 588 (8th Cir. 1997) (citing Missouri v Jenkins, 115 S.Ct. 2038, 2043, 2044, 2045 (1995)).

37. Ibid., 1154.

38. Green & Baker, *Urban Legends*, 90–91.

39. Hsiu-Fang Hsieh, *Three Approaches to Qualitative Content Analysis*, 15 QUALITATIVE HEALTH RESEARCH 1277 (2005).

40. Jenkins v. Missouri, 78 F.3d 1270 (8th Cir. 1996) (affirming the order of the district court refusing to add proposed interveners to the litigation); 115 F.3d 554 (8th Cir. 1997) (attorney fee dispute), rehearing en banc granted and judgment vacated by 124 F.3d 1310 (8th Cir. 1997) (en banc); 127 F.3d 709 (8th Cir. 1997) (attorney fee dispute).

41. Missouri v. Jenkins, 516 F.3d 1074 (8th Cir. 2008), as corrected (March 27, 2008).

42. Missouri v. Jenkins, 122 F.3d 588, 590–91 (8th Cir. 1997).

43. Jenkins v. Missouri, 103 F.3d 731, 738–39 (8th Cir. 1997).

44. Missouri v. Jenkins, 959 F. Supp. 1151, 1155 (W.D. Mo. 1997), affirmed, 122 F.3d 588 (8th Cir. 1997).

45. Ibid., 1154.

46. Ibid., 1158.

47. Missouri v. Jenkins, 965 F. Supp. 1295, 1304 (W.D. Mo. 1997).

48. Ibid., 1303.

49. Missouri v. Jenkins, 122 F.3d 588, 595 (8th Cir. 1997)

50. Jenkins v. School District of Kansas City, Missouri, 73 F.Supp.2d 1058 (W.D. Mo. 1997), reversed under a different name, Jenkins v. Missouri, 216 F.3d 720 (8th Cir. 2000) (en banc).

51. Ibid., 1060–61.

52. Jenkins v. Missouri, 216 F.3d 720, 724 (8th Cir. 2000) (en banc).

53. Ibid., 728 (Judge Heany, concurring), 736–37 n.16 (Judge Beam, dissenting)

54. Danielle Holley-Walker, *After Unitary Status: Examining Voluntary Integration Strategies for Southern School Districts*, 88 NORTH CAROLINA LAW REVIEW 877 (2010).

55. Lee v. Tallapoosa County Board of Education, 2002 WL 31757973, *1 (M.D. Ala. 2002); Lee v. Alexander City Board of Education, 2002 WL 31102679, *1 (M.D. Ala. 2002); Lee v. Lee County Board of Education, 2002 WL 1268395, *1 (M.D. Ala. 2002).

56. Lee v. Autauga County Board of Education, 2004 WL 2359667, *4 (M.D. Ala. 2004).

57. Lee v. Tallapoosa County, 2002 WL 31757973 at *5; Lee v. Alexander City, 2002 WL 31102679, *6; Lee v. Lee County, 2002 WL 1268395, *6.

58. Hampton v. Jefferson County Board of Education, 102 F. Supp.2d 358, 366 (W.D. Ky. 2000).

59. Hoots v. Pennsylvania, 118 F. Supp.2d 577, 602–603 (W.D. Pa. 2000).

60. Parents Involved in Community Schools v. Seattle School District No. 1, 426 F.3d 1162, 1204 (9th Cir. 2005), reversed, 127 S.Ct. 2738 (2007); NAACP, Jacksonville Branch v. Duval County Schools, 273 F.3d 960,966 (11th Cir. 2001); Gensaw v. Del Norte County Unified School District, 2008 WL 1777668, *7 (N.D. Cal. 2008); McFarland v. Jefferson County

Public Schools, 330 F.Supp.2d 834 (W.D. Ky. 2004), consolidated with Parents Involved in Community Schools v. Seattle School District No. 1 and reversed 127 S.Ct. 2738 (2007); Davis v. School District of City of Pontiac, 95 F.Supp.2d 688, 697 (E.D. Mich. 2000); Manning v. School Bd. of Hillsborough County, 1997 WL 33479029, *29 (M.D. Fla. 1997), report of magistrate judge adopted in part and rejected in part, 24 F.Supp.2d 1277 (M.D. Fla. 1998), reversed, 244 F.3d 927 (11th Cir. 2001).

61. Fisher v. Tucson Unified School District, 652 F.3d 1131 n.27 (9th Cir. 2011); Liddell by Liddell v. Board of Education of City of St. Louis, 126 F.3d 1049, 1058–59 n.13 (8th Cir. 1997); Gensaw v. Del Norte County Unified School District, 2008 WL 1777668 n.4 (N.D. Cal. 2008).

62. James E. Ryan, Sheff, *Segregation, and School Finance Litigation*, 74 NEW YORK UNIVERSITY LAW REVIEW 529, 563 n.108 (1999); Goodwin Liu, *The Parted Paths of School Desegregation and School Finance Litigation*, 24 LAW & INEQUALITY 81, 82 (2006); Kristi L. Bowman, *A New Strategy for Pursuing Racial and Ethnic Equality in Public Schools*, 1 DUKE FORUM FOR LAW & SOCIAL CHANGE 47 (2009).

63. Green & Baker, *Urban Legends*, at 82–84.

64. DeRolph v. State, 677 N.E.2d 733, 793 (Supreme Court of Ohio 1997) (Chief Justice Moyer, dissenting) (In this decision, the Ohio Supreme Court struck down the state's school finance system as violating the state constitution. Dissenting, Chief Justice Moyer relied on *Jenkins* to support the statement that "There simply is no proof that changing Ohio's funding system or infusing additional funds will improve education"), opinion clarified by 678 N.E.2d 419 and order clarified by 699 N.E.2d 518.

65. City of Pawtucket v. Sundlun, 662 A.2d 40 (Rhode Island Supreme Court 1995).

66. Ibid., 59.

67. Leandro v. State, 488 S.E.2d 249, 260 (Supreme Court of North Carolina 1997).

68. Green & Baker, *Urban Legends*, 58, 82–84

69. Committee for Educational Equality v. State., 294 S.W.3d 477 n.36 (Supreme Court of Missouri 2009) ("just 30 years ago . . . for example, in the Kansas City school desegregation case, schools for black students were found to have received hand-me-down books from the schools for whites as recently as the late 1970s"); Green & Baker, *Urban Legends* (discussing both cases in detail).

70. U.S. v. LULAC-GI Forum, 2007 WL 2177369, *9 (E.D. Texas 2007); vacated by 572 F.Supp.2d 726, 754–55 (2008); reversed by 601 F.3d 354 (5th Circuit 2010).

71. Parents Involved, 551 U.S. 701.

72. Kristi L. Bowman, *Seeing Government Purpose Through the Objective Observer's Eyes: The Evolution–Intelligent Design Debates*, 29 HARVARD JOURNAL OF LAW & PUBLIC POLICY 417 (2006).

73. Parents Involved, 551 U.S. 750, 752, 756, 764 n. 6.

74. Horne v. Flores, 557 U.S. 433 (2009).

75. Equal Educational Opportunities Act of 1974, Public Law 93-380, 88 Statutes 514.

76. Ibid., 448.

77. Ibid., 454–55.

78. Ibid., 470.

Parents Involved in Community Schools v. Seattle School District No. 1 and Meredith v. Jefferson County Board of Education

551 U.S. 701 (2007)

BYRON E. LEET

Meredith v. Jefferson County Board of Education
A Community Committed to Diverse Schools

THE MORNING OF DECEMBER 4, 2006, BROKE CLEAR BUT COLD IN WASHINGTON, DC. The overnight low temperature had been 29 degrees, which made it a cold night to sleep outside the Supreme Court building, yet that is precisely where a number of people had spent the night in anticipation of arguments in the high court on the constitutionality of voluntary race-conscious student assignment plans in Louisville and Seattle. As we made our way past citizens crying out that morning for the Supreme Court to honor the promise of *Brown v. Board of Education*[1] and affirm the lower courts' rulings that Jefferson County, Kentucky's student assignment plan was constitutional, I was humbled that a case I had been called upon to try would be argued before the highest court in the land. The full story behind how our case—*Meredith v. Jefferson County Board of Education*[2]—brought us to that historic morning begins long before the lawsuit was even filed.

The history of desegregation in Jefferson County dates back to 1971, when parents filed suit against the former Louisville Board of Education and the separate Jefferson County Board of Education, a lawsuit that was initially dismissed by the federal district court, but on appeal the Sixth Circuit Court of Appeals reversed and ordered the elimination of all vestiges of state-imposed segregation in both school districts. In 1975, the Louisville and Jefferson County school districts were merged and the district court ordered the new school board to implement a desegregation plan for the merged district.

The first indication that 25 years of desegregation in Jefferson County was under attack came in 1998 when a lawsuit was filed by black parents who claimed that the school district's racial guidelines at Central High School—a historically black Louisville school before the 1975 desegregation decree—violated the Constitution. Black students were being turned away from Central High because the school was attracting an insufficient number of white students to keep it within the school district's race guidelines. Although the plaintiffs in *Hampton v. Jefferson County Board of Education*[3] only challenged their children's denial of admission to Central High School, the lawsuit called into question the validity of student assignment throughout Jefferson County and highlighted what became the single most fascinating aspect of this dispute: the political and societal issues associated with considerations of race in the era after the desegregation decrees have been lifted.

In the mid-1970s, desegregation, or "forced busing," in Louisville was met with considerable unrest and violence. But by the late 1990s, large segments of our community had come to accept race-conscious student assignment and our school board's commitment to avoiding a return to racial isolation. Yet with the passage of some twenty-five years, many citizens were probably unaware how our public schools in Louisville had become some of the most integrated schools in America. In defending our client and trying the case, it was our obligation to tell a story and explain—not only to the federal judge who would decide this case but also to the community that was now following the case closely—just how Jefferson County came to be where it was.

The Jefferson County, Kentucky school district is a county-wide, urban/suburban district. It is the 31st largest in the United States with approximately 100,000 students—52% of them are white, 37% are African American, and 11% are in other racial or ethnic groups. Nearly two-thirds of the students in the Jefferson County public schools qualify for free or reduced price lunch. Our law firm has represented the school board for many years.

In *Hampton*, the Central High case, district judge John Heyburn eventually ruled in 2000 that a school district that is not subject to a desegregation decree can still use race in its general student assignments, even to the extent of some racial guidelines, because assignment to one or another school imposes no burden and confers no benefit. However, Judge Heyburn ruled that the school board could not use race to assign students to Central High because it offered magnet programs not otherwise available within Jefferson County. The school board modified student assignment to comply with Judge Heyburn's decision but maintained the race guidelines at all schools except Central and three other magnet schools that offered programs not generally available. Anyone who was concerned about this issue knew that perhaps it was only a matter of time before another plaintiff challenged student assignment in Jefferson County more generally.

That challenge came in 2002 when a white parent filed suit claiming that his sons had been denied admission to schools on the basis of race in violation of the Constitution. An additional white parent (Ms. Meredith) was added to the lawsuit in 2003 and it would be that parent, who claimed her child had been denied admission to a nonmagnet elementary school, who would become the sole plaintiff on appeal. I would be called upon again to serve as lead trial counsel for the school board in this case, as I had in the Central High case. On behalf of the school board, we repeated many of the arguments made in the *Hampton* case: the compelling governmental interest served by efforts in Jefferson County to avoid a return to racial isolation in the schools and the ways in which the Jefferson County plan was narrowly tailored to achieve that purpose.

In 2003, the United States Supreme Court decided *Gratz v. Bollinger*[4] and *Grutter v. Bollinger*.[5] The following year, in *Meredith*, Judge Heyburn held that except for certain race-separate lists in the application process at traditional magnet schools the Jefferson County school board plan was constitutional.[6] He based his ruling on his prior analysis in *Hampton* and the Supreme Court's recent decisions in *Gratz* and *Grutter*. Jefferson County's plan was intact; only Meredith appealed; the Sixth Circuit affirmed and then denied Meredith's motion for rehearing.[7]

Meredith filed a timely petition for a writ of certiorari. But something significant had happened on the Supreme Court: Justice O'Connor retired. The Supreme Court had previously denied certiorari in a case presenting this same issue and the Court repeatedly postponed deciding whether to accept our case or not. It was on the very last day for a decision that the Supreme Court granted Meredith's petition for writ of certiorari and the petition filed by the plaintiffs in the similar Seattle case. Coincidentally, I was in Washington, DC, the day the certiorari petitions were granted. Heading to the airport the following morning, I read the editorials in the *Washington Post* and the *Washington Times*. Not surprisingly, the *Post* supported the student assignment plans in Louisville and Seattle, while the *Times* called for both plans to be struck down. The battle lines were drawn.

One of my law partners had argued our case in the Sixth Circuit and would argue again in the United States Supreme Court. The practical effect of that for me was to allow me to relax in the days immediately leading up to the argument and to enjoy the trip to Washington and the build up to this historic argument. The scene that we all witnessed on the morning of the argument—with citizens standing in the cold calling for our case and the promise of *Brown* to be affirmed—was one I do not expect to duplicate in my legal career.

The decision was every bit as close as many experts had predicted.[8] Four justices found a compelling governmental interest in the Jefferson County plan *and* found the plan was narrowly tailored to satisfy that interest. In other words, four justices upheld our client's plan in all respects. Four justices voted to strike down the plan. Justice Kennedy would break the tie: he agreed there was a compelling governmental interest in maintaining racial diversity in the schools—a majority of the United States Supreme Court had found a compelling governmental interest—but he found the plan was not narrowly tailored to satisfy that interest.

The story does not end there. The Jefferson County school board proceeded to develop a multifactor plan where the race of individual students as a basis for measuring diversity has been replaced by a mix of demographic and socioeconomic factors. The elected members of the Jefferson County school board reaffirmed their commitment to avoiding a return to the segregated schools of the 1970s and took to heart Justice Kennedy's opinion that:

> This Nation has a moral and ethical obligation to fulfill its historic commitment to creating an integrated society that ensures equal opportunity for all of its children. A compelling interest exists in avoiding racial isolation, an interest that a school district, in its discretion and expertise, may choose to pursue. Likewise, a district may consider it a compelling interest to achieve a diverse student population. Race may be one component of that diversity, but other demographic factors, plus special talents and needs, should also be considered.[9]

A number of candidates ran for election to our school board touting anti-student assignment campaign themes. Every single one of them lost; most did not even come close. The citizens of Jefferson County continue to elect and reelect school board members who are committed to achieving diverse schools.

Byron E. Leet is a partner at Wyatt Tarrant & Combs, LLP.

NOTES

1. Brown v. Board of Education, 347 U.S. 483 (1954).
2. Meredith v. Jefferson County Board of Education, 547 U.S. 1178 (2006) (certiorari granted), consolidated with Parents Involved in Community Schools v. Seattle School District No. 1, 547 U.S. 1177 (certiorari granted) for argument, and decided as Parents Involved in Community Schools v. Seattle School District No. 1, 551 U.S. 701 (2007).
3. Hampton v. Jefferson County Board of Education, 72 F. Supp. 2d 753 (W.D. Ky. 1999).

4. Gratz v. Bollinger, 539 U.S. 244 (2003).

5. Grutter v. Bollinger, 539 U.S. 306 (2003).

6. McFarland v. Jefferson County Public Schools, 330 F. Supp. 2d 834, 864 (W.D. Ky. 2004) (on appeal, *McFarland* became *Meredith*).

7. McFarland *ex rel.* McFarland v. Jefferson County Public Schools, 416 F.3d 513 (6th Cir. 2005), rehearing denied, 2005 U.S. App. LEXIS 22940 (6th Cir. Oct. 21, 2005).

8. Parents Involved, 551 U.S. 701.

9. Ibid., 798–99.

ERWIN CHEMERINSKY

Making Schools More Separate and Unequal

Parents Involved in Community Schools v. Seattle School District No. 1

AMERICAN PUBLIC SCHOOLS ARE INCREASINGLY SEPARATE AND UNEQUAL. BY every measure public schools are becoming more racially segregated.[1] Historically, much less has been spent on education for African American and Latino students than for white students. The Supreme Court deserves a great deal of the blame for this. In *San Antonio Independent School District v. Rodriguez*[2] the Court held that inequalities in school funding do not deny equal protection and the Court concluded that education is not a fundamental right under the Constitution. While *Rodriguez* meant that there would be unequal schools, another decision a year later, *Milliken v. Bradley*,[3] ensured that they would be racially separate.

In *Milliken*, the Supreme Court ruled that it is generally unconstitutional for courts to order interdistrict remedies for school segregation, such as transferring white students from suburban schools to city schools and minority students from city schools to suburban schools. Without the ability to assign students from city schools to suburban ones, and from suburban schools to city ones, there is no practical way to achieve desegregation in almost every metropolitan area. If 90% of a city's school system is comprised of minority students, no amount of busing or shifting students can achieve desegregation. *Milliken* thus has had a devastating effect on the ability to achieve desegregation in many areas. Duke professor Charles Clotfelter, in a careful study of American schools, concluded that 60% of segregation is a result of *Milliken v. Bradley*; or put another way, American schools would be 60% less segregated if interdistrict remedies were possible.[4] The combined effect of *Milliken* and *Rodriguez* has been enormous. American public education is characterized by wealthy white suburban schools spending a great deal on education surrounding much poorer black and Latino city schools that spend much less on education. The promise of *Brown* of equal educational opportunity has been unfulfilled because of the Supreme Court's failures.

After these decisions, the Court continued to limit the ability of courts to remedy racial segregation in schools. For example, in *Board of Education of Oklahoma City v. Dowell*,[5] the issue was whether a desegregation order should continue when its end would mean a resegregation of the public schools. There the Supreme Court held that federal court desegregation orders should be ended once a school system has achieved "unitary status" even when it will mean the resegregation of the public schools. The result has been the end of many successful desegregation orders. These cases—*Rodriguez, Milliken, Dowell*, and others like them—have limited the ability of courts to create equal educational opportunity. But many school boards on their own implemented plans to enhance racial diversity and desegregate their schools. In 2007, *Parents Involved in Community Schools v. Seattle School Dist. No. 1*[6] imposed significant, new limits on the ability of school systems to adopt such voluntary desegregation programs.

The first part of this chapter describes the Court's decision in *Parents Involved*, the second describes the effects of the decision on American public education, and the third explains why the decision is fundamentally flawed in its premises and its conclusions. *Parents Involved* must be understood in the context of 40 years of Supreme Court decisions that have contributed to the current condition of increasingly separate and unequal schools. Indeed, there has not been a single Supreme Court decision since *Rodriguez* in 1973 that has furthered desegregation or enhanced the equality of American public education.

The Court's Decision

Parents Involved in Community Schools v. Seattle School Dist. No. 1 involved public school systems in Louisville, Kentucky, and Seattle, Washington, that had adopted plans that used race as one factor in assigning students to schools to achieve greater racial diversity. Louisville, which had a program that included all students from kindergarten through 12th grade, had previously been a system segregated by law and had been subject to a judicial desegregation order that had been lifted not long before it adopted its own desegregation plan. Seattle never had been segregated by law and had a plan that used race as a factor in assigning students to high schools to achieve greater racial diversity.

The Court, in a 5–4 decision, found both plans to be unconstitutional. Chief Justice Roberts' opinion was joined in its entirety only by Justices Scalia, Thomas, and Alito. Justice Kennedy concurred in part, but also concurred only in the judgment in part, and his separate opinion is thus crucial to determining the scope and impact of the decision.

All five Justices in the majority agreed that the government must meet strict scrutiny, its actions must be necessary to achieve a compelling purpose, even if it is using race to achieve school desegregation. Chief Justice Roberts, writing for the majority, declared: "It is well established that when the government distributes burdens or benefits on the basis of individual racial classifications, that action is reviewed under strict scrutiny."[7] In the part of Chief Justice Roberts' opinion that Justice Kennedy did not join, Roberts, writing for a plurality of four, found that Seattle and Louisville lacked a compelling interest for their desegregation efforts. He stressed that the school systems were not seeking to remedy constitutional violations and he rejected the argument that diversity in classrooms was an interest sufficient to meet strict scrutiny, stating:

> However closely related race-based assignments may be to achieving racial balance, that itself cannot be the goal, whether labeled "racial diversity" or anything else. To the extent the objective is sufficient diversity so that students see fellow students as individuals rather than solely as members of a racial group, using means that treat students solely as members of a racial group is fundamentally at cross-purposes with that end.[8]

By contrast, Justice Kennedy and the four dissenters said that desegregating schools is a compelling government interest. Justice Kennedy stated: "In the administration of public schools by the state and local authorities it is permissible to consider the racial makeup of schools and to adopt general policies to encourage a diverse student body, one aspect of which is its racial composition."[9]

But all five Justices in the majority agreed that the school districts failed to show that race neutral means could not achieve desegregation—in other words, the school districts failed to show that race-conscious means were necessary. Justice Kennedy, like the four Justices in the plurality, said that race can be used in assigning students only if there is no other way of achieving desegregation. He identified several alternatives that school systems can use to achieve greater racial diversity in their schools:

School boards may pursue the goal of bringing together students of diverse backgrounds and races through other means, including strategic site selection of new schools; drawing attendance zones with general recognition of the demographics of neighborhoods; allocating resources for special programs; recruiting students and faculty in a targeted fashion; and tracking enrollments, performance, and other statistics by race. These mechanisms are race conscious but do not lead to different treatment based on a classification that tells each student he or she is to be defined by race, so it is unlikely any of them would demand strict scrutiny to be found permissible.[10]

Justice Breyer wrote a lengthy dissent joined by Justices Stevens, Souter, and Ginsburg.[11] He described how American public schools are increasingly racially segregated and lamented that the Court's decision will have the effect of placing many effective desegregation plans in jeopardy. Justice Breyer attached an appendix to his dissent which listed the many voluntary desegregation plans which will be in jeopardy in light of the invalidation of the Louisville and Seattle programs. The dissent questioned whether these efforts can be effective in achieving meaningful desegregation.

The majority and the dissent have dramatically different views about the importance of diversity in public schools and the meaning of *Brown*. Chief Justice Roberts sees in the Constitution a command for color-blindness and concluded his opinion by declaring:

Before *Brown*, schoolchildren were told where they could and could not go to school based on the color of their skin. The school districts in these cases have not carried the heavy burden of demonstrating that we should allow this once againeven for very different reasons. For schools that never segregated on the basis of race, such as Seattle, or that have removed the vestiges of past segregation, such as Jefferson County, the way to achieve a system of determining admission to the public schools on a nonracial basis, is to stop assigning students on a racial basis. The way to stop discrimination on the basis of race is to stop discriminating on the basis of race.[12]

By contrast, Justice Breyer and the dissent express the need for deference to school boards in desegregating schools and see the majority as abandoning the promise of *Brown*. Justice Breyer concludes his dissent by stating:

The last half century has witnessed great strides toward racial equality, but we have not yet realized the promise of *Brown*. To invalidate the plans under review is to threaten the promise of *Brown*. The plurality's position, I fear, would break that promise. This is a decision that the Court and the Nation will come to regret.[13]

The Impact of *Parents Involved*

Parents Involved thus limits the ability of school systems to adopt voluntary desegregation plans. In assessing this decision, it is important to put this in the context of a general unwillingness in so many places across the country to adopt voluntary desegregation plans at all. *Parents Involved* thus reinforces and provides an excuse for what school boards do not want to do anyway. Education professor Erica Frankenberg and lawyer Chinh Q. Le point out that, "the law alone cannot account for the scores of school districts and communities that have essentially offered no strategy for or even intention of addressing racial, ethnic, and socioeconomic isolation in their schools, despite the growing segregation they are and have been witnessing."[14]

There is very little federal incentive encouraging school districts to pursue integration. The Obama Administration's recent efforts with regard to the nation's education system have focused mainly on encouraging the proliferation of charter schools.[15] Many proponents of desegregation worry that charter schools may actually hamper and undermine integration efforts, given the increasingly segregated nature of such schools.[16] Indeed, several school districts in Georgia sued their state over the establishment of charter programs for this very reason.[17] Also, the remaining federal efforts do not do very much to encourage integration efforts. Political science professor Stephen Samuel Smith thus concluded that:

> To be sure, court opinions such as those in *Parents Involved* will have important consequences for school districts around the country. . . . But insofar as (i) there is looser coupling between local venues and Congress and the executive branch on desegregation issues than there was in the civil rights era, and (ii) the federal government has largely abandoned its efforts to promote desegregation, the new politics of desegregation is likely to be more piecemeal than it was in the civil rights era and more likely to occur on a district-by-district basis, since it is more dependent on local conditions and developments.[18]

It is in this context that the effects of *Parents Involved* need to be assessed. The decision has most obviously affected the desegregation efforts of the school districts pursuing existing integration plans fatally similar to those of Seattle and Jefferson County that were struck down by *Parents Involved*. While estimates on the actual number of such districts vary considerably (from "more than 1,000" to "possibly less than ten"), they still undoubtedly exist, and "the efforts of the . . . school districts that presently pursue racial integration will undoubtedly impact the lives of a significant number of schoolchildren, even if only some of those districts continue their efforts after *Parents Involved*."[19] These districts are left with two choices: risk future litigation by relying on the Kennedy concurrence to craft desegregation plans centered on factors other than race or that consider race as only one of many factors, or simply abandon previous desegregation efforts.[20]

To be sure, some districts are taking the former route. According to law professor Kimberly Jenkins Robinson, "[d]espite the *Parents Involved* decision, many school districts remain committed to pursuing diversity and avoiding racial isolation."[21] She cites as one of her examples the new student assignment plan adopted in May 2008 by the district in Jefferson County, Kentucky, which seeks to increase economic and racial diversity by employing socioeconomic factors.[22] But the reality also is that many school districts are simply abandoning their desegregation efforts.[23] This is exactly the effect that Justice Breyer predicted in his dissent in *Parents Involved* and it has occurred across the country. In this way, the school experiences of thousands of children have been adversely affected by the *Parents Involved* decision.

Parents Involved has also likely affected the decisions of school districts that are considering adopting measures to ameliorate the issue of segregation, similar to the way it affected the districts with an existing plan discussed in the previous section. The *Parents Involved* decision operates to scare away schools from adopting desegregation measures, and provides ammunition to litigious parents. As *Parents Involved* supporter and President of the Center for Equal Opportunity Roger Clegg puts it, the effect of *Parents Involved* will be significant, and is already visible.

> School-board members across the country will pick up the paper and read what the Court did, and they will conclude that using skin color to determine school assignments is a bad idea. . . . On top of all this, school-board members now know that, when their counterparts in Seattle and Louisville used race-based student assignments, they enmeshed their respective school districts in years of litigation, ultimately losing and ultimately requiring them to pay, not just their own lawyers, but the opposing side's lawyers as well. . . . "No thanks," other school boards will say. The Seattle and Louisville plans were not atypical and were not particularly sloppy or badly thought out, and they were skillfully defended. But they lost.[24]

In Smith's words, "Thus, in Clegg's view, the potential harm of litigation costs, along with an unclear standard established by Justice Kennedy, will serve to deter school districts from implementing any race-conscious policies to support desegregation."[25]

Furthermore, the efforts of the Office of Civil Rights in the Department of Education under the Bush Administration only served to make matters worse in discouraging school systems from adopting voluntary desegregation plans:

> [I]n the wake of the 2007 *Parents Involved* decision, OCR issued a "Dear Colleague" letter misinterpreting the court decision as antithetical to the very goal of integrated education,

and warned districts against the pursuit of any type of voluntary, race-conscious student assignment strategies. The goal of racially integrated education, according to the Bush-era Education Department, was to be realized without direct consideration of race.[26]

Misinformation and uncertainty about the decision, then, coupled with the difficulty associated with altering community views enough to elect a school board majority committed to an integration plan, and the very real possibility that an upset parent may initiate expensive and potentially successful litigation if a plan is adopted, ensure that only the communities that are overwhelmingly steadfast in their commitment to diversity will continue to pursue integration.

The effects are especially apparent when one considers the impact of *Parents Involved* on the many school districts that have had their desegregation orders lifted and been declared "unitary" since the decision. For the most part, *Parents Involved* operates to prohibit these districts from carrying over their existing desegregation plans.[27] One of the first federal courts to react to *Parents Involved* was in Tucson, Arizona. On August 21, 2007, federal district judge David C. Bury, a George W. Bush nominee, relied heavily upon *Parents Involved* in stating that the court intended to let the Tucson Unified School District (TUSD) out of a desegregation order issued in 1978 following a class action suit from Latino and black parents. Attorneys at the Mexican American Legal Defense and Educational Fund (MALDEF) responded the same day and submitted a Motion to Reconsider arguing that Judge Bury's ruling was based upon a misunderstanding of *Parents Involved*, which allowed for race-conscious measures in remedying de jure segregation, which was exactly the case in Tucson. The Tucson school board, however, responded to Judge Bury's order by ending their school desegregation program by a 3–2 vote.[28]

The events in the Charlotte-Mecklenburg, North Carolina, school district (CMS) are probably most illustrative of what happens to integration plans in the post–*Parents Involved* landscape. Superintendent Eric Smith was selected in 1996 while CMS was still under a desegregation order, and during his job interview promised to the school board "that the one thing I would not do as superintendent was intentionally re-segregate the Charlotte-Mecklenburg schools."[29] Smith initially acted in complete accordance with this promise by vigorously defending his school system's desegregation goals from a legal challenge by white parents in 1999.[30] However, when that trial resulted in a court order declaring CMS unitary, Smith largely abandoned his commitment to desegregation. Political scientist Stephen Samuel Smith writes about the superintendent:

> [T]he 1999 trial altered his perspective. Although a majority of the board still wanted to preserve as much as possible of CMS's historic commitment to desegregation, Smith was much more focused on adopting a plan that would be sure to avoid any additional legal

challenges, would appeal to advocates of neighborhood schools, could be implemented quickly, and would satisfy a Charlotte business elite worried that uncertainty in pupil assignment was jeopardizing corporate relocations to Charlotte. Thus, Smith rejected proposals that CMS consider [free and reduced lunch status] or other socioeconomic criteria in developing its new plan even though such criteria were legal, and without such criteria, the new plan was sure to increase the number of high-poverty schools. Smith was aware of the many problems posed by high-poverty schools, but he felt that CMS and the broader community had the resources and will to deal with these problems. Indeed, when asked by a local journalist "whether concentrating low-income kids in inner city schools made the job harder," he replied, "I don't think it matters."[31]

Mr. Smith, a superintendent with a demonstrated commitment to desegregation goals, abandoned integration efforts due a combination of economic, political, and legal pressures.

One of the most important things lost because of *Parents Involved* is hope, specifically the hope that the federal judiciary would assist the nation's schools fight the rising trends of segregation and fulfill its promise in *Brown*. The effect of *Parents Involved* is that the federal government, through the federal courts, is standing in the way, instead of facilitating, desegregation efforts. James Ryan—formerly a law professor at the University of Virginia and now dean of the Harvard Graduate School of Education—makes this observation:

> To be sure, the Court's decision does not take away much that is tangible, as it will not affect many current student assignment plans. But it takes away some hope. Hope that the Court would stand firmly on the side of school integration. Hope that, despite past disappointments, new ways could be found to integrate schools, ways that were acceptable to local citizens of every color and ethnicity. Hope that schools would be places where students go not just to improve their test scores but also to become better citizens and better people. Hope that integrated schools would lead, slowly but finally, to an integrated society. So, yes, the decision is in one sense not terribly significant. But it is no small thing to dash hope.[32]

Conclusion: A Misguided Decision

Chief Justice Roberts's plurality opinion in *Parents Involved*, quoted at length earlier, is based on the premise that the Constitution requires that the government be color-blind in its actions. But nowhere does the Fourteenth Amendment say or imply that the government must be color-blind. I certainly do not believe that the meaning of a constitutional provision is determined by the intent of its framers, but it is clear that the drafters of the Fourteenth Amendment meant to allow the government to use race in its programs to benefit minorities. As professor Stephen A. Siegel powerfully demonstrated, the Congress that ratified the Fourteenth Amendment adopted a plethora of race-based programs to benefit especially former slaves.[33]

The premise for both Chief Justice Roberts and Justice Kennedy is that government actions that use race for beneficial ends, such as desegregating schools, are the same under the Constitution as the use of race to disadvantage minorities. But this is wrong. There is a fundamental difference between using race to harm students of color and using race to benefit all by enhancing racial diversity and desegregation. Justice Sotomayor recently powerfully replied to Chief Justice's Roberts conclusion in *Parents Involved* by declaring:

> This refusal to accept the stark reality that race matters is regrettable. The way to stop discrimination on the basis of race is to speak openly and candidly on the subject of race, and to apply the Constitution with eyes open to the unfortunate effects of centuries of racial discrimination. As members of the judiciary tasked with intervening to carry out the guarantee of equal protection, we ought not sit back and wish away, rather than confront, the racial inequality that exists in our society. It is this view that works harm, by perpetuating the facile notion that what makes race matter is acknowledging the simple truth that race *does* matter.[34]

The Supreme Court's decision in *Parents Involved* is based on the majority's view that race does not matter in terms of the composition of classrooms or for children's education. The decision's effect is to end many voluntary desegregation plans and to discourage others. In this way, it is contributing to the separate and unequal schools that exist throughout the United States.

Erwin Chemerinsky is the Dean and Distinguished Professor of Law, Raymond Pryke Professor of First Amendment Law at the University of California, Irvine School of Law. This chapter is adapted from an essay by the same title forthcoming in the MICHIGAN STATE UNIVERSITY LAW REVIEW.

NOTES

The author would like to thank Hikmat Chehabi and James Miller for their excellent research assistance.

1. Gary Orfield & Chungmei Lee, The Civil Rights Project, *Racial Transformation and the Changing Nature of Segregation*, 8–14 (2006) (analyzing data from the United States Department of Education's Common Core of Data, 2003–2004); Regina Rosenello, *School Integration in the Wake of* Parents Involved *and* Meredith, 40 RUTGERS LAW JOURNAL 535, 536 n.3 (2009).

2. San Antonio Independent School District v. Rodriguez, 411 U.S. 1 (1973).

3. Milliken v. Bradley, 418 U.S. 717 (1974).

4. CHARLES T. CLOFELTER, AFTER *BROWN*: THE RISE AND RETREAT OF SCHOOL DESEGREGATION (Princeton University Press 2004).

5. Board of Education of Oklahoma City Public Schools, Independent School District No. 89, Oklahoma County, Oklahoma v. Dowell, 498 U.S. 237 (1991).

6. Parents Involved in Community Schools v. Seattle School District No. 1, 551 U.S. 701 (2007).

7. Ibid., 720.

8. Ibid., 733.

9. Ibid., 788 (Justice Kennedy, concurring in part and concurring in the judgment in part).

10. Ibid., 789.

11. Ibid., 803 (Justice Breyer, dissenting).

12. Ibid., 747–48 (Chief Justice Roberts)

13. Ibid., 868 (Justice Breyer, dissenting).

14. Erica Frankenberg & Chinh Q. Le, *The Post-*Parents Involved *Challenge: Confronting Extralegal Obstacles to Integration*, 69 OHIO STATE LAW JOURNAL 1015, 1021 (2008); James E. Ryan, *The Supreme Court and Voluntary Integration*, 121 HARVARD LAW REVIEW 131, 132 (2007) ("The truth is that racial integration is not on the agenda of most school districts and has not been for over twenty years. . . . Modern education reform efforts might still share the goal of equalizing educational opportunities for minority students, which the Court in *Brown* embraced. But integration is not generally the means of choice to achieve that goal, nor is the Supreme Court the key arena"); Danielle Holley-Walker, *Educating at the Crossroads:* Parents Involved, *No Child Left Behind and School Choice*, 69 OHIO STATE LAW JOURNAL 911, 926 (2008) (expressing the opinion that, given the pressures and emphasis placed on student performance by No Child Left Behind, school integration may not be a top priority for the majority of schools).

15. Greg Toppo, *Ready, Set, Race for Education Money: States Rush to Make Changes to Get Part of Stimulus Grant*, USA TODAY 7D (November 4, 2009) (illustrating how the Obama Administration has prioritized further expansion of the charter movement by tying eligibility for stimulus funds from Race to the Top grants to the loosening of legal caps on the number of charters).

16. Alyssa M. Simon, *"Race" to the Bottom? Addressing the Student Body in Diversity in Charter Schools After* Parents Involved, 10 CONNECTICUT PUBLIC INTERST LAW JOURNAL 399, 403–404 ("While charter schools theoretically have the potential to reduce segregation by drawing from larger attendance zones and crafting missions that might appeal to a diverse cross section of students, they are in fact more racially isolated than their public counterparts. Seventy percent of black charter school students attend "intensely segregated" schools. The average white charter school student attends a charter school that is over 70 percent white, despite the fact that white students comprise only 43 percent of charter school enrollees" (internal citations omitted)).

17. Adai Tefera, Erica Frankenberg, & Genevieve Siegel-Hawley, *School Integration Efforts After* Parents Involved, 37 HUMAN RIGHTS 10, 11 (2010).

18. Stephen Samuel Smith, *Still Swimming Against the Resegregation Tide? A Suburban Southern School District in the Aftermath of* Parents Involved, 88 NORTH CAROLINA LAW REVIEW 1145, 1175 (2010).

19. Frankenberg & Le, *The Post-*Parents Involved *Challenge*, 1021 n. 29; Kimberly Jenkins Robinson, *The Constitutional Future of Race-Neutral Efforts to achieve Diversity and Avoid Racial Isolation in Elementary and Secondary Schools*, 50 BOSTON COLLEGE LAW REVIEW 277, 279 (2009). In a forthcoming article, Erica Frankenberg estimates that the number of districts using a voluntary integration policy in 2014 is about 70. Erica Frankenberg, *Assessing the Status of School Desegregation Sixty Years After* Brown, MICHIGAN STATE LAW REVIEW (forthcoming 2015).

20. Parents Involved, 551 U.S. 788–89 (Justice Kennedy, concurring) (suggesting various strategies to avoid racially isolated schools and to create diverse ones including: "strategic site selection of new schools; drawing attendance zones with general recognition of the demographics of neighborhoods; allocating resources for special programs; recruiting students and faculty in a targeted fashion; and tracking enrollments, performance, and other statistics by race").

21. Robinson, *The Constitutional Future*, 279; Emily Bazelon, *The Next Kind of Integration*, NEW YORK TIMES § MM, 38 (July 20, 2008); Mark Walsh, *Use of Race Uncertain for Schools*, EDUCATION WEEK 1 (July 18, 2007) (quoting an attorney for numerous school boards who stated that "she was hearing a commitment [from school districts] to do whatever could pass legal muster to keep schools racially diverse"); Susan Eaton, *Diversity's Quiet Rebirth*, EDUCATION WEEK (August 18, 2008).

22. Robinson, *The Constitutional Future*, 280–81; Genevieve Siegel-Hawley, Initiative on School Integration at The Civil Rights Project/Proyecto Derechos Civiles, *The Integration Report, Issue 4*, (February 25, 2008) (school districts were ordered by the Iowa Department of Education to revise decades-old desegregation plans to comply with *Parents Involved*, and all five chose to develop "new diversity plans that consider socio-economic status, academic skill levels, race and ethnicity, and language background" as opposed to simply abandoning desegregation efforts).

23. Abbey Coffee & Erica Frankenberg, The Civil Rights Project, *Two Years After the* PICS *Decision: Districts' Integration Efforts in a Changing Climate* 5–8 (June 30, 2009) (in Arkansas, the Fort Smith Public School District voted to abolish its previous practice of multicultural transfers, specifically in response to the 2007 Supreme Court ruling regarding "racially based" transfer policies); Matthew C. Greene, *Unsuspected Shoals in Equal Protection: Adapting Wisconsin's Special Transfer Program to Survive* Parents Involved, 2008 WISCONSIN LAW REVIEW 1201 (2008) (charting the history of Wisconsin's decades-old voluntary desegregation plan (Chapter 220), explaining how it was rendered unconstitutional by the *Parents Involved* decision, and advocating for policymakers to revise the program in compliance with Justice Kennedy's concurrence). Sadly for Mr. Greene and the children involved in Wisconsin's public schools, it appears the program is being phased out. Erin Richards, *As School Options Expand, Landmark Chapter 220 Integration Program Fade*, MILWAUKEE WISCONSIN JOURNAL SENTINEL (December 24, 2013); Genevieve Siegel-Hawley, Initiative on School Integration at The Civil Rights Project/Proyecto Derechos Civiles, *The Integration Report*, issue 2 (January 21, 2008) (noting that "in the months following the June 2007 *Seattle/Louisville* decision, we have seen a disturbing pattern develop among school districts deciding that the easiest and safest response to the ruling is to eliminate existing

desegregation plans altogether").

24. Roger Clegg, *A Good—If Mixed Bag*, THE NATIONAL REVIEW (July 5, 2007).

25. Smith, *Still Swimming*, 1150.

26. Genevieve Siegel-Hawley, Initiative on School Integration at The Civil Rights Project/Proyecto Derechos Civiles, *The Integration Report, Issue* 23 (January 13, 2010); Tefera, Frankenberg, & Siegel-Hawley, *School Integration Efforts*, 13 ("In 2008, the Bush administration sent a letter to school districts inaccurately interpreting the *Parents Involved* decision in a way that suggested only race-neutral means of pursuing integration would be legal. As President Obama took office, civil rights groups and other stakeholders anticipated that his administration would be more supportive of integration efforts, including issuing new guidance to replace the previous 2008 letter. In the third year of the Obama administration, however, no such guidance about voluntary integration has been issued").

27. Parents Involved, 721 (noting that Jefferson County's recently dissolved desegregation order could not operate as a the requisite compelling interest to satisfy strict scrutiny); Coffee & Frankenberg, *Two Years After the* PICS *Decision*, 10 (listing 44 districts to have been declared unitary two years since the *Parents Involved* decision).

28. Charles J. Ogletree, Jr. & Susan Eaton, *From Little Rock to Seattle and Louisville: is "All Deliberate Speed" Stuck in Reverse*, 30 UNIVERSITY OF ARKANSAS AT LITTLE ROCK LAW REVIEW 279, 290–91 (2008).

29. Eric Smith, *Achieving Equity: Why Diversity, High Expectations Matter*, CHARLOTTE OBSERVER 13A (March 9, 1999).

30. STEPHEN SAMUEL SMITH, BOOM FOR WHOM? EDUCATION, DESEGREGATION, AND DEVELOPMENT IN CHARLOTTE, 161–71 (SUNY Press 2004); Capacchione v. Charlotte-Mecklenburg Schools, 57 F. Supp. 2d 228, 242 (W.D.N.C. 1999).

31. Smith, *Still Swimming*, 1177.

32. Ryan, *The Supreme Court and Voluntary Integration*, 132–33.

33. Stephen A. Siegel, *The Federal Government's Power to Enact Color Conscious Laws: An Originalist Inquiry*, 92 NORTHWESTERN UNIVERSITY LAW REVIEW 477 (1998).

34. Schuette v. Coalition for Affirmative Action, 134 S.Ct. 1623, 1676 (2014) (Justice Sotomayor, dissenting).

MICHAEL J. DUMAS

Contesting White Accumulation in Seattle

Toward a Materialist Antiracist Analysis of School Desegregation

SEATTLE PARENT KATHLEEN BROSE WAS OUTRAGED WHEN HER DAUGHTER was assigned to Franklin High School, rather than her first choice, the oversubscribed Ballard High School, which had recently undergone a $35 million renovation. For Brose, the school district's use of race as a factor in school assignment, although intended to achieve racial balance, penalized her daughter for being white, and prevented her from enrolling at Ballard, the family's local community high school. "She was told basically, 'You have no value to us, except your skin color. We don't care if it's going to be a burden to have you get on that school bus every day.'"[1] Ultimately, Brose would form a group, Parents Involved in Community Schools, which would successfully sue the Seattle School District over this "racial tiebreaker" policy, leading to a declaration by the Supreme Court that the policy violated students' constitutional rights. The ruling also invited greater scrutiny of any effort to consciously address racial (re)segregation in public schools. The majority opinion would effectively deny the significance of material advantages whites enjoy as a result of long-standing policies and practices intended to do exactly that—assist whites in gaining and maintaining access to property and resources (including schooling) not available to people of color.

In this chapter, I argue that Parents Involved in Community Schools (PICS)—both the Seattle parents' organization and the Supreme Court decision of the same name—offer a defense of white *material* advantage in school assignment, even as they invoke appeals to fairness, choice, and colorblindness. In Seattle, as in cities across the nation, historical white entitlement to privileged urban spaces continues to reproduce inequities in access to educational facilities, programs, and prestige. Thus, in school assignment, to adopt colorblind policies is to allow whites to continue to benefit from what legal scholar Daria Roithmayr calls the "locked-in advantages" of racial discrimination, in which whites come by their school (and racial-spatial) advantages innocently.[2] By contrast, a decidedly materialist and antiracist analysis of school desegregation, as put forth in this chapter, importantly refocuses our attention on the racialized distribution (and maldistribution) of economic resources in the city, and proffers a different plot in the story of school desegregation—one that shifts our gaze to the accumulation and maintenance of white wealth.[3] Through this lens, we understand that "community" schools in historically segregated white neighborhoods areas are hardly innocent institutions, and may serve to reproduce white material advantage for generations to come.

This chapter is at once a theoretical intervention and a reflection on this moment in school desegregation politics. I begin with a detailed explanation of materialist approaches to the analysis of race and racism. I then offer an historical overview of housing discrimination in Seattle, in which racially segregated neighborhoods led inevitably to racially segregated schools. This creates the context for a critical materialist analysis of the white defense of racial advantage in school assignment, which I offer here using the specific language of Brose herself and also Chief Justice Roberts's plurality opinion and Justice Thomas's concurring opinion in *Parents Involved in Community Schools v. Seattle School District No. 1*.[4] Finally, I consider the future of white privilege and material advantage in access to public education resources, and attempt to identify priorities for antiracist cultural and political responses.

Racial Materialism and Antiracist Politics

Racial materialism asserts that race and racism function to serve the interests of wealth accumulation. As Robert Young explains,

> Race signals a marking for exploitation, and this economic assignment, in turn, generates an accompanying ideological machinery to justify and increase that exploitation. . . . Race represents not just a cultural or political category as many critics attest to, but it

represents an historic apparatus for the production, maintenance, and legitimation of the inequalities of wage-labor.[5]

An antiracist materialism, then, is deeply concerned with countering the maldistribution of economic resources, specifically as these policies and practices are motivated by racism and intentionally or unintentionally lead to racially disparate outcomes. To formulate a materialist racial critique of white advantage, it is first necessary to understand the interconnected cultural and political-economic processes through which white advantage is made to seem normal, even inevitable, and always innocent. Below, I explain how theorizing neoliberal multiculturalism and white material and ideological dominance help us more clearly understand conditions on the ground in Seattle.

NEOLIBERAL MULTICULTURALISM IN A POSTRACIAL UNITED STATES

After World War II, the U.S. instituted a new racial order, and in a radical departure from history, adopted a formal, state-supported antiracism in response to critiques from around the globe, and particularly from the Soviet Union.[6] This was done to blunt the ascendancy of communism and solidify the legitimacy of the United States as an imperial power, and as the global leader in capitalist expansion. Whereas white supremacy formed the dominant governmental and ideological regime prior to World War II, after the war, the U.S. formally adopted the liberal stance that resolving the "Negro problem" would both facilitate, and serve as evidence of the nation's democratic ideals, and therefore, its right to lead the (free) world. In short, "African American economic success would prove capitalism to be neutral to race rather than structured by it."[7]

A few decades later, the rise of neoliberalism in the 1980s and 1990s shifted the relationship between government and race. After World War II and throughout the 1960s, to be sure, the state positioned itself as the leader in advancing antiracism. But, under neoliberal multiculturalism, it is neoliberal economic policies and ideological formations that resolve the problem of racism. In other words, because the market is ostensibly colorblind and equally accessible to all, it is regarded as best suited to facilitate racial equality. Neoliberal multiculturalism promises to usher in the postracial period, by nurturing a new global citizenship centered on economic participation. In doing so, neoliberal multiculturalism abandons any explicit mention of race.[8]

Neoliberal multiculturalism is still attentive to racial difference, however, and recognizes inequitable outcomes, but explains these differences as essentially not about race or (in)justice, but rather as the result of individual and group choices.[9]

Through the neoliberal-multicultural lens, we can still feel sympathy to the extent that racialized subjects are perceived as being prevented from participating in the market. However, if they (seemingly) reject opportunities to participate in the market, no matter how rigged that system may be, then our sympathies can be justifiably withheld. Any argument that the economic sphere is already regulated by racial privilege will fall on deaf ears, as the market is already presumed to be multicultural and racially ethical (i.e., *post*racial) on its face.

In the next section, we see how this recent (post-)racial order creates the cultural context in which white accumulation of resources is seen as having nothing to do with race at all, and at the same time, continues to allow "race" and racialized spaces of people of color to be considered anachronisic holdovers from an earlier time, and impediments to social progress.

WHITE SPATIAL IMAGINATIONS, COLORBLINDNESS AND "THE URBAN"

In pursuit of economic stability and advantage, homeowners in metropolitan areas often support policies that protect their wealth, most often in ways that further segregate themselves off from areas deemed less desirable, and encourage disproportionate public and private spending in their own areas, at the expense of others.[10] These are universal strategies that in the U.S. take on a peculiarly racial pattern (although scholars have also noted similarly racial dynamics in other nations).[11] Importantly, this racial imagination is also compounded by a desire for financial profit, which has the material consequence of limiting access for those racialized bodies whose very presence is understood to depreciate the value of the territory.[12] Those few who are allowed in must be exceptional (or exceptionally wealthy) in some way, or may gain entry as part of a political effort to undermine claims of racial bias, which, in the officially antiracist state, may be penalized, either directly or through loss of community status.

This community status under neoliberal multiculturalism is linked to a white imagination of the metropolis as an ideal dwelling place and playground. That is, "the urban" is imagined as sophisticated, technologically and culturally.[13] Thus, while urban whites may dismiss multicultural projects that open up "their" geographic spaces to people of color in any significant number, multiculturalism is valued as a signifier of a certain tolerance and sophistication, as a way to be, or appear to be more interesting and worldly. In contrast to this imagination of the "sophisticated city," the white spatial imaginary (as George Lipsitz terms it) understands itself as necessarily pushing back against the possibility of "the urban jungle."[14] Here, urban spaces are constructed as sites of violence, laziness, and decay, inhabited by (mostly) people of color whose various pathologies lead them to reproduce these conditions on their own. The "jungle" is thereby deemed unworthy of investment, justifying a shift of resources away from these spaces and toward whiter "sophisticated" areas of the city.[15] It is not thought that these political-economic decisions reproduce inequities, but that the inequities are simply the result of a natural, albeit unfortunate defect in the people who are somehow accustomed to, and—in a free market—choose to live in the "jungle."

Not all whites condone or seek to advance the white spatial imaginary, and it is not only whites who capitalize on it. However, as Lipsitz maintains, "every white person benefits from the association of white places with privilege, from the neighborhood race effects that create unequal and unjust geographies of opportunity."[16] These race effects include access to more highly resourced schools, less exposure to environmental pollution, proximity to more public transportation options, and the availability of higher-quality nutrition and superior health services. In short, the imagination of white spaces generates value by attracting more material advantages. As Lipsitz explains, "It is not that suburban [and I would add, urban] whites are innately racist and consequently favor land use policies that increase the racial gap, but rather that prevailing land use policies produce a certain kind of whiteness that offers extraordinary inducements and incentives for a system of privatization that has drastic racial consequences."[17]

Important for the analysis I offer here is to understand that very little of this happens with explicit mention of race. Even as white racial privilege is maintained, actors speak primarily as homeowners, as taxpayers, as Americans, who have no racial interests. It is, as Eduardo Bonilla-Silva puts it, "racism without racists."[18] To be sure, there are those who consciously and unconsciously embrace white supremacy, but under neoliberal multiculturalism, even those who advocate racist ideas have adopted a language of colorblindness, allowing them to speak on behalf of whiteness without evidence that they are doing so. Thus, white advantage is maintained by a collusion between those who honestly have no racial animus and those who still harbor it. This colorblind racism, which became hegemonic in the late 1960s, "explains contemporary racial inequality as the outcome of nonracial dynamics."[19] Consistent with our current racial order, colorblindness ushered in an era in which "whites rationalize minorities' contemporary status as the product of market dynamics, naturally occurring phenomena, and blacks' imputed cultural limitations."[20]

The white spatial imaginary invokes a seemingly virtuous colorblindness that is racially innocent and defensible, at least or especially in court. Its interests are framed as simply an effort to ensure fairness and freedom for all, by *not* attending to racial difference. In practice, this means either refusing to acknowledge disproportionate race effects at all, or explaining them (away) as the choice by racial minorities to hold on to an unsophisticated racial identification that ultimately impedes economic progress for those groups, and if we are not careful—if we let them in (to *our* spaces)—will doom us all.

WHITE CARTELS: "LOCKING IN" RACIAL ADVANTAGES (WITHOUT RACIAL ANIMUS)

Postracial ideologies refuse to recognize white accumulation of economic resources as a specifically racial phenomenon, because this would mean having to acknowledge that race effects are, in fact, a product of racism. Within this ideological context, social policies continue to reproduce economic inequality along racial lines. However, none of this occurred accidentally. Daria Roithmayr suggests framing racial discrimination in the United States as the activity of what she calls "racial cartels."[21] Here, race "pays off" with economic advantage, secured through formal and informal processes that profit one racial group by excluding others.[22] "In theoretical terms," Roithmayr explains, "racial cartels generated profit in the same way that market cartels do—by restricting supply and manipulating price."[23] In housing policy, for example, state policies condoned discrimination well into the 1960s, redlining policies limited the ability of black homeowners to secure home improvement loans, and racially restrictive housing covenants allowed, and even compelled, white homeowners to refuse to sell their homes to people of color. These racially exclusionary policies and practices created coveted "white neighborhoods" and increased the property values of homes in those areas, all while guaranteeing that the areas open to black people and other people of color were deprived of resources, thereby driving down the value of homes in those communities. "Far from costing whites to discriminate," Roithmayr notes, "exclusion paid significant dividends."[24]

Racial monopolies on economic resources "lock in" advantages such that there need be no racial animus for these benefits to continue, and continue to accrue payoffs for white citizens and their children, across generations. Roithmayr maintains that whites "engage in racial exclusion not because they have a taste for discrimination or because they are irrational, but because they derive significant economic, social and political benefits."[25] To be sure, Roithmayr's point about the economic advantage is well taken; even so, we have ample evidence that whites rarely own up to the racism they harbor. Here is where colorblindness comes into play. As Eduardo Bonilla-Silva found in his research, "whites, for the most part, do not interpret their racial isolation and segregation from blacks as racial."[26] Instead, he notes, they "either do not see any need to explain this or explain it as a nonracial matter ('Race has nothing to do with it' or 'That's the way things are')."[27]

Such colorblindness, as is clear in Seattle, leaves little legal recourse, since we have little evidence of what the courts might recognize as racial animus. I still want to identify these practices as instantiations of white supremacy, as provocative as that may seem to some readers. However, I would suggest that in our current historical moment—informed by neoliberal multiculturalism—what we are witnessing is perhaps less racial animus and more a resolved racial entitlement. That is, whites have developed a rational basis for discrimination, one rooted in a belief that they deserve more, either because they have worked harder, or simply made better choices. To the extent that there are clear racial patterns, this is either incidental (what Bonilla-Silva indicates as race having "nothing to do with it") or due to the cultural deficiencies of black people and other people of color. In other words, to use Bonilla-Silva's description, that's just "the way things are."[28]

The theoretical discussion of white advantage I have offered in this section makes clear that there is little that is racially innocent about the distribution of material resources in US society. In the next section, I turn to Seattle, specifically, to explain how housing and education policy choices intentionally and unintentionally reproduce segregated neighborhoods and schools in the city.

De jure Inequality: Intentionally Segregated Housing and Schools in Seattle

When the Seattle School Board voted in 1977 to implement the Seattle Plan for the Elimination of Racial Imbalance, Board President Dan Olson made clear why it was necessary to implement a city-wide mandatory desegregation plan in the first place.[29] "I would like to address these comments to the city officials, to the federal officials, and to real estate people," said Olson, who had won his seat over an antibusing candidate and whose son was one of the white students who had participated in the relatively unsuccessful voluntary busing program:

> Now that the School District has acted within its power to rectify a situation that has been created by segregated housing patterns, we look now to the city government to do those kinds of things that can help alleviate this situation. We look to the federal government to do those kinds of things that can help alleviate segregated housing patterns and we look thirdly to the real estate industry and to all of us who buy and sell houses as individuals to do those things that will alleviate segregation in housing patterns. We certainly can make the whole situation a lot better if we all take actions in this regard.[30]

The Supreme Court affirmed the constitutionality of racially restrictive housing covenants in 1926 and did not declare those covenants unenforceable until 1948.[31] Like many cities, Seattle had its own prolonged struggle against racist housing practices. When new jobs in the growing manufacturing sector brought a sharp increase in Seattle's black population in the 1930s, a significant number of the city's white homeowners, particularly in the city's north end, began to include such covenants in their property deeds.[32] A common phrase found in many deeds of homes on Seattle's Queen Anne Hill read, "No person or persons of Asiatic, African or Negro blood, lineage, or extraction shall be permitted to occupy a portion of said property."[33] In the Wedgewood neighborhood, one such covenant instructed that "no persons of any race other than the white race shall use or occupy any building or any lot" but graciously allowed that "this covenant shall not prevent occupancy by domestic servants of a different race domiciled with an owner or tenant."[34]

Between 1940 and 1960, the city's black population increased from 1% to 4.8%.[35] However, by 1960, almost 80% of Seattle's black residents lived in one community, the Central District. By 1957, Garfield High School, located in the center of the Central District, would be more than 50% African American; the vast majority of black youth in the entire city attended this one high school. In 1961, the NAACP's local affiliate proposed that Seattle adopt an ordinance forbidding housing discrimination. While their proposal found support among civil rights advocates, it was opposed by organizations representing the real estate industry and apartment property owners. The City Council neglected to take up the issue.[36]

A fair housing ordinance came before the Council again in 1963, as the new Seattle Human Rights Commission put forth a new measure that would impose criminal charges on those who discriminated on the basis of race, ethnicity, or creed.[37] As it became clear that the majority of the Council would not support the proposed law, Rev. John Adams, chair of the Central Area Committee on Civil Rights, warned that racial discrimination was a "moral problem of the white community."[38] This prompted a rebuke from one of the white City Council members, who suggested that Adams and the other activists could not determine what the moral decision was in this case. In fact, they argued that the proposed measure violated other moral standards—fairness, choice, and freedom of association. Led once again by real estate interests, opponents lambasted fair housing as "forced housing."[39] Seattle finally passed a fair housing ordinance in 1968, around the same time as the federal Fair Housing Act, and just weeks after the assassination of Martin Luther King Jr.[40] The success of advocates this time was due in part to changing attitudes, locally and nationally, but also because of black urban rebellions the previous summer. Some feared that failure to respond to activists' demands could result in more uprisings, particularly in the wake of King's murder.

Segregated neighborhoods inevitably produced segregated neighborhood schools, placing the city in an untenable legal position. The mandatory school desegregation plan passed in 1977—characterized by opponents as "forced busing"—was itself the result of the failure of the "voluntary racial transfer" program of the 1960s.[41] While a significant number of black residents in the Central District had volunteered to have their children attend predominantly white schools in the north end, very few white parents had opted to send their children to the more racially diverse schools in the Central District and south end of the city.[42] Faced with the likelihood of a federal lawsuit, the school board hoped to implement a plan that would satisfy the ACLU, NAACP, and other civil rights groups.[43] The Seattle Plan for the Elimination of Racial Imbalance promised to do just that, throughout the city.[44] White opposition was immediate and fierce; a large percentage of families left the city for suburban districts or placed their children in private schools.[45] An antibusing initiative was placed on the ballot.[46]

By the mid-1980s, white rejection of school desegregation was joined by growing black disillusionment, as a number of black leaders, educators, and activists concluded that the district's plan placed a disproportionate burden on children of color, without a marked improvement in academic outcomes.[47] More, culturally ill-equipped teachers and administrators in predominantly white schools seemed unable to create welcoming learning environments for the children being bused in from the Central District and the south end.[48] This decrease in support coincided with the development of an increasingly right-leaning Supreme Court, which had indicated its willingness to curtail the use of race in school assignment (and hiring and university admissions as well). During the 1990s, Seattle's municipal and school board leaders worked together to dismantle much of the unpopular busing program.

By the time Kathleen Brose first raised her objections to the racial tiebreaker policy in 2000, the policy was one of the last vestiges of the district's effort to diversify the city's schools. The objective of the racial tiebreaker was to give preference in high school assignment to those students whose enrollment contributed toward bringing a given school closer to the district average of 40% white students and 60% students of color.[49] The tiebreaker was only necessary for schools that are oversubscribed—that is, schools where more students wished to attend than there were seats available. Not coincidentally, every one of these highly desirable schools was located in the city's predominantly white north end, except for Garfield High, the historically black school in the now quickly gentrifying Central District. As poor and working class, and even lower middle-class black families found themselves priced out of the neighborhood, and even out of the city altogether, and as Garfield perfected its magnet programs designed almost solely to attract white families, the percentage of black students at the school declined sharply from the days when it was one of the only high schools in the city to welcome black students.[50]

Defensive Discourses: Reproducing White Innocence and Advantage

Material race effects of social and educational policy belie the racial innocence asserted by Kathleen Brose and her organization in Seattle, and by Supreme Court Chief Justice John Roberts and Justice Clarence Thomas. For these political actors, the use of race comes as an assault on white families and on the nation's values, even as both PICS and the high court fail to account for the viciousness of the historical structuration of state-sponsored white supremacy. I turn now to a critical analysis of four of these defensive discourses, so powerfully employed in creating a benign "common sense" narrative about white resource accumulation.

THE MYTH OF DE FACTO SEGREGATION

Shortly after the 2007 Supreme Court ruling, Kathleen Brose returned to complete her bachelor's degree in history at the University of Washington. One of the courses she took was Professor Quintard Taylor's "Blacks in the West."[51] She notes, "This class enhanced my knowledge of the struggles of black people in the West as well as the Civil Rights movement in Seattle. I now have a much greater appreciation of their trials and tribulations."[52] Even so, she emphasizes, her view of the case has not changed: she still believes that the school district "implemented forced integration to combat the de-facto [sic] segregation of Seattle's neighborhoods that developed during the use of housing covenants."[53] Of course, housing covenants were first enforced *by law*, and then, even after declared unenforceable, were permitted *by law* until the late 1960s. Even in the decades that followed, weak enforcement of existing housing discrimination law meant that homeowners and real estate agents continued to discourage people of color from purchasing homes in predominantly white neighborhoods.[54] As such, residential segregation in Seattle was not, in fact, de facto; rather, it was cruelly and decidedly de jure. The "trials and tribulations" of black people in the West included a long history of legal exclusion from purchasing or renting property in certain neighborhoods and, as a result, limited access to schools in these neighborhoods. Yet, Brose's new "appreciation" of this history does not lead to a reevaluation of her position.

Chief Justice Roberts goes so far as to suggest that there is no evidence of white racism in Seattle schools. "Seattle has never operated segregated schools," Roberts notes, ". . . nor has it ever been subject to court-ordered desegregation."[55] Thus, Roberts is able to dismiss claims of historical racial bias in school assignment because civil rights activists in Seattle conceded to the desegregation plan developed by the school board, rather than subject the district to a long court case in which a judge would have likely imposed a desegregation plan, in recognition of the clear racial segregation in Seattle schools.

THE DENIAL OF WHITE PRIVILEGE

In Quintard Taylor's book on Seattle's Central District, the historian writes:

> As a self-proclaimed politically progressive city, Seattle celebrated its image as a multicultural, multiracial democracy where opportunity was open to all. The reality for the entire century between 1870 and 1970 was vastly different for most of black Seattle . . . the forces arrayed against black aspirations were supported sometimes consciously, and often unwittingly, by the vast majority of Seattleites who chose to ignore the plight of the impoverished, the uneducated, the economically disadvantaged—particularly if they were of a different color.[56]

To the extent that white Seattle residents acknowledge these historical "forces arrayed against Black aspirations," they are able to position themselves as progressive and multicultural. Yet, this is a kind of (neoliberal) multiculturalism that fails to make any connection between the past and racial effects in the present. It flattens the difference between unequally advantaged racial groups, such that it then becomes possible to speak with fervor about the need to protect *all* citizens' rights, and take into account *all* families' desires in school assignment, as if all residents are situated similarly in relation to race and racism. In a city whose spatial imagination and access to privileged properties has been and continues to be determined so heavily by race, the primary effect of this colorblind discourse is a shift of attention and concern away from black residents and toward protecting and advancing whites.

Justice Thomas also warns of what he regards as a maligning of whites, by suggesting that they enjoy white privilege. As part of his argument that Seattle educators cannot be trusted to administrate or educate around race, Thomas recounts an incident in which the district's diversity chief found herself on the receiving end of national right-wing criticism after posting a definition of cultural racism on the district's website. Her explanation cautioned educators to be wary about attributing value and normality to whiteness, while regarding people of color as different and less than.[57] Thomas dismisses this concept altogether, along with the district's clarification, which offered a critique of the "melting pot" as still insisting that the cultural practices of people of color must be melted down, in a process of assimilation.[58] For Thomas, this is proof that the Seattle schools have no credibility in thinking about race.

Thomas then goes on to more directly deride the existence of white privilege or advantage: "The school district sent a delegation of high school students to a 'White Privilege Conference.' One conference participant described 'white privilege' as 'an invisible package of unearned assets which I can count on cashing in each day, but about which I was meant to remain oblivious.'"[59] Thomas was so certain that the public would share his distaste of the idea of white privilege—and the idea that a school district might take it seriously—that he simply cited this one example without further comment, as if the very incident were damning enough.

ROMANTICIZING THE (SEGREGATED) NEIGHBORHOOD

For Brose, neighborhood schools are preferable because they allow parents to be more involved in their children's educations, and prevent children from having to spend so much time commuting across the city to distant schools. More, she asserts, "the high schools have different curricula and certain schools are not a good academic fit for a particular learning style."[60] For example, Brose's daughter wished to participate in orchestra; Ballard High School offered this program, while Franklin did not. However, differences in curricular and extracurricular program offerings are also a reflection of disparities in resources available to schools. While schools in the north end are more likely to have more honors and AP courses, for example, these have often been limited in south end schools.[61] Also, in Seattle, as schools have resegregated by class and race, schools in more affluent areas have amassed large endowments that allow them to pay for more teachers, counselors, and arts and science programs, and to make improvements to their physical infrastructure beyond that which is covered in the general allocation to each school.[62] Thus, what Brose refers to as "academic fit" belies a desire to secure a spot at the schools with the most resources; rather than a certain learning style, what is usually offered at the more privileged schools are more rigorous courses, the kind necessary for students to gain admission to selective universities. In other words, these are not simply schools that are different in kind; more importantly, they are different in capital. Although Brose maintains that the priority now, after the *Parents Involved* ruling, should be to ensure that all schools in Seattle are able to provide a high-quality education, there is little guidance on how to do this beyond advocating for strong leadership and parent involvement. And notably, Brose never allows that white families may have secured access to more material educational resources through exercising racial advantage and dominance.

"The Seattle schools had never been segregated," Brose insists.[63] What she means here is that there were never any explicit racially discriminatory district attendance policies. And indeed, she is right. Seattle does not have a history of vitriolic resistance to school desegregation. However, it is disingenuous to suggest that the schools were never racially segregated, given that most black students were historically concentrated in schools in the Central District and south end prior to implementation of the city-wide desegregation plan, and more recently, as the city retreated from this plan, many schools in the south end became majority students of color, in a city that is nearly 80% white.[64] Unfortunately, as I will discuss in the next section, since civil rights activists never followed through on their threat to sue the city over school segregation, and instead pressured the district to adopt a city-wide plan "without a court order," it is possible for Brose (and Supreme Court Justices) to assert that Seattle schools were never *illegally* segregated.[65] It is only in this context, and by bracketing off the discussion of school desegregation from the reality of de jure housing segregation, that neighborhood schools can be romanticized, and their history of racial exclusion made invisible.

Chief Justice Roberts, in his opinion, also rejects the idea that racism had anything to do with racial patterns, either in schools or neighborhoods. He acknowledges that the district pursued the racial tiebreaker "to address the effects of racially identifiable housing patterns on school assignments," and even goes so far as to note that "most white students live in the northern part of Seattle, most students of other racial backgrounds in the southern part."[66] Yet, Roberts is seemingly disinterested in how these patterns emerge, or is perhaps unconvinced that these patterns signify anything about racial intent.

Justice Thomas is more transparent in defending segregated neighborhoods and the segregated schools that result from them:

> Racial imbalance is not segregation. Although presently observed racial imbalance might result from past de jure segregation, racial imbalance can also result from any number of innocent private decisions, including voluntary housing choices. Because racial imbalance is not inevitably linked to unconstitutional segregation, it is not unconstitutional in and of itself.[67]

Again, I am not contesting Thomas's point about the constitutionality of racial imbalance. However, there is ample evidence that housing segregation in Seattle and across the nation is deeply impacted by a history of racial animus and bias, enshrined in law. Thomas's rush to proclaim such racial patterns as "innocent" in effect constructs whiteness as innocent, and thus white people can be seen as not only the innocent victims of race-conscious policies, but arguably, the *first* victims. The history of racist housing policy effectively erased—and in the case of Seattle, no specific court desegregation order—it is as if the harm to whites is the original sin in school assignment.

THE "ANTIRACIST" MIDDLE GROUND

Although joining with the majority, Justice Anthony Kennedy offered his own opinion, almost entirely because Roberts and Thomas denied the existence of racism. As he notes, "The enduring hope is that race should not matter; the reality is that too often it does."[68] Kennedy describes Roberts's opinion as "imply[ing] an all-too-unyielding insistence that race cannot be a factor in instances when, in my view, it may be taken into account. The plurality opinion is too dismissive of the legitimate interest government has in ensuring all people have equal opportunity regardless of their race."[69] Here, as in the rest of his opinion, Kennedy is concerned about access to material educational resources, and, unlike Roberts and Thomas, suggests that racial patterns in access to resources are indeed troubling. He proposes that, even as the use of race in assigning specific students is illegal, school boards may pursue racial diversity through other means, by taking race and other demographics into account when constructing new schools and allocating resources. Thus, Kennedy allows for strategic initiatives that correct material inequities that are a result of racist policies and practices. Even here, however, there is no mandate that government remedy racial inequality—just a concession that it may, if the people so wish. But how likely is it that local or state governments will muster the political will to address the maldistribution of educational resources along racial lines? And can this be done simply by allocating more money to racially segregated or resegregating schools serving people of color, without addressing the concentration of white students and wealth in public schools across town (and in some cities, even down the street)? To answer these questions, I consider what it would mean to operationalize a material antiracist school desegregation politics.

De/re-centering Whiteness: Toward a Material Analysis of Race in School Desegregation Policy and Politics

Materialist antiracisms, almost by definition, require projects that call constant attention to and seek to eradicate the economic foundation of racial inequality. Colorblindness cannot accomplish this, and neither can neoliberal state antiracism, as advanced here in Justice Kennedy's "middle-ground" concurrence, with its focus on opening up markets without addressing generations of maldistribution. As David Theo Goldberg cautions, "Equal access to unequal resources and possibilities from positions of unequal preparation and power ultimately entails a third-class ticket to nowhere."[70] In Seattle, black leaders, educators and advocates in Seattle pursued school desegregation as a way to correct inequities in access to educational resources.[71] This alone proved insufficient to overcome the race effects of housing discrimination.

We also have evidence that, given the choice, whites will choose not to live in racially diverse neighborhoods that might then be more likely to produce racially diverse schools. In a recent article, researchers asked whether the end of a federally mandated school desegregation plan in Charlotte-Mecklenburg, North Carolina—that is, the end of court-ordered busing—would lead families to make different choices related to housing.[72] While homeowners' current neighborhood schools might be more diverse, reflecting the demographics of the local area, would a return to "community schools" cause them to look for more racially homogenous communities to live in? And indeed, researchers found that, for those who moved after the policy ended, white families were more likely to move to neighborhoods with a higher concentration of white people.[73] Although they concede that they have no evidence to prove that race was the primary motivating factor, their data does indicate that whites moved in segregative ways.[74] They conclude that, to the extent desegregation policy shifts precipitate increased housing segregation (and thus, exacerbate school segregation) we may open up new opportunities to insist on the constitutionality of using race in school assignment.[75] As they note, a causal relationship between government policy decisions and racialized housing choice patterns may mean "the line is not clear between formalized de jure segregation and informal de facto segregation resulting from residential choices."[76]

Other school desegregation researchers have also pointed out the link between housing and school segregation. Erica Frankenburg, for example, noting the increase in black-white residential segregation in the previous decade, and the judicial retreat from school desegregation, argues, "Despite the policy focus of the last 50 years on designing school desegregation plans, residential segregation today reflects vestiges of government action and should be the focus of more concerted policy efforts to both eliminate racial discrimination and affirmatively further residential integration."[77]

Proclaiming that "education policy is housing policy," Richard Rothstein contends that "residential segregation's causes are both knowable and known—twentieth century federal, state and local policies explicitly designed to separate the races and whose effects endure today."[78] He advocates such corrective measures as changing exclusionary zoning codes, locating housing for low and moderate income residents in predominantly white areas, and prohibiting landlord discrimination against poor people with housing vouchers.

All of these proposals acknowledge that what counts as school desegregation policy will need to include some attention to correcting material inequities, and specifically, pushing back against the accumulation and hoarding of economic and educational resources by white homeowners. However, the question is how to actually make this happen. A materialist antiracist analysis of the *Parents Involved* case suggests several hurdles. First, as Jodi Melamed explains, we are living in a moment in which a firmly neoliberal multicultural ideology has taken hold.[79] In this context, white activists like Kathleen Brose can present racial patterns in school assignment as mere reflections of individual parents' choices. Thus, because some black parents would prefer their children to attend Franklin High School because it is closer to their homes in the south end, Brose can shift attention away from material differences between Franklin and Ballard, and instead herald herself as the protector of all parents' ability to exercise their freedom in the marketplace. The conservative justices similarly advance the neoliberal-multicultural fantasy that racial patterns are not really about racism, but simply the result of where different racial and ethnic groups choose to live and send their children to school. And to the extent that racism might be acknowledged, the market is put forth as the corrective.

Second, a materialist antiracism calls attention to the sense of white entitlement over certain spaces in the city. This racial imagination leads some residents of north end Seattle neighborhoods to imagine their neighborhoods, and the public schools in their neighborhoods, as their own. Brose argued that her daughter should have priority in enrolling at Ballard High School, largely because of the proximity of the school to their home in the nearby predominantly white Magnolia neighborhood. Families in the south end should, in this imagination, send their children to Franklin and the other high schools on that end of town. North end residents, whose wealth and race already secure for them political advantage, are more effectively able to advocate for and secure monies for improvements to their neighborhoods and also for their schools. This, in turn, increases their property values, and their ability to attract the most experienced teachers. Since teacher salaries are paid by the central district office, more money goes to the north end schools as senior teachers move to these more heavily resourced schools.[80] None of these practices are overtly racial; however, the history of white claims to certain spaces of the city sets all of this into motion, and thus culturally reproduces the racialization and racial imagination of urban spaces long after the laws have been changed.

Third, and following from this, the *Parents Involved* decision reveals how white racial advantage becomes "locked in," to use Roithmayr's term. Because Seattle had never been found legally culpable for operating segregated schools, the Supreme Court and Kathleen Brose could repeatedly insist that Seattle never segregated students by race, despite ample evidence to the contrary. Brose complains that some of her critics accused her and her organization of racism, but insists that she holds no racial animus. And to be sure, I do not mean to suggest that here. However, the locked-in advantages of whiteness do not require animus. Even so, there is a sense of entitlement to advantage that takes the place of animus. This entitlement is never articulated as, or even imagined as, a *racial* entitlement; it is simply a set of economic advantages that continue to accrue as a result of historical racial advantages. As noted above, white people are not the only ones to benefit from the economic advantages of living in north end neighborhoods; however, these neighborhoods were created and their boundaries determined with the accumulation of white wealth in mind.

Conclusion

In this chapter, I have emphasized the link between generations of legal housing discrimination and the inevitability of school segregation following from residential segregation policies and practices intended to benefit and placate white Seattle residents. Segregated schools are not inherently unequal, but they almost always are, because whites enjoy greater economic wealth and political power, which, in Seattle, contributes to sharp differences in the resources and social capital available in north and south end schools. Thus, a return to what advocates call "community" or "neighborhood" schools is quite likely to contribute to greater racial and economic inequality.[81]

However, in the current neoliberal multicultural context, the inevitability of inequality is seen as the result of wise (or poor) choices made by individual consumers to live in this neighborhood or that one, or different levels of abilities leading to different levels of income, which then facilitates the ability of more skilled (and therefore better compensated) citizens to purchase properties in more exclusive areas. If, then, they are able to provide better schools for their children, this is simply the reward for their ability to compete in the marketplace.

Under this logic, there is a certain innocence to neighborhood schools, regardless of how segregated they may be, or how unequal their resources. In fact, as evident in the defense offered by Brose, Roberts, and Thomas, this innocence is apparently under attack by those who would inject consideration of the history of (structural) racial advantage into policy discourse on racial advantage.

From a materialist antiracist perspective, school desegregation is a worthy, yet altogether inadequate project. If our aim is to address the racial maldistribution of educational resources, rather than simply bring people together to create racially diverse schools, then our politics must attend to the root causes of material social and educational inequities.[82] With regard to school desegregation, specifically, a materialist antiracism demands that we attend to the relationship between housing policy and the concentration of white wealth and educational resources. Given entrenched interests in maintaining economic advantage, and a nearly hegemonic commitment to a colorblind neoliberal multiculturalism, it will likely prove difficult to convince those with advantage that they came by that advantage through a system of white supremacy and laws which were put in place to secure it.

What we need is a school desegregation politics that both recenters and decenters whiteness. We need to recenter whiteness in the sense that we shift our political gaze from concern about students of color or achieving student diversity toward a concern about how white families and communities hoard educational resources for themselves, and create exclusive educational spaces that limit access to others. This attention to what Roithmayr calls racial cartels promises to keep our school desegregation discourse focused on remedying a long history of greed and presumed entitlement. In this way, whiteness is necessarily decentered. That is, we recommit to an understanding of public education in which we are no longer obligated to defend and protect white advantage simply because it has always been so, and in which educational resources are no longer commodities available to those with the most purchasing power.

Michael J. Dumas is an Assistant Professor in the Graduate School of Education and Department of African American Studies at University of California, Berkeley.

NOTES

This research was supported by dissertation fellowships from the Spencer Foundation and from The Graduate School and University Center of The City University of New York.

1. Lee Hochberg, *Supreme Court Revisits Race in Public Schools*, PBS NEWSHOUR (December 4, 2006).

2. DARIA ROITHMAYR, REPRODUCING RACISM: HOW EVERYDAY CHOICES LOCK IN WHITE ADVANTAGE (New York University Press 2014).

3. Thomas Shapiro, Tatjana Meschede, & Sam Osoro, Institute on Assets and Social Policy, *The Roots of the Widening Racial Wealth Gap: Explaining the Black-White Economic Divide* (2013); THOMAS SHAPIRO & MELVIN L. OLIVER, BLACK WEALTH/ WHITE WEALTH: A NEW PERSPECTIVE ON RACIAL INEQUALITY (Routledge 1997); DOUGLAS S. MASSEY, AMERICAN APARTHEID: SEGREGATION AND THE MAKING OF THE UNDERCLASS (Harvard University Press 1998).

4. 551 U.S. 701 (2007).

5. Robert Young, *Putting Materialism Back into Race Theory: Toward a Transformative Theory of Race*, http://www.redcritique.org/WinterSpring2006/ puttingmaterialismbackintoracetheory.htm (2006).

6. JODI MELAMED, REPRESENT AND DESTROY: RATIONALIZING VIOLENCE IN THE NEW RACIAL CAPITALISM (University of Minnesota Press 2009).

7. Ibid., x.

8. Ibid., 42.

9. Ibid., 44.

10. GEORGE LIPSITZ, HOW RACISM TAKES PLACE 28 (Temple University Press 2011).

11. KALERVO GULSON, EDUCATION POLICY, SPACE AND THE CITY: MARKETS AND THE (IN)VISIBILITY OF RACE (Routledge 2011).

12. LIPSITZ, HOW RACISM TAKES PLACE.

13. Zeus Leonardo & Margaret Hunter, *Imagining the Urban: The Politics of Race, Class, and Schooling*, in WILLIAM PINK & GEORGE NOBLIT, INTERNATIONAL HANDBOOK OF URBAN EDUCATION, 779, 783 (Springer 2007).

14. Ibid.

15. STEPHEN N. HAYMES, RACE, CULTURE AND THE CITY: A PEDAGOGY FOR BLACK URBAN STRUGGLE (State University of New York Press 1995); MINDY FULLILOVE, ROOT SHOCK: HOW TEARING UP CITY NEIGHBORHOODS HURTS AMERICA, AND WHAT WE CAN DO ABOUT IT (One World/Ballantine Publishing 2005).

16. LIPSITZ, HOW RACISM TAKES PLACE, 28.

17. Ibid., 35.

18. EDUARDO BONILLA-SILVA, RACISM WITHOUT RACISTS: COLOR-BLIND RACISM AND THE PERSISTENCE OF RACIAL INEQUALITY IN AMERICA (Rowman & Littlefield 2014).

19. Ibid.

20. Ibid., 2.

21. ROITHMAYR, REPRODUCING RACISM; Daria Roithmayr, *Racial Cartels*, 16 MICHIGAN JOURNAL OF RACE & LAW 45 (2010).

22. Roithmayr, *Racial Cartels*, 51.

23. Ibid., 48.

24. Ibid.

25. Ibid., 52.

26. BONILLA-SILVA, RACISM WITHOUT RACISTS.

27. Ibid., 171.

28. Ibid.

29. ANN LAGRELIUS SIQUELAND, WITHOUT A COURT ORDER: THE DESEGREGATION OF SEATLLE'S SCHOOLS (Madrona 1981).

30. Seattle School Board Meeting (December 14, 1977), Seattle Public Schools Archives, Seattle, Washington.

31. Corrigan v. Buckley, 271 U.S. 323 (1926); Shelley v. Kraemer, 334 U.S. 1 (1948).

32. Kate Davis, *Housing Segregation in Seattle* (Master's thesis, University of Washington (2005)).

33. James Gregory, Seattle Civil Rights and Labor History Project, *Racial Restrictive Covenants* http://depts.washington.edu/civilr/covenants.htm (2007).

34. Ibid.

35. QUINTARD TAYLOR, THE FORGING OF A BLACK COMMUNITY: SEATTLE'S CENTRAL DISTRICT FROM 1870 THROUGH THE CIVIL RIGHTS ERA, 159–84 (University of Washington Press 1994).

36. Ibid.

37. Anne Frantilla, *The Seattle Open Housing Campaign, 1959-1968: Housing Segregation and Open Housing Legislation*, http://www.blackpast.org/history-seattle-open-housing-campaign.

38. Ibid.

39. Ibid.

40. TAYLOR, THE FORGING OF A BLACK COMMUNITY, 203–209.

41. Doris H. Pieroth, *Desegregating the Public Schools: Seattle, Washington, 1954–1968*, 12, 15–16 (Doctoral dissertation, University of Washington (1979)).

42. Michael J. Dumas, *Theorizing Redistribution and Recognition in Educational Research: "How do we get dictionaries at Cleveland?,"* in JEAN ANYON, THEORY AND EDUCATIONAL RESEARCH: TOWARD CRITICAL SOCIAL EXPLANATION, 81, 84 (Routledge 2009); Michael J. Dumas, *What Is this 'Black' in Black Education? Imagining a Cultural Politics without Guarantees*, in ZEUS LEONARDO, HANDBOOK OF CULTURAL POLITICS AND EDUCATION, 403 (Sense Publishers 2010); Michael J. Dumas, *A Cultural Political Economy of School Desegregation in Seattle*, 113 TEACHERS COLLEGE RECORD 703, 720 (2011).

43. Dumas, *A Cultural Political Economy*, 711; Dumas, *Theorizing Redistribution*, 84.

44. Dumas, *A Cultural Political* Economy, 709–11.

45. Ibid., 712; Dumas, *Theorizing Redistribution*, 84.

46. Dumas, *A Cultural Political Economy*, 720–21; Dumas, *Theorizing Redistribution*, 84.

47. Terry Tang, *Busing runs into a black backlash*, THE WEEKLY [Seattle] 21-22 (December 4, 1985).

48. Michael J. Dumas, *"Losing an Arm": Schooling as a Site of Black Suffering*, 17 RACE, ETHNICITY AND EDUCATION 1 (2014).

49. *How the Racial-Tiebreaker Began*, THE SEATTLE TIMES (June 29, 2007).

50. Dumas, *A Cultural Political Economy*, 714–16.

51 Kathleen Brose, *The Tie Breaker Ruling in Perspective: A Plaintiff Looks Back on the Historic U.S. Supreme Court Decision of 2007*, (2011), http://www.blackpast.org/perspectives/09-30-2009-tie-breaker-ruling-perspective-plaintiff-looks-back-historic-u-s-supreme-cou

52 Ibid.

53. Ibid.

54. JEAN ANYON, GHETTO SCHOOLING: A POLITICAL ECONOMY OF URBAN EDUCATIONAL REFORM, 105 (Teachers College 1997); JEAN ANYON, RADICAL POSSIBILITIES: PUBLIC POLICY, URBAN EDUCATION, AND A NEW SOCIAL MOVEMENT, 2nd ed. (Routledge 2014); Janet L. Smith & David Stovall, *"Coming Home" to New Homes and New Schools: Critical Race Theory and the New Politics of Containment*, 23 JOURNAL OF EDUCATION POLICY 135, 148–49 (2008).

55. Ibid., 712.

56. TAYLOR, THE FORGING OF A BLACK COMMUNITY, 239.

57. Parents Involved, 551 U.S. 781 n.30 (Justice Thomas, concurring).

58. Ibid.

59. Ibid.

60. Allie Holly-Gottlieb, *A Tale of Two Schools*, http://www.thestranger.com/seattle/a-tale-of-two-schools/Content?oid=3774&ref=twitter (2000).

61. Ibid.

62. Brian M. Rosenthal, *As Parents Raise Cash, Schools Confront Big Gap*, THE SEATTLE TIMES (January 28, 2012); Tan Vinh, *Schools Go beyond the Bake Sale as Tax Support Wanes*, THE SEATTLE TIMES (January 11, 2004).

63. Brose, *The Tie Breaker Ruling in Perspective.*

64. Dumas, *A Cultural Political Economy*, 711–20.

65. SIQUELAND, WITHOUT A COURT ORDER, 86–93.

66. Parents Involved, 551 U.S. at 712.

67. Ibid., 749-50 (Justice Thomas, concurring).

68. Ibid., 787 (Justice Kennedy, concurring in part and concurring in judgment).

69. Ibid., 788.

70. DAVID THEO GOLDBERG, THE THREAT OF RACE: REFLECTIONS ON RACIAL NEOLIBERALISM 19 (Blackwell Publishing 2009).

71. Dumas, *Theorizing Redistribution and Recognition*, 84; Dumas, *A Cultural Political Economy*, 705.

72. David D. Liebowitz, & Lindsay C. Page, *Does School Policy Affect Housing Choices? Evidence From the End of Desegregation in Charlotte-Mecklenburg*, 51 AMERICAN EDUCATIONAL RESEARCH JOURNAL 671 (2014).

73. Ibid., 696.

74. Ibid., 696–98.

75. Ibid., 697–99.

76. Ibid., 699.

77. Frankenberg, *The Role of Residential Segregation*, 561.

78. Rothstein, *Modern Segregation*, 5.

79. MELAMED, REPRESENT AND DESTROY, 137–40.

80. Marguerite Roza & Paul Hill, *Equalizing Education Dollars.* THE WASHINGTON POST (August 21, 2005).

81. GARY ORFIELD & SUSAN E. EATON, DISMANTLING DESEGREGATION: THE QUIET REVERSAL OF *BROWN V. BOARD OF EDUCATION* (The New Press 1996); Gary Orfield & Chungmei Lee, The Civil Rights Project, Brown *at 50: King's Dream or Plessy's Nightmare?* (2004).

82. ANYON, GHETTO SCHOOLING 151–86; ANYON, RADICAL POSSIBILITIES, 113–14, 148–69, 170–87.

PART III

Looking to the Future

DANIELLE R. HOLLEY-WALKER

After Unitary Status
Examining Voluntary Integration Strategies for Southern School Districts

IN THE YEARS SINCE THE SUPREME COURT'S 2007 DECISION IN *PARENTS INVOLVED in Community Schools v. Seattle School District No. 1*,[1] scholars have speculated on the long-term impact of the case.[2] The argument has been made that *Parents Involved* will have little practical effect on school districts because racial integration is off the agenda of most school districts.[3] Others have predicted that the case will lead to fewer school districts utilizing race-conscious student assignment plans.[4]

This chapter enters this debate and the larger conversation about the future of racially integrated public schools by providing empirical data on student assignment plans that were used by Southern school districts prior to 2010, after they attained unitary status.[5] As the facts of *Parents Involved in Community Schools* demonstrate, Southern school districts will likely continue to be at the forefront of the struggle over voluntary integration efforts. Many such districts are being released from desegregation orders that allowed them to use race-conscious remedies to address previous de jure racial segregation. Without those court orders, school districts are faced with a choice about whether to continue to make racial integration a priority and what legally permissible strategies they may employ. The main goal of this chapter is to provide a snapshot of how many Southern school districts are facing this dilemma and what choices they are making. This chapter also presents an overview of strategies to encourage voluntary racial integration in Southern school districts.

Post-Unitary Status in Southern School Districts

BACKGROUND AND METHODOLOGY

In a series of cases in the 1990s, the Supreme Court explained that in order for a school district to demonstrate that it is entitled to have its desegregation decree lifted, the district court should examine (1) whether the school board "complied in good faith with the desegregation decree since it was entered"; and (2) "whether the vestiges of past discrimination had been eliminated to the extent practicable."[6] In determining the latter, the district court "should look not only at student assignments, but 'to every facet of school operations—faculty, staff, transportation, extra-curricular activities and facilities.'"[7] The Supreme Court's decisions in the early 1990s cases *Board of Education of Oklahoma City Public Schools v. Dowell*,[8] *Freeman v. Pitts*,[9] and *Missouri v. Jenkins*[10] made it easier for school districts to achieve unitary status and resulted in more school districts across the country having their desegregation decrees lifted.[11]

The Appendix to this chapter identifies school districts in Southern states that achieved unitary status between 2004 and 2009. The year 2004 was chosen as the starting date for this study for a couple of reasons. First, it provided a five-year period to study to be able to identify a significant sample of cases. Second, the litigation in *Parents Involved* took place during this period, so in order to be able to identify school districts that might be making decisions based on that case, it was important to choose a time period that encompassed when the case was pending and after the Supreme Court rendered its decision.

The list of school districts displayed in the Appendix was compiled using two methods, first, by referencing *Becoming Less Separate? School Desegregation, Justice Department Enforcement, and the Pursuit of Unitary Status*, a study completed by the United States Commission on Civil Rights in September 2007.[12] *Becoming Less Separate* included in its data Southern school districts that were granted unitary status from 2004 to 2007 and also identified school districts that planned to seek unitary status. A Westlaw search was then conducted for any school districts on the "plan to seek unitary status" list in order to determine whether unitary status had been reached prior to 2010. Once the unitary school districts were identified, searches were conducted in the Public Access to Court Records ("PACER") database for federal courts in order to gather the court filings (e.g., motions for unitary status, opposition motions, court orders) related to the unitary status proceedings.[13]

TRENDS IN THE DISSOLUTION OF DESEGREGATION ORDERS

There are 89 school districts in Alabama, Florida, Georgia, Louisiana, Mississippi, North Carolina, and South Carolina that had their desegregation decrees lifted between 2004 and 2009. There are two important trends that are evident from these unitary status cases: the integral role of the U.S. Department of Justice (DOJ) in the cases and the racially homogenous demographics of many of these districts.

First, in many of the cases where the school district achieved unitary status after 2004, the DOJ played an integral role in having the desegregation order dissolved. Often the unitary status proceedings commenced only after a review conducted by the DOJ.[14] After these status reviews were completed, often the DOJ and the school district made a joint motion to the district court for unitary status.[15] In these motions, the DOJ and school district typically argued that the school district had complied with all six of the *Green* factors (student assignment, faculty, staff, transportation, extracurricular activities, and facilities), indicating that the school district had eliminated the vestiges of the formerly de jure segregated school system.[16] The key role of the DOJ in the unitary status cases is not surprising because in many instances the United States was the original plaintiff in the desegregation case.[17] The timing, however, is noteworthy. Many of the school districts analyzed in this chapter were under desegregation orders since the late 1970s, but the DOJ under President George W. Bush undertook an affirmative review of many desegregation cases, and these reviews led to motions for unitary status.[18]

The Hampton County school district in South Carolina provides an example of the DOJ's key role in the recent unitary status cases. In Hampton County, the United States filed the desegregation action against the school district in 1970. The district court ordered a desegregation plan that focused on combining all schools in the district into one elementary school, one middle school, and one high school.[19] The school district continued this plan through the 2003–2004 school year. In 2003, the DOJ initiated a review of the desegregation order and, after review, informed the school district that it had met its obligations under the desegregation order. The DOJ and school district filed a joint motion for unitary status in February 2005, which was granted by the district court.[20]

The role of the DOJ in the school desegregation cases has a long and complex history that will not be fully explored here, but two key points are worth mentioning. For one, the sitting president strongly impacts the tone of the executive branch—and thus the DOJ—regarding desegregation cases.[21] The eight years of George W. Bush's

presidency did not mark the first time the executive branch has been hostile toward
desegregation litigation and the race-conscious remedies that are often associated
with these cases.[22] During the Nixon administration, the President spearheaded
the passage of the Equal Educational Opportunities Act of 1974,[23] "which set forth
the federal government's policy favoring neighborhood schools and rejecting racial
balance as the goal of school desegregation."[24] Under the Reagan administration,
"[p]olitical operatives from the White House formulated a civil rights policy that
consisted of a resistance to traditional school desegregation remedies in favor of
voluntary transfer programs, magnet schools, and neighborhood schools; opposition
to race-conscious remedies; [and] minimal civil rights enforcement . . . ."[25]

The integral role of the Bush DOJ in the Southern school district cases identified
in this study has important implications for the future of desegregation in Southern
schools. Although the standards for unitary status have eased under the Supreme
Court desegregation cases of the 1990s, without the assistance of the federal government many school districts will not seek unitary status.[26] This may be due to a lack
of school district or private party resources, or to a perception that the lingering
desegregation case is unimportant to the daily operations of the school district.
This suggests that the activity and philosophy of the DOJ will be a crucial aspect of
the future of desegregation cases. If the DOJ continues to take an active and hostile
approach to continuing Southern desegregation cases, it is likely that more school
districts will have their desegregation orders lifted.

Additionally, a pro-unitary status DOJ calls for a balancing arm of the executive
branch to assist in maintaining integrated schools. If the DOJ utilizes its resources to
assist school districts in achieving unitary status, then other agencies in the federal
government, particularly the Department of Education, should use their resources
to counsel and assist school districts in maintaining integrated schools.[27] In school
districts where demographics make racial integration difficult because the entire
district is single-race, the U.S. Department of Education should assist school district
officials in developing strategies for positive educational outcomes in these racially
isolated settings.[28] The Department of Education's Office of Civil Rights should
also provide support for states and school districts that want to combat racially
isolated school districts by adopting interdistrict remedies.[29] The federal government
should not view its role as solely focused on ending desegregation cases, but should
instead take a comprehensive approach to providing a vision and resources for high
quality education for students in every school district that was previously under a
desegregation order.

The second important trend, another commonality in the recent unitary
status cases in Southern states, is that many of the school districts are populated
predominately by one race.[30] In many of the small school districts in this study that

achieved unitary status since 2004, the African American student population is approximately 80% or higher. This trend comports with national research on the shifting nature of school segregation. "[R]ecent research shows that racial composition differences across district boundary lines contribute more to segregation today than do differences within them. Charles Clotfelter, for example, estimated that 69% of segregation in metropolitan areas was due to segregation between districts."[31]

These findings validate the suggestion of some scholars that the Supreme Court's decision in *Parents Involved* may not significantly impact racial desegregation because integration is "not on the radar" of many school districts.[32] Integration may be off the radar in these school districts because the racial demographics of the school districts do not lend themselves to an obvious integration strategy.

Student Assignment Plans in Post-Unitary Status Districts

This part focuses on the types of student assignment plans that are being adopted by Southern school districts that have recently achieved unitary status. The goals here are two-fold: to identify and examine the most frequently used types of student assignment plans, and to identify trends in the type of student assignment plans adopted and isolate some of the key reasons why certain assignment plans are becoming most prevalent.

STUDENT ASSIGNMENT PLANS: FOUR MAJOR METHODS

Post-unitary status school districts use four major methods of student assignment plans: attendance zones, racial diversity transfers, socioeconomic status (SES) transfers, and magnet schools. Student assignment plans that rely on attendance zones are plans that divide the school district along residential lines and then assign students to a school that is close to their home.[33] Most of the "racial diversity transfer" plans identified below (meaning all race-conscious student assignment plans) use attendance zones as the first method for assigning students to schools, and then allow students to transfer on a voluntary basis to a school in which they are not of the majority race in that school. The "SES diversity transfer" plans include student assignment plans where the school district allows students to transfer based on their socioeconomic status.[34] Some school districts that no longer use race as a factor in student assignment have begun to examine SES as a factor in student assignment to produce a more diverse learning environment.[35] Nationally, in 2010, about forty school districts serving 2.5 million students pursued some form of socioeconomic integration.[36]

One of the leading districts to pursue socioeconomic school integration has been Wake County, North Carolina, a dynamic and growing jurisdiction of more than 120,000 students, which includes the city of Raleigh and its surrounding suburbs. In 2000, the Wake County School Board voted to replace a longstanding racial integration plan with a goal that no school in the district should have more than 40 of students eligible for free and reduced-price lunch, and no school should have more than 25 of students performing below grade level. Wake County's plan has received considerable national attention because the initial results suggested it was working to raise achievement of all students and narrow the gap between socioeconomic groups.[37]

Another method used in student assignment plans is a magnet school structure. "Magnet schools are those that offer a specialized school curriculum organized around a particular subject matter . . . or theme, or that use a distinctive teaching methodology, and seek to attract both white and minority students from all parts of the city, and away from their neighborhood schools or private schools."[38] Magnet schools are also being used in settings that employ socioeconomic status diversity initiatives. For example, in Cambridge, Massachusetts, each school is a magnet school, and all schools must have "comparable percentages of students who are eligible for free or reduced-price lunch."[39]

The Appendix indicates what type of student assignment plan a school district currently had in place in 2010 and when that plan was adopted. If a school district used a combination of the methods listed above, the chart indicates each method used by the district.

METHODOLOGY AND FINDINGS

There were several methods used for compiling the information on student assignment plans displayed in the Appendix. Internet searches were performed to identify the student assignment plan used by the school district. When an Internet search did not reveal the student assignment plan, the school district was sent a survey that asked the school district official to submit a copy of a student assignment plan and to answer questions about the motivations. In circumstances where it was difficult to obtain an e-mail address for school district officials, phone interviews were conducted with an appropriate school district official to answer the survey questions. In a few instances, the student assignment plan was not available through public searches and school district officials did not answer the research survey. In those cases, the Appendix indicates that the plan is not available.

THE TRENDS IN POST-UNITARY STATUS STUDENT ASSIGNMENT PLANS

1. SMALL DISTRICTS. A key commonality that is clear from the study is the large number of post-unitary status school districts that are "small districts," which are defined as districts that have a single school for each grade level. Thirty-eight of the school districts in this study were identified as small districts. That means that the racial integration of individual schools in the district will not be impacted by shifting students from one school to another school because there is only one school for each grade level. Also, the level of integration in the individual schools depends solely on the racial makeup of the school district as a whole.

For a second significant group of the post-unitary status school districts, the district may have more than one school for each grade level, but is still too small for student assignment plans to have a significant impact on the integration of individual schools.[40] Many of these districts have fewer than five elementary schools, one middle school, and one high school. In Alabama, three school districts (Alexander City, Bessemer City, and Bibb County) are in this category. In Georgia, three school districts fall into this category (Brooks County, Butts County, and Lowndes County).

The school district in Wakulla County, Florida, is an example of a smaller district that utilized an attendance zone student assignment plan.[41] In the 2007–2008 school year, the district had a student population of 84.7% white, 10.5% black, 1.5% Latino, and 0.6% Asian.[42] The district had four elementary schools, two middle schools, and one high school. The school district had residential attendance zones, and students were required to attend the school in the attendance zone of their residence.[43] The only reasons for student transfer under the policy were educational needs, physical health needs, and discipline or emotional problems.[44] The Wakulla County School District acquired unitary status in 2008 after a review of the desegregation order initiated by the DOJ.[45] It appears that, even prior to unitary status, the Wakulla County schools used an attendance zones plan. The school district adopted a student assignment plan in 1999 and revised it in 2000, 2005, and 2007.[46] There is no indication that *Parents Involved* impacted the student assignment plan during the 2007 revision. For the small districts identified in this study, interdistrict remedies may prove to be the most effective method for increasing racial diversity.

2. SOCIOECONOMIC STATUS AS A REPLACEMENT FOR RACE. Another trend in post-unitary school district assignment plans is to replace racial criteria for student assignments with SES criteria. The Jefferson County school district—the district involved in one of the *Parents Involved* cases—is a large, metropolitan district with a multiracial population. During the 2008–2009 school year, at the elementary school

level, there were 48,404 students, 48% white and 36% African American.[47] The school district had approximately 90 elementary schools, 24 middle schools, and 21 high schools.[48] Therefore, the school district choices regarding student assignment could actually impact the integration of the public schools.

The following school districts in this study resemble Jefferson County, Kentucky, in that the school district size and demographics allow student assignment to impact the integration of the schools: Marion County, Florida; Seminole County, Florida; Bibb County, Georgia; and Lafayette Parish, Louisiana.

The Seminole County, Florida, school district provides an example of how SES can be used to achieve successfully integrated schools. The district is located in the middle portion of the state, in the I-4 corridor. The school district is large and racially diverse, in 2009–2010 enrolling 64,977 students, of whom 57.3% are white, 13.6% are African American, and 18.5% are Hispanic.[49] The district included 37 elementary schools, 13 middle schools, and nine high schools.[50]

The attendance zone and SES transfer program in Seminole County were clearly crafted with an eye toward compliance with the Supreme Court's decision in *Parents Involved*.[51] Prior to the decision, Seminole County used race as a consideration in the drawing of attendance zones and approving transfers.[52] The district stated that its post-unitary status student assignment policy "promotes and supports the Board's Excellence and Equity policy, minimizes overcrowding conditions, [and] promotes and maintains diverse student enrollment consistent with Constitutional requirements."[53] The policy also adopted a broad definition of "diversity by including socioeconomic status, gender, race/ethnicity, English Speakers of Other Languages (ESOL), and disability."[54] This broad definition of diversity is the type that the Supreme Court approved in the Michigan Law School affirmative action case, *Grutter v. Bollinger*.[55]

The Seminole County school district has operated primarily under an attendance zone student assignment plan. The school board organized the schools into "attendance zones" and "cluster zones" that "reflect the diversity of the community."[56] "If the residential areas surrounding a school site did not provide diversity, and/or if a proposed change in attendance zones created less diverse student enrollments, the Board could merge several geographic areas into a cluster zone, and/or establish a magnet program."[57] The Seminole County student assignment plan also allowed for SES diversity student transfers. The school board approved transfers that help align schools with the average percentage of free or reduced lunch students in the entire district. According to the Seminole County school student attendance zones policy, "students qualifying for free/reduced price lunch who attend a school with a high percentage of free/reduced price lunch students may transfer to any school with a low percentage of free/reduced price lunch students."[58] The policy also allowed students who do not qualify for free or reduced lunches and who are in "low percentage" schools to transfer to a "high percentage" school. The policy provided for free transportation if the transfer is within the student's attendance zone.

On the whole, the Seminole County student assignment plan could prove to be a model program for other school districts seeking integration after *Parents Involved*. The policy considered racial integration, SES, and other forms of diversity in a manner that seems likely to achieve integrated schools.

3. SOME SCHOOL DISTRICTS CONTINUE TO CONSIDER RACE AS A FACTOR. Despite the Supreme Court's ruling in *Parents Involved*,[59] a few school districts in this study continued to maintain race-conscious student assignment plans. These school districts were in a very small group regionally and nationally based on the fact that a "vast majority" of school districts across the nation do not use race as a factor in student assignment.[60] The Marion County school district—a large school district in north central Florida serving approximately 43,000 students—continued to use a race-conscious student assignment plan even after *Parents Involved*.[61] During the 2009–2010 school year, the school district was also racially diverse, with approximately 52% white students, 20% black, and 16% Latino in 2008.[62] It had 28 elementary schools, eight middle schools, two combined elementary and middle schools, and eight high schools.[63]

The Marion County schools used a neighborhood school assignment plan, with the availability of racial majority-to-minority transfers. The policy "authorizes and supports diversity transfers, which are the voluntary transfer of a student from a school in which his/her race is in the majority to a school in which his/her race is in the minority."[64] As of 2009, the current plan was virtually the same as the student assignment plan in place before the district achieved unitary status.[65] The school board was concerned that after unitary status the district would revert to predominately one-race schools, and therefore the district decided to maintain the racial diversity transfer policy.[66]

The Marion County majority-to-minority transfer provision may face a legal challenge under *Parents Involved*. The plurality opinion in the case held that the voluntary integration plans in question violated the Equal Protection Clause because they were not narrowly tailored.[67] The plurality offered a broad condemnation of the use of race in student assignment plans: "For schools that never segregated on the basis of race, such as Seattle, or that have removed the vestiges of past segregation, such as Jefferson County, the way to achieve a system of determining admission to the public schools on a nonracial basis, is to stop assigning students on a racial basis."[68] The plurality also offered a more specific critique as to why the types of racial classifications used by school districts were not narrowly tailored: they had a limited view of racial diversity by "viewing race exclusively in white/nonwhite terms in Seattle and black/other terms in Jefferson County."[69]

The Marion County plan differed, however, in some key ways from the Seattle and Jefferson County plans that were struck down by the Supreme Court in *Parents Involved*. Most important, the Marion County plan did not have racial guidelines or numeric targets.[70] A majority of the Court was highly critical of the use of specific numeric targets for racial composition of schools.[71] In Marion County, the focus of the student assignment plan was on attendance zones, with a transfer option. Also, in the Seattle and Jefferson County plans, schools became oversubscribed and some students were prevented from attending the school of their choice or the school closest to their residence.[72] The Marion County policy only guaranteed majority-to-minority transfer where there is space available at the school to which the student seeks to transfer.[73] This would likely make it more difficult for potential plaintiffs to establish that they were injured by the majority-to-minority transfer policy.

In light of *Parents Involved* a school district with a student assignment policy like that in Marion County would reduce Equal Protection Clause concerns by including in its written policy the goals and purposes of the entire policy and how the majority-to-minority transfer policy assists in achieving these goals. To achieve greater integration results, the school district should also consider race-neutral alternatives—such as socioeconomic transfers—and make formal, specific findings as to why the school district prefers to maintain a race-conscious transfer policy instead of a race-neutral policy.[74]

4. STRATEGIC ATTENDANCE ZONES. Another important trend evident from the study is the need to reimagine the traditional attendance zone student assignment plans. Justice Kennedy, in his key concurrence in *Parents Involved*, suggested that one constitutional method of considering race would be for school districts to study the racial makeup of their district as they draw the attendance zone boundaries.[75]

In 2006–2007, Lafayette Parish school district, located in southern Louisiana, included 21 elementary schools, 12 middle schools, and 11 high schools.[76] In 2008, the district served approximately 30,000 students.[77] At that time, its student assignment plan was primarily based on attendance zones.[78] Students were required to attend school in the attendance area where they resided, and the Lafayette Parish school district considered racial demographic concentrations in the drawing of attendance zone boundary lines.[79]

The school district also included a number of magnet schools (schools of choice) that favor the admission of "low income, low performing students" and are not based on attendance zones.[80] According to the district, the purpose of these schools was to "give students a more exciting and fulfilling educational experience and improve the ethnic diversity of [the] schools."[81] The student assignment policy also allowed for "student educational advantage" (SEA) transfers. This policy was essentially an SES diversity transfer program that allowed students who receive free or reduced lunch to transfer to any school in the district provided there was space available.[82] In sum, Lafayette Parish was an example of a school district that used attendance zones in combination with other student assignment strategies to allow for the possibility of racially diverse student bodies.

All of the trends identified from this study—the prevalence of small districts, the use of socioeconomic status as a factor, the continued but limited use of race as a factor, and the possibility of strategic attendance zones—suggest the types of considerations that may influence school districts in creating or maintaining racially diverse schools.

Strategies for Racial Integration after Unitary Status

This part briefly canvasses a number of possible strategies that may allow Southern schools to promote racially integrated learning environments after unitary status. It is intended to provide only a brief overview and synopsis based on the trends identified in the two-part study above.

SCHOOL DISTRICT INITIATIVE

School districts will be the primary source for the creation and adoption of student assignment plans that foster racial diversity. As noted above, many school districts have been experimenting with methods such as socioeconomic diversity to improve student achievement and create more racially diverse student bodies. Despite these experiments, if the goal of a school district is to reap the benefits of racially diverse schools, then more school districts may want to consider using race as a factor in student assignment.[83]

Race-conscious student assignment plans will have to be carefully crafted to ensure that they comply with *Parents Involved*. This will likely mean that school districts crafting such plans will need considerable assistance from academics and practicing lawyers.[84] Jefferson County, Kentucky, provides an example of the type of effort that will be necessary if school districts seek to implement race-conscious student assignment plans. After the Supreme Court struck down Jefferson County's plan, the school district received considerable assistance in crafting a new race-conscious student assignment plan.[85]

THE NEED FOR INTERDISTRICT REMEDIES

Many of the post-unitary status school districts in this study were small school districts with a student population of predominately one race. The issue for these school districts has been how to promote racially integrated schools when the demographics of the school district do not allow for effective intradistrict voluntary integration. For these school districts, interdistrict remedies have become a crucial option. Since the Supreme Court's decision in *Milliken v. Bradley*,[86] the availability of interdistrict remedies has been severely limited.[87] The Supreme Court has even limited some intradistrict remedies that the Court found were effectively interdistrict in nature. In *Missouri v. Jenkins*,[88] for instance, the Supreme Court struck down a plan to improve schools in Kansas City, Missouri, by making them more attractive to the surrounding suburbs.[89] "[T]he Court found that the purpose motivating these seemingly intra-district remedies exceeded the scope of the constitutional violation because they were effectively interdistrict in nature."[90]

Despite the obstacles presented by these Supreme Court rulings, there may still be avenues for producing racially integrated schools by using interdistrict and state-wide remedies.[91] One example of these possibilities is demonstrated in *Sheff v. O'Neill*,[92] where the Connecticut Supreme Court ruled that de facto racial segregation of the Connecticut public schools violated the state's constitution.[93] The plaintiffs in *Sheff* argued that the Hartford schools were racially and ethnically segregated and that de facto segregation violated the two equal protection provisions in the state constitution and the state's education clause.[94] The initial response by the State to the Connecticut Supreme Court ruling was to recommend voluntary integration and the increase of targeted funds to programs in the urban school districts and to carefully avoid interdistrict remedies like busing. Eventually, after significant debate, the Connecticut legislature adopted an "Open Choice" program that would "allow students in certain urban school districts to transfer to suburban schools where space was available."[95] The new legislation also established grants to fund the creation of "racially diverse interdistrict magnet schools."[96] After the passage of this legislation, the plaintiffs felt there was little actual progress being made toward desegregating the Hartford schools, so in a settlement between the parties in January 2003, the State agreed to set specific goals for reducing racial isolation and committed to building new magnet schools to reach this goal.[97]

There are important lessons to derive from *Sheff* for proponents of racial integration in the public schools. In order to secure the interdistrict remedies that provide meaningful desegregation when school districts are racially isolated, there is a need for a new round of desegregation litigation under state constitutional provisions. If plaintiffs are successful in disrupting de facto racial segregation through findings of state constitutional violations, they may gain access to interdistrict remedies like the Open Choice plan in Connecticut.

THE FEDERAL GOVERNMENT

School district initiatives and continuing desegregation litigation will play a key role in the future of racial integration in Southern schools. Beyond these two avenues, the federal government also has a key role to play in revitalizing the movement for racial diversity.

1. THE DEPARTMENT OF JUSTICE. As discussed above, the DOJ has played an active role in dismantling desegregation decrees. The Department should make a wholesale change in its approach to ongoing desegregation cases to ensure the integration goals can actually be achieved. The DOJ should not actively assist school districts in achieving unitary status, for without its assistance many school districts will remain under their desegregation orders.[98]

Why should the DOJ encourage the status quo in desegregation cases? After *Parents Involved*, it is clear that once a desegregation case has ended, the school district will have significantly less flexibility to take affirmative steps to maintain racially integrated schools.[99] Desegregation cases have also provided the impetus for school districts to invest additional resources for the education of minority students.[100] Due to the requirements of desegregation decrees, school districts have built magnet schools, increased teacher pay, and modernized facilities.[101] Thus, in order to provide resources for students and to preserve school districts' option for race-conscious student assignment plans, the DOJ should view ongoing desegregation cases as positive for students and school districts.

The desegregation case in Tangipahoa Parish, Louisiana, is an example of the opportunities that may arise from an ongoing desegregation case. Tangipahoa Parish is located in the eastern tip of Louisiana.[102] The school district has been under a desegregation order since 1965.[103] Recently, African American plaintiffs filed a motion requesting that school district officials be required to meet certain requirements under the desegregation order.[104] In response, the school district has proposed $187.4 million dollars in school construction and $12 million in operating costs to develop magnet schools with the goal of further desegregation and improving school quality.[105]

2. THE ROLE OF THE DEPARTMENT OF EDUCATION. The Department of Education (DOE) should also begin to play a more active role in this area by assisting post-unitary status school districts in developing constitutional voluntary integration

policies. First, the DOE should provide funding to study voluntary integration policies that produce educational and social benefits for students. In many areas of school policy, the DOE's Office of Innovation and Improvement funds studies to identify and gather data on effective school reforms and policies.[106] The DOE's Office of Innovation and Improvement should begin a "best practices" project to identify voluntary integration programs that meet the parameters described by the Supreme Court in *Parents Involved*.[107] This program would be important for a number of reasons. A DOE best practices study would send a clear message from the federal government to school districts that racial integration is back on the agenda and is important for student outcomes and the promotion of crucial societal and educational values. Federally funded data collection and model programs for voluntary education would provide valuable information and guidance to many school districts that may not have the resources to develop voluntary integration policies.[108] Research funded by the federal government would be able to provide a blueprint for voluntary integration, and a blueprint that the executive branch endorses as in compliance with *Parents Involved*.

Conclusion

A significant number of Southern school districts declared unitary status between 2004 and 2009. In a few of these districts, student assignment plans have played a key role in helping to maintain racial integration and to sustain the benefits that flow from racial diversity. As discussed earlier, school districts have provided socioeconomic transfer plans, magnet schools, and carefully tailored race-conscious student assignment plans to ensure continued integration. These schools—and their successful practices maintaining integration—have become important models for other school districts.

For the majority of Southern school districts, where size and demographics may prevent racial integration, additional strategies must be developed to ensure that students receive the quality education that they deserve. The post-unitary status prospects of the school district should become a more central focus of the DOE's and DOJ's efforts in desegregation cases.

Danielle Holley-Walker is Dean and Professor of Law at Howard University School of Law. This chapter is adapted from a law review article by the same title, published in 88 NORTH CAROLINA LAW REVIEW 877 (2010).

Appendix: Student Assignment Plans Adopted in Southern School Districts that Attained Unitary Status, 2004–2009

School District	Student Assignment Plan	Year Unitary Status Granted
Alabama[1]		
Alexander City	Attendance zones with out-of- district transfer option	2004
Attalla City	Attendance zones (small district)[2]	2006
Autauga County	Attendance zones, transfer option	2005
Bessemer City	N/A[3]	2006
Bibb County	N/A	2006
Blount County	Attendance zones	2005
Cherokee County	Attendance zones	2005
Coffee County	Attendance zones	2004
Coosa County	Attendance zones (small district)	2006
Covington County	Attendance zones	2006
Crenshaw County	Attendance zones	2006
Cullman City	Attendance zones, transfer option	2004
Dale County	N/A	2005
Dekalb County	Attendance zones	2006
Dothan City[4]	Attendance zones, magnet schools	2007
Elba City	Attendance zones (small district)	2004
Elmore County	Attendance zones (small district)	2004
Gadsden City	Attendance zones	2005
Henry County	Attendance zones	2006
Houston County[5]	Attendance zones	2008
Lee County	Attendance zones	2005
Macon County	Attendance zones	2006
Midfield City	Attendance zones	2006
Mountain Brook City	Attendance zones	2005
Oneonta City	Attendance zones (small district)	2005
Phoenix City	Attendance zones, magnet school	2005
Pike County	Attendance zones	2007
Roanoke City	Attendance zones (small district)	2007
Tallapoosa County	Attendance zones	2004
Troy City	Attendance zones (small district)	2005
Winston County	N/A	2004
Florida[6]		
Marion County	Attendance zones, racial diversity transfer, magnet schools	2007

Seminole County	Attendance zones, SES diversity transfer, magnet schools	2006
Wakulla County[7]	Attendance zones	2009

Georgia[8]

Baker County	Attendance zones (small district)	2007
Bibb County[9]	Attendance zones	2007
Bleckley County	Attendance zones (small district)	2006
Brooks County	Attendance zones, transfer option	2005
Butts County	Attendance zones, race, SES considered in attendance zones	2005
Chattahoochee County	Attendance zones (small district)	2006
Clay County	Attendance zones (small district)	2006
Echols County	Attendance zones (small district)	2005
Hancock County	Attendance zones (small district)	2007
Jasper County	Attendance zones (small district)	2006
Lowndes County	Attendance zones, hardship transfer option	2006
McIntosh County	Attendance zones (small district)	2006
Morgan County	Attendance zones (small district)	2006
Pelham City	Attendance zones (small district)	2006
Putnam County	Attendance zones (small district)	2007
Quitman County	Attendance zones (small district)	2006
Schley County	Attendance zones (small district)	2005
Seminole County	Attendance zones (small district)	2006
Thomas County	Attendance zones (small district)	2006
Treutlen County	Attendance zones (small district)	2007
Webster County	Attendance zones (small district)	2006
Wilkes County	Attendance zones (small district)	2005

Louisiana[10]

Ascension Parish	Attendance zones	2004
Grant Parish	Attendance zones	2007
Lafayette Parish	Attendance zones, SES transfer, magnet schools (diversity)	2006
Rapides Parish	Attendance zones	2006
Red River Parish	Attendance zones	2005
Saint Bernard Parish	Attendance zones	2006
Tensas Parish	Attendance zones (small district)	2005
West Feliciana Parish	Attendance zones	2007

Mississippi[11]

Calhoun County	Attendance zones	2007
Coffeeville	Attendance zones (small district)	2007
Hazlehurst City	Attendance zones (small district)	2005
Indianola[12]	Attendance zones (small district)	2008

Leflore County	Attendance zones	2005
Madison County	Attendance zones	2006
Marshall County	Attendance zones	2005
Noxubee County	Attendance zones	2004
South Delta	Attendance zones (small district)	2004
Tishomingo Co. Special Municipal	Attendance zones	2005
West Tallahatchie	Attendance zones (small district)	2006
Wilkinson County	N/A	2004
North Carolina[13]		
Alamance-Burlington Schools[14]	Attendance zones	2009
Bertie County[15]	N/A	2009
South Carolina[16]		
Anderson County Dist. 03	Attendance zones	2005
Bamberg County Dist. 02	Attendance zones (small district)	2004
Berkeley County	Attendance zones (small district)	2004
Clarendon County Dist. 02	Attendance zones (small district)	2004
Colleton County	Attendance zones, transfer option	2004
Fairfield County	Attendance zones	2006
Florence County Dist. 04	Attendance zones (small district)	2005
Hampton County Dist. 01	Attendance zones	2004
Hampton County Dist. 02	Attendance zones (small district)	2005
Lexington County Dist. 01	Attendance zones	2005
Orangeburg County Dist. 03	Attendance zones	2006

APPENDIX NOTES

1. U.S. Commission on Civil Rights, *Becoming Less Separate? School Desegregation, Justice Department Enforcement, and the Pursuit of Unitary Status*, 111–13 (2007).

2. The term "small district" is used to indicate that these school districts have a single elementary, middle, and high school. This is important because it means a student assignment plan would not enhance racial integration given that there is only one school for all students in the district.

3. The designation "N/A" indicates the author was unable to obtain the student assignment plan for this district.

4. Abbie Coffee & Erica Frankenberg, The Civil Rights Project, *Two Years After the* PICS *Decision: Districts' Integration Efforts in a Changing Climate*, 11 (2009).

5. Lee v. Houston County Board of Education, 1:70CV1058-WHA, 2008 WL 166954 (M.D. Ala. Jan. 16, 2008).

6. U.S. Commission on Civil Rights, Becoming *Less Separate*, 121.

7. Minutes of Wakulla County School Board Meeting, November 17, 2008; Coffee & Frankenberg, *Two Years After*, 12; Dave Weber, *Vestiges of Segregation? After 50 Years,*

Lawsuits over the Integration of Florida's Public Schools Still Linger, ORLANDO SENTINEL B1 (February 15, 2009).

8. U.S. Commission on Civil Rights, *Becoming Less Separate,* 127–28.

9. Adams v. Board of Public Education of Bibb County, 5:63-CV-1926(WDO), 2007 WL 841945 (M.D. Ga. Mar. 20, 2007).

10. U.S. Commission on Civil Rights, *Becoming Less Separate,* 139–40.

11. Ibid., 139–40.

12. Coffee & Frankenberg, *Two Years After,* 12; U.S. Commission on Civil Rights, *Becoming Less Separate,* 150 (noting that the district was seeking unitary status as of September 2007).

13. In Pitt County, North Carolina, the Eastern District of North Carolina approved a consent decree that delayed a decision on unitary status until 2012. Everett v. Pitt County Board of Education, 6:69-CV-702-H, slip opinion at 4 (E.D.N.C. Nov. 4, 2009).

14. Mike Wilder, *Law Limits Schools' Racial Balance,* TIMES-NEWS (BURLINGTON, N.C.) A1 (August 14, 2009).

15. Thadd White, *Bertie Gains Unitary Status,* ROANOKE-CHOWAN NEWS-HERALD (AHOSKIE, N.C.) A1 (September 1, 2009).

16. U.S. Commission on Civil Rights, *Becoming Less Separate,* 167.

NOTES

The author would like to thank the UNC Center for Civil Rights, the UCLA Civil Rights Project, and the University of Georgia Education Policy and Evaluation Center for organizing the "Looking to the Future" conference at which an earlier draft of this chapter was presented. The author would like to thank Elise Boddie, Eboni Nelson, Susan Kuo, and Jacqueline Fox for their thoughtful comments on drafts of this chapter. The author would also like to thank her co-panelists at the "Looking to the Future" conference for their helpful comments and collaboration. The author is grateful for the research assistance of Jessica Martin, Jill Yarsely, and Michael Mannering.

1. Parents Involved in Community Schools v. Seattle School District No. 1, 551 U.S. 701 (2007).

2. Erica Frankenberg & Chinh Q. Le, *The Post-Parents Involved Challenge: Confronting Extralegal Obstacles to Integration,* 69 OHIO STATE LAW JOURNAL 1015, 1015 (2008) (noting that commentators are beginning to assess *Parents Involved* to determine its impact on student assignment plans).

3. James E. Ryan, *The Supreme Court and Voluntary Integration,* 121 HARVARD LAW REVIEW 131, 132 (2007).

4. Derek W. Black, *The Uncertain Future of School Desegregation and the Importance of Goodwill, Good Sense, and a Misguided Decision,* 57 CATHOLIC UNIVERSITY LAW REVIEW 947, 980 (2008); Sharon L. Browne & Elizabeth A. Yi, *The Spirit of Brown in* Parents Involved *and Beyond,* 63 UNIVERSITY OF MIAMI LAW REVIEW 657, 672–73 (2009).

5. The term "unitary status" is given to school districts that have had their desegregation decrees lifted, thus closing the desegregation case. Green v. County School Board of

New Kent County, 391 U.S. 430, 436 (1968) (articulating the goal of Brown v. Board of Education, 347 U.S. 483 (1954), as a "transition to a unitary, nonracial system of public education"); Wendy Parker, *The Decline of Judicial Decisionmaking: School Desegregation and District Court Judges*, 81 NORTH CAROLINA LAW REVIEW 1623, 1631 n.50 (2003).

6. Board of Education of Oklahoma City Public Schools v. Dowell, 498 U.S. 237, 249–50 (1991); Freeman v. Pitts, 503 U.S. 467, 491 (1992); Dowell, 498 U.S. at 250; Parker, *The Decline of Judicial Decisionmaking*, 1645.

7. Dowell, 498 U.S. 250 (quoting Green, 391 U.S. 435).

8. Dowell, 498 U.S. 237.

9. Freeman, 503 U.S. 467.

10. Missouri v. Jenkins, 515 U.S. 70 (1995).

11. Jenkins, 515 U.S. at 100 (holding that school districts can achieve unitary status with student achievement levels below national norms); Freeman, 503 U.S. 471 (permitting district courts to grant unitary status in some categories and cease to supervise a school system in those categories); Dowell, 498 U.S. 248 (emphasizing the importance of local control of schools and that a desegregation decree should be dissolved once a school district has demonstrated compliance for a reasonable period of time); Gary Orfield & Chungmei Lee, The Civil Rights Project, Brown *at 50: King's Dream or Plessy's Nightmare*, 9 (2004); Wendy Parker, *The Future of School Desegregation*, 94 NORTHWESTERN UNIVERSITY LAW REVIEW 1157, 1158 (2000).

12. U.S Commission on Civil Rights, *Becoming Less Separate? School Desegregation, Justice Department Enforcement, and the Pursuit of Unitary Status*, 111–71 (2007).

13. PACER provides online access to opinions for federal cases. PACER, Administrative Office of the U.S. Courts, Overview, http:// pacer.psc.uscourts.gov/pacerdesc.html.

14. United States v. Hampton County School District No. 2, No. 70-611, slip opinion at 1 (D.S.C. Feb. 15, 2005) (noting that the DOJ commenced a review of the desegregation case in August 2003 and then informed the school district that it believed the school district had met its obligations under the desegregation order); Albert v. Denmark-Olar School District No. 2, Nos. 68-830 & 69-44, slip op. 1–2 (D.S.C. July 6, 2004) (noting that in September 2002 the DOJ began a review of the desegregation case by seeking information from the school district). After the review was complete, the DOJ informed the district that it believed it had met its obligations under the desegregation order. Ibid.

15. Joint Memorandum in Support of Declaration of Unitary Status and Dismissal 1, United States v. Fairfield County School District, No. 70-608 (D.S.C. Sept. 11, 2006).

16. Ibid., 2–6; Green, 391 U.S. at 435 (1968).

17. Fairfield County School District, No. 70-608, slip opinion at 1 (noting that the United States filed the initial desegregation case); Hampton County School District, No. 70-611, slip opinion at 1 (noting that the United States filed the initial desegregation case); Denmark-Olar School District, Nos. 68-830 & 69-44, slip opinion 2 (noting that a private plaintiff and the United States both filed desegregation cases against the school district in 1968 and 1969 respectively, and the cases were consolidated in 1969).

18. U.S. Commission on Civil Rights, *Becoming Less Separate*, 28 ("Since FY [fiscal year] 2000, the DOJ has actively pursued the closure of school desegregation case").

19. Hampton County, No. 70-611, 1.

20. Joint Memorandum in Support of Declaration of Unitary Status and Dismissal at 1,

Hampton County, No. 70-611.

21. Chinh Q. Le, *Racially Integrated Education and the Role of the Federal Government*, 88 NORTH CAROLINA LAW REVIEW 725, 731–48 (2010).

22. Ibid., 748.

23. Equal Educational Opportunities Act of 1974, Pub. L. No. 93-380, 88 Stat. 515.

24. Le, *Racially Integrated Education*, 739.

25. Ibid., 742; GARY ORFIELD & SUSAN E. EATON, EDS., DISMANTLING DESEGREGATION: THE QUIET REVERSAL OF *BROWN V. BOARD OF EDUCATION*, 16–18 (New Press 1997) (detailing the handling of school desegregation cases during the Reagan administration and in particular the DOJ's opposition to race-conscious remedies such as busing).

26. Parker, *The Decline of Judicial Decisionmaking*, 1192.

27. Le, *Racially Integrated Education*, 769 (arguing that the Department of Education should help "educate the public about the benefits of integration and the harms of racial isolation").

28. Eboni S. Nelson, *Examining the Costs of Diversity*, 63 UNIVERSITY OF MIAMI LAW REVIEW 577, 625 (2009).

29. Le, *Racially Integrated Education*, 775 (arguing that the Department of Education's Office of Civil Rights should actively encourage school districts to explore legally permissible strategies that expand educational opportunities by exposing students to diverse educational settings).

30. Frankenberg & Le, *The Post*-Parents Involved *Challenge*, 1027–28.

31. Ibid.

32. Ryan, *The Supreme Court*, 132.

33. Leland Ware, *Turning Back the Clock: The Assault on Affirmative Action*, 54 WASHINGTON UNIVERSITY JOURNAL OF URBAN AND CONTEMPORARY LAW 3, 21 (1998) (stating that school attendance zones are based on residential districts).

34. Kimberly Jenkins Robinson, *The Constitutional Future of Race-Neutral Efforts to Achieve Diversity and Avoid Racial Isolation in Elementary and Secondary Schools*, 50 BOSTON COLLEGE LAW REVIEW 277, 337 (2009).

35. Craig R. Heeren, *"Together at the Table of Brotherhood" Voluntary Student Assignment Plans and the Supreme Court*, 24 HARVARD BLACKLETTER LAW JOURNAL 133, 183 (2008).

36. Richard D. Kahlenberg, *Socioeconomic School Integration*, 85 NORTH CAROLINA LAW REVIEW 1545, 1551–52 (2007).

37. The situation in Wake County has continued to change. Erica Frankenberg & Sarah Diem, *School Board Leadership and Policymaking in Changing Political Environments*, 45 URBAN REVIEW 117 (2013).

38. MARK G. YUDOF ET AL., EDUCATIONAL POLICY AND THE LAW, 414 (Wadsworth Cengage Learning 2002); Frankenberg & Le, *The Post*-Parents Involved *Challenge*, 1047 ("What makes a magnet school different from the typical specialty school . . . is its explicit desegregative purpose").

39. Kahlenberg, *Socioeconomic School Integration*, 1553.

40. For the purposes of this chapter, including the Appendix, districts in this second group

are not considered "small districts." Nevertheless, they are discussed in this section due to their similar characteristics with small districts.

41. Wakulla County is located in north Florida, just south of Tallahassee. Wakulla County School District, *WCSB School List*, http:// wakulla.fl.schoolwebpages.com/education/ components/scrapbook/default.php? sectiondetailid=1458& (indicating four elementary schools, two middle schools, one high school, and one charter school).

42. Florida Department of Education, *NCLB School District and State Public Accountability Report for Wakulla County Superintendent's Office* (2007–2008).

43. Wakulla County School District, *WCSB School List*.

44. Wakulla County School District School Board, *Student Assignment Policy*, 2–3 (2007).

45. Weber, *Vestiges of Segregation?*

46. Wakulla County School District School Board, *Student Assignment Policy*, 7 (2007).

47. Department of Accountability Research & Planning, Jefferson County Public Schools, 2008–2009 *School Profiles*. For the 2008–2009 school year, Jefferson County middle schools enrolled 20,439 students, with 54% of them White and 36.2% Black. For the same year, the high school statistics show 26,375 students enrolled, with 56.3% being white and 35.5% black.

48. Jefferson County Public Schools, *About Us*, http:// www.jefferson.k12.ky.us/AboutUs/ About.html.

49. Seminole County Public Schools, *Seminole County Public Schools Facts 2009–2010*, http:// www.scps.k12.fl.us/community_involvement/_doc/SCPSFacts.pdf.

50. Seminole County Public Schools, *Schools*, http:// www.scps.k12.fl.us/index7b. cfm?portalid=schools7 (listing nine schools in the "High Schools" drop-down menu).

51. Parents Involved, 551 U.S. 789 (2007) (Justice Kennedy, concurring) (noting that school districts may pursue racial diversity by drawing attendance zones with recognition of demographics, and that districts may use race neutral means).

52. Dave Weber, *Mixing Rich and Poor is New Goal—Seminole Schools, Among Others, Seek to Supplant Racial Integration with Socioeconomic Diversity*, ORLANDO SENTINEL B1 (Aug. 5, 2007) (quoting Seminole County school board attorney as pleased that the new socioeconomic status diversity plans, adopted as part of the consent decree that ended the desegregation case, also are in line with *Parents Involved*).

53. Seminole County School District School Board, School Board Policy Manual for the Seminole County School Board § 5.30 (2009) [hereinafter Seminole Assignment Plan].

54. Ibid.

55. Grutter v. Bollinger, 539 U.S. 306, 325 (2003) ("[T]he diversity that furthers a compelling state interest encompasses a far broader array of qualifications and characteristics of which racial or ethnic origin is but a single though important element").

56. Seminole Assignment Plan, 4.

57. Ibid.

58. Ibid.

59. Parents Involved, 551 U.S. 710.

60. Ryan, *The Supreme Court*, 144–45 (noting that even the highest estimates for school districts considering race as a factor in student assignment would be 1,000 school districts nationally, leaving 15,000 school districts that do not consider race).

61. Marion County Public Schools, *Schools*, http:// www.marion.k12.fl.us/schools/ (reporting system-wide enrollment at 41,826 students as of October 20, 2009).

62. Florida Department of Education, Florida Comprehensive Assessment Test, Student Performance Results: District Reading Demographic Report, https:// app1.fldoe.org/ FCATDemographics/Selections.aspx?level=District&subj=Reading (for Year, select "2009," for Grade, select "3," then select "Continue"; on resulting screen, select "Total Students," for Ethnicity, select "Asian/Pacific Islander," "Black," "Hispanic," and "White," for Statistics, select "Number of Students," for District, select "MARION," then choose "View Report").

63. Marion County Public Schools, Schools, http:// www.marion.k12.fl.us/schools/.

64. Marion County School Board, *School Board Policies – Student Assignment*, 2 (2007) [hereinafter Marion Assignment Plan], available at http:// www.marion.k12.fl.us/dept/ hrm/docs/policies/Board%20Policy%205_20.pdf.

65. Telephone Interview with Anthony Burke, Supervisor of Student Assignment and Records, Marion County Public Schools (February 12, 2009) (transcript on file with the NORTH CAROLINA LAW REVIEW).

66. Ibid.

67. Parents Involved, 551 U.S. at 735.

68. Ibid., 747–48 (quoting Brown v. Board of Education, 349 U.S. 294, 300–01 (1955)).

69. Ibid., 723.

70. Marion Assignment Plan, 3.

71. Parents Involved, 551 U.S. 729 ("This working backward to achieve a particular type of racial balance, rather than working forward from some demonstration of the level of diversity that provides the purported benefits, is a fatal flaw under our existing precedent").

72. Ibid., 711–13.

73. Marion Assignment Plan, 3.

74. Parents Involved, 551 U.S. 735 ("The districts have also failed to show that they considered methods other than explicit racial classifications to achieve their stated goals. Narrow tailoring requires 'serious, good faith consideration of workable race-neutral alternatives.'" (quoting Grutter v. Bollinger, 539 U.S. 306, 339 (2003))).

75. Ibid., 789 (Kennedy, J., concurring).

76. Lafayette Parish School System, *LPSS Schools*, http:// www.lpssonline.com/schools.

77. Lafayette Parish School System, *2006–2007 Annual Report*, http:// www.lpssonline.com/ site3165.php.

78. Lafayette Parish School System, *School Board Policies: Assignment of Schools*, 1 (2008), available at http:// www.lpssonline.com/uploads/JBCCAAssignmentofSchools.pdf.

79. Ibid; Stephen J. Caldas, Roslin Growe & Carl L. Bankston III, *African American Reaction to Lafayette Parish School Desegregation Order: From Delight to Disenchantment*, 71 JOURNAL OF NEGRO EDUCATION 43, 47 (2002).

80. Lafayette Parish School System, *School Board Policies: Assignment of Schools*, 1 (2008), available at http:// www.lpssonline.com/uploads/JBCCAAssignmentofSchools.pdf.

81. Ibid., 4.

82. Ibid.

83. Erica Frankenberg & Liliana M. Garces, *The Use of Social Science Evidence in* Parents Involved *and* Meredith: *Implications for Researchers and Schools*, 46 UNIVERSITY OF LOUISVILLE LAW REVIEW 703, 748 (2008).

84. Frankenberg & Le, *The Post*-Parents Involved *Challenge*, 1021.

85. Danielle Holley-Walker, *Educating at the Crossroads:* Parents Involved, *No Child Left Behind and School Choice*, 69 OHIO STATE LAW JOURNAL 911, 928 (2008).

86. Milliken v. Bradley, 418 U.S. 717 (1974).

87. Milliken v. Bradley centered on a plan to use interdistrict remedies to reduce segregation in the Detroit, Michigan, schools. Ibid., 721–23; Frankenberg & Le, *The Post*-Parents Involved *Challenge*, 1030.

88. Missouri v. Jenkins, 418 U.S. 717 (1974).

89. Ibid., 97–98.

90. Frankenberg & Le, *The Post*-Parents Involved *Challenge*, 1031.

91. Rachel F. Moran, *Milo's Miracle*, 29 CONNECTICUT LAW REVIEW 1079, 1090 (1997).

92. Sheff v. O'Neill, 678 A.2d 1267 (Connecticut Supreme Court 1996).

93. Ibid., 1270–71; John C. Brittain, *Why* Sheff v. O'Neill *Is a Landmark Decision*, 30 CONNECTICUT LAW REVIEW 211, 211 (1997).

94. Lauren A. Wetzler, *Buying Equality: How School Finance Reform and Desegregation Came to Compete in Connecticut*, 22 YALE LAW & POLICY REVIEW 481, 496 (2004); Connecticut Constitution, Article 1, §§ 1, 20; Connecticut Constitution, Article VIII, §1.

95. Ibid., 502.

96. Ibid.

97. Ibid., 504–505.

98. Parker, *The Future of School Desegregation*, 1187–206.

99. Ibid.

100. For example, after the Connecticut Supreme Court's decision in *Sheff*, the state increased education funding by $200 million. Wetzler, *Buying Equality*, 503.

101. Wendy Parker, *The Supreme Court and Public Law Remedies: A Tale of Two Kansas Cities*, 50 HASTINGS LAW JOURNAL 475, 570–74 (1999); David S. Tatel, *Desegregation Versus School Reform: Resolving the Conflict*, 4 STANFORD LAW & POLICY REVIEW 61, 64 (1992–93).

102. Tangipahoa Parish School System, www.tangischools.org/info.html.

103. Moore v. Tangipahoa Parish School Board, 594 F.2d 489, 491 (Louisiana Supreme Court 1979).

104. David J. Mitchell, *Tangipahoa School Desegregation Hearing Set*, ADVOCATE (Baton Rouge, LA.) B4 (June 9, 2009).

105. Ibid.

106. Frankenberg & Le, *The Post*-Parents Involved *Challenge*, 1050–52 (describing the federal government's effort to conduct research and provide support for magnet schools through the Magnet School Assistance Program).

107. Danielle Holley-Walker, *The Accountability Cycle: The Recovery School District Act and New Orleans' Charter Schools*, 40 CONNECTICUT LAW REVIEW 125, 159–61 (2007).

108. Orfield & Eaton, ORFIELD & EATON, DISMANTLING DESEGREGATION, 353.

ERICA FRANKENBERG and SARAH DIEM

Voluntary Integration and School Board Leadership in Louisville, Kentucky

And what of respect for democratic local decisionmaking by States and school boards? For several decades this Court has rested its public school decisions upon *Swann*'s basic view that the Constitution grants local school districts a significant degree of leeway where the inclusive use of race-conscious criteria is at issue. Now localities will have to cope with the difficult problems they face (including resegregation) deprived of one means they may find necessary.

> —Justice Breyer, dissenting in *Parents Involved in Community Schools*
> *v. Seattle School District No. 1 (PICS)*, 551 U.S. 701, 866 (2007).

THE ROLE OF SCHOOL BOARDS TODAY IS INCREASINGLY COMPLEX, AS MULTIPLE stakeholders and interest groups have become more influential in the education policy-making process, including local and state actors with no formal jurisdiction over education policy. An added complication is that federal court decisions, most notably *PICS*, have hamstrung local efforts to maintain or create racially and ethnically diverse schools. In the years since *PICS*, Jefferson County Public Schools (JCPS), one of the districts involved in the case, has developed a new student assignment policy and already subsequently revised this policy; its process illustrates the considerable effort school boards must expend to adopt policies that are effective in achieving the board's goals, comply with the Court's decision, and satisfy parental preferences to the extent possible.

School boards are, by definition, part of the political process. They create policy in response to players inside and outside of the education arena who wish to see their perspectives mirrored in the policies governing schools, and they must be representative of all individuals without explicitly pandering to their political bases.[1] As the demographic makeup of public schools (and neighborhoods) shift and schools become more segregated, and as school desegregation lawsuits come to a close across the country, the role of school boards becomes critically important in maintaining policies designed to remedy segregation and promote equal opportunity, policies that may challenge the status quo.[2] Today, only about 70 school districts across the country that are not currently under a desegregation court order employ voluntary integration policies designed to maintain or increase racial and ethnic diversity in their schools.[3] Grounded in the literature about school boards and school diversity, this chapter studies one of those districts, Jefferson County (Louisville), Kentucky, seeking to understand the factors that enable that district to continue to pursue integration amid legal and political challenges. This chapter is part of our larger project exploring the pursuit of racial and ethnic diversity in public schools in Jefferson County, Kentucky, and Wake County, North Carolina.[4]

School Boards and Policy-making in a Shifting Sociopolitical Context

SCHOOL BOARDS AND EQUITY

While the tradition of local control of schools is a long-held value in public education, the body charged with oversight—school boards—may, for a variety of reasons, be limited in their ability to pursue equal opportunity for students.[5] First, though the lowest level of democracy, which should theoretically make school boards the most accessible to the public, democratic participation is minimal. Often there are negligible turnout rates for school board elections, due in part to the sizable share of districts that hold elections apart from other elections.[6] Perhaps related, there is little preparation for becoming a school board member and no required training. As Jennifer Hochschild points out, the responsibilities of school boards are numerous and they spend a small fraction of their time devoted to policy.[7]

More significantly for our purposes here, in a society with racial and economic segregation, the local nature of school boards may make them likely to *increase* inequality because their actions as policy-makers will be focused on furthering the interests of the students within their prescribed district. And because of racial and ethnic enclaves within districts, "democratic control of locally-based school boards works against equal educational opportunities or outcomes even within a single district."[8] As is the case with other elected leaders, evidence suggests that community members from historically disadvantaged groups have limited influence over school board decision-making.[9]

Nationally, school board members have a disproportionately higher white percentage as compared to the racial composition of public school students, although they have become more representative than they once were.[10] Even in diverse districts with the most diverse boards, the average share of minority board members is less than 30%.[11] A ward-based election system is significantly more likely to increase black representation but not that of Hispanics.[12] A study of Texas districts found that ward-based school board elections hurt Latino representation in predominantly Latino districts.[13] This matters for many reasons, including black residents reporting more satisfaction with the district when its school board has at least one black representative.[14]

Finally, another factor that can affect school boards' decisions to adopt equity policies is when broader networks, including national and state school boards associations, provide support and technical assistance to school boards. For example, because the *PICS* decision did not have a clear majority, districts were understandably confused about what the decision meant, and the Bush Administration's arguably overly restrictive reading of the decision did not help matters.[15] The National School Boards Association held sessions at its annual conferences to help inform member districts about the decision and has also produced two manuals since the decision reviewing case law and social science evidence, as well as drawing upon case studies of districts' approaches to integration after *PICS*. Additionally, the Council of Great City Schools, along with the NAACP Legal Defense Fund, lobbied Congress for a federal grant program to provide technical assistance to school districts to design student assignment plans that would comply with *PICS*.[16] This grant program was authorized in summer 2009 and provided funding for 11 districts' diversity efforts (including JCPS).

RACIAL AND ETHNIC DIVERSITY IN COMMUNITIES AND PUBLIC SCHOOLS TODAY

Nationally, school segregation is growing even as residential segregation slowly declines.[17] While the segregation of black and Latino students continues to increase, the isolation of white students is the highest of any group.[18] For many reasons, school segregation is connected to residential segregation. Demographic patterns show the rapid move to suburban communities, creating pockets of exclusivity in metropolitan areas.[19] White families have moved further away from the central city and affluent, outer-ring suburbs are growing.[20] While a growing number of minority and poor residents are moving to the suburbs, these groups tend to cluster in a subset of suburban areas, often adjacent to the central city, characterized as older, inner-ring suburbs.[21] Segregation is also increasing within metropolitan area suburbs.[22] In countywide districts, disparate demographic groups are still contained within one district, but are increasingly distant from households that differ by race or income. As these demographics shift, policies may shift away from issues of equity.[23]

One of the ways in which school segregation has changed over the last several decades is the growing role that school district boundary lines play in overall segregation. Charles Clotfelter refers to this as shifting from a *Brown* era to a *Milliken* one.[24] The Supreme Court's *Milliken* decision was the first post-*Brown* decision limiting the extent of desegregation remedies.[25] In *Milliken*, the Court held that separate suburban jurisdictions could not be part of a desegregation remedy unless they had contributed to the central city district's segregation.[26] Such action was virtually impossible to prove and meant that majority-minority urban districts would likely lack enough white students to create integrated schools. Today, by most measures, at least 70% of overall segregation is due to segregation between districts, and segregation is highest in the regions of the country where there are small, municipal-only districts.[27]

By contrast, reports have also found that some of the highest levels of black and Latino exposure to white students occur in countywide metropolitan areas.[28] One way to accomplish broad school integration is to have a school desegregation plan that covers a large geographical area, which is often the case in countywide school districts.[29] A comparison of four metropolitan areas found the countywide district with a comprehensive desegregation plan had more substantial reduction in housing segregation trends.[30] Countywide districts are better able to maintain diverse schools,[31] have less white flight where enclaves don't exist, and maintain political support for high-quality, equitable schools in ways very different from the politics existing in metro areas where city schools are separate from neighboring suburbs.[32] While demographic diversity may be an advantage in accomplishing integration, as court oversight for desegregation fades and enclaves within countywide districts grow, will the advantage of countywide districts persist if diversity results in more opposition to pursuing voluntary integration? The larger disparity among constituencies within a countywide district may make it more difficult to sustain a consensus supportive of integration if it reallocates resources in ways perceived to hurt certain groups.[33]

POLICY-MAKING POST-*PICS*

A likely cause of the existence of enclave schools today—a factor that also imbues these enclaves with more significance—is the growing hostility of the judicial system to school desegregation efforts as well as race-conscious policymaking more generally. Beginning in the 1990s, the Supreme Court issued a series of decisions that collectively defined how lower courts should judge school districts' desegregation efforts and when districts subject to court oversight should be released from supervision.[34] These decisions emphasized the importance of returning governance of school districts to school boards and removing the involvement of federal courts. Additionally, in the late 1990s, influenced by Supreme Court decisions in non-educational cases, lower federal courts began to rule against voluntary use of race by school districts in magnet school admissions.[35] Thus, even prior to the Court's most recent ruling on desegregation in *PICS*,[36] a judicial pattern of questioning governmental use of race had emerged, although the 2003 *Grutter v. Bollinger*[37] decision affirming the use of race in higher education was counter to this overall trend.

In June 2007, the Supreme Court found that the Seattle Public Schools and JCPS violated students' rights because of how their policies attempted to increase diversity.[38] The *PICS* decision was the latest in a recent trend of federal court decisions to express hesitance about using race, and it has forced districts to think of new ways to integrate schools without relying on race as the sole factor in their assignment policies. The decision was significant because it declared that there are compelling reasons that school boards would want to implement policies designed to integrate schools and reduce racial isolation. Yet at the same time a majority of the justices determined that the policies used by Seattle and JCPS (e.g., race-conscious controlled choice plans) were unconstitutional in their use of a student's race/ethnicity.

Judicial implementation literature questions the extent to which Supreme Court decisions will be complied with, particularly when decisions are controversial. An example is communities' response to the *Brown* decision—few African American students were attending majority white schools in the South even a decade after the decision.[39] In the immediate aftermath of *PICS*, James Ryan argued that the decision would not have much impact on the ground, as relatively few districts had voluntary integration plans in place.[40]

Kevin Welner has argued that the courts can shape the terms of debate on a particular issue by influencing which policy alternatives are viable and, in fact, research suggests varied political responses around the country.[41] As feared by Justice Breyer in his *PICS* dissent, one response has been to end voluntary integration efforts, which when coupled with the ending of court-ordered desegregation plans, may help explain why school segregation is rising even as housing segregation slowly declines.[42] Other work suggests that race-neutral alternatives to race-conscious integration may be less effective at creating racial integration and that they are no less politically divisive.[43] Finally, preliminary evidence also finds that the *PICS* decision may be prompting a redefinition by districts of "diversity," in ways that still use race to some extent but dilute or de-emphasize race by including other factors.[44]

Jefferson County Public Schools

While JCPS—and many of its parents—values diversity and the many benefits that result from it, it has faced a political climate that has made it challenging at times to maintain its current student assignment plan.[45] Early in 2010, the school board suggested it would entertain the idea of altering the plan's diversity guidelines to give parents as much choice as possible; alterations were adopted and implemented by the 2013–14 school year.[46] State politicians have tried to influence plan modifications, and the plan was also challenged in state court. Yet, the school board has remained committed to integration.

COMMUNITY AND SCHOOL DISTRICT DEMOGRAPHICS

In 1974, JCPS was formed through a merger of the city and county school systems that were both de jure segregated.[47] Today, JCPS is a 399-square-mile urban-suburban district that serves the city of Louisville and its surrounding suburbs. The demographics of Jefferson County and JCPS have not changed much since school desegregation was enforced after *Brown*: since 1970, the black population in Jefferson County has increased slightly while the white population has remained stable and a small Latino population has emerged. JCPS students mirror the county population; today, JCPS enrolls approximately 101,000 students; 48.5% are white, 36.8% black, and 14.7% other.[48] About 64% of JCPS students receive free or reduced-price lunch.[49]

The district has remained committed to creating diversity in its schools; however, Jefferson County neighborhoods remain segregated. In 2010, one-quarter of black residents lived in block groups that were 90–100% minority and more than half lived in predominantly minority block groups even though whites were 71% of the population.[50] More than 60% of Jefferson County's 86 communities have populations that are 90–100% white.[51] This residential segregation has important implications for school diversity in a post-*PICS* era in which school districts' policy options, if they wish to pursue integration, are limited.[52] Ironically, though the demographic diversity of the countywide districts makes school integration more possible than central city districts, where diversity exists alongside enclaves, it may be harder to maintain district-wide political support for policies aimed at creating middle-class, integrated schools.[53]

JCPS: MAINTAINING VOLUNTARY INTEGRATION THROUGH JUDICIAL DECISIONS

The district operated under a court order to desegregate from the 1970s through 2000, when as a result of the *Hampton v. Jefferson County Board of Education*[54] litigation, JCPS was declared unitary. Although no longer required to desegregate its schools—which it had vigorously resisted during the 1970s—the district decided to continue using largely the same integration assignment plan that it had been required to use when under court oversight.

Litigation ensued several years later when a handful of students were not permitted to enroll in their first-choice school. After the Supreme Court struck down JCPS's use of an individual student's race/ethnicity to determine student assignment in *PICS*, JCPS (in contrast to Seattle) immediately vowed to continue integrating students—noting the Supreme Court affirmed the importance of such plans—in a way that complied with the Court's decision. In fact, the district had begun studying what other school districts' voluntary integration plans looked like. After consultation with national experts and numerous community listening sessions, the JCPS board in spring 2008 unanimously adopted the plan proposed by the superintendent that sought to integrate by race, socioeconomic status, and educational attainment.

After the second year under the new, post-*PICS* student assignment plan, JCPS faced considerable criticism from parents primarily about the length of bus rides (and higher than usual transfer requests). Further, approximately half of the elementary schools in JCPS were not in compliance under the new plan, suggesting the existence of school enclaves.[55] In addition to the administrative team's review of the policy, which had delayed the implementation of changes to the middle school student assignment plan from 2010–11 to 2011–12, the school board brought in outside experts to evaluate the student assignment plan and transportation operations.[56] Despite the consultants' recommendations to delay implementation of the middle school boundary changes another year, the board moved forward with them in fall 2011 to assuage any concern that the board was "reneging" on its commitment to the diversity plan.[57] In January 2012, the board approved a plan for the 2012–13 school year, which altered the definition of diversity and improved the flow of information to all households.[58] Additional changes in 2013–14 altered which schools students could select, moved the school application process online, and implemented other changes to improve the plan's mechanics.

While continuing to study whether it can improve its existing student assignment plan to lower bus times and improve diversity, the district has continued to defend its specific student assignment policies, and its general ability to determine policy. In 2010, after challenges in federal court to the JCPS integration plan failed, lawyer Teddy Gordon (who represented the plaintiffs in *Meredith*) filed a lawsuit in state court citing a Kentucky state law that applied only to consolidated school districts requiring them to allow students to enroll in the school nearest their house.[59] The lower court opinion ruled against the plaintiffs, finding JCPS's student assignment policy to be legal because the original law had been amended from "attend" to "enroll" and because parents were allowed to submit applications at their nearby school, the policy was within the law's bounds.[60] An appellate panel in fall 2011, however, reversed this opinion in a fractured decision in which the majority was deeply critical of the school board and the current policy.[61] The school board appealed this decision to the Kentucky Supreme Court, which in 2012 ruled in favor of the district and its ability to determine student assignment policy.[62]

SCHOOL BOARD: INTERGOVERNMENTAL INFLUENCE ON INTEGRATION POLICY

Studying the local political climate and the changes in student assignment policy does not present the whole picture, though. It is also important to consider whether the structure of the school board as a governmental body influences a district's equity policies. Specifically, the ward-based nature of district elections—or at least the way in which wards are currently constructed within these school districts—may work against equity-based policies if school board members (and motivated voters in their election district) narrowly conceive of their interests. Ironically, the move from at-large elections to ward-based elections often occurred in the South as a way to increase minority representation, although such representation is currently limited on JCPS's school board.

The JCPS school board is comprised of seven members, each elected for a four-year term from a geographic area within the district. Several members of the JCPS school board have served for a long time, as far back as when JCPS operated under court-ordered desegregation. In 2012, the board included both graduates of JCPS and former employees of the school district. Joe Hardesty and Carol Haddad were elected in 1990 (Haddad also served a term during the 1970s). Four other members were on the school board prior to the *PICS* decision. Only Diane Porter, whose district is mostly African American, joined the board after the Supreme Court decision (she was appointed in 2010 and elected to a full term in fall 2010). The board had six white members and one African American board member.

In the 2010–11 school year, white enclave (and disproportionately non-white) schools existed in JCPS. District 2 experienced a sharp increase in white enclaves during the decade after unitary status with over half of the elementary schools comprised of white populations 61% or higher. The other board district where a majority of elementary schools were white enclaves, district 3, was the only district to not have any largely non-white schools. Conversely, district 1 had no white enclaves and the vast majority of schools were disproportionately non-white. District 7 had consistently experienced high levels of white enclaves since 2000 with 70% of the elementary schools made up of predominately white students.

In 2010, after a second straight tumultuous school opening that was blamed on the integration plan, there was concern about whether sitting school board members might not survive their reelection campaign. Of the four seats up for election, only Linda Duncan (elected in 2006) in district 5 was unopposed. In district 1, there were three challengers to Diane Porter who had been appointed to her seat earlier in the year, all of whom supported of the integration plan despite some concerns over its operation.[63] Debbie Wesslund, in district 3, was seen as potentially vulnerable due to the existence of white enclaves in her district. Her two opponents favored returning to neighborhood schools, while Wesslund suggested modifications were needed.[64] However, all incumbent board members were reelected. (Although the mayor has no formal power with regard to the school district, the integration plan was also discussed during the 2010 mayoral race. Hal Heiner, the Republican candidate, was critical of the student assignment policy and lost the election.) Shortly thereafter, by a 5–2 vote, the district voted not to renew the superintendent's contract, with the rationale that there had not been enough "urgency" in improving student performance.[65] The superintendent was seen, particularly in the media, as the champion of integration and he had overseen the development and implementation of the post-*PICS* plan. Newspaper editorials questioned the school board's commitment to integration, adding to criticism earlier in 2010 from some Louisville civil rights organizations.

In 2011, although no school board elections were held, the JCPS integration plan and the school board supporting it remained a focus of electoral politics. The Republican candidate for governor, David Williams, repeatedly raised the issue of JCPS's "busing" policy as a concern. Jefferson County is the most populous county in Kentucky and is home to the largest share of African Americans in the state. As a state legislator, Williams was the cosponsor of a bill introduced in the 2010–11 session called the Neighborhood Schools Act that would have guaranteed JCPS students could attend the public school closest to where they lived. Hearings were held in January 2011, which included testimony from several JCPS school board members. While the Senate narrowly passed the bill, it was never voted on by the Kentucky House; a similar bill was introduced and went nowhere in 2012. Williams identified JCPS board members as standing in the way of the state's most important economic development "crisis"—apparently concluding that the student assignment plan was related to the high numbers of JCPS schools that were failing.[66] He also called for dissolving the JCPS school board, suggesting that it would be better to have the metro Louisville mayor appoint a superintendent and have the metro council act as school board. His rationale was that these individuals would be more responsive to the public than the current board, which he repeatedly argued was beholden to the teachers union.[67] Williams finished a distant second to sitting governor Steve Beshear in the November 2011 election and received an even lower share of the votes (27%) in Jefferson County.[68]

In 2012, three JCPS school board seats were on the ballot, and the three incumbents, who each have served at least a dozen years, did not run for reelection. The plaintiff in the state court case, Chris Fell, ran for Larry Hujo's seat in district 7.[69] Teddy Gordon, who has litigated cases against JCPS's integration policies, lives in district 2 and unsuccessfully ran for board election against Steve Imhoff in 2004. Imhoff responded to Gordon's request for the school board to drop the litigation defending the district's right to determine its own student assignment policies, "When he gets on the school board, he can vote whichever way he wants."[70] Given the sharp increase in the enclave schools in district 2 (and elsewhere), the integration plan was a topic of debate in the 2012 election. However, in each of the three seats that were contested, none of the "neighborhood schools" candidates won election,[71] bringing a bit of stability to the board after many years of legal and political challenges. Advocates for the student assignment plan viewed the election results as a win for the student assignment plan, providing the board the ability to focus more of their efforts on student achievement across the district.[72]

While the 2012 election brought the first significant turnover to the board since before *PICS,* the board remained committed to integration generally and student assignment became less of a focal point as district staff continued to implement recommended changes to the existing policy. Additionally, pending legal cases had been resolved. Yet, as we have learned through our fieldwork in the district, the leadership remains vigilant knowing that support can quickly change. Indeed, in fall 2014, a majority of school board seats are up for election. One board member, Debbie Wesslund in district 3, decided to not run; her district is one in which there are many new schools and neighborhoods with some of the highest concentrations of white and wealthy homeowners who would prefer their children attend one of these nearby schools. Diane Porter in district 1, containing Louisville and the West End, which is predominantly nonwhite, was unopposed. Carol Haddad and Linda Duncan ran against several challengers each.

In the current legal climate, the JCPS school board has been a model of stability and commitment to pursuing, and defending, voluntary integration plans. The JCPS board criticized a state court for acting like a school board in its appellate decision (which has often been an issue in desegregation cases). Despite this politically contentious climate and the fact that not all school board members represent districts that may see desegregation in their individual self-interest, the board has been resolute in its commitment to pursuing school integration. It selected a new superintendent, Donna Hargens, who began in August 2011, and who had been interim superintendent in Wake County, North Carolina, amid the turmoil after its school board ended its diversity policy and moved to a policy based on their home address; Wake County now tries to minimize concentrations of low-performing and low-income students at each school while also prioritizing proximity and stability.[73]

Conclusion

JCPS has a long history of desegregation efforts, and has been seen as a national model because of the success of and support for its voluntary diversity policies. Unlike many other communities, JCPS has experienced a significant amount of stability in its school board membership and despite being the target of extensive legal action, has managed to maintain political stability in support of its integration policy. In fact, there has been enough support to revise the integration plan to improve its effectiveness. In part, this may be because the design of diversity policies the school board has implemented has changed the politics of diversity in the district. JCPS's policy was a controlled choice plan, which offers more choice to appease parents. While parents could not be assured of what school their child(ren) would attend, allowing some choice may have diffused the frustration of parents who preferred an enclave school. Additionally, the school board and district administration in this county-wide district have been resolute in their responses to state and federal legal cases as well as state and local political challenges to integration policy.

However, moving forward, the district has a new superintendent, meaning that school board leadership will be critical. The candidates for Louisville mayor and Kentucky governor who have sought to interfere with the JCPS's school board's decision-making lost their respective elections in 2010 and 2011. Additionally, at a time of considerable upheaval—with three board slots up for election in 2012, pending revisions to the existing desegregation plan, and their appeal of the state court's decision about student assignment—JCPS ended 2012 with a board still committed to its diversity policy, district administrators implementing changes to improve the desegregation plan, and a victory in a state court allowing them to determine student assignment policy. As the dust has settled from five tumultuous years after *PICS*, JCPS's integration efforts remain in place due to the board's stable commitment thus far and the electoral defeat of opponents of integration efforts. In 2014, a majority of JCPS school board seats were on the ballot, and only one of the members (from district 1) up for re-election was unopposed.[74] While to date JCPS represents a case of school board stability and has experienced a time of relative calm related to student assignment and a shifting focus on improving student achievement, even here we see the importance of school board elections. Specifically, in the current legal and political context, districts must remain aware that electoral change may be on the horizon thereby shifting support for the diversity policy. The reality may be that student assignment policy might never be "calm" in a district like JCPS that has been at the center of the integration debate since *PICS.*

Erica Frankenberg is an Assistant Professor in the Department of Education Policy Studies in the College of Education at the Pennsylvania State University. **Sarah Diem** is an Assistant Professor in the Department of Educational Leadership & Policy Analysis at the University of Missouri. This chapter is adapted from *School Board Leadership and Policymaking in Changing Political Environments,* originally published in 45 URBAN REVIEW 117 (2012).

NOTES

1. Jacqueline P. Danzberger, *Governing the Nation's Schools: The Case for Restructuring Local School Boards,* 75 PHI DELTA KAPPAN 67 (1994); Frederick Hess & Olivia Meeks, The National School Boards Association, The Thomas B. Fordham Institution, & The Iowa School Board Foundation, *School Boards Circa 2010: Governance in the Accountability Era* (2011); Jennifer L. Hochschild, *What School Boards Can and Cannot (Or Will Not) Accomplish,* in WILLIAM G. HOWELL, ED., BESIEGED: SCHOOL BOARDS AND THE FUTURE OF EDUCATION POLITICS 324 (Brookings Institution Press 2005).

2. CHARLES T. CLOTFELTER, AFTER *BROWN*: THE RISE AND RETREAT OF SCHOOL DESEGREGATION (Princeton University Press 2004); Gary Orfield, The Civil Rights Project/Proyecto Derechos Civiles, *Reviving the Goal of an Integrated Society: A 21st Century Challenge* (2009).

3. Erica Frankenberg, *Assessing the Status of School Desegregation Sixty Years After* Brown, MICHIGAN STATE UNIVERSITY LAW REVIEW (forthcoming 2014).

4. Sarah Diem & Erica Frankenberg, *The Politics of Diversity: Integration in an Era of Political and Legal Uncertainty,* 115 TEACHERS COLLEGE RECORD 1 (2013); Sarah Diem, Erica Frankenberg, Nazneen Ali, & Colleen Cleary, *The Politics of Maintaining Diversity Policies in Demographically Changing Urban-Suburban School Districts,* 120 AMERICAN JOURNAL OF EDUCATION 351 (2014); Erica Frankenberg & Sarah Diem, *School Board Leadership and Policymaking in Changing Political Environments,* 45 THE URBAN REVIEW 117 (2013).

5. Jennifer L. Hochschild & Bridget Scott, *Trends: Governance and Reform of Public Education in the United States,* 62 PUBLIC OPINION QUARTERLY 79 (1998).

6. Hochschild, *What School Boards Can and Cannot Accomplish*; Gene I. Maeroff, *The Future of School Boards*, EDUCATION WEEK 30 (January 12, 2011).

7. Hochschild, *What School Boards Can and Cannot Accomplish*; Frederick M. Wirt & Michael W. Kirst, *Local School Boards, Politics, and the Community*, in FREDERICK M. WIRT & MICHAEL W. KIRST, EDS., THE POLITICAL DYNAMICS OF AMERICAN EDUCATION (McCutchan Publishing Corporation 2005).

8. Hochschild, *What School Boards Can and Cannot Accomplish*, 329.

9. Kara S. Finnigan & Mark Lavner, *A Political Analysis of Community Influence Over School Closure*, 44 URBAN REVIEW 133 (2011); Clarence N. Stone, *Social Stratification, Nondecision-Making and the Study of Community Power*, 10 AMERICAN POLITICS QUARTERLY 275 (1982); SIDNEY VERBA, KAY L. SCHLOZMAN, & HENRY E. BRADY, VOICE AND EQUITY: CIVIC VOLUNTARISM IN AMERICAN POLITICS (Harvard University Press 1995).

10. Maeroff, *The Future of School Boards*.

11. Hess & Meeks, *School Boards Circa 2010*.

12. Melissa J. Marschall, *Minority Incorporation and Local School Boards*, in WILLIAM G. HOWELL, BESIEGED: SCHOOL BOARDS AND THE FUTURE OF EDUCATION POLITICS, 173 (Brookings Institution Press 2005).

13. Kenneth J. Meier & Eric Gonzalez Juenke, *Electoral Structure and the Quality of Representation on School Boards*, in HOWELL, BESIEGED, 199.

14. Marschall, *Minority Incorporation*.

15. Chinh Q. Le, *Racially Integrated Education and the Role of the Federal Government*, 88 NORTH CAROLINA LAW REVIEW 725 (2010). In December 2011 the Obama Administration rescinded this letter and issued comprehensive guidance regarding the ways in which school districts could use race to pursue diversity or avoid racial isolation.

16. Kathryn A. McDermott, Elizabeth DeBray, & Erica Frankenberg, *How Does Parents Involved in Community Schools Matter? Legal and Political Influence in Education Politics and Policy*, 114 TEACHERS COLLEGE RECORD 1 (2012).

17. Orfield, *Reviving the Goal*; Sean F. Reardon & John T. Yun, *Integrating Neighborhoods, Segregating Schools*, in JOHN C. BOGER & GARY ORFIELD, EDS., SCHOOL RESEGREGATION: MUST THE SOUTH TURN BACK?, 51 (University of North Carolina Press 2005).

18. Orfield, *Reviving the Goal*.

19. Erica Frankenberg, *Splintering School Districts: Understanding the Link Between Segregation and Fragmentation*, 34 LAW AND SOCIAL INQUIRY 869 (2009).

20. The Brookings Institution Metropolitan Policy Program, *State of Metropolitan America: On the Front Lines of Demographic Transformation* (2010); MYRON ORFIELD, AMERICAN METROPOLITICS (Urban Institute Press 2002).

21. WILLIAM H. FREY, MELTING POT SUBURBS: A CENSUS 2000 STUDY OF SUBURBAN DIVERISTY (Brookings Institution Press 2001); ORFIELD, AMERICAN METROPOLITICS.

22. Chad R. Farrell, *Bifurcation, Fragmentation or Integration? The Racial and Geographic Structure of U.S. Metropolitan Segregation, 1990–2000*, 45 URBAN STUDIES 467 (2008).

23. CLARENCE N. STONE, CHANGING URBAN EDUCATION (University Press of Kansas 1998).

24. CLOTFELTER, AFTER *BROWN*.

25. Milliken v. Bradlley, 433 U.S. 267 (1977).

26. Ibid.

27. CLOTFELTER, AFTER *BROWN*; Reardon & Yun, *Integrating Neighborhoods*.

28. Erica Frankenberg, Chungmei Lee, & Gary Orfield, The Civil Rights Project, *A Multiracial Society with Segregated Schools: Are We Losing the Dream?* (2003).

29. Erica Frankenberg, *The Impact of School Segregation on Residential Housing Patters: Mobile, AL and Charlotte, NC*, in BOGER & ORFIELD, SCHOOL RESEGREGATION, 261; Frankenberg, *Splintering School Districts*.

30. Genevieve Siegel-Hawley, *City Lines, County Lines, Color Lines: An Analysis of School and Housing Segregation in Four Southern Metropolitan Areas, 1990–2010* (Doctoral dissertation, University of California, Los Angeles (2011)).

31. Gary Orfield, *Metropolitan School Desegregation*, in JOHN A. POWELL, GAVIN KEARNEY, & VINA KAY, EDS., IN PUSUIT OF A DREAM DEFERRED, 121 (Peter Lang 2001).

32. DIANA PEARCE, BREAKING DOWN THE BARRIERS: NEW EVIDENCE ON THE IMPACT OF METROPOLITAN SCHOOL DESEGREGATION ON HOUSING PATTERS (National Institute of Education 1980); CLOTFELTER, AFTER *BROWN*; Sarah Diem, *The Relationship Between Policy Design, Context, and Implementation in Integration Plans*, 20 EDUCATION POLICY ANALYSIS ARCHIVES 1 (2012); JAMES E. RYAN, FIVE MILES AWAY, A WORLD APART: ONE CITY, TWO SCHOOLS, AND THE STORY OF EDUCATIONAL OPPORTUNITY IN MODERN AMERICA (Oxford University Press 2010).

33. Kathryn A. McDermott, Erica Frankenberg, & Sarah Diem, *The "Post-Racial" Politics of Race: Student Assignment Policy in Three School Districts*, EDUCATIONAL POLICY, published online before print (January 30, 2014).

34. Board of Education of Oklahoma v. Dowell, 498 U.S. 237 (1991); Freeman v. Pitts, 503 U.S. 467 (1992); Missouri v. Jenkins, 515 U.S. 70 (1995); ORFIELD & EATON, DISMANTLING DESEGREGATION.

35. Jacinta S. Ma & Michal Kurlaender, *The Future of Race-Conscious Policies in K–12 Schools: Support from Recent Legal Opinions and Social Science Evidence*, in BOGER & ORFIELD, SCHOOL RESEGREGATION, 239.

36. Parents Involved in Community Schools v. Seattle School District No. 1, 551 U.S. 701, 866 (2007).

37. Grutter v. Bollinger, 539 U.S. 306 (2003).

38. Parents Involved in Community Schools, 551 U.S. 701.

39. CLOTFELTER, AFTER *BROWN*.

40. James E. Ryan, *The Supreme Court and Voluntary Integration*, 121 HARVARD LAW REVIEW 131 (2007).

41. KEVIN WELNER, LEGAL RIGHTS, LOCAL WRONGS: WHEN COMMUNITY CONTROL COLLIDES WITH EDUCATIONAL EQUITY (State University of New York Press 2001).

42. McDermott, DeBray, & Frankenberg, *How Does Parents Involved in Community Schools Matter?*; Le, *Racially Integrated Education*.

43. Sean F. Reardon, John T. Yun, & Michal Kurlaender, *Implications of Income-Based School*

Assignment Policies for Racial School Segregation, 28 EDUCATION EVALUATION AND POLICY ANALYSIS 49 (2006); Kathryn A. McDermott, Erica Frankenberg, Sarah Diem, & Elizabeth DeBray, *The New Race-Neutrality and the Changing Urban Education Regime* (September 2010). Paper presented at the annual meeting of American Political Science Association, Washington, DC.

44. Genevieve Siegel-Hawley & Erica Frankenberg, *Redefining Diversity: Political Responses to the Post-*PICS *Environment*, 86 PEABODY JOURNAL OF EDUCATION 529 (2011).

45. Gary Orfield & Erica Frankenberg, The Civil Rights Project/Proyecto Derechos Civiles, *Experiencing Integration in Louisville: How Parents and Students See the Gains and Challenges* (2011).

46. Antoinette Konz, *JCPS Denies 70 Percent of Transfer Requests for Fall*, THE COURIER-JOURNAL (July 18, 2010).

47. Newburg Area Council, Inc. v. Board of Education of Jefferson County, 510 F.2d 1358 (6th Cir. 1974).

48. Jefferson County Public Schools Department of Accountability, Research and Planning, *2013–2014 Data Books* (2013).

49. Ibid.

50. Siegel-Hawley, *City Lines, County Lines, Color Lines.*

51. U.S. Census Bureau, *Jefferson County, KY, 2010 Community Facts*, http://factfinder2.census.gov/faces/nav/jsf/pages/index.xhtml.

52. Reardon & Yun, *Integrating Neighborhoods.*

53. Orfield, *Metropolitan School Desegregation.*

54. Hampton v. Jefferson County Board of Education, 102 F. Supp. 2d 358, 360 (W.D. Ky. 2000).

55. McDermott, DeBray, & Frankenberg, *How Does* Parents Involved in Community Schools *Matter?*

56. The first author was part of the team evaluating the student assignment policy.

57. Antoinette Konz, *No Delay for JCPS Middle School Boundary Changes*, THE COURIER-JOURNAL (March 14, 2011).

58. Chris Kenning, *JCPS Urges Changes in Student Assignment Plan*, THE COURIER-JOURNAL (December 12, 2011).

59. Jefferson County Board of Education v. Fell, 391 S.W.3d 713 (Supreme Court of Kentucky 2012). Fell v. Jefferson County Board of Education, 2011 WL 4502673 (Kentucky Court of Appeals 2011).

60. Ibid.

61. Ibid.

62. Antoinette Konz, *Kentucky High Court Agrees to Hear Jefferson School-Assignment Case*, THE COURIER-JOURNAL (December 3, 2011).

63. Antoinette Konz, *Four Candidates for JCPS District 1 Share Major Issues*, THE COURIER-JOURNAL (October 20, 2010).

64. Sean Rose, *District 3 School Board Candidates Talk Student Achievement*, THE COURIER-JOURNAL (October 20, 2010).

65. Antoinette Konz, *JCPS Superintendent Sheldon Berman to be Replaced*, THE COURIER-JOURNAL (November 22, 2010).

66. Bennett Haeberle, *House Leaders: Williams' Legislative Agenda Likely Dead*, WDRB News (January 12, 2011).

67. Phillip M. Bailey, *Williams Praises Ruling Against JCPS Student Assignment Plan*, WFPL NEWS (September 30, 2011).

68. *Kentucky's County-by-County Results for Governor*, THE COURIER-JOURNAL (November 9, 2011).

69. Chris Kenning, *Lawyer Tells JCPS: End Litigation Now*, THE COURIER-JOURNAL (October 3, 2011).

70. Ibid.

71. Antoinette Konz, *David Jones Jr., Chuck Haddaway and Chris Brady All Win Seats on JCPS School Board*, THE COURIER-JOURNAL (November 7, 2012).

72. Antoinette Konz, *With Neighborhood Schools Candidates Defeated, JCPS Shifts Focus to Student Achievement*, THE COURIER-JOURNAL (November 10, 2012).

73. Wake County Public School System, *Student Assignment, 2013–2014*, http://www.wcpss.net/policy-files/series/policies/6200-bp.html (2013).

74. Antoinette Konz, *Wesslund Won't Seek Re-election to JCPS School Board*, THE COURIER-JOURNAL (March 29, 2014).

DAVID HINOJOSA and KAROLINA WALTERS

How Adequacy Litigation Fails to Fulfill the Promise of *Brown* (But How it Can Get Us Closer)

A QUALITY EDUCATION IS OFTEN SEEN AS THE POTENTIAL EQUALIZER IN THE pursuit of the "American Dream" between the "haves" and the "have-nots." There is nary a sane person who would say that he or she is against equal educational opportunities. Indeed, all 50 states have articles specifically addressing the states' obligations to provide a public education.[1] Through school desegregation and school finance litigation, the quest for equal educational opportunities through court action has continued for well over a century.

At the heart of early school desegregation cases was the legal, social, and educational lesson needed to be taught: Segregating students on the basis of race in schoolhouses was not only "perhaps the most virulent form of this polity-threatening corruption," but was also detrimental to the learning of students and to our greater society by denying equal educational opportunities.[2] Our highest court waited until 1954 in *Brown v. Board of Education*[3] to hold that the ill-conceived notion enunciated in *Plessy v. Ferguson*[4] and other cases—that segregating people on the basis of race was acceptable so long as equal services and facilities were available—deserved no cover under the Equal Protection Clause. As former NAACP Legal Defense Fund attorney Jack Greenberg said of the *Brown* decision, "*Brown* led to the sit-ins, the freedom marches . . . the Civil Rights Act of 1964. . . . If you look at *Brown* as . . . the icebreaker that broke up . . . that frozen sea, then you will see it was an unequivocal success."[5] *Brown* also "reminded the nation that there are limits to majoritarianism that the courts are obliged to . . . enforce in . . . the spirit and letter of the United States Constitution" and "contributed an unprecedented expansion of the American economy, consumer and tax base, created a more informed citizenry, and strengthened substantive democracy."[6]

Indeed, the success of *Brown* cannot reasonably be questioned when considering that it struck down as unconstitutional hundreds of policies and practices aimed specifically at excluding African American and other minority students from all-white schools.[7] As the years passed, however, the courts often scaled back efforts to desegregate public schools. Indeed, many say the watering-down of the *Brown* decision began in 1955 when the Supreme Court announced in *Brown II* that responsible actors need only address illegal segregation with "all deliberate speed."[8] Saddled with de facto segregated schools, some advocates and civil rights organizations turned their attention to federal and state courts to enforce constitutional rights to equitable access to educational opportunities between school districts.[9]

The resulting school finance litigation has been extensive. School finance litigation is generally considered to have three "waves," and much has been said about the impact of the latest wave, often referred to as "adequacy" cases. Some researchers criticize the justiciability of such claims, suggesting that the courts should stay out of the fray and allow legislators, policymakers, and voters to decide freely how to fund schools.[10] At the same time, others suggest that adequacy cases are the only remaining type of education cases capable of rooting out inequalities in public education and thus fulfilling *Brown*'s promise of equal educational opportunities for children of color.[11] While there should be no question whether courts can appropriately rule on state constitutional adequacy claims, the answer to the question of whether adequacy cases have realized equitable opportunities for children of color and at-risk children on the whole remains elusive, at best.[12] On the school segregation aspect of *Brown*, adequacy litigation has made no inroads to achieving desegregated schools, nor does it claim to pursue such. Although one could plausibly argue that having adequate funding in transportation includes taking into account some of the costs related to magnet and diverse cluster schools, that issue is typically not raised in adequacy lawsuits. However, yielding equal educational opportunities for minority and at-risk children, especially in high poverty schools, remains largely an aspirational goal, and one perhaps more important than ever before, given the increase in the number of minority and at-risk students served in public schools across the U.S. coupled with the increase in high-stakes testing and accountability measures.

Accordingly, this chapter provides a snapshot of some of the systemic challenges facing school finance advocates in the courts, as well as some suggestions that should be considered to positively affect minority and at-risk student achievement and access. It begins by briefly discussing the school finance equity cases; turns to an analysis of the school finance adequacy cases, with a focus on three all-too common problems encountered in this type of litigation; and then discusses future strategies, litigation and otherwise.

"Equity" Litigation

For more than 45 years and counting, public education advocates have filed several actions in courts seeking equitable and adequate resources for all school children, lending credence to the mission of *Brown*.[13] The first "wave" of school finance litigation entails federal claims filed under the equal protection clause of the Fourteenth Amendment and typically begins with a discussion of the *Rodriguez v. San Antonio Independent School District* case.[14] Although a handful of other cases were filed before *Rodriguez*, it is the seminal federal school finance case.[15]

Rodriguez began as a student protest in 1968, when approximately 400 students attending Edgewood High School on the proud but impoverished west side of San Antonio, Texas, walked out of school protesting the quality of education and the condition of their school.[16] The evidence of inequalities was largely irrefutable. In a survey of 110 school districts in Texas, the ten wealthiest districts with property values above $100,000 per pupil received $585 per pupil for a property tax of only $0.31. The students in the four poorest districts with property values below $10,000 per pupil received only $60 per pupil—despite taxing their residents at a rate nearly 250% higher, $0.70.[17] The groups of districts also differed along racial lines: the ten wealthiest districts enrolled 8% minority students compared to 79% in the poorest districts.[18] The lack of resources caused high-minority, property-poor districts like Edgewood to struggle in recruiting and retaining qualified teachers.[19]

Following the trial, the three-judge panel issued its decision finding the Texas school finance system unconstitutional, and, relying partly on *Brown*, held that education was a fundamental right under the U.S. Constitution.[20] But the victory was short-lived. On March 21, 1973, in a 5–4 decision, the Supreme Court reversed the lower court's opinion.[21] Although the Supreme Court agreed with the lower court that "'the grave significance of education both to the individual and to our society' cannot be doubted," it refused to hold that the importance of education elevated it to a fundamental right, concluding that education was neither explicitly nor implicitly a right guaranteed under the Constitution.[22] Emphasizing the importance of "local control" over education, the Court applied the rational basis standard of review to the Texas system and found that the grossly inequitable system passed constitutional muster.[23] In a stinging dissent, Justice Thurgood Marshall berated the majority for retreating from the foundation of *Brown* and suggested that the plaintiffs turn to state courts for recourse.[24]

Thus, the "second wave" of school finance litigation followed, asserting similar equity claims, but largely under state constitutional equal protection clauses.[25] At the center of the claims in these cases were the unequal educational opportunities afforded to students based on where they lived and where they went to school, which stemmed from disparate access to resources due to state education funding that relied heavily on local property taxes. While race was not central to many of the claims, because many minority students lived in the lower property-wealth districts, minority students were often impacted disparately by starkly unequal funding systems.

In California, students and parents sued in state court under both the United States and California constitutions in 1968, challenging the grossly unequal California school finance system that also relied on disparate property values and property tax rates.[26] Following *Rodriguez*, the California Supreme Court revisited its earlier decision in *Serrano I* and pronounced once again that under the California Constitution, education was a fundamental right.[27] The court ultimately struck down the California school finance system as unconstitutional. However, voters in property-wealthy districts retaliated and passed an initiative that capped raises on property taxes; consequently, the legislature was forced to level-down resources allocated for public education.[28]

Similarly, in New Jersey, plaintiffs filed suit challenging the school funding inequalities under the state constitution requiring a "thorough and efficient system of free public schools."[29] The New Jersey Supreme Court ultimately found the system unconstitutional after determining that the state failed "to fulfill[] its obligation to afford all pupils that level of instructional opportunity which is comprehended by a thorough and efficient system of education for students" as required under its state constitution.[30] In separate litigation filed in 1981, *Abbott v. Burke*,[31] plaintiffs challenged the constitutionality of the New Jersey school funding system because of the significant disparities in expenditures between poor urban school districts and wealthy suburban districts, and the lack of adequate funds.

Other state courts upheld similar equity challenges in the early years following *Rodriguez*, including challenges in Arkansas, Connecticut, and Wyoming.[32] The relatively simple notion behind these complex equal protection cases was captured well by the Vermont Supreme Court when it held, "[m]oney is clearly not the only variable affecting educational opportunity, but it is one that government can effectively equalize."[33] The success of these state equity cases slowed in the 1980s with 15 courts denying challenges up to that period, many relying on similar reasoning found in *Rodriguez*, but the pendulum again swung back in favor of the plaintiffs in the late 1980s.[34] In Texas, property-poor school districts, including Edgewood Independent School District (ISD), and parents such as Demetrio Rodriguez, again challenged the inequities in the Texas school finance system. This time they won, with the Supreme Court of Texas holding in 1989 that the state's education clause requires that "children who live in poor districts and children who live in rich districts . . . be afforded a substantially equal opportunity to have access to educational funds."[35] Like the built-in advantages for the former all-white schools in *Brown*, the *Edgewood* court noted that the Texas school finance system favored high-wealth districts, allowing those districts "to provide their students broader educational experiences including more extensive curricula, more up-to-date technological equipment, better libraries and library personnel, teacher aides, counseling services, lower student-teacher ratios, better facilities, parental involvement programs, and drop-out prevention programs. They are also better able to attract and retain experienced teachers and administrators."[36]

Although these cases importantly brought attention to the arbitrary and inequitable systems that typically based funding on a student's zip code, and led to significant school finance reforms in states where successful cases were brought, the success was limited. First, for states where equity claims were denied outright as nonjusticiable, or as violating the separation of powers doctrine, there was no recourse other than local advocacy efforts. Second, even in those states where equity claims were successful, success was limited to guaranteeing near-equal funding compared to other wealthier school districts in the state but did not ensure that the funding was adequate to meet the educational needs of at-risk and minority students. And with testing and accountability reforms beginning to take place in states across the country, the need to ensure not only equitable funding, but also adequate funding to deliver equal educational opportunities for all children became equally important.

"Adequacy" Litigation

The struggle for equal educational opportunities in school desegregation litigation was rooted not only in the need to integrate students of different races, but relatedly, in the widely held belief that white-only schools offered a higher quality education. If the white-only schools were in disrepair, poorly resourced, and staffed by teachers lacking certification, for example, there may not have been such a strong desire to integrate the schools.[37] However, that often was not the case. Thus, achieving a certain quality of education through desegregation remained a central theme, though courts were often reluctant to impose monetary orders.[38]

Thus, on the heels of increasingly challenging attempts to reduce inequalities in school funding for public school children based on federal and state constitutional equal protection claims, plaintiffs began to assert adequacy claims under the education clauses of state constitutions as a means to improve educational opportunities and achievement for all children.[39] This "third wave" of school finance litigation—adequacy litigation—shifted the focus away from trying to equalize the amount spent on each student and instead began questioning the sufficiency of school funding for students based on need.[40] Adequacy litigation is seen as a means of ensuring that all public-school children (regardless of race or zip code) receive an adequate level of education, with one court describing adequacy litigation as establishing "a constitutional floor of minimally adequate education to which public-school students are entitled."[41]

In some states, such as New York and Colorado, advocates turned to adequacy litigation in part because previous attempts at remedying the state's school finance system based on equity claims had failed.[42] But generally there was a growing belief that equalizing expenditures per student alone did not always result in equalizing educational opportunities for all public school children.[43] Indeed, other factors, including socioeconomic status and race, tended to impact educational achievement, essentially requiring certain school districts "to spend more than average simply to provide average educational opportunities."[44] How courts would address the disparities among school districts and, particularly, the special needs of at-risk student populations in primarily low-wealth districts that enroll high concentrations of minority and low income children, would come to mark the success of adequacy litigation at securing equal educational opportunities for minority and at-risk students.

As we reflect on the decades of adequacy litigation, and particularly as we consider how to employ adequacy litigation in pursuit of *Brown*'s promise of equal educational opportunities for all schoolchildren, three major issues present themselves. First, defining an adequate education is complex and problematic. By applying the lowest level of academic achievement to the definition of an "adequate education," state courts essentially gut the constitutional rights at stake. Second, the identity of the plaintiffs can affect the outcome of adequacy litigation substantially. Evidence of mixed success in higher funded districts enrolling smaller numbers of at-risk students may mask the real challenges high poverty schools and at-risk students face, leaving courts uncertain how to receive and weigh evidence of achievement in determining adequacy claims. Third, courts can be reluctant to exercise their broad remedial powers, even when fully justified in doing so. Each of these shortcomings, however, can be effectively addressed by both litigants and the courts, bringing us closer to *Brown*'s promise of equal educational opportunities for all.

PROBLEMS WITH DEFINING AN ADEQUATE EDUCATION

Adequacy claims originate from the education clauses of state constitutions, which require state legislatures to provide for a public education system using terms such as "thorough and efficient," "adequate," or "ample."[45] While few can legitimately dispute that all children deserve a minimally adequate education, the real challenges in trying to achieve equal educational opportunities through adequacy litigation begin with defining what constitutes an adequate education.[46]

Some states turn to their own state-established standards when interpreting the meaning of an adequate education. But one of the inherent problems in using states' educational standards to define a constitutionally adequate education is that states may set the bar low for an accredited education and, in turn, fund high-poverty, high-minority schools only up to that level.[47] In 1995, the Texas Supreme Court equated the provision of an adequate education with state accreditation standards.[48] This was particularly problematic because the state created the accreditation standards to ensure that most school districts met them, not to ensure that students were receiving an adequate education.[49] The court did hold that the Texas Legislature's discretion was not limitless, stating the legislature could be held liable if it "define[d] what constitutes a general diffusion of knowledge so low as to avoid its obligation to make suitable provision imposed by article VII, section 1" of the Texas Constitution (the Education Clause).[50] Nevertheless, in 2005, despite a vast record showing significant underperformance of minority and at-risk students, the Texas Supreme Court found compelling the fact that most plaintiff school districts were accredited and held the system constitutionally adequate.[51] Similarly, the Kansas Supreme Court employed this perspective until 2003, when it held the legislature did not have unfettered discretion and the plaintiffs should be able to prove that achievement gaps based on race and socioeconomic status—among other evidence—demonstrate an inadequate and unsuitable education.[52]

Courts that have had greater success in weighing educational opportunities in adequacy cases tend to invoke prudential-type standards for an adequate education that may rely on state standards but that, importantly, invoke meaningful standards that withstand the test of time.[53] One of the early, landmark adequacy decisions was *Rose v. Council for Better Education* out of Kentucky. There, plaintiffs representing poor school districts alleged that the Kentucky school finance system was so inadequate and inequitable as to result "in an inefficient system of common school education in violation" of the Kentucky Constitution and the equal protection and due process clauses of the Fourteenth Amendment.[54] In *Rose*, the Supreme Court of Kentucky credited the trial court's findings that Kentucky's school financing system was unconstitutional because "students in property poor school districts are offered a minimal level of educational opportunities, which is inferior to those offered to students in more affluent districts."[55] The trial court referred to this disparate treatment as "'invidious' discrimination, based on the place of a student's residence."[56]

However, what distinguishes *Rose* from earlier school finance litigation based on equal protection claims is that the Supreme Court of Kentucky further recognized that problems within Kentucky's school system could not simply be addressed through financial equalization between districts.[57] For example, the court noted that "a substantial difference in the curricula offered in the poorer districts contrasts with that of the richer districts, particularly in the areas of foreign language, science, mathematics, music and art."[58] This recognition that providing an adequate education included more than just accounting for particular financial inputs into a given school district led the court to establish a standards-based definition of what it would mean for a child in Kentucky to achieve an "efficient" education for state constitutional purposes. Other state courts later adopted Kentucky's definition of an "efficient" education or referenced it as a basis when defining what constitutes an adequate education.[59] Using such prudential standards not only avoids arbitrarily setting accreditation standards too low, but also gives clearer and lasting guidance to state legislatures, litigants, and the courts when addressing the important issue of adequate funding.

CHOOSING THE "RIGHT" PLAINTIFFS

Critics of school finance cases often lament the fact that advocates fail to be more selective in choosing the plaintiffs and claims that more closely align with the denial of equal educational opportunities.[60] This can be a great concern where claims that the education of all students in a given state or school district is insufficiently funded for purposes of achieving an adequate education may cloud the reality that low-wealth districts with high concentrations of minority and low-income children are facing serious challenges to provide the caliber of education that wealthier plaintiff districts are already achieving.[61] Of course, with substantial education budget cuts made by state legislatures in recent years forcing all districts in a given state to cut teachers and educational programs while imposing additional mandates and raising educational demands on students, the delivery of an adequate education to all students may be at risk.[62] However, when courts are receiving evidence of mixed success in public schools based on the performance of non-at-risk students, the compelling case for economically disadvantaged, English-language learner, and minority students can be lost.

For example, the Texas Supreme Court dismissed an overwhelming record of contrasting achievement between at-risk and minority students and non-at-risk and majority students in a case brought by over 300 school districts asserting general adequacy claims. There, the school districts challenged the adequacy of the Texas school finance system, ranging from the property-poor Edgewood ISD plaintiff-intervenor districts to the property-wealth districts located in Alamo Heights, Plano, and Highland Park.[63] The court acknowledged the wide achievement gaps between white students and their Latino, black, and economically disadvantaged peers, as well as large gaps in dropout and graduation rates.[64] The court also noted that the number of state-standardized tests administered also increased, as well as the punitive measures applied to students through the expansion of high-stakes testing.[65] As a result, districts incurred significant costs for remediation, including "summer school, remedial class, curriculum specialists, [and] reduced class-size."[66] The court then put aside this striking evidence, self-selecting evidence of two outputs to hold that the system was adequate: finding that Texas scores on the National Assessment for Educational Progress (NAEP) had improved relative to other states and overall state-standardized test scores (Texas Assessment of Knowledge and Skills, or TAKS).[67] Ultimately, on the adequacy claim, the court held: "we cannot conclude that the Legislature has acted arbitrarily in structuring and funding the public education system so that school districts are not reasonably able to afford all students the access to education and the educational opportunity to accomplish a general diffusion of knowledge."[68]

Because some adequacy cases have proven more effective in fulfilling the promise of *Brown* by bringing specific claims on behalf of at-risk and minority students, in 2011, the Mexican American Legal Defense and Educational Fund (MALDEF) filed suit against Texas again, bringing stronger, more specific adequacy claims on behalf of economically disadvantaged and ELL plaintiff students. Following a three-month trial, the district court held in favor of the at-risk students' adequacy claim.[69] The Travis County district court reaffirmed its seminal ruling in favor of the at-risk students' adequacy claim after re-opening the evidence to consider the impact of 2013 legislative changes and holding a three-week evidentiary hearing.[70] The court supported its conclusions with 364 single-spaced pages of findings, including hundreds of findings highlighting the educational challenges facing at-risk students and the schools serving the growing at-risk population. Undoubtedly, this decision will be appealed, but the trial court's decision is an important step.[71]

Litigation victories based on similar theories have occurred in California and North Carolina, among others. In *Williams v. California*,[72] economically disadvantaged and minority students enrolled in mostly segregated schools filed suit under the California Constitution arguing that they were being provided unequal tools to acquire a fundamental education. These included qualified teachers, adequate facilities in both condition and space, and instructional materials. After four years of litigation, the case eventually settled with five bills signed into law that guaranteed California's students "appropriate teacher assignment, sufficient instructional materials, and facilities in good repair."[73] The settlement also created standards and accountability measures, which included school district oversight and assistance to the lowest performing schools, which led to increased student performance in those schools.[74]

In North Carolina, plaintiffs representing property-poor school districts and plaintiff-intervenors representing wealthy school districts both alleged that the North Carolina school finance system was inadequate and that the state denied students "their fundamental constitutional right to equal educational opportunities."[75] The trial court determined that the North Carolina school finance system "is valid, sound and flexible enough to provide for the delivery of adequate funding to all school systems in North Carolina . . . so that they may provide each child with the equal opportunity to obtain a sound basic education," but at the same time recognized that "[e]conomically disadvantaged children, more so than economically advantaged children, need opportunities and services over and above those provided to the general student population in order to put them in a position to obtain an equal opportunity to receive a sound basic education."[76] The trial court specifically identified poverty, racial/ethnic minority status, and lack of English language proficiency among the socioeconomic factors that "place students at risk of educational failure."[77] As the court found, in "1998–1999, the [end of grade] test results for mathematics and reading combined for the third grade by race showed that . . . 46.4% (680) of American Indian children scored below Level III; 56.1% (17,728) of black children scored below Level III; [and] 49.8% (1,462) of Hispanic children scored below Level III," while only "25.6% (16,068) of white children scored below Level III."[78] For the same school year, in grades 3–8, "79.2% of white students . . . were performing at grade level (Level III or above) in reading and math as compared to 48.5% of black students, 55.5% of Native American students and 55.6% of Hispanic Students."[79]

The court next identified quality pre-kindergarten programs as "an effective means of increasing the performance of low-income and otherwise at-risk students."[80] Based on the facts presented, the court ultimately concluded that at-risk children in North Carolina were "being denied their fundamental constitutional right to receive the equal opportunity to a sound basic education" because of "the failure of the State to provide early childhood education in the form of quality pre-kindergarten educational programs."[81] The trial court ordered that the state provide pre-kindergarten educational programs for all at-risk children that qualify for the program.[82] These cases, along with other targeted adequacy cases in states like New Jersey, Kansas, Wyoming, and South Carolina, demonstrate that courts may be more receptive to stronger, more focused claims filed on behalf of minority and at-risk students than more generalized adequacy claims.

THE PROBLEMS WITH REMEDIES

A major problem with remedying the lingering inequalities and inadequacies in state school finance systems is the courts' concern with overstepping their judicial power and encroaching upon the legislature's power to enact laws. Typically, courts have broad remedial powers to address legal wrongs. Where a constitutional violation is proven, courts have the power to declare the acts in question unconstitutional, to order injunctive relief, and to ensure that any harm proven is redressed.[83] However, in education cases, state courts often defer substantially (if not wholly) to state legislatures in remedying the constitutional violation.[84] Like the federal courts in *Brown* and other school desegregation cases, state courts in school finance cases are reluctant to issue injunctions specifying remedies. Although state courts should defer to the legislative branch in enacting a remedy because they are the branch of government principally assigned to establishing public school finance systems, courts can appropriately influence those remedies by: first, issuing more specific declaratory and injunctive relief aimed at the harms shown in court; and second, by reviewing the legislative remedies to ensure that they correct the violations found, as opposed to back-door deals that typically influence remedies. These actions are not uncommon practices of the courts and should help ensure that those students harmed by the inequitable and inadequate school finance systems are provided with relief that ultimately leads to the provision of equal educational opportunities.

Critics of school finance cases often argue that the courts are ill-prepared to oversee school finance reform because of the inherent politics and varying interests involved.[85] They point to protracted litigation as a sign of the ineffectiveness of school finance cases as a remedy to ensuring equal educational opportunities. However, none of these arguments have merit. First, virtually every legislative act is subject to political wagering and diverse interests. Whether the issue involves redistricting, regulation of public utilities, driver's licenses, employment, taxes, or the like, these matters are subject to public debate. However, if a state legislature adopts a redistricting plan that purposefully draws boundaries to dilute minority voting strength, should those actions be subject to judicial review under federal or state constitutions and statutes? If a state legislature arbitrarily and unnecessarily regulates private companies offering public utilities, should those actions be subject to review? Certainly, the answer is *"yes,"* and the same logic applies to school finance litigation.

Similarly, the fact that a small minority of states have engaged in protracted school finance litigation does not mean that courts are ill-prepared to handle and resolve school funding cases. If that were the case, we possibly could have seen a reversion to "separate but equal" de jure segregation in public schools. Instead, we have witnessed some courts relying on strong, judicially manageable standards and then enforcing those standards when necessary either in the remedial phase or in separate litigation filed years later.

The Kansas school finance cases illustrate courts effectively exercising their judicial powers to interpret state actions against the constitution, identify judicially manageable standards, and enforce their orders when necessary to ensure equal educational opportunities for at-risk and minority students. The *Mock* case was the first among the contemporary school funding cases alleging that the state had failed to "make suitable provision" for education as required by the Kansas Constitution for students in lower-wealth school districts.[86] In a pretrial opinion, in 1991, the district court held that each child must be given an educational opportunity that is equal to that made available to every other child under the state constitution.[87] The legislature responded by adopting a new school finance system in 1992 that provided low-wealth school districts with additional revenue while cutting taxes, but various groups of plaintiffs sued, some alleging that the reforms did not go far enough, others that they went too far. In 1994, the Kansas Supreme Court upheld the constitutionality of the school finance system and established standards to weigh future challenges. In defining a "suitable" education, the Kansas Supreme Court relied on the legislature's goals and a constitutional provision requiring the legislature to "provide for intellectual, educational, vocational and scientific improvement by establishing and maintaining public schools."[88] The court also held that "the issue of suitability is not stagnant" and "must be closely monitored."[89]

These standards appropriately guided the Kansas courts in subsequent cases. Each time that the legislature defaulted on its constitutional obligation to provide a suitable education, the courts held the state responsible.[90] And each time the courts held the evidence demonstrated that the state had satisfied the standard, the courts denied plaintiffs relief.[91]

The Kansas courts also steadfastly ensured that the remedies targeted the violations. Following the *Mock* case, the legislature's new school finance system lowered property taxes 38% and reduced the equity gaps between property-poor and property-rich districts.[92] By 2003, the state legislature had scaled back its school funding formulas and the Kansas Supreme Court affirmed a lower court ruling finding the system inadequate and unsuitable for mid- and large-size school districts with high proportions of minority, at-risk, and special education students.[93]

The court also cited the state for basing its formulas on "former spending levels and political compromise," instead of actual costs, which particularly impacted weighting factors for bilingual education, special education and at-risk students, among others.[94] When the state failed to increase the funding sufficiently, and failed to base funding on actual costs, the Court ordered the legislature to commit $285 million for the 2005–06 school year and retained jurisdiction pending a legislative cost study.[95] In 2006, Kansas passed legislation intended to increase funding for at-risk and ELL students, among others, and decrease inequities between school districts over a three-year period.[96] The Kansas Supreme Court concluded that these targeted increases, though not perfect, substantially complied with its mandates and relinquished jurisdiction.[97]

Kansas is not alone. The Wyoming courts have also established clear judicially manageable standards for the state legislature to follow in order for the state to meet its constitutional obligation of providing "a complete and uniform system of public instruction" and retained jurisdiction when necessary to monitor the remedy.[98] New Jersey is often criticized for its litigious history, but in fact, it represents a dogged approach by the New Jersey Supreme Court in holding the legislature to its duty of curing constitutional deficiencies identified by the court.[99]

However, other courts have struggled to ensure equal educational opportunities in school finance lawsuits by failing to maintain strong judicial standards and/or to enforce or apply effectively their standards. For example, in Texas, the state supreme court established a strong standard for equity claims in *Edgewood v. Kirby*[100] and dutifully applied this standard when the legislature's next school finance plan arbitrarily exempted 132 extremely wealthy school districts from the plan, holding the system again unconstitutional.[101] But over the years, the Texas Supreme Court seemingly watered down this standard by first requiring equity only up to the cost of providing an adequate education;[102] then accepting a nine-cent tax advantage in favor of property-wealthy school districts as satisfying the equity standard;[103] and exempting the extremely property-wealthy school districts who were held harmless from the imposition of the *Edgewood I* mandate based on the state's word that it would eventually phase out those school district's substantial equity advantage.[104] For the substantial number of at-risk and minority school children enrolled in the state's poorest school districts, the promise of competing on a level playing field remains just that—a promise, unfulfilled.

Texas's handling of adequacy claims also provides little recourse due to the courts' application of the standard. Like the Kansas court, the Texas Supreme Court created a strong, judicially enforceable standard for adequacy claims tied to state statutory goals for public education and holding that the legislature cannot set the bar for adequacy so low that students do not acquire a general diffusion of knowledge.[105] But as with the equity claims, the court struggled to apply the standard appropriately to the facts in the case. The court first dismissed glaring inequities and inadequacies related to educational inputs, holding that the adequacy of the system depended on outputs.[106] Then, after acknowledging stark achievement gaps among minority students and special populations and depressing dropout and graduation rates, the court noted slight improvements in student scores on the state and national standardized tests, ultimately ruling "we cannot conclude that the Legislature has acted arbitrarily in structuring and funding the public education system so that school districts are not reasonably able to afford all students the access to education and the educational opportunity to accomplish a general diffusion of knowledge."[107] The Court ultimately held the system unconstitutional under a separate constitutional provision outlawing statewide property taxes, but that led to a remedy that cut property taxes but did not necessarily increase access to educational opportunities.[108]

The latest school finance lawsuit filed in Texas may signal whether the Texas Supreme Court intends to emphasize the importance of providing equal educational opportunities for all students. This case includes a more specific challenge to the arbitrary and inadequate funding for at-risk students filed by the Edgewood ISD plaintiffs, as well as a claim that the system is inequitable for property-poor school districts. The district court applied the *Edgewood V* standards to the substantial record evidencing large and growing achievement gaps between minority and at-risk students and deepening equity gaps between property-poor and property wealthy districts. In its 2013 ruling following a three-month trial, the state trial court held the system unconstitutionally inequitable for property-poor districts and inadequate for at-risk students, and it reaffirmed this ruling in August 2014 after considering 2013 legislative changes and conducting an extensive evidentiary hearing.[109]

The New York court's difficulty with ensuring equal educational opportunities through its adequacy ruling resulted largely from its deference to the New York Legislature, as seen in the *Campaign for Fiscal Equity v. State* litigation.[110] Arkansas also struggled to effectuate a timely and effective remedy through adequacy litigation. In *Lake View School District No. 25 v. Huckabee,* plaintiff school districts successfully challenged Arkansas's failure to provide its students with an adequate education as guaranteed by the state constitution.[111] However, as in New York, the Supreme Court of Arkansas hesitated in ordering targeted, concrete remedies to address the constitutional deprivation, despite plaintiffs' request for "specific remedies against the State."[112] Only after the court recalled its mandate because the legislature had failed to persist with its own remedy, did the legislature comply over the long term.[113]

Finally, North Carolina's courts have struggled with providing the legislature too much leniency, ultimately reversing the trial court's order that the state provide pre-kindergarten educational programs to all at-risk children who qualify and, instead, deferring to the legislature's plan.[114] The Superior Court did, however, later intervene again when the state cut education funding and scaled back on its pre-K program for at-risk students.

In sum, when courts retreat from targeted remedial orders, they run the risk that state legislatures will fail to address the true disparities that keep school finance systems from providing the constitutional guarantees of an adequate education to all public school children, particularly at-risk students, and, worse, that these unaddressed disparities will increase the divide between those students receiving an adequate education and those left behind—leading to more litigation.[115] Even those courts that have deferred remedies to state legislatures have recognized that if a state legislature fails to remedy constitutional deprivations "or ha[s] consistently shown an inability to do so," then a court "is empowered to provide relief by imposing a specific remedy and instructing the recalcitrant state actors to implement it."[116] By doing so, courts can help finally achieve the equality of educational opportunity promised in *Brown* and the constitutional right to an adequate education for all school children, regardless of race or background, as guaranteed by the states.

¿Dónde Vamos? (Where Do We Go From Here?)

Many commentators would likely agree that if we had both integrated schools and equalized and adequately funded school finance systems, achievement and opportunity gaps would close and we would be closer to realizing the dream of *Brown* than ever before.[117] Unfortunately, given the current precedents in both school desegregation and school finance litigation, that is not likely to occur. However, none of the efforts should be abandoned either. In 2006, when a Dallas ISD school principal used English as a Second Language classes as a proxy to segregate Latino and African American students, it was *Brown* and its progeny that stopped the within-school segregation.[118] When Kansas and Texas, among others, cut education funding and funded students differently based on the zip code they lived in, it was, and will be, the state courts that restored, and will continue to restore, the rights to an equitable and adequate education for impoverished and minority students through the state education clauses.[119]

For school integration advocates, race-neutral efforts to integrate schools must be considered alongside active school desegregation litigation. And, while the impact of school finance litigation may be improved by being tried by those students truly injured and remedied more appropriately by the courts as described further above, practitioners and advocates must begin to think beyond the box of dollars and cents. A promising educational opportunity case was filed recently by MALDEF, *Martinez v. New Mexico*.[120] The plaintiffs are 51 parents and at-risk public school students. Their complaint presents adequacy claims centered on economically disadvantaged, ELL, and special education students; substantive due process claims; equal protection claims; claims based on the deprivation of a multicultural education; claims calling for the monitoring of expenditures; and claims targeting teacher evaluations and school accountability systems that are driving quality teachers and administrators away from high need students and schools. If successful, the *Martinez* lawsuit could result in the most comprehensive remedy to date.

Conclusion

Although adequacy litigation has made important advances, it also has substantial limitations. First, courts often establish a minimal floor when defining an adequate education and its funding component, which does nothing to address the disparities in access to resources between low-wealth districts that often enroll high concentrations of minority and low income children, and high-wealth districts. By applying the lowest level of academic achievement to the definition of an "adequate education," especially when relying on minimal state accreditation standards or no standards at all, state courts essentially gut the constitutional rights at stake. Second, adequacy lawsuits are often brought by a plethora of school districts and school children ranging widely in demographics and funding. While this may seem like a logical political maneuver, evidence of success in higher-funded plaintiff districts enrolling few at-risk students may mask the real challenges high poverty schools and at-risk students face, leaving courts uncertain how to receive and weigh evidence of achievement in determining adequacy claims. Third, favorable court decisions holding school finance systems unconstitutional often leave it up to state legislatures to remedy the violations, which, in turn, can politicize the ruling. Consequently, where the evidence presented during trial often highlights the struggles of at-risk and minority students, the remedy stage seldom addresses those students' specific educational needs with, for example, increased funding and opportunities targeted at those students. As a result, many of the cyclical problems with unequal educational opportunities and arbitrary, inadequate funding systems are never addressed.

Thus, 60 years after *Brown*, equal educational opportunities remain elusive and achievement gaps remain a grave concern. But neither school finance litigation nor school desegregation litigation, standing alone, was ever meant to close the achievement gaps. The fact is that the courts can only do so much, and much more must be done by policymakers, advocates, civil rights leaders, educators and parents—in conjunction with litigation when necessary—to prioritize public education and level up the playing field so that all students have the opportunity to reach their full potential. While *Brown* indeed operated as the icebreaker, it was, and remains, an unfulfilled promise but one that the public can ill afford to give up.

David Hinojosa is the Regional Counsel for MALDEF's Southwest Office in San Antonio, Texas. **Karolina Walters** is a former staff attorney for MALDEF's Southwest Office in San Antonio, Texas. The chapter is excerpted from a law review article by the same title forthcoming in the MICHIGAN STATE LAW REVIEW (2014–2015).

NOTES

David Hinojosa has served as MALDEF's lead counsel for the "Edgewood ISD Plaintiffs" in the last two Texas school finance cases, in the first statewide adequacy/educational opportunity challenge filed by 51 parents and at-risk children in New Mexico, *Martinez v. State of New Mexico*, and on behalf of Plaintiff-Intervenor at-risk students and parents in Colorado's first adequacy case, *Lobato/Ortega v. Colorado*. He also serves as MALDEF's lead counsel in a number of school desegregation, equal educational opportunity language, and higher education access cases. During Karolina Walters' tenure at MALDEF, she served as counsel to amici defending the University of Texas-Austin's holistic admissions policy against a Fourteenth Amendment Equal Protection challenge, *Fisher v. University of Texas*. She also worked on school desegregation and equal educational opportunity language cases. The opinions expressed in this article are those of the authors alone.

1. Molly Hunter, *Requiring States to Offer a Quality Education to All Students*, HUMAN RIGHTS MAGAZINE (2005).

2. James S. Liebman, *Desegregating Politics: "All-Out" School Desegregation Explained*, 90 COLUMBIA LAW REVIEW 1463, 1475 (1990).

3. Brown v. Board of Education, 347 U.S. 483 (1954).

4. Plessy v. Ferguson, 163 U.S. 537 (1896).

5. Ellis Case, *A Dream Deferred*, NEWSWEEK 1 (May 11, 2004).

6. Lynn Huntley, *Foreword*, in ROBERT L. CARTER, ON THE RIGHT SIDE OF HISTORY: LESSONS FROM *BROWN*, 3 (Southern Education Foundation 2004).

7. Michael Heise, *Litigated Learning and the Limits of Law*, 57 VANDERBILT LAW REVIEW 2417, 2421 (2004) ("*Brown* rendered state-enforced 'whites only' public schools to little more than a painful relic of American history").

8. James Ryan, *The Supreme Court and Voluntary Integration*, 121 HARVARD LAW REVIEW 131, 132 (2007) (citing Brown v. Board of Education, 349 U.S. 294, 301 (1955) ("Brown II")).

9. Fisher v. Tucson Unified School District, 652 F.3d 1131 (9th Cir. 2011) (reversing the lower

court's declaration of unitary status due to evidentiary record replete with evidence showing school district's lack of good faith compliance); NAACP Legal Defense and Educational Fund, *Fifth Circuit Refuses to Dismiss Longstanding School Desegregation Case in St. Martin Parish, Louisiana* (June 24, 2014) (discussing the case and also the fact that the NAACP LDF currently has 100 school desegregation cases on its docket). James Ryan, *Schools, Race, and Money*, 109 YALE LAW JOURNAL 249, 252 (1999) ("School finance litigation is . . . often depicted both as a means of moving beyond race as the salient issue in education reform and as an effective way to achieve educational equity and adequacy for disadvantaged students from all racial and ethnic backgrounds"). Other areas of education law litigated to ensure substantial reforms and equal educational opportunities—not discussed in this chapter—include enforcement of the Equal Educational Opportunities Act of 1974, Section 1703(f), which requires that states and local education agencies take appropriate action to ensure that ELL students have access to quality language programs implemented with the necessary resources so that the students can "overcome their language barriers"; and enforcement of the Individuals with Disabilities Education Act, which ensures services to children with disabilities and governs how states and local education agencies provide intervention and services to students with disabilities.

10. William S. Koski, *Courthouses vs. Statehouses?* 109 MICHIGAN LAW REVIEW 923, 926 (2011) (citing ERIC A. HANUSHEK & ALFRED A. LINDSETH, SCHOOLHOUSES, COURTHOUSES, AND STATEHOUSES: SOLVING THE FUNDING-ACHIEVEMENT PUZZLE IN AMERICA'S PUBLIC SCHOOLS (Princeton University Press 2009).

11. See, for example, Michael A. Rebell, *Educational Adequacy, Democracy, and the Courts*, in NATIONAL RESEARCH COUNCIL, ACHIEVING HIGH EDUCATIONAL STANDARDS FOR ALL: CONFERENCE SUMMARY, 218, 221 (National Academy Press 2002).

12. Michael W. Combs & Gwendolyn M. Combs, *Revisiting* Brown v. Board of Education: *A Cultural, Historical-Legal, and Political Perspective*, 47 HOWARD LAW JOURNAL 627, 628 (2004) (discussing three different research camps on influence of Supreme Court's decision in *Brown*); Orley Ashenfelter, William J. Collins, & Albert Yoon, *Evaluating the Role of* Brown vs. Board of Education *in School Equalization, Desegregation, and the Income of African Americans*, NBER Working Paper No. 11394 (June 2005) (noting that Southern-born black male workers who completed their education in the years immediately preceding desegregation earned less income compared to those who followed behind them in school by just a few years).

13. Despite the complementary goals of securing equal educational opportunities for schoolchildren of color and of poverty, advocates in school desegregation cases have often failed to collaborate on joint efforts on school finance advocates. Kristi Bowman, *A New Strategy for Pursuing Racial and Ethnic Equality in Public Schools*, 1 DUKE FORUM FOR LAW & SOCIAL CHANGE 47, 52 (2009). This may be due to the fact that school desegregation advocates see school finance supporters as essentially arguing for separate but equal, or separate but adequate, schools. Jeannie Oakes & Martin Lipton, *"Schools That Shock the Conscience"*: Williams v. California *and the Struggle for Education on Equal Terms Fifty Years After* Brown, 15 BERKELEY LA RAZA LAW JOURNAL 25, 26 (2004) (comparing the arguments for equal educational tools essential for a fundamental education in the school finance case, *Williams v. California*, to the arguments of school desegregation lawyers in the era of separate but equal). This may also occur because some actors in school finance cases, as well as school desegregation litigators, fail to see school finance as a civil rights issue; or because school finance advocates often must "accept and

ignore" segregated schools, which detracts attention away desegregating and integrating schools. Greg Winter, *50 Years After* Brown, *the Issue Is Often Money*, NEW YORK TIMES 1 (May 17, 2003) (quoting *Brown* attorney Jack Greenberg as discounting financing cases as not being adequate and that "[i]ntegration is the only way to do that"; and quoting Campaign for Fiscal Equity's school finance attorney Michael Rebell as countering that "[t]he fact that school districts remain very separate is a reality that the Supreme Court has allowed. . . . This is the world we're living in"). MALDEF is one of the very few organizations to combat lack of equal educational opportunities using state constitutional clauses for school finance cases, Title VI and the Fourteenth Amendment for school desegregation cases, and the Equal Educational Opportunities Act of 1974 for language discrimination. James A. Ferg-Cadima, Mexican American Legal Defense and Educational Fund, *Black, White, and Brown: Latino School Desegregation Efforts in the Pre- and Post-*Brown v. Board of Education *Era*, 29–30 (2004).

14. The authors are unsure if this description as a "first wave" is accurate because only a handful of cases were filed in federal court during this era, and those ceased—in large part—in 1973 following the Rodriguez decision. James E. Ryan, *Standards, Testing, and School Finance Litigation*, 86 TEXAS LAW REVIEW 1223, 1229 (2008).

15. Rebell, *Educational Adequacy* at 224 (citing McInnis v. Shapiro, 293 F. Supp. 327 (N.D. Ill. 1968), where the plaintiffs argued that the Illinois school funding system's minimum foundational funding was inadequate for disadvantaged urban students).

16. The number of students and protestors was estimated between 300 and 3,000. Cynthia E. Orozco, Rodriguez v. San Antonio ISD, Texas State Historical Association (2013) (estimating 400 protestors); Ron White, *3000 Ask Reforms in Walkout*, SAN ANTONIO LIGHT 1 (May 16, 1968) (estimating 3,000 protestors); Doris Wright, *Edgewood Students Protest*, SAN ANTONIO EXPRESS NEWS 1 (May 17, 1968) (estimating 300 protestors).

17. Rodriguez v. San Antonio Independent School District, 337 F. Supp. 280, 282.

18. Ibid., 282 n.3.

19. JOSÉ A. CÁRDENAS, TEXAS SCHOOL FINANCE REFORM: AN IDRA PERSPECTIVE, 9 (Intercultural Development and Research Association 1997) (noting that in 1969, less than half of Edgewood's teachers met minimum certification requirements and the teacher turnover rate was 33%).

20. Rodriguez, 337 F. Supp. 281–82.

21. San Antonio Independent School District v. Rodriguez, 411 U.S. 1 (1973).

22. Ibid., 35.

23. Ibid., 50–55.

24. Ibid., 71, 133 n.100.

25. Ryan, *Standards*, 1229. Plaintiffs in *Serrano I* asserted both state and federal constitutional claims. Serrano v. Priest, 18 Cal. 3d 728 (Cal. 1976) (Serrano II).

26. Serrano v. Priest, 5 Cal.3d 584, 585, 589–90 (1971) (Serrano I).

27. Serrano II, 18 Cal. 3d 765–66.

28. Rebell, *Educational Adequacy*, 227.

29. New Jersey Constitution, art. 8, § IV, ¶ 1.

30. Robinson v. Cahill, 62 N.J. 473, 515 (N.J. 1973).

31. Education Law Center, *The History of* Abbott v. Burke (2013).

32. Rebell, *Educational Adequacy*, 226.

33. Brigham v. State, 166 Vt. 246, 256 (Vermont Supreme Court 1997) ("[W]e are simply unable to fathom a legitimate governmental purpose to justify the gross inequities in educational opportunities evident from the record. The distribution of a resource as precious as educational opportunity may not have as its determining force the mere *fortuity* of a child's residence. It requires no particular constitutional expertise to recognize the capriciousness of such a system").

34. Rebell, *Educational Adequacy*, 227; Unified School District 229 v. Kansas, 885 P.2d 1170, 1184–85 (Kansas Supreme Court 1994) (citing 12 state court opinions rejecting equity claims). It has been reported that the "adequacy" movement overtook the "equity" movement in the late 1980s. Rebell, *Educational Adequacy*, 228. However, this statement is not entirely accurate. Many of the cases termed "adequacy" cases were more like "equity" cases because fundamental to the claims and evidence at issue in many of those cases was the disparate access to resources between school districts. Edgewood Independent School District v. Kirby, 777 S.W.2d 391, 397 (Texas Supreme Court 1989) (Edgewood I) (holding that students in all school districts must have substantially equal access to similar revenue at similar tax effort—a ruling based on equity); Ryan, *Standards*, 1235-37 (describing the evidence and analysis of unequal educational opportunities in "adequacy" cases, including those in Montana, Texas, Tennessee, Arizona, New Jersey, Arkansas, and Vermont. As Ryan notes, "[t]he mislabeling of some cases, moreover, has given the false impression that almost all school finance decisions since 1989 have been about adequacy as opposed to equity").

35. Edgewood I, 777 S.W.2d 397.

36. Ibid., 393

37. Although undoubtedly the inherent evil of separating children on the basis of race alone would have been attacked.

38. The Kansas City, Missouri desegregation case is a notable exception. The Supreme Court discussed the expenditures in its third opinion in the *Jenkins* case. Missouri v. Jenkins 515 U.S. 70 (1995).

39. Campaign for Fiscal Equity ("CFE") v. State, 719 N.Y.S. 2d 475, 481 (2001) (describing how the previous school finance litigation in New York "was among the majority of cases that found that unequal funding of school districts did not violate state equal protection clauses"); Jared S. Buszin, *Beyond School Finance: Refocusing Education Reform Litigation to Realize the Deferred Dream of Education Equality and Adequacy*, 62 EMORY LAW JOURNAL 1613, 1620–21 (2013).

40. CFE, 719 N.Y.S. 2d 481; Buszin, *Beyond School Finance*, 1621.

41. CFE, 719 N.Y.S. 2d 481; Buszin, *Beyond School Finance*, 1621 (describing adequacy litigation as litigation wherein "courts have interpreted the education clauses in state constitutions to require states to provide a substantive education that does not fall below a minimally adequate level"); Paul L. Trachtenberg, *Beyond Educational Adequacy: Looking Backward and Forward Through the Lens of New Jersey*, 4 STANFORD JOURNAL OF CIVIL RIGHTS & CIVIL LIBERTIES 411, 420–21 (2008) (describing New Jersey's definition of a "thorough and efficient" or "adequate" education as "requir[ing] . . . an equal educational opportunity for all that 'must be understood to embrace that educational opportunity which is needed in the contemporary setting to equip a child for his role as a citizen and as a competitor in the labor market,' but not the best possible education" (quoting Abbott v. Burke ("Abbott I"), 495 A.2d 376, 382 (New Jersey Supreme Court 1985)).

42. CFE, 719 N.Y.S. 2d at 479; Buszin, *Beyond School Finance*, 1620; James E. Ryan, *The*

Influence of Race in School Finance Reform, MICHIGAN LAW REVIEW 432, 450 (1999).

43. Rebell, *Educational Adequacy*, 227; Buszin, *Beyond School Finance*, 1630; Hoke County Board of Education v. State, 2000 WL 1639686, *56 (North Carolina Superior Court 2000) affirmed in part as modified and reversed in part under a different name, Hoke County Board of Education v. State, 358 N.C. 605 (North Carolina Supreme Court 2004) (crediting expert opinion "that throwing money at an education problem without having goals in place for the spending and a system of accountability to measure the effectiveness of the spendings is wasteful and not likely to result in improving student performance").

44. Ryan, *The Influence of Race*, 435 ("The greater needs of poor children, coupled with the greater costs of operating urban schools, virtually guarantee that urban schools will have to spend more than average simply to provide average educational opportunities"); Rebell, *Educational Adequacy*, 227; Buszin, *Beyond School Finance*, 1631.

45. Rebell, *Educational Adequacy*, 232; Buszin, *Beyond School Finance*, 1621–22.

46. Buszin, *Beyond School Finance*, 1622; Rebell, *Educational Adequacy*, 231.

47. Ryan, *Schools, Race, and Money*, 260 (stating that "[m]any school finance and school desegregation cases thus have become primarily concerned with obtaining sufficient funds to finance a basic level of education in the poorest and/or most racially isolated school districts").

48. Edgewood v. Meno, 917 S.W.2d 717, 730 (Texas Supreme Court 1995) (Edgewood IV).

49. Neeley v. West Orange Cove Consolidated Independent School District, 176 S.W.3d 746, 788 (Texas Supreme Court 2005) (noting that "the requirements for an 'academically acceptable' rating are set to assure, not that there will be a general diffusion of knowledge, but that almost every district will meet them").

50. Ibid., 784.

51. Neeley, 176 S.W.3d 791-92 (discussing the implications of accredited schools in striking down efficiency/ equity claims). Curiously though, the same court held the fact that school district were providing an accredited education did not preclude the court from holding the system in violation of article VIII, § 1(e) claim.

52. Montoy v. Kansas, 275 Kan. 145, 151–53 (Kansas Supreme Court 2003) (Montoy I).

53. Other courts use neither state nor prudential standards, serving no interest to the claims and evidence. In *Lobato v. Colorado*, the state supreme court used neither state standards nor prudential standards in determining what constitutes an adequate education. The trial court accepted the higher court's suggestion in a prior interlocutory appeal that it may "rely on the legislature's own pronouncements to develop the meaning of a 'thorough and uniform' system of education" and ultimately held the system "irrational, arbitrary, and severely underfunded." Lobato v. State, Case No. 2005CV4794, District Court Findings of Fact and Conclusions of Law at 182; 218 P.3d 358, 363 (Colorado Supreme Court 2009). Ignoring both the history surrounding the education clause and the standards and goals imposed by the Colorado General Assembly, the state supreme court used selective definitions to interpret the words "thorough" and "uniform," ultimately concluding the current system met the mandate because it was "of a quality marked by completeness, is comprehensive, and is consistent across the state." Compare Lobato v. State, 304 P.3d 1132, 1140 (Colorado Supreme Court 2013) (majority opinion) with Lobato, 218 P.3d 1151-60 (J. Hobbs dissenting) (criticizing majority for selective definitions for thorough and uniform).

54. Rose v. Council for Better Education, Inc., 790 S.W. 2d 186, 190 (Kentucky Supreme Court 1989).

55. Rose, 790 S.W. 2d 192.

56. Ibid.

57. Ibid., 197.

58. Ibid.

59. Rebell, *Educational Adequacy*, 235–36.

60. Martin R. West & Paul E. Peterson, *The Adequacy Lawsuit: A Critical Appraisal*, in SCHOOL MONEY TRIALS: THE LEGAL PURSUIT OF EDUCATIONAL ADEQUACY, 2 (Brookings Institution Press 2007) (arguing that even after judicial relief ordered, there is no guarantee that the funds will reach the students).

61. Buszin, *Beyond School Finance*, 1627 ("The academic performance of an average black or Hispanic student is equivalent to the performance of an average white student in the lowest quartile of white achievement").

62. Lobato, 304 P.3d 1150 (recognizing $1 billion cut to education); Patrick Michel, *5.4 Billion Spending Cut Already Takings a Toll on Schools*, TEXAS OBSERVER (March 19, 2012) (describing a $5.4 billion cut to the Texas education budget).

63. Neeley, 176 S.W.3d 751–52.

64. Ibid., 765–68.

65. Ibid., 765.

66. Ibid., 769.

67. Ibid., 789. The court apparently disregarded the fact that Texas ranked 37th among states.

68. Ibid., 789–90.

69. The Texas Taxpayer & Student Fairness Coalition v. Williams, 2013 WL 459357 (Travis County District Court 2013).

70. The Texas Taxpayer & Student Fairness Coalition v. Williams, 2014 WL 4243277 (Travis County District Court 2014).

71. The trial court also held the system overall was inadequate and unsuitable as a result of the increasing academic and testing standards, the substantial budget cuts, and growing economically disadvantaged and ELL student populations in Texas, but independently concluded the system was unconstitutional for at-risk students. Ibid.

72. Jeannie Oakes & Martin Lipton, *"Schools That Shock the Conscience": Williams v. California and the Struggle for Education on Equal Terms Fifty Years After Brown*, 15 BERKELEY LA RAZA LAW JOURNAL 25, 25–26 (2004).

73. Sally Chung, ACLU Foundation of Southern California, Williams v. California, *Lessons from Nine Years of Implementation*, 6 (2013).

74. Ibid., 7 (report also finding that thousands of textbooks were being provided in the classroom, and a decrease in the number of classes taught by "misassigned teachers").

75. Hoke County Board of Education, 2000 WL *1.

76. Ibid., *91, 97.

77. Ibid., *94.

78. Ibid., *99, *10 (determining that academic performance less than Level III "is a constitutionally unacceptable minimum standard").

79. Ibid.

80. Ibid., *106.

81. Ibid., *107; ibid., *107 ("The absence of such pre-school intervention for at-risk children materially affects their being able to have the equal opportunity to obtain a sound basic education from the start of their academic ladder").

82. Ibid.

83. Montoy III, 112 P.3d 931 ("Nor should doubts about the court's equitable power to spur legislative action or to reject deficient legislation impede judicious over-sight. An active judicial role in monitoring remedy formulation is well-rooted in the courts' equitable powers. As long as such power is exercised only after legislative noncompliance, it is entirely appropriate.") (citing *Unfulfilled Promise: School Finance Remedies and State Courts*, 104 HARVARD LAW REVIEW 1072, 1087–88 (1991)).

84. Buszin, *Beyond School Finance*, 1624-25; United States v. State of Texas, 680 F.2d 356, 372-74 (5th Cir. 1982) (holding injunctive relief moot in EEOA language rights case where district court's injunctive relief should have given deference to consideration of new laws passed by Texas Legislature in addressing statutory violations).

85. For example, consider Koski, *Courthouses & Statehouses*, and HANUSHEK & LINDSETH, SCHOOLHOUSES, COURTHOUSES, AND STATEHOUSES.

86. Kansas has been the subject of approximately eight separate school finance lawsuits, and about ten state supreme court opinions, over the past 45 years. United School District 229 v. Kansas, 885 P.2d 1170, 1175-78 (Kansas Supreme Court 1994) (describing history of school finance litigation up to 1994); John Robb & Alan Rupe, *School Finance Case File* (describing additional cases of *Montoy/Robinson, Gannon,* and *Petrella*). The Kansas Constitution's education clause provides: The legislature shall make suitable provision for finance of the educational interests of the state. Kansas Constitution art. 6, § 6(b).

87. Mock v. State of Kansas, 91CV1009 (Shawnee County District Court, slip opinion October 14, 1991).

88. United School District 229 v. Kansas, 885 P.2d 1170, 1186 (Kansas Supreme Court 1994) ("USD 229"); Kansas Constitution art. 6, § 1.

89. USD 229, 256 Kan. 257-58; Montoy I, 275 Kan. 155 (holding that the suitability provision may also be violated when the state funds education "so low that regardless of what the State says about accreditation, it would be impossible to find that the legislature has made 'suitable provision for finance of the educational interest of the state.'").

90. Montoy v. Kansas, 120 P.3d 306 (Kansas Supreme Court 2005) (holding the system unconstitutional following legislative modifications to the school finance system); Gannon v. State, 319 P.3d 1196 (Kansas Supreme Court 2014) (finding the system inequitable for its failure to provide school districts with "reasonably equal access to substantially similar educational opportunity through similar tax effort" and remanding the adequacy claim to the trial court for further findings).

91. Unified School District 229 v. State, 885 P.2d 1170 (Kansas Supreme Court 1994) (finding the system suitable and constitutional); Montoy v. Kansas, 138 P.3d 755 (Kansas Supreme Court 2006) (Montoy IV) (finding the state substantially complied with the Supreme Court's mandates).

92. Robb & Rupe, *Case File*.

93. Montoy II, 120 P.3d 310.

94. Ibid. Even when the Kansas Legislature attempted to extract the cases from the courts, the courts responded strongly in judging the legislature's failure to fulfill its constitutional duty. "The mountain labored and brought forth nothing at all," the judge wrote on May

11, referring to the Legislature's inaction. "In fact, rather than attack the problem, the Legislature chose instead to attack the court." Greg Winter, *50 Years After* Brown, *the Issue Is Often Money*, NEW YORK TIMES (May 17, 2004).

95. Montoy III, 112 P.3d 941 (basing this figure on the 2001 cost study ordered by the legislature and taking into account current budget levels).

96. Montoy IV, 138 P.3d 760–65.

97. Ibid.

98. National Education Access Network, *School Funding Cases in Wyoming* (2012) (citing Campbell County School District v. State, 907 P.2d 1238 (Wyoming Supreme Court 1995)). The Washington Supreme Court has also held that its education article, Washington Constitution art. IX, § 1, imposes a judicially enforceable affirmative duty on the State to make ample provision for the education of all children residing within its borders" and relies, in part, on statutes. McCleary v. State of Washington, Case No. 84362-7 (Washington Supreme Court 2014). The Washington Supreme Court defines education as the means to acquire the basic knowledge and skills needed to compete in today's economy and meaningfully participate in this state's democracy. In describing the substantive content of the knowledge and skills, the court uses the State's "broad educational concepts outlined in Seattle School District, the four learning goals in Engrossed Substitute House Bill (ESHB) 1209, 53d Leg., Reg. Sess. (Washington 1993), and the State's essential academic learning requirements (EALRs)." Ibid., 2–3. In January 2014, the Washington Supreme Court found the state had not fulfilled its constitutionally duty in amply providing an education. Ibid.

99. As the Texas Supreme Court aptly stated "the continued litigation over public school finance cannot fairly be blamed on constitutional standards that are not judicially manageable; the principal cause of continued litigation, as we see it, is the difficulty the Legislature has in designing and funding public education in the face of strong and divergent political pressures. Neeley, 176 S.W.3d 779.

100. Edgewood I, 777 S.W.2d 397.

101. Edgewood Independent School District v. Kirby (Edgewood II), 804 S.W.2d 491, 498 (Texas Supreme Court 1991).

102. Edgewood II, 804 S.W.2d 491.

103. Edgewood Independent School District v. Meno (Edgewood IV), 917 S.W. 2d 717, 732 (Texas Supreme Court 1995).

104. Ibid., 731 n.12.

105. Holding that "[t]he public education system need not operate perfectly; it is adequate if districts are *reasonably* able to provide their students the access and opportunity the district court described." Neeley, 176 S.W.3d 752 (emphasis in original).

106. Ibid., 788.

107. Neeley, 176 S.W.3d 789-90.

108. Ibid., 794.

109. The Texas Taxpayer & Student Fairness Coalition, 2013 WL 459357; 2014 WL 4243277. In the 2013 legislative session following the court's ruling, the Texas Legislature enacted some educational reforms and replaced $3.4 billion of the $5.4 billion previously cut from public education and the court reopened the evidence.

110. CFE, 719 N.Y.S. 2d, 481, 549. The trial court's disparate impact claim was subsequently overturned by the Appellate Division and that decision was affirmed by the Court of

Appeals. Campaign for Fiscal Equality, Inc. v. State, 801 N.E. 2d 326, 329 (New York Supreme Court 2003).

111. Lake View School District No. 25 of Phillips County v. Huckabee, 91 S.W. 3d 472, 495 (Arkansas Supreme Court 2002).

112. Ibid., 507.

113. Lake View School District No. 25 of Phillips County v. Huckabee, 210 S.W.3d 28 (Arkansas Supreme Court 2005); 257 S.W.3d 879 (Arkansas Supreme Court 2007).

114. Hoke County Board of Education, 599 S.E. 2d 393-95, 398.

115. National Education Access Network, *N. Carolina Plaintiffs File Major Non-Compliance Motion* (May 28, 2014) (demonstrating that the percentage of at-risk students in North Carolina has increased over the time period that the state has failed to fulfill its remedial commitments).

116. Hoke County Board of Education, 599 S.E. 2d 393.

117. PETER SCHRAG, FINAL TEST: THE BATTLE FOR ADEQUACY IN AMERICA'S SCHOOLS, 1 (New Press 2003) (stating that integration and equalized funding programs would lead to closing the achievement gaps).

118. Santamaria v. Dallas Independent School District, 2006 WL 3350194, *2, *31–33 (N.D. Tex. Nov. 16, 2006). Indeed, the court took on Defendants' "separate but equal" defense head on, stating: "Defendants' contention that no constitutional violation is taking place, since non-LEP minority students in ESL classes are receiving an equal educational opportunity as non-LEP Anglo students in General Education classrooms, because all classes at Preston Hollow follow DISD's mandated curriculum, and the same scope and sequence. The court is baffled that in this day and age, Defendants are relying on what is, essentially, a 'separate but equal' argument. The court cannot help but be reminded of the Supreme Court's decision over one hundred and ten years ago in *Plessy v. Ferguson*, 163 U.S. 537 (1896)."

119. Although equity and adequacy cases are, for the most part, discussed in this article separately, there should be no mistake that the preferred method of advocacy is to push for both equitable and adequate education in order to arrive closer to *Brown's* doorstep. Texas, Kansas, Washington, New Jersey, Wyoming, Montana, and Kentucky—among others—have the precedent to ensure an equitable and adequate education. The only question remains whether the right plaintiffs will marshal forward the right claims and get the court to enforce a favorable judgment.

120. Martinez v. New Mexico, Case No. D-101-CV201400783, First Amended Complaint (June 12, 2014).

BENJAMIN M. SUPERFINE and JESSICA J. GOTTLIEB

Teacher Evaluation and Collective Bargaining

The New Frontier of Civil Rights

THE 50TH ANNIVERSARY OF THE CIVIL RIGHTS ACT[1] AND 60TH ANNIVERSARY of *Brown v. Board of Education*[2] merit both celebration for how far we have come and critical evaluation of how far we have left to go. Since *Brown* was decided in 1954, the United States has engaged in a vast array of reforms undertaken at least partly in the name of educational equality.[3] These reforms are often designed to address persistent problems in education, such as the achievement gap between white students and students of color and unequal access to educational opportunities. Desegregation, school finance reform, the education of students with disabilities and English language learners (ELLs), the various iterations of the Elementary and Secondary Education Act (ESEA), standards- and accountability-based reforms, and school choice round out only the most high-profile of these reform efforts. These reforms have spanned the judicial, legislative, and executive branches, have involved federal and state governments and school districts, and sometimes have been undertaken with the ambitious aim of transforming teaching and learning at the school and classroom levels.

Despite this persistent commitment to the ideal of racial and ethnic equality in educational opportunities, such reforms have reflected a range of ideas about the place of education in our broader society and, in turn, what an equal and high-quality education actually means.[4] Large-scale education reform in the period immediately following *Brown* and the civil rights era was largely aimed at providing students with equal educational access and learning opportunities for two main purposes: maintaining an inclusive and robustly functioning democracy, and facilitating social mobility.[5] Since then, other goals have become central as well, such as supporting the international economic competitiveness of the U.S. in an increasingly globalized world,[6] and ensuring that parents have the individual freedom to make educational choices for their children.[7] While it is important to keep these newer goals in mind and critically consider their place in the history of education reform, it is also important for us to understand our current efforts in relation to the conceptions of equality underlying civil rights era reforms. Indeed, although equalizing educational opportunities for students has been a primary aim of education law and policy since at least *Brown*, we now risk taking an overly narrow view of why we educate students.

Grounded in a commitment to the goals historically underlying *Brown* and the Civil Rights Act, addressing racial and ethnic disparities in education and providing equal educational opportunities to all students, this chapter analyzes two of the most important types of education reforms currently being undertaken: states' development of teacher evaluation and accountability systems, and changes to states' collective bargaining laws for teachers. Reformers have framed both of these changes as necessary for increasing and equalizing teachers' effectiveness and ultimately equalizing learning opportunities for students.[8] Furthermore, these reforms may provide an avenue for providing more equal learning conditions for all students, a key goal of *Brown* and the Civil Rights Act.

Since the late 2000s, a wave of state-level laws aimed at enhancing teacher evaluation and accountability has emerged across the U.S. These laws generally increase the frequency of teacher evaluation, specify in detail how teachers must be evaluated, and increase accountability for teachers' performance. New requirements formally tying teacher evaluation to student performance on standardized tests and anchoring decisions about teacher employment and tenure on these evaluations constitute central elements of these laws. From 2009 to 2013, as many as 26 states put in place new legislation requiring teacher evaluations to include student achievement data.[9] Although states have been the primary sites for teacher evaluation and accountability reform, the federal government also has pushed states in this direction, primarily through the Race to the Top Fund (RTT) and waivers releasing states from requirements of the No Child Left Behind Act.[10]

Given that modern teacher evaluation and accountability systems are generally aimed at identifying and removing poorly performing teachers, and form the basis for alterations to teacher compensation policies, these reforms directly intersect with collective bargaining laws for teachers. A large majority of states has long had in place laws that allow teachers unions to require school districts to engage in collective bargaining over a range of issues, including teacher salaries, layoff procedures, and grievance and dismissal procedures.[11] These laws form the foundation and ultimately the boundaries for the collective bargaining agreements that can be made between school districts and local teachers' unions. As such, these laws generally frame the tenure and employment decisions that are implicated by recently enacted teacher evaluation systems. However, many of these laws have been weakened recently in concert with the enactment of teacher evaluation systems, specifically with respect to the abilities of teachers unions to bargain over issues such as teacher employment, compensation, and dismissal.[12] Together, states' enactment of teacher evaluation and accountability systems and modifications of laws governing collective bargaining form the centerpiece of reforms aimed at equalizing and increasing teachers' effectiveness.

Although these intertwined reform efforts have some promise for improving and equalizing students' learning opportunities, a deep examination of them reveals that they are not well designed to fulfill the goals historically underlying *Brown* and the Civil Rights Act, namely, providing equal educational opportunities for all students regardless of race or ethnicity. On one hand, the broad aim of improving teachers' effectiveness reflects an important advance over many education reforms of the past. A growing consensus among education researchers indicates that teacher quality and effectiveness are two of the most important factors that influence student learning.[13] Moreover, while teacher quality and effectiveness are especially important for improving the performance of poor and minority students, they are inequitably distributed among students.[14] Exacerbating such issues, most traditional teacher evaluation systems have resulted in almost every teacher receiving a high rating.[15] Recent reforms aimed at improving teacher effectiveness accordingly reflect an effort to improve, at least in part, the inequitable distribution of students' learning opportunities.

On the other hand, these reforms are poorly designed to provide all students with the educational opportunities they need to engage deeply with the democratic process and facilitate their social mobility. The teacher evaluation and accountability reforms suffer from a range of problems, including technical issues with the design of testing systems, the likely effects of these systems on teachers' motivation, and the ultimately watered-down vision of teaching and learning underlying these systems. Indeed, the vision underlying these laws of what it means to teach effectively is one closely aligned with industrial work, in which teaching is treated as mechanistic and routine. Such industrial work stands in stark contrast to that of a "professional" teacher who can skillfully and flexibly engage with a variety of students to promote rigorous and analytical thinking. This type of thinking is precisely what is needed to support a highly functioning democracy and facilitate social mobility among students in the twenty-first century. Compounding such problems, the primary legal defenses available to teachers who have been terminated under teacher evaluation and accountability systems protect teachers the most when they act more like industrial workers than professionals.

State laws governing collective bargaining with teachers unions generally drive teaching and learning in a similar direction. While there are important differences among states' collective bargaining laws for teachers, they are fundamentally grounded in a vision of teaching as industrial labor.[16] Under the conditions put in place by these laws, teachers unions and school districts are incentivized to bargain in a way that foregrounds "bread and butter" issues involving the protection of teachers against the decisions of management. On a broader level, such collective bargaining laws weaken the possibility of robust teacher input into the design of teacher evaluation, which is critical for a highly functioning school environment characterized by collaboration and professional relationships. The net result of such reform is that the quality of teaching and learning, which is critical for achieving our most fundamental social goals, is being driven in the wrong direction.

In order to analyze recent developments in teacher evaluation and their relationship with collective bargaining, this chapter is divided into three primary parts. The first part examines recent developments in teacher evaluation and the legal protections teachers potentially have available to them, and the research on teacher evaluation. This part focuses on the major problems these systems involve and highlights the form of teaching and learning such systems incentivize. The second part analyzes the terrain of laws governing collective bargaining for teachers. This part particularly covers the issues over which teachers unions and school districts can and must bargain, and the potential effects on schools. The third part offers recommendations for moving forward more productively and in a way that is sensitive to the historical goals underlying *Brown* and the Civil Rights Act. Finally, this chapter offers concluding thoughts.

Teacher Evaluation Laws

The enactment of teacher evaluation and accountability systems has quickly become a strategy employed by both state and federal governments to improve teacher effectiveness and, in turn, student learning opportunities and performance. By 1992, 38 states had in place legislation with specific requirements for teacher evaluation.[17] Under most of these early teacher evaluation systems, principals and administrators were completely responsible for evaluating teachers, and almost all teachers were rated as performing satisfactory.[18] By the mid-2000s, some states had begun to focus more intensely on teacher evaluations and their relationship to student performance, and by 2003, at least nine states had enacted laws encouraging teachers to be paid for performance, although only two states had in place policies that tied teacher evaluation to student achievement.[19] Spurred in part by RTT, states adopted teacher evaluation and accountability policies more quickly in the late 2000s and early 2010s. In 2009, only 14 states required annual evaluations of all teachers, and four states required student achievement to be an important factor in assessing teacher performance. But by 2013, 41 states required teacher evaluations to include student achievement data, 20 states required student growth to be the preponderant criterion, and 19 states tied evaluation to tenure decisions.[20] The teacher evaluation systems that incorporate student achievement data often rely on value-added modeling (VAM), a statistical calculation that ties student growth on standardized achievement tests to particular teachers.

While student achievement data is central in most recently enacted teacher evaluation systems, these systems include several other components as well. Many of these systems incorporate classroom observations conducted by administrators, who are generally the teachers' principals.[21] Some of these systems also use direct assessments of teacher knowledge and student ratings of teachers.[22] Some of these systems include other sources of information, such as ratings of teachers' commitment to the school community, measures of teacher professionalism (such as unexcused teacher absences and late arrivals), and student test score improvements for a teacher's school.[23]

Notably, there has been strong political pushback to many of these changes, particularly from teachers unions. Randi Weingarten, president of the American Federation of Teachers (AFT), has repeatedly argued that teacher evaluation systems can improve student learning opportunities only when they are aimed at continually developing teachers' skills instead of teacher accountbaility.[24] Echoing historical criticisms of efforts to restrict teachers' autonomy, Chicago Teachers Union (CTU) president Karen Lewis stressed during the 2012 CTU teacher strike that teacher evaluation and accountbility systems narrowly focused on student achievment deskill teachers and make them less able to help students learn important knowledge and skills.[25] At the very least, such criticisms from high-profile teachers union leaders underscore the contentious nature of these systems and the potential not just for political blowback but legal blowback as well.

TEACHER EVALUATION LITIGATION

Because new teacher evaluation and accountability systems threaten teachers' job security in ways they have not previously faced, there is the strong potential for adversely affected teachers to engage in litigation. Teachers who feel they have been unfairly disciplined or fired as a result of poor ratings on evaluations may sue schools or school districts in response to such actions. As professors Preston Green, Bruce Baker, and Joseph Oluwole argue, there are several potential approaches teachers might take in such lawsuits, but a few stand out as the most likely: lawsuits involving Due Process Clause challenges, Equal Protection Clause challenges, and claims under Title VII of the Civil Rights Act.[26] Because tenured teachers have explicitly articulated job protections under both state statute and collective bargaining agreements, they are the most likely to sue if adversely affected by teacher evaluation and accountability systems.

Given the legal frameworks used by courts to evaluate such claims, it appears increasingly difficult for such litigation to succeed.[27] Due Process Clause challenges focusing on the loss of teachers' tenure appear to have the best chance of success. The Supreme Court found that teacher tenure derived from state statute provides teachers with a property right to continued employment.[28] Tenured teachers in several states would be able to establish property interests under such an approach.[29] However, Supreme Court cases from the last two decades indicate that the approach for identifying property interests under the Due Process Clause may change.[30] In education, this change would potentially require courts to focus on whether teacher evaluation systems were enacted primarily for the benefit of students or teachers. As Karl Camillucci argues, "Because none of the schemes primarily intend to benefit tenured teachers, dismissal of public teachers based on performance evaluations would not impose an atypical and significant hardship on those teachers, and they would not have a property interest in employment protected by due process."[31] So while such litigation may have some potential to protect teachers in the near term, it appears that shifting Supreme Court jurisprudence may make such protection increasingly difficult to obtain.

If teachers adversely affected by recently enacted teacher evaluation and accountability systems choose to engage in such litigation, their decisions would be understandable. Such litigation would serve as a potential form of protection against what many teachers will likely perceive to be unfair decisions. However, this type of litigation would reflect and even exacerbate the problems already inherent in teacher evaluation systems. First, the litigation would only act as a shield against the problems of teacher evaluation systems and would do little for quickly improving them so as to actually enhance students' learning opportunities. In this way, the litigation would pit teachers against schools and districts instead of more directly acting toward school improvement.

Second, the analytic frameworks used in Due Process litigation could actually encourage teachers to act in ways that treat education reform as a zero-sum game between teacher benefits and student benefits. Because teachers' claims may be at their strongest when reforms are intended to benefit them rather than students, teachers may be encouraged to push for reforms that solely protect them from the unfair actions of administrators. But as discussed below, such an approach does not square with the kind of reform needed to generate stronger learning opportunities for students in line with the demands of the twenty-first century. Teachers and administrators must work together to create an environment in schools that supports the kind of professional behavior needed to create these learning opportunities.[32] As such, litigation generated in response to teacher evaluation systems has the potential to paradoxically degrade students' learning opportunities.

RESEARCH ON TEACHER EVALUATION SYSTEMS

Although there is not much empirical research that directly relates to teacher evaluation and accountability systems, the extant research indicates that they likely will not improve or equalize students' learning opportunities in the intended fashion. On one hand, these reforms are based on the theory that they will help schools and districts make data-driven personnel decisions informed by student achievement gains and administrators' observations. As noted above, there is a strong consensus among educational researchers that teachers are one of the most important factors influencing student learning, especially for poor and minority students.[33] However, teachers traditionally have not received robust evaluations on any consistent basis, and teacher evaluation systems have generally failed at identifying effective and ineffective teachers.[34]

Despite the potential of recently enacted teacher evaluation and accountability systems to resolve such problems, these systems have several serious weaknesses. These systems often employ VAM, which uses data from student achievement tests that have not been validated for this use.[35] Such test data especially may involve "floor" or "ceiling" effects, which means that they are ineffective at determining scores for low- or high-achieving students. There is also a large range of factors other than teachers that drive student performance.[36] For example, VAM generally does not account for such influences on student progress in students' achievement like family income, ethnicity, and ability. As such, teachers who teach many English language learners or students with disabilities have shown lower student achievement gains than when they teach other students.[37]

There are also many influences within schools that affect student achievement gains other than teachers. For example, a science teacher who emphasizes mathematical modeling and computation may influence how a student scores on a mathematics achievement test. As a result, it would be very difficult to pin that student's mathematics score gains to a particular teacher.[38] The observational components of teacher evaluation systems also involve several potential problems. For example, in an early study of the implementation of an observational rubric, principals' scores for teachers were often more lenient or severe than the external evaluators.[39] Given such problems, estimates of teachers' performance have proven very unstable across tests, classes, and years.[40] The National Research Council's Board on Testing and Assessment accordingly stated, "VAM estimates of teacher effectiveness should not be used to make operational decisions because such estimates are far too unstable to be considered fair or reliable."[41]

In addition to the problems of conducting the actual evaluations, teacher evaluation and accountability systems likely will not have their intended effect of motivating teachers to perform better. Although there is some logic that data from these systems can help administrators employ incentives to motivate stronger performance, the evidence supporting this notion is mixed at best.[42] Because there are so many influences on student learning aside from teachers, teacher evaluation and accountability reforms can discourage teachers from working in schools with poor and minority students.[43] These reforms could reinforce the common practice of assigning inexperienced teachers to these students.[44] Moreover, these reforms restrict teachers' autonomy by intensifying teachers' focus on particular learning objectives and tests. Yet, teachers highly value self-determinism, discretion, and authority over classroom work.[45] Increasing external evaluation and controls therefore tends to minimize the intrinsic rewards and perceived meaningfulness of teaching.[46]

Perhaps most importantly, teacher evaluation and accountability systems emphasize data from student assessments that involve a problematic vision of what students should learn. As the Gordon Commission on the Future of Assessment in Education argued, assessments serve as statements about what educators, policymakers, and parents want their students to learn. Yet, current assessments generally fail to assess the knowledge and skills students need to succeed in the twenty-first century. These assessments fail to assess whether students can evaluate the validity and relevance of different pieces of information and draw conclusions from them, make conjectures and seek evidence to test them, contribute to their job or community networks, and generally make sense of the world. Moreover, they fail to provide teachers with actionable information about their students and support high-quality instructional practices.[47] In short, while recently enacted teacher evaluation and accountability systems are aimed at the laudable goal of improving and equalizing students' learning opportunities, they involve several serious problems that weaken their potential to do so and reinforce a view of teaching and learning that serves students poorly.

Collective Bargaining and Teaching

Given the recent focus on increasing teacher effectiveness through enhanced teacher evaluation and accountability, many reforms have also focused on modifying states' collective bargaining laws. In most states that have experienced such reforms, collective bargaining laws frame the tenure and employment decisions that are implicated by teacher evaluation and accountability systems. In some of these states, the legal requirements regarding collective bargaining with teachers unions have simply been modified to align with recently enacted teacher evaluation and accountability laws. However, laws governing collective bargaining for teachers have been more drastically modified and severely weakened in other states. Such changes include the prohibition of bargaining over the placement of teachers, structure of performance evaluation systems, and the implementation of policy regarding teacher firing and discipline.

The wave of reforms aimed at scaling back collective bargaining for teachers reflects the broader political pressure that teachers unions currently face. Teachers unions have both strong critics and supporters. Critics generally argue that teachers unions harm education by hamstringing administrative authority, preventing administrators from creating flexible staffing arrangements, protecting ineffective teachers, failing to reward effective teaching, and creating huge inefficiencies.[48] Advocates of teachers unions argue that collective bargaining results in agreements produced by fair negotiations that protect teachers from unfair or unwise treatment from administrators. Some advocates further argue that collective bargaining is in fact a strong tool for enhancing teacher effectiveness—it provides the space for collaboration to promote teacher professionalism, peer review, differentiated compensation, and professional development.[49]

Given the deep influence that the landscape of laws governing collective bargaining between teachers unions and schools districts can ultimately have on student learning opportunities, it is critical to examine these changes and claims about them with closer attention to what we actually know and what we do not. However, it is worth noting that, while this debate has been highly politicized, it generally does not rest on strong attention to evidence, despite the high profile and often highly politicized debates about collective bargaining in education. Little is actually known about the effects of collective bargaining in education.[50] While there is not sufficient data to support conclusions about its effect on the quality of the teacher workforce as a whole, there is some evidence that collective bargaining does impact key teacher workforce policies, especially compensation and teaching assignments.[51] This section accordingly examines the collective bargaining landscape for teachers, with a particular focus on how this landscape is rooted in a vision of teaching as industrial labor.

THE CURRENT LANDSCAPE OF COLLECTIVE BARGAINING LAW IN EDUCATION

Almost every state has in place laws permitting collective bargaining for teachers. Only five states—Georgia, North Carolina, South Carolina, Texas, and Virginia—do not permit collective bargaining for teachers.[52] Twenty-four states (including these five) have in place "right-to-work" provisions under state constitution or statute.[53] In a right-to-work state, labor unions and employees may not require employees to join unions or pay union dues as a condition of employment. Consequently, the power of unions to form and bargain collectively is significantly weakened in these states. At the same time, collective bargaining is required by school districts if requested by a teachers union in 30 states, and 15 states permit but do not require districts to engage in collective bargaining.[54] In these states, bargaining can occur over a potentially wide range of issues, including teacher salaries, healthcare, grievance and dismissal procedures, class size, length of the school day and year, and transfer and layoff procedures.[55] Moreover, bargaining may occur over issues that border on those that are sometimes left to administrators, such as class size, professional development, coaching, and student discipline.[56] Independent of a teacher union's ability to engage in collective bargaining, the First Amendment guarantees teachers the right to join a union and engage in certain union activities without being disciplined.[57]

In states that at least permit collective bargaining with teachers unions, statutes widely vary over the scope of what can and cannot be bargained. Moreover, many of the relevant provisions in state collective bargaining statutes are vague, which has paved the way for judicial and labor board interpretations of this scope. Under such state statutes and judicial decisions, the potential issues for collective bargaining generally fall into three categories: mandatory, permissive, and excluded.[58] Mandatory issues are those that primarily relate to employee working conditions over which teachers unions and school districts must bargain.[59] In the case of teaching, mandatory issues directly affect teacher compensation and working conditions, and generally include salary, hours, pension, and healthcare.[60]

Permissive issues are those that can be bargained over if a school district and union choose. These issues are generally those that do not primarily relate to working conditions but are not solely set aside for management.[61] Permissive issues may begin to touch upon matters of education policy, such as defining educational objectives and textbook selection.[62] It is worth noting that placement of an issue in the permissive category often means in practice that a school district will refuse to bargain over the issue, essentially foreclosing bargaining and teacher input over the issue.[63]

Finally, issues that are excluded cannot be bargained over, regardless of the wishes of a union or a school district. Some excluded issues are those defined by statute to protect certain terms of conditions and teacher employment, such as due process protections for teacher tenure, rules governing the compensation schedule for teachers (often requiring that teachers are paid on the basis of experience, training, and education), and layoff procedures.[64] Other excluded issues are those considered to relate to education policy and require managerial discretion, such as staffing and principal appointment.[65]

Despite this framework, many potential issues for bargaining do not clearly fall into one of these three categories under state statutes. As a result, issues that are excluded in one state may be permissive in another. Such issues include class size, workload, student discipline, calendar, professional development, and guidelines for promotion, tenure, and retrenchment.[66] Where state statutes are vague, courts and administrative boards often decide the categories into which certain issues fall. These decisions often depend on the extent to which an issue is related to teacher working conditions or managerial discretion or public policy.[67] As discussed above, an issue should be classified as mandatory the closer it relates to working conditions, while an issue should be classified as excluded the closer it relates to managerial discretion or public policy.[68] Indeed, this classification scheme reflects how collective bargaining law is historically rooted in industrial labor. As the Supreme Court noted when interpreting the National Labor Relations Act, decisions about the core operations of business must be left entirely in the hands of management, while workers only have the right to force bargaining over "wages, hours, and other terms and conditions of employment."[69] However, it is worth noting that classifying issues as either relating to working conditions or managerial authority or policy is complex and laden with value judgments. As the Court of Appeals of Maryland stated, "[E]very managerial decision in some way relates to 'salaries, wages, hours and other working conditions,' and is therefore negotiable."[70] As the court also noted, virtually every such decision also involves education policy considerations and is arguably nonnegotiable.

Teacher evaluation particularly reflects the problems in this classification scheme as it applies to education. As professor Martin Malin argues, "[E]valuations can affect job security, pay, and assignments. However, how evaluations are conducted also raises questions of educational policy."[71] As such, states have classified teacher evaluation differently. For example, courts and labor boards in Connecticut, Maine, and New Hampshire found that teacher evaluation systems are a permissive subject of bargaining.[72] On the other hand, states such as Florida, Michigan, and Wisconsin have prohibited bargaining over the process and substance of teacher evaluations.[73] Kansas takes a more nuanced approach by requiring bargaining over procedures for evaluating teachers but only permitting bargaining over evaluation criteria.[74] Teacher evaluation has also become a central issue in *Doe v. Deasy*, a case decided in 2012 in which the California Superior Court ordered Los Angeles Unified School District (LAUSD) to include student progress in teacher evaluations.[75] Although the court ruled that LAUSD had some discretion about how to include student progress, the court emphasized that such inclusion is required by state statute and cannot be ignored because of the collective bargaining process.

Decisions about how to classify potential issues for bargaining can fundamentally shape the relationships between teachers and schools. If an issue is not classified as mandatorily negotiable, a district can unilaterally cut out a teachers union from decision-making over that issue.[76] A district or school can then go even further by selecting individual teachers and administrators to provide input. At the same time, teachers unions may engage in "impact bargaining"; that is, even if an issue is excluded, unions may bargain over facets of that issue that impact employee terms and working conditions. For example, although some courts have found that the length of the school day is not mandatory, the exact hours and compensation associated with extended hours could be bargained over.[77] Given both impact bargaining and the principle that matters of educational policy and managerial discretion should not be mandatory, collective bargaining is channeled toward "bread and butter" issues. As a result, collective bargaining agreements often focus on shielding teachers against decisions imposed by schools and districts and deemphasize the broader policy facets of an issue.

Some critics have noted the potentially harmful effects of such legal principles. According to these critics, collective bargaining law in education does not provide an environment that facilitates that development of high-performance schools.[78] In high-performance workplaces, employees generally take responsibility in an organization for decision-making in their areas of expertise. Although collective bargaining law does not necessarily prevent teachers and administrators from developing such a relationship, it provides a foundation for a more industrial-style relationship. Similarly, although teacher "buy-in" to education policy and administrative decision-making are critical factors in school performance, collective bargaining law does little to facilitate relationships that engender this sort of support.[79] Moreover, when teachers unions are blocked from negotiating over issues, they in turn often focus on blocking the implementation of reforms in ways available to them.[80]

In short, collective bargaining laws in education are present in a majority of states, but they often narrowly circumscribe the role of teachers unions. While these laws are written differently, they are generally rooted in the conception of industrial labor. They focus on protecting teachers from the whims and potentially unwise decisions of educational administration. But as discussed below, they also create a legal environment that does not naturally support the development of high-performing schools that provide high quality and equal learning opportunities for students. Especially in concert with recent teacher evaluation legislation, current collective bargaining laws may actually work against this goal.

RECENT CHANGES TO COLLECTIVE BARGAINING LAWS FOR TEACHERS

Several states recently have made significant changes to their collective bargaining laws. Since 2011, at least 12 states have modified their laws governing the extent to which public employees can bargain over a range of different issues.[81] In education, these issues include tying teacher compensation to evaluation, lengthening the time it takes for teachers to achieve tenure, and streamlining procedures for teacher discipline and firing.[82] In some cases, these laws entirely prohibit bargaining over such issues. In addition, while some states that had recently enacted teacher evaluation systems focused on aligning their collective bargaining laws with these systems, other states made more sweeping changes to their collective bargaining laws.

For example, Idaho restricted collective bargaining for teachers to issues of compensation, which were defined as salary and benefits, including insurance and leave.[83] However, Idaho voters rejected this law in November 2012.[84] Indiana made similar changes by restricting collective bargaining for teachers to wages, salary, and issues related to fringe benefits like insurance.[85] The state prohibited bargaining for teachers over everything else and expressly prohibited bargaining over teacher evaluation, dismissal procedures and criteria, the school calendar, and restructuring options.[86] Although collective bargaining was already limited in Michigan, the state recently prohibited bargaining over a range of issues, including teacher placement, reductions in the teaching force, performance evaluation systems, policy regarding teacher discipline or firing, and the role of evaluation in performance-based compensation.[87] Tennessee replaced the possibility of collective bargaining with a process called "collaborative conferencing," in which the district and teachers meet to discuss the terms and conditions of professional employee service over issues such as salaries, grievance procedures, and payroll deductions.[88] However, the state does not require the parties to reach an agreement and allows a school board to set the terms and conditions if no agreement can be reached.[89] Moreover, collaborative conferencing cannot occur over teacher evaluation, staffing decisions, and differential pay plans and incentive compensation.[90]

Perhaps the most high-profile attack on collective bargaining in education occurred in Wisconsin. Under the leadership of Governor Scott Walker, the state passed a law limiting teachers unions from bargaining on issues other than base wages for approximately two-thirds of the school districts.[91] The law also required teachers to significantly increase their contributions to their pensions and health insurance premiums.[92] This law was passed without any support from state Democrats and sparked vicious political fights during its consideration, including the flight of 14 Democratic members of the Wisconsin State Senate from the state to delay a vote on the law. Similar efforts emerged in Ohio: the law there limited bargaining between teachers unions and school boards over salary.[93] However, this law was quickly repealed by voter referendum by a 22-point margin. So, although many states have recently modified their collective bargaining laws to align with the recent enactment of teacher evaluation systems, some states have significantly weakened the power of teachers unions to bargain over a range of other issues as well.

PROFESSIONAL UNIONISM

Although collective bargaining in education is typically characterized as a zero-sum game that treats teaching much like industrial labor, the concept of professional, or reform, unionism offers a different view of bargaining. Under this concept, teachers unions are characterized by an emphasis on "teacher professionalism in service of student learning."[94] Professional unionism in education is focused on issues of teaching and learning to a much greater extent than traditional unionism in education. The first core tenet of professional unionism is joint custody, shared by the union and the district, of any reform.[95] The second tenet is union and management collaboration, characterized by collegial working relations and ongoing problem-solving, rather than periodic negotiations. The final tenet is a shared concern for public interest, in which the union assumes partial responsibility for the long-term success of the institution and is not solely focused on bread and butter issues for its members. In contrast, industrial unionism has been characterized by separation between labor and management, adversarial bargaining, and an emphasis on self-interest and protection of teachers.[96]

Professional unionism accordingly involves an approach to bargaining known as interest-based bargaining. Professor Julia Koppich describes this type of bargaining as taking a collaborative approach rather than an adversarial approach, in which both parties are positioned as working together to address common issues.[97] Interest-based bargaining is integrative, rather than distributive, in which "union and management [seek] common roads for mutual benefit"[98] and use what is best for students as the "litmus test" for any proposed idea.[99] The contracts that stem from interest-based bargaining potentially include a larger range of issues than traditional contracts and have been described as "living contracts" in which problems are addressed as they arise instead of every few years when it becomes time to renew the contract.[100]

Professional unionism potentially offers several benefits that may foster conditions that promote high-performance schools and increased learning opportunities for all students. First, as reflected by its name, professional unionism could increase the professionalism, both in reality and perception, of the teaching workforce. By replacing rigid work rules with more expansive and flexible contracts, teachers arguably have increased freedom to teach in ways that best meet the learning needs of their students. Professional unionism also could encourage a less adversarial bargaining process, especially if issues are being negotiated as they arise, rather than attempting to resolve several years' worth of issues each time a contract needs to be renegotiated. Finally, professional unionism could allow districts to have more flexibility to adapt to changing policy environments.

Despite these potential benefits, there are strong barriers to engaging in professional unionism. First, it would require new skills and training for union leaders and their district counterparts.[101] Furthermore, there are few incentives for unions to adopt a more professional type of unionism or practice interest-based bargaining.[102] To adopt professional unionism would mean putting the common interests of the school system and the students above the interests of the members. As professor Terry Moe argues, "The unions are not in the business of representing children. It is not their goal to create a school system that is organized for truly effective performance. They are driven by their own interests, and those special interests are in the driver's seat even when the unions engage in 'reform.'"[103] Under this logic, it is unlikely that widespread professional unionism will ever prevail because it would require unions to shift their focus away from bread and butter issues to the promotion of reforms and policies that may not be popular with their members.

Finally, empirical research on the effects of interest-based bargaining in education is fairly limited, but there are several case studies of cities that have used interest-based bargaining. For example, Cincinnati implemented some aspects of interest-based bargaining during its 1988 contract negotiations, including monthly meetings to address contract implementation issues and joint committees to address many aspects of schooling (e.g. curriculum, professional development, and allocation of federal funds).[104] However, these efforts had mixed results and later negotiations assumed much of the negative tone and relationships of prior negotiations. Greece, New York, also implemented interest-based bargaining in 1987.[105] The 1989 contract increased the flexibility of teacher work rules, created new roles for teacher-leaders, and encouraged school level shared decision-making. So, while interest-based bargaining may reduce the sheer number of gains made by teachers unions during negotiation and may be difficult to implement, it may be more likely to produce contracts that satisfy both parties and are seen as mutually beneficial.

Reinvigorating the Principles of *Brown* and the Civil Rights Act

Large-scale education reform in the period immediately following *Brown* and through the civil rights era was largely aimed at providing students with equal educational access to schools and learning opportunities in order to address existing racial and ethnic disparities. In doing so, such reforms were ultimately focused on maintaining an inclusive and robustly functioning democracy and facilitating social mobility. Other important goals for education reform, such as maintaining the international economic competitiveness of the U.S., have also emerged since the civil rights era. While these goals are also important to keep in mind when developing and implementing education reforms, it is critical that we do not forget the goals underlying the civil rights era reforms as well, especially given the persistence of the achievement gap.

Given some of the primary education reform goals of the civil rights era, the current slate of reforms focused on teacher evaluation and collective bargaining has some promise. These reforms respond to major problems that other large-scale reforms have faced in the past. Perhaps most importantly, they focus on teachers, who are one of the most important influences in schools on students' learning opportunities. Indeed, teacher quality and effectiveness are especially important for improving the learning opportunities of poor and minority students.

However, these reforms are poorly designed on balance to provide all students with the learning opportunities they need to engage deeply with the democratic process and facilitate their social mobility in the twenty-first century. There are several problems in the design of current teacher evaluation and accountability systems that generally weaken their ability to improve teaching, such as widespread sources of invalidity. On a more fundamental level, the learning opportunities encouraged by laws governing collective bargaining and teacher evaluation laws are not well aligned with primary education goals underlying civil rights era education reform. Today, all students need to master not only specific content knowledge and skills in disciplines like mathematics and language arts; they must also master broader competencies, such as knowledge creation, working with abstractions, thinking systemically, cognitive persistence, and collective cognitive responsibility. Indeed, the legal environment structuring recent reforms in both teacher evaluation and collective bargaining reflects a vision of teaching that is more closely aligned with industrial work than the sort of more "professional" work that is more attuned to such knowledge and skills.

Recommendations to improve teacher evaluation and collective bargaining in line with the goals underlying civil rights era education reforms could take any number of forms. Here, we aim at laying out fundamental principles to guide such improvement. First, these reforms must grow from a vision of teaching and learning that is at least partly attuned to the goals of civil rights era education reforms while remaining relevant to the demands of the modern era. As discussed above, learning opportunities for all students should be focused not only on skills and knowledge in certain disciplines, but also certain broad competencies that go beyond those currently assessed under large-scale testing practices.

In turn, the laws governing teacher evaluation and accountability should be restructured. On a surface level, issues such as the validity of testing practices should be resolved to the extent possible. More fundamentally, assessment practices should be better aligned to a robust policy image of teachers and teaching. Moreover, the construction of teacher evaluation and accountability systems should be a more collaborative process that draws on input from the teacher workforce. As it currently stands, teacher evaluation and accountability systems are not well designed to motivate teachers. A more collaborative process would engender more "buy-in" from teachers, which is critical for ensuring that any reform aimed at improving teaching is effectively implemented.[106] This process should be aimed not only at incentivizing teachers to work harder, but also developing their skills and knowledge. If teachers are to engage in a more professional form of teaching more consistently, the legal environment should provide the necessary support.[107]

Collective bargaining laws for teachers should be restructured around a similar set of principles. Although the actual research on the effects of collective bargaining is limited and mixed, the law in this area flows from a conception of teaching as industrial labor and typically treats bargaining as a zero-sum game between school districts and unions. Instead, the legal environment structuring collective bargaining for teachers should focus parties more on collaboration over issues that directly affect students. Indeed, as discussed above, teacher evaluation and accountability systems sit at the heart of the issues that should be bargained. By tilting bargaining away from such issues, the law fails to encourage the creation of robust learning opportunities for students.

Accordingly, state laws governing collective bargaining should encourage interest-based bargaining to a greater extent. Moreover, the law should encourage bargaining over issues that involve education policy to a greater extent. By bringing teachers unions into issues of education policy, the law would have a greater chance of supporting the development of high-performing schools that provide high-quality and equal learning opportunities for students. To be sure, such a shift in the nature of bargaining in education would require a massive reconstruction in many areas of the very idea of collective bargaining in education and appropriate union action. The politics characterizing the relationship between schools and unions is thick, and it is structured by the attitudes of several entrenched stakeholders, ranging from those in unions and schools to politicians and the general public. Restructuring bargaining in this fashion would be very difficult, especially given the current political climate. However, it would be a crucial step in shaping unions into more professional organizations that can consistently contribute to the improvement of student learning opportunities.

Conclusion

The 50th anniversary of the Civil Rights Act and 60th anniversary of *Brown* represent an important occasion to consider our current trajectory in education reform. By looking back to these landmark events, we can gain a vantage point to help us better understand the nature of current reform efforts, and to consider how we might continue to progress towards providing equal educational opportunities to all students, regardless of race or ethnicity. Teacher evaluation and accountability systems and states' collective bargaining laws for teachers are two of the most important and widespread types of education reforms currently being undertaken. While these intertwined reforms have promise for improving and equalizing students' learning opportunities, much work still needs to be done to help these reforms have significant and lasting effects at scale. By critically considering what types of teaching and learning are needed in the twenty-first century in light of civil rights era goals, we can begin to effect such changes and ultimately provide all students with the learning opportunities they deserve.

Benjamin M. Superfine is an Associate Professor and Director of the Research on Urban Education Policy Initiative in the College of Education at the University of Illinois at Chicago. **Jessica J. Gottlieb** is a is a post-doctoral research associate at the Center for STEM Education at the University of Notre Dame. The ideas in this chapter are further developed in an article by the same title forthcoming in the MICHIGAN STATE LAW REVIEW.

NOTES

1. Civil Rights Act of 1964, Public Law No. 88–352, §§ 401–410, 78 Stat. 241, 246–49 (1964) (codified as amended 42 U.S.C. §§ 2000c–2000c-9 (2006)).
2. Brown v. Board of Education, 347 U.S. 483 (1954).

3. BENJAMIN M. SUPERFINE, EQUALITY IN EDUCATION LAW AND POLICY: 1954–2010 (Cambridge University Press 2013).

4. David F. Labaree, Public Goods, *Private Goods: The American Struggle over Educational Goals*, 34 AMERICAN EDUCATION RESEARCH JOURNAL 39 (1997).

5. AMY GUTMANN, DEMOCRATIC EDUCATION (Princeton University Press 1999) (analyzing the political purposes of education); CARL KAESTLE, PILLARS OF THE REPUBLIC (Hill and Wang 1983).

6. National Commission on Excellence in Education, U.S. Department of Education, *A Nation at Risk: The Imperative for Educational Reform*, 5 (1983).

7. Christopher A. Lubienski, *Redefining "Public" Education: Charter Schools, Common Schools, and the Rhetoric of Reform*, 103 TEACHERS COLLEGE RECORD 634 (2001).

8. Liana Heitin, *Chicago Dispute Puts Spotlight on Teacher Evaluation*, EDUCATION WEEK (September 19, 2012).

9. National Council on Teacher Quality, *Prep Review: A Review of the Nation's Teacher Preparation Programs* (2013).

10. American Recovery and Reinvestment Act of 2009, Pub. L. No. 111-5, § 3, 123 Stat. 115, 115–16 (2009); Alyson Klein, *"Race to the Top" Standards Link Questioned; Some in Congress Worry Federal Intrusion Ahead Through Money for Testing*, EDUCATION WEEK (August 12, 2009).

11. Benjamin A. Lindy, *The Impact of Teacher Collective Bargaining Laws on Student Achievement: Evidence from a New Mexico Natural Experiment*, 120 YALE LAW JOURNAL 1130 (2011).

12. Ibid.

13. Eric A. Hanushek et al., National Bureau of Economic Research, *Teachers, Schools, and Academic Achievement* (1998).

14. U.S. Department of Education, *Our Future, Our Teachers: The Obama Administration's Plan for Teacher Education Reform and Improvement* (2011).

15. Daniel Weisberg et al., *The New Teacher Project, The Widget Effect: Our National Failure to Acknowledge and Act on Differences in Teacher Effectiveness* (2009).

16. David M. Rabban, *Can American Labor Law Accommodate Collective Bargaining by Professional Employees?*, 99 YALE LAW JOURNAL 689 (1990).

17. Carole A. Veir & David L. Dagley, *Legal Issues in Teacher Evaluation Legislation: A Study of State Statutory Provisions*, 2002 BRIGHAM YOUNG UNIVERSITY EDUCATION AND LAW JOURNAL 1 (2002).

18. Weisberg, *The New Teacher Project*.

19. EdCounts Database, EDUCATION WEEK.

20. National Council on Teacher Quality, *Prep Review*.

21. Steven Glazerman et al., Brown Center on Education Policy, Brookings Institute, *Passing Muster: Evaluating Teacher Evaluation Systems* (2011).

22. Ibid.

23. Ibid.

24. Randi Weingarten, American Federation of Teachers, *Press Release: Statement by Randi Weingarten on the NCTQ Report on Teacher Evaluation* (2011).

25. Monica Davey, *Teachers End Chicago Strike on Second Try*, NEW YORK TIMES

(September 18, 2012).

26. Preston C. Green et al., *The Legal and Policy Implications of Value-Added Teacher Evaluation Policies*, 2012 BRIGHAM YOUNG UNIVERSITY EDUCATION AND LAW JOURNAL 1 (2012).

27. Ibid.

28. Cleveland Board of Education v. Loudermill, 470 U.S. 532 (1985).

29. Karl D. Camillucci, *Regretting* Roth? *Why and How the Supreme Court Could Deprive Tenured Public Teachers of Due Process Rights in Employment*, 44 LOYOLA UNIVERSITY OF CHICAGO LAW JOURNAL 591, 594 (2013).

30. Ibid.

31. Ibid., 637.

32. Jennifer A. Mueller & Katherine H. Hoyde, *Theme and Variation in the Enactment of Reform: Case Studies*, in JONATHAN A. SUPOVITZ & ELLIOT H. WEINBAUM, EDS., THE IMPLEMENTATION GAP: UNDERSTANDING REFORM IN HIGH SCHOOLS (Teachers College Press 2008).

33. Linda Darling-Hammond, *Teacher Quality and Student Achievement: A Review of State Policy Evidence*, 8 EDUCATION POLICY ANALYSIS ARCHIVES 1 (2000).

34. Steven Glazerman et al., Brown Center on Education Policy, Brookings Institute, *Passing Muster: Evaluating Teacher Evaluation Systems* (2011).

35. Audrey Amerin-Beardsley, *Methodological Concerns about the Educational Value Added Assessment System*, 32 EDUCATION RESEARCH 65 (2008).

36. Rodney S. Whiteman et al., Center for Evaluation and Education Policy, *Revamping the Reacher Evaluation Process* (2011).

37. Linda Darling-Hammond, Stanford Center for Opportunity Policy in Education, Stanford University, *Creating a Comprehensive System for Evaluating and Supporting Effective Teaching* (2012).

38. Gene V. Glass, Education Policy Research Unit, Arizona State, *Teacher Evaluation* (2004).

39. Lauren Sartain et al., Consortium on Chicago School Research, University of Chicago, *Rethinking Teacher Evaluation: Findings From the First Year of the Excellence in Teaching Project in Chicago Public Schools* (2010).

40. Eva L. Baker et al., Economic Policy Institute, *Problems With the Use of Student Test Scores to Evaluate Teachers* (2010).

41. Board on Testing and Assessment & National Research Council, National Academy of Sciences, *Letter Report to the U.S. Department of Education on Race to the Top* (2009).

42. Thomas Dee & James Wyckoff, National Bureau of Economic Research, *Incentives, Selection, and Teacher Performance: Evidence from Impact* (2013).

43. Whiteman, *Revamping the Teacher Evaluation Process.*

44. Darling-Hammond, *Creating a Comprehensive System.*

45. LARRY CUBAN, HOW TEACHERS TAUGHT: CONSTANCY AND CHANGE IN AMERICAN CLASSROOMS, 1890–1980 (Longman Publishing 1984).

46. Linda Darling-Hammond and Elle Rustique-Forrester, *The Consequences of Student Testing for Teaching and Teacher Quality*, in USES AND MISUSES OF DATA FOR EDUCATIONAL ACCOUNTABILITY AND IMPROVEMENT. THE 104th YEARBOOK OF THE NATIONAL SOCIETY FOR THE STUDY OF EDUCATION, PART 2 (Blackwell

Publishing 2005).

47. Gordon Commission, *A Statement Concerning Public Policy* (2013).

48. Frederick M. Hess & A. P. Kelly, *Scapegoat, Albatross, or What? The Status Quo in Teacher Collective Bargaining*, in COLLECTIVE BARGAINING IN EDUCATION: NEGOTIATING CHANGE IN TODAY'S SHOOLS (Harvard Education Press 2006).

49. Ibid.

50. Susan M. Johnson & Morgaen L. Donaldson, *The Effects of Collective Bargaining on Teacher Quality*, in COLLECTIVE BARGAINING IN EDUCATION (Harvard Education Press 2006).

51. Charles T. Kerchner, *Union-Made Teaching: The Effects of Labor Relations on Teaching Work*, 13 REVIEW OF RESEARCH IN EDUCATION 317 (1986); Katharine O. Strunk & Jason A. Grissom, *Do Strong Unions Shape District Policies?: Collective Bargaining, Teacher Contract Restrictiveness, and the Political Power of Teachers' Unions*, 10 EDUCATION EVALUATION AND POLICY ANALYSIS 389 (2010).

52. Gus Lubin, *The Five States Where Teachers Unions Are Illegal Have the Lowest Test Scores in America*, FORBES (February 23, 2011).

53. National Right to Work Legal Defense Foundation, *Right to Work States*, http://www.nrtw.org/rtws.htm (2013).

54. Lubin, *Five States Where Teachers Unions Are Illegal*.

55. Lindy, *Impact of Teacher Collective Bargaining Laws*.

56. William S. Koski, *Teacher Collective Bargaining, Teacher Quality, and the Teacher Quality Gap: Toward a Policy Analytic Framework*, 6 HARVARD LAW & POLICY REVIEW 67 (2012).

57. Federacion de Maestros de Puerto Rico v. Acevedo-Vila, 545 F. Supp. 2d 219, 229 (D.P.R. 2008).

58. Charles J. Russo, *A Cautionary Tale of Collective Bargaining in Public Education: A Teacher's Right or Tail Wagging the Dog*, 37 UNIVERSITY OF DAYTON LAW REVIEW 317 (2012).

59. Mark Paige, *Applying the "Paradox" Theory: A Law and Policy Analysis of Collective Bargaining Rights and Teacher Evaluation Reform from Selected States*, 2013 BRIGHAM YOUNG UNIVERSITY EDUCATION AND LAW JOURNAL 21 (2013).

60. Koski, *Teacher Collective Bargaining*.

61. Paige, *Applying the "Paradox" Theory*.

62. Koski, *Teacher Collective Bargaining*.

63. Rabban, *Can American Labor Law Accommodate Collective Bargaining*, 714 (stating, ". . . declaring governance a permissive subject . . . can also undermine traditional means of professional influence").

64. Koski, *Teacher Collective Bargaining*.

65. Russo, *A Cautionary Tale*.

66. Rabban, *Can American Labor Law Accommodate Collective Bargaining*.

67. Paige, *Applying the "Paradox" Theory*.

68. Montgomery County Education Association v. Board of Education, 534 A.2d 980, 986 (1987).

69. First National Maintenance Corporation v. National Labor Relations Board, 452 U.S. 666 (1981).

70. Montgomery County Education Association, 534 A.2d 986.

71. Martin H. Malin, *Sifting through the Wreckage of the Tsunami that Hit Public Sector Collective Bargaining*, 16 EMPLOYEE RIGHTS & EMPLOYMENT POLICY JOURNAL 533 (2012).

72. Wethersfield Board of Education v. State Board of Labor Relations, 519 A.2d 41 (Connecticut Supreme Court 1986); In re Pittsfield School District, 744 A.2d 594 (New Hampshire Supreme Court 1999); Saco-Valley Teachers Association v. MSAD 6, No. 79-56 (Maine Labor Relations Board, August 7, 1979).

73. Paige, *Applying the "Paradox" Theory.*

74. Unified School District No. 314 v. Kansas Department of Human Resources, 856 P.2d 1343 (Kansas Supreme Court 1993); Unified School District No. 352 v. NEA-Goodland, 785 P.2d 993 (Kansas Supreme Court 1990).

75. Doe v. Deasy, Tentative Decision on Petition for Writ of Mandate: BS 134604 (California Superior Court 2012).

76. Martin H. Malin, *The Paradox of Public Sector Labor Law*, 84 INDIANA LAW JOURNAL 1369, 1385, 1389 (2009).

77. Paige, *Applying the "Paradox" Theory*, 27.

78. Malin, *The Paradox of Public Sector Labor Law*, 1380, 1385.

79. Jennifer A. Mueller & Katherine H. Hoyde, *Theme and Variation in the Enactment of Reform: Case Studies*, in THE IMPLEMENTATION GAP: UNDERSTANDING REFORM IN HIGH SCHOOLS (Teachers College Press 2008).

80. Paige, *Applying the "Paradox" Theory*, 28.

81. Malin, *Sifting through the Wreckage*, 533. This article was used extensively in this section to identify states that had recently changed their teacher collective bargaining laws.

82. Koski, *Teacher Collective Bargaining*, 96.

83. Section 1108, 61st Legislature § 17 (Idaho 2011).

84. Idaho Secretary of State, Election Division, November 6, 2012 General Election Results, Proposition 1.

85. 2011 Indiana Acts 575 § 14.

86. Ibid., § 15.

87. Section 1108, 61st Legislature § 17 (Idaho 2011).

88. 2011 Tennessee Public Acts 378, § 49-5-605(b)(1).

89. Ibid., § 49-5-609(d).

90. Ibid., § 49-5-608(b).

91. Russo, *A Cautionary Tale*, 334.

92. Ibid. (citing Amy Merrick, *Wisconsin Union Law to Take Effect*, WALL STREET JOURNAL A2 (June 15, 2011)).

93. Notably, the law continued to allow bargaining over health care, sick time, and pension benefits.

94. Daniel F. Jacoby & Keith Nitta, *The Bellevue Teachers Strike and Its Implications for the Future of Postindustrial Reform Unionism*, 26 EDUCATION POLICY 533, 535 (2011).

95. CHARLES T. KERCHNER & JULIA E. KOPPICH, A UNION OF PROFESSIONALS: LABOR RELATIONS AND EDUCATIONAL REFORM (Teachers College Press 1993).

96. Julia E. Koppich, *Addressing Teacher Quality Through Induction, Professional Compensation, and Evaluation: The Effects on Labor-Management Relations*, 19 EDUCATION POLICY 90 (2005).

97. Ibid.

98. Ibid., 94.

99. Adam Urbanski, *Improving Student Achievement through Labor-Management Collaboration in Urban School Districts*, 17 EDUCATION POLICY 503 (2003).

100. Ibid.

101. KERCHNER & KOPPICH, A UNION OF PROFESSIONALS.

102. Koppich, *Addressing Teacher Quality*.

103. TERRY M. MOE, SPECIAL INTEREST: TEACHERS UNIONS AND AMERICA'S PUBLIC SCHOOLS (Brookings Institution Press 2011).

104. Byron King, *Cincinnati: Betting on an Unfinished Season*, in CHARLES T. KERCHNER & JULIA E. KOPPICH, A UNION OF PROFESSIONALS (Teachers College Press 1993).

105. Anthony M. Cresswell, *Greece Central School District: Stepping Back from the Brink*, in KERCHNER & KOPPICH, A UNION OF PROFESSIONALS.

106. Mueller & Hoyde, *Theme and Variation in the Enactment*.

107. DAVID K. COHEN & HEATHER C. HILL, LEARNING POLICY: WHEN STATE EDUCATION REFORM WORKS, 1–12 (Yale University Press 2001).

GARY ORFIELD

Education and Civil Rights
Lessons of Six Decades and Challenges of a Changed Society

THE *BROWN v. BOARD OF EDUCATION*[1] DECISION CREATED A NEW VISION FOR American education. African American students who had been segregated by law in 17 states and Washington, DC, in schools that never were "separate but equal" were suddenly told that their schools were "inherently unequal" and promised that the courts would end segregation in their educations. The passage of six decades since means that we have had ample time to learn what actually happened, how it worked, and to observe the conditions under which we made major progress toward the goal of integrated schools and those that have pushed us backward. It is also a very good time to think about how to apply the positive lessons of the desegregation experience to a society that has been profoundly transformed by huge demographic changes and massive nonwhite immigration and is now deeply multiracial and highly segregated with schools that will soon have a white minority on a national level. Our courts and our elected officials have too often forgotten the lessons of *Brown* and tacitly assumed that "separate but equal" schools can be equal and that we can dispose of the tools created in the civil rights revolution to deal with issues of racial inequities. The "colorblind" assumptions of current law are largely blind to the historical and social nature of today's segregation. In assuming that racial problems have been solved courts and legislatures take away rights that research shows are still badly needed and justify assumptions by dominant groups that since discrimination has ended and things are still unequal, white dominance reflects "merit" and that black and Latino inequality reflects the failure of the historically excluded groups to take advantage of the opportunities in a colorblind society.

We can start our analysis with the immediate present. We are far past the peak of desegregation in this country, which came in the late 1980s for African Americans, and has been going continuously backward for a quarter century. There never was any substantial effort to desegregate Latino students and there has been a continuing rise in their educational segregation since data were first collected nationally in 1968.[2] In major parts of the country, there is little evidence today of any enduring impact of the movement to desegregate schools. For example, the state of New York is now the nation's most segregated for black students, yet there are no significant desegregation court orders still in effect; there never was a desegregation plan in New York City (which now has more than a million highly segregated students); and recently created New York charter schools with no civil rights policies are segregated even more intensely than the regular public schools.[3] Additionally, California, where there was actually a pre-*Brown* victory against Latino segregation in the *Mendez v. Westminster*[4] case in 1946, now has the most segregated Latino students in the U.S.[5]

School segregation today is rarely only by race, though—it is usually double segregation by race and poverty. To make things more complicated, blacks and Latinos are often concentrated together in the same impoverished schools, isolated from whites, Asians, and the middle class. In a society where postsecondary education has become the only reliable path to the middle class, students in doubly segregated high schools are more likely to drop out, to have fewer advanced classes to choose from, and to have much less information from their peer group about college possibilities.[6] Typically, selective colleges do not even visit the doubly segregated high schools to recruit students since it is very unlikely that they will have students who have been adequately prepared. Increasingly in the great centers of immigration we have schools that are segregated by ethnicity, poverty, *and* language, with few native English speakers in these schools of triple segregation. In sum, segregation not only persists, it is expanding. In the South, where most desegregation occurred, black students are still far less segregated than the absolute separation before *Brown*, but the gains of the last 45 years have been lost.

How We Got Here

Brown is a wonderful case celebrated by lawyers everywhere—but an almost complete failure in desegregating Southern schools. When President Kennedy asked for a major civil rights act in 1963, it was nine years after *Brown* and 99% of the black students in the South were still in 100% black schools. Very few Southern districts had obeyed the Supreme Court even though individual plaintiffs were soon exhausting all of their remedies and their appeals. There were no black teachers teaching Southern white students. The overwhelming burden of enforcing *Brown* was being carried by a small group of private lawyers (the NAACP Legal Defense fund and a few other groups), since almost no lawyers in any of those states would take the cases.[7]

In reality, nothing had been done because the *Brown* decision did not create clear goals, standards, measurement, accountability, or help in making the difficult transition of desegregation. Each federal judge overseeing a desegregation case, all of whom were appointed with the advice and consent of segregationist senators, was given the job of figuring out what to do on his own "with all deliberate speed."[8] The Supreme Court did not even clearly define the goal of *Brown* until 1968, in the *Green v. Board of Education of New Kent County*[9] decision. That was the situation before the 1964 Civil Rights Act,[10] which gave the federal executive branch critical new tools to enforce civil rights. The Act allowed the federal government to create a coherent policy of education civil rights. Along with the first major federal general aid education legislation in American history—the 1965 Elementary and Secondary Education Act (ESEA)[11]—the Civil Rights Act answered the questions that *Brown* had not. It provided authority for the Justice Department to sue school districts. It obliged the federal government to take action against any recipient of federal aid that was discriminating. It empowered the government to cut off funds to school districts and, in fact, it mandated a funding cutoff unless there was some other remedy. It also provided technical assistance in terms of helping to deal with the community relations problems, and money to help school districts think about how to change.[12] Later on, in the Emergency School Aid Act,[13] the government would provide federal desegregation assistance of up to a billion dollars per year to help school districts deal with race relations, retrain teachers, develop more diverse curricular materials, create magnet schools, and other strategies.

In 1965, the ESEA created the largest federal funding for public education in American history. The Johnson Administration, which was responsible for the enactment of both the Civil Rights Act and ESEA, tied them together in a way that was extremely powerful: Many Southern school districts received a 20–25% supplement to their budget because ESEA was focused on high poverty schools. The

Figure 1: Southern Desegregation and Resegregation for Black Students, 1954–2011

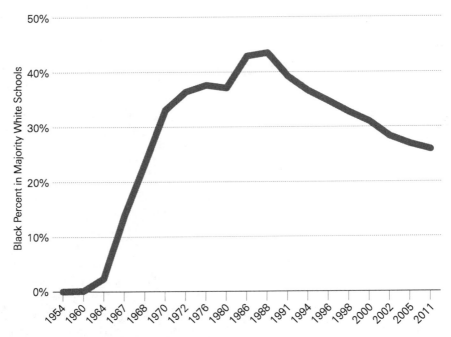

Source: U.S. Department of Education, National Center for Education Statistics, Common Core of Data (CCD), Public Elementary/Secondary School Universe Survey Data. Data prior to 1991 obtained from the analysis of the Office of Civil Rights data in Gary Orfield, *Public School Desegregation in the United States, 1968–1980* (Joint Center for Political Studies 1983). First published in Gary Orfield and Erica Frankenberg, The Civil Rights Project, Brown *at 60: Great Progress, a Long Retreat, and an Uncertain Future* (2014), as were all subsequent figures and tables in this chapter.

Johnson Administration, however, made the receipt of funds contingent on seriously starting to desegregate. It also established the school desegregation guidelines and when more than 100 districts in the South did not comply with the guidelines, the federal government cut off their funding. When funding was lost because of lack of compliance, the Justice Department sued the school districts under the power granted to it via the Civil Rights Act—and it won all of these cases. Nothing like this has ever been done in any other federal aid program in American history.[14] Schools had extremely powerful incentives to comply.

As a result of this combination of forces, every district in the South started desegregating. As figure 1 demonstrates, desegregation more than doubled the year after the Civil Rights Act and then ascended faster after that. But, there were only five years in American history, 1964–1969, when all three branches of the federal government were working actively towards desegregating schools. Congress had given the executive branch broad authority via the Civil Rights Act; the Johnson Administration implemented the sanctions and enforced the rules (not perfectly, but much better than anybody had ever done before or since); and, the Supreme Court strongly supported the executive branch's actions. Southern schools went from virtual apartheid to being the most integrated schools in the United States in about five years, and they remain the most integrated now.[15] When *Brown* was decided, there was virtually unanimous white opposition to school integration in the South. After integration was forced via federal action, creating a new reality and disproving many fears and stereotypes, attitudes changed dramatically.[16]

One of the other things the Civil Rights Act did was to commission what became known as the Coleman Report, the only national study that has ever been done by the federal government on school segregation.[17] This report, *Equality of Educational Opportunity*, was based on a unique national survey of a large sample of students in schools across the U.S. and was published in 1966. It found that the most important influences on student achievement were not funding disparities (which turned out to be less unequal and less related to outcomes than people thought), but rather differences in family background, in one's peer group at school, and in teacher quality. Since those factors strongly favored white schools, the Report's conclusions offered a major social science argument for the "inherent inequality" the Supreme Court found in *Brown*. The skills of fellow students and teachers made central impacts on educational opportunity and they were systematically different in segregated schools. The study also showed a tremendous inequality in educational outcomes by race. Average black and Latino students were graduating, if they made it to high school at all, with a three- or four-year achievement gap compared to white students.[18] Subsequent research has confirmed that segregated schools are unequal in deep and powerful ways that reach far beyond the simple test scores that were at the center of the Coleman analysis.[19]

In the late 1960s, the process of desegregation was proceeding rapidly, supported by a unanimous Supreme Court that embraced the Johnson Administration's guidelines, when President Nixon came into office. During his campaign, however, Nixon had gone to Charlotte, North Carolina, to promise voters that he was going to reverse course on desegregation. He pledged to change the Supreme Court and he created the Southern coalition that embraced Strom Thurmond and white segregationists.[20] The first year of the Nixon Administration, I visited the Republican headquarters for the state of South Carolina. A staff member told me their plan regarding race relations, which appears to have been Nixon's plan, as well: he said that they had figured out that there was going to be a black party and a white party in the future of the Deep South and the GOP was going to be the white party.[21]

During July 1969, the first summer of the Nixon Administration, I was in the Atlanta regional office of the U.S. Department of Education's Office for Civil Rights when the federal government stopped the fund cutoff mechanism of the 1964 Civil Rights Act. The director of the office called the staff together for a meeting and read a telegram from Washington announcing the change. Federal bureaucrats who were in that room started crying. They knew they were losing their authority; they were losing the leverage with which they had helped produce desegregation in most of the schools in the South. One of them told me that afternoon that they still had a couple of little rural districts that were coming in with desegregation plans and surmised that those district must not know any Republican political leaders in Washington. The Justice Department was turned over to officials who believed it was their job to slow things down. They went to the Supreme Court in *Alexander v. Holmes County Board of Education*[22] and asked that desegregation be delayed in Mississippi, but the Court refused this request and instead ordered immediate integration. For the first time since the civil rights revolution, Justice Department lawyers sat at the table on the side of white segregationists. Many Justice Department lawyers resigned. In 1970, the White House abruptly announced the firing of the director of the Office for Civil Rights, Leon Panetta (who would much later become famous as White House Chief of Staff under President Clinton, and later head of the CIA under President Obama) for enforcing the desegregation rules.[23]

That shift was the beginning of the end of the "second reconstruction" created by the civil rights movement and civil rights law. President Nixon filled four Supreme Court appointments, including a new Chief Justice, replacing Earl Warren with Warren Burger. Until that point, all of the Court's decisions on school desegregation from *Brown* forward had been unanimous. By 1973, however, the Court was divided when it decided *Keyes v. School District No. 1*,[24] which extended desegregation to the North. In *Keyes*, the Court held that if plaintiffs prove a violation in a significant part of a Northern city school district, the violation is presumed to affect the entire district unless the school district can prove there were other causes of the remainder of the segregation.[25] As the saying goes, whoever has the burden of proof in a complex civil rights case is very likely to lose. Thus, at first glance, the *Keyes* holding seemed very positive for plaintiffs—if they could generate enough money to investigate a city's history, it turned out that they were almost certain to document sufficient local violations to get a desegregation order inside the city. One problem, however, was that the decision, two decades after *Brown*, was already too late. Most major U.S. cities were already becoming heavily minority and impoverished because we were already a quarter-century into the extraordinary postwar white suburbanization of baby boom white America. We had already become a suburban society, and city school districts had lost much of their white enrollment in that process.[26] Another problem was that it took much more money than civil rights groups had to sue a big school district and prove the history of violations by examining very complex patterns of attendance boundary changes, selection of sites for schools, race-based assignment of teachers, discriminatory transfer plans, and related violations by local housing authority—and nobody ever had enough money to bring a serious federal case in Chicago, New York, Los Angeles, or a number of other communities.[27]

Also in *Keyes*, the Court recognized the history of discrimination against Latinos and ruled that they have the same kind of rights that blacks have regarding desegregation.[28] Latinos had been discriminated against in the Southwest, as documented by the Civil Rights Commission and in numerous court cases. Unfortunately, *Keyes* was decided during the Nixon Administration, which did nothing to enforce the change in law. In fact, the Nixon Administration was found guilty by federal courts of intentionally not enforcing the 1964 Civil Rights Act.[29] It was put under court order itself and that was the driving force for what little enforcement occurred in the South after this period. But, there was never any real desegregation enforcement for Latinos. Major cases in Las Vegas and Denver were exceptions to the rule; most of the rest of the country basically just accepted the existing and increasing residential and educational isolation of Hispanics. Efforts to use state law in California, which had the largest Latino population, were frustrated by the passage of Proposition 1 in 1979.[30]

After *Keyes*, the Court decided *Milliken v. Bradley*[31] in 1974 and turned against school desegregation for the first time since it had decided *Brown* 20 years earlier. In *Milliken*, a conservative district court judge had decided that the only viable solution to the racial isolation in Detroit's public schools would be to involve students from surrounding school districts in the remedy.[32] This determination produced a constitutional and political crisis. The court of appeals affirmed the decision.[33] When the case was appealed to the Supreme Court, President Nixon said that if the Court were to also affirm the decision, the Constitution should be amended.[34] Scores of attorneys general from across the country intervened on behalf of the Detroit suburbs.[35]

By a 5–4 decision in *Milliken*, the Court decided that it was more important to preserve the local autonomy of the suburban school districts than to desegregate children in Detroit, who the Court admitted had been unconstitutionally segregated and discriminated against by both the Detroit School Board and the state of Michigan.[36] The Court pretended there was some alternative inside Detroit, which was already 70% black and changing very rapidly in the aftermath of terrible riots and a terrible housing crisis caused by massive mismanagement of housing subsidy programs.[37] Justice Thurgood Marshall predicted the decision would mean that millions of children all over the country were doomed to segregated education.[38]

He was correct. The *Milliken* decision stated that the court could not require suburban districts to participate in the remedy because plaintiffs could not prove that the Detroit suburbs had discriminated against minority students. Of course, the suburban districts had few minority students because housing across the Detroit metropolitan area was among the most hypersegregated in the U.S., so there was no one to segregate in suburban schools.[39] The judge who cast the deciding vote in that case, Justice Potter Stewart, added a footnote stating that the causes of housing segregation are unknown or unknowable, although a great deal of evidence on the official action causing housing segregation in greater Detroit was in the record.[40]

Milliken is a tragic decision in terms of illogic, false description of a country, deliberate dismissal of a long legal tradition of state sovereignty over local governments (especially school districts), and the purposeful evasion of an analysis of the housing evidence that had helped convince the trial court of the consequences of decades of racially motivated state actions. It did not deny the violation but commanded prompt desegregation within the city, which the lower courts had found to be impossible. After the case was remanded to the district court, the judge made the same conclusion again and ordered, instead, state funds for some remedial programs, an idea that was sustained by the Supreme Court in 1977 in *Milliken II*.[41] That plan, however, did not succeed and th e district court abandoned the effort after 12 years, with the judge saying he did not know what to do as the city schools continued their long decay.[42] *Milliken II* remedies would later be strongly limited by the Supreme Court in the *Missouri v. Jenkins*[43] case in 1995, creating a true dead end for "separate but equal" desegregation remedies.

Milliken was effectively the end of the expansion of desegregation law, although desegregation for blacks continued to have a little momentum through 1988, particularly in the South, where residential segregation was decreasing. For Latinos, who were strongly concentrated in poorer, heavily nonwhite districts in metropolitan areas, desegregation was pretty much a dead letter. By the 1980s, 90% of Latinos and blacks were concentrated in residentially segregated metropolitan areas, which were usually broken into many school districts.[44]

By this point, the impetus for further urban desegregation was basically gone. Since desegregation was limited to central cities only, it was possible to prove violations in nearly any central city but impossible to get any remedy that would work over time. I do not know of any federal court that ever looked seriously at a major urban school district and did not find it intentionally segregated. Almost all major cities had gerrymandered their public housing in a segregated way. They created optional school attendance zones so whites could transfer out of black or Latino areas. They assigned teachers on racial grounds and had differential curricula by race of school. There was a whole pattern of inequality of schooling that was not accidental. With a great deal of effort, plaintiffs could prove a violation after *Milliken* but would often be denied a remedy worth the effort.[45]

Voluntary desegregation was also already under attack. The school desegregation assistance program in the Emergency School Aid Act of 1972 had been a compromise between Senator Walter Mondale and President Richard Nixon at the time major urban desegregation was taking place in the South. Liberals had wanted to support successful integration and the Nixon Administration had wanted money to ease the transition in the South, where it had many political allies, when the courts gave it no choice. This law devoted a lot of money to helping teachers and schools adapt to a historic racial change; it was very popular with school districts; and research showed that it had positive race relations and academic achievement impacts.[46] Unfortunately, it was the largest federal education program terminated in President Reagan's first budget, and these efforts have had almost no resources since that time. Many Americans believe that vast sums were spent on failed desegregation that would have been better spent on compensatory education. In fact, hundreds of billions of dollars have been spent on compensatory education by the federal government, usually with disappointing results, and almost nothing on desegregation in the last third of a century.

When it was adequately funded, the school desegregation assistance program produced the flourishing of magnet schools.[47] Because of the limitations of *Milliken*, many cities with heavily minority populations were being asked to desegregate inside a central city with a declining white enrollment surrounded by segregated white suburban districts. In order to try to retain the middle-class and white population of the city while desegregating, many districts moved towards magnet schools, which were intended to offer unique academic programs with mechanisms to provide integration. Magnet school policies include providing information to all parents, transporting students free of charge, not screening to keep students out of the schools, and so forth. Magnet schools became the largest choice system in the United States and still enroll roughly four million students—more than charter schools.[48] A number of magnet schools with civil rights policies became very popular in the cities where they were located and drew students of different racial and ethnic groups together.[49]

Unfortunately, as the early 1960s had made clear when hundreds of Southern school districts embraced "freedom of choice" plans that left school system segregation virtually untouched, choice without any kind of equity provisions will not work. Not very many parents will choose if choice is purely optional and the schools are segregated, which is why the Office for Civil Rights and the Supreme Court found "freedom of choice" plans inadequate a half century ago.[50] Choices made in an uncontrolled choice system will often only increase inequity. This has been well established all over the world in comparative studies of choice programs, including voucher programs. In 1991, a new form of choice, charter schools, emerged in Minnesota. By and large, charter schools are usually choice systems without equity provisions, and, as a result, end up being another highly segregated kind of neighborhood school, in most cases.[51] In fact, many of them have turned out to be the most segregated part of the public schools for black children.[52] For example, a recent Civil Rights Project report examined charter schools in New York City, which were actively expanded under Mayor Bloomberg's administration. In Manhattan in 2011–12, 97% of the charter schools were intensely segregated, as were 100% of charter schools in the Bronx.[53]

In the 1990s, the Supreme Court made three decisions that made things even worse. In *Board of Education v. Dowell*[54] in 1991, the Court held that desegregation remedies were a temporary punishment, not a long-term enforcement for cities that had a history of segregation. If a school district obeyed a court order for a certain period of time—even if conditions were still segregated and unequal, and even if return to neighborhood schools would produce high levels of segregation—a district court could still declare the school district unitary and close the case. A school district would not be judged on the basis of what would happen if unitary status was granted; it would be stopped only if civil rights lawyers could prove the policy was adopted with the *intention* to segregate, which is extremely hard to prove. Thus, a school district could return to neighborhood schools based on what they said were families' desire for the children to attend schools close to home, even if substantial racial isolation also would result.[55] The second decision, *Freeman v. Pitts*,[56] concluded the following year that even if a school district's court order had never been complied with in some major aspects, the courts could end parts that had never been followed. In the third decision, *Missouri v. Jenkins*,[57] a trial court and Court of Appeals had found the state of Missouri liable for fostering segregation in Kansas City, Missouri, but the Supreme Court permitted state funding to end and limited its purposes even though the inequalities had not been remedied. At this point, an increasingly conservative judiciary took a very unusual activist approach to dissolving desegregation plans in a number of school districts. Although I know of no federal judge who ordered a district to comply with the Supreme Court decision on busing in a long-standing school case without any party filing a motion to desegregate the schools, and although courts almost always wait for a party to file a motion to change a constitutional ruling, a number of judges decided to initiate action to end desegregation efforts. The Supreme Court's decisions had given federal district judges broad authority to decide whether the districts had done what they thought was "practicable" and they tended to give the districts the benefit of the doubt.[58] Some courts just decided to clear their dockets of these cases.

The return to neighborhood schools after districts were released from court order had many consequences. Then as now, in most of our cities, neighborhood schools in which blacks or Latinos are concentrated are also concentrated poverty schools. Table 1 illustrates this correlation today. The neighborhood schools for whites and most Asians are middle-class schools.[59] As schools resegregate, teachers tend to leave high-minority, high-poverty schools—particularly teachers with experience or high credentials who have other options—and move to middle-class schools.[60] Policies and practices systematically send teachers from schools where they are badly needed to schools where kids are much more privileged. Accountability policies accentuate that movement by punishing the most disadvantaged schools for not accomplishing things that are beyond their power to accomplish, which gives teachers and administrators a strong incentive to move to a school with more privileged students from more educated families which will be proclaimed a success whether or not the teachers are better because of the excellent preparation of the students and the educational capital and resources of their families.

As many researchers have found, the school is only part of the story. Children are in school for only one-fifth or one-sixth of their time during the year. The rest of their lives are very important for their education; so much is outside of the school's control.[61] For example, children come to kindergarten with already very large gaps in skills and knowledge.[62] A combination of social and economic policies would be necessary to truly achieve equality of outcomes. Desegregation is only one of those policies; it cannot by itself end difference that has many roots, but how students are segregated in weak schools or gain access to more successful schools still matters a lot. How students are assigned to classes, how they are treated inside classes, what they are exposed to, what they learn or lose during the summer, what kind of support systems they have, what kind of counseling is available to them—all of those things matter. This means, of course, that school integration is only part of a broader strategy that would be needed to truly equalize opportunity, although it is a crucial part of that strategy.

Finally, and most recently, in 2007 the Supreme Court held in *Parents Involved in Community Schools v. Seattle School District No. 1*[63] that most of the major voluntary desegregation plans in the country that were being implemented without court orders (mostly magnet schools and transfer plans) were unconstitutional. The Court held, in a 5–4 decision, that because an intradistrict voluntary transfer program had a specific integration goal and sometimes held seats for students of an underrepresented racial group, it was unconstitutional because all applicants were not always treated the same. It did not matter if spaces were set aside in a voluntary program that local officials saw as necessary to achieve integration, if no students were required to attend the program, or if the program was voluntarily enacted by

Table 1. Relationship Between Segregation by Race and by Poverty, 2011–12

% Poor in Schools	Percent Black and Latino Students in Schools									
	0–10%	11–20%	21–30%	31–40%	41–50%	51–60%	61–70%	71–80%	81–90%	91–100%
0–10	11.4	10.0	3.6	1.9	2.2	2.2	2.1	2.9	2.1	2.2
11–20	11.8	16.2	11.3	4.2	2.8	1.9	1.8	1.6	1.5	1.3
21–30	13.4	14.7	14.4	10.1	5.2	3.7	2.5	2.2	1.7	1.5
31–40	16.1	15.0	15.2	14.8	10.7	7.2	4.8	2.7	2.2	1.8
41–50	16.3	14.3	15.5	16.5	15.1	12.7	8.6	4.9	3.0	2.4
51–60	13.4	12.7	14.9	17.1	16.7	16.9	13.4	8.0	4.6	3.5
61–70	9.0	9.3	12.5	15.7	19.1	17.8	18.5	15.5	9.2	5.4
71–80	4.7	4.7	7.7	11.3	16.0	18.8	20.8	22.0	18.3	10.5
81–90	2.0	1.9	3.4	5.7	8.7	13.2	17.5	23.2	29.3	20.6
91–100	1.9	1.2	1.5	2.6	3.4	5.6	10.0	17.0	28.0	50.8
Total	100	100	100	100	100	100	100	100	100	100
% of U.S. Schools	33.2	13.9	9.0	6.9	5.9	4.9	4.4	4.2	5.0	12.7

Note: Excluded schools with 0% FRL (Free and Reduced Lunch) students.

Source: U.S. Department of Education, National Center for Education Statistics, Common Core of Data (CCD), Public Elementary/Secondary School Universe Survey Data (2011–12).

the local officials. At the time of this decision, Justice Stevens said that no member of the Court when he was appointed by President Ford (which had four justices appointed by President Nixon) would have signed that decision because it would have been unimaginable to undermine desegregation in such a callous way and to forbid the kind of voluntary desegregation that the courts had been urging and approving for generations.[64]

Many school districts have learned that segregation is related to massive educational problems quite obvious in the accountability data and in the identification of "failing schools," since the schools on the list of "failing schools" and "dropout factories" were very commonly schools segregated by race and poverty. Because *Parents Involved* prohibited any voluntary desegregation plan that made choices about student enrollment on the basis of a student's race (a fundamental part of almost all desegregation plans), many districts saw no feasible alternatives since assignment on the basis of social class often does not produce racial desegregation.[65] Districts seeking post-2007 voluntary plans considering race—including Louisville-Jefferson County, which had been part of the *Parents Involved* case—found both parents and students desiring to continue desegregation and resorted to very detailed analyses of the racial/ethnic composition of neighborhoods, which were used as a factor in student assignment.[66] The work-around was a complicated and costly process and most school districts did not do it. Thus, dropping desegregation standards in choice plans often brought rapid resegregation.

While the courts have been dismantling successful court orders and limiting even voluntary plans, the stakes have risen enormously. At the end of the civil rights era, the country was about one-seventh black and about one-twentieth Latino. At the present time, the country's public school enrollment is more than one-quarter Latino, about one-sixth black, about one-twentieth Asian, and just barely half white.[67] We have had a major transition in our population and the enrollment of our schools without corresponding major policy developments.

Congress passed a number of measures limiting desegregation efforts at the peak of the busing conflict in the early to mid-1970s,[68] and no significant Congressional action supporting desegregation has occurred since 1972. Congress has not passed a major education law since No Child Left Behind in 2002. Long periods of social change have come and gone with no policy response. The courts have been eliminating the admittedly inadequate but significant tools to desegregate schools that remained in constitutional law. During the peak of the Great Recession, the Obama Administration had a great deal of stimulus money to initiate educational programs and great discretion in spending it. It made a few million dollars available one year to help school districts think about how to deal with diversity and desegregation after the Supreme Court's 2007 *Parents Involved* decision. It did not know whether any districts would be interested. Even though the federal government was flooded with applications, the Administration put no more money in that coffer, did not seriously enforce the desegregation goal, did not expand magnet schools, and instead very actively pushed the expansion of charter schools—fostering the most segregated sector of public education and doing nothing for the one that held the most potential for integration. The Obama Administration did not put anything in the Race to the Top about integration or diversity, nor did they provide any help for diverse communities to remain diverse.[69]

At this point, the jurisprudence and public policies that embrace "colorblindness" assume that systemic racial problems have been resolved and that individuals have equal opportunities and a fair chance in a postracial society. Although there has never been a day in which students of color have attended equal and integrated schools or that the outcomes of public schooling have been equal, the assumption is that the passage of time and the brief serious enforcement of civil rights laws cured the historic violations of minority rights and ended the prejudice of local officials. The profound inequalities that remain then must be either the fault of the victims or insolvable by the courts, which are assumed to have done everything that can feasibly be done. These assumptions are delusions. If they were not, we would not have seen the systematic resegregation that has occurred since the courts retreated from the goal of *Brown*. We would not have seen the discrimination in housing and mortgage finance that left middle-class black and Latino families stuck with failing predatory mortgages in highly vulnerable communities, which produced vast and highly unequal losses in the Great Recession. We would not have drastic difference in graduation rates and success in college for students from resegregated high schools. Teachers would not systematically leave schools that resegregate. In other words, if those assumptions held true, we would be in a different, truly colorblind society and we could turn to other problems. Unfortunately, we are not. When we believe or pretend that is the case, we are engaging in the kinds of rhetorical tricks the Supreme Court used in *Plessy v. Ferguson*[70] when it expressed the belief that local officials would be fair and that discrimination was only a problem in the minds of the minority groups, and thus set the stage for full-scale implementation of apartheid policies in 17 states. Being "colorblind" in a society where racial inequalities are still deeply entrenched amounts to officially legitimating the privileges of the dominant groups and disposing of the civil rights of those locked into isolation and inequality.

What Can Come Next

COMPLEX PROBLEMS AND COMPLEX SOLUTIONS

Recently, a coalition of leading civil rights groups in Washington and research centers across the nation has been pressuring the Obama Administration consistently to try to do something positive in response to these challenges.[71] Thousands of suburban school systems are going through racial change and have no real help either from the government or from the education profession. The Civil Rights Project and a team of scholars from the universities of California, Texas, Minnesota, South Florida, and Harvard, have studied a number of these communities.[72] Most of the school districts studied had no plan, no help, and were resegregating. Some are in total denial and assume that the resegregation process can be reversed by improving test scores and ignoring race (in spite of strong evidence that white parents and teachers withdraw from schools that resegregate).[73] The dynamic of resegregating neighborhoods and of some resegregating suburbs is that resegregation tends to be first by race and then by class. A whole series of things happen to schools, neighborhoods, investment structures, employment, and really to all aspects of a community as resegregation takes place.[74] One would think, in a suburban society, that the fear of replicating the destructive ghettoization process that went on in central cities a half-century ago would be seen as very threatening. Unfortunately, today's policymakers do not even have a language to talk about these changes or tools to work on them since the language with which we have been talking for three decades about educational quality has been based on accountability and the assumption that we can create greater racial equality in society by having higher standards, more sanctions, and better tests without changing anything about the society or which schools children have access to. That language ignores the failures of the accountability policies to achieve end racial gaps and their irrelevance to the goals of achieving stable integration.

There have been vast changes in American society since World War II, and they are continuing; figure 2 and table 2 illustrate some of these changes. At the time of *Brown* we were experiencing a great baby boom, a massive move of blacks from the South to Northern and Western cities, and an explosion of virtually all-white suburbanization. Latinos were a serious presence only in the Southwest and in a few cities. As the civil rights era ended in the mid-1970s, the white middle class was already gone from many cities and the white birthrate was dropping rapidly. Blacks were beginning to move back to the South. The immigration reform of 1965 was beginning to show what would become monumental changes in Latino and Asian

Figure 2. Public School Enrollment from 1968 to 2011

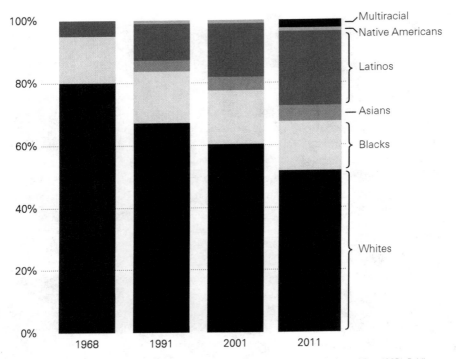

Source: U.S. Department of Education, National Center for Education Statistics, Common Core of Data (CCD), Public Elementary/Secondary School Universe Survey Data. Data prior to 1991 obtained from the analysis of the Office of Civil Rights data in GARY ORFIELD, PUBLIC SCHOOL DESEGREGATION IN THE UNITED STATES, 1968–1980 (Joint Center for Political Studies 1983).

population. Magnet schools were growing very rapidly and charter schools had not been invented yet. Integration was still growing slowly for African Americans and shrinking steadily for Latinos.

We are now in a different world. The white population is shrinking and has not been reproducing itself for a number of years. Across the Southwest, Latinos are moving into historically black areas and sometimes displacing the black population. In schools in the West there are more Latinos than whites, who account for only two-fifths of the total enrollment. There are few whites and few middle-class families of any race enrolling children in the public schools of many central cities, and the big cities have significantly more Latino than African American students. The once-isolated Latino and Asian populations are spreading out across the country,

Table 2. Public School Enrollment by Race/Ethnicity and Region, 2011–2012

	Total Enrollment	White	Black	Asian	Latino	Native American	Multiracial
				Percent			
South	15,957,201	44.7%	24.1%	3.1%	25.3%	0.5%	2.3%
West	11,310,045	40.2%	5.3%	8.3%	41.4%	1.7%	3.1%
Northeast	7,731,000	60.1%	14.4%	6.4%	17.3%	0.3%	1.4%
Border	3,548,325	63.7%	19.1%	2.8%	8.2%	3.4%	2.8%
Midwest	9,451,340	68.1%	13.5%	3.1%	11.2%	0.9%	3.1%
Alaska	113,093	48.2%	3.7%	8.7%	6.4%	25.3%	7.6%
Hawaii	182,529	14.3%	2.4%	68.1%	6.4%	0.5%	8.2%
Other	489,846	0.2%	2.5%	8.4%	88.6%	0.1%	0.2%
U.S. Total	48,783,379	51.5%	15.4%	5.1%	24.3%	1.1%	2.5%

Note: Our definition of the regions is as follows: **South**: Alabama, Arkansas, Florida, Georgia, Louisiana, Mississippi, North Carolina, South Carolina, Tennessee, Texas, and Virginia; **Border**: Delaware, District of Columbia, Kentucky, Maryland, Missouri, Oklahoma, and West Virginia; **Northeast**: Connecticut, Maine, Massachusetts, New Hampshire, New Jersey, New York, Pennsylvania, Rhode Island, and Vermont; **Midwest**: Illinois, Indiana, Iowa, Kansas, Michigan, Minnesota, Nebraska, North Dakota, Ohio, South Dakota, and Wisconsin; **West**: Arizona, California, Colorado, Montana, Nevada, New Mexico, Oregon, Utah, Washington, and Wyoming.

Source: U.S. Department of Education, National Center for Education Statistics, Common Core of Data (CCD), Public Elementary/Secondary School Universe Survey Data, 2011–12.

especially in areas of economic growth. Black residential segregation, which peaked about 1970, has declined modestly, while Latino segregation has risen. There has been a huge migration of nonwhite families to suburban communities and schools, and the suburban schools in our largest metros were only half-white by 2011. There is now as large a percent of Asians in the school population as there were Latinos in the late 1960s, and they are, on average, by far the most educationally and economically successful racial group. A rapidly growing number of school districts have significant populations of three or four racial/ethnic groups and complex patterns of racial inequality.[75] It is not surprising that principles framed in a black-white context more than a half century ago are not adequate for current situations. The desegregation plans of the past were built on integrating one minority group with whites and on the assumption that a plan that addressed the pattern of segregation that existed at the time of the trial would hold over time. Neither of these assumptions is true. City populations have never been stable and that is why good policy requires continuous updating along many dimensions. Rather than developing new solutions for a changing society and learning from the dramatically different patterns in various states and metropolitan areas, politicians and administrators have ignored the issues and there has been a severe increase in school segregation by race and poverty as a result.

Because of these changes, we now must think about multiracialism in a creative way. We must think about integration in a situation where whites are the minority, or where whites are one of several minorities because everybody is a minority. This is the last generation of a white majority in this country and there is no longer a white majority in public schools.[76] The West and the South have been predominantly nonwhite in school enrollment for years. In a series of reports the Civil Rights Project is producing about the Eastern seaboard states right now, Latinos and Asians are the growing populations in every part of New England and the Middle Atlantic regions, many of which have white outmigration. The South, which has been a white-black polarized society throughout its history, is now triracial and the Latino school enrollment has recently surpassed black enrollment. Both middle-class black and Latino families are primarily living in suburbs—but they are attending increasingly segregated suburban schools. Whites remain in other suburban sectors, but clearly dominate school populations only in small towns and rural areas.[77] We are in the middle of a great transition yet we do not have stable multiracial communities or stable multiracial schools. Nobody is really using the schools in some central cities except poor minorities. New Orleans has no more traditional public schools. That is not a viable structure for the future of our society and we must figure out something better.

Interestingly, positive changes are happening with regard to housing segregation. Specifically, housing discrimination is decreasing and a recent study by HUD shows that overt discrimination in housing is going down quite a lot.[78] These changes create more possibilities for residential integration and for addressing issues without tremendous demographic pressure as when African Americans and Latinos were confined to segregated neighborhoods that were overcrowded and overpopulated, in desperate need of housing, and with no capacity to move except in a straight line out of those communities. Now, different residential patterns create opportunities such as expanding magnet schools and putting some civil rights requirements on our charter schools so that they are schools of equitable choice.

Similarly, some neighborhoods in central cities are now gentrifying. This is happening across the country—in Los Angeles and Boston, in Philadelphia and Washington, in San Francisco and Seattle, and in many other locations.[79] In fact, Washington, DC, has been becoming whiter for the last three censuses; it has declined 40% in black population from its peak and is up 30% in white population from its bottom.[80] Public schools there are almost totally segregated, though, and a large parallel system of segregated charter schools have been added without engaging the white population in either system.[81] It is possible to draw these families back into traditional public schools, but we cannot do this unless we can figure out a way to talk about and respond to the racial dimension that parents seldom mention but are seriously concerned about. The conventional wisdom of school administrators seems to be, "Well, if we get the tests up, everybody will be happy," but that is not true and gentrifiers seldom use public schools in many communities. A parent will not be happy if his or her child is the only one of a certain racial or ethnic group in the school, or if they are not treated well or provided the courses that prepare them for college. Where the schools are resegregated by race and poverty, few white or middle-class families of any race will consider buying into a neighborhood and raising their children there. To solve this problem and create integrated schools attractive to all families there must be plan to welcome all, to create real diversity, and to meet the educational needs of the parents with choices. The result of such an effort can create the kind of schools that all children deserve and build the community and support for public education.

Integration does not happen by accident. If a nice suburban community is becoming diverse, and 60% of the housing market is African American or Latino and 40% is white, in a relatively few years a lot of resegregation can occur. That should be one of the basic things city planners, school administrators, and school board members think about. It is much easier to create lasting integration if there are collaborative early efforts to attract families of all races to the community and the school and create a positive image of a rich multiracial future. In important ways, communities are self-fulfilling prophecies. If people believe that a community is not integrated but in transition to a ghetto, that prophecy is likely to become reality within a few years. Yet, often mostly poor and mostly minority school districts do not provide the middle-class families any credible reason to stay in the community or in the school, and whites clearly tend to move to whiter areas.

If we put all of these trends together and aim to engage them in a way that will produce lasting diversity on multiple levels, the result will have to be a combined integration-conscious school and housing policy approach, and we will have to think about that approach in the long-run in multiple minority settings because that is where we are going as a society.[82] There is going to continue to be a racial change in this country, and how it is shaped is going to be determined by several things. One of them is housing policy. HUD studies, for example, in Denver, Phoenix, and Columbus, Ohio, back in the 1980s showed that if public housing had been placed differently or rented out differently, the school segregation problem would have mostly disappeared. Public housing is not a very large sector of the housing market, but it is a substantial sector of the black housing market and also important for Latinos in some areas. Now, we are largely subsidizing housing through vouchers. If we gave vouchers and money and counseling in locations that produce integration, for example, we could produce much more stability in neighborhoods than if we let them all be targeted in places that are going to be in transition, which is what we have usually done. We must think about housing and schools in concert.

If we plan successfully, we will realize substantial benefits in addition to the clear benefits of understanding each other and learning how to work together effectively. For example, the United States is a largely monolingual country. There is no other advanced country where educated people only know one language. Very few learn how to speak another language fluently in this country unless the family brought the second language with them as immigrants or students go abroad to study. But, we have many millions of native speakers of other languages who are in this country as a result of immigration. We can bring them together voluntarily with native English speakers in schools where they can learn each other's language—that makes what is now considered a deficit (the English language learners in our schools) into a potential advantage for all as students each gain fluency and understanding of the other's language and culture.[83] There are actually hundreds of examples of this now around the country and, of course, many private schools promise this as a great asset. The mindset in education planning must shift: Being fluent in Spanish is an asset in the right setting and is an advantage in the United States labor market already.[84] Properly done, such schools can create positive social and educational gains in an integrated situation of equal status interaction, where each group respects and learns from the other.

EVERYONE'S RESPONSIBILITY

We can have a multiracial future, but we do not have a successful multiracial present. We are at dismal point in terms of policy and leadership. From a civil rights perspective, this is the worst Supreme Court in 80 years. The Court seems determined to take away the relatively modest tools that we have to deal with racial and ethnic inequality. The Obama Administration has many officials who do understand these issues, but they are not proposing any significant initiatives. Social and educational policies have narrowed and offer little. We have schools of education, schools of law, and other institutions that could contribute to the challenge that are devoting little energy to these challenges, instead tacitly accepting the idea that we can safely ignore questions of race. Those of us who are in the academic world should be ready to develop and present findings that show the realities of the society that is emerging and propose ideas that schools and communities can implement. Researchers should conduct experiments that help us think about what would be a really good Asian/Hispanic/white school or a school with African Americans and Native Americans and Asians, many of the combinations that will exist in our future as the nation continues to change.

We have been facing deepening segregation now for a quarter-century. There are costs: vulnerable students are attending increasingly impoverished and isolated schools and have fewer chances as competition for college and jobs gets harder. That means their families and communities will suffer seriously and that their chances for mobility in the next generation will be severely narrowed. It means society will not maximize the creative and economic capacity of our country. Many communities in our viable urban centers are reviving to some extent, but only partially because they do not have viable interracial schools. There are hundreds of suburban communities where white and middle-class people would like to stay, and would not mind diversity, but do not want to experience resegregation, which is often the likely outcome in the absence of positive policies. If those communities resegregate by race and then by poverty, everyone loses.

Most of the people who are in control of this country and a great many of the voters are from an older population who grew up in a far less diverse society. They do not really understand the transformation and many hope it can be stopped. This relates to the intensity of anti-immigrant feelings and to wedge-issue politics playing on public fears that society is changing. But the transformation cannot be stopped; it would continue even if the border were completely sealed—it is built into the composition and the age structure of our population. The change to a majority-nonwhite country can be done well, or it can be done badly, but it will happen. We are on the path for taking away the tools that could make it come out better and adopting policies that will almost surely make it worse.

Our educational leaders and our courts need to focus seriously on what we have learned, where we are now, and what can be done. Our political leaders need the courage to recognize the changes in our society and the mounting costs of inaction. There is much in our six decades of experience since *Brown* to indicate what could work and how we would benefit. Passive acceptance of growing racial and economic polarization of our schools has been a great failure of vision. A half-century ago, America accomplished what had seemed to be unimaginable changes in the South. Now, it is giving up much of the progress and ignoring the issues in the North and West that were never addressed. We need to find the courage and commitment to create and work for a vision of successfully diverse schools helping to build and create opportunities in a profoundly multiracial future.

Conclusion

People sometimes say, "Desegregation can't be done," or "Desegregation failed." It did not fail, though. When it was done properly, it succeeded and it lasted until it was dismantled. It was not miraculous and it did not change everything, but it did change a lot. A black or Latino child's chances of graduating from high school went up, her chances of going to college increased, her chances of living and working successfully in an interracial setting expanded. A lot of important things happened, and they were important not just for minorities, but for all parts of society. White and Asian students who experienced desegregated schools were much better prepared for the very diverse society in which they will live and work for the rest of their lives. Sixty years after *Brown*, we have learned that desegregation is really hard, but we learned during six decades of *Plessy* that equality within segregation is impossible on any significant level. We are learning that again as we lapse back to segregation.

The U.S. has been living in a seemingly hopeful but truly dangerous delusion—that the country can go through a great transformation of our highly polarized society and the problems will simply solve themselves. Nothing in our history says that this is so. Ignoring the issues only intensifies separation and stratification. By seriously facing our new realities and taking the best lessons of the civil rights era we can create the only secure future for the multiple minorities, including whites, who must find ways to live and work together if our institutions are to flourish in a nation with no majority group. It could be a kind of society new to the world: an integrated society built in part on integrated schools where the vision of *Brown* is a daily reality.

Gary Orfield is a Distinguished Research Professor of Education, Law, Political Science and Urban Planning at the University of California, Los Angeles, and co-director of the Civil Rights Project.

NOTES

1. Brown v. Board of Education, 347 U.S. 485 (1954).
2. Gary Orfield & Erica Frankenberg, The Civil Rights Project, Brown *at 60: Great Progress, a Long Retreat, and an Uncertain Future* (2014).
3. John Kucsera & Gary Orfield, The Civil Rights Project, *New York State's Extreme. School Segregation. Inequality, Inaction and a Damaged Future* (2014).
4. Mendez v. Westminster, 64 F. Supp. 544 (S.D. Cal. 1946), affirmed, 161 F.2d 774 (9th Cir. 1947) (en banc).
5. Gary Orfield and Jongyheon Ee, The Civil Rights Project, *Segregating California's Future. Inequality and Its Alternative. 60 Years after* Brown v. Board of Education (2014).
6. Robert Linn & Kevin Welner, National Academy of Education, *Race-conscious policies for assigning students to schools: Social science research and the Supreme Court cases* (2007).
7. REED SARRATT, THE ORDEAL OF DESEGREGATION: THE FIRST DECADE (Harper and Row 1966); JAMES E. RYAN, FIVE MILES AWAY, A WORLD APART, 27 (Oxford

University Press 2010); BRUCE ACKERMAN, WE THE PEOPLE, VOLUME 3: THE CIVIL RIGHTS REVOLUTION, 233 (Harvard University Press 2014).

8. The long-standing tradition of the Senate was that the senior senator of the president's party from the state affected had a veto over the nomination of federal district judges during this period. JACK WALTER PELTASON, FIFTY-EIGHT LONELY MEN (Harcourt, Brace & World 1961); Brown v. Board of Education, 349 U.S. 294 (1955) (Brown II).

9. Green v. Board of Education of New Kent County, 391 U.S. 430 (1968).

10. Civil Rights Act of 1964, Public Law No. 88-352, 78 Stat. 241 (codified as amended in scattered sections of 2 U.S.C., 28 U.S.C., and 42 U.S.C.).

11. Elementary and Secondary Education Act of 1965, Public Law No. 89-10, 78 Stat. 241 (codified as amended in scattered sections of 20 U.S.C.).

12. 42 U.S.C. §§ 2000c-2 to c-6, 2000d to d-1 (2006).

13. Emergency School Aid Act, Public Law No. 89-10, 92 Stat. 2252 (enacted no currently effective sections). The legislative history is reported in GARY ORFIELD, CONGRESSIONAL POWER: CONGRESS AND SOCIAL CHANGE, 173–88 (Harcourt Brace Jovanovich 1975).

14. GARY ORFIELD, THE RECONSTRUCTION OF SOUTHERN EDUCATION: THE SCHOOLS AND THE 1964 CIVIL RIGHTS ACT (John Wiley 1969).

15. Orfield & Frankenberg, Brown *at 60.*

16. Gary Orfield, *Public Opinion and School Desegregation,* 96 TEACHERS COLLEGE RECORD 654 (1995) (discussing Gallup Poll data).

17. James S. Coleman, Ernest Q. Campbell, Carol J. Hobson, James McPartland, Alexander M. Mood, Frederic D. Weinfeld & Robert L. York, United States Department of Health, Education, and Welfare, *Equality of Educational Opportunity* (1966).

18. Coleman et al., *Equality of Educational Opportunity,* 21.

19. Brief of 553 Social Scientists as Amici Curiae in Support of Respondents, Parents Involved in Community Schools v. Seattle School District No. 1, 2006 WL 2927079 (U.S.), 10-12, 32a-3a (U.S. 2006).

20. HARRY S. DENT, THE PRODIGAL SOUTH RETURNS TO POWER, 82–82, 111–12 (Wiley 1978); LEON FRIEDMAN & WILLIAM F. LEVANTROSSER, EDS., RICHARD M. NIXON: POLITICAN, PRESIDENT, ADMINISTRATOR, 143 (Greenwood Press 1991).

21. Gary Orfield, *The Politics of Resegregation,* SATURDAY REVIEW, 58–60, 77, 79 (September 20, 1969); DENT, THE PRODIGAL SOUTH. Dent was Deputy White House Counsel for President Nixon.

22. Alexander v. Holmes County Board of Education, 396 U.S. 19 (1969).

23. LEON PANETTA & PETER GALL, BRING US TOGETHER: THE NIXON TEAM AND THE CIVIL RIGHTS RETREAT (Lippincott 1971).

24. Keyes v. School District No. 1, 413 U.S. 189 (1973).

25. Keyes, 413 U.S. at 208.

26. DOUGLAS MASSEY & NANCY DENTON, AMERICAN APARTHEID, 44–45 (Harvard University Press 1993).

27. GARY ORFIELD, MUST WE BUS?: SEGREGATED SCHOOLS AND NATIONAL POLICY, 151–97 (Brookings Institution 1978).

28. Keyes, 413 U.S. 197–98.

29. Adams v. Richardson, 356 F. Supp. 92 (D.D.C. 1973).

30. Chungmei Lee, Harvard Civil Rights Project, *Denver Public Schools: Resegregation, Latino Style* (2006); Proposition 1, Primary Election (November 6, 1979) (regarding the "School Assignment and Transportation of Pupils").

31. Milliken v. Bradley, 418 U.S. 717 (1974).

32. Bradley v. Milliken, 345 F. Supp. 914 (E.D. Mich. 1972).

33. Bradley v. Milliken, 484 F.2d 215 (6th Cir. 1973).

34. *Nixon Interested in Busing Amendment*, THE PALM BEACH POST, A1, A7 (February 21, 1972).

35. PAUL DIMOND, BEYOND BUSING: REFLECTIONS ON URBAN SEGREGATION, THE COURTS, AND EQUAL OPPORTUNITY (University of Michigan Press 2005); ORFIELD, MUST WE BUS?, 31–32.

36. Milliken, 418 U.S. 741–42, 753.

37. BRIAN D. BOYER, CITIES DESTROYED FOR CASH: THE FHA SCANDAL AT HUD (Follett 1973). Detroit was one of the cities most damaged by the Nixon Administration's reliance on unsupervised private business to manage a gigantic home ownership program which financed white flight from Detroit and left thousands of blacks holding overpriced housing, fraudulently marketed in poor condition they could not maintain and that was soon abandoned.

38. Milliken v. Bradley, 418 U.S. 717, 783 (1974) (Marshall, J., dissenting).

39. Massey & Denton, AMERICAN APARTHEID, 75–77.

40. Milliken v. Bradley, 418 U.S. 717, 756 n.2 (1974) (Justice Stewart, concurring); DIMOND, BEYOND BUSING, 55–56.

41. Milliken v. Bradley, 433 U.S. 267 (1977) (Milliken II).

42. GARY ORFIELD & SUSAN EATON, DISMANTLING DESEGREGATION: THE QUIET REVERSAL OF *BROWN V. BOARD OF EDUCATION*, 149–51 (New Press 1996) (quoting Bradley v. Milliken, 476 F. Supp. 257, 258 (E.D. Mich 1979).

43. Missouri v. Jenkins, 515 U.S. 70 (1995).

44. Orfield & Frankenberg, Brown *at 60*, 14.

45. ORFIELD, MUST WE BUS?, 20–22 (listing the violations found in many Northern desegregation cases through the mid-1970s).

46. Robert L. Crain, National Opinion Research Center, *Southern Schools: An Evaluation of the Effects of the. Emergency School Assistance Program and of School Desegregation* (1973).

47. JEFFREY A. RAFFEL, HISTORICAL DICTIONARY OF SCHOOL SEGREGATION AND DESEGREGATION: THE AMERICAN EXPERIENCE, 94 (Greenwood Press 1998).

48. Genievieve Siegel-Hawley & Erica Frankenberg, The Civil Rights Project, *Reviving Magnet Schools: Strengthening a Successful Choice Option*, 9 (2012).

49. Siegel-Hawley & Frankenberg, *Reviving Magnet Schools*, 7–8.

50. U.S. Commission on Civil Rights, *Southern School Desegregation, 1966–67*, 74 (1967); Green v. New Kent Company, 391 U.S 430, 439–41 (1968).

51. Kucsera & Orfield, *New York's Extreme School Segregation*.

52. Genevieve Siegel-Hawley & Erica Frankenberg, *A Segregating Choice? An Overview of Charter School Policy, Enrollment Trends, and Segregation*, in GARY ORFIELD & ERICA FRANKENBERG, EDUCATIONAL DELUSIONS? WHY CHOICE CAN DEEPEN INEQUALITY AND HOW TO MAKE SCHOOLS FAIR, 129–44 (University of California Press 2013).

53. Kucsera & Orfield, *New York's Extreme School Segregation*, viii, 86.

54. Board of Education of Oklahoma City v. Dowell, 498 U.S. 237, 248–49 (1991).

55. Ibid.

56. Freeman v. Pitts, 503 U.S. 467, 489 (1992).

57. Missouri v. Jenkins, 515 U.S. 70, 101–2 (1995); Jenkins by Agyei v. Missouri, 11 F.3d 755, 765 (8th Cir. 1993); Jenkins v. Missouri, 77-0420-CV-W-4, 1993 WL 566488, *2 (W.D. Mo. July 30, 1993).

58. Gary Orfield, *Conservative Activists and the Rush toward Resegregation*, in JAY HEUBERT, ED., LAW AND SCHOOL REFORM, 39–87 (Yale University Press 1999).

59. Orfield & Frankenberg, Brown *at* 60.

60. Catherine E. Freeman, Benjamin Scafidi, & David L. Sjoquist, *Racial Segregation in Georgia Public Schools, 1994–2001*, in JOHN CHARLES BOGER & GARY ORFIELD, SCHOOL RESEGREGATION: MUST THE SOUTH TURN BACK? (University of North Carolina Press 2005).

61. PRUDENCE L. CARTER & KEVIN G. WELNER, EDS., CLOSING THE OPPORTUNITY GAP: WHAT AMERICA MUST DO TO GIVE EVERY CHILD AN EVEN CHANCE (Oxford University Press 2013).

62. David Shenk, *The 32-Million Word Gap*, THE ATLANTIC (March 9, 2010).

63. Parents Involved in Community Schools v. Seattle School District No. 1, 551 U.S. 701, 732–35, 798 (2007) (Chief Justice Roberts, plurality opinion) (Justice Kennedy, concurring).

64. Parents Involved, 551 U.S. 701, 803 (2007) (Justice Stevens, dissenting).

65. Justice Kennedy had suggested boundary changes and school site selection, but these methods are often ineffective in large school districts and can even speed resegregation by focusing racial change on a small part of a school district and leaving outlying white areas untouched. On the feasibility of social class integration see Sean F. Reardon, John T. Yun, & Michal Kurlaender, *Implications of Income-Based School Assignment Policies for Racial School Segregation*, 28 EDUCATIONAL EVALUATION AND POLICY ANALYSIS 49 (2006).

66. Lisa Chavez & Erica Frankenberg, The Civil Rights Project, *Integration Defended: Berkeley Unified's Strategy to Maintain School Diversity* (2009).

67. Orfield & Frankenberg, Brown *at* 60.

68. Including a serious limitation on Title VI of the 1964 Civil Rights Act sponsored by Senator Joseph Biden to try to block desegregation efforts in the Wilmington, Delaware, area; ORFIELD, MUST WE BUS?, 272–73; *Wilmington Morning News* (July 10, 1974).

69. National Coalition of School Diversity, *NCSD Issue Brief #4*, 2 (2012); National Coalition of School Diversity, *Education, Equity and Opportunity in the Obama Administration's FY 2015 Budget* (2014).

70. Plessy v. Ferguson, 163 U.S. 537, 550–51 (1896).

71. National Coalition, *NCSD Issue Brief #4*, 2. National Coalition, *Education, Equity and Opportunity*.

72. ERICA FRANKENBERG & GARY ORFIELD, EDS., THE RESEGREGATION OF SUBURBAN SCHOOLS: A HIDDEN CRISIS IN AMERICAN EDUCATION (Harvard Education Press 2012).

73. CHARLES T. CLOTFELTER, AFTER *BROWN*: THE RISE AND RETREAT OF SCHOOL DESEGREGATION (Princeton University Press 2004).

74. FRANKENBERG & ORFIELD, THE RESEGREGATION OF SUBURBAN SCHOOLS.

75. Orfield & Frankenberg, Brown *at 60*, 2, 6–8, 13, 17, 22–23.

76. Sam Roberts, *In a Generation, Minorities May Be the U.S. Majority*, THE NEW YORK TIMES (Aug. 13, 2008).

77. Orfield & Frankenberg, Brown *at 60*, 9, 13–14; The Civil Rights Project, School Segregations Trends in the Eastern States (2014).

78. U.S. Department of Housing and Urban Development, *Housing Discrimination Against Racial And Ethnic Minorities 2012* (2013).

79. Kucsera & Orfield, *New York State's Extreme School Segregation*; Daniel Hartley, Federal Reserve Bank of Cleveland, *Gentrification and Financial Health* (2013).

80. United States Census Bureau, *District of Columbia Quickfacts Sheet* (2013); United States Census Bureau, *District of Columbia—Race and Hispanic Origin: 1880 to 1990* (2002).

81. National Alliance for Public Charter Schools, *District of Columbia Public Schools— Students by Race and Ethnicity* (2012).

82. Gary Orfield, *Housing Segregation Produces Unequal Schools: Causes and Solutions*, in CARTER & WELNER, CLOSING THE OPPORTUNITY GAP, 40–60.

83. Patricia C. Gándara & Gary Orfield, *Moving from Failure to a New Vision of Language Policy*, in PATRICIA C. GÁNDARA & MEGAN HOPKINS, ENGLISH LEARNERS AND RESTRICTIVE LANGUAGE POLICIES, 216–25 (Teachers College Press 2010).

84. REBECCA M. CALLAHAN & PATRICIA C. GÁNDARA, THE BILINGUAL ADVANTAGE: LANGUAGE, LITERACY, AND THE U.S. LABOR MARKET (Multilingual Matters 2014).

Contributing Authors

Frederick P. Aguirre is a California Superior Court Judge in Orange County, a position he has held since 2002. He began his legal career by working as a Reginald Heber Smith Fellow and VISTA Volunteer with the Legal Aid Society of Santa Clara County for three years, which was followed by 28 years in private practice in Orange County. Judge Aguirre is the co-author of several books profiling Mexican American veterans from World War I through our most recent wars in the Middle East. He received a BA from the University of Southern California and a JD from UCLA.

Joyce A. Baugh is a Professor in the Department of Political Science at Central Michigan University where she teaches courses in constitutional law, civil rights and liberties, judicial process, American government, and the Civil Rights Movement. She is the author of *The Detroit School Busing Case:* Milliken v. Bradley *and the Controversy over Desegregation* (2011) and *Supreme Court Justices in the Post-Bork Era: Confirmation Politics and Judicial Performance* (2002). Dr. Baugh is also the co-author of *The Changing Supreme Court: Constitutional Rights and Liberties* (1997, with Thomas R. Hensley and Christopher E. Smith) and *The Real Clarence Thomas: Confirmation Veracity Meets Performance Reality* (2000, with Christopher

E. Smith). She received a BA from Clemson University and an MA and PhD from Kent State University.

Derek W. Black is a Professor of Law at the University of South Carolina School of Law. His scholarship focuses on educational equality and intentional discrimination in education. He is the author of *Education Law: Equality, Fairness, and Reform* (2013). Previously, he taught at American University, the University of North Carolina, and Howard University where he founded and directed the Education Rights Center. Prior to teaching, Professor Black litigated issues relating to school desegregation, diversity, school finance equity, student discipline, and special education at the Lawyers' Committee for Civil Rights Under Law. He received a BA from the University of Tennessee and a JD from the University of North Carolina.

Kristi L. Bowman is a Professor of Law at Michigan State University College of Law and a faculty associate at the MSU College of Education's Education Policy Center. Previously, she taught at Drake University and the University of Mississippi. Much of her scholarship focuses on racial and ethnic equality in education and, relatedly, the fiscal stability of school districts. She also has written extensively about students' First Amendment rights and is a co-author of the fifth edition of *Educational Policy and the Law* (2012, with Mark Yudof, Betsy Levin, Rachel Moran, and James Ryan). In 2009, Professor Bowman received the Education Law Association's Goldberg Award for Distinguished Scholarship in Education Law. Before teaching, she represented school districts as an attorney at Franczek Sullivan (now Franczek Radelet) in Chicago. She received a BA from Drake University and an MA and JD from Duke University.

Allison R. Brown is a Program Officer for the Racial Justice portfolio at the Open Society Foundations. She is a civil rights attorney, founder of Allison Brown Consulting (ABC), and host of the online radio show *Know-it-All: The ABCs of Education*. Ms. Brown worked as a trial attorney for the United States Department of Justice in the Educational Opportunities Section of the Civil Rights Division, where she enforced federal statutes that prohibit discrimination in public education. She received a BA from Howard University and a JD from Harvard Law School.

Erwin Chemerinsky is the founding Dean and Distinguished Professor of Law, and Raymond Pryke Professor of First Amendment Law, at the University of California, Irvine School of Law, with a joint appointment in Political Science. Previously, he taught at Duke University, the University of Southern California, UCLA, and DePaul University. His areas of expertise are constitutional law, federal practice, civil rights and civil liberties, and appellate litigation. He is the author of eight books and more than 200 articles in law reviews. He frequently argues cases before the nation's highest courts, including the Supreme Court. In January 2014, *National Jurist* magazine named Dean Chemerinsky as the most influential person in legal education in the United States. He received a BA from Northwestern University and a JD from Harvard Law School.

Charles T. Clotfelter is the Z. Smith Reynolds Professor of Public Policy and Professor of Economics and Law at Duke University. At Duke, he has served as Vice Provost for Academic Policy and Planning, Vice Chancellor, Vice Provost for Academic Programs. Currently, he is the Associate Dean of Academic Programs at the Sanford School of Public Policy. Among his books are *Big-Time Sports in American Universities* (2011), *After* Brown: *The Rise and Retreat of School Desegregation* (2004), *Buying the Best: Cost Escalation in Elite Higher Education* (1996), *Selling Hope: State Lotteries in America* (1989, with Philip J. Cook), and *Federal Tax Policy and Charitable Giving* (1985). He received a BA from Duke University and an MA and PhD from Harvard University.

Sarah Diem is an Assistant Professor in the Department of Educational Leadership & Policy Analysis at the University of Missouri. Her research focuses on the sociopolitical and geographic contexts of education, paying particular attention to how politics, leadership, and implementation of educational policy affect diversity outcomes. Dr. Diem has published in the *American Journal of Education, Educational Administration Quarterly, Teachers College Record, Educational Policy, Race Ethnicity and Education, The Urban Review, Education Policy Analysis Archives*, and the *Journal of School Leadership*, among other journals. She received a BA and JD from the University of Texas at Austin and an MPA from the University of Oregon.

Michael J. Dumas is an Assistant Professor in the Graduate School of Education and the Department of African American Studies at University of California, Berkeley. Previously, he taught at New York University. His work has been published in a number of journals, including *Teachers College Record; Race, Ethnicity and Education;* and *Education Policy Analysis Archives,* and he is the editor of a forthcoming special issue of the *Journal of Educational Policy* about the cultural politics of race in educational policy. He is also a contributor to the *Handbook of Critical Race Theory in Education* (2013). He received a BA from Fairhaven College at Western Washington University, an MEd from the University of Maryland at College Park, and a PhD from The Graduate Center of The City University of New York.

Patricia A. Edwards, a member of the Reading Hall Fame, is a Professor of Language and Literacy in the Department of Teacher Education at Michigan State University. Dr. Edwards is a nationally and internationally recognized expert in family/ school/ community partnerships, especially among poor and minority children. She served as President of the International Reading Association and as the first African American President of the Literacy Research Association (formerly the National Reading Conference). Among her numerous publications are *Change is Gonna Come: Transforming Literacy for African American Students* (2010, with Gwendolyn Thompson McMillon, and Jennifer D. Turner) and *Bridging Literacy and Equity: The Essential Guide to Social Equity Teaching* (2012, with Althier M. Lazar and Gwendolyn Thompson McMillon). She received a BS from Albany State University, an MS from North Carolina A&T University, an EdS from Duke University, and a PhD from the University of Wisconsin–Madison.

John J. (Jack) Feeheley is the retired Senior Vice President of Michigan Con Gas Company and a former FBI agent. After joining the Bureau in 1952, his assignments included the Criminal Division on Organized Crime, the Counter-Soviet Espionage Division, the Communist Party-USA activities, and the civil rights investigations in the 1950s. In 1962, Mr. Feeheley became a Deputy Director of Blue Cross-Blue Shield of Michigan, and in 1969 he took a position with Mich Con Gas Company, where he worked until retiring in 1993. He received a BS from Monmouth College and is a veteran of the U.S. Navy.

Erica Frankenberg is an Assistant Professor in the Department of Education Policy Studies at The Pennsylvania State University. Her current research includes studying suburban racial change, policy, and the politics of response to the Supreme Court's decision about voluntary integration, and how school choice policies affect racial stratification. Her work has been published in leading education policy journals and law reviews. Dr. Frankenberg has co-authored or co-edited several books, including *Educational Delusions? Why Choice Can Deepen Inequality and How to Make it Fair* (2013, with Gary Orfield) and *The Resegregation of Suburban Schools: A Hidden Crisis in American Education* (2012, with Gary Orfield). She was formerly a researcher at the Civil Rights Project at Harvard and UCLA. She received an AB from Dartmouth College, and a MEd and EdD from Harvard University.

Kevin Fox Gotham is Professor of Sociology and Associate Dean of Academic Affairs in the School of Liberal Arts at Tulane University. He has research interests in postdisaster redevelopment, real estate and housing policy, and the political economy of tourism. He is author of *Race, Real Estate and Uneven Development*

(2014), *Authentic New Orleans* (2007), *Critical Perspectives on Urban Redevelopment* (2001), and *Crisis Cities: Disaster and Redevelopment in New York and New Orleans* (2014, with Miriam Greenberg). He received a BA, MA, and PhD from the University of Kansas.

Jessica J. Gottlieb is a postdoctoral research associate at the Center for STEM Education at the University of Notre Dame. Her research interests include the effect of accountability-based policies on teacher quality and the social construction of teachers and teaching in education policy. She received a BS from the University of Southern California and a PhD from the University of Illinois at Chicago.

Jack Greenberg is the Alphonse Fletcher Jr. Professor of Law at Columbia Law School, where he has been a member of the faculty since 1984. Between 1949 and 1961 he was Assistant Counsel at the NAACP Legal Defense and Education Fund, and in 1961 he became the Director-Counsel, succeeding Thurgood Marshall. As an attorney at NAACP-LDF, Professor Greenberg argued 40 cases before the Supreme Court, including *Brown v. Board of Education*. He has taught at law schools around the country and the world, received numerous honorary degrees, and published extensively about constitutional, civil, and human rights issues, particularly education rights. He is a founding member of the Mexican American Legal Defense Fund. In 2001, Professor Greenberg received the Presidential Citizens Medal. He received a BA, LLB, and LLD from Columbia University.

Cheryl Brown Henderson is the Founding President of The Brown Foundation for Educational Equity, Excellence and Research, and owner of Brown & Associates, an educational consulting firm. Since its establishment in 1988, the Foundation has provided scholarships to more than 100 minority students, established libraries for children in low-income communities, developed curriculum on *Brown v. Board of Education* for educators across the country, and worked with Congress and the National Park Service to preserve sites associated with the landmark Supreme Court ruling of 1954. Ms. Henderson has received various awards and recognition for work in education and her community service. She received a BA from Baker University, an MA from Emporia State University, and an honorary PhD from Washburn University.

David Hinojosa is the Regional Counsel for MALDEF's Southwest Office in San Antonio, Texas. He has served as MALDEF's lead counsel for the "Edgewood ISD Plaintiffs" in the last two Texas school finance cases; in the first statewide adequacy/educational opportunity challenge filed by 51 parents and at-risk children in New Mexico, *Martinez v. State of New Mexico*; and on behalf of Plaintiff-Intervenor at-risk students and parents in Colorado's first adequacy case, *Lobato/Ortega v. Colorado*. Mr. Hinojosa also serves as MALDEF's lead counsel in a number of school desegregation, equal educational opportunity language, and higher education access cases. Mr. Hinojosa is also a former air traffic controller in the U.S. Air Force. He received a BA from New Mexico State University and a JD from the University of Texas at Austin.

Danielle R. Holley-Walker is Dean and Professor of Law at Howard University School of Law. She has taught at the University of South Carolina School of Law and Hofstra University School of Law. Prior to teaching, she practiced civil litigation at Fulbright & Jaworski, LLP, in Houston. Dean Holley-Walker has published articles on a range of civil rights and education issues, including the No Child Left Behind Act, charter school policies, desegregation plans, and affirmative action in higher education. She received a BA from Yale University and a JD from Harvard University.

Nathaniel R. Jones is Of Counsel at Blank Rome, LLP. He has served as an Assistant United States Attorney for the Northern District of Ohio and as Assistant General Counsel to President Johnson's National Advisory Commission on Civil Disorders. He held the position of general counsel of the NAACP from 1969 to 1979 before being appointed to the U.S. Court of Appeals for the Sixth Circuit in 1979 by President Jimmy Carter. He retired from that position in 2002. Judge Jones's work as a national and international civil rights activist has been recognized by numerous awards and by 19 honorary degrees. Additionally, the federal building and U.S. Courthouse in Youngstown, Ohio, is named in his honor. He received a BA and LLB from Youngstown State University.

Byron E. Leet is a partner at Wyatt, Tarrant & Combs, LLP, where he serves as cochair of the firm's Litigation & Dispute Resolution service team. He has more than 30 years of experience litigating in state and federal court, is included in Woodward/White's *The Best Lawyers in America* and *Kentucky Super Lawyers*, and is a Louisville "Lawyer of the Year." Mr. Leet served as trial counsel for the Jefferson County, Kentucky, public school system in the litigation challenging the constitutionality of the Jefferson County student assignment plan. He received a BA from the University of Louisville and a JD from Vanderbilt University.

John R. Munich is a partner at Stinson Leonard Street LLP, where he chairs the firm's Business and Commercial Litigation I division. He represents businesses in trial and appellate tribunals and in commercial arbitrations across the country. He also assists companies in conducting internal investigations and in responding to governmental investigations. In addition to his business litigation practice, Mr.

Munich also represents state agencies and officials in education finance lawsuits. Prior to joining Stinson Leonard, he served as an Assistant United States Attorney for the District of Columbia and as Deputy Attorney General for the state of Missouri. He received an AB and JD from St. Louis University.

Gary Orfield is the Distinguished Research Professor of Education, Law, Political Science & Urban Planning at the University of California-Los Angeles and the Co-Director of the Civil Rights Project/ Proyecto Derechos Civiles, which he co-founded at Harvard University with Christopher Edley Jr. in 1996. He is the author or editor of many books, academic articles, and reports. Dr. Orfield has been involved in the development of governmental policy and has served as an expert witness or special master in several dozen court cases. He has received the American Political Science Association's Charles Merriam Award, the American Educational Research Association's Social Justice in Education Award, and is a member of the National Academy of Education. He received a BA from the University of Minnesota and an MA and PhD from the University of Chicago.

Wendy Parker is a Professor at Wake Forest University School of Law. She joined the Wake Forest faculty in 2003 from the University of Cincinnati College of Law, where she began teaching in 1996. Before teaching law, Professor Parker litigated school desegregation cases as a Skadden Arps Fellow and staff attorney for the Lawyers' Committee for Civil Rights and as a trial attorney for the U.S. Department of Justice, Civil Rights Division. She received a BA and a JD from the University of Texas at Austin.

James E. Ryan is the Dean and Charles William Eliot Professor at the Harvard Graduate School of Education. He is an expert on law and education, constitutional law, and constitutional theory. He is the co-author of the textbook *Educational Policy and the Law* (2012, with Mark Yudof, Betsy Levin, Rachel Moran, and Kristi L. Bowman), and the author of *Five Miles Away, A World Apart* (2010). Before coming to Harvard, Dean Ryan was the William L. Matheson & Robert M. Morgenthau Distinguished Professor at the University of Virginia School of Law. He also served as academic associate dean from 2005–09, and founded and directed the school's Program in Law and Public Service. He received an AB from Yale University and a JD from the University of Virginia.

Philippa Strum is a Senior Scholar at the Woodrow Wilson International Center for Scholars. She also is the former Director of the Division of U.S. Studies at the Wilson Center and Professor of Political Science Emerita, CUNY. Her books include *Women* *in the Barracks: The VMI Case and Equal Rights* (2002), *When the Nazis Came to Skokie: Freedom for the Speech We Hate* (1999), and *Louis D. Brandeis: Justice for the People* (1984). She is a frequent expert lecturer in the Middle East and Central Asia for the Department of State. In 1994, Dr. Strum received the Hughes-Gossett Award for scholarly writing about the U.S. Supreme Court, and in 2013 she presented a lecture about the *Mendez* case at the Court. She received a BA from Brandeis University, an EdM from Harvard University, and a PhD from the Graduate Faculty of The New School.

Benjamin M. Superfine is an Associate Professor in the Educational Policy Studies Department at the University of Illinois at Chicago, and the Director of the Research on Urban Education Policy Initiative there. His research focuses on the history of education law and policy, school finance reform, standards-based reform and accountability, and teacher evaluation. His work has been published such educational and legal journals as the *American Educational Research Journal, American Journal of Education, Cardozo Law Review, Educational Policy*, and *Teachers College Record*. He is the author of two books, *The Courts and Standards-based Education Reform* (2008) and *Equality in Education Law and Policy: 1954–2010* (2013). He received a BA from the University of Pennsylvania, and a JD and PhD from the University of Michigan.

Karolina Walters is a former staff attorney for MALDEF's Southwest Office in San Antonio, Texas. During her tenure there, she served as counsel to *amici* defending the University of Texas at Austin's holistic admissions policy against a Fourteenth Amendment Equal Protection challenge: *Fisher v. University of Texas at Austin*. She also worked on school desegregation and equal educational opportunity language cases. She received a BA from Boston University, an MID from the University of Pittsburgh, and a JD from American University, Washington College of Law.

Index